Implementing and Administering Cisco Solutions 200-301 CCNA Exam Guide

Second Edition

Everything you need to pass the 200-301 CCNA v1.1 exam and advance your career as a network engineer

Glen D. Singh

Neil Anderson

Implementing and Administering Cisco Solutions 200-301 CCNA Exam Guide

Second Edition

Portfolio Director: Vijin Boricha

Project Manager: Gandhali Raut

Relationship Leads: Sneha Shinde and Deepak Kumar

Content Engineer: Kalyani S.

Technical Editor: Simran Ali

Copy Editor: Safis Editing

Proofreader: Safis Editing

Presentation Designer: Salma Patel

Growth Lead: Ankita Thakur

First Published: November 2020

Second Edition: July 2025

Production Reference: 1250725

Published by Packt Publishing Ltd.
Grosvenor House
11 St Paul's Square
Birmingham
B3 1RB

ISBN: 978-1-83588-748-6

www.packtpub.com

I would like to dedicate this book to the people in our society who have always worked hard in their field of expertise and who have not been recognized for their hard work, commitment, sacrifices, and ideas, but who, most importantly, believed in themselves when no one else did. This book is for you. Always have faith in yourself. With commitment, hard work, and focus, anything is possible. Never give up because great things take time.

- Glen D. Singh

Contributors

About the Authors

Glen D. Singh is a cybersecurity author, educator, and industry professional who specializes in Cyber Operations, Red and Blue Teaming, and Enterprise Networking. He holds a Master of Science (MSc) in Cybersecurity and multiple industry certifications from renowned awarding bodies such as EC-Council, Cisco, and Check Point.

With a passion for teaching and mentoring, Glen generously imparts his extensive knowledge and experience through his role as an author. His books cover a spectrum of topics, including vulnerability discovery, threat detection, intrusion analysis, incident response, network security, and enterprise networking. As an aspiring game changer, Glen is dedicated to elevating cybersecurity awareness in his homeland, Trinidad, and Tobago.

LinkedIn profile: `https://www.linkedin.com/in/glen-singh/`

I would like to thank God, the preserver of the universe, for all His divine grace and guidance. I would also like to thank Sneha Shinde, Kalyani S., Gandhali Raut, and the wonderful team at Packt Publishing, who have provided amazing support throughout this journey. To the technical reviewers, thank you for your outstanding contribution to making this an amazing book.

Neil Anderson has been passionate about IT for over 20 years.

Since 2007, Neil has specialized in developing and delivering technical training while also offering consultancy services and mentoring IT professionals. He has trained engineers responsible for designing and implementing some of the largest Cloud and Data Center deployments across the Asia Pacific region and beyond.

Neil's commitment to quality training and personalized support has earned him the trust of leading companies and countless IT professionals. He takes pride in hearing how his training has helped others advance their careers and achieve industry-recognized certifications.

Having experienced the challenges of the IT industry firsthand, Neil understands what it takes to succeed. His mission is to empower IT professionals with the skills and confidence they need to reach the next level in their careers.

About the Reviewers

Amir Shetaia is a passionate engineer and researcher currently pursuing a Master of Applied Science (MASc) in Electrical and Computer Engineering at Queen's University. At Queen's, he serves as both a Teaching Assistant and Research Assistant in the Kauffman Lab for Safety-Critical Software Engineering (CritLab), under the mentorship of Dr. Sean Kauffman.

A graduate in Mechatronics Engineering from Mansoura University, Amir has built extensive expertise in embedded systems, robotics, AI, computer vision, and cloud computing. His leadership experience includes serving as the Club Leader of the Mansoura Robotics Club, where he empowered over 1,000 students and spearheaded initiatives to advance robotics education.

Amir has cultivated a strong technical foundation through internships at leading organizations, including Siemens Digital Industries Software, Huawei, Valeo, and the Information Technology Institute (ITI). These experiences equipped him with advanced skills in AUTOSAR, RTOS, Automotive Protocols, Embedded Linux, cloud computing, and embedded systems. His dedication to innovation and teamwork was recognized when he led his team to win first place at the Huawei ICT Competition Global Final.

With a steadfast commitment to technology and innovation, Amir Shetaia strives to make meaningful contributions to the fields of engineering and computing.

Joseph Tindi is a seasoned IT professional with a diploma in Information Technology and an impressive array of certifications, including A+, CCNA, Security+, and CySA+. His diverse background encompasses roles in PC support, network engineering, cybersecurity analysis, penetration testing, forensic analysis, malware analysis, cloud computing, and digital marketing. Joseph brings a unique blend of technical expertise and hands-on experience to every project. He currently works as a freelance penetration tester, helping organizations strengthen their cybersecurity defenses. When he's not uncovering vulnerabilities, Joseph enjoys playing soccer.

LinkedIn profile: `https://www.linkedin.com/in/joseph-tindi-57244b169`

Table of Contents

5

Practical Subnetting 179

6

Wireless Architectures and Virtualization 201

7

Implementing VLANs and Interswitch Connectivity 227

8

EtherChannels and Layer 2 Discovery Protocols 269

9

Understanding and Configuring Spanning Tree 287

15

Device Access Controls and VPNs 499

16

Implementing Access Controls Lists (ACLs) 539

17

Implementing Layer 2 and Wireless Security 577

18

Network Automation and Programmability Techniques 633

Preface

Implementing and Administering Cisco Solutions 200-301 CCNA Exam Guide, Second Edition, focuses on a range of Cisco technologies that will help you gain a firm understanding of networking, IP connectivity, IP services, security, network programmability, and automation.

Throughout this book, you will be exposed to various networking components and discover how they all work together in an enterprise network. You will also learn how to configure Cisco devices using the **command-line interface** (**CLI**) to provide network access, services, security, connectivity, and management.

During the course of this book, you will come across different hands-on labs with real-world scenarios that are designed to help you gain essential on-the-job skills and experience. Furthermore, this book will teach you networking technologies and solutions to implement and administer enterprise networks and infrastructure using Cisco solutions.

By the end of this book, you will have gained the confidence to pass the *200-301 CCNA* examination and be well versed in a variety of network administration and security engineering solutions.

Who This Book Is For

This book is designed for beginners who are interested in starting a career in the field of networking and students who are pursuing the *Cisco Certified Network Associate (CCNA) 200-301 v1.1 certification.* In addition, this book is also for any IT professional who is interested in gaining a career boost and learning how to implement and administer Cisco solutions in small to medium-sized networks.

What This Book Covers

Chapter 1, Introduction to Networking, introduces the concepts of network models and the role and function of common networking devices.

Chapter 2, Getting Started with Cisco IOS Devices, demonstrates how to set up a small Cisco environment, perform basic device configurations, and set up remote access.

Chapter 3, Network Architectures and Physical Infrastructure, covers the fundamentals of common network architectures such as the 2-Tier, 3-Tier, and Spine-Leaf models. In addition, this chapter covers common cabling types and interface issues.

Chapter 4, IPv4 and IPv6 Addressing, explores the fundamentals of IPv4 and IPv6 addresses, types of addresses, and how to convert an IPv4 address between binary and decimal.

Chapter 5, Practical Subnetting, provides an in-depth and practical discussion on how to get started with designing an IPv4 address scheme for an organization and demonstrates how to perform subnetting.

Chapter 6, Wireless Architectures and Virtualization, covers the fundamentals of Cisco wireless architectures and common operating modes of access points. Additionally, this chapter explores the importance of using virtualization within an IT environment.

Chapter 7, Implementing VLANs and Interswitch Connectivity, introduces the concepts of creating virtual local area networks and the importance of logically segmenting a physical network. This chapter also covers how to extend VLANs over a Layer 2 network and how to set up inter-VLAN routing.

Chapter 8, EtherChannels and Layer 2 Discovery Protocols, explores the importance of using link aggregation between switches such as EtherChannels. This chapter also covers common Layer 2 protocols used by network professionals to discover connected networking devices.

Chapter 9, Understanding and Configuring Spanning Tree, covers the role and function of Spanning Tree within a network and demonstrates how to configure and troubleshoot Spanning Tree within a Cisco environment.

Chapter 10, Interpreting Routing Components, explains the fundamentals of routing and the various components of a routing table within a Cisco router.

Chapter 11, Understanding Static Routing, Dynamic Routing, and First Hop Redundancy, explains how to configure static routing and dynamic routing within a Cisco environment. In addition, this chapter explains the importance and use cases of first-hop redundancy on a network.

Chapter 12, Configuring Network Address Translation (NAT), explains the importance of NAT within an organization and provides the hands-on skills needed to administer and troubleshoot various NAT implementations.

Chapter 13, Implementing Network Services and IP Operations, explains and demonstrates how to set up common network services such as **Dynamic Host Configuration Protocol** (**DHCP**), **Domain Name System** (**DNS**), **Simple Network Management Protocol** (**SNMP**), and Syslog on a Cisco network.

Chapter 14, Exploring Network Security, explores the fundamentals and importance of network security concepts.

Chapter 15, Configuring Device Access Controls and VPNs, demonstrates how to secure Cisco IOS devices and establish site-to-site and remote access VPNs using Cisco devices.

Chapter 16, Implementing Access Control Lists (ACLs), covers the importance of using ACLs on a network to perform Layer 3 and Layer 4 traffic filtering between networks using Cisco IOS routers.

Chapter 17, Implementing Layer 2 and Wireless Security, covers how to set up common Layer 2 security features on Cisco IOS switches to prevent common attacks such as man-in-the-middle, CAM table flooding, MAC address spoofing, and rogue DHCP on a network.

Chapter 18, Network Automation and Programmability, broaches the fact that the world of networking is moving toward automation, and network engineers will now need to learn how automation can improve efficiency in network deployment and management. This chapter introduces you to network automation techniques and programmability.

How to Get the Most Out of This Book

This book is crafted to equip you with the knowledge and skills necessary to excel in the *200-301 CCNA v1.1* exam through memorable explanations of major domain topics. It covers the five critical core domains for implementing and administering Cisco solutions that candidates must be proficient in to pass the exam. For each domain, you'll work through content that reflects real-world network administration challenges. At certain points in the book, you will assess your understanding by taking chapter-specific quizzes. This not only prepares you for the *200-301 CCNA v1.1* exam but also allows you to dive deeper into a topic as needed based on your results.

Online Practice Resources

With this book, you will unlock unlimited access to our online exam-prep platform (*Figure 0.1*). This is your place to practice everything you learn in the book.

How to Access These Materials

To learn how to access the online resources, refer to *Chapter 19, Accessing the Online Practice Resources*, at the end of this book.

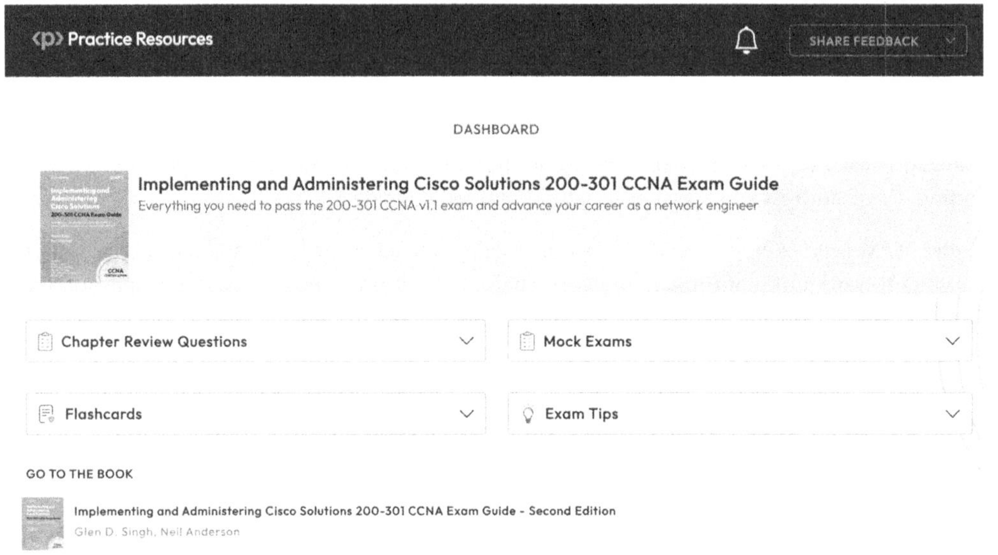

Figure 0.1: Online exam-prep platform on a desktop device

Sharpen your knowledge of CCNA concepts with multiple sets of mock exams, interactive flashcards, and exam tips accessible from all modern web browsers.

Download the practice lab files

You can download the practice lab files for this book from GitHub at `https://github.com/PacktPublishing/Implementing-and-Administering-Cisco-Solutions-200-301-CCNA-Exam-Guide-Second-Edition`. If there's an update to the lab files, it will be updated in the GitHub repository.

We also have other code bundles from our rich catalog of books and videos available at `https://github.com/PacktPublishing/`. Check them out!

Conventions Used

There are several text conventions used throughout this book.

`Code in text`: Indicates code words in text, database table names, folder names, filenames, file extensions, pathnames, dummy URLs, user input, and X (formerly Twitter) handles. Here is an example: "Assign DHCP snooping for either a single VLAN or a range of VLANs by using the `ip dhcp snooping vlan vlan-id` command in global configuration mode.

A block of code is set as follows:

```
GigabitEthernet0/1 is up, line protocol is up (connected)
  Description: Connected to Wide Area Network (WAN)
  Internet address is 172.16.1.1/24
```

Bold: Indicates a new term or an important word. Here is an example: "Since DHCP clients are expected to send only **DHCP Discover** and **DHCP Request** messages into an untrusted port, if an untrusted port receives a **DHCP Offer** or **DHCP Acknowledgement** message, then a violation will occur."

> **Tips or important notes**
> Appear like this.

Get in Touch

Feedback from our readers is always welcome.

General feedback: If you have any questions about this book, please mention the book title in the subject of your message and email us at `customercare@packt.com`.

Errata: Although we have taken every care to ensure the accuracy of our content, mistakes do happen. If you have found a mistake in this book, we would be grateful if you could report this to us. Please visit `www.packtpub.com/support/errata` and complete the form. We ensure that all valid errata are promptly updated in the GitHub repository at `https://packt.link/u5hFk`.

Piracy: If you come across any illegal copies of our works in any form on the internet, we would be grateful if you could provide us with the location address or website name. Please contact us at `copyright@packt.com` with a link to the material.

If you are interested in becoming an author: If there is a topic that you have expertise in and you are interested in either writing or contributing to a book, please visit `authors.packtpub.com`.

Share Your Thoughts

Once you've read *Implementing and Administering Cisco Solutions 200-301 CCNA Exam Guide, Second Edition*, we'd love to hear your thoughts! Scan the QR code below to go straight to the Amazon review page for this book and share your feedback.

https://packt.link/r/183588749X

Your review is important to us and the tech community and will help us make sure we're delivering excellent quality content.

Download a Free PDF Copy of This Book

Thanks for purchasing this book!

Do you like to read on the go but are unable to carry your print books everywhere? Is your eBook purchase not compatible with the device of your choice?

Don't worry! With every Packt book, you now get a DRM-free PDF version of that book at no cost.

Read anywhere, any place, on any device. Search, copy, and paste code from your favorite technical books directly into your application.

The perks don't stop there. You can get exclusive access to discounts, newsletters, and great free content in your inbox daily.

Follow these simple steps to get the benefits:

1. Scan the QR code or visit the link below:

`https://packt.link/free-ebook/9781835887486`

2. Submit your proof of purchase.
3. That's it! We'll send your free PDF and other benefits to your email directly.

1

Introduction to Networking

The *Cisco Certified Network Associate (CCNA) 200-301* certification is designed to prepare you for associate-level networking roles in the **information technology** (**IT**) industry. CCNA is one of the most popular certification requirements for almost every network engineering job, and there is a very good reason why. The CCNA certification is a foundational-level certification with a lot of essential information. Although part of the name contains the word "associate," it is simply a part of the Cisco certification hierarchical structure since the next level is *Cisco Certified Network Professional (CCNP)* and at the top is *Cisco Certified Internetwork Expert (CCIE)*.

The *CCNA* certification is one of the most highly recommended certifications in the field of network engineering that you can acquire to either break into the industry or gain a career boost. The *CCNA* certification will provide you with the foundational knowledge and skills necessary for roles involving the design, implementation, configuration, and troubleshooting of small to medium-sized enterprise networks. You will learn how to efficiently implement network access, IP connectivity, IP services, and network security configuration on an enterprise network. Additionally, gaining the *CCNA* certification will open up a whole new world of career opportunities as the certification is well respected in the networking field.

Making the Most of This Book – Your Certification and Beyond

This book and its accompanying online resources are designed to be a complete preparation tool for your **CCNA**.

The book is written in a way that means you can apply everything you've learned here even after your certification. The online practice resources that come with this book (*Figure 1.1*) are designed to improve your test-taking skills. They are loaded with timed mock exams, chapter review questions, interactive flashcards, case studies, and exam tips to help you work on your exam readiness from now till your test day.

Before You Proceed

To learn how to access these resources, head over to *Chapter 19, Accessing the Online Practice Resources*, at the end of the book.

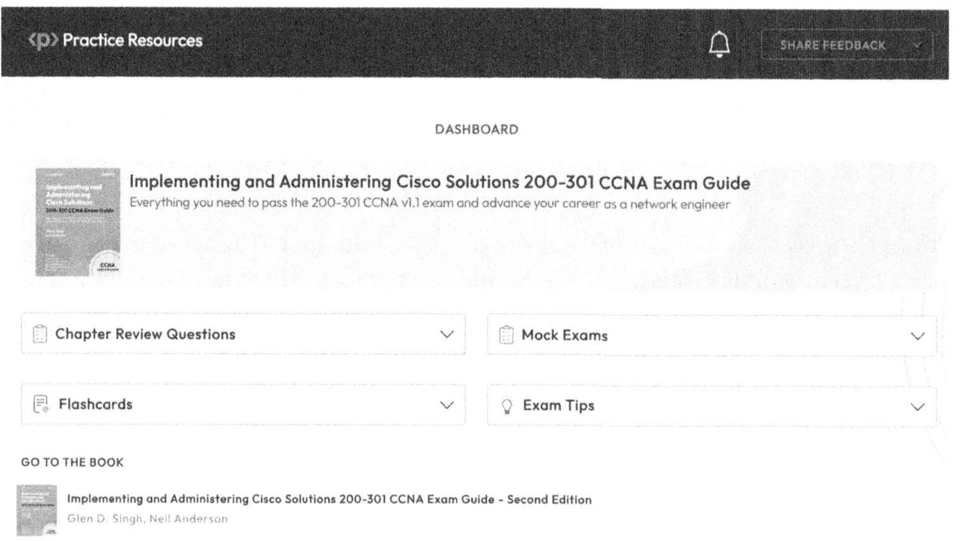

Figure 1.1: Dashboard interface of the online practice resources

Here are some tips on how to make the most of this book so that you can clear your certification and retain your knowledge beyond your exam:

1. Read each section thoroughly.
2. **Make ample notes**: You can use your favorite online note-taking tool or use a physical notebook. The free online resources also give you access to an online version of this book. Click the `BACK TO THE BOOK` link from the dashboard to access the book in **Packt Reader**. You can highlight specific sections of the book there.
3. **Chapter review questions**: At the end of this chapter, you'll find a link to review questions for this chapter. These are designed to test your knowledge of the chapter. Aim to score at least **75%** before moving on to the next chapter. You'll find detailed instructions on how to make the most of these questions at the end of this chapter in the *Exam Readiness Drill - Chapter Review Questions* section. That way, you're improving your exam-taking skills after each chapter, rather than at the end of the book.
4. **Flashcards**: After you've gone through the book and scored **75%** or more in each of the chapter review questions, start reviewing the online flashcards. They will help you memorize key concepts.

5. **Mock exams**: Revise by solving the mock exams that come with the book till your exam day. If you get some answers wrong, go back to the book and revisit the concepts you're weak in.
6. **Exam tips**: Review these from time to time to improve your exam readiness even further.

In this chapter, you will learn about various network models and how they are used in real-world devices to enable systems to communicate with each other. You will also learn about the role and function of common networking devices, including how they are used to interconnect users and systems and forward traffic between a sender and receiver. Lastly, you will learn about the role and function of common networking devices and gain a better idea of their placement within a network.

This chapter covers *Domain 1: Network Fundamentals*, objectives *1.1 Explain the role and function of network components*, *1.5 Compare TCP to UDP*, and *1.13 Describe switching concepts*, of the *200-301 CCNA v1.1* certification exam.

In this chapter, you will learn about the following exam topics:

- Network models
- OSI reference model
- TCP/IP network model
- The role and function of networking devices

You can now dive in!

Network Models

Commonly asked questions among aspiring network professionals are what is a network and why is a network important? A network can be defined as having two or more computing devices interconnected while using a set of communication protocols (rules) that enables them to share a resource with each other. Resources can be anything from a file server, **network-attached storage** (**NAS**), a network-connected printer, or even a media server with offline copies of your favorite movies and TV shows.

In the world of computer networking, communication between systems is not possible without using a set of guidelines or rules to ensure data is efficiently delivered between a source (sender) and a destination (receiver) host over a network. For instance, imagine you are currently using your smartphone to access the `www.cisco.com` website to learn more about the CCNA certification, such as the exam objectives. To ensure you are connected to the internet, there are multiple network components that exist between your smartphone and the destination web server that is hosting Cisco's website. In addition, before your smartphone sends a web request message to the destination website, a lot of different rules are used to ensure that your device has network connectivity and access to the internet, and even that you can download Cisco's home page on the web browser on your mobile phone. These sets of rules are commonly referred to as network protocols.

The following are the roles and functions of network protocols:

- **Addressing**: Addressing helps with identifying the sender and receiver of a message. Addressing in this context refers to logical addressing such as **Internet Protocol version 4 (IPv4)** and **Internet Protocol version 6 (IPv6)** addresses. In addition, it also involves physical addressing, such as the **media access control (MAC)** address.
- **Reliability**: Reliability helps ensure the guaranteed delivery of messages between a sender and receiver.
- **Flow control**: Flow control mechanisms help control the rate at which data is transmitted and received.
- **Sequencing**: Sequencing mechanisms ensure each message is uniquely assigned a label for easy identification and classification by systems.
- **Error detection**: Error detection helps a receiving device to identify whether the incoming message is corrupted.
- **Application interface**: Application interfaces ensure process-to-process mapping between a sender and receiver.

In the networking world, there are a lot of network protocols. Whether you find it intimidating or it piques your curiosity to learn about them all, as an aspiring network professional, you can start by learning about the ones that are essential to you and those that are important for the CCNA certification.

In the early days, prior to the internet, there was an early prototype known as the **Advanced Research Projects Agency Network (ARPANET)** that was developed by the US **Department of Defense (DoD)** with the intention to enable US-based educational institutions such as universities and government-funded research centers to establish a long-distance network over the traditional telephone lines in early connections. However, packet-switching was preferred as it provided more efficient and resilient communication over long distances.

To enable network communication over systems that were connected to ARPANET, the **Network Control Protocol (NCP)** defined the rules for communication, and they were used until January 1, 1983. Due to various issues, such as sustainability and scalability, the ARPANET project was decommissioned in 1990. NCP was used to enable systems to communicate over ARPANET; nowadays, there are many different network protocols, with unique roles and functions in modern networks.

Network models were created to ensure each network-connected device (such as computers, servers, network-attached printers, **Internet of Things** (**IoT**) devices, and smartphones) has all the essential protocols to ensure the communication and transmission of data from one system to another. The following are common network models:

- **Open Systems Interconnection** (**OSI**)
- **Transmission Control Protocol/Internet Protocol** (**TCP/IP**)

The upcoming section will cover the characteristics of both the OSI and TCP/IP network models and the roles and functions of their layers. It will also compare the differences between both of these network models.

OSI Reference Model

The **International Organization for Standardization** (**ISO**) started developing the seven-layer OSI model back in the late 1970s, and it became a working model in the 1980s. This OSI model was intended to be a fully operational network model with all the essential networking protocols packed into a unified stack, enabling network-connected devices to communicate and share resources.

Each layer of the OSI model has a unique role and function and enables network professionals to better understand what is happening during the exchange of data from one system to another and identify network-related issues while performing troubleshooting.

Table 1.1 shows the seven layers of the OSI model:

<table>
<tr><th>Layer</th><th>Name</th><th>Protocol Data Unit (PDU)</th></tr>
<tr><td>7</td><td>Application</td><td rowspan="3">Data</td></tr>
<tr><td>6</td><td>Presentation</td></tr>
<tr><td>5</td><td>Session</td></tr>
<tr><td>4</td><td>Transport</td><td>Segment</td></tr>
<tr><td>3</td><td>Network</td><td>Packet</td></tr>
<tr><td>2</td><td>Data Link</td><td>Frame</td></tr>
<tr><td>1</td><td>Physical</td><td>Bits</td></tr>
</table>

Table 1.1: OSI model

As shown in *Table 1.1*, the Application layer is where data is created by an application (software) that is running on the host device, such as the web browser on a computer that creates a web request message. Once the web request message is created, it is sent down the network model to the lower layers. The lower layers are responsible for inserting additional information, such as the logical and physical addressing parameters for the delivery of the message to the destination. This principle is similar to writing a traditional letter and adding addressing details to ensure the postal service is able to locate and deliver the letter to the intended recipient.

> **Note**
>
> An easy method to remember the layers of the OSI model is using the mnemonic *All People Seem To Need Data Processing*, where the first letter of each word in the sentence corresponds with the first letter of each layer in the model, from top to bottom. While this mnemonic has been used for quite a long time, you can develop your own technique of remembering the order of the layers.

Whenever an application, whether it is a web browser or an email application, creates a message, it is commonly referred to as **application data**. This **data** is the raw message, like the body of a traditional letter, without any addressing information such as the destination address or the sender's address. The Application layer passes this raw data down to the lower layers, where each layer has a unique role and responsibility to ensure the appropriate addressing details, such as that the sender's and destination addresses are correctly appended to the data to ensure it is transported and delivered to the intended recipient using the most efficient route (path).

As you will have noticed, in *Table 1.1*, there is a column with the name **Protocol Data Unit** (**PDU**). A PDU is used at various layers of the OSI model to refer to the form of data as it passes through each layer. As the application data is created at the Application layer, the PDU is referred to as **data**. As data travels downward to the Transport layer, it is appended with a Layer 4 header, which controls specific details to ensure the delivery of the message between the sender and destination hosts. At this point, the PDU will be referred to as a **segment**. The process of appending headers onto the PDU at the Transport, Network, and Data Link layers is referred to as **encapsulation**.

> **Note**
>
> As the PDU moves down to the lower layers and is encapsulated with a Layer 3 header, it is referred to as a **packet**. A PDU with a Layer 2 header and trailer is referred to as a **frame**. Lastly, when the PDU is converted into an electrical, light, or radio frequency signal for the network media on the Physical layer, it is called **bits**.

To put it simply, whenever a host device such as a computer is sending data, the data is created at the Application layer. It travels down the OSI model stack until it arrives at the Data Link layer. Then, it is placed on the Physical layer, that is, the network media, which is wired (copper or fiber) or wireless (radio frequency).

When a host receives a message on a network, it is received on the Physical layer and travels upward to the Application layer. While moving up the OSI model, each layer, such as the Data Link, Network, and Transport layers, will remove the headers until the raw datagram is delivered to the Application layer at the top. This process is commonly referred to as **de-encapsulation**.

Figure 1.2 shows a high-level visual representation of a computer sending application data to a server over a network. Here, the OSI network model is used as a reference:

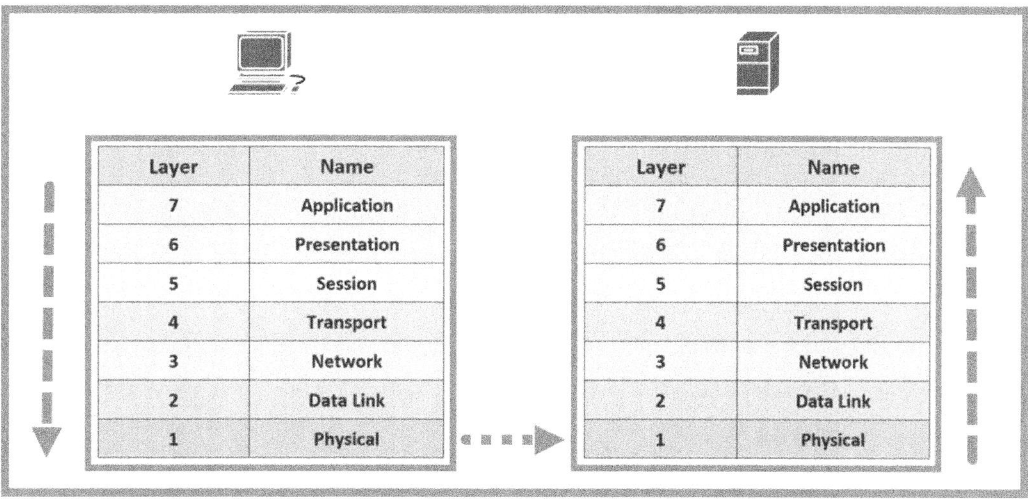

Figure 1.2: Sending and receiving messages

Within the OSI model, the upper layers, such as the Application, Presentation, and Session layers, are used to provide support for application functions such as enabling a web browser on your computer to create and process web requests from a web server. The lower layers, such as the Transport, Network, and Data Link layers, are responsible for inserting the appropriate header with addressing and control information to ensure that the data is delivered to the intended destination over a network.

Application Layer

The Application layer is found closest to the end user within the OSI model. This layer provides an interface for enabling communication between applications that are running on the host operating system of your computer and the underlying network protocols that are responsible for delivering your message (data) to the intended destination.

For instance, you may be interested in learning about the *200-301 CCNA v1.1* exam objectives. Typically, you would open the web browser application and go to `https://learningnetwork.cisco.com/s/ccna-v1-1-exam-topics`, as shown in *Figure 1.3*:

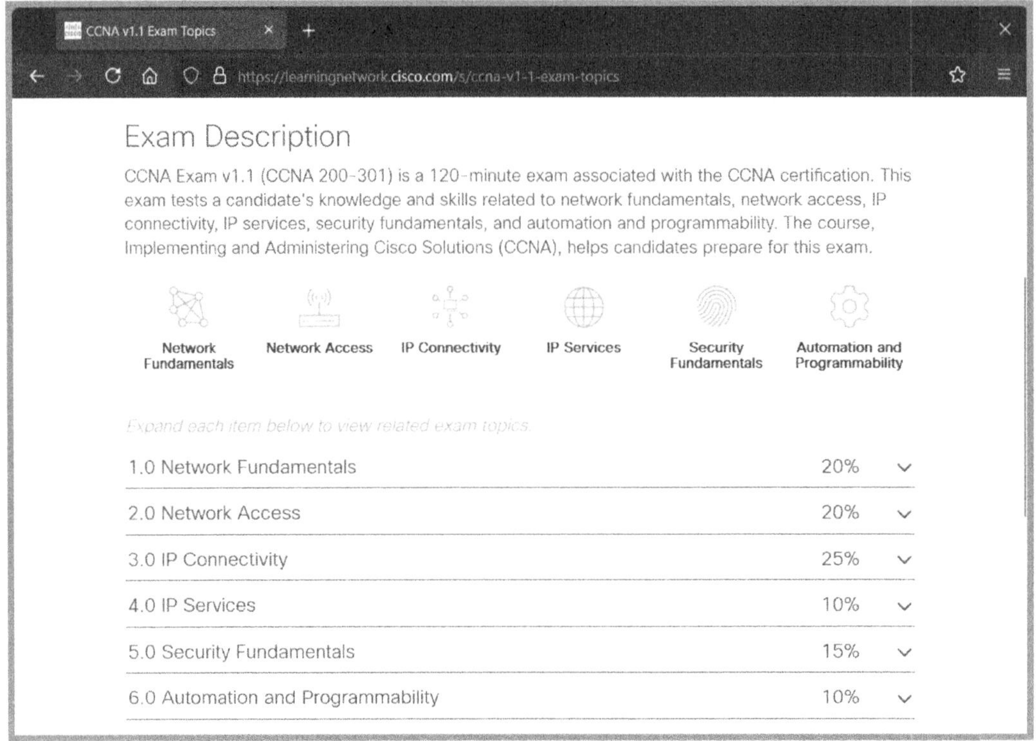

Figure 1.3: Cisco learning network website

As shown in *Figure 1.3*, the web browser uses **Hypertext Transfer Protocol Secure** (**HTTPS**), an Application-layer protocol that enables the web browser to communicate with the web application that is running on Cisco's web server. In this scenario, it is important to remember that the end user, such as yourself, will not directly interface with an Application layer such as HTTPS, but would rather use an application that is installed on your host device such as the web browser.

Figure 1.4 shows an example of an HTTP header that is created by a sender device such as a Windows computer using Mozilla Firefox as the web browser application:

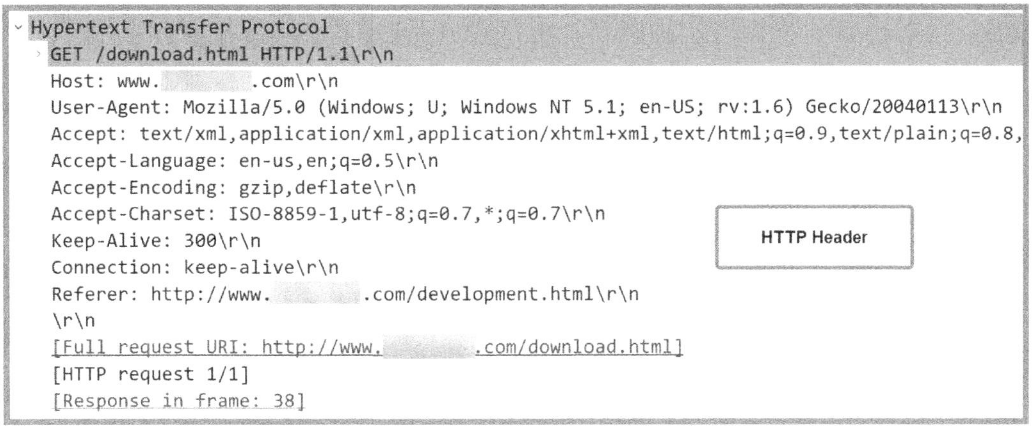

```
Hypertext Transfer Protocol
  GET /download.html HTTP/1.1\r\n
  Host: www.        .com\r\n
  User-Agent: Mozilla/5.0 (Windows; U; Windows NT 5.1; en-US; rv:1.6) Gecko/20040113\r\n
  Accept: text/xml,application/xml,application/xhtml+xml,text/html;q=0.9,text/plain;q=0.8,
  Accept-Language: en-us,en;q=0.5\r\n
  Accept-Encoding: gzip,deflate\r\n
  Accept-Charset: ISO-8859-1,utf-8;q=0.7,*;q=0.7\r\n
  Keep-Alive: 300\r\n
  Connection: keep-alive\r\n
  Referer: http://www.        .com/development.html\r\n
  \r\n
  [Full request URI: http://www.        .com/download.html]
  [HTTP request 1/1]
  [Response in frame: 38]
```

HTTP Header

Figure 1.4: HTTP header

The following are some common Application-layer protocols:

- **Domain Name System** (**DNS**): Used to resolve hostnames to IP addresses over a network.
- **Dynamic Host Configuration Protocol** (**DHCP**): Used to distribute IP addresses to connected hosts on a network.
- **Hypertext Transfer Protocol** (**HTTP**): Enables web browsers to retrieve web pages and interact with a web application over a network.
- **Simple Mail Transfer Protocol** (**SMTP**): SMTP is used to send emails from an email application to an email server, and to send emails from one email server to another over a network.
- **Post Office Protocol** (**POP**): POP is used to download a copy of emails from an email server onto an email application on the host, then deletes the emails from the email server.
- **Internet Message Access Protocol** (**IMAP**): IMAP synchronizes the email messages between an email server and an email application.
- **File Transfer Protocol** (**FTP**): This Application-layer protocol allows the transferring of files between an FTP client on a host and an FTP server.

As shown in *Figure 1.5*, these are just some of the many Application-layer protocols:

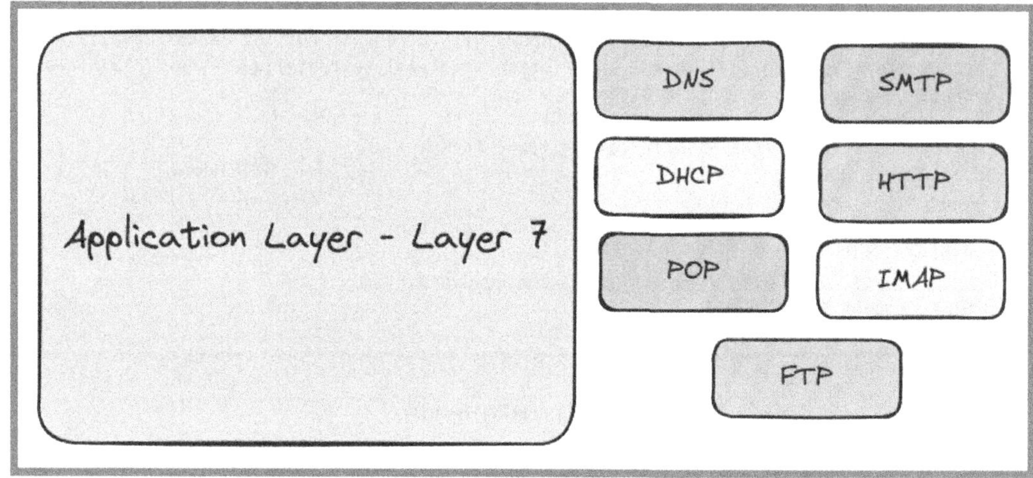

Figure 1.5: Application-layer protocols

Keep in mind that when data is created by an Application-layer protocol, it can only be interpreted by the same Application-layer protocol on another system. For instance, if you are using the web browser application on your smartphone to view websites, your smartphone uses HTTPS to communicate with the web server, which also uses HTTPS to interpret the data.

Figure 1.6 shows a visual representation of this analogy:

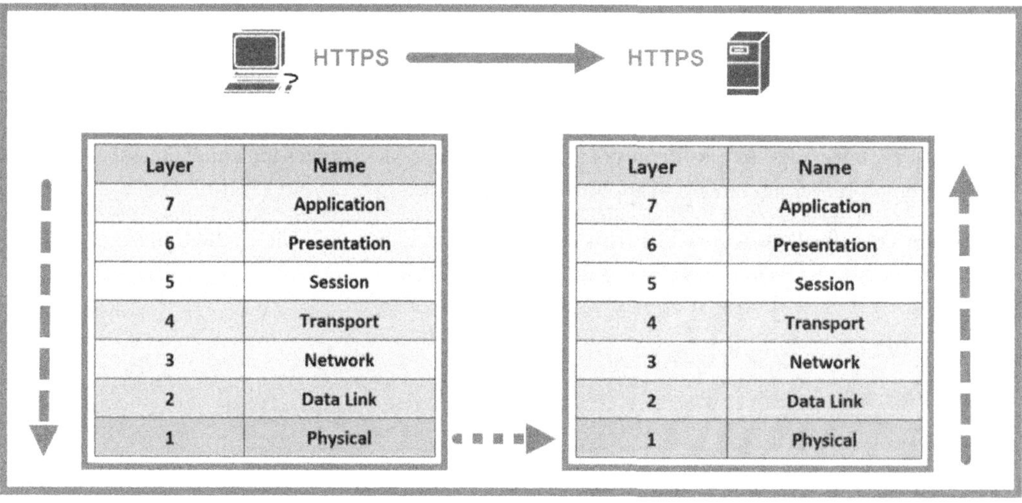

Figure 1.6: Process-to-process mapping

Since the Application-layer protocols generate the raw datagram without any addressing or formatting that is recognized by the lower layers of the OSI model, the data created in the Application layer is sent down to the Presentation layer.

Presentation Layer

For hosts that are sending data, such as a computer to a web server, the Application-layer protocols in the sender device are responsible for creating system-dependent data such as ASCII and other unique data types. The Presentation layer is responsible for transforming this system-dependent data into an independent format that is recognizable by the lower layers of the OSI model and systems on a network. On the destination device (the web server), the Presentation layer will be responsible for reversing the transformation of the independent format back to the system-dependent data before sending it upward to the appropriate Application-layer protocol, as shown in *Figure 1.7*:

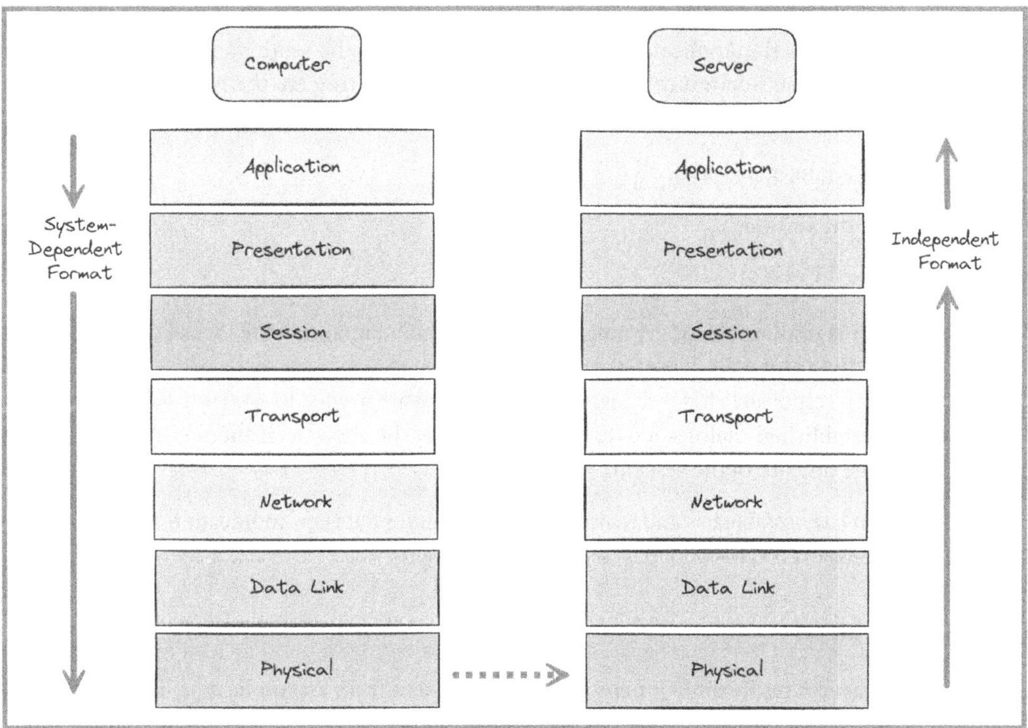

Figure 1.7: Presentation layer

The following are the main functions of the Presentation layer:

- **Data formatting**: Ensuring the data that is created by a sender device is encoded in a compatible format for receipt by the intended destination device over the network
- **Data compression and decompression**: Responsible for compressing data before transmission and decompression upon receipt
- **Data encryption and decryption**: Encrypts data before transmission to ensure confidentiality over network communication, and decrypts the encrypted message on the recipient device

During this time, the PDU will still be referred to as data, and once the Presentation layer completes its tasks, the PDU will be sent down to the next layer.

Session Layer

The Session layer helps the Application-layer protocols between the sender and receiver devices to set up and maintain their communication efficiently. The following are the main functions of the Session layer:

- Create or establish a session
- Maintain the session
- Terminate the session

The Session layer is responsible for creating/establishing and maintaining the logical dialogs between the Application-layer protocols of both the sender and receiver devices over the network. In addition, the Session layer is responsible for exchanging the details that are needed to establish a dialog, maintain or keep those established dialogs active, and even restart the sessions if there is any unexpected disruption or idle timeout of the session.

After the Session layer establishes and maintains the session for data communication, the PDU is sent down to the Transport layer, where data encapsulation begins.

Transport Layer

The Transport layer is responsible for ensuring that data sent from an Application-layer protocol is delivered to the same Application-layer protocol on the destination host. Imagine if your computer was sending HTTPS messages to a destination server on the internet, and the destination server is hosting multiple server roles, such as web and email services. How will the OSI model and its layers then know which Application-layer protocol created the datagram on the sender device, and which Application-layer protocol should the datagram be delivered to on the recipient's system?

Figure 1.8 shows a visual representation of this scenario:

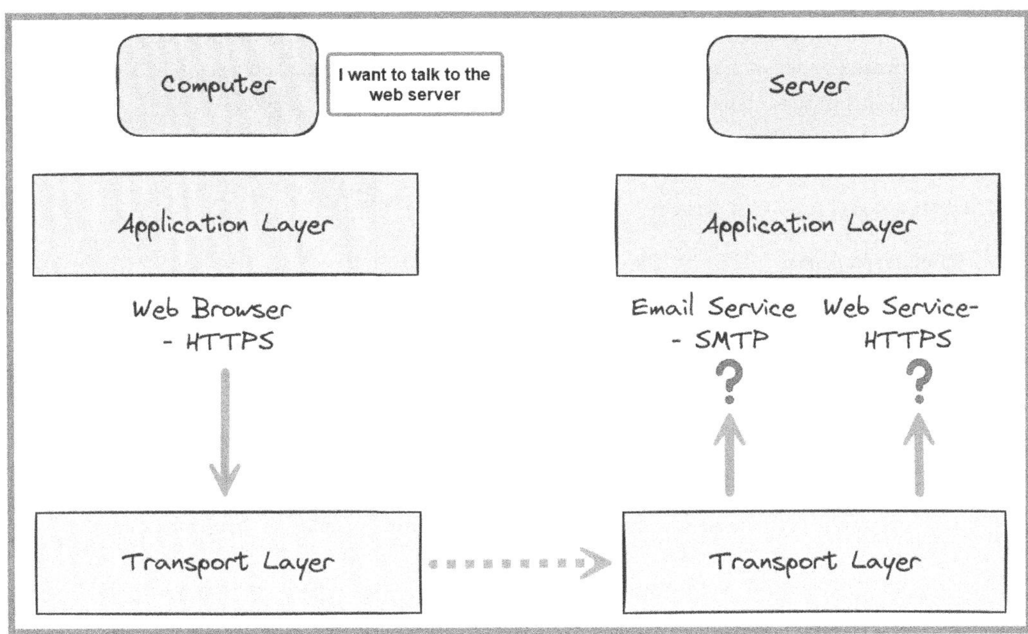

Figure 1.8: Transport layer

As shown in *Figure 1.8*, there is a problem that needs to be solved. How can the Transport layer ensure that HTTPS messages from the sender are delivered to the same Application-layer protocol or services on the server side?

To better understand the solution to this issue, you will need to take a dive into understanding service port numbers on a system. On a sender device such as a computer or a smartphone, when the Transport layer receives data from the Application layer, it identifies the Application-layer protocol, such as HTTPS, and encapsulates a Layer 4 header onto the PDU.

Figure 1.9 shows a visual representation of encapsulating a Layer 4 header onto the datagram:

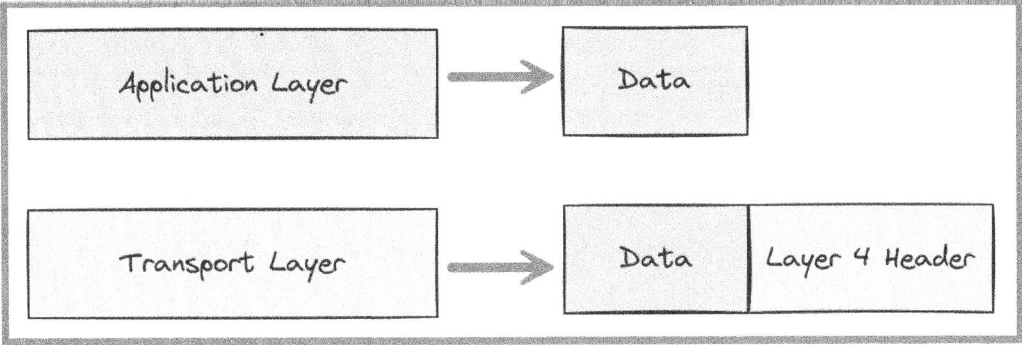

Figure 1.9: Layer 4 header encapsulation

Within the Layer 4 header, the Transport layer inserts the source and destination service port numbers. Within a network model such as the OSI and TCP/IP network models, there are 65,535 service port numbers, and each is associated with an Application-layer protocol or service.

These service ports are grouped into the following categories:

- **Well-known port**: 0–1,023
- **Registered ports**: 1,024–49,151
- **Dynamic or private ports**: 49,152–65,535

Since many Application-layer protocols operate in a client-server model, whereby a computer has a client application that requests services or resources from another device on a network, such as a server that provides the services and resources, the sender (client) device is usually assigned an ephemeral, random source port number and a destination port that is associated with the Application-layer protocol.

Figure 1.10 shows the role the source and destination port numbers play at the Transport layer:

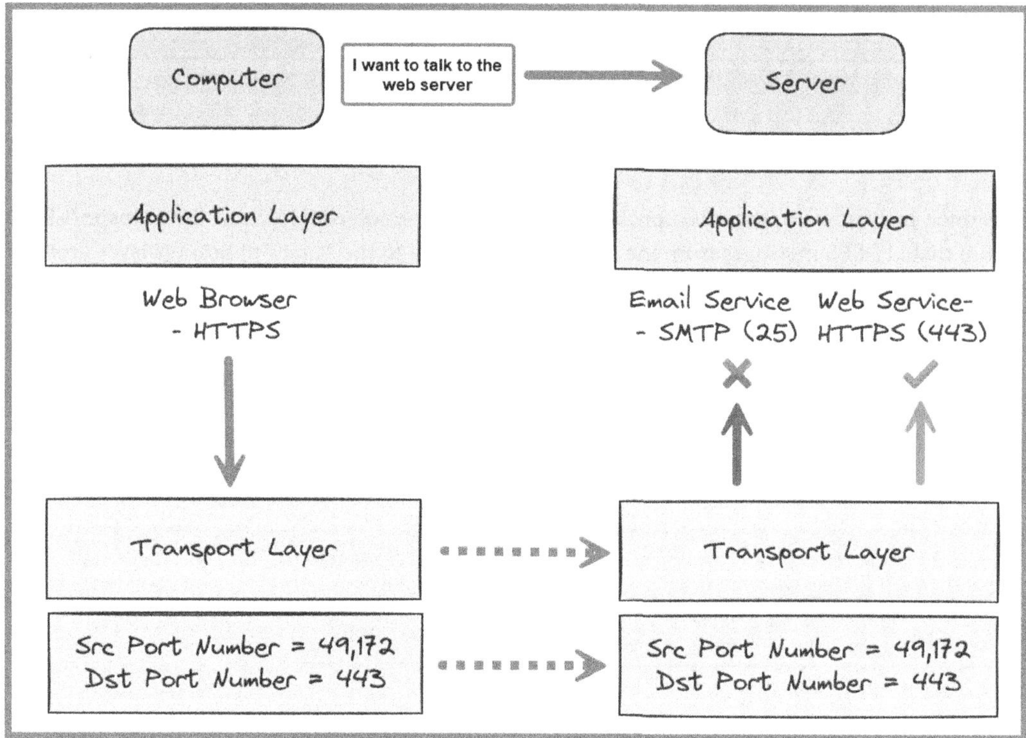

Figure 1.10: Service port numbers

As shown in *Figure 1.10*, the Transport layer on the sender (computer) inserted the destination service port number `443`, which is associated with HTTPS, and a randomly generated (ephemeral) source service port number. The destination port number helps the Transport layer on the recipient (server) to determine which Application-layer protocol the message should be sent to.

The source port number plays an important role when a recipient is responding to the sender. For instance, the sender device creates and sends an **HTTP request** message to the web server. This message contains the instructions to retrieve the web page from the web server. However, before the server responds to the computer (sender), it switches the source and destination port numbers on the Layer 4 header, using the original source port number as the new destination port.

Figure 1.11 shows a visual representation of the flipping of the service port numbers on the Layer 4 header by the server to ensure the message is delivered to the appropriate Application-layer protocol or process on the computer:

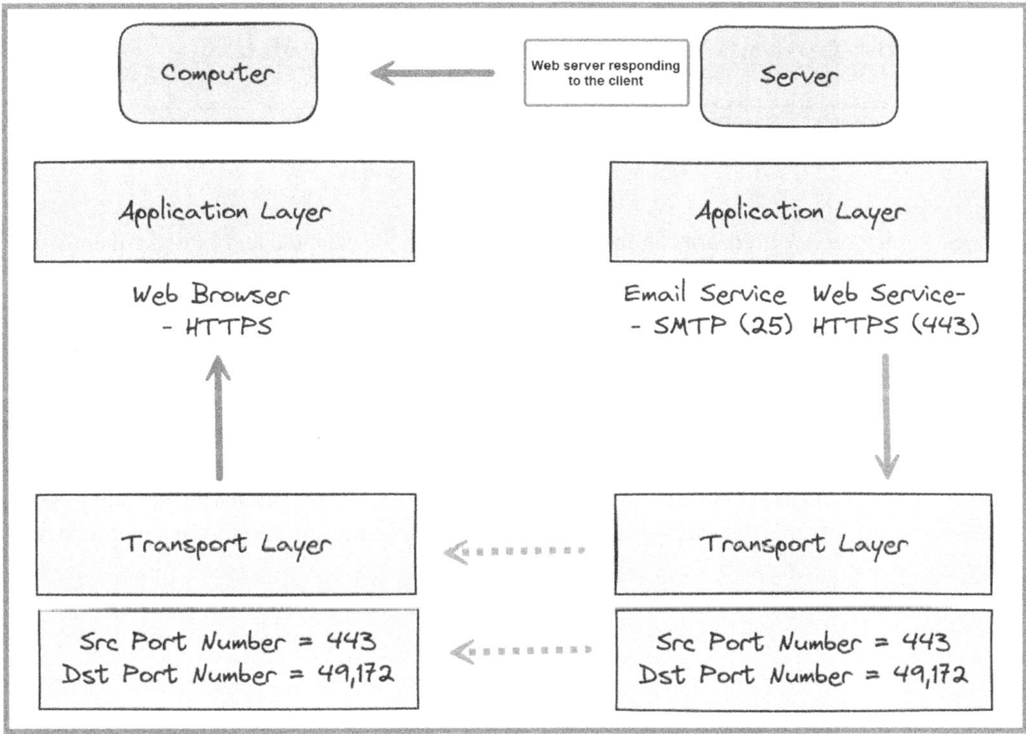

Figure 1.11: Reverse port numbers

As previously mentioned, there are 65,535 service port numbers. These service port numbers are categorized as shown in *Figure 1.12*:

Category	Port numbers
Well-known ports	1-1,023
Registered ports	1,024-49,151
Private/dynamic ports	49,152-65,535

Figure 1.12: Port number categories

The well-known service ports are commonly associated with the essential and most frequently used application and network services. Some of these are HTTP, HTTPS, SMTP, FTP, and IMAP. Registered port numbers are usually used by organizations that have officially registered their applications to operate on a specific number. The private/dynamic port numbers are used for temporary communication between systems on a network.

These service ports are not physical ports that are seen on networking devices; rather, they are logical ports opened by the operating system of a device for sending and receiving data on a network. Think of them as the logical doorways of your operating system. If a port is open, it means the operating system is either sending data to a destination or expecting incoming communication from a remote device.

Table 1.2 shows a list of common Application-layer protocols and their associated service port numbers:

Application-Layer Protocol	Service Port Number
File Transfer Protocol (FTP)	20 (Data), 21 (Control)
Secure Shell (SSH)	22
Telnet	23
Simple Mail Transfer Protocol (SMTP)	25
Domain Name System (DNS)	53
Hypertext Transfer Protocol (HTTP)	80
HTTP Secure (HTTPS)	443
Post Office Protocol (POP)	110
Internet Message Access Protocol (IMAP)	143

Table 1.2: Common Application-layer protocols

> **Note**
>
> For a list of protocols and their associated port numbers, please see `https://www.iana.org/assignments/service-names-port-numbers/service-names-port-numbers.xhtml`.

So far, you have read about the importance of service port numbers and how they are leveraged by the Transport layer to ensure process-to-process mapping between Application-layer protocols. The Transport layer is also responsible for ensuring the delivery of the Application-layer datagrams to the intended recipients over a network.

The following are the Transport-layer protocols that assist with the delivery of a datagram:

- **Transmission Control Protocol** (**TCP**)
- **User Datagram Protocol** (**UDP**)

As mentioned earlier, Application-layer protocols and processes are not responsible for ensuring that datagrams are delivered to the intended destination. They are only concerned with the creation of data. Both TCP and UDP have their advantages, disadvantages, and use cases. In the next sub-section, you will learn more about TCP.

Transmission Control Protocol

TCP is a connection-oriented protocol that establishes a logical connection between a sender and receiver over a network, before allowing the transmission of data from the Application-layer protocols or processes.

If an Application-layer protocol uses TCP as the Transport-layer protocol, a TCP Layer 4 header is encapsulated onto the data. *Table 1.3* shows the various fields of a TCP header:

<table>
<tr><th colspan="2">Source Port</th><th colspan="2">Destination Port</th></tr>
<tr><td colspan="4">Sequence Number</td></tr>
<tr><td colspan="4">Acknowledgment Number (if ACK is set)</td></tr>
<tr><td>Data Offset</td><td>Reserved</td><td>Flags</td><td>Window Size</td></tr>
<tr><td colspan="2">Checksum</td><td colspan="2">Urgent Pointer (if URG is set)</td></tr>
<tr><td colspan="4">Options</td></tr>
</table>

Table 1.3: TCP header

The following is a description of each field shown in *Table 1.3*:

- `Source Port`: This is a 16-bit field that identifies the source service port number.
- `Destination Port`: This is a 16-bit field that identifies the destination service port number.
- `Sequence Number`: This is a 32-bit field that is used during the reassembly process on the recipient's device.
- `Acknowledgment Number`: This is a 32-bit field used to indicate the message has been received by the recipient and contains the acknowledgment number (sender's sequence number + 1).
- `Data Offset`: This is a 4-bit field, sometimes referred to as the header length. It is commonly used to specify the length of the TCP header.
- `Reserved`: This is a 6-bit field that's reserved for future use.
- `Flags`: This field contains eight sub-fields, each being 1 bit in size and used to specify various TCP flags, such as the following:
    - `CWR`: Congestion flag, used by the sender to indicate it has received a message with a TCP **Explicit Congestion Notification** (**ECN**) flag set and responded to the congestion control
    - `ECE`: ECN echo flag, used to indicate whether a device is ECN capable or the congestion experienced flag is set to identify network congestion

    - `URG`: Urgent flag, indicates the significance of the `Urgent Pointer` field
    - `ACK`: Acknowledgment flag, indicates the significance of the `Acknowledgment Number` field
    - `PSH`: Push flag, indicates the push function is significant
    - `RST`: Reset flag, indicates to reset the logical network connection
    - `SYN`: Synchronization flag, used to synchronize the sequence numbers
    - `FIN`: Finish flag, indicates the last message from the sender device
- `Window Size`: This is a 16-bit field that specifies the number of bits or bytes that can be received.
- `Checksum`: This is a 16-bit field that's used for error checking.
- `Urgent Pointer`: Used if the TCP URG flag is set. This 16-bit field is used to indicate the last urgent data byte.
- `Options`: This is an optional field and ranges between 0 and 320 bits.

Figure 1.13 shows a TCP header using Wireshark, a network protocol analyzer application used by network and cybersecurity professionals:

```
˅ Transmission Control Protocol, Src Port: 3372, Dst Port: 80, Seq: 0, Len: 0
    Source Port: 3372
    Destination Port: 80
    [Stream index: 0]
  > [Conversation completeness: Complete, WITH_DATA (31)]
    [TCP Segment Len: 0]
    Sequence Number: 0    (relative sequence number)
    Sequence Number (raw): 951057939
    [Next Sequence Number: 1    (relative sequence number)]
    Acknowledgment Number: 0
    Acknowledgment number (raw): 0
    0111 .... = Header Length: 28 bytes (7)
  > Flags: 0x002 (SYN)
    Window: 8760
    [Calculated window size: 8760]
    Checksum: 0xc30c [unverified]
    [Checksum Status: Unverified]
    Urgent Pointer: 0
  > Options: (8 bytes), Maximum segment size, No-Operation (NOP), No-Operation (NOP), SACK permitted
  > [Timestamps]
```

Figure 1.13: TCP header in Wireshark

Before data is sent, the sender device, such as a computer, initiates the TCP three-way handshake between itself and the intended destination, as shown in *Figure 1.14*:

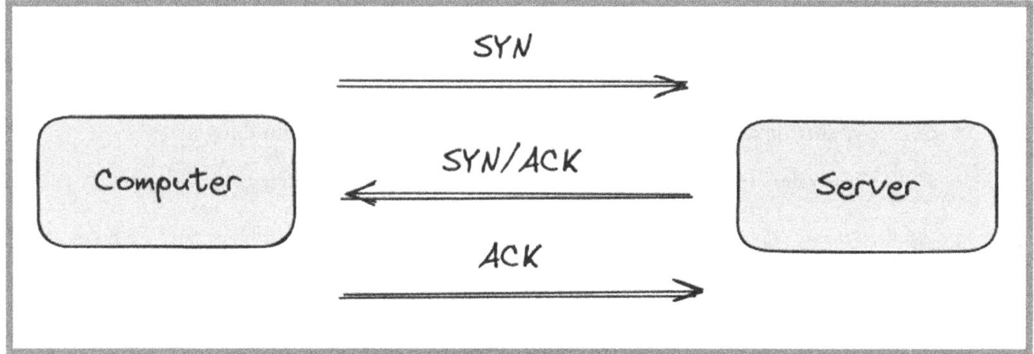

Figure 1.14: TCP three-way handshake

The following is a technical breakdown of this process:

1. The computer wants to communicate with the destination server using HTTPS as the Application-layer protocol. Since HTTPS is designed to use TCP as the preferred Transport-layer protocol, the Transport layer of the computer sends a TCP **Synchronization** (**SYN**) message to the server with the following details in the Layer 4 header:

    - **Source port number**: This is a dynamic service port number used by the computer.
    - **Destination port**: The destination service port number for the Application-layer protocol or process on the server.
    - **Randomly generated sequence number**: The sequence number is used to initialize the starting sequence number for data that belongs to the same data stream.
    - **Window size**: The window size helps both the sender and recipient to mutually agree upon the amount of data to transmit.

    Figure 1.15 shows the TCP SYN message, including a sequence number:

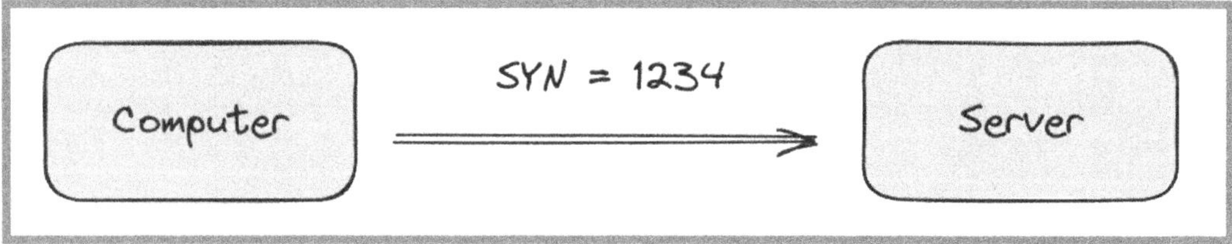

Figure 1.15: TCP SYN

2. Next, the server receives the TCP SYN message and responds with a TCP **Synchronization/ Acknowledgment** (**SYN/ACK**). In this response, an acknowledgment sequence number is set. This is the sender's sequence number + 1. In addition, the response message contains a randomly generated sequence number that informs the sender it also wants to establish a logical connection for communication, as shown in *Figure 1.16*:

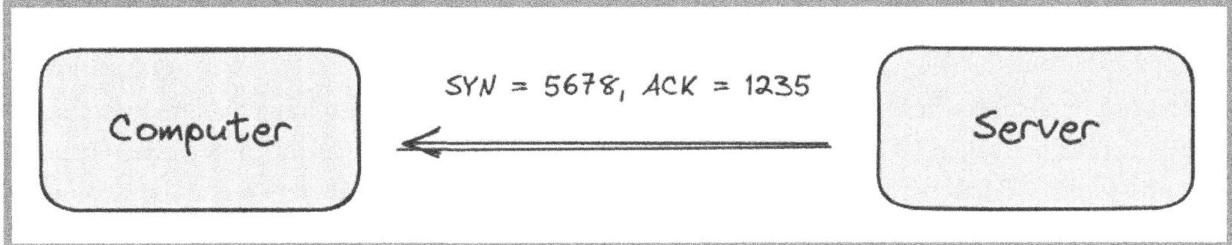

Figure 1.16: TCP SYN/ACK

3. Lastly, when the computer receives the TCP SYN/ACK message from the server to complete the TCP three-way handshake, it responds with a TCP ACK message, which contains an incremented value based on the server's SYN sequence number, as shown in *Figure 1.17*:

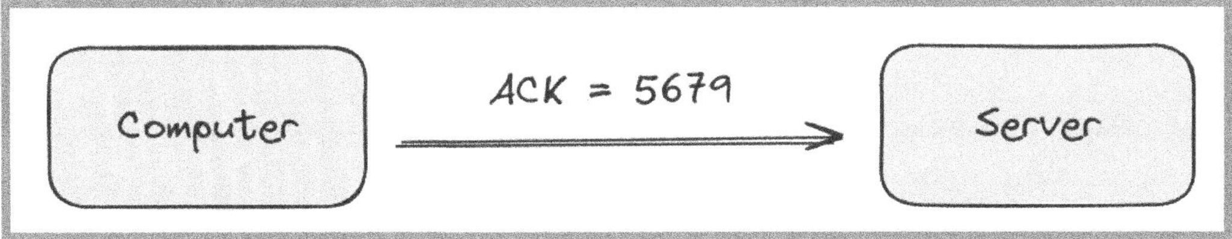

Figure 1.17: TCP ACK

After the TCP three-way handshake is established between the sender and the destination host, data transmission occurs between the Application-layer protocols of the computer and server.

Figure 1.18 shows the TCP three-way handshake of a packet capture within Wireshark:

No.	Source	Destination	Protocol	Info
1	145.254.160.237	65.208.228.223	TCP	3372 → 80 [SYN] Seq=0 Win=8760 Len=0 MSS=1460
2	65.208.228.223	145.254.160.237	TCP	80 → 3372 [SYN, ACK] Seq=0 Ack=1 Win=5840 Len
3	145.254.160.237	65.208.228.223	TCP	3372 → 80 [ACK] Seq=1 Ack=1 Win=9660 Len=0
4	145.254.160.237	65.208.228.223	HTTP	GET /download.html HTTP/1.1

Figure 1.18: Packet capture

As shown in *Figure 1.18*, packets 1, 2, and 3 show the TCP three-way handshake. Once the handshake has been established, the Application-layer protocol HTTP sends data to the destination web server over the network. TCP is a Transport-layer protocol that provides a guarantee of the delivery of data between the sender and destination. When the destination host receives a message, it will respond with a TCP ACK packet to inform the sender it has received the message. If the sender does not receive the TCP ACK response, it will attempt to re-transmit the message until the Application-layer protocol or process experiences a timeout.

What if the Application-layer protocol on either the computer or server no longer wants to exchange data? What happens then? If the Application-layer protocol is using TCP as the preferred Transport-layer protocol, TCP will perform a TCP FIN/ACK handshake to gracefully terminate the session, as shown in *Figure 1.19*:

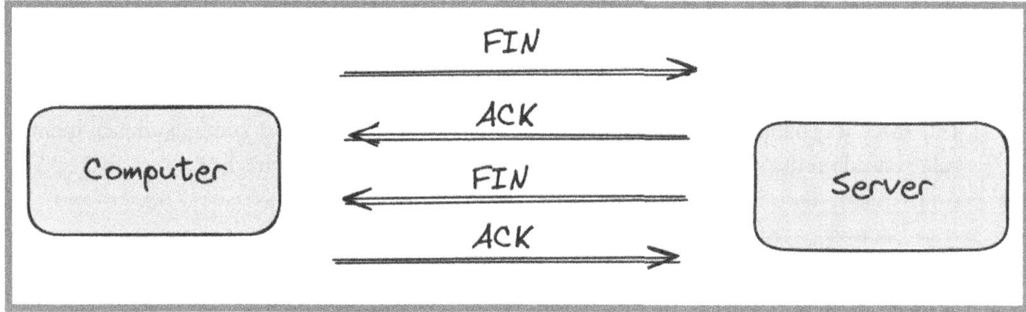

Figure 1.19: TCP FIN/ACK handshake

As shown in *Figure 1.19*, the computer initiates the graceful termination by sending a TCP **finish** (**FIN**) message to the server. Then, the server responds with TCP ACK and TCP FIN messages back to the computer. Lastly, the computer sends a TCP ACK to the server to confirm the termination from the server.

Figure 1.20 shows the TCP FIN/ACK messages being exchanged between a sender and receiver host to gracefully terminate their sessions:

No.	Source	Destination	Protocol	Info
40	65.208.228.223	145.254.160.237	TCP	80 → 3372 [FIN, ACK] Seq=18365 Ack=480
42	145.254.160.237	65.208.228.223	TCP	3372 → 80 [FIN, ACK] Seq=480 Ack=18366

Figure 1.20: TCP graceful termination

The following are the advantages of using TCP as the preferred Transport-layer protocol:

- It is a connection-oriented protocol that establishes a TCP three-way handshake before exchanging data.
- It provides a guarantee of delivery of data between Application-layer protocols and processes that use TCP.
- TCP delivers the data using the same order in which it was placed on the physical network and reassembled on the receiver's device.
- It uses the window size to manage flow control between a sender and receiver device over a network.

The following are the disadvantages of using TCP over a network:

- The receiver device responds with a TCP ACK message to acknowledge receipt of the data. This introduces additional overhead on the network.
- If a host is sending multiple messages to another device, all the messages from the sender are not placed on the network for transmission. TCP will send some of the messages and wait for an acknowledgment from the recipient before proceeding to send another batch. This process is repeated, and therefore, TCP is not suitable for time-sensitive communication.

Up next, you will learn about the fundamentals of UDP.

User Datagram Protocol

Not all Application-layer protocols use TCP. Some use UDP. UDP is a connectionless Transport-layer protocol that does not guarantee the delivery of messages from a sender to a receiver over a network but is preferred for transporting time-sensitive data between hosts over a network. Unlike TCP, UDP uses best-effort techniques when sending messages and does not provide any reassurance to the sender.

Therefore, no acknowledgment is returned to the sender on whether a message is received by the intended destination host or not. If a message were to be lost or dropped along the way, the sender would not be aware of it, and as a result, they would not retransmit any lost or dropped messages to the intended destination host.

If an Application-layer protocol uses UDP as the preferred Transport-layer protocol, a UDP Layer 4 header is encapsulated onto the data. *Table 1.4* shows the various fields of a UDP header:

Source Port	**Destination Port**
Length	Checksum

Table 1.4: UDP header fields

The following is a description of each field shown in *Table 1.4*:

- `Source Port`: This is a 16-bit field that indicates the source service port number.
- `Destination Port`: This is a 16-bit field that indicates the destination port number.
- `Length`: This is a 16-bit field that indicates the length of the header.
- `Checksum`: This is a 16-bit field used for error detection.

Figure 1.21 shows the UDP header using Wireshark:

```
˅ User Datagram Protocol, Src Port: 61125, Dst Port: 53
    Source Port: 61125
    Destination Port: 53
    Length: 39
    Checksum: 0xbad9 [unverified]
    [Checksum Status: Unverified]
    [Stream index: 0]
  › [Timestamps]
    UDP payload (31 bytes)
```

Figure 1.21: UDP header in Wireshark

While many Application-layer protocols and processes use TCP, the following are the advantages of using UDP as the preferred Transport-layer protocol:

- UDP does not need to wait for an acknowledgment from the recipient before sending more data on the network to the destination host. As the data is ready, UDP sends it. This is a benefit of using UDP for time-sensitive and real-time data such as **Voice over IP** (**VoIP**) and Video over IP technologies.
- Since the recipient does not send any acknowledgment messages when using UDP, there is less overhead on the network.

The following are the disadvantages of using UDP on a network:

- It does not provide a guarantee of the delivery of data between a sender and receiver.
- If data is lost during transmission, the sender does not retransmit lost messages.
- UDP does not assist in reassembling incoming messages if they are received in an out-of-order sequence.

Once either a TCP or UDP Layer 4 header is encapsulated onto the datagram from the upper layers, it is referred to as a **segment**. The segment is sent down to the Network layer of the OSI model for logical addressing.

Network Layer

The Network layer of the OSI model is responsible for assigning the logical addresses, which are the IP addresses, and inserts the source and destination IP addresses in the packet header. At the Network layer, either an IPv4 or an IPv6 header is encapsulated onto the datagram. This Layer 3 header, whether it is IPv4 or IPv6, enables the message (data) to travel across different networks until it reaches the intended destination host. To put it simply, when the segment is received from the upper Transport layer, the source and destination IP addresses are appended to the message to ensure devices such as routers and firewalls are able to route the messages to a remote device or the internet if needed.

Figure 1.22 shows a visual representation of encapsulating the Layer 3 header:

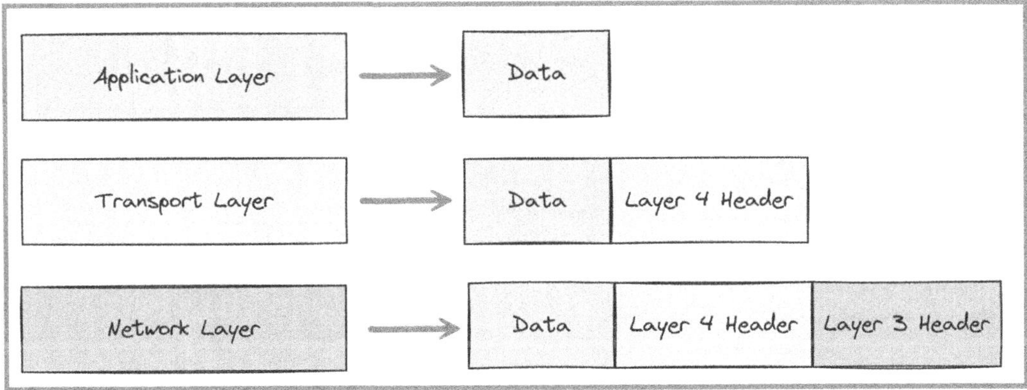

Figure 1.22: Layer 3 header encapsulation

On a network, each device is assigned or configured with an IPv4 or IPv6 address, which enables them to communicate outside their local network. For instance, if a destination host is located on the internet, the source and destination IP addresses play an important role as the destination address helps the router determine how to forward the message, while the source IP address helps the recipient to identify and reply to the sender.

Figure 1.23 shows the computer (sender) inserting the source and destination IPv4 addresses to ensure the server (recipient) receives the message and verifying that the destination IPv4 address matches the IPv4 address of the server. Once the Network layer of the server verifies the destination IPv4 address, it de-encapsulates the Layer 3 header of the packet before sending it upward to the Transport layer:

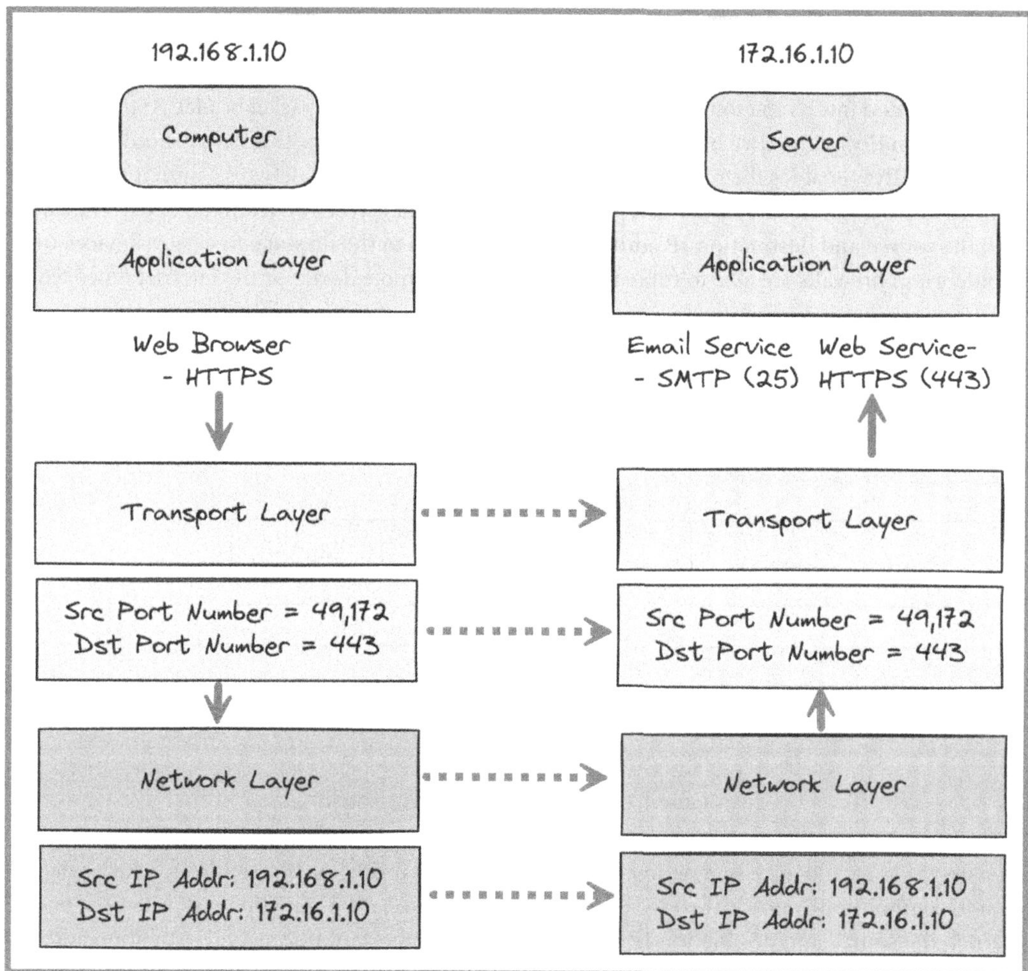

Figure 1.23: Importance of the IP header

> **Note**
>
> When an IPv4 or IPv6 header is encapsulated at the Network layer, the PDU is referred to as a **packet**. Additionally, IP is a connectionless Network-layer protocol that uses best effort to deliver packets to their destination. Therefore, it relies on the Transport-layer protocols for delivery.

Table 1.5 shows the various fields within an IPv4 header:

<table>
<tr><td rowspan="2">Version</td><td rowspan="2">Internet Header Length</td><td colspan="2">Differentiated Services (DS)</td><td colspan="2" rowspan="2">Total Length</td></tr>
<tr><td>DSCP</td><td>ECN</td></tr>
<tr><td colspan="4">Identification</td><td>Flag</td><td>Fragment Offset</td></tr>
<tr><td colspan="2">Time to Live (TTL)</td><td colspan="2">Protocol</td><td colspan="2">Header Checksum</td></tr>
<tr><td colspan="6">Source IP Address</td></tr>
<tr><td colspan="6">Destination IP Address</td></tr>
<tr><td colspan="6">Options</td></tr>
</table>

Table 1.5: IPv4 header

The following are the roles and functions of each field within an IPv4 header:

- `Version`: A 4-bit field used to identify it as an IPv4 packet.
- `Internet Header Length`: A 4-bit field that indicates the end of the header and the beginning of the data section.
- `Differentiated Services (DS)`: An 8-bit field used to identify the priority of the packet on the network. This was originally known as the **Type of Service** (**TOS**) field and contains the following sub-fields:
  - `DSCP`: This field, which stands for **Differentiated Services Code Point**, identifies the classification and management of the packet on networks that use **Quality of Service** (**QoS**).
  - `ECN`: This field indicates network congestion without discarding packets.
- `Total Length`: A 16-bit field that's used to indicate the total size of the packet.
- `Identification`: A 16-bit field that is used for identifying a group of fragments that belong to a single IP datagram.
- `Flag`: A 3-bit field used to control or identify whether the packet is part of a fragment group.
- `Fragment Offset`: A 13-bit field used to identify the sequencing position of a fragmented packet.
- `Time to Live (TTL)`: An 8-bit field that contains a TTL value that determines the lifespan of the packet on a network and prevents routing loops. The TTL value decreases by 1 when it arrives at a router along the path from the sender to the receiver. When TTL = 0, the packet is discarded.
- `Protocol`: An 8-bit field used to identify the payload type that's within the packet.
- `Header Checksum`: A 16-bit field used for error checking of the packet.

- `Source IP Address`: A 32-bit field indicating the sender's IPv4 address.
- `Destination IP Address`: A 32-bit field indicating the intended recipient's IPv4 address.
- `Options`: This 32-bit field is not always used by the Network layer.

A network protocol analyzer such as Wireshark enables you to inspect the fields and values of an IPv4 packet, as shown in *Figure 1.24*:

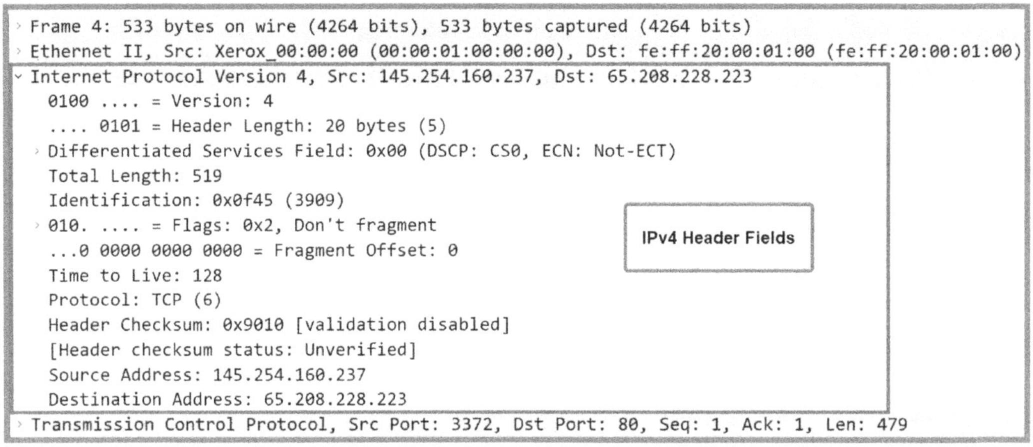

```
› Frame 4: 533 bytes on wire (4264 bits), 533 bytes captured (4264 bits)
› Ethernet II, Src: Xerox_00:00:00 (00:00:01:00:00:00), Dst: fe:ff:20:00:01:00 (fe:ff:20:00:01:00)
˅ Internet Protocol Version 4, Src: 145.254.160.237, Dst: 65.208.228.223
    0100 .... = Version: 4
    .... 0101 = Header Length: 20 bytes (5)
  › Differentiated Services Field: 0x00 (DSCP: CS0, ECN: Not-ECT)
    Total Length: 519
    Identification: 0x0f45 (3909)
  › 010. .... = Flags: 0x2, Don't fragment
    ...0 0000 0000 0000 = Fragment Offset: 0
    Time to Live: 128
    Protocol: TCP (6)
    Header Checksum: 0x9010 [validation disabled]
    [Header checksum status: Unverified]
    Source Address: 145.254.160.237
    Destination Address: 65.208.228.223
› Transmission Control Protocol, Src Port: 3372, Dst Port: 80, Seq: 1, Ack: 1, Len: 479
```

IPv4 Header Fields

Figure 1.24: IPv4 header using Wireshark

Some networks use IPv6 and the Network layer is responsible for encapsulating the right version of the IP header onto the datagram to ensure it is delivered to the intended destination host. Unlike IPv4, IPv6 has a lot fewer fields within its header, as shown in *Table 1.6*:

<table>
<tr><td>Version</td><td>Traffic Class</td><td colspan="2">Flow Control</td></tr>
<tr><td colspan="2">Payload Length</td><td>Next Header</td><td>Hop Limit</td></tr>
<tr><td colspan="4">Source IP Address</td></tr>
<tr><td colspan="4">Destination IP Address</td></tr>
</table>

Table 1.6: IPv6 header

The following are the roles and functions of each field within an IPv6 header:

- `Version`: A 4-bit field that identifies it's an IPv6 packet
- `Traffic Class`: An 8-bit field that has the same function as the `DS` field of an IPv4 packet, used to identify the priority of the packet on the network
- `Flow Control`: A 2-bit field, also referred to as the **Flow Label**, used to inform the routers on the network to apply the same handling for IPv6 packets that have the same flow control label
- `Payload Length`: A 16-bit field used to identify the length of the payload (data)
- `Next Header`: An 8-bit field used to indicate the payload type
- `Hop Limit`: An 8-bit field used to specify the TTL value
- `Source IP Address`: A 128-bit field indicating the sender's IPv6 address
- `Destination IP Address`: A 128-bit field indicating the destination host's IPv6 address

Figure 1.25 shows an IPv6 header and its field using Wireshark:

```
v Internet Protocol Version 6, Src: 2001:0:4137:9e50:8000:f12a:b9c8:2815, Dst: 2001:4860:0:2001::68
   0110 .... = Version: 6
 > .... 0000 0000 .... .... .... .... .... = Traffic Class: 0x00 (DSCP: CS0, ECN: Not-ECT)
   .... 0000 0000 0000 0000 0000 = Flow Label: 0x00000
   Payload Length: 12
   Next Header: ICMPv6 (58)
   Hop Limit: 21
   Source Address: 2001:0:4137:9e50:8000:f12a:b9c8:2815
   Destination Address: 2001:4860:0:2001::68
```

IPv6 Header

Figure 1.25: IPv6 header using Wireshark

Once the Network layer encapsulates the Layer 3 header on the data, it is sent down to the Data Link layer.

Data Link Layer

The Data Link layer is responsible for placing the datagram it receives from the upper layers onto the physical network. This layer of the OSI model takes care of managing how much data is placed on the wired or wireless network media for transmission and performing error detection for incoming messages from the physical network.

When the datagram is received from the upper Network layer, the Data Link layer encapsulates a Layer 2 header and trailer onto the datagram, as shown in *Figure 1.26*:

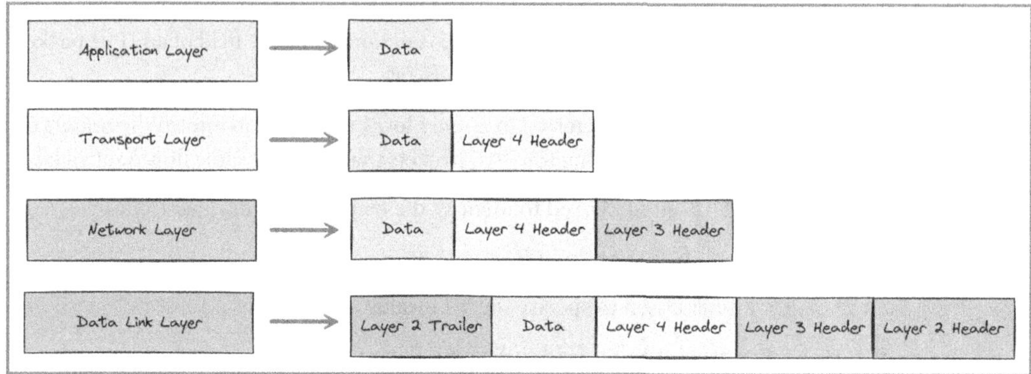

Figure 1.26: Layer 2 header and trailer

Figure 1.27 shows the various fields found within a Layer 2 header:

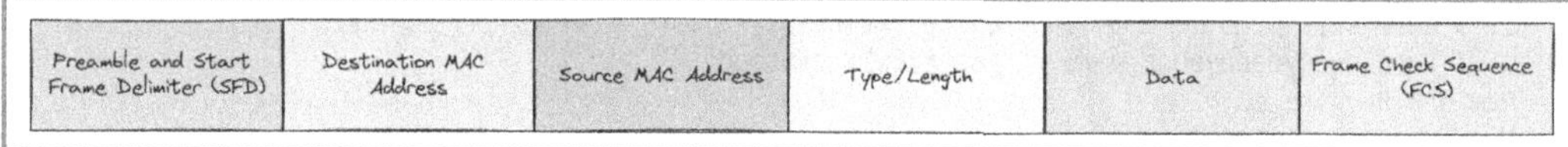

Figure 1.27: Layer 2 header fields

Now, take a look at the description of each field within the Layer 2 header:

- `Preamble and Start Frame Delimiter (SFD)`: The preamble is a 56-bit (7-byte) field used to indicate the start of the frame to the receiver and the SFD is an 8-bit (1-byte) field that's used for synchronizing messages during transmission from a sender to a receiver.
- `Destination MAC Address`: A 48-bit (6-byte) field that contains the Ethernet (MAC) address of the destination device on the local network.
- `Source MAC Address`: A 48-bit (6-byte) field that contains the Ethernet (MAC) address of the sender on the local network.
- `Type/Length`: This is a 16-bit (2-byte) field used for identifying the upper-layer protocol such as IPv4 or IPv6.
- `Data`: This is a 46–1,500-byte field that contains the data from the Application-layer protocol.
- `Frame Check Sequence (FCS)`: This is a 32-bit (4-byte) field that's used for error detection and integrity checking.

Within the Data Link layer, there are two sub-layers that are responsible for assigning Layer 2 addressing information and managing flow control. These are **Logical Link Control** (LLC) and **MAC**, as shown in *Figure 1.28*:

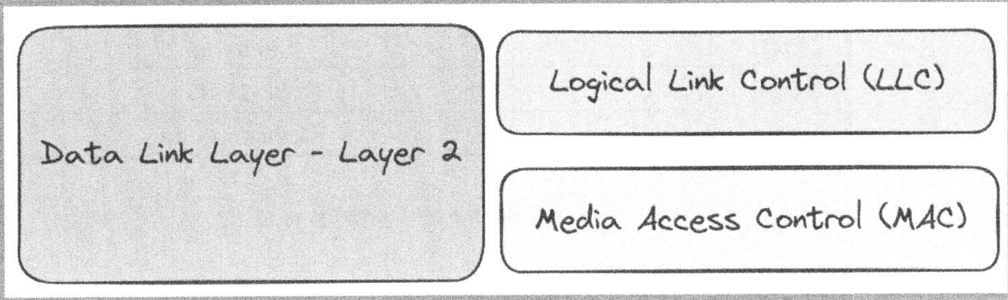

Figure 1.28: Layer 2 sub-layers

When the packet is received from the Network layer, LLC encapsulates it with a Layer 2 header that contains the Ethernet source and destination MAC addresses. In addition, LLC also appends a Layer 2 trailer to the end of the packet that contains the **Frame Check Sequence** (**FCS**). Once the packet is encapsulated with the Layer 2 header and trailer, it is referred to as a **frame**.

In addition, a mathematical representation of the contents of the frame, known as the **Cyclic Redundancy Check** (**CRC**), is stored within the `FCS` field of the Layer 2 trailer. The CRC enables the receiver device to perform integrity checks to determine whether the frame was altered or corrupted during transmission.

The MAC sub-layer of the Data Link layer is responsible for inserting the Ethernet addresses, known as the MAC addresses, into the Layer 2 header of the frame before placing the datagram onto the physical network.

> **Note**
>
> The Ethernet address is commonly referred to as the MAC address, **burned-in address** (**BIA**), and physical address. The Ethernet address of a host is commonly found on the **network interface card** (**NIC**) or network adapter.

A MAC address is uniquely assigned to each NIC on a device and it is unique globally. It is a 48-bit (6-byte) address that is embedded into the firmware of the NIC by the vendor who made the NIC or the device, such as a computer. This 48-bit MAC address is written in the form of hexadecimal, which ranges from 0 to 9, A to F. The first 24 bits of the MAC address are known as the **organizational unique identifier** (**OUI**), which helps network and cybersecurity professionals determine the vendor of a device once the MAC address is known. The other 24 bits are uniquely generated by the vendor of the network adapter.

Table 1.7 shows the various representations of a MAC address:

Organizational Unique Identifier (OUI)	Assigned by the Vendor
3 bytes	3 bytes
24 bits	24 bytes
00-E0-F7	58-1E-83
Cisco Systems	Device specific

Table 1.7: OUI portion of a MAC address

The following are common representations of MAC addresses from various vendors:

- `0060.5c3d.d901`: Format used on Cisco devices
- `00-60-5c-3d-d9-01`: Format used on Microsoft Windows operating systems
- `00:60:5c:3d:d9:01`: Format used on Linux-based operating systems

To easily identify the vendor of a MAC address, you can perform a lookup using any of the following online MAC address databases:

- `https://macvendors.com/`
- `https://www.wireshark.org/tools/oui-lookup.html`

Figure 1.29 shows an example of performing a MAC address lookup using the OUI lookup tool on the Wireshark website:

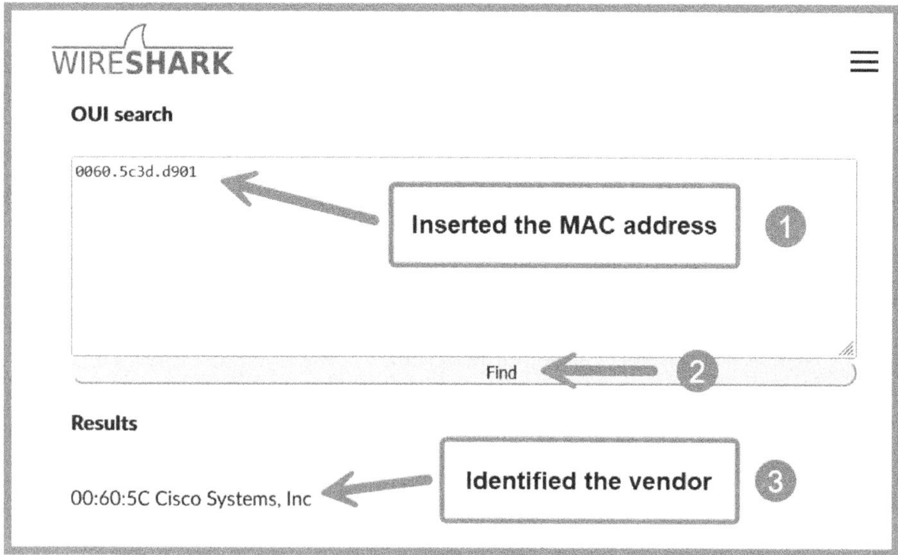

Figure 1.29: OUI lookup

Figure 1.30 shows the Ethernet header (Layer 2 header) of a frame using Wireshark:

```
˅ Frame 4: 533 bytes on wire (4264 bits), 533 bytes captured (4264 bits)
    Encapsulation type: Ethernet (1)
    Arrival Time: May 13, 2004 06:17:08.222534000 SA Western Standard Time
    UTC Arrival Time: May 13, 2004 10:17:08.222534000 UTC
    Epoch Arrival Time: 1084443428.222534000
    [Time shift for this packet: 0.000000000 seconds]
    [Time delta from previous captured frame: 0.000000000 seconds]
    [Time delta from previous displayed frame: 0.000000000 seconds]
    [Time since reference or first frame: 0.911310000 seconds]
    Frame Number: 4
    Frame Length: 533 bytes (4264 bits)
    Capture Length: 533 bytes (4264 bits)
    [Frame is marked: False]
    [Frame is ignored: False]
    [Protocols in frame: eth:ethertype:ip:tcp:http]
    [Coloring Rule Name: HTTP]
    [Coloring Rule String: http || tcp.port == 80 || http2]
˅ Ethernet II, Src: Xerox_00:00:00 (00:00:01:00:00:00), Dst: fe:ff:20:00:01:00 (fe:ff:20:00:01:00)
  › Destination: fe:ff:20:00:01:00 (fe:ff:20:00:01:00)
  › Source: Xerox_00:00:00 (00:00:01:00:00:00)
    Type: IPv4 (0x0800)
```

Ethernet Frame

Figure 1.30: Ethernet header

Once the Data Link layer completes its task, it sends the frame to the Physical layer of the OSI model.

Physical Layer

Before the frame is sent to the Physical layer, the Data Link layer hands over the frame to the network adapter or NIC of the sender's device such as a computer. The sender's network adapter is responsible for ensuring the frame is placed on the network media, whether the media is a copper cable, fiber optic cable, or radio frequency. Therefore, the entire frame is converted into bits that are represented as electrical signals on a wire or the radio frequency that is being transmitted on a wireless network. These bits are also represented as ones and zeroes when written in binary format.

Figure 1.31 shows the responsibility of the Physical layer:

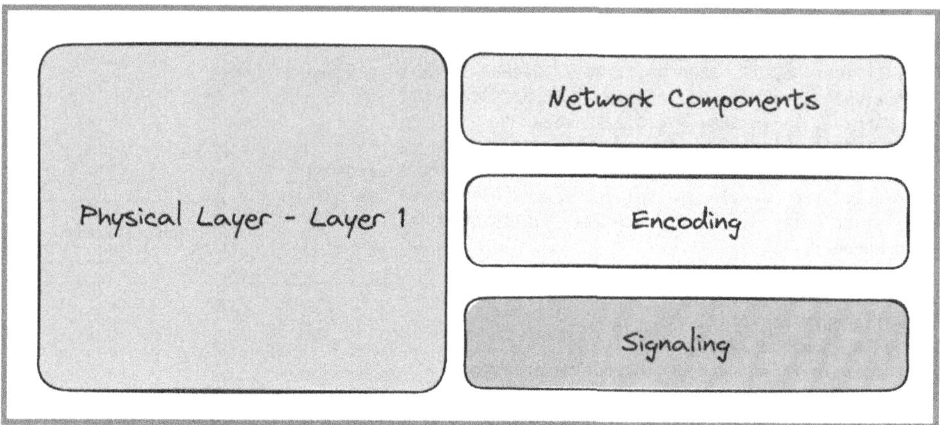

Figure 1.31: Physical layer

To put it simply, the ensure frame is not placed on the physical media. It is broken down into ones and zeroes. However, these ones and zeroes are sent as high and low voltages over a copper cable from the sender device, such as a computer to a network device. On the sender's device, the network adapter is responsible for encoding the frame into bits, creating a data stream that is recognizable by both the sender and receiver devices. Additionally, the network adapter is responsible for ensuring that the bits are converted into the appropriate signal to be transported over the network media.

For instance, if the network media is using a copper cable, then the signal is converted into electrical signals by the network adapter. If the network media is a fiber optic cable, then the network adapter converts the bits into light signals. Lastly, if the network media is using wireless communication, then the network adapter converts the signal into radio frequency for transmission.

The OSI network model did not gain enough traction to be widely adopted and eventually became a reference model. Hence, many network professionals commonly refer to the OSI network model as the **OSI reference model**.

TCP/IP Network Model

The TCP/IP network model was developed back in the 1970s and was adopted as the standard network model when the internet was officially launched on January 1, 1983.

Unlike the OSI model, which is a seven-layer model, TCP/IP has four layers, as shown in *Figure 1.32*:

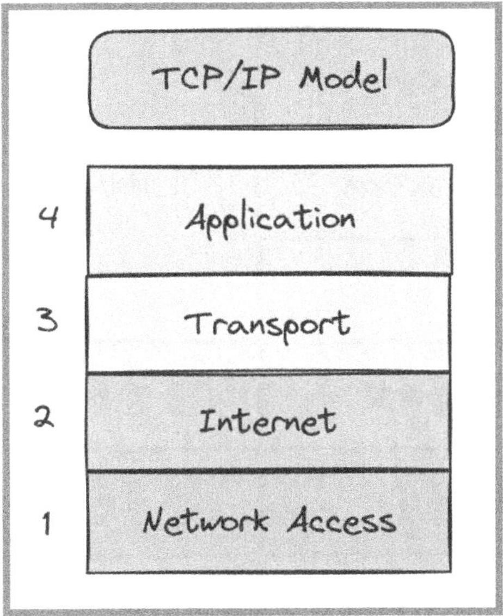

Figure 1.32: TCP/IP network model

When you compare TCP/IP with the OSI reference model, you will see that the Application layer of TCP/IP combines the role and function of the Application, Presentation, and Session layers of the OSI model. However, the role and function of the Transport layer in both TCP/IP and the OSI models remain the same. The Internet layer of TCP/IP is responsible for the **Internet Protocol** (**IP**) and routing, whereas the Network layer of the OSI model encompasses a broader range of Layer 3 protocols. Lastly, the Network Access layer of TCP/IP combines the roles and functions of the Data Link and Physical layers of the OSI model.

Figure 1.33 shows how the layers of the OSI reference model aligned with the layers of TCP/IP:

OSI Model	TCP/IP Model
7 Application	Application 4
6 Presentation	
5 Session	
4 Transport	Transport 3
3 Network	Internet 2
2 Data Link	Network Access 1
1 Physical	

Figure 1.33: TCP/IP network model

Lastly, keep in mind that TCP/IP is implemented on all network-connected devices, such as your computers, servers, laptops, IoT devices, smartphones, and networking devices. Next, you will learn about the role and function of common networking devices.

The Role and Function of Networking Devices

Networking devices are the essential components that help connect your systems, such as computers, laptops, servers, and even IoT devices, to the network and share resources. In this section, you will explore the role and function of various networking devices.

Network Hubs

In today's world, you will not find too many legacy networking devices such as network hubs. In the early days of networks, hubs were used to interconnect computers and servers to create a network for sharing resources. However, hubs are now obsolete and are no longer recommended to be used in any modern network.

You can now take a look at the operation of hubs to better understand the issues that made them obsolete. Whenever a connected host, such as a computer, sends an electrical signal over the wire to an interface on a hub, the hub will re-broadcast that same signal out of all other interfaces, except the interface that is connected to the sender.

To get a better understanding of how a hub forwards traffic on a network, take a look at *Figure 1.34*:

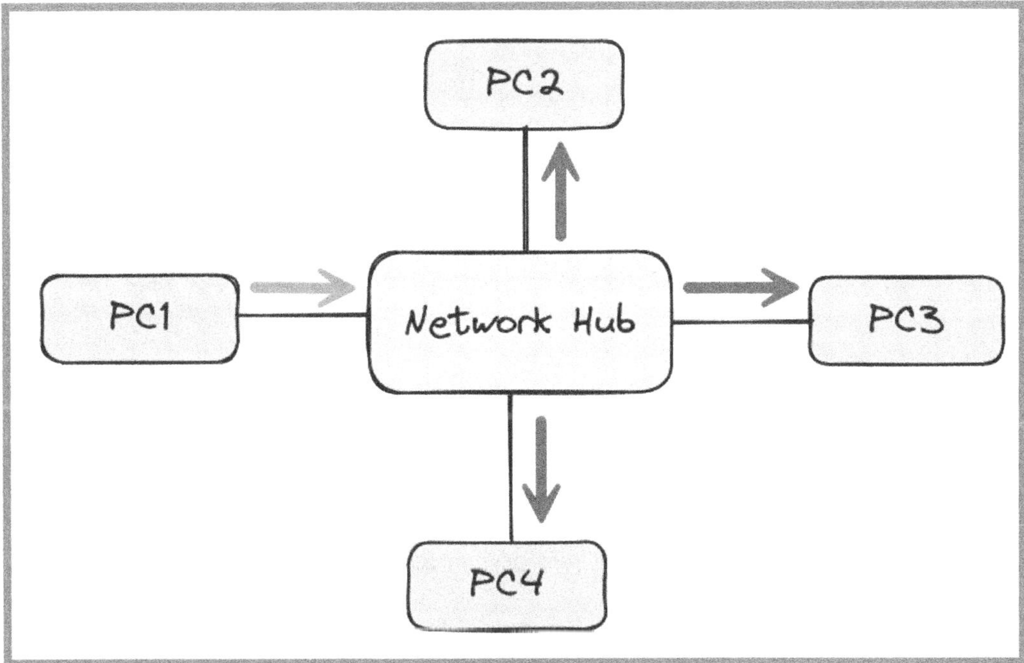

Figure 1.34: Operations of a network hub

As shown in the preceding diagram, there are four computers that are connected to a unique interface on the hub. In our scenario, **PC1** wants to send a message to **PC4** only. When **PC1** sends the message, in the form of an electrical signal on the network media, to the hub, it will accept the incoming electrical signal and repeat/re-broadcast the same signal out of all other interfaces such as those connected to **PC2**, **PC3**, and **PC4**. This means the message from **PC1** is also sent to unintended destination devices, such as **PC2** and **PC3**, on the network, which then creates both a networking and security concern.

First, try to understand the network performance issues you may encounter if there are too many hubs within a larger network. Any signal a hub receives is simply re-broadcasted out of its other interfaces. For instance, if a network professional were to implement multiple hubs that are interconnected to extend the local, internal network of an organization, each time one of the hubs receives an incoming electrical signal, it then sends the same signal out on all other interfaces, and this process is repeated on other connected hubs.

Figure 1.35 shows the replication of the broadcast traffic through a small network:

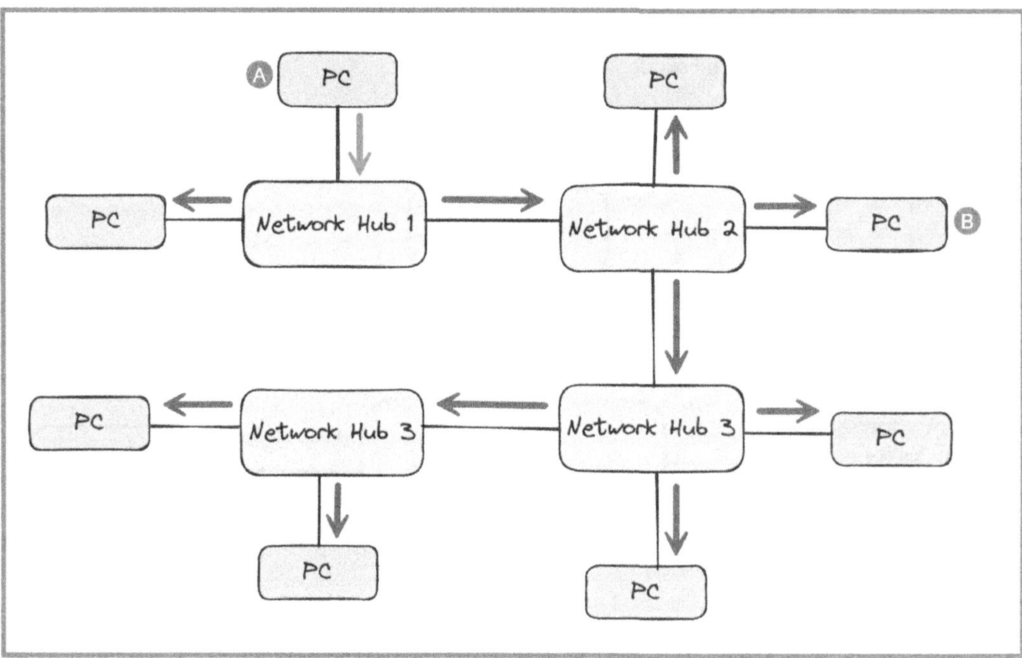

Figure 1.35: Broadcast messages propagating the network

As shown in *Figure 1.35*, the electrical signal from hub 1 will propagate to all the other interconnected hubs in the same manner, thus causing unnecessary broadcast (noise) traffic, which, in turn, will create network congestion and consume the available network bandwidth. Think of it as a roadway being filled with too many vehicles, resulting in heavy traffic.

What if two or more devices, such as computers, decide to transmit messages at the same time over a hub-based network? The result is the same as two vehicles colliding; in a network, this is known as **packet collision**. This results in packets being corrupted and requiring the sender to re-transmit the message again over the network.

To ensure no collisions occur over a hub-based network, only one computer can send their message at a time on the network. This creates a challenge because all other computers on the same network will be contending to use the network medium, thus creating a **contention-based network**.

To overcome such challenges, **Carrier-Sense Multiple Access with Collision Detection** (**CSMA/CD**) is implemented within computers and servers. CSMA/CD ensures that a computer checks the network media, such as the network cable, to identify whether an electrical signal is present or not. If it detects an electrical signal, it means another device is using the network and that it should wait until the network is signal-free. The computer will check again; if no electrical signal is detected on the network media (cable/wire), the computer will proceed to send its signal to the hub.

Network switches were developed to overcome these problems. Layer 2 switches are considered to be smarter devices than hubs. You can now take a look at the reasons for this.

Layer 2 Switches

Layer 2 switches are considered to be smarter devices than hubs. Switches are intermediary networking devices that operate at Layer 2 of the OSI reference model and are commonly used by network professionals for interconnecting end devices such as computers, printers, and servers and extending the network infrastructure within a building.

Unlike network hubs that re-broadcast an incoming signal out of all other interfaces, network switches create a logical network connection between the sender and destination devices to ensure that the messages are exchanged between the sender and recipient.

Figure 1.36 shows a small network where **PC 1** is transmitting a message to **PC 3** and the switch forwards the message only to **PC 3**:

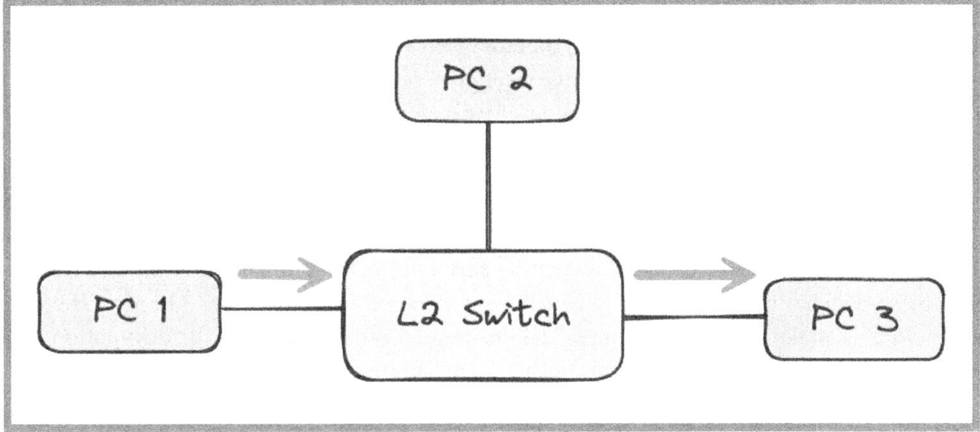

Figure 1.36: Functions of a switch

Since most network switches operate at Layer 2 of the OSI reference model, switches learn and store the source MAC addresses found in the Layer 2 header of a frame. These source MAC addresses are stored in the **Content Addressable Memory** (**CAM**) table on Cisco switches. However, the CAM table is commonly referred to as the MAC address table in general discussions.

Whenever a frame enters a switch's interface, the source MAC address of the frame is stored in the CAM table and is associated with that interface. To further understand how a switch populates the CAM table, take a look at *Figure 1.37*, with three computers that are connected to the same switch on different interfaces:

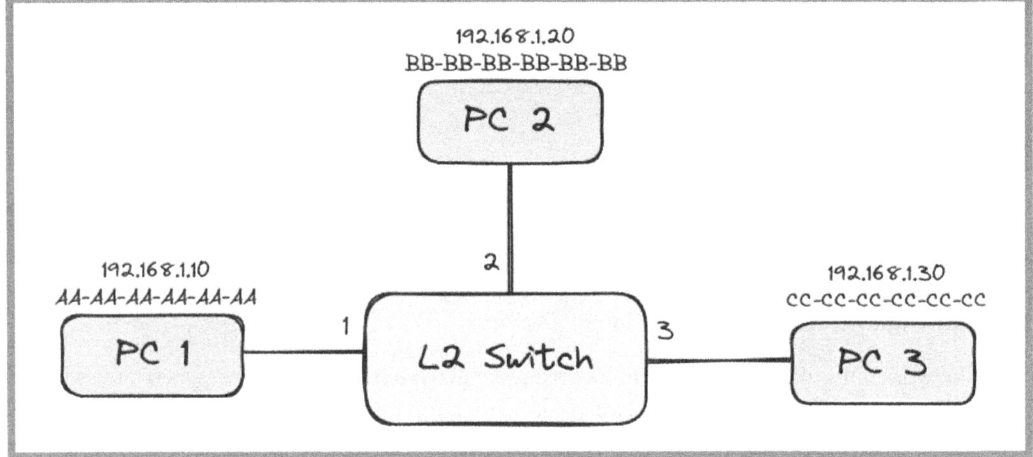

Figure 1.37: Devices interconnected using a switch

When a switch is powered on, the CAM table does not contain any entries because the contents of the CAM table are stored in **random access memory** (**RAM**). As you'll know, the content of RAM is temporary and it is cleared whenever a device loses power or reboots.

Assume **PC 1** wants to send a message over to **PC 3**. For many beginners in the field of networks, it's easy to think the IP addresses of both the sender and receiver are important to the switch, but they are not. While **PC 1** will insert the Layer 3 header with the source and destination IP addresses, the Layer 2 header will contain the source and destination MAC addresses and these Layer 2 addresses will be read by the switch. Since Layer 2 switches operate at the Data Link layer of the OSI reference model, these switches will not be able to read the information from the Layer 3 header. Therefore, Layer 2 switches make their forwarding decisions based on the contents of the destination MAC address found in a frame and the contents of their MAC address table.

Switching Concepts: Understanding the MAC Address Table and ARP

In this scenario, if **PC 1** already knows the IP address of **PC 3** but not its MAC address, what happens? In this situation, **PC 1** will send an **Address Resolution Protocol (ARP) request** message on the network, requesting any other device on the network with the IP address `192.168.1.30` to respond and provide its MAC address.

> **Note**
>
> ARP is a Layer 2 network protocol used to resolve IP addresses to MAC addresses on a local network. An ARP request message sets the destination MAC address as `FF:FF:FF:FF:FF:FF`, which informs the switch to broadcast this message to all other devices, except the sender.

Figure 1.38 shows the ARP request being sent through a network:

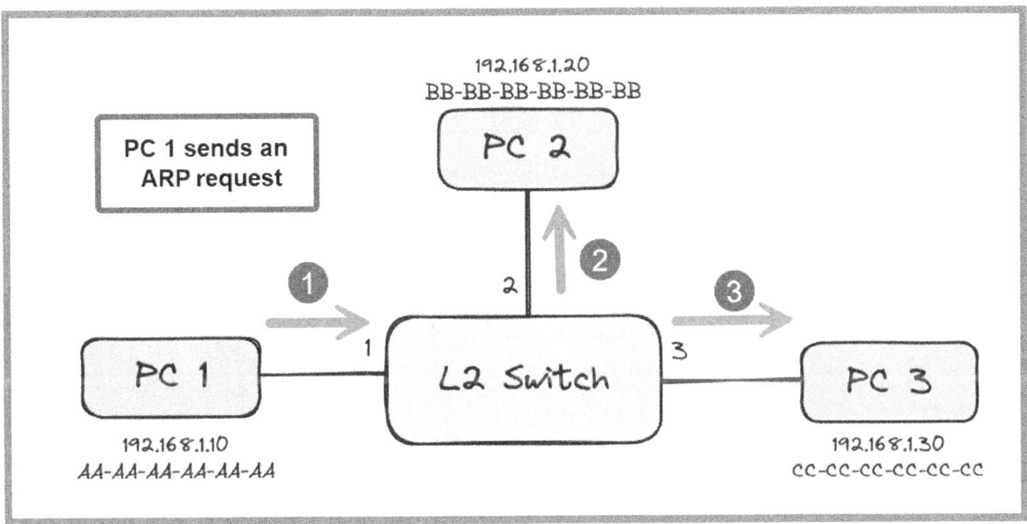

Figure 1.38: ARP request message

Each device on the LAN will receive the ARP request message. At this point, the switch receives the ARP request message on interface 1 and populates the source MAC address on the CAM table (MAC address table), as shown in *Table 1.8*:

Interface	MAC Address
Port 1	AA-AA-AA-AA-AA-AA
Port 2	
Port 3	

Table 1.8: MAC address table

The device that is assigned the IP address `192.168.1.30` will respond with an ARP reply message only to the sender, which is **PC 1**, as shown in *Figure 1.39*:

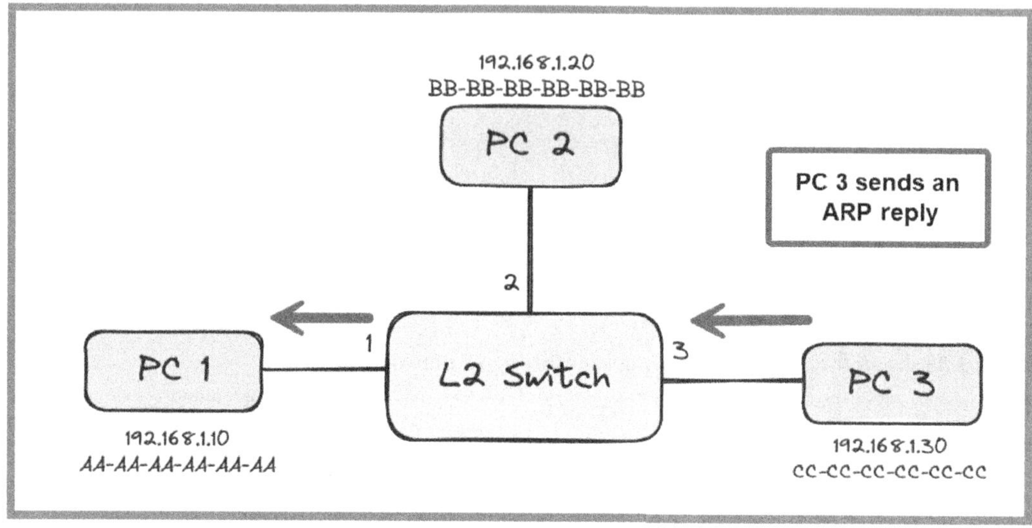

Figure 1.39: ARP reply

The ARP reply message is a unicast transmission (one-to-one) and is sent directly to **PC 1**. The ARP reply is sent only to the sender due to the following reasons:

- The ARP reply message contains the destination MAC address of **PC 1**.
- The switch already learned **PC 1**'s MAC address on interface 1 and recognizes that the destination MAC in the Layer 2 header of the ARP reply is associated with interface 1, as shown in *Table 1.9:*

Interface	MAC Address
Port 1	AA-AA-AA-AA-AA-AA
Port 2	
Port 3	CC-CC-CC-CC-CC-CC

Table 1.9: MAC address table

When **PC 1** receives the ARP reply from **PC 3**, it also temporarily stores **PC 3**'s MAC address with the associated IP address within its local ARP cache for 300 seconds, or 5 minutes. Once the destination MAC is known, it is inserted within the destination MAC address field of the Layer 2 header that is created by **PC 1**.

> **Note**
>
> On Cisco devices, the CAM table maintains a default inactivity timer of 300 seconds (5 minutes); this value can be modified. The default inactivity timer on Windows is also 300 seconds (5 minutes).

Switching Concepts: Frame Flooding

In this scenario, there are three computers connected to the same switch. **PC 1** already knows the destination MAC address and destination IP address of the recipient, that is, **PC 3**, but the switch MAC address table is empty and does not know which interface **PC 3** is connected to.

Figure 1.40 shows a visual representation of the network diagram:

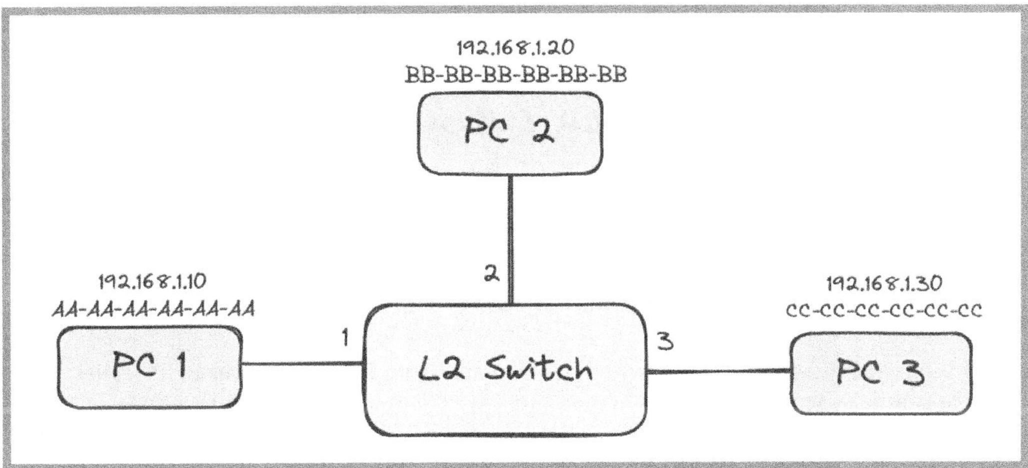

Figure 1.40: Network diagram

PC 1 will create the message and ensure that all the fields within Layer 2 and Layer 3 headers are filled with the appropriate destination addresses for **PC 3**. When the switch receives the incoming message from **PC 1**, it inspects Layer 2 and records the source MAC address under interface 1 within its MAC address table, as shown in *Table 1.10*:

Interface	MAC Address
Port 1	AA-AA-AA-AA-AA-AA
Port 2	
Port 3	

Table 1.10: MAC address table

Next, the switch will inspect the destination MAC address of the Layer 2 header and check its MAC address table to determine the location of the recipient. In this situation, the destination MAC address, which belongs to **PC 3**, does not exist in the switch's MAC address. Therefore, the switch will forward the message out of all other interfaces, except the interface that is connected to the sender (**PC 1**), as shown in *Figure 1.42*:

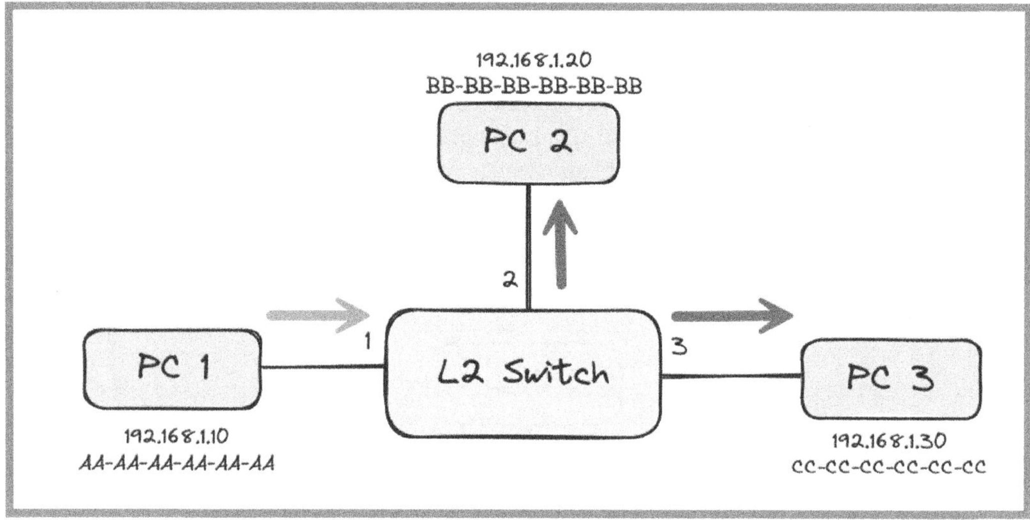

Figure 1.41: Switch sends traffic to all devices

If **PC 1** sends a request message that requires a response from **PC 3**, whenever **PC 3** replies, **PC 3** will include its own MAC address within the source MAC address field on the Layer 2 header. As a result, the switch will record the source MAC address from the incoming message and associate it to interface 3, as shown in *Figure 1.42*:

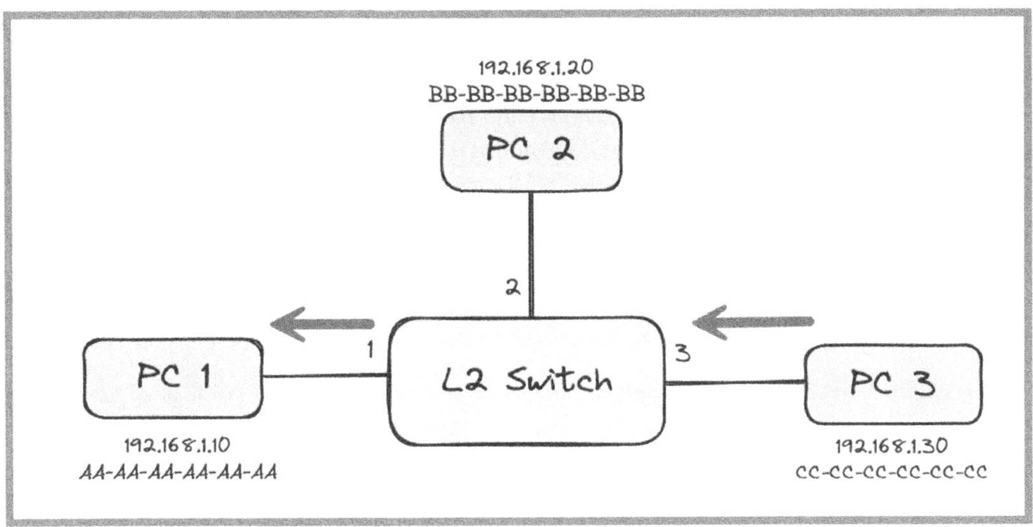

Figure 1.42: PC 3 responds

Table 1.11 shows that the switch has recorded **PC 3**'s MAC address under interface 3:

Interface	MAC Address
Port 1	AA-AA-AA-AA-AA-AA
Port 2	
Port 3	CC-CC-CC-CC-CC-CC

Table 1.11: MAC address table

Note

To view the ARP cache on a Cisco device, use the `show arp` command. To view the MAC address table on a Cisco device, use the `show mac-address-table` or `show mac address-table` command. To view the ARP cache on a Windows-based system, use the `arp -a` command. To view the ARP cache on Linux-based systems, use the `arp` command.

Next, you will learn about Layer 3 switches.

Layer 3 Switches

Layer 3 switches have all the same functionalities as Layer 2 switches. However, these devices have additional features. Since they operate at Layer 2 and Layer 3 of the OSI reference model, they are able to inspect the Layer 3 header of a packet and make their forwarding decisions based on the destination IP address of the message.

By default, the interfaces of a Layer 3 switch are configured to operate in Layer 2 mode. This means that they will inspect only the Layer 2 header of any incoming message and will make their forwarding decisions like a typical Layer 2 switch. However, these interfaces of a Layer 3 switch can be configured as Layer 3 interfaces, enabling network professionals to configure an IP address on each interface.

This enables the Layer 3 switch to perform both Layer 2 and Layer 3 operations within an organization's internal network, reducing the need for a dedicated router to forward traffic between networks.

Figure 1.43 shows a scenario with two interfaces, configured to operate in Layer 3 mode with IP addresses:

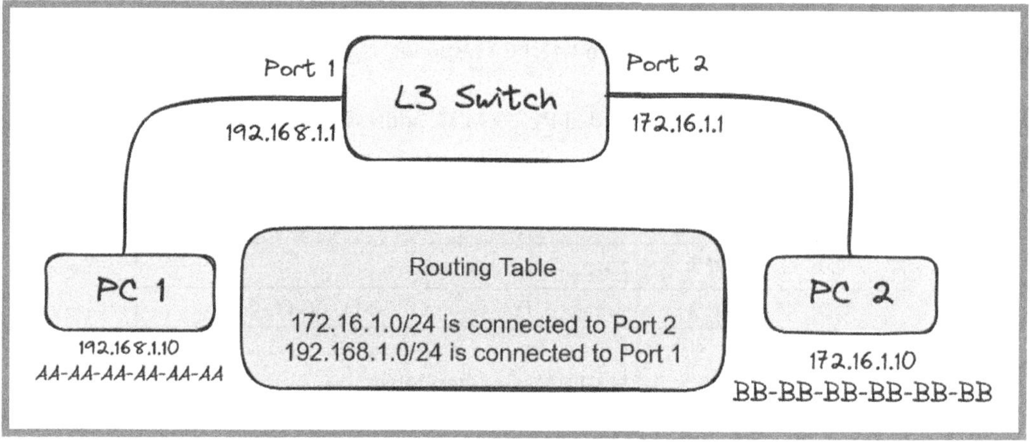

Figure 1.43: Layer 3 switching

As shown in *Figure 1.43*, **PC 1** is connected to the `192.168.1.0/24` network with a range of usable addresses from `192.168.1.1` to `192.168.1.254` and **PC 2** is connected to the `172.16.1.0/24` network with a range of usable addresses from `172.16.1.1` to `172.16.1.254`. In addition, **Port 1** of the Layer 3 switch is configured with `192.168.1.1`, which also acts as the default gateway address for any device within the `192.168.1.0/24` network, including **PC 1**. Similarly, **Port 2** of the Layer 3 switch is configured with the default gateway address for any device within the `172.16.1.0/24` network.

> **Note**
> In the world of IPv4 addressing, the network ID and broadcast addresses are not assignable to any device.

Therefore, when **PC 1** wants to send a message to a recipient that does not belong to its own network, such as **PC 2**, which is on `172.16.1.0/24`, it will forward the packet to the default gateway, such as the Layer 3 switch or a router.

Similar to a router, the Layer 3 switch has a **routing table** that contains routes to known destination networks. The Layer 3 switch will inspect the destination IP address within the incoming message, and will then perform a **route lookup** to identify whether the routing table has a valid destination route. Once a route is found, it will process the route and forward the packet out of the connected interface. If a route is not found, the Layer 3 switch informs the sender that the destination host or destination network is unreachable.

Lastly, Layer 3 switches can also perform Layer 2 switching functions based on MAC addresses. This provides dual functionality and distinguishes them from traditional routers on a network.

Routers

A router is a networking device that is used to interconnect two or more different networks together. Whether the networks are different based on their IP addressing scheme or media type, such as copper cables and fiber optic cables, routers are the specialized devices for connecting them and ensuring network traffic can be routed between them.

Routers operate at Layer 3 of the OSI reference model and inspect the destination IP address of the Layer 3 header of a packet. Routers then perform a route lookup in the routing table to identify a valid route to the destination host. As previously mentioned, the router has a **routing table** that contains routes to known destination networks. The router will inspect the destination IP address within the incoming message and perform a **route lookup** to identify whether the routing table has a valid destination route. Once a route is found, it will process the route and forward the packet out of the connected interface. If a route is not found, the router informs the sender that the destination host or destination network is unreachable.

The following diagram shows two different IP networks, `192.168.1.0/24` and `172.16.1.0/16`. Devices on the `192.168.1.0/24` network will only be able to intercommunicate with other devices that belong to the same IP segment, but not another IP segment; the same goes for devices on the `172.16.1.0/24` network, as shown in *Figure 1.44*:

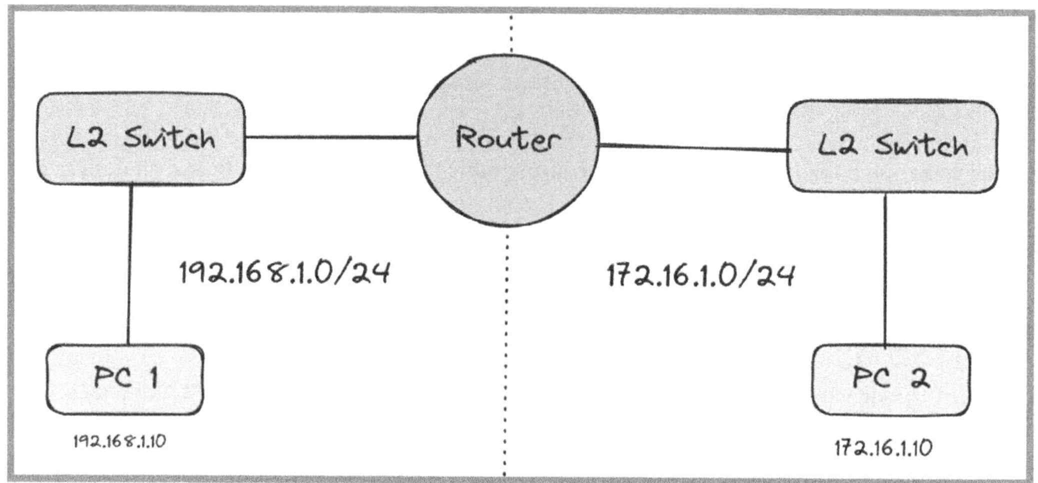

Figure 1.44: Router interconnecting different networks

To enable both IP networks to intercommunicate, that is, to enable devices from the `192.168.1.0/24` network to share resources with devices on the `172.16.1.0/24` network and vice versa, a Layer 3 device such as a router is required. The router enables interconnection between these different networks. Additionally, the router acts as the default gateway for each of the networks. This means that if **PC 1** wants to send a message to **PC 2**, the message must be sent to the default gateway address that is usually configured on the router's interface, which is directly connected to the same IP network as **PC 1**. Additionally, the default gateway address needs to be configured on **PC 1**. If **PC 1** does not have a default gateway configured on its network adapter, it will not be able to communicate with devices outside the `192.168.1.0/24` network.

You will read more about IP connectivity, such as static and dynamic routing, later in this book, in *Chapter 11, Understanding Static and Dynamic Routing*.

Next-Generation Firewalls and Intrusion Prevention Systems

A firewall is a network security appliance that is designed to filter malicious traffic between networks. These network security appliances are typically installed on the network edge of an organization's network and configured and tuned to carefully inspect all inbound and outbound traffic, looking for any security-related threats and violations of policies to help protect the organization from cyber-attacks and threats.

It is highly recommended that a **next-generation firewall** (**NGFW**) network edge is implemented. The internet contains millions of useful resources, from training videos to tutorials and community forums, to help you get started. However, there are many threats, such as malware and threat actors, that roam the internet and attempt to infect and compromise targeted systems and organizations. The firewall will act as the first line of defense against these threats that originate from the internet. However, it is a single line of defense, and a **defense-in-depth** approach is needed to ensure multiple layers of protection are implemented to safeguard an organization's assets.

Figure 1.45 shows the typical deployment of a firewall on a network:

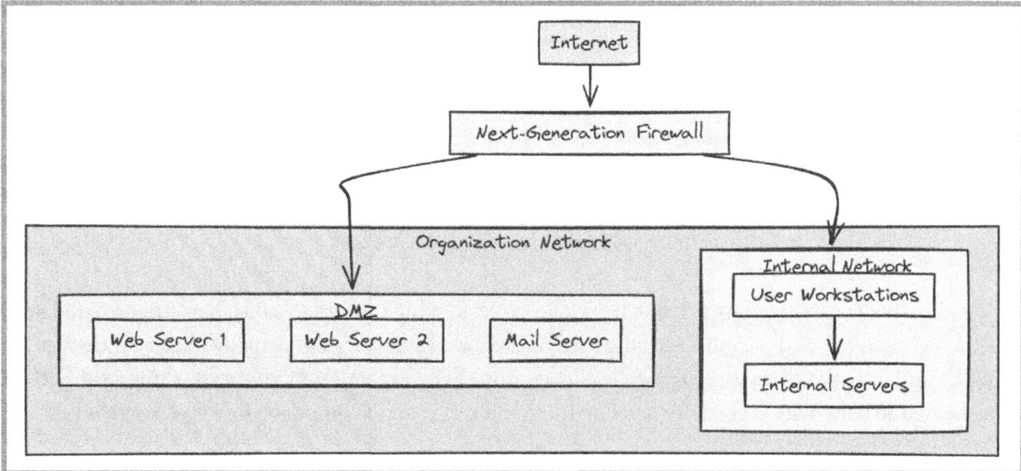

Figure 1.45: Perimeter firewall deployment

As shown in *Figure 1.45*, the NGFW is deployed between the internet and the organization's network infrastructure. In addition, one of the internal interfaces of the firewall is connected to the internal network, where the end users and internal servers are located. Therefore, another internal interface of the firewall is connected to the **demilitarized zone** (**DMZ**), a semi-trusted area of the network that enables external users or systems to access the devices within the DMZ while protecting the internal network from attacks and threats.

An NGFW is designed to be superior in many ways, such as protecting the network and users from advanced threats, providing **deep packet inspection** (**DPI**), which enables the firewall to decrypt messages and inspect the application data found within a packet, preventing ransomware from entering the network, and having **virtual private network** (**VPN**) features.

A firewall, by default, will allow traffic originating from the internal private network to all other networks, such as the internet. However, any traffic that is initiated from the internet to the internal network is blocked by default. The Cisco firewall uses the concept of identifying a **security zone** to help it determine the level of trust it has for a network. When deploying a Cisco firewall, the security engineer must assign each configured interface to a security zone and assign a trust-level value.

Figure 1.46 shows the default security level for a legacy Cisco **Adaptive Security Appliance** (**ASA**) firewall:

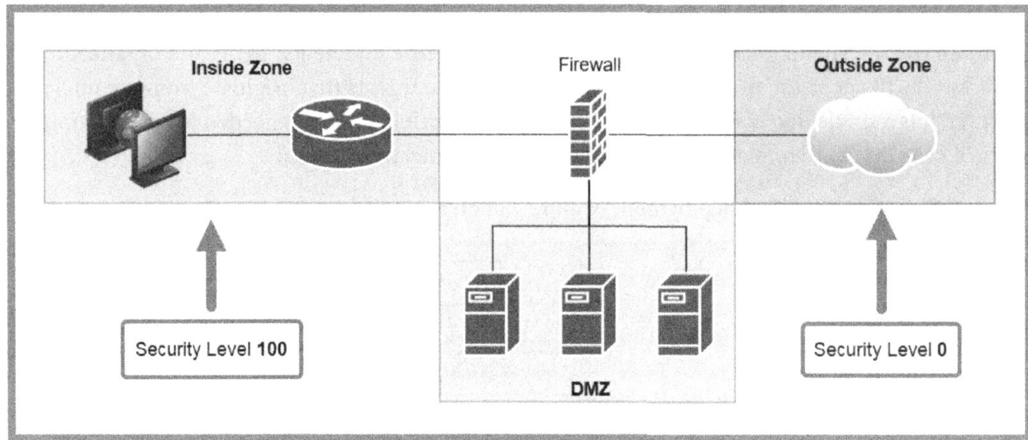

Figure 1.46: Security zones of a firewall

The **inside zone** is usually your private, internal network, which is supposed to be a fully trusted and safe environment for all devices in the corporate network. This zone will normally have a security level of 100 to indicate that it is a fully trusted security zone. The firewall will allow all traffic originating from the inside zone with a security level of 100 to all other zones that have lower security levels.

The internet, as you know, is the most unsafe network in existence, filled with extremely malicious malware and hackers. The internet-connected interface is usually assigned a security level of 0 and is known as the **outside zone**. Any traffic that has been initialized from the outside zone to the inside zone will be blocked by default on the firewall. However, keep in mind that if a user on the inside zone has initialized a connection to the outside zone, the firewall will allow it by default, and if there is any returning traffic, the firewall will allow it.

Note

The security-level schemes mentioned in this book are based on the Cisco security technologies.

The DMZ is a semi-trusted zone that is attached to the firewall on the corporate network. This zone is created to place servers that are accessible from the internet and the inside zone. The following are some guidelines for creating a DMZ on your network:

- The traffic initiating from the DMZ should not be allowed to access the inside zone.
- Rules should be created on the firewall to allow specific traffic to flow to the servers that are located in the DMZ.

- Ensure traffic initiating from the inside zone can access the DMZ.
- The security level of the DMZ should be between the values of the inside and outside zones.

However, within an organization, there may be multiple trusted zones that have a security level closer to 100. Therefore, you can consider assigning a security level of 50 to the DMZ.

Intrusion Prevention Systems

An **intrusion prevention system** (**IPS**) was previously a dedicated network security appliance that sat between the firewall and the internal network. However, as technology evolved, the IPS was integrated into the NGFWs and it now requires a subscription-based license to be enabled on commercial firewalls. An IPS is used to detect and block network-based intrusion attacks that are undetectable by firewalls.

Figure 1.47 shows how a firewall sends traffic for inspection to the integrated IPS module:

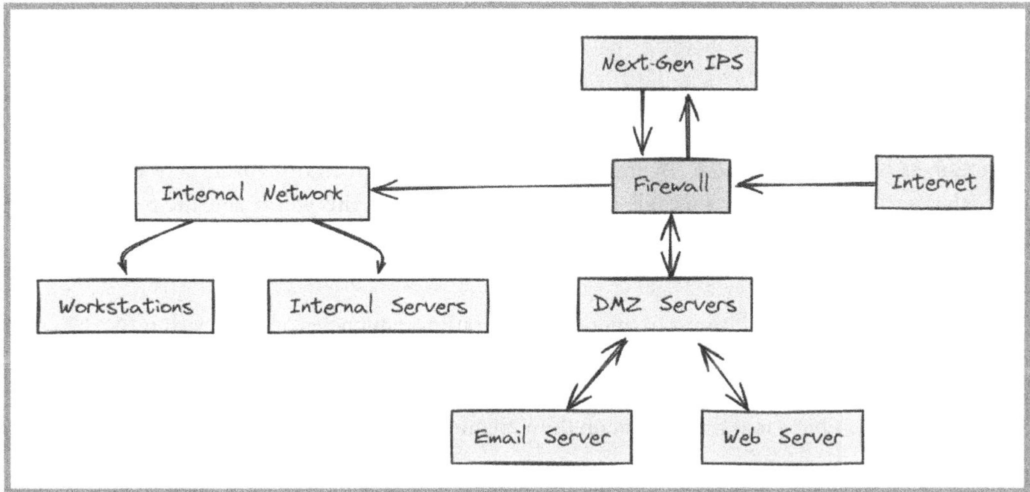

Figure 1.47: Traditional IPS deployment

With the advancement of technologies and innovation, Cisco has integrated their IPS into their NGFW appliances as a module. The benefits of this are reduced physical footprints, such as having fewer physical appliances and using a unified management dashboard for both the Cisco IPS and firewall.

The Cisco IPS downloads a database of malware signatures and **cyber threat intelligence** (**CTI**) from Talos, Cisco's security intelligence and research group. It uses this information to closely inspect all traffic flowing through it and identify any malicious traffic or anomalies. Additionally, the IPS can be manually configured with predefined rules created by a network security engineer. It also automatically learns the behavior of the network to catch suspicious traffic types. The benefit of having an IPS on a network is to detect malicious traffic and proactively stop it in real time, preventing the attack from entering the internal network of an organization.

> **Note**
>
> If you are interested in building your own IPS device, check out Snort at `www.snort.org`. Snort is an open source IPS application.

Unlike IPS, an **intrusion detection system** (**IDS**) is considered to be a reactive security solution. An IDS is configured to receive a copy of the network traffic, detect security threats, and send alerts.

An IDS is not implemented in line with network traffic like an IPS and does not have the capability to stop an attack as it happens in real time. Furthermore, the IDS sends an alert only after a threat is detected, which makes it reactive.

Now that you have learned about the functions of firewalls and IPSs, you can dive into understanding the role and function of access points.

Access Points

A **wireless access point** (**WAP**) is a networking device that enables users with mobile devices such as smartphones, IoT devices, and even laptops with a wireless network adapter to connect and access the resources on a wired network. By implementing WAPs within an organization, the mobility of users who perform work using a mobile device can be increased. This will enable the mobile user to roam around within the building and use any free office rooms. Additionally, implementing a wireless infrastructure within an organization reduces the need to install network cables.

WAPs use antennas that emit radio frequency. These radio frequencies operate within the 2.4 GHz and 5 GHz spectrum based on the **Institute of Electrical and Electronics Engineers** (**IEEE**) 802.11 standard for wireless networking. The IEEE 802.11 standard enables mobile devices with compatible wireless network adapters to transmit data on these frequencies between itself and an associated WAP.

The 2.4 GHz spectrum provides a lower frequency and provides greater distance. As there are many buildings and homes with WAPs that operate on the 2.4 GHz range, the radio airways of 2.4 GHz are now very saturated. Each device tries to transmit its data to clients without causing interference, but this has become almost impossible now. The 2.4 GHz band uses a total of 14 channels. While it was once recommended to use channels 1, 6, and 11 to minimize overlap and interference between WAPs, this strategy is no longer as effective due to the increasing number of devices and networks competing for the same limited frequency space. *Figure 1.48* shows the recommended clean channels of 2.4 GHz:

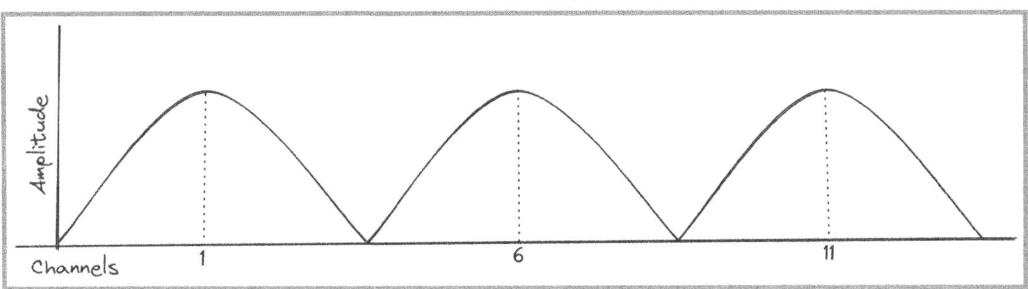

Figure 1.48: Wireless channels range

However, even this recommendation is no longer beneficial. A WAP can use channel 2, 4, or even 8, which will create an overlap (interference) between the recommended channels (1, 6, and 11).

The 5 GHz frequency provides a lot more channels, with 23 non-overlapping channels, thus creating less interference among nearby WAPs that are also operating on the 5 GHz frequency. The downside of using 5 GHz is the short distance the signal can travel. However, this may be a benefit. Imagine an organization that uses multiple floors to implement a 5 GHz wireless infrastructure to serve employees. Since the 5 GHz frequency travels much shorter distances as compared to the 2.4 GHz, this reduces the likelihood for the signal of a WAP to interfere (overlap) with another WAP that is within the same vicinity that is also using the same 5 GHz band.

More on wireless networking and architecture will be covered in later chapters of this book. Next, you will learn about the role and function of network controllers.

Controllers

Network controllers assist network professionals with centrally managing and optimizing the performance of their network infrastructure and improving their security posture. For instance, network controllers function as the brain of each network device within an organization. This means that the brain functionality of each switch, router, and even WAP is centrally managed by a single network controller.

The following are some common roles and functions of using a network controller:

- Centralize the device management of routers, switches, WAPs, and firewalls.
- Improve configuration management throughout the entire network infrastructure.
- Monitor and improve network performance.
- Monitor and improve the security management of networking devices.
- Monitor and diagnose network performance issues and assist with troubleshooting issues.

By implementing network controllers such as **Cisco Digital Network Architecture** (**Cisco DNA**) and a **Cisco wireless local area network controller** (**Cisco WLC**), network professionals are better equipped to closely monitor their network infrastructure and ensure that it is fully optimized, reliable, and secure at all times. Using network controllers also helps with automating configurations on network devices, monitoring network performance, and troubleshooting issues.

The Cisco DNA platform is an IP-based software solution designed by Cisco Systems to provide network professionals with applications they can use to manage, automate, and gather intelligence analytics, as well as monitor security, on a Cisco network across multiple devices and platforms.

A WLC provides a centralized management dashboard for the entire wireless infrastructure. This system enables network and security professionals to manage all associated WAPs on the network. For instance, a network professional can simply log in to the web interface of the WLC and configure the entire wireless network, and then the WLC will push the configurations to each connected WAP within a few minutes.

Endpoints and Servers

An end device or an endpoint is simply any device that is used by an end user, such as a desktop, a laptop, a smartphone, or even a tablet computer. End devices usually request services or access to resources that are usually located on a centralized system such as a server. Servers are dedicated systems on a network that provide resources and services to all endpoints and users on a network.

Power over Ethernet

Power over Ethernet (**PoE**) enables network media that supports electrical signals such as copper cables to carry sufficient electrical power from a source such as a PoE-enabled switch to a low-powered, PoE-supported end device such as a VoIP phone, an IP camera, or even a WAP. PoE allows both data and electrical signals to flow through a single network cable from the PoE switch to the receiver. Using PoE technologies helps reduce the need for additional power outlets within a room or building.

The following are some common PoE standards:

- **IEEE 802.3af** (**PoE**): This version of PoE provides up to 15.4 watts of power over a Cat 5 network cable and is commonly used to power up devices such as VoIP phones and WAPs.
- **IEEE 802.3at** (**PoE+**): This version of PoE provides up to 25.5 watts of power to support more power-consuming devices.
- **IEEE 802.3bt** (**PoE++ or 4PPoE**): This version of PoE is available in Type 3, which provides up to 60 watts of power, and Type 4, which provides up to 100 watts of power.

Figure 1.49 shows how powered devices such as VoIP phones and IP cameras are connected to a PoE switch:

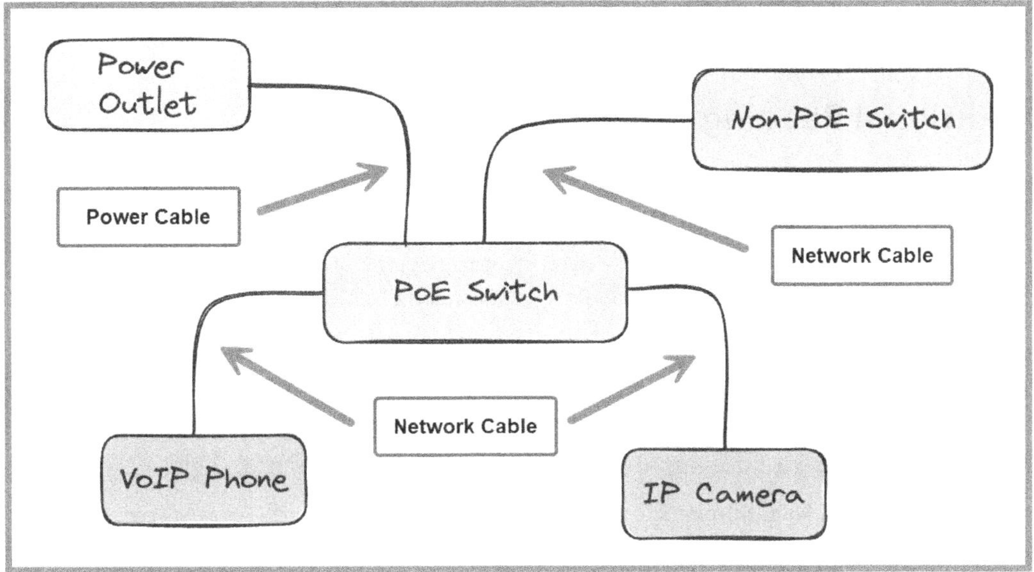

Figure 1.49: PoE switch

Having completed this section, you have learned about the role and function of various network components and systems.

Summary

In this chapter, you learned about the roles and functions of key network components, such as routers, which use IP addresses to forward packets to their destinations; Layer 2 switches, which manage the forwarding of frames and use MAC addresses to determine their forwarding decisions; and even Layer 3 switches, which perform both Layer 2 and Layer 3 switching and routing functions.

Furthermore, you've learned how NGFW and IPS solutions enhance the network security of organizations. You also gained a better understanding of their placement within a network topology. Additionally, you've discovered how various controllers, such as Cisco DNA, assist with network management and automation, while Cisco WLCs provide centralized management of a wireless network architecture.

Lastly, you've learned the function of each layer of the OSI and TCP/IP network models and what occurs as application data travels between a sender and a destination host over a network.

This chapter will help in your journey toward learning how to implement and administrate Cisco solutions and prepare for the *200-301 CCNA v1.1* certification. In the next chapter, *Chapter 2, Getting Started with Cisco IOS Devices*, you will learn about the common network designs, network interface types, and cables.

Additional Reading

- OSI model reference chart: `https://learningnetwork.cisco.com/s/article/osi-model-reference-chart`
- *Understanding TCP/IP*: `https://www.cisco.com/E-Learning/bulk/public/tac/cim/cib/using_cisco_ios_software/linked/tcpip.htm`
- The foundation of networking devices: `https://www.cisco.com/c/en/us/solutions/small-business/resource-center/networking/networking-basics.html`
- *What Is Power over Ethernet (PoE)?*: `https://www.cisco.com/c/en/us/solutions/enterprise-networks/what-is-power-over-ethernet.html`
- *What Is a WLAN Controller?*: `https://www.cisco.com/c/en/us/products/wireless/wireless-lan-controller/what-is-wlan-controller.html`
- Cisco DNA Center: `https://www.cisco.com/c/en/us/products/collateral/cloud-systems-management/dna-center/nb-06-dna-center-data-sheet-cte-en.html`

Exam Readiness Drill – Chapter Review Questions

Apart from mastering key concepts, strong test-taking skills under time pressure are essential for acing your certification exam. That's why developing these abilities early in your learning journey is critical.

Exam readiness drills, using the free online practice resources provided with this book, help you progressively improve your time management and test-taking skills while reinforcing the key concepts you've learned.

HOW TO GET STARTED

- Open the link or scan the QR code at the bottom of this page
- If you have unlocked the practice resources already, log in to your registered account. If you haven't, follow the instructions in *Chapter 19* and come back to this page.
- Once you log in, click the START button to start a quiz
- We recommend attempting a quiz multiple times till you're able to answer most of the questions correctly and well within the time limit.
- You can use the following practice template to help you plan your attempts:

Working On Accuracy		
Attempt	**Target**	**Time Limit**
Attempt 1	40% or more	Till the timer runs out
Attempt 2	60% or more	Till the timer runs out
Attempt 3	75% or more	Till the timer runs out
Working On Timing		
Attempt 4	75% or more	1 minute before time limit
Attempt 5	75% or more	2 minutes before time limit
Attempt 6	75% or more	3 minutes before time limit

The above drill is just an example. Design your drills based on your own goals and make the most out of the online quizzes accompanying this book.

First time accessing the online resources? 🔓

You'll need to unlock them through a one-time process. **Head to** *Chapter 19* **for instructions**.

Open Quiz	
`https://packt.link/ccnachap1`	
OR scan this QR code →	

2
Getting Started with Cisco IOS Devices

This chapter is where you start your journey learning about Cisco technologies, in particular, learning how to implement and administer Cisco solutions in an enterprise organization. One of the key components to ensure your success is gaining a lot of hands-on experience with Cisco devices. This hands-on experience helps you understand essential Cisco concepts (those that are covered in this book) easily and demonstrates the effect configurations have during the implementation phases.

However, a major challenge for most beginners is gaining hands-on experience during their learning and examination preparation phases. Another concern is getting access to Cisco equipment after classroom training hours or even when a training session has ended. To solve these challenges, this is a dedicated chapter to demonstrate how to build a Cisco lab environment that allows you to get the hands-on experience you need to get started with Cisco IOS devices.

In this chapter, you will learn how to get started with a Cisco IOS device by setting up a personal lab environment for honing your skills, accessing a Cisco IOS device, and building a small Cisco network.

In this chapter, you will read about the following topics:

- Getting started with Cisco IOS
- Accessing a Cisco IOS device
- Setting up a Cisco lab environment
- Configuring your first Cisco network
- Performing troubleshooting procedures

Time to dive in!

Technical Requirements

Lab files for this chapter can be found at: `https://packt.link/CCNArepoCh02`

Getting Started with Cisco IOS

Cisco enterprise devices, such as their routers and switches, have a networking operating system known as the Cisco **Internetwork Operating System** (**IOS**). Cisco IOS enables network professionals to easily manage and control the hardware components within Cisco IOS devices. Furthermore, Cisco IOS also provides the necessary software features to support a wide range of network functionalities, including routing, switching, and security. However, unlike most network operating systems and firmware that provide the user with a **graphical user interface** (**GUI**), Cisco IOS provides **command-line interface** (**CLI**) access only.

Additionally, the Cisco routers and switches have similar hardware components to computers, such as the following:

- **Processor**: A **central processing unit** (**CPU**) to execute network operations on the device
- **Memory**: Has limited **random access memory** (**RAM**) to temporarily store data and configurations while awaiting instructions from the CPU
- **Storage**: Uses either external or integrated flash memory
- **Network adapters**: Different models of routers and switches have various port densities (support for a number of ports)
- **Power supply unit** (**PSU**): The PSU is usually integrated into the motherboard of the device and is responsible for converting **alternating current** (**AC**) to **direct current** (**DC**)
- **Motherboard**: The motherboard interconnects all hardware components of the device and enables Cisco IOS to operate the hardware

> Note
>
> Cisco IOS is stored in flash memory. Using the `show flash` command will show all the contents in flash.

System administrators are required to understand each phase of the boot process of computers and servers, as this information is useful when troubleshooting any issues that may prevent the operating systems from loading properly. Similarly, both aspiring and seasoned network professionals are required to understand the boot process of Cisco IOS devices.

The following is the boot process of a Cisco IOS device:

1. **Power-on self-test** (**POST**): POST performs a check on all the hardware components to ensure they're all functioning correctly.
2. **Bootstrap**: Bootstrap is a simple application that's stored in **read-only memory** (**ROM**) that turns on the hardware components and locates Cisco IOS.
3. **Locating and loading Cisco IOS**: The bootstrap checks the following locations for Cisco IOS in the following sequential order:
    I. Flash memory (default location for Cisco IOS) – once Cisco IOS is found, it's loaded into RAM.
    II. **Trivial File Transfer Protocol** (**TFTP**) server – once Cisco IOS is found on a remote TFTP server, the Cisco device downloads it and runs it in RAM.
    III. If Cisco IOS is not found in flash memory or the TFTP server, then the bootstrap loads a scaled-down version of Cisco IOS into RAM, which provides the network professional with the capability to reload a full version of Cisco IOS into flash memory.
4. Providing the bootstrap locates Cisco IOS either in flash memory or on the TFTP server, it loads it into RAM.
5. **Loading configurations**: Once the full version of Cisco IOS is loaded into RAM, the device checks for the `startup-config` file that is stored in **non-volatile RAM** (**NVRAM**) and loads it into `running-config` in RAM.
6. If the `startup-config` file is not found, the device will enter the setup mode, which prompts the user to configure the device.
7. **Initializing services and operations**: Once Cisco IOS and the configuration files are loaded, the device will start various services and enable interfaces for operation.

Through these steps, you have learned how a Cisco IOS device boots into the operating system and loads its configurations into RAM.

> **Note**
>
> When configuring Cisco IOS, the configurations are stored within the `running-config` file in RAM. Since RAM is volatile and loses its contents when the device is powered off, it's important to save the configurations in the `startup-config` files that are located in NVRAM. However, saving `running-config` in `startup-config` is a manual process, which you will learn about in a later section of this chapter.

Figure 2.1 shows the boot process of a Cisco IOS device:

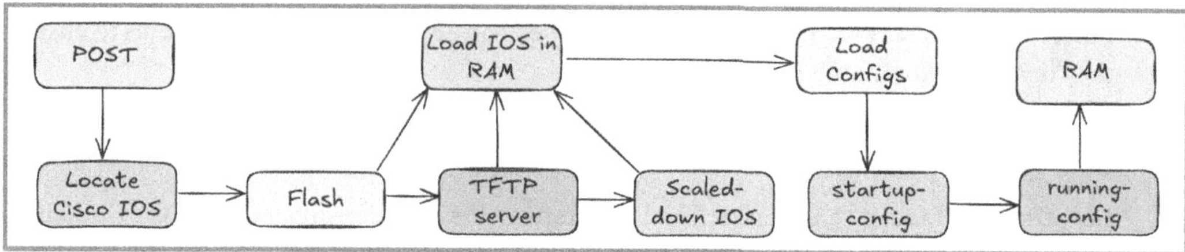

Figure 2.1: Boot process

Cisco IOS Modes and Levels of Access

Cisco IOS is a full-fledged network operating system that enables network professionals to control the hardware and other components of a Cisco device. In addition, Cisco IOS provides advanced security features to help network professionals improve their network security and prevent unauthorized access to Cisco routers and switches.

Cisco IOS has many modes or levels of access and each of these enables network professionals to execute specific commands. These levels of access/modes are as follows:

- **User Exec**: Upon accessing a Cisco device, Cisco IOS places the network professional into this mode. This mode has very limited capabilities and access to the device. With this mode, the network professional can execute commands such as `ping` and `traceroute` to troubleshoot connectivity issues.
- User Exec mode can be easily identified by the > prompt, as shown here:

```
Router>
```

- **Privilege Exec**: This mode provides higher privileges and enables the network professional to view the device's configurations and access the global configuration mode of Cisco IOS.
- The Privilege Exec mode can be easily identified by the # prompt, as shown here:

```
Router#
```

- **Global Configuration**: This mode enables network professionals to apply configurations and changes to the entire device and access interface, line, and router modes.
- The Global Configuration mode can be easily identified by the `(config)#` prompt, as shown here:

```
Router(config)#
```

- **Interface mode**: Interface mode enables network professionals to apply configurations on specific interfaces of the device, such as configuring the IP address and subnet mask on the interface.
- Interface mode is easily identified by the `(config-if)#` prompt, as shown here:

```
Router(config-if)#
```

- **Line mode**: This mode enables network professionals to apply configurations on the console port and the **Virtual Teletype** (**VTY**) lines for remote access.
- Line mode is easily identified by the `(config-line)#` prompt, as shown here:

```
Router(config-line)#
```

Figure 2.2 shows the various levels of access or modes of Cisco IOS:

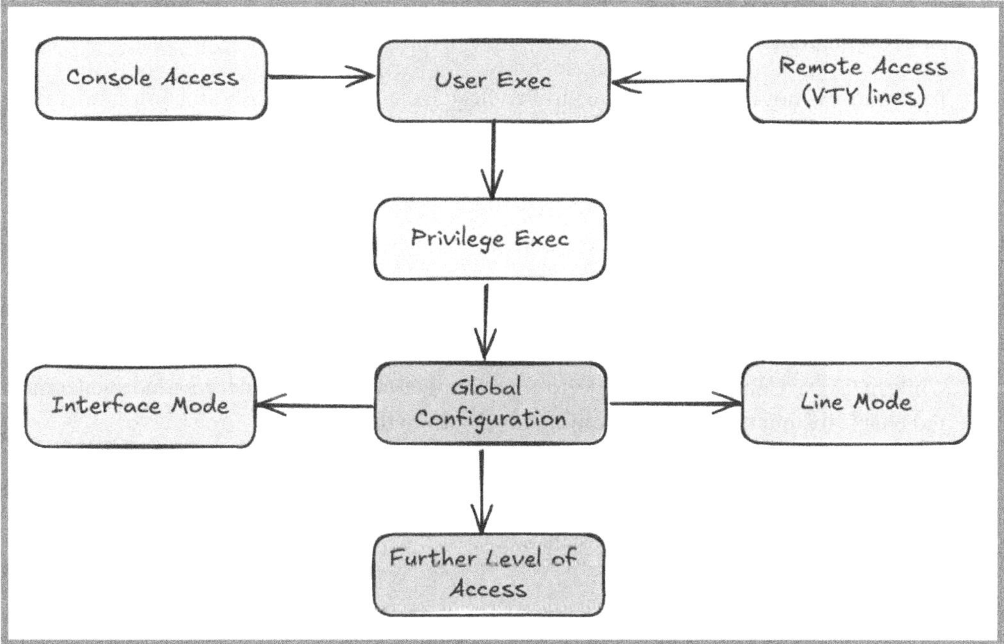

Figure 2.2: Cisco IOS modes

As shown in *Figure 2.2*, network professionals usually gain access to the User Exec mode via the console port or remote access through a VTY line using **Secure Shell** (**SSH**) or Telnet.

> **Note**
>
> SSH is a secure remote access protocol that enables network protocols to securely connect to a remote device over the network and obtain terminal access. By default, SSH encrypts the data between the SSH client on the network professional's computer and the SSH service that's running on the remote network device. Telnet is an unsecured remote access protocol that provides terminal access to networking devices. However, Telnet does not encrypt the data between the user and the Telnet service on the network device.

The following are examples of some common Cisco IOS commands for getting started with configuring a Cisco IOS device and moving around the different modes, such as User Exec, Privilege Exec, and even Global Configuration mode:

1. To elevate or move from User Exec to Privilege Exec, use the `enable` command and hit `Enter`, as shown here:

   ```
   Router> enable
   ```

2. To move from Privilege Exec to Global Configuration mode, use the `configure terminal` command and hit `Enter`, as shown here:

   ```
   Router# configure terminal
   ```

3. While in Global Configuration mode, to access an interface, set an IP address and subnet mask, and enable the interface, use the commands shown here:

   ```
   Router(config)# interface gigabitEthernet 0/1
   Router(config-if)# ip address 192.168.1.1 255.255.255.0
   Router(config-if)# no shutdown
   Router(config-if)# exit
   ```

> **Note**
>
> The `exit` command will return you to the previous mode. Therefore, if you're in Interface mode, you will return to Global Configuration mode. After typing a command, hit `Enter` on the keyboard to execute the command within Cisco IOS.

4. If you're in Global Configuration mode, use the `exit` command to return to Privilege Exec mode, as shown here:

   ```
   Router(config)# exit
   ```

5. Once you're in Privilege Exec mode, use the `disable` command to return to User Exec mode, as shown here:

   ```
   Router# disable
   ```

6. To save `running-config` into `startup-config`, use the following command:

   ```
   Router# copy running-config startup-config
   ```

The following shows an example of using all the commands in the preceding steps:

```
Router> enable
Router# configure terminal
Router(config)# interface gigabitEthernet 0/1
Router(config-if)# ip address 192.168.1.1 255.255.255.0
Router(config-if)# no shutdown
Router(config-if)# exit
Router(config)# exit
Router# copy running-config startup-config
Router# disable
Router>
```

> **Note**
>
> If you are in Router, Interface, or Line mode, using the `exit` command will return you to Privilege Exec mode.

Having completed this section, you have learned about the boot process of Cisco IOS devices and the fundamentals of navigating between various modes of Cisco IOS. Next, you will learn how to perform initial device access on a new Cisco IOS router or switch.

Accessing a Cisco IOS Device

Unlike computers and smartphones, networking devices do not support video output, which makes it necessary for network professionals to use alternative methods, such as remote access, to interact with Cisco IOS for administration and troubleshooting. Whenever you purchase a new Cisco IOS device, you will find a special blue cable within the box, known as a **console cable**. The console cable enables network professionals to gain initial access to Cisco IOS from a computer using a terminal emulator application.

Figure 2.3 shows a Cisco console cable:

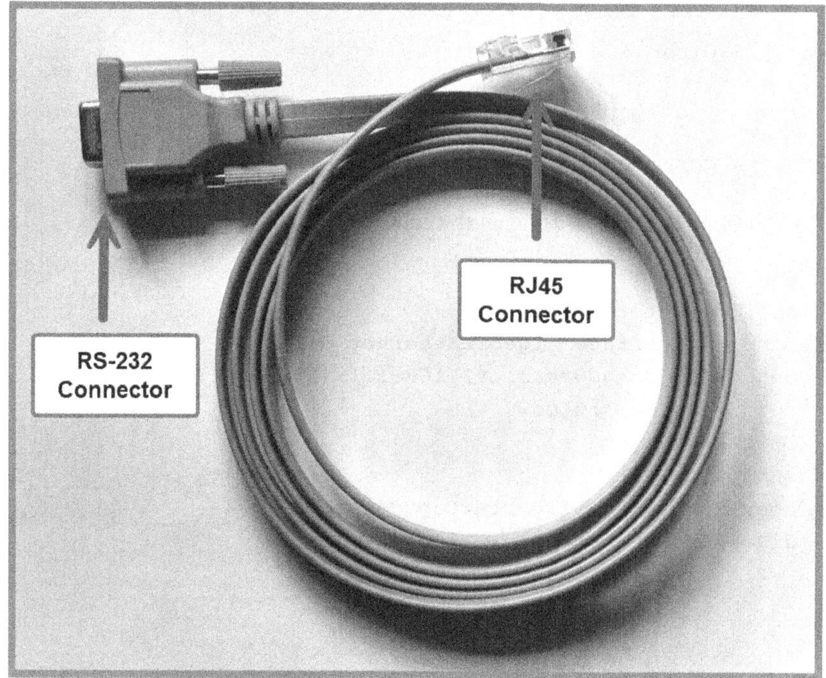

Figure 2.3: Cisco console cable

As shown in the preceding figure, there's an RS-232 connector that connects to a serial interface (DB-9) on a computer. However, modern computers and laptops no longer have a DB-9 interface to support the RS-232 connector. Therefore, network professionals may need to acquire an RS-232-to-USB converter cable to bridge the connection.

Figure 2.4 shows an RS-232-to-USB converter cable:

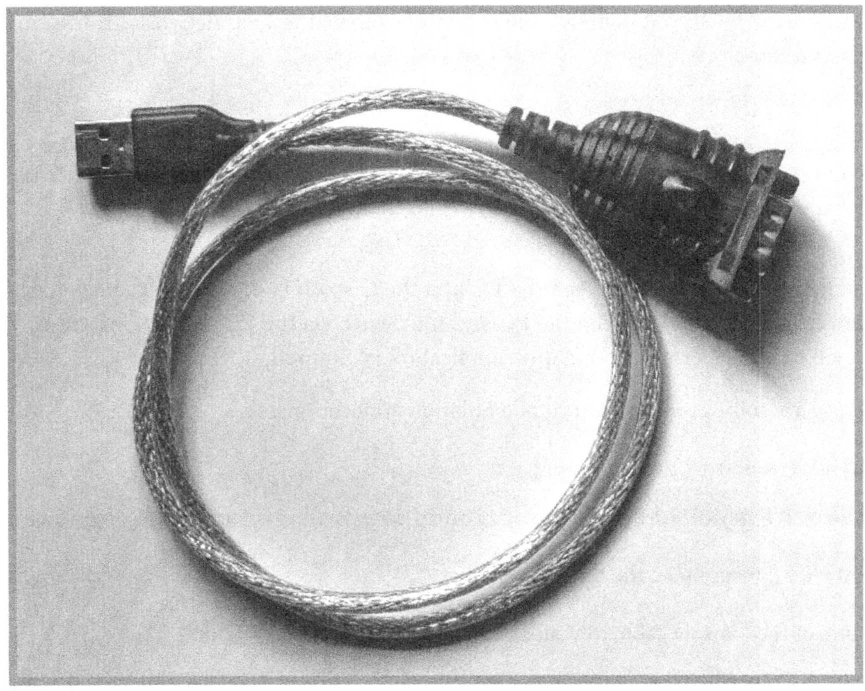

Figure 2.4: RS-232 converter cable

Additionally, the RJ45 connector on the console cable connects to the console port of a Cisco IOS device, as shown:

Figure 2.5: Console port

The console port of a Cisco IOS device will always be labeled to help network professionals easily identify the interface.

> **Note**
>
> Keep in mind that you will need to use a console cable to gain initial access to a device that has not been configured for remote access and management.

Upon making the connection between the PC and the Cisco IOS device using the console cable, a serial connection is created between the PC and the device via the RS-232-to-USB cable. To access the CLI of Cisco IOS, a terminal emulation application is required.

The following are some common terminal emulation applications:

- **PuTTY (free)**: `https://www.putty.org/`
- **SecureCRT (paid)**: `https://www.vandyke.com/products/securecrt/`

To access the CLI, please take the following steps:

1. Connect the console cable to your laptop and the Cisco IOS device.
2. If you're using Microsoft Windows, open `Control Panel` and click on `Device Manager`.
3. Expand the `Port (COM & LPT)` category to view which COM interface is assigned to the cable.
4. *Figure 2.6* shows COM3 is being utilized on the computer:

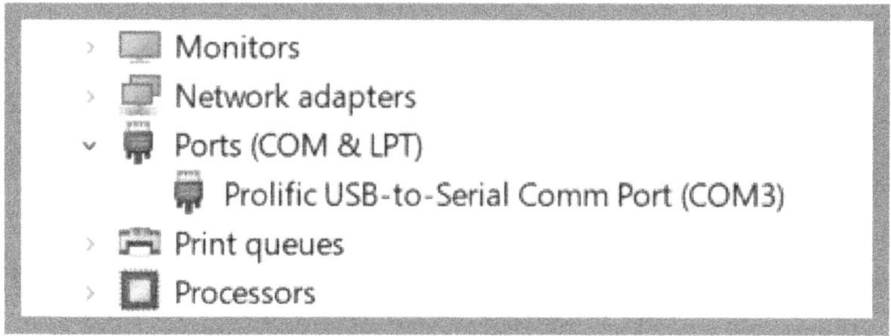

Figure 2.6: Device Manager on Windows

> **Note**
>
> If the serial connection does not appear, ensure the latest drivers are installed for the cable on your computer. Additionally, the COM port number may be different when the cable is connected to your computer.

5. Next, download PuTTY on your computer and launch the application. Once PuTTY opens, use the following settings:

    - `Connection type`: `Serial`
    - `Serial line`: `COM3` (change this accordingly)
    - `Speed`: `9600`
    - `Data bits`: `8`
    - `Parity`: `None`
    - `Stop bit`: `1`
    - `Flow control`: `None`

> **Note**
>
> PuTTY can be downloaded via the Microsoft Store application on Microsoft Windows operating systems.

6. *Figure 2.7* shows the PuTTY Configuration window:

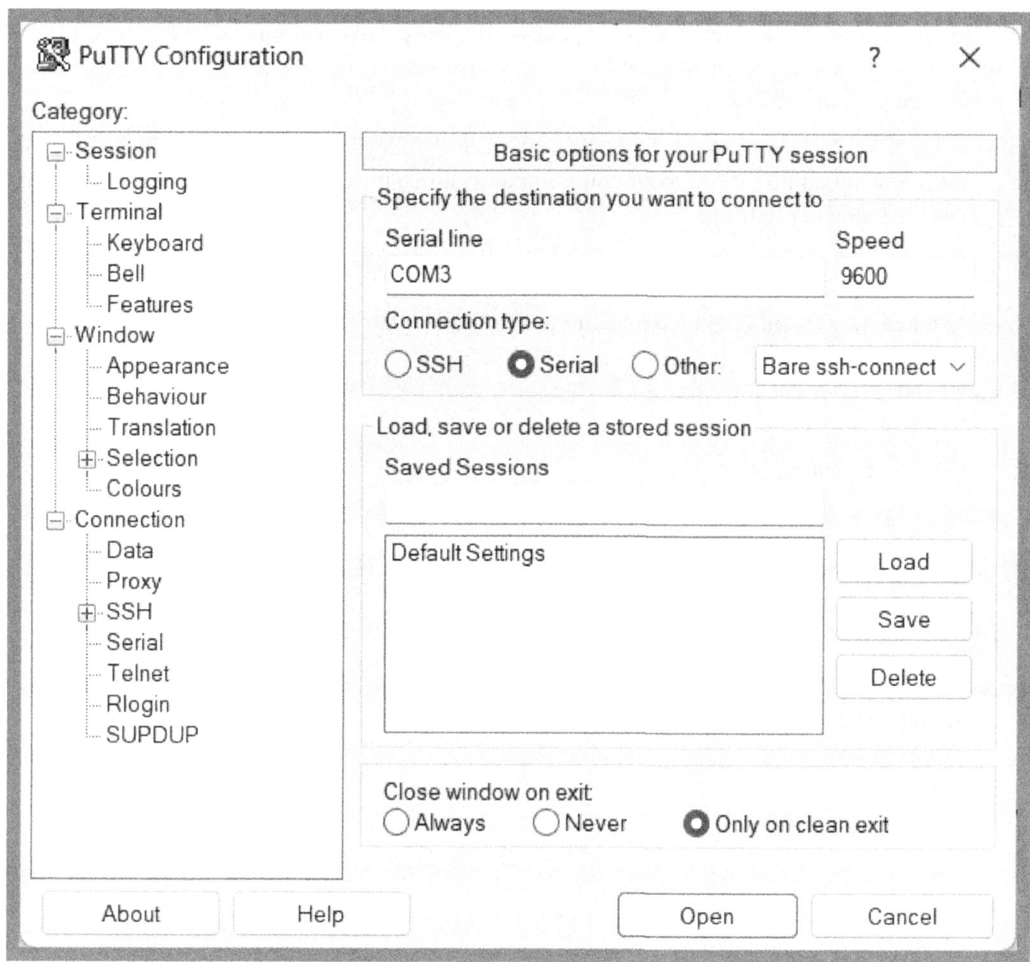

Figure 2.7: PuTTY on Windows

7. Next, click on `Open` to establish the serial connection from PuTTY through the console cable to Cisco IOS.

8. *Figure 2.8* shows the typical welcome screen when connecting to Cisco IOS:

```
C2960 Boot Loader (C2960-HBOOT-M) Version 12.2(25r)FX, RELEASE SOFTWARE (fc4)
Cisco WS-C2960-24TT (RC32300) processor (revision C0) with 21039K bytes of memory.
2960-24TT starting...
Base ethernet MAC Address: 0002.1600.1603
Xmodem file system is available.
Initializing Flash...
flashfs[0]: 1 files, 0 directories
flashfs[0]: 0 orphaned files, 0 orphaned directories
flashfs[0]: Total bytes: 64016384
flashfs[0]: Bytes used: 4670455
flashfs[0]: Bytes available: 59345929
flashfs[0]: flashfs fsck took 1 seconds.
...done Initializing Flash.

Boot Sector Filesystem (bs:) installed, fsid: 3
Parameter Block Filesystem (pb:) installed, fsid: 4


Loading "flash:/2960-lanbasek9-mz.150-2.SE4.bin"...
########################################################################## [OK]
Smart Init is enabled
smart init is sizing iomem
                  TYPE      MEMORY_REQ
                TOTAL:      0x00000000
Rounded IOMEM up to: 0Mb.
Using 6 percent iomem. [0Mb/512Mb]

              Restricted Rights Legend
Use, duplication, or disclosure by the Government is
subject to restrictions as set forth in subparagraph
(c) of the Commercial Computer Software - Restricted
Rights clause at FAR sec. 52.227-19 and subparagraph
(c) (1) (ii) of the Rights in Technical Data and Computer
Software clause at DFARS sec. 252.227-7013.
           cisco Systems, Inc.
```

Figure 2.8: CLI of a Cisco IOS router

Now that you have learned how to access a Cisco IOS device using the console cable, take a look at acquiring the Cisco Packet Tracer application, a network simulator built by Cisco for learning for the **Cisco Certified Network Associate** (**CCNA**) certification.

Setting Up a Cisco Lab Environment

Learning about networking can be a lot of fun and leveraging your imagination enables you to design, configure, and troubleshoot complex network architectures. However, as an aspiring network professional and candidate for the CCNA certification, it is important to gain a lot of practical, hands-on experience in implementing and administering Cisco devices. This means that everything you learn, in theory, should be applied to a practical lab to help you gain a solid understanding of the topic.

To assist with creating a lab environment, Cisco has created a very powerful network simulator application for students who are pursuing the CCNA certification. It is called **Packet Tracer** and it is available to anyone for free. The Cisco Packet Tracer application helps students design, configure, and troubleshoot real-world Cisco architectures without the need to acquire expensive physical devices. Most importantly, the Cisco Packet Tracer commands used on devices within the application can be easily copied and pasted into real Cisco devices.

Lab: Getting the Cisco Packet Tracer Application

To get your hands on the Cisco Packet Tracer application, please follow the given steps:

1. On your host computer, go to `https://www.netacad.com/courses/getting-started-cisco-packet-tracer` and click on the `Get Started With Self-Paced` button, as shown in *Figure 2.9*:

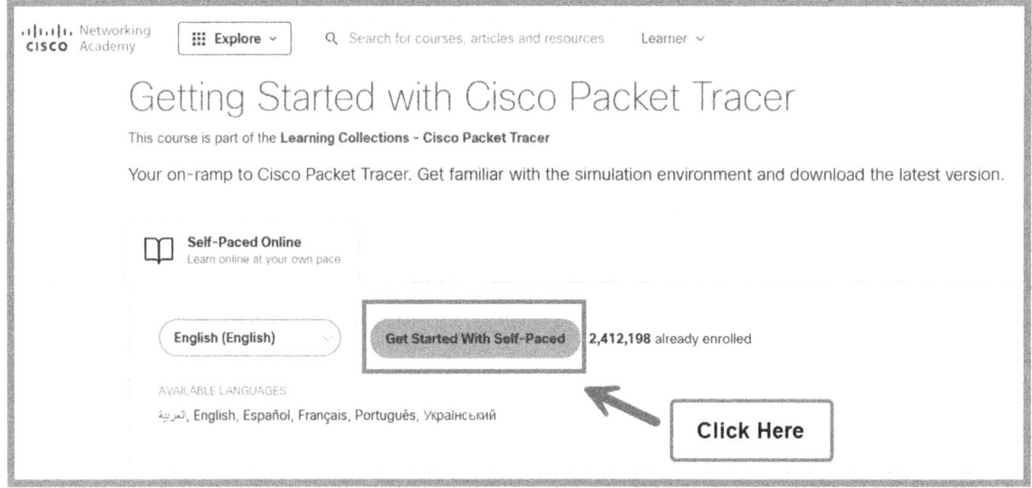

Figure 2.9: Packet Tracer course

2. Next, click on the `Sign up` link to register for a free user account on the platform, as shown in *Figure 2.10*:

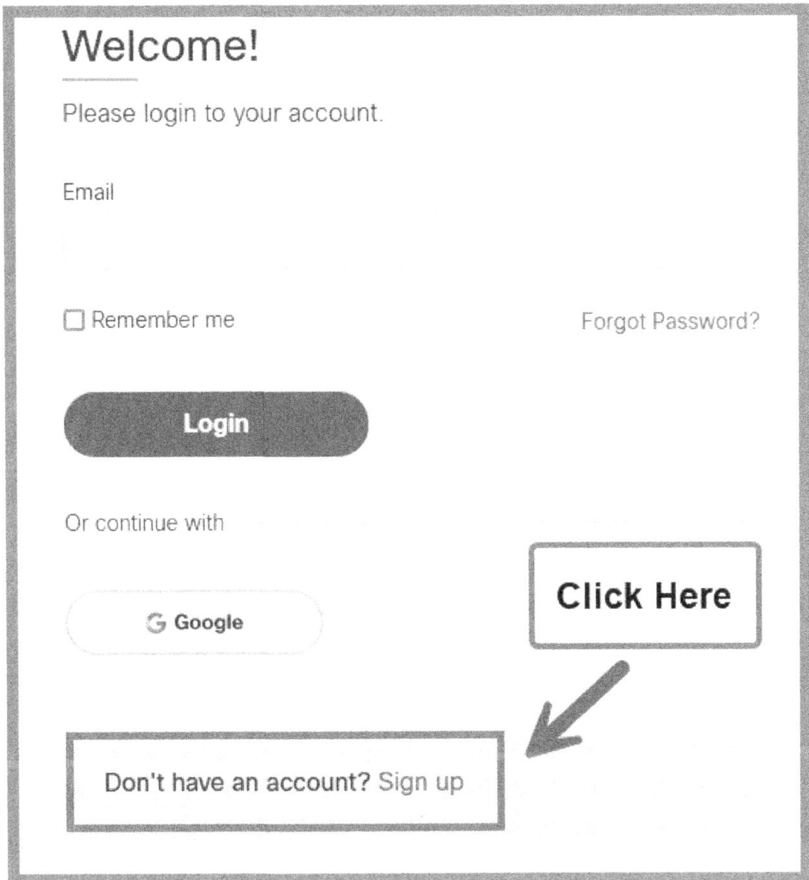

Figure 2.10: Login portal

3. Complete the sign-up form to create a new account.
4. Once the account is created, the `Terms and Conditions` window will appear. Ensure you read and accept them to proceed to the next step.

5. On the `Course Outline` tab, click on `1.0.3 Download Cisco Packet Tracer` to access the download link for the Cisco Packet Tracer application, as shown in *Figure 2.11*:

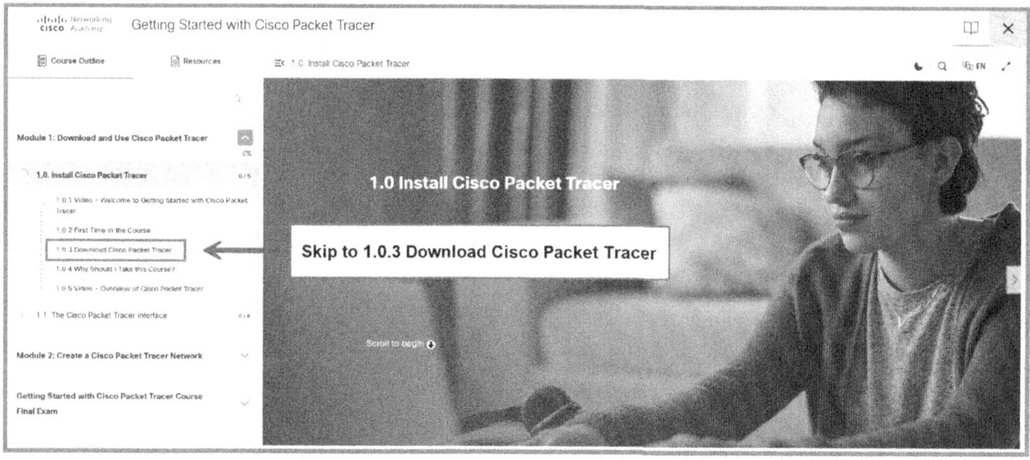

Figure 2.11: Course platform

> **Note**
>
> I strongly suggest that you complete the `Getting Started with Cisco Packet Tracer` course at *step 5* before proceeding further. The course will help you become familiar with the user interface to ensure you can find your way around the application.

6. Alternatively, you can go to `https://www.netacad.com/resources/lab-downloads` to download the version of Packet Tracer that's compatible with your computer's operating system, as shown in *Figure 2.12*:

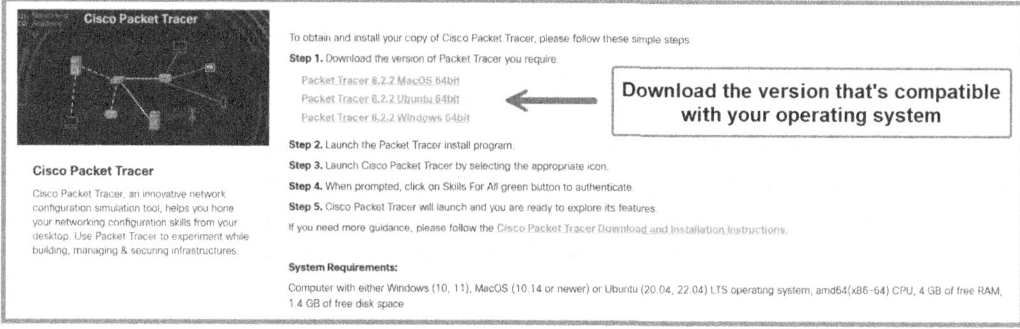

Figure 2.12: Locating Cisco Packet Tracer

> **Note**
>
> For the exercises throughout this book, I'll be using `Packet Tracer 8.2.2 Windows 64bit`.

7. After downloading Packet Tracer, ensure you have installed it on your computer.
8. After the installation is complete, launch the application and it will prompt you to log in. Select the `Cisco Skills For All` option, as shown in *Figure 2.13*:

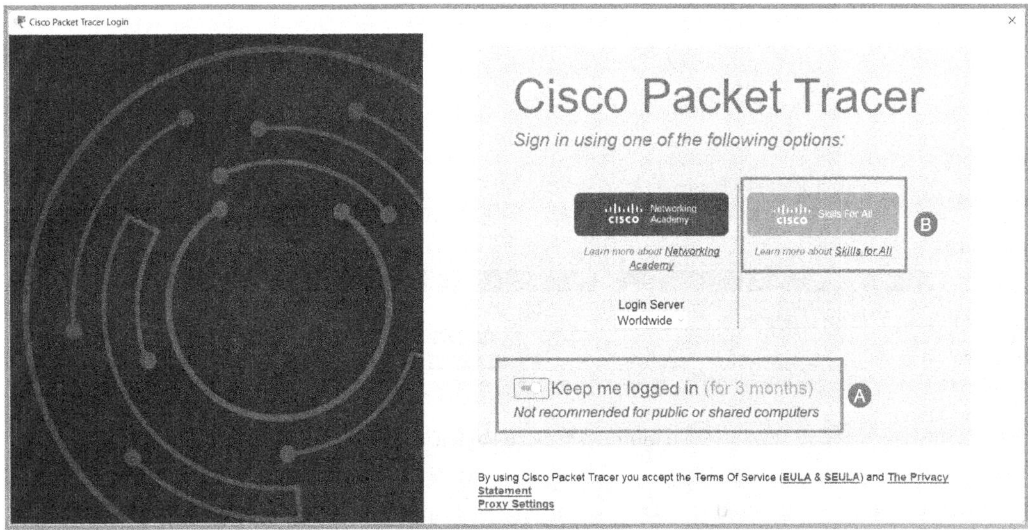

Figure 2.13: Sign-in portal

9. Enter your newly created user credentials to authenticate yourself to the Packet Tracer application and unlock its features. Once you've logged in to the Packet Tracer application, its user interface will load, as shown in *Figure 2.14*:

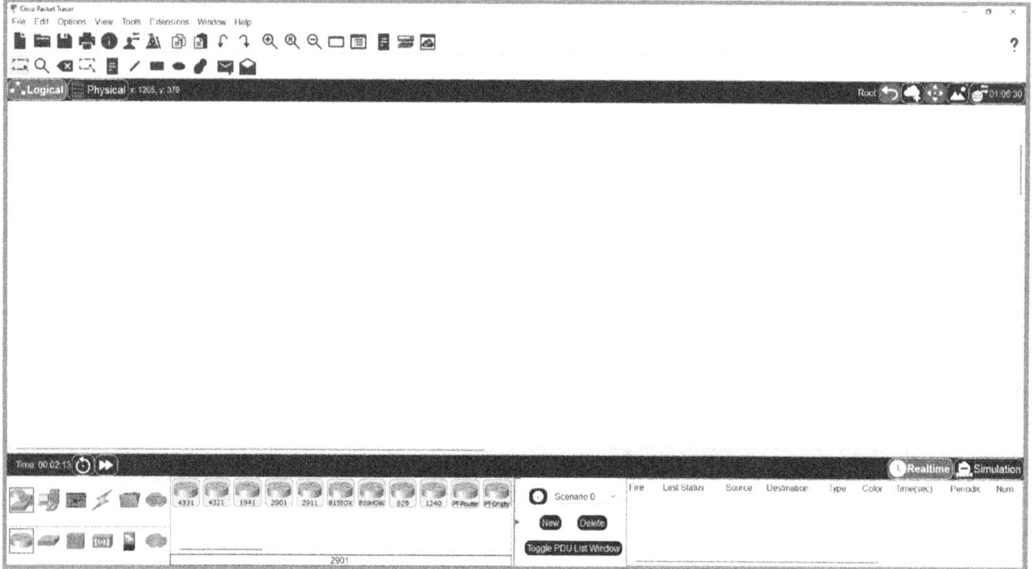

Figure 2.14: Cisco Packet Tracer

Now that you have completed this exercise and have acquired a copy of the Cisco Packet Tracer application, you will learn how to use the Packet Tracer interface.

Lab: Understanding the Cisco Packet Tracer Interface

Now that you have installed Packet Tracer on your PC, the following instructions will help you become a bit more familiar with the user interface and locate items easily:

1. Launch the Packet Tracer application as shown in *Figure 2.15*:

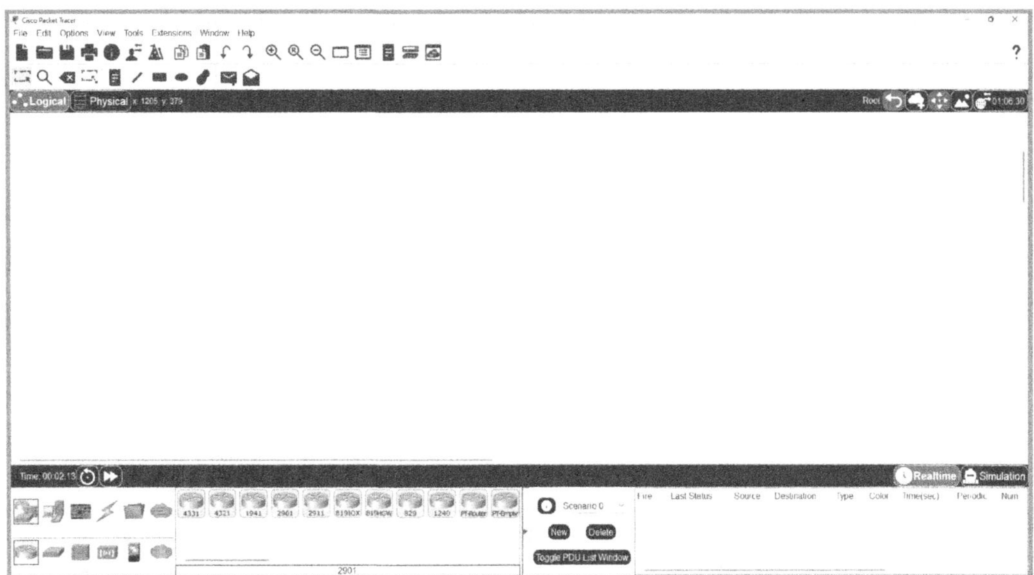

Figure 2.15: Cisco Packet Tracer user interface

2. The bottom toolbar contains all the network devices and components. The upper row represents various categories of networking devices and components, such as `Networking Devices`, `End Devices`, `Components`, `Connections`, `Miscellaneous`, and `Multiuser Connection`, as shown in *Figure 2.16*:

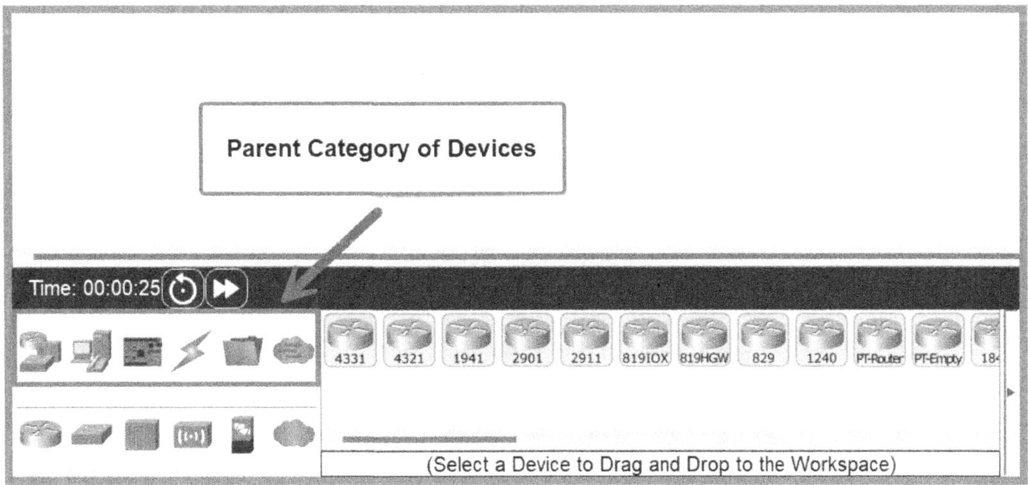

Figure 2.16: Cisco Packet Tracer device categories

> **Note**
>
> Hovering the mouse cursor over each icon shows you the name of the category or component.

3. Select the `Networking Devices` category to display the sub-category on the lower row, as shown in *Figure 2.17*:

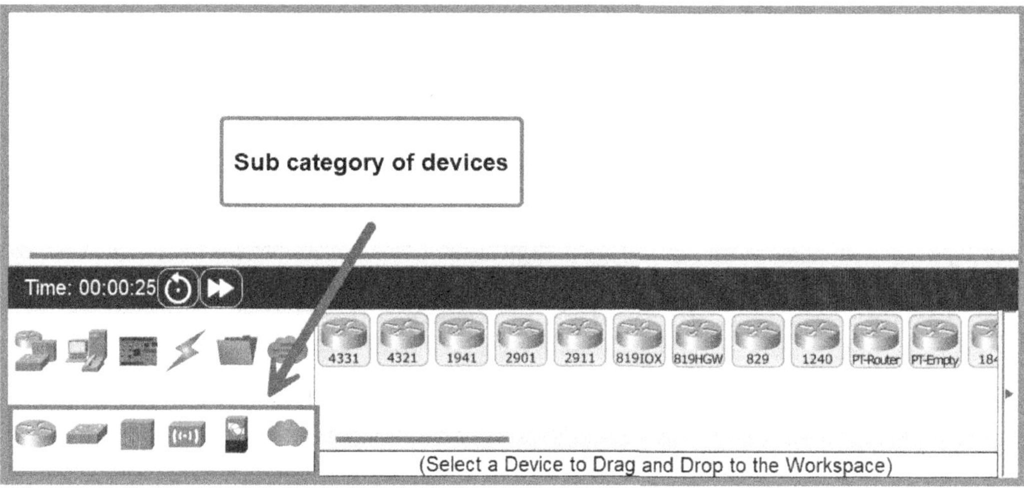

Figure 2.17: Device sub-categories

4. As shown in the preceding screenshot, the sub-categories display various components, such as routers, switches, hubs, wireless devices, security, and WAN emulation.

5. Select `Routers` within the sub-categories to display various models of Cisco routers that are integrated into the Packet Tracer application, as shown in *Figure 2.18*:

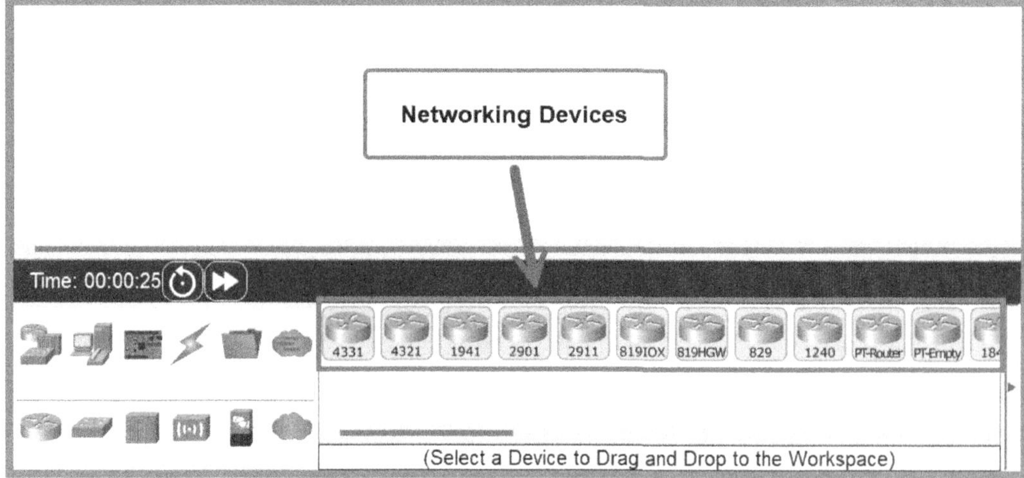

Figure 2.18: Network devices in Cisco Packet Tracer

6. To place a device in the logical space, click on the `2911` router and drag it anywhere within the space.
7. Select the `End Devices` category, click on `PC0`, and drag it onto the logical space, as shown in *Figure 2.19*:

Figure 2.19: PC and router within Cisco Packet Tracer

8. Click on the `Connections` category, select the `Console` cable, then click on `PC0` and attach it to the `RS-232` port. To connect the other end of the cable, click on the `2911` router and select the `Console` port, as shown in *Figure 2.20*:

Figure 2.20: PC to router using a console cable

9. When a cable is selected and you click on a device, a list of available ports will appear. Then, clicking on a port will logically connect the cable to the selected port.

> **Note**
>
> If you're having difficulties setting up the lab, you can download the pre-built lab file from `https://packt.link/CCNArepoCh02` and select the `Lab 1 - Accessing the Cisco IOS CLI.pkt` file to download and open it with Packet Tracer on your computer.

10. To access the CLI of Cisco IOS on the router, click on `PC0` and select `Desktop` | `Terminal`, as shown in *Figure 2.21*:

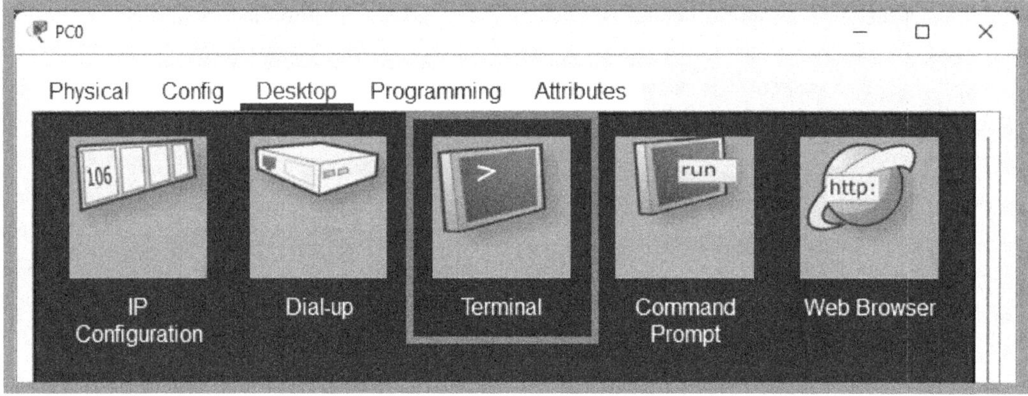

Figure 2.21: Terminal within Cisco Packet Tracer

11. When the `Terminal` application opens, click on `OK` to access the CLI on the router, as shown in *Figure 2.22*:

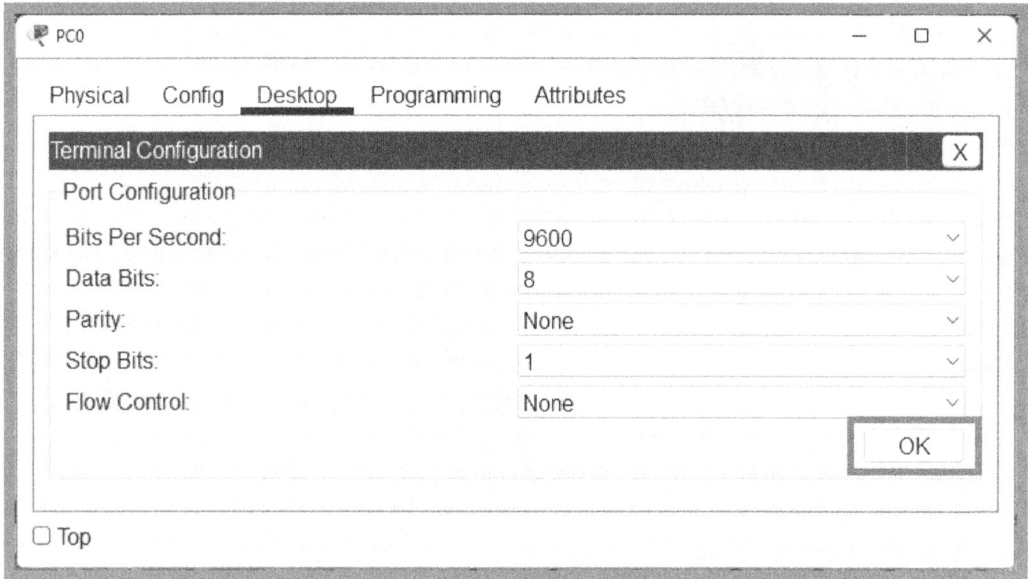

Figure 2.22: Terminal settings

12. You will notice Cisco IOS is decompressed and loaded into RAM. When a router is powered on without a `startup-config` file, it will prompt the user with the following question:

    ```
    Would you like to enter the initial configuration dialog? [yes/
    no]:
    ```

13. Type `no` and hit *Enter* twice to continue, as shown in *Figure 2.23*:

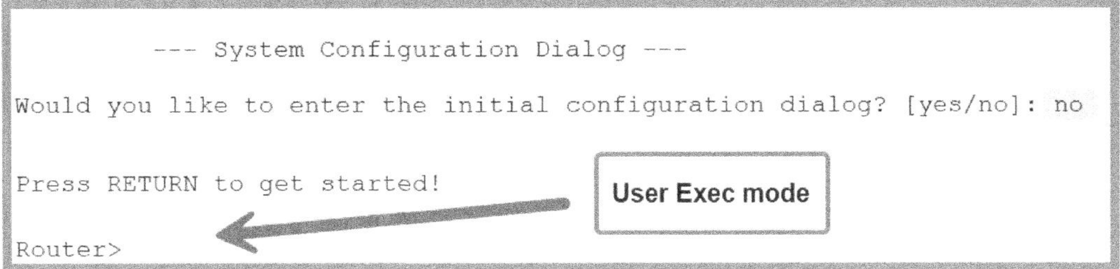

Figure 2.23: CLI of a Cisco IOS device

14. Typing `yes` will enable the initial configuration dialog; however, this option is not recommended for an aspiring network engineer pursuing the CCNA certification. Hence, always type `no` and hit *Enter* to access the User Exec mode.

Now that you have learned how to access a new Cisco IOS device using the console cable, next, you will learn how to set up a small Cisco network and test end-to-end connectivity.

Configuring Your First Cisco Network

When building a network, it is always recommended to start with a network diagram called a network topology. A topology is used to show the logical and physical connections between devices on a network, as well as basic IP addressing assignments.

Figure 2.24 shows the first lab topology:

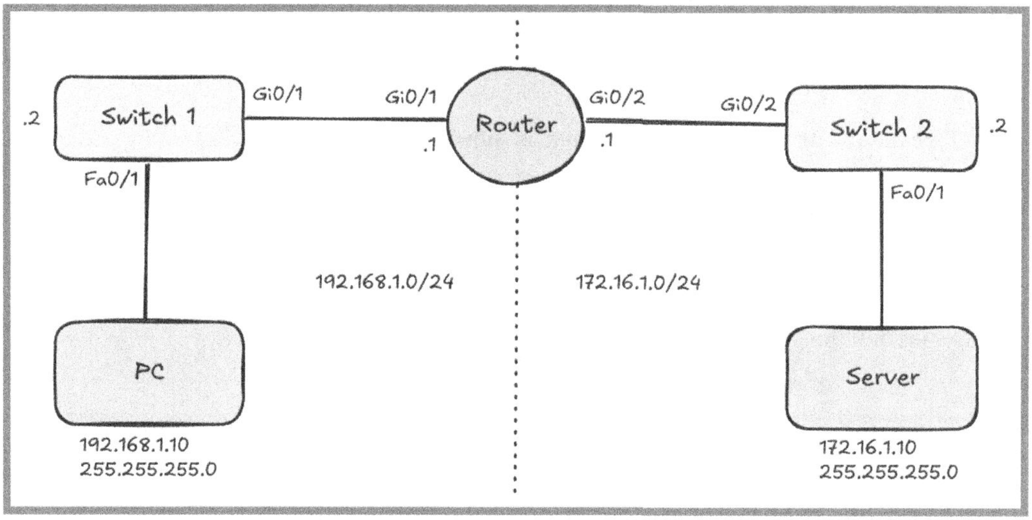

Figure 2.24: Lab topology

As you can see, there are two networks: `192.168.1.0/24` and `172.16.1.0/24`. These are interconnected using a Cisco 2911 model router. Each of these networks has a Cisco 2960 model switch to allow the PC and server to interface with the network.

Table 2.1 shows the IP addressing scheme for each device in the lab topology:

Device	Interface	IP Address	Subnet Mask	Default Gateway
Router	GigabitEthernet 0/1	192.168.1.1	255.255.255.0	N/A
	GigabitEthernet 0/2	172.16.1.1	255.255.255.0	N/A
Switch 1	Interface VLAN 1	192.168.1.2	255.255.255.0	192.168.1.1
Switch 2	Interface VLAN 1	172.16.1.2	255.255.255.0	172.16.1.1
PC	FastEthernet 0	192.168.1.10	255.255.255.0	192.168.1.1
Server	FastEthernet 0	172.16.1.10	255.255.255.0	172.16.1.1

Table 2.1: IP addressing table

If you are up for the challenge, you can choose to build this lab topology within Cisco Packet Tracer or download a pre-built file by taking the following steps:

1. Go to `https://packt.link/CCNArepoCh02`
2. Download the `Lab 2 - Configuring Cisco IOS Devices.pkt` file and open it with Cisco Packet Tracer on your computer to follow along.
3. *Figure 2.25* shows the contents of the file when it is opened using Cisco Packet Tracer:

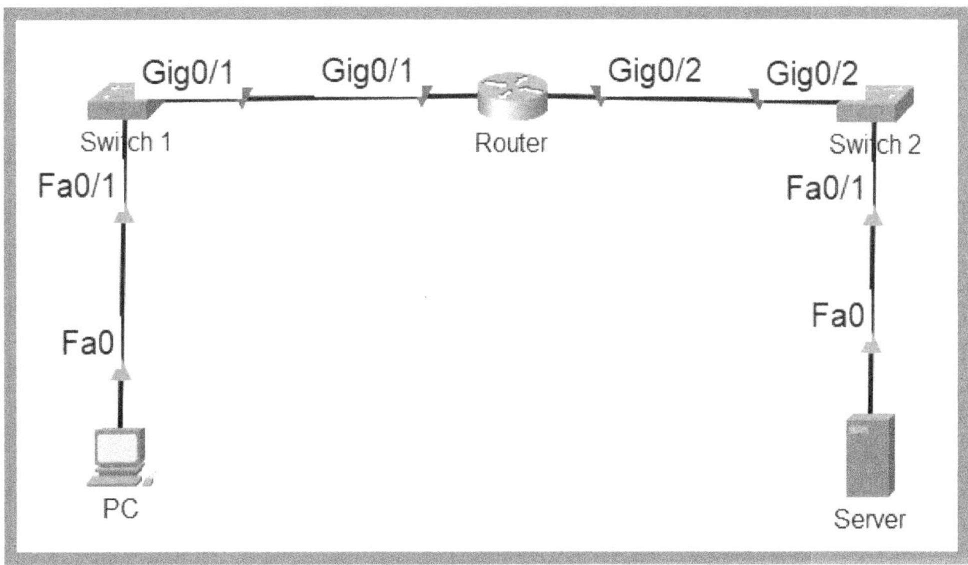

Figure 2.25: Lab file

> **Note**
>
> To display the interface labels in Packet Tracer, click on `Options` | `Preferences`, then select the `Interface` tab and check `Always Show Port Labels in Logical Workspace`.

Once you have opened the `Lab 2 - Configuring Cisco IOS Devices.pkt` file using Cisco Packet Tracer on your computer, you can proceed to the next steps.

Task 1: Navigating Cisco IOS

Understanding how to interact with Cisco IOS is essential for performing various configuration and management tasks. In this task, you will become familiar with the basics of navigating Cisco IOS:

1. You can start with the Cisco router. Click on the `Router` icon and select the `CLI` tab, as shown in *Figure 2.26*:

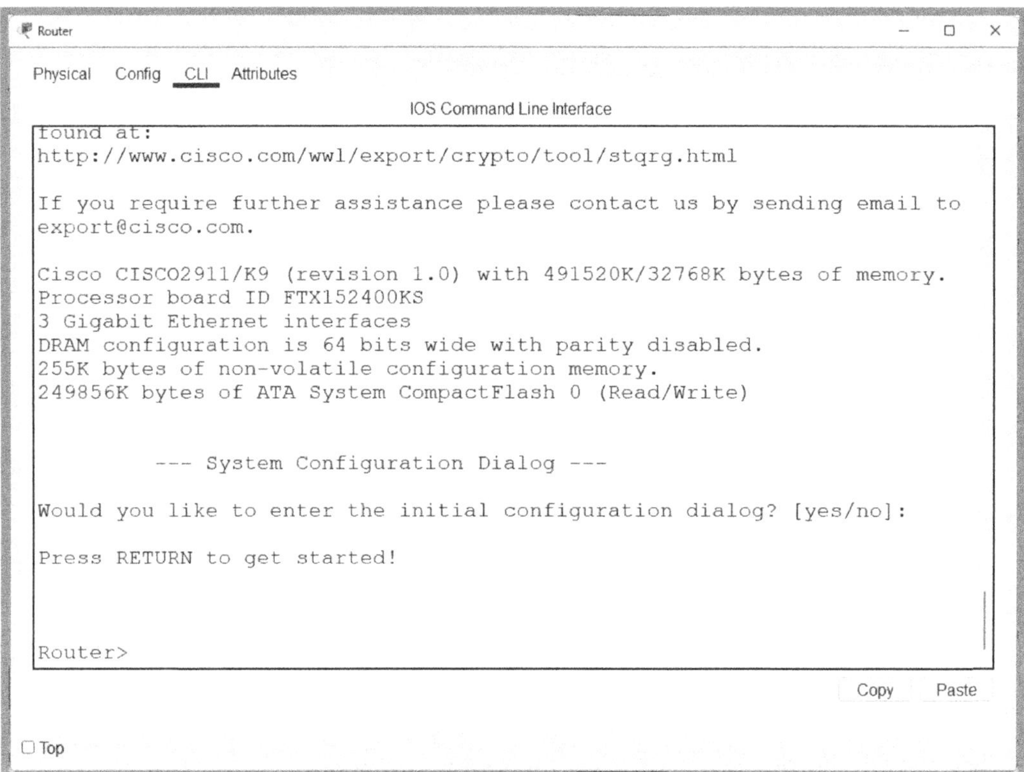

Figure 2.26: Router CLI

> **Note**
>
> In a real-world scenario, you'll need to connect the console cable between your computer and the console port of the router. Then, use a terminal emulator application such as PuTTY or SecureCRT to access the CLI of the Cisco router running Cisco IOS.

2. Since the bootstrap on the router did not find a `startup-config` file within NVRAM, the following prompt appears:

```
--- System Configuration Dialog ---
Would you like to enter the initial configuration dialog? [yes/
no]:
```

3. Type no and hit *Enter* twice to access User Exec mode, as shown in *Figure 2.27*:

```
        --- System Configuration Dialog ---

Would you like to enter the initial configuration dialog? [yes/no]: no


Press RETURN to get started!



Router>
```

Figure 2.27: Router CLI

4. Now, you should be in the User Exec mode (>). To access Privilege Exec mode, use the `enable` command, as shown here:

```
Router> enable
```

5. As shown in *Figure 2.28*, the prompt has changed from > to #, which indicates you are no longer in User Exec mode and are now in Privilege Exec mode:

```
Router> enable
Router#
```

Figure 2.28: Elevating to Privilege Exec mode

6. To move from Privilege Exec to User Exec mode, use the `disable` command:

```
Router# disable
```

7. As shown in *Figure 2.29*, the prompt has changed from # to >, which now indicates that you are back in User Exec mode:

```
Router# disable
Router>
```

Figure 2.29: Moving to User Exec mode

> **Note**
>
> Cisco IOS is able to temporarily store the last 15 commands executed on the device. Using the up and down keys on your keyboard, you can cycle through recently used commands for each mode. Therefore, if you are in Privilege Exec mode, you will only see the most recent commands used in that mode.

8. Cisco IOS allows network professionals to enter the shorthand version of a command provided Cisco IOS is able to recognize most parts of the command itself. While in User Exec mode, type `en` and hit `Enter`:

```
Router> en
```

9. As shown in *Figure 2.30*, Cisco IOS automatically recognizes the `enable` command and executes it:

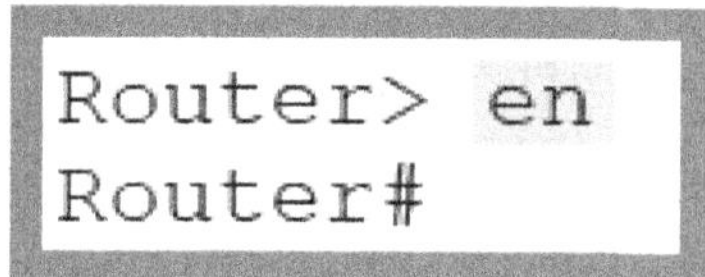

Figure 2.30: Shorthand commands

> **Note**
>
> If Cisco IOS is unable to recognize a shorthand command, it will provide an error message such as `% Ambiguous command: " e"`.

10. Cisco IOS supports context-sensitive help and a command syntax checker feature for verifying the accuracy of a command entered by a user.
11. If you want to determine all the commands that begin with `sh`, then type `sh?` as shown here:

```
Router# sh?
```

12. As shown in *Figure 2.31*, Cisco IOS returns the `show` command:

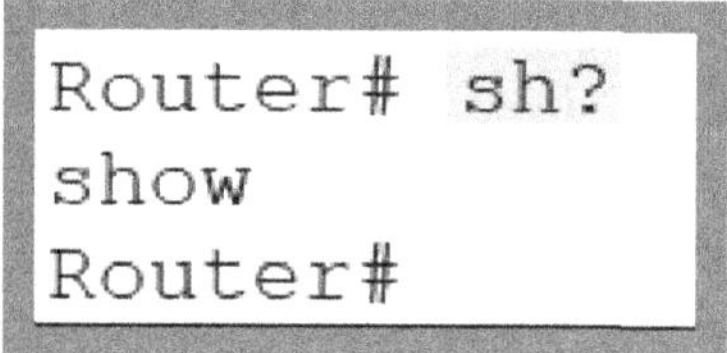

Figure 2.31: Using the context-sensitive help

13. Additionally, if you want to view a list of commands that are supported by `show`, use the `show ?` command, shown in *Figure 2.32*:

```
Router# show ?
  aaa                  Show AAA values
  access-lists         List access lists
  arp                  Arp table
  cdp                  CDP information
  class-map            Show QoS Class Map
  clock                Display the system clock
  controllers          Interface controllers status
  crypto               Encryption module
  debugging            State of each debugging option
  dhcp                 Dynamic Host Configuration Protocol status
  dot11                IEEE 802.11 show information
  file                 Show filesystem information
  flash:               display information about flash: file system
```

Figure 2.32: Using the context-sensitive help

14. As shown in *Figure 2.32*, the left column shows the various commands to append after the `show` command, such as `show clock`, while the right column shows their descriptions.

> **Note**
>
> When Cisco IOS displays multiple lines, it temporarily breaks by indicating a `--More--` syntax at the end of a page. Using the `Enter` key on your keyboard will display an additional line of output, while the spacebar will display another page of output on your screen.

Cisco IOS is filled with a lot of commands that enable you to perform many tasks, such as routing, switching, and security. However, you do not need to learn about every command, only those that are applicable to the CCNA certification.

Now that you have a better idea of how to navigate Cisco IOS, you can dive into configuring your small network topology.

Task 2: Checking the IOS Version

As an aspiring network professional, it is important to identify the current IOS version on your Cisco device. By identifying the IOS version, you will be able to determine whether there is a newer version of the operating system and whether there are security vulnerabilities and bugs, as well as getting help with asset management.

Use `show version` on the Cisco IOS router to view the device's operating system, hardware components, and system uptime, as shown in *Figure 2.33*:

```
Router# show version
Cisco IOS Software, C2900 Software (C2900-UNIVERSALK9-M), Version (A)
15.1(4)M4, RELEASE SOFTWARE (fc2)
Technical Support: http://www.cisco.com/techsupport
Copyright (c) 1986-2012 by Cisco Systems, Inc.
Compiled Thurs 5-Jan-12 15:41 by pt_team

ROM: System Bootstrap, Version 15.1(4)M4, RELEASE SOFTWARE (fc1)
cisco2911 uptime is 38 minutes, 2 seconds (B)
System returned to ROM by power-on                        (C)
System image file is "flash0:c2900-universalk9-mz.SPA.151-1.M4.bin"
Last reload type: Normal Reload
```

Figure 2.33: The show version command

Figure 2.33 shows the following:

- The version of Cisco IOS as `15.1(4)M4`.
- The system uptime since the last boot. This helps network professionals determine whether the device lost power, triggering a network outage.
- The location and filename of Cisco IOS on the device.

Task 3: Best Practices for Securing Devices

By default, anyone with physical access can use a console cable that is connected to their computer and the console port of a Cisco IOS device to access the User Exec mode of the device.

Securing the Console Port

To password-protect and enable authentication on the console port, use the following commands on the router:

```
Router> enable
Router# configure terminal
Router(config)# line console 0
Router(config-line)# password mySecurePassword
Router(config-line)# login
Router(config-line)# exec-timeout 5 0
Router(config-line)# exit
```

If you are already in Privilege Exec mode, you can simply start with line #2 and move from there. The following is a description of each line of the command:

- The `enable` command allows elevation to Privilege Exec mode
- The `configure terminal` command allows elevation to Global Configuration mode.
- The `line console 0` command enters the console line mode
- The `password [your_password]` command allows you to set a password

> **Note**
> The `password` command sets your password in plaintext within the configuration files. It's not recommended to use this command unless there's no other choice. The `secret` command automatically encrypts your password and stores the encrypted version, but the `secret` command is not available in Line mode.

- The `login` command enables authentication on the console line and, therefore, prompts the user to enter a password that's set within the Line mode. In this scenario, the user will be required to enter `MySecurePassword` to access Cisco IOS via the console port.
- The `exec-timeout [minutes] [seconds]` command specifies the exec-timeout period to automatically terminate an idle session on the console line.
- The `exit` command is used to exit the line mode and return to the Global Configuration mode.

Figure 2.34 shows the execution of the preceding commands on the router:

```
Router>enable
Router#configure terminal
Enter configuration commands, one per line.  End with CNTL/Z.
Router(config)#line console 0
Router(config-line)#password mySecurePassword
Router(config-line)#login
Router(config-line)#exec-timeout 5 0
Router(config-line)#exit
Router(config)#
```

Figure 2.34: Securing the console port

> **Note**
> To remove the password from the line console mode, use the `no password` command.

Securing the Privilege Exec Mode

By default, users move from User Exec to Privilege Exec mode without restrictions. To secure administrative access to the Privilege Exec mode, use the following instructions:

1. To restrict unauthorized access in the Privilege Exec mode, use the `enable password [your_password]` command within Global Configuration mode, as shown here:

    ```
    Router(config)# enable password myNotSecurePassword
    ```

> **Note**
>
> The `enable password` command does not encrypt the actual password when it is stored in the `running-config` or `startup-config` file.

2. *Figure 2.35* shows how the preceding command sets the password and shows how the user will be prompted to enter the correct credentials to access Privilege Exec mode:

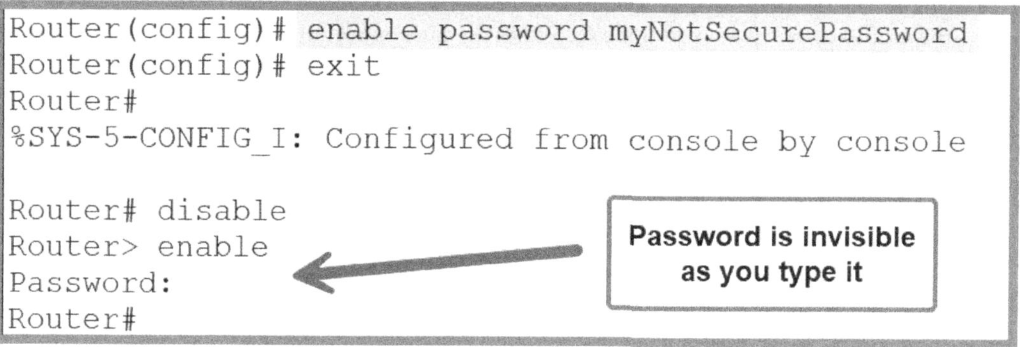

Figure 2.35: Using the enable password command

3. As shown in *Figure 2.35*, when prompted to enter the password to access Privilege Exec mode, it is invisible as you type it for security reasons.
4. *Figure 2.36* shows the contents of the `running-config` file and displays `enable password` in plaintext:

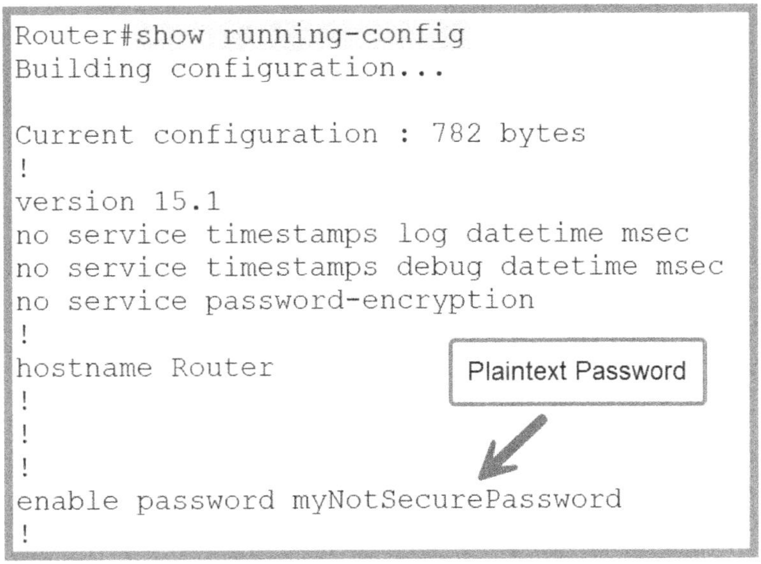

```
Router#show running-config
Building configuration...

Current configuration : 782 bytes
!
version 15.1
no service timestamps log datetime msec
no service timestamps debug datetime msec
no service password-encryption
!
hostname Router
!
!
!
enable password myNotSecurePassword
!
```

Plaintext Password

Figure 2.36: Plaintext password

5. However, it is highly recommended to use the `enable secret [your_password]` command to set an encrypted password, which is more secure, by using the following commands:

```
Router(config)# enable secret myEncryptedPassword
```

6. *Figure 2.37* shows the execution of the preceding command and verifies the `enable secret` command stores the encrypted form of the password in the `running-config` file:

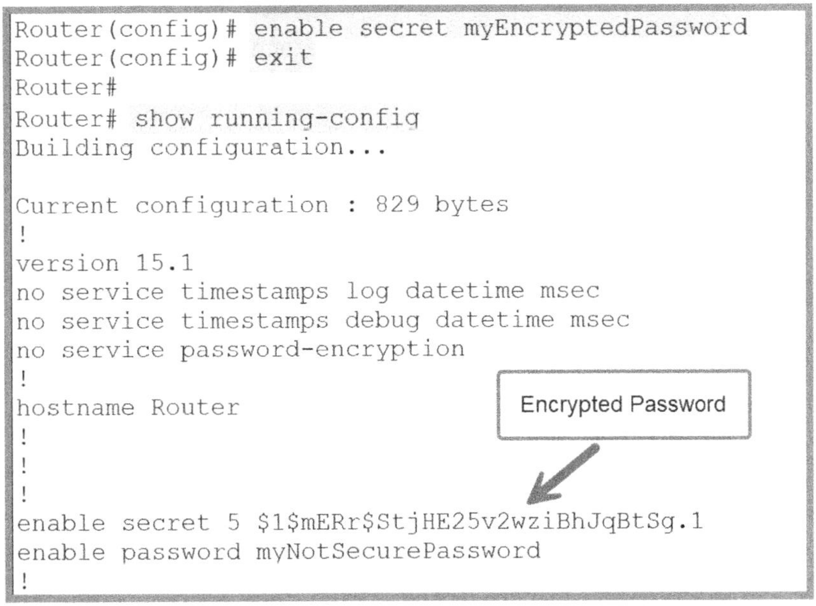

```
Router(config)# enable secret myEncryptedPassword
Router(config)# exit
Router#
Router# show running-config
Building configuration...

Current configuration : 829 bytes
!
version 15.1
no service timestamps log datetime msec
no service timestamps debug datetime msec
no service password-encryption
!
hostname Router
!
!
!
enable secret 5 $1$mERr$StjHE25v2wziBhJqBtSg.1
enable password myNotSecurePassword
!
```

Encrypted Password

Figure 2.37: Plaintext password

7. As shown in *Figure 2.37*, both the `enable secret` and `enable password` passwords are stored in the `running-config` file. However, if both exist on a Cisco IOS device, `enable secret` will take precedence when the user is moving from User Exec to Privilege Exec mode. This means `enable password` will no longer be enforced when the `enable secret` password is set.
8. It's recommended to remove the less secure password from the configurations by using the following command:

   ```
   Router(config)# no enable password
   ```

9. *Figure 2.38* shows the execution of the preceding command and verifies that `enable password` is no longer saved within the `running-config` file on the router:

```
Router(config)# no enable password
Router(config)#
Router(config)# exit
Router#
Router# show running-config
Building configuration...

Current configuration : 793 bytes
!
version 15.1
no service timestamps log datetime msec
no service timestamps debug datetime msec
no service password-encryption
!
hostname Router
!
!
!
enable secret 5 $1$mERr$StjHE25v2wziBhJqBtSg.1
!
!
```

The 'enable password' is no longer present

Figure 2.38: Removing enable password

As shown in *Figure 2.38*, the encrypted form of the password is stored in the `running-config` file on the router.

Task 4: Changing the Hostname and Setting a Banner

One of the very first tasks when provisioning a new router, switch, access point, or even a firewall is changing the default hostname of the device. Each device on your network should have a unique hostname. Many organizations usually implement a naming convention that's used for assigning hostnames to systems and devices on the network.

Displaying a legal banner whenever someone logs in to your network device is highly recommended. Such notifications can be used as an official legal warning to anyone who is either attempting to gain or has gained unauthorized access to the device.

Setting a Hostname

Hostnames help network professionals to easily identify and manage their network devices. When a network professional remotely connects to a device, the hostname quickly helps the user recognize and determine whether they have connected to the right device, especially if there are multiple devices in a large network architecture.

The following are general guidelines when configuring a hostname on a Cisco IOS device:

- The hostname should not have any spaces. For instance, `BLD RTR 01` is not acceptable. However, using the underscore (_) or period (`.`) character to represent a space is acceptable - `BLD_RTR_01`.
- Hostnames should not be more than 64 characters in length.
- It's recommended that hostnames begin with a letter and not a number.
- Hostnames can end with either a letter or a number.

To change the hostname of the router from the Global Configuration mode, use the following commands:

```
Router(config)# hostname TT-RTR-01
```

As shown in *Figure 2.39*, the hostname of the router changed immediately after executing the `hostname` command.

```
Router(config)# hostname TT-RTR-01
TT-RTR-01(config)#
```

Figure 2.39: Changing the hostname

If you need to reset the hostname of a device to the default, use the `no hostname` command within the Global Configuration mode of the Cisco IOS device.

Setting a Banner

To set a banner on the Cisco IOS device, use the `banner` command. There are different banners, such as the **message of the day (MOTD)** banner, the login banner, and the Exec banner.

To set the MOTD banner from Global Configuration mode, use the following command on the router:

```
TT-RTR-01(config)# banner motd #Unauthorized Access is Prohitbited.#
```

The following is a breakdown of the preceding command:

- The `banner motd` command sets the message of the day that will be shown to anyone who administratively attempts to access Cisco IOS on the router.
- The # character represents an opening and closing delimiter with the message enclosed between them. A delimiter can be #, $, @, !, %, or &. Delimiters work in pairs. If you use $ as the opening delimiter, you should use the same as the closing delimiter.

Figure 2.40 shows the banner that appears during a console connection:

```
Unauthorized Access is Prohitbited.

User Access Verification

Password:
```

Figure 2.40: Displaying the banner

Legal statements in banners should be crafted by the legal team of an organization and placed on company-owned devices to notify unauthorized users about the consequences of unauthorized access.

Task 5: Configuring IP Addresses

Before configuring IP addresses on a router's interfaces, it is essential to verify which interfaces are available and which ones are in use. Privilege Exec mode enables you to run your `show` commands to verify the device's operating status, hardware components, and configurations.

The `show ip interface brief` command displays a summary of all interfaces on the router, as shown in *Figure 2.41*:

```
TT-RTR-01# show ip interface brief
Interface              IP-Address      OK? Method Status                Protocol
GigabitEthernet0/0     unassigned      YES NVRAM  administratively down down
GigabitEthernet0/1     unassigned      YES NVRAM  administratively down down
GigabitEthernet0/2     unassigned      YES NVRAM  administratively down down
Vlan1                  unassigned      YES unset  administratively down down
```

Figure 2.41: Summary of interfaces

The following provides a description of each column of the output in *Figure 2.41*:

- `Interface`: Specifies the interface type (Ethernet, FastEthernet, or GigabitEthernet) and the interface ID.
- `IP-Address`: Specifies whether an IP address is assigned to an interface.
- `OK?`: Validates whether the assigned IP address on the interface is valid. If the address is valid, it will show `YES`. If there's an issue with the address, it will show `NO`.
- `Method`: Tells you how the IP address was assigned to the interface. The following are the different methods indicated by Cisco IOS:
    - `manual`: The IP address was manually configured on the interface
    - `DHCP`: The interface was automatically assigned the IP address from a DHCP server on the network
    - `unset`: No IP address was assigned on the interface
- `Status`: Specifies the line protocol status of the interface. The following are the different status types indicated by Cisco IOS:
    - `up`: The interface is administratively up and in operation
    - `down`: The interface is administratively down
    - `administratively down`: The interface is manually shut down by a network professional using the `shutdown` command within Interface mode
- `Protocol`: Verifies the status of the IP protocol on the interface. The following are the different protocol statuses that are indicated by Cisco IOS:
    - `up`: The IP protocol on the interface is running
    - `down`: The IP protocol is not running due to a misconfiguration on the interface or other issues

To configure an IP address, subnet mask, and description on a router's interface, use the following instructions:

1. From the Global Configuration mode, use the following commands to configure the `GigabitEthernet0/1` interface of the router with a description and IP address with a subnet mask, and administratively enable the interface:

```
TT-RTR-01(config)# interface gigabitEthernet 0/1
TT-RTR-01(config-if)# description connected to LAN_1
TT-RTR-01(config-if)# ip address 192.168.1.1 255.255.255.0
TT-RTR-01(config-if)# no shutdown
TT-RTR-01(config-if)# exit
```

2. Next, from the Global Configuration mode, use the following commands to configure the `GigabitEthernet0/2` interface of the router:

```
TT-RTR-01(config)# interface gigabitEthernet 0/2
TT-RTR-01(config-if)# description connected to LAN_2
TT-RTR-01(config-if)# ip address 172.16.1.1 255.255.255.0
TT-RTR-01(config-if)# no shutdown
TT-RTR-01(config-if)# exit
```

3. Then, use the `show ip interface brief` command to view the status changes of the interfaces, as shown in *Figure 2.42*:

```
TT-RTR-01# show ip interface brief
Interface              IP-Address      OK? Method Status                Protocol
GigabitEthernet0/0     unassigned      YES NVRAM  administratively down down
GigabitEthernet0/1     192.168.1.1     YES manual up                    up
GigabitEthernet0/2     172.16.1.1      YES manual up                    up
Vlan1                  unassigned      YES unset  administratively down down
```

Figure 2.42: Summary of interfaces

4. The following are additional commands to verify the status and configurations of an interface:
   - `show interfaces`: Displays all information about all interfaces
   - `show interfaces gigabitEthernet 0/1`: Displays all information about a specific interface
   - `show interfaces status`: Displays a summary of interfaces and their duplex, speed, and VLAN status
   - `show running-config`: Displays the configurations on the interfaces

5. Next, use the `show running-config` command to display the configurations that were applied on each interface of the router, as shown in *Figure 2.43*:

```
!
interface GigabitEthernet0/1
 description connected to LAN_1
 ip address 192.168.1.1 255.255.255.0
 duplex auto
 speed auto
!
interface GigabitEthernet0/2
 description connected to LAN_2
 ip address 172.16.1.1 255.255.255.0
 duplex auto
 speed auto
!
```

Figure 2.43: Interface configurations

6. As shown in the preceding screenshot, each interface contains the default configurations for both the duplex and speed modes – both are set to automatic mode.

Task 6: Setting up Secure Remote Access

Remote access enables network professionals to remotely monitor, manage, and troubleshoot devices. There are two common remote access protocols that are supported on Cisco IOS devices:

- **Telnet**: An unsecured protocol that transmits data in plaintext and operates on port 23 by default
- **SSH**: A secure protocol that establishes a secure communication channel and operates on port 22 by default

Both Telnet and SSH allow you to remotely access a device via a terminal, allowing you to gain shell access. However, Telnet is an unsecured method to remotely access and manage a device as traffic can be seen in plaintext. SSH is the recommended method for remote access. All SSH traffic is encrypted by default. If a hacker is intercepting SSH traffic over a network, the attacker will not be able to see the actual contents of the traffic flowing between the SSH client and the SSH server.

Setting Up Telnet

To configure Telnet on the router from Global Configuration mode, use the following commands:

```
TT-RTR-01(config)# line vty 0 4
TT-RTR-01(config-line)# password myTelnetPassword
TT-RTR-01(config-line)# exec-timeout 10 0
TT-RTR-01(config-line)# login
TT-RTR-01(config-line)# exit
```

The following are descriptions of the preceding commands:

- `line vty 0 4`: The command will be applied to the VTY lines 0 to 4, which are used for remote access
- `password myTelnetPassword`: Sets the Telnet password for the VTY lines 0 to 4
- `login`: Enables password-checking and prompts the user to enter the Telnet password
- `exec-timeout 10 0`: Sets an exec inactivity timeout of 10 minutes and 0 seconds

However, to disable Telnet and prevent any incoming Telnet connections to the router, use the following commands from Global Configuration mode:

```
TT-RTR-01(config)# line vty 0 4
TT-RTR-01(config-line)# transport input ssh
TT-RTR-01(config-line)# no password
TT-RTR-01(config-line)# exit
```

The following are descriptions of the preceding commands:

- `line vty 0 4`: The commands will be applied to the VTY lines 0 to 4, which are used for remote access
- `transport input ssh`: Ensures the router accepts incoming SSH connections only
- `No password`: The password that's set in Line mode is applicable to Telnet connections

By disabling Telnet and configuring SSH, any password that is configured under Line mode will no longer be applicable as users are prompted to enter a valid username and password combination during the SSH authentication process to the Cisco IOS router.

Configuring SSH

To configure SSH on the router from Global Configuration mode, follow the given instructions:

1. Change the default hostname of the device. This was completed during *Task 4* already.
2. Configure an `enable secret` password. This was completed during *Task 3*.

3. Set the domain name of the router as it's required for creating the RSA encryption keys. Use the `ip domain-name [your_domain_name]` command in Global Configuration mode:

```
TT-RTR-01(config)# ip domain-name ccnalab.local
```

4. Create the RSA encryption keys for data encryption with SSH:

```
TT-RTR-01(config)# crypto key generate rsa
```

5. The key (modulus) size should be at least `1024` or greater to improve security, as shown in *Figure 2.44*:

```
TT-RTR-01(config)# ip domain-name ccnalab.local
TT-RTR-01(config)#
TT-RTR-01(config)# crypto key generate rsa
The name for the keys will be: TT-RTR-01.ccnalab.local
Choose the size of the key modulus in the range of 360 to 4096 for
your
  General Purpose Keys. Choosing a key modulus greater than 512 may
take
  a few minutes.

How many bits in the modulus [512]: 1024
% Generating 1024 bit RSA keys, keys will be non-exportable...[OK]

TT-RTR-01(config)#
*Mar 1 0:15:13.112: %SSH-5-ENABLED: SSH 1.99 has been enabled
TT-RTR-01(config)#
```

Figure 2.44: Configuring SSH

6. Create a local user account for the SSH user:

```
TT-RTR-01(config)# username User1 secret mySSHpassword
```

Note

The `secret` command will store the encrypted form of the password within the `running-config` file. Instead, if you use the `password` command, the password will be stored in plaintext. This command is not recommended unless it's the only available option.

7. Enable SSHv2 and configure SSH on the VTY lines:

```
TT-RTR-01(config)# ip ssh version 2
TT-RTR-01(config)# line vty 0 4
TT-RTR-01(config-line)# transport input ssh
TT-RTR-01(config-line)# login local
TT-RTR-01(config-line)# exit
```

8. The `login local` command is commonly used on the VTY and console lines, which specifies the local authentication should be used, that is, check for a valid username and password only.
9. When this command is applied, the authentication mechanisms will not acknowledge any password that's configured under Line mode. For instance, if the previous Telnet password is still present, the `login local` command will only check for the user accounts that were created in *step 4*.

> **Note**
>
> In Privilege Exec mode, the `show users` command enables device administrators to identify which users are remotely connected.

Task 7: Configuring the Console to Use Local User Accounts

Now that you have created a local user account, you can also configure the console line to check for a local user account, instead of a password only.

To perform this task, use the following commands:

```
TT-RTR-01(config)# line console 0
TT-RTR-01(config-line)# login local
TT-RTR-01(config-line)# no password
TT-RTR-01(config-line)# exit
```

Task 8: Disabling Domain Lookup and Encrypting All Plaintext Passwords

If you have incorrectly entered a command, Cisco IOS may attempt to perform a domain lookup, as shown in *Figure 2.45*:

```
TT-RTR-01#cisco
Translating "cisco"...domain server (255.255.255.255) % Name lookup aborted
TT-RTR-01#
```

Figure 2.45: Domain lookup

To prevent or disable automatic domain name or **Domain Name System** (**DNS**) lookup on a Cisco IOS device, use the following command in Global Configuration mode:

```
TT-RTR-01(config)# no ip domain-lookup
```

There are various modes within Cisco IOS that do not support the `enable secret` or the `secret` command for storing the encrypted form of a password, and only the `password` command is available.

To automatically encrypt all existing and future plaintext passwords that are stored in the configuration file, use the following command in Global Configuration mode:

```
TT-RTR-01(config)# service password-encryption
```

Task 9: Saving Configurations and Rebooting Systems

All the configurations that were performed in the previous steps and tasks are stored in the `running-config` file. To view the `running-config` file, use the `show running-config` command, as shown in *Figure 2.46*:

```
TT-RTR-01# show running-config
Building configuration...

Current configuration : 1041 bytes
!
version 15.1
no service timestamps log datetime msec
no service timestamps debug datetime msec
service password-encryption
!
hostname TT-RTR-01
!
!
!
enable secret 5 $1$mERr$StjHE25v2wziBhJqBtSg.1
!
!
```

Figure 2.46: Current configuration

Use the following steps to properly save the current configurations such that these configurations are loaded into memory when the device reboots:

1. If the device loses power or reboots, the configurations are lost. Therefore, to save the current configurations in the `startup-config` file, use the following commands in Privilege Exec mode:

   ```
   TT-RTR-01# copy running-config startup-config
   ```

2. After executing the preceding command, the following prompt will appear:

   ```
   Destination filename [startup-config]?
   ```

3. Simply hit `Enter` again to use the default name of the configuration file.
4. To test whether your configurations save properly, use the `show startup-config` command within Privilege Exec mode and compare it with the `running-config` file.
5. Lastly, use the `reload` command to reboot the device from the CLI.

Keep in mind that the configurations of `running-config` are lost if the device reboots or loses power. Therefore, it's essential to save the current configurations after completing and testing the functionality of a system change.

Task 10: Configuring Switch 1

This sub-section covers the instructions for configuring `Switch 1` within your lab topology:

1. To secure Privilege Exec mode, use the following commands to restrict unauthorized access:

```
Switch> enable
Switch# configure terminal
Switch(config)# enable secret myEncryptedPassword
```

2. Use the following commands to configure the hostname and banner on the switch:

```
Switch(config)# hostname TT-SW-01
TT-SW-01(config)# banner motd #Unauthorized Access is
Prohitbited.#
```

3. A **switch virtual interface** (**SVI**) enables a network professional to configure an IP address on a management **virtual local area network** (**VLAN**) interface for the purposes of remote management and troubleshooting. To configure an SVI on `Switch 1`, use the following commands:

```
TT-SW-01(config)# interface vlan 1
TT-SW-01(config-if)# ip address 192.168.1.2 255.255.255.0
TT-SW-01(config-if)# no shutdown
TT-SW-01(config-if)# exit
```

4. To ensure that the switch is reachable outside its own IP network, a default gateway should be configured on the switch. Use the following command to set a default gateway on the switch:

```
TT-SW-01(config)# ip default-gateway 192.168.1.1
```

5. To configure a domain name and generate RSA keys for setting up SSH, use the following commands:

```
TT-SW-01(config)# ip domain-name ccnalab.local
TT-SW-01(config)# crypto key generate rsa
```

6. To create a local user account and enable SSHv2 to improve security, use the following commands:

```
TT-SW-01(config)# username User1 secret mySSHpassword
TT-SW-01(config)# ip ssh version 2
```

7. To configure VTY lines for SSH input only, use the following commands:

```
TT-SW-01(config)# line vty 0 4
TT-SW-01(config-line)# transport input ssh
TT-SW-01(config-line)# login local
TT-SW-01(config-line)# exit
```

8. To configure the console line for local authentication, use the following commands:

```
TT-SW-01(config)# line console 0
TT-SW-01(config-line)# login local
TT-SW-01(config-line)# exit
```

9. To disable domain name lookup, encrypt all plaintext passwords, and save configurations on the device, use the following commands:

```
TT-SW-01(config)# no ip domain-lookup
TT-SW-01(config)# service password-encryption
TT-SW-01(config)# exit
TT-SW-01# copy running-config startup-config
```

Now that you have configured `Switch 1` within the lab, you can move on to the next section within the topology.

Task 11: Configuring Switch 2

In this sub-section, you will be configuring `Switch 2` within the lab topology:

1. To secure Privilege Exec mode on `Switch 2`, use the following commands:

```
Switch> enable
Switch# configure terminal
Switch(config)# enable secret myEncryptedPassword
```

2. To configure the hostname and banner on `Switch 2`, use the following configurations:

```
Switch(config)# hostname TT-SW-02
TT-SW-02(config)# banner motd #Unauthorized Access is
Prohitbited.#
```

3. To configure an SVI on the switch, use the following commands:

```
TT-SW-02(config)# interface vlan 1
TT-SW-02(config-if)# ip address 172.16.1.2 255.255.255.0
TT-SW-02(config-if)# no shutdown
TT-SW-02(config-if)# exit
```

4. To ensure the switch is reachable outside its own IP network, a default gateway should be configured on the switch. Use the following commands to set a default gateway on the switch:

```
TT-SW-02(config)# ip default-gateway 172.16.1.1
```

5. To configure a domain name and generate RSA keys for setting up SSH, use the following commands:

```
TT-SW-02(config)# ip domain-name ccnalab.local
TT-SW-02(config)# crypto key generate rsa
```

6. To create a local user account and enable SSHv2 for better security, use the following commands:

```
TT-SW-02(config)# username User1 secret mySSHpassword
TT-SW-02(config)# ip ssh version 2
```

7. To configure VTY lines for SSH access, use the following:

```
TT-SW-02(config)# line vty 0 4
TT-SW-02(config-line)# transport input ssh
TT-SW-02(config-line)# login local
TT-SW-02(config-line)# exit
```

8. To configure the console line for local authentication, use the following commands:

```
TT-SW-02(config)# line console 0
TT-SW-02(config-line)# login local
TT-SW-02(config-line)# exit
```

9. To disable domain name lookup, encrypt all plaintext passwords, and save configurations, use the following commands:

```
TT-SW-02(config)# no ip domain-lookup
TT-SW-02(config)# service password-encryption
TT-SW-02(config)# exit
TT-SW-02# copy running-config startup-config
```

Having completed this section, you have learned how to set up a small Cisco environment and apply common device configurations. Next, you will learn how to perform common troubleshooting procedures.

Performing Troubleshooting Procedures

During and after configuring your devices on a network, it is best practice to verify the IP addresses on each device.

Table 2.2 shows the IP address scheme for the lab topology:

Device	Interface	IP Address	Subnet Mask	Default Gateway
Router	GigabitEthernet 0/1	192.168.1.1	255.255.255.0	N/A
	GigabitEthernet 0/2	172.16.1.1	255.255.255.0	N/A
Switch 1	Interface VLAN 1	192.168.1.2	255.255.255.0	192.168.1.1
Switch 2	Interface VLAN 1	172.16.1.2	255.255.255.0	172.16.1.1
PC	FastEthernet 0	192.168.1.10	255.255.255.0	192.168.1.1
Server	FastEthernet 0	172.16.1.10	255.255.255.0	172.16.1.1

Table 2.2: IP addressing scheme

Up next, you will learn about various troubleshooting commands for both end devices and Cisco devices.

Verifying IP Configurations on End Devices

The following commands are commonly used by network professionals in their troubleshooting process to identify whether they've assigned the appropriate IP address on a host device:

- `ipconfig`: A Windows-based command for displaying the IP address, subnet mask, and default gateway addresses of each interface
- `ipconfig /all`: A Windows-based command that displays additional addressing such as the **media access control** (**MAC**) address and DNS server addresses on each interface
- `ifconfig`: A Linux-based command for displaying the IP addresses and interfaces
- `ip address`: A Linux-based command for displaying IP addresses and interfaces on Linux systems

Verifying IP Configurations on Cisco Devices

The following are useful Cisco IOS commands for verifying IP configurations on Cisco devices:

- `show ip interface brief`: Displays a summary of all interfaces, their status, and assigned IP addresses
- `show ip interface [interface-ID]`: Shows IP-related information for a specific interface
- `show interfaces [interface-ID]`: Shows detailed information about a specific interface
- `show running-config`: Displays the device's current configurations, including the IP addresses that are configured on each interface

Verifying End-to-End Connectivity

The `ping` and `traceroute` utilities are software-based tools that are integrated into many operating systems, such as Windows, Linux, macOS, and even Cisco IOS. The `ping` utility leverages **Internet Control Message Protocol** (**ICMP**) for checking end-to-end connectivity between a sender and a destination host. ICMP is a Layer 3 network protocol that is integrated within the OSI and TCP/IP network model that sends error and operational messages to identify whether there is a failure or a successful connection between devices over a network. Additionally, the `traceroute` utility also leverages ICMP for checking each hop along the path from a sender to a destination host.

Figure 2.47 shows how to use the `ping` utility on a Windows-based system:

```
C:\> ping 172.16.1.10

Pinging 172.16.1.10 with 32 bytes of data:

Reply from 172.16.1.10: bytes=32 time=7ms TTL=127
Reply from 172.16.1.10: bytes=32 time<1ms TTL=127
Reply from 172.16.1.10: bytes=32 time<1ms TTL=127
Reply from 172.16.1.10: bytes=32 time<1ms TTL=127

Ping statistics for 172.16.1.10:
    Packets: Sent = 4, Received = 4, Lost = 0 (0% loss),
Approximate round trip times in milli-seconds:
    Minimum = 0ms, Maximum = 7ms, Average = 1ms
```

Figure 2.47: ping results on a Windows device

As shown in the preceding screenshot, the PC sent four `ping` requests to `172.16.1.10` (server) and got four `ping` replies, which indicates the destination host is online and has end-to-end connectivity.

> **Note**
>
> The `ping [destination host]` command is applicable to Windows, Linux, macOS, and Cisco IOS devices.

Figure 2.48 shows the `ping` output on a Cisco IOS router:

```
TT-RTR-01> ping 192.168.1.10

Type escape sequence to abort.
Sending 5, 100-byte ICMP Echos to 192.168.1.10, timeout is 2 seconds:
!!!!!
Success rate is 100 percent (5/5), round-trip min/avg/max = 0/0/0 ms

TT-RTR-01>
```

Figure 2.48: ping results on a Cisco device

Cisco IOS does not provide a similar output to Windows or Linux operating systems – rather, it provides various symbols with different meanings, such as the following:

- `!`: Successful – `ping` requests are sent and received.
- `.`: Request timeout – the `ping` request is sent to the destination but no response is received. This is caused by a return path being missing from the destination host or ICMP responses being disabled on the recipient device.
- `U`: Destination unreachable – the sender or default gateway does not have a route to the destination host or network. This is caused by a missing route from the routing table of the sender or default gateway.

Additional Troubleshooting Tips

The following are common troubleshooting tips:

- Verify the destination device is powered on
- Verify the cables are connected to the correct interfaces
- Ensure the IP addresses are configured on the correct interfaces
- Ensure the interfaces are administratively up

Having completed this section, you have learned about the fundamental checks to perform. As you progress further in this book, you will learn about more technologies and their troubleshooting procedures.

Summary

Having completed this chapter, you have gained hands-on experience in performing initial device configurations on a Cisco router and two Cisco switches to build a small network. During these exercises, you've learned about the commands needed to change the hostname, set a banner, configure interfaces with IP addresses, and even set up remote access using SSH. Most importantly, the knowledge gained from this chapter will help you to better understand the CLI of Cisco IOS devices when performing advanced configurations in later chapters of this book.

I hope this chapter has been informative for you and is helpful in your journey toward learning how to implement and administer Cisco solutions and prepare for the 200-301 CCNA v1.1 certification. In the next chapter, *Chapter 3, Network Architectures and Physical Infrastructure*, you will learn about some common network topologies and their architectures, and how they are implemented in various types of organizations.

Additional Reading

- *8 Steps to Configure Your Network Switch*: `https://www.cisco.com/c/en/us/solutions/small-business/resource-center/networking/how-to-setup-network-switch.html`
- Configuring a Cisco router: `https://www.cisco.com/c/en/us/td/docs/routers/access/800M/software/800MSCG/routconf.html`

Exam Readiness Drill – Chapter Review Questions

Apart from mastering key concepts, strong test-taking skills under time pressure are essential for acing your certification exam. That's why developing these abilities early in your learning journey is critical.

Exam readiness drills, using the free online practice resources provided with this book, help you progressively improve your time management and test-taking skills while reinforcing the key concepts you've learned.

HOW TO GET STARTED

- Open the link or scan the QR code at the bottom of this page
- If you have unlocked the practice resources already, log in to your registered account. If you haven't, follow the instructions in *Chapter 19* and come back to this page.
- Once you log in, click the START button to start a quiz
- We recommend attempting a quiz multiple times till you're able to answer most of the questions correctly and well within the time limit.
- You can use the following practice template to help you plan your attempts:

Working On Accuracy		
Attempt	Target	Time Limit
Attempt 1	40% or more	Till the timer runs out
Attempt 2	60% or more	Till the timer runs out
Attempt 3	75% or more	Till the timer runs out
Working On Timing		
Attempt 4	75% or more	1 minute before time limit
Attempt 5	75% or more	2 minutes before time limit
Attempt 6	75% or more	3 minutes before time limit

The above drill is just an example. Design your drills based on your own goals and make the most out of the online quizzes accompanying this book.

First time accessing the online resources?

You'll need to unlock them through a one-time process. **Head to** *Chapter 19* **for instructions.**

Open Quiz	
https://packt.link/ccnachap2 OR scan this QR code →	

3

Network Architectures and Physical Infrastructure

It is important for network professionals such as engineers to be familiar with various network designs and architectures that are commonly used within organizations. Learning about network architectures will provide you with the fundamentals necessary to understand, design, and implement a resilient network infrastructure that supports scalability, redundancy, and security and improves network management.

In this chapter, you will learn about common network topologies and their architectures, and how they are implemented in various types of organizations. Lastly, you will learn the fundamentals of physical interfaces on networking devices and cabling types.

This chapter covers *Domain 1: Network Fundamentals*, objectives *1.2 Describe characteristics of network topology architectures*, *1.3 Compare physical interface and cabling types*, and *1.4 Identify interface and cable issues*, of the *200-301 CCNA v1.1 Certification* exam.

In this chapter, you will cover the following topics:

- Network topologies and architectures
- Physical interface and cabling types

You can now dive in!

Network Topologies and Architectures

A network topology is an arrangement of common networking devices, such as routers and switches, security appliances (e.g., firewalls), and network connections, that shows how devices are interconnected. Network topologies and their diagrams help network professionals to better understand, improve, and troubleshoot issues more efficiently.

Network topologies play an important role in that they have the potential to directly affect the overall performance and security of interconnected devices within an organization. For instance, network topologies help design and improve scalability for ever-expanding organizations to meet their customers' needs. With a better understanding of architecture, network professionals are better equipped to identify whether their network infrastructure has any points of failure and assist with improving the redundancy and reliability of network resources and services to users.

A poorly designed network can compromise the overall performance of data transmission between devices. However, by adopting industry best practices and design models, professionals can implement an architecture that supports improved performance, resilience, availability, and network security.

> **Note**
>
> The **Cisco Validated Design Zone** provides various proof-of-concept network design guides to help aspiring and seasoned network professionals with designing and implementing an architecture that supports Cisco best practices; these design guides can be found at `https://www.cisco.com/c/en/us/solutions/design-zone.html`.

In the upcoming sub-sections, you will learn about various network topologies and architectures, such as three-tier, two-tier, spine-leaf, small office/home office, wide area network, on-premises, and cloud architectures.

Three-Tier Architecture

The Cisco three-tier architecture is a hierarchical network design that supports the scalability needed for network professionals to expand the network infrastructure without compromising network performance. It also supports redundancy and fault tolerance to ensure that there are multiple paths between a sender and destination host within the organization, such that, if a primary path is faulty or unavailable, the network traffic can be forwarded through an alternate path to the destination.

In addition, the three-tier architecture makes it easier to implement network security solutions that prevent various types of cyber-attacks and threats from compromising the network and its users. Lastly, this architecture improves the overall manageability of the network by enabling network professionals to replace legacy devices with new systems to support users.

Figure 3.1 shows an overview of the three-tier architecture:

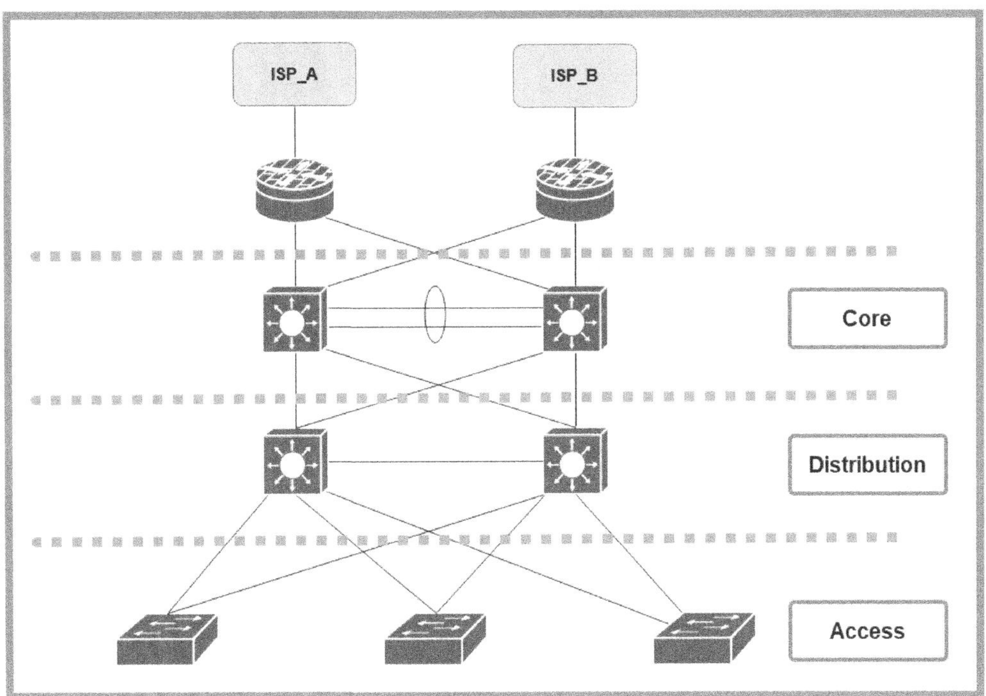

Figure 3.1: Cisco three-tier architecture

As shown in *Figure 3.1*, the following are the roles and functions of each layer:

- **Core**: The core layer functions as the high-speed backbone of the network and is used to connect the distribution layer blocks with the rest of the network.
- **Distribution**: The distribution-layer functions are the intermediary between the core and access layers of the network and provide redundancy between the access layer switches. The distribution layer is also responsible for layer 3 routing, **quality of service** (**QoS**), and aggregating network traffic from the access layer switches to the core layer of the network. QoS is a network service that enables network professionals to prioritize and allocate network bandwidth to specific traffic types.
- **Access**: The access layer block provides network access for end devices to interface with the network resources and services. At the access layer, network security controls are implemented to ensure authorized users and devices are permitted to access the network and its resources.

In a real-world scenario, each branch office of an organization will consist of both an access block and a distribution block, as shown in *Figure 3.2*:

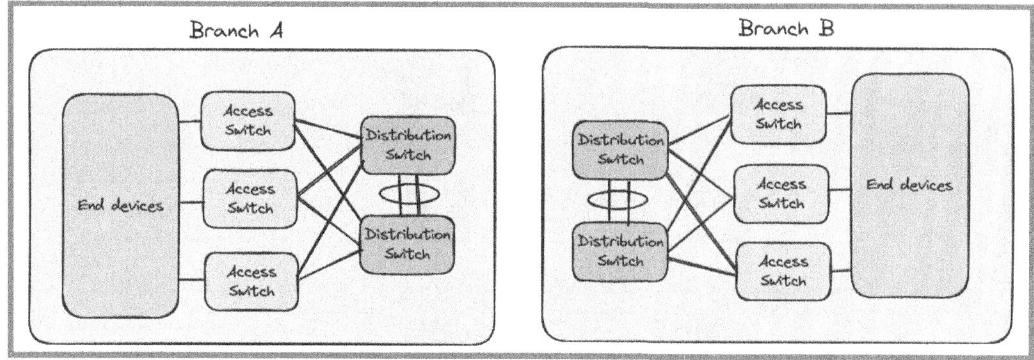

Figure 3.2: Access and distribution blocks

As shown in *Figure 3.2*, each branch location has both the distribution and access layer switches.

The core layer plays a vital role in an enterprise network. To get a better idea of how the connections are made in a real-world scenario, take a look at *Figure 3.3*:

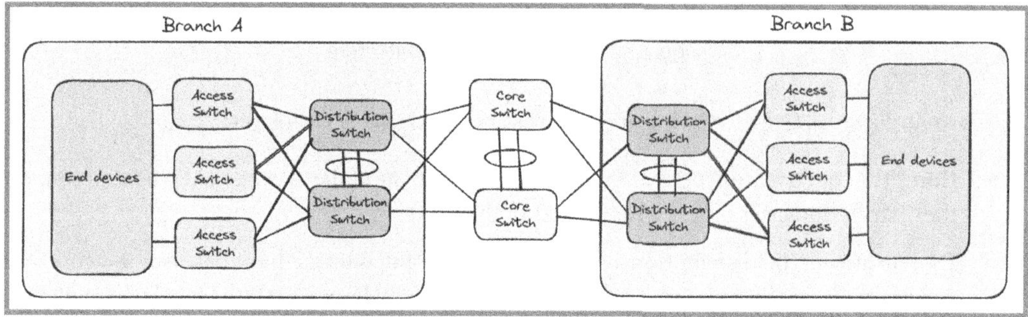

Figure 3.3: Connecting branch offices

As shown in the preceding diagram, the core layer ensures each branch network is connected to the campus network. For instance, traffic between the hosts of a branch network will travel between the access and distribution blocks only. However, if a host on one branch wants to request or access resources located in another branch network, the distribution block on the source network will be responsible for forwarding traffic to the core network.

Two-Tier Architecture

The two-tier architecture is a simpler network design than the three-tier architecture and combines the role and function of the core and distribution layers into a single network block known as the **collapsed core**. This type of network architecture is usually implemented within smaller networks than the large networks that the three-tier architecture uses.

Figure 3.4 shows the two-tier architecture, which consists of only the access and distribution switches and not the core switches:

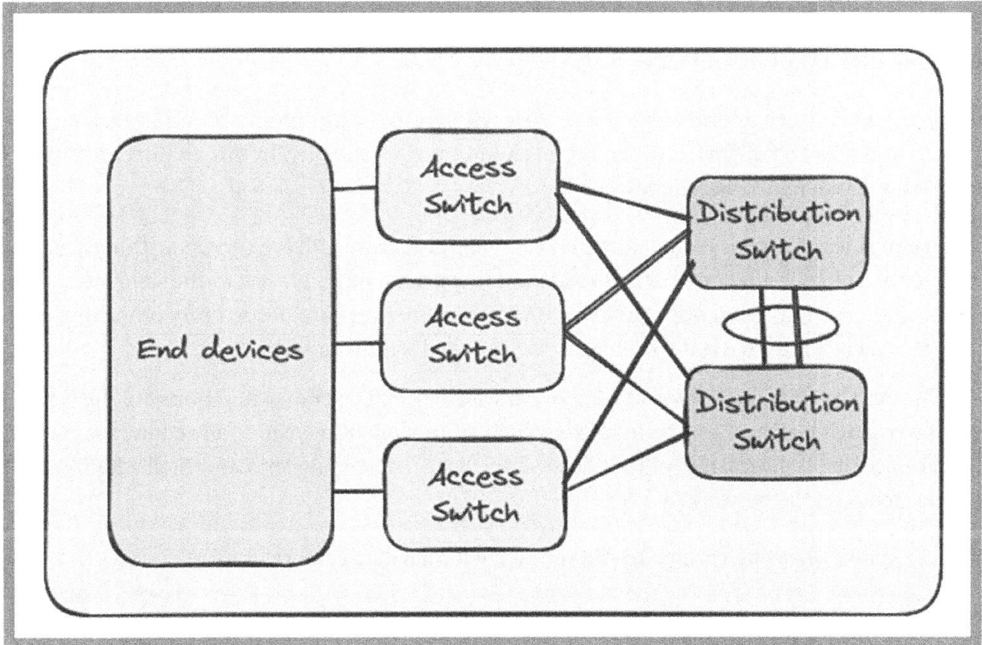

Figure 3.4: Cisco two-tier architecture

As shown in *Figure 3.4*, the two-tier architecture consists of the access and distribution blocks of a branch network. However, it is important to understand the role and function of each layer:

- **Collapsed core**: The collapsed core uses distribution-layer switches and combines the functions of both the core and distribution layers. In addition, this layer is responsible for providing high-speed bandwidth, performing layer 3 routing, and handling traffic aggregation from the access-layer switches.
- **Access**: The access layer block provides network access for end devices to interface with the network resources and services. At the access layer, network security controls are implemented to ensure that authorized users and devices are permitted to access the network and its resources.

> **Note**
>
> Combining the core and distribution functions can lead to scalability and redundancy issues in larger networks. The distribution layer is more than just aggregation; it often handles policy enforcement, security filtering, and other functions that could be overloaded if combined with core functions.

The two-tier architecture provides a cost-effective design that is more suited to smaller organizations with smaller networks without compromising network performance and support scalability.

Spine-Leaf Architecture

The spine-leaf network architecture is a two-tier design that's commonly found in data centers; it supports east-west traffic flow between servers and improves stability. In this architecture, there are two layers of Cisco network switches:

- **Leaf**: A leaf switch is installed within each server rack and all the servers within the rack are connected to it. If a server wants to communicate with other servers in the same rack, the leaf switch provides interconnectivity for them. If more ports are needed for connecting servers on a rack, additional leaf switches can be installed within a rack.
- **Spine**: The spine switch installed above the lead switch layer and functions are the backbone layer. Each leaf switch is connected to each spine switch to ensure full redundancy within a data center. If more bandwidth is needed, the data center engineers can install additional spine switches on the network.

Figure 3.5 shows leaf switches on each server rack within a data center:

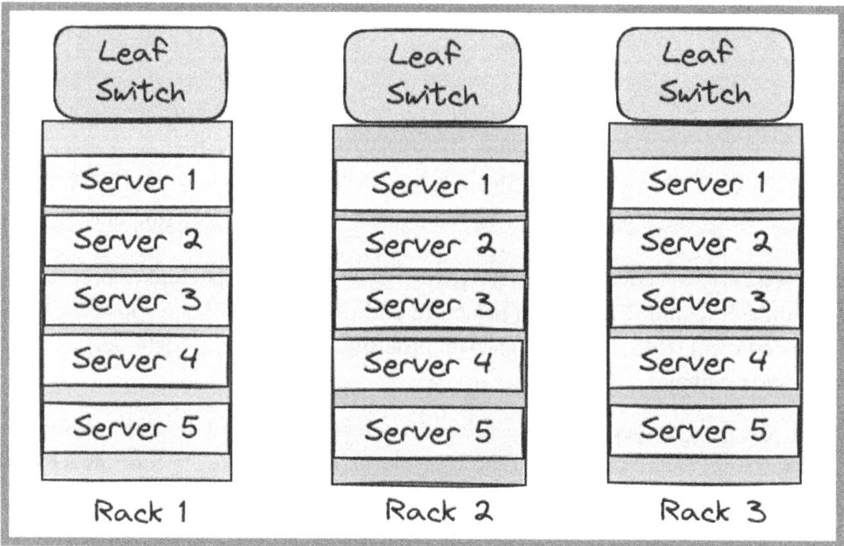

Figure 3.5: Leaf switches

> **Note**
>
> Leaf switches are commonly referred to as **top-of-rack** (**ToR**) switches.

Figure 3.6 shows how each leaf switch interconnects with each spine switch to create a full mesh for redundancy:

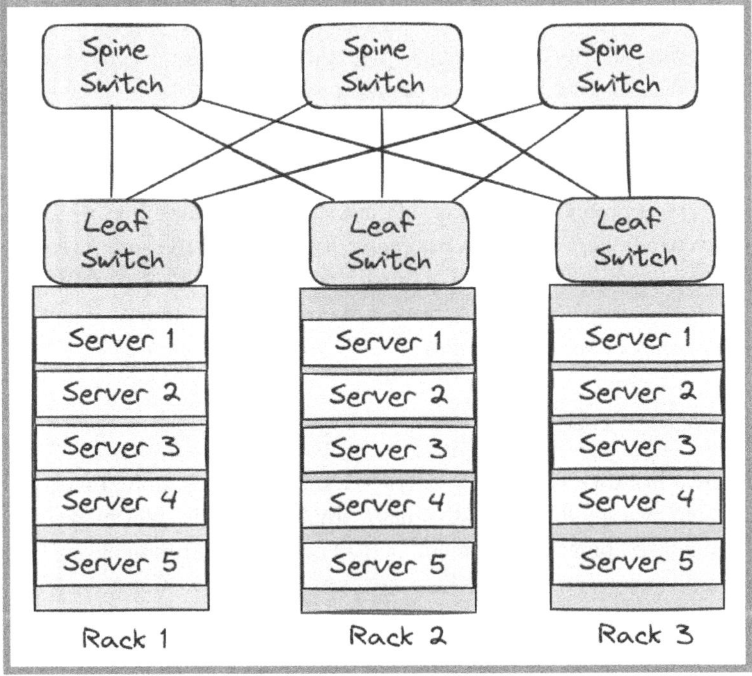

Figure 3.6: Spine-leaf switches

As shown in *Figure 3.6*, each leaf switch is connected to each spine switch. This design enables data center engineers to easily expand the network if additional servers are installed. For instance, if a new server rack is installed with a few servers, a leaf switch or ToR switch is also installed on the new rack. The leaf switch is then connected to each spine switch within the network architecture.

> **Note**
>
> **East-West** traffic typically refers to data moving laterally within the data center, while **North-South** traffic refers to data moving in and out of the data center.

In addition, the spine-leaf switches are not the typical layer 2 switches that are commonly found within organizations. These spine-leaf switches are designed specifically for data center environments and are configured to operate using a Layer 3 technology known as **virtual extensible LANs (VXLANs)**.

VXLAN enables data center engineers to leverage a virtualization technology that surpasses the limitation of the traditional **virtual LAN (VLAN)**, enabling the creation of a Layer 2 network over a Layer 3 network infrastructure, while the spine-leaf switches operate as Layer 3 switches and use dynamic routing protocols in the data center. In addition, VLANs are limited to 4,096 unique IDs within a network as compared to VXLAN supporting 16+ million unique segments on a large network. While VLANs operate at Layer 2, VXLANs operate at Layer 3.

Data center engineers implement VXLANs within their network architecture as this allows Layer 2 frames to be encapsulated within a Layer 3 packet. These Layer 3 packets use **User Datagram Protocol (UDP)**, a transport layer protocol for delivering the encapsulated Layer 2 frames over an IP network between one switch to another within the data center. It also creates an overlay network that can span multiple physical networks and has the capability of integrating with **software-defined networking (SDN)** solutions such as using network controllers to improve the automation and programmability of networking devices in a large organization.

Small Office/Home Office

Small office/home office (SOHO) usually refers to a small network infrastructure that is designed for and implemented by a small business that has a physical footprint of a single office space within a building or even a home office environment. SOHO network environments are usually simpler to manage as compared to enterprise networks in medium and large organizations.

Unlike larger networks that contain a lot of routers, switches, access points, and even firewalls, within a SOHO setting, you will commonly find all-in-one devices such as a wireless router or even a **unified threat management (UTM)** firewall for small businesses. UTM firewalls are configured to detect and prevent known malware and filter network traffic between the internet and your internal networks.

A wireless router is an all-in-one device because it has a built-in router for connecting different IP networks and physical networks (wired and wireless), a switch for allowing users to connect their computers using a wired connection to the back of the wireless router, and an access point for providing wireless connectivity to mobile devices such as smartphones, laptops, and **internet of things (IoT)** devices.

Figure 3.7 shows a typical SOHO environment with the essential network components, such as a wireless router, a network switch, and a UTM firewall:

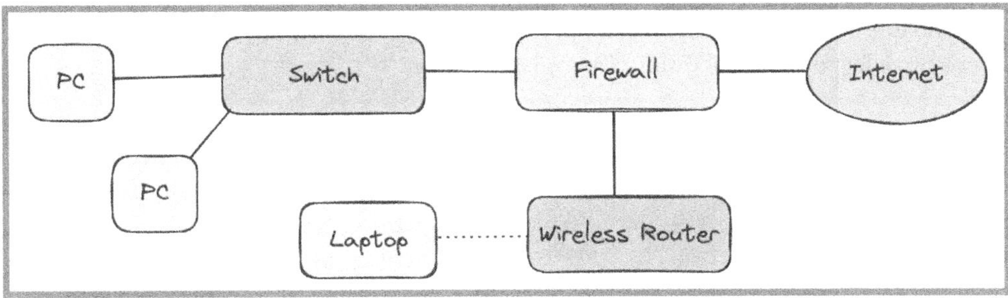

Figure 3.7: SOHO network

The Cisco Firepower 1010 firewall is a small-business firewall appliance with an integrated switch that is most suitable for SOHOs and small branch offices. Therefore, by using a small Cisco firewall with a wireless router, or even just by using switch, you can set up a SOHO architecture quickly and easily.

Wide Area Network Architectures

A **wide area network** (**WAN**) is a network architecture that enables an organization to extend its LAN over a large geographic distance. For instance, an organization might host a few critical servers on-premises at their head office location but want their employees who are working at a remote office to access those same servers. The organization can contact a **telecommunication provider** (**telco**) who can set up and manage the WAN infrastructure that connects the organization's remote offices. Keep in mind that the customer, that is, the organization, does not set up or maintain the WAN infrastructure. Telcos usually offer various types of WAN services using a subscription-based model.

There are various types of WAN topologies, such as the following:

- Point-to-point
- Hub-and-spoke
- Dual-home
- Fully meshed
- Partially meshed

In a **point-to-point** topology, the service provider sets up and maintains a dedicated connection between two edge routers, as shown in *Figure 3.8*:

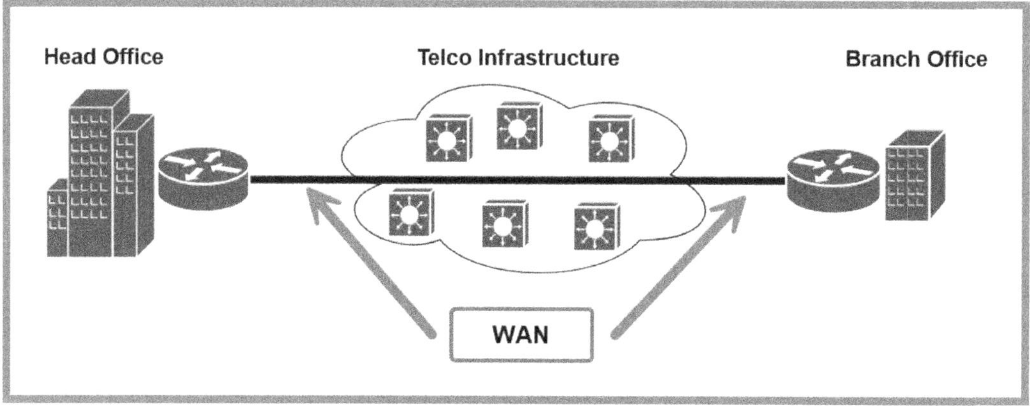

Figure 3.8: Point-to-point WAN topology

As shown in *Figure 3.8*, the organization has two branches that are connected using a traditional WAN solution from a telco.

In a **hub-and-spoke** architecture, the telco establishes point-to-point links between the head office and branch locations, connecting the edge device of the head office to the edge device at each remote office. In addition, the network professionals of the organizations are responsible for configuring each edge device, whether it is a router or firewall, to forward traffic using the following guidelines:

- The edge device at the head office should be configured to forward traffic to each branch location
- Each edge device at each remote office should be configured to forward traffic to the head office

These guidelines will ensure that the head office functions as the centralized reference point for all network traffic between remote offices. *Figure 3.9* shows the hub-and-spoke architecture:

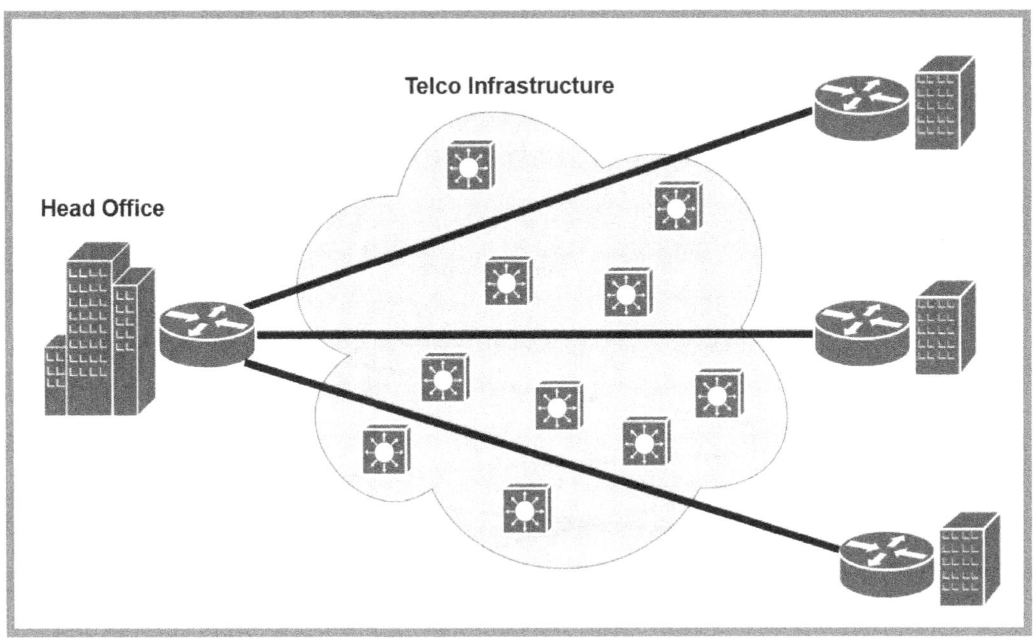

Figure 3.9: Hub-and-spoke topology

As shown in *Figure 3.9*, the head office router is a single device that functions as the hub, and all network traffic from all other branch routers must go through it. That makes this type of architecture a **single-home topology**.

In a **dual-home** topology, there are two hub routers that provide redundant connections between each spoke router at the branch locations and the head office location. This architecture provides better redundancy than a traditional hub-and-spoke architecture. While dual-homed provides redundancy, it increases complexity and potential costs, as it requires additional hardware and possibly different service providers to ensure true redundancy.

In addition, this network design ensures that organizations are able to easily implement a backup (redundancy) service provider connection. For instance, one hub router can be connected to one telco service, while the other hub router is connected to another telco service.

Figure 3.10 shows a dual-home architecture, where each remote office has two connections to both routers at the head office:

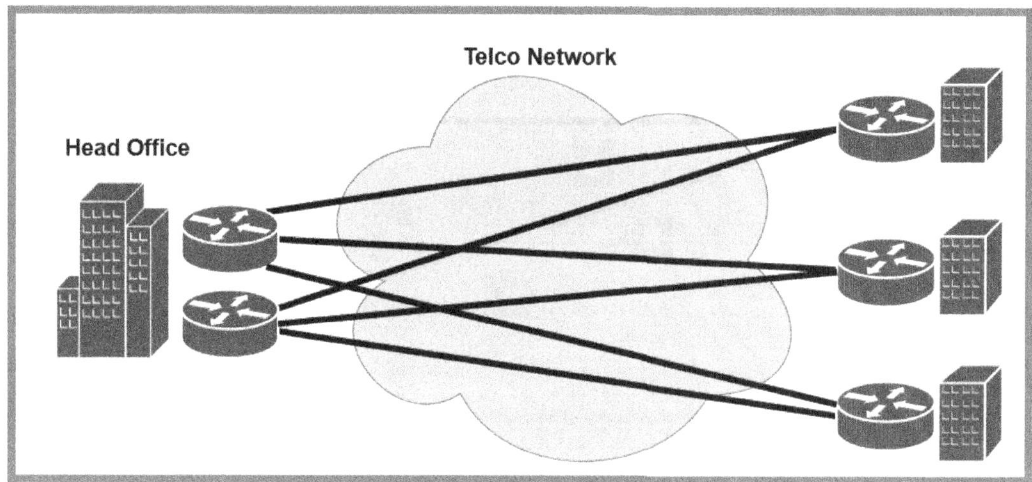

Figure 3.10: Dual-home

A **fully meshed** architecture provides the most redundancy as the edge device of a branch office is directly connected with all branch office's edge devices. Therefore, if a path is unavailable between a source and destination, a redundancy path can be used to forward traffic between branch locations.

However, as more edge devices are added to the WAN topology, more WAN connections are required to connect with all other remote offices, and this increases the overall cost of using the telco. As the mesh expands, the complexity of maintaining and troubleshooting any issue that arises becomes more challenging.

Figure 3.11 shows a fully meshed architecture:

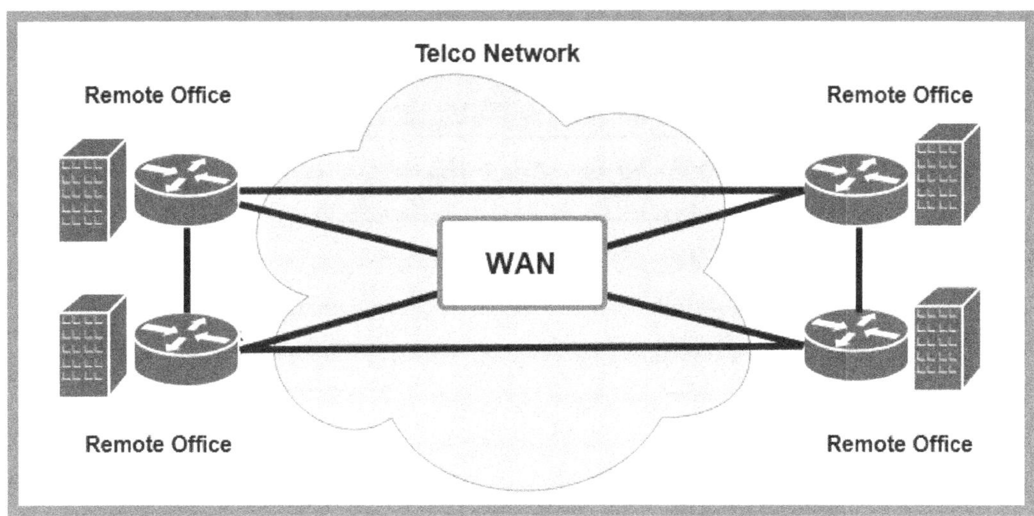

Figure 3.11: Fully meshed

In a **partially meshed** architecture, not all edge devices are directly connected with each other; only some are. For instance, an edge router of one branch office might be directly connected to all other locations, but an edge device at another branch office might be directly connected to only one other remote office.

Figure 3.12 shows a partially meshed architecture, where not all of the branch routers have a connection to all other routers:

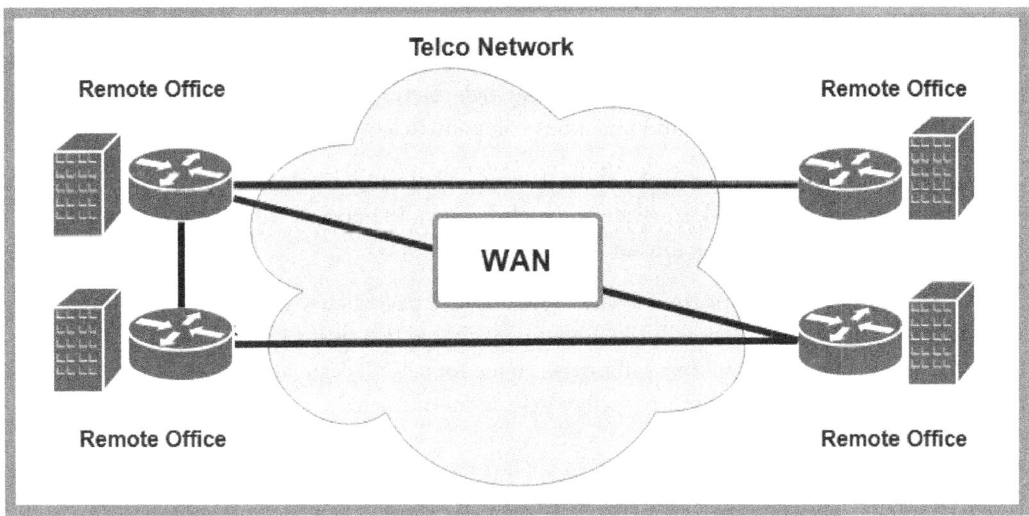

Figure 3.12: Partially meshed

As technology continues to evolve, new and emerging technologies appear in the telecommunication industry, such as dedicated and switched WAN services from telcos, as shown in *Figure 3.13*:

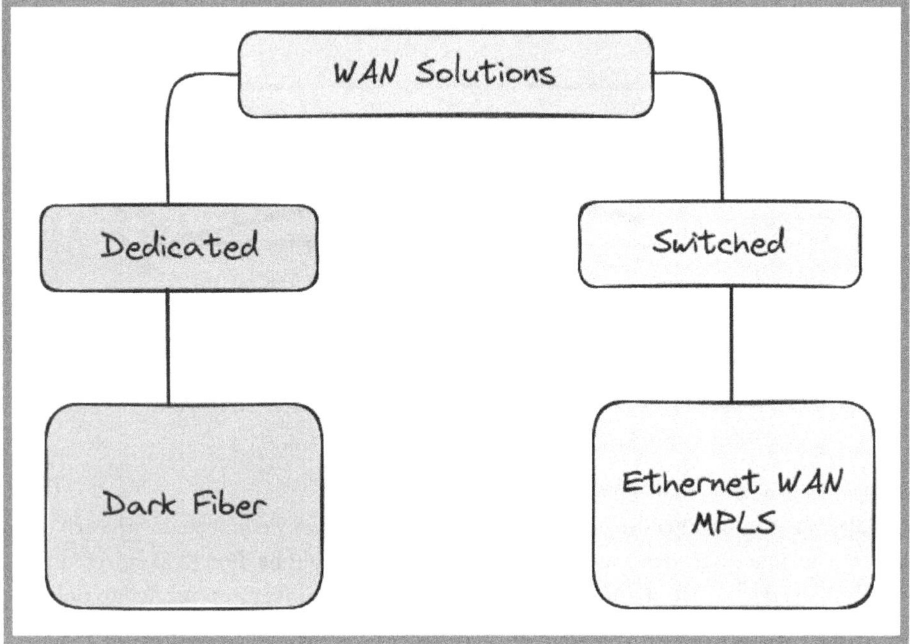

Figure 3.13: WAN solutions

Dedicated WAN connections are usually more expensive than other WAN solutions since the telco ensures that the customer receives the fixed/dedicated bandwidth based on the **service-level agreement** (**SLA**) between the provider and the customer. One such solution is a **dark fiber** infrastructure, which is owned and installed by a telecommunications company (telco) but is not currently activated.

Dark fiber is leveraged by a telco in the event that an organization wants to either lease or purchase this fiber connection to establish a private and high-bandwidth network with complete management of and control over the infrastructure and equipment.

Unlike dedicated WAN connections, which ensure that packets use the same path between the sender and receiver, in packet-switched (sometimes referred to as just switched) WAN connections, individual packets travel via multiple paths between the source and destination. Using packet-switched technologies ensures faster and more efficient delivery of messages.

Ethernet is a technology that was created for LANs and was not originally intended to be used on WAN connections due to the maximum support distance of a copper cable, which is up to 100 meters. However, with the advancement of Ethernet and fiber optic cables, Ethernet over fiber cables supports distances from 5 kilometers to even 70 kilometers, depending on the Ethernet standard for fiber optic cables. This enhancement to Ethernet standards has enabled telcos to offer Ethernet WAN connections to their customers.

> **Note**
>
> Within the networking industry, there are various names for Ethernet WAN, such as **metropolitan Ethernet** (**MetroE**), **Ethernet over MPLS** (**EoMPLS**), and **virtual private LAN service** (**VPLS**).

Multiprotocol label switching (**MPLS**) is another packet-switched WAN connection offered by telcos. MPLS allows telcos to support high-performance routing capabilities for connecting their customers without compromising the method of access. Simply put, the network connection between the customer's network and the telco's network is independent of the interface, which permits the use of MetroE and **digital subscriber line** (**DSL**).

> **Note**
>
> MetroE is a managed WAN solution from telcos that supports both point-to-point and multi-point connections, enabling organizations to interconnect their branch offices. DSL is provided by telcos to both residential and business customers and allows data transmission over traditional telephone lines.

Within a telco network, the engineers set up and maintain a logical connection for interconnecting the branch offices of the customer without relying on the type of connection used at each branch office.

Figure 3.14 shows a typical MPLS architecture:

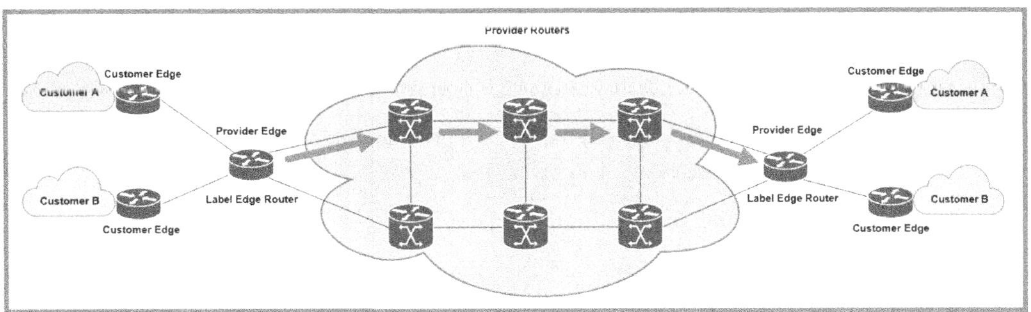

Figure 3.14: MPLS network

As shown in the preceding diagram, the following are the various components of an MPLS network:

- **Customer edge (CE) router**: The CE router is located on the customer's edge and terminates the access method (MetroE or DSL) from the telco. It's also responsible for forwarding network traffic to the LER.
- **Label edge router (LER)**: The LER operates as both the entry and exit nodes for all MPLS traffic that's entering or leaving the telco's MPLS network. The ingress LER is responsible for assigning a label to the incoming customer's traffic, while the egress LER removes the labels for outgoing network traffic that's leaving the MPLS network.
- **Label switch router (LSR)**: These are the intermediate routers within the MPLS network and they're managed by the telco. These LSRs inspect the labels on the network traffic, swap the labels based on the label forwarding table, and forward the packet to the next hop/router.

MPLS is a common solution from telcos as it's also used to provide services such as **virtual private network (VPN)** connectivity, QoS for prioritizing traffic types, and network redundancy to support availability.

On-Premises and Cloud Architectures

On-premises architecture is simply the traditional network topologies, components, network security appliances, and network management and monitoring solutions that exist in many enterprise networks.

The following are the common network components within an enterprise network:

- **Routers**: Responsible for connecting different networks and forwarding packets between IP networks
- **Switches**: Responsible for connecting devices on a LAN
- **Access points**: Allows mobile devices to connect and access resources on the network
- **Network-attached storage (NAS)**: A dedicated device on the LAN that provides file-level storage for users
- **Storage area network (SAN)**: A dedicated, high-performance network designed for data storage
- **Uninterruptible power supplies (UPSs)**: A UPS provides limited backup power to connected devices and systems in the event of a power loss
- **Heating, ventilation, and air conditioning (HVAC)**: A dedicated system for managing cooling, airflow, and ventilation

In addition, there are some common network topologies that describe how devices are connected within a network architecture: star, bus, ring, and mesh.

In a star topology, all devices are connected to a centralized device, such as a network switch. Therefore, all end devices send their traffic to the switch. The switch makes its forwarding decision based on the destination **medium access control** (**MAC**) address found within the Layer 2 header of the frame.

Figure 3.15 shows a star topology with PCs as end devices, which are connected to a centralized intermediary networking device (in this case, a switch):

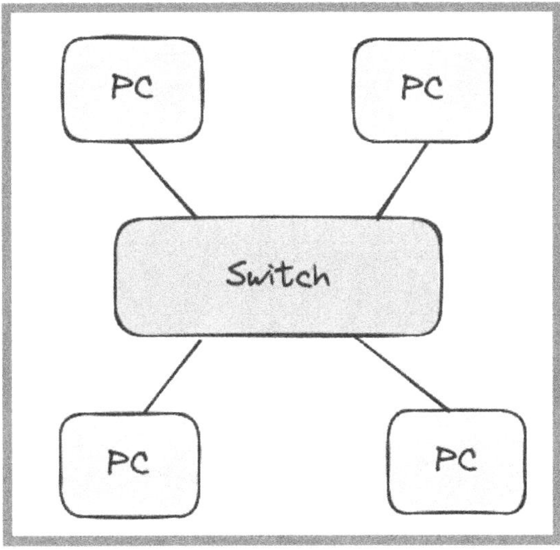

Figure 3.15: Star topology

In a bus topology, all devices are connected to a centralized cable known as a bus. This topology does not support redundancy; the entire network goes down if there's a break in the cable. Additionally, only one device can transmit at a time as the entire topology operates as a single contention-based network and a single broadcast domain.

Figure 3.16 shows a bus topology with terminals connected to a centralized cable, such as a coaxial cable that's used for sending electrical signals to the server and other systems on the network:

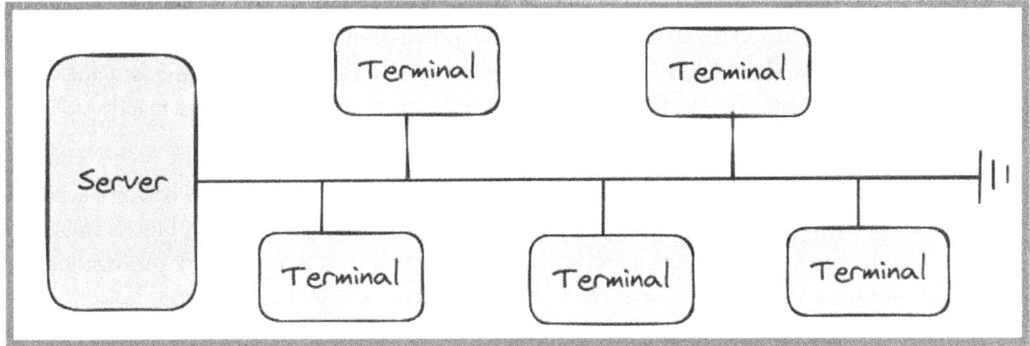

Figure 3.16: Bus topology

In a ring topology, devices are connected in a circular fashion and only one device can send a message at a time, as the topology is a content-based network.

Figure 3.17 shows a ring topology with multiple end devices that are each connected to the neighboring device:

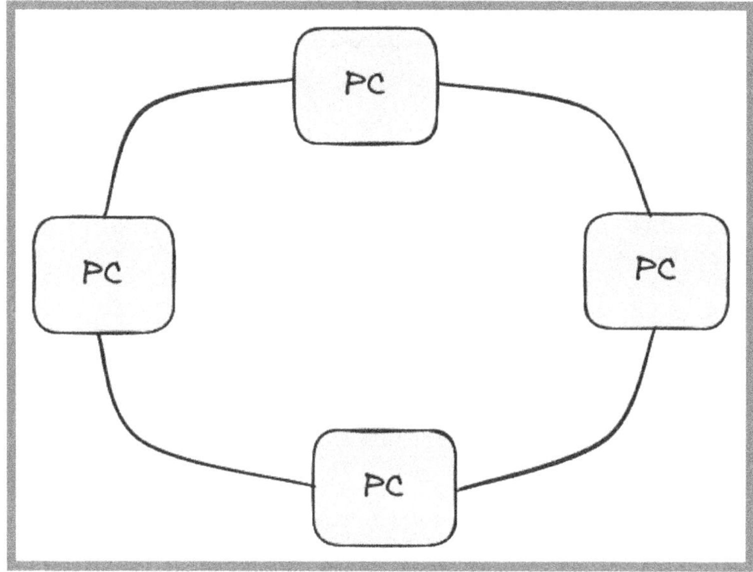

Figure 3.17: Ring topology

In a mesh topology, all devices are connected to create multiple paths between all devices and provide the most redundancy. Lastly, a hierarchical topology usually consists of two or more different network topologies that are interconnected, for instance, a star and a bus topology, or even a ring and a star topology.

Within many network architectures, professionals implement security solutions to reduce the risk of cyber-attacks and threats. Some of these solutions are security appliances and network management tools, such as network-based firewalls used to monitor and filter malicious traffic between networks. This can be done to implement an **intrusion detection system** (**IDS**) for detecting and analyzing network traffic for potential threats that are not recognizable by firewalls. An IDS is a reactive solution as it will alert after a threat is identified but does not contain the threat.

Furthermore, implementing an **intrusion prevention system** (**IPS**) helps network and security professionals to monitor and analyze network traffic for threats, and it proactively blocks and alerts when a threat is detected. Lastly, using network monitoring tools enables network professionals to closely monitor the availability and performance of network devices within their organization. These tools help network professionals to identify failures in their network and assess the health of their network components.

Cloud Computing and Technologies

Cloud computing enables you to use computing resources that are located in someone else's data center via the internet. In today's world, the need to have physical servers in an organization is slowly decreasing.

Having physical servers within an organization has disadvantages. It means that organizations are generally required to have a dedicated and available IT team ready to configure, support, and troubleshoot any issues with on-premises servers. Additionally, physical servers usually increase the physical footprint of the organization. Each physical server requires its own supply of electricity to operate. A power outage could compromise the availability of the servers and the resources it provides users. Furthermore, as more servers become clustered within the same room and continuously run, they will generate heat, meaning dedicated cooling systems are needed, and if a hardware failure occurs on a server, it may disrupt network services.

With cloud computing, an organization can reduce the need for physical servers and simply pay only for the resources they use from a cloud computing service provider such as Microsoft Azure or **Amazon Web Services** (**AWS**).

On the backend of the cloud computing service provider, a lot of virtualization and automation technologies are leveraged to quickly spin up resources for their customers in as little as a couple of minutes.

Cloud computing has many advantages. Cloud computing service providers usually guarantee over 99% uptime annually, which means that organizations do not need to worry a lot about downtime due to power outages or hardware failures. Cloud computing services are accessible anywhere and at any time. An internet connection is all a user needs to access virtual machines and applications hosted within the cloud. Furthermore, cloud computing helps reduce the number of physical services within an organization, and therefore, the space can be better utilized by the IT team.

Cloud computing providers are responsible for all hardware maintenance on virtual servers and services, so IT teams need no longer be concerned about monitoring hardware failures and procuring additional hardware components. Furthermore, customers only pay for what they use from a cloud provider. Lastly, cloud computing service providers allow the customer to scale their platform or services at any time. This is particularly beneficial as it enables IT teams to easily adjust the amount of resources they need to implement new solutions and sustain existing applications and services.

Though there are many benefits to using cloud computing, there are also some disadvantages. When using a cloud computing platform, you do not have full control of the backend platform as it is managed by the service provider. You need to secure your cloud services and resources just as you would for local servers in your organization. An internet connection is always required from the user's end to access resources online.

There are various services offered by cloud computing providers to their customers:

- **Software as a service (SaaS)**
- **Platform as a service (PaaS)**
- **Infrastructure as a service (IaaS)**

In a SaaS solution, the cloud provider grants access to the applications and services that are delivered over the internet and made available to the customer. The customer is not responsible for the management or administration of the underlying architecture, such as the networking, server configuration, or even the hardware of the virtual server within the data center. An example of SaaS is Microsoft 365 or Google Workspace.

In a PaaS solution, the cloud provider grants access to the development tools and services that are needed for application development. This cloud service allows the developer to have some control over the configuration or development environment on the virtual servers.

In an IaaS solution, the cloud provider grants access to everything on a virtual server to the customer. For instance, the customer will be able to allocate additional hardware resources to a virtual machine, choose the operating system and its version for the installation on a virtual machine, and deploy applications on a virtual machine.

In the world of cloud computing, there are four main types of cloud models:

- Private cloud
- Public cloud
- Hybrid cloud
- Community cloud

In a public cloud, the cloud provider offers applications and services to the public using a pay-as-you-go model. This allows customers/tenants to pay for the resources they use in the cloud provider's data center. Examples of public cloud providers are Microsoft Azure, AWS, and Google Cloud.

In a private cloud, the applications and services within the data center are made available to a specific user or organization only. For instance, if your organization builds a data center to host critical systems, applications, and services for their employees only, then it would be considered a private cloud environment.

The hybrid cloud model merges the private and public cloud models. Organizations usually have a private cloud hosting their applications and data. The private cloud provides faster data transfer rates between the users within the organization as it is locally hosted. However, the organization also pays for a public cloud service. This allows them to ensure they continuously replicate the private cloud onto the public cloud for redundancy and availability.

A community cloud is created for a specific community. For instance, a dedicated cloud infrastructure can be created for healthcare providers to ensure that they are compliant with various industry standards and regulatory standards such as the **Health Insurance Portability and Accountability Act** (**HIPAA**).

Having completed this section, you have learned about various network topologies, architectures, and cloud computing services and models. In the next section, you will learn about physical interface connections, issues, and cabling types.

Physical Interface and Cabling Types

In this section, you will learn about the fundamentals of fiber and copper cables, how to identify interface and cabling issues, and how to resolve them on a Cisco device.

Fiber Optic Cables

Fiber optic cables are quickly replacing copper cables and many areas of modern network infrastructure. Fiber optic cables use light signals to transmit data along a plastic or glass core. Before an end device, such as a server, or networking device, such as a switch, sends data over a fiber optic cable, the NIC of the device is responsible for converting the frame into a signal that can be transmitted over the network media. The NIC uses either a laser or a **light-emitting diode** (**LED**) to create light signals that can travel along the core of the fiber optic cable. The cores of fiber optic cables are very fragile and can break very easily if the cable is bent or too much physical pressure is applied to it.

Since fiber optic cables use light signals from lasers and LEDs, these light signals can be transmitted a lot faster than electrical signals over a copper cable. Fiber optic cables are less susceptible to attenuation as compared to copper cables but are not immune to it, since all transmission media experience some degree of signal loss over distance. Copper cables are highly susceptible to attenuation. Fiber optic cables are immune to **electromagnetic interference** (**EMI**) and **radio frequency interference** (**RFI**). Fiber optic cables are usually more expensive as compared to copper cables, and the fragile core of fiber optic cables means a high risk of damage.

There are two common categories of fiber optic cables: single-mode fiber and multi-mode fiber.

Single-mode fiber (**SMF**) uses a single path of light when transmitting the light signal through the core. This technique reduces the attenuation and dispersion of the signal. Additionally, the SMF core is only 9 microns in diameter and is smaller when compared with the core of multi-mode fiber. Furthermore, SMF uses a laser as the light source, which enables the signal to travel at longer distances with higher precision.

While it's said that SMF provides data transmission over 10 kilometers with no signal quality issues, that isn't always true, as there are many factors that can affect the bandwidth, including the quality of the fiber, the type of transceivers used, and the data rate. Even so, SMF does provide higher bandwidth and is suitable for long-distance transmission. SMF is more expensive than multi-mode fiber.

Multi-mode fiber (**MMF**) uses multiple paths of light when transmitting light signals through the core. This technique increases the likelihood of attenuation and dispersion. The cores of MMF cables are larger than those of SMF cables. The core size of MMF is between 50–62.5 microns in diameter to allow multiple light paths. Additionally, MMF uses LEDs or a **vertical cavity surface emitting laser** (**VCSEL**) to generate light signals. MMF has a shorter range as compared to SMF (only 2 kilometers as the light signals experience attenuation). Keep in mind that MMF provides less bandwidth and is commonly used on internal networks within organizations; it is less expensive than SMF.

The following are some common fiber connectors for terminating the ends of the cable:

- **Lucent connector** (**LC**): This a small-form-factor connector used on fiber optic cables that are commonly implemented within high-density applications. One of the notable features of this connector is the simple push-and-latch design, which makes it easy to install and remove. This connector is commonly used on both SMF and MMF cables.
- **Straight tip** (**ST**): This connector provides a secure connection as it leverages a bayonet-style coupling mechanism. This fiber connector is commonly used on both SMF and MMF cables and is commonly installed within commercial and industrial environments.
- **Subscriber connector** (**SC**): This connector has a square form factor and leverages a push-pull mechanism. This connector is also used on both SMF and MMF cables.
- **Mechanical transfer registered jack** (**MT-RJ**): The MT-RJ connector is designed for two fibers for duplex connections to a networking device. This connector is also used on both SMF and MMF cables.

Next, you will learn about some common copper cables.

Copper Cables

Copper cables are one of the most common types of network cable you will find in medium-sized and large organizations. Copper cables are inexpensive and easy to install within office spaces and buildings. There are two popular types of copper cables: **unshielded twisted pair** (**UTP**) and **shielded twisted pair** (**STP**).

UTP cables consist of four pairs of twisted wires without any shielding from EMI or RFI and are used to transmit electrical signals. The wires are twisted to prevent EMI from being absorbed by copper conductors, and it also helps reduce crosstalk. In addition, UTP cables are inexpensive and easy to install as compared to STP cables.

Figure 3.18 shows a UTP cable:

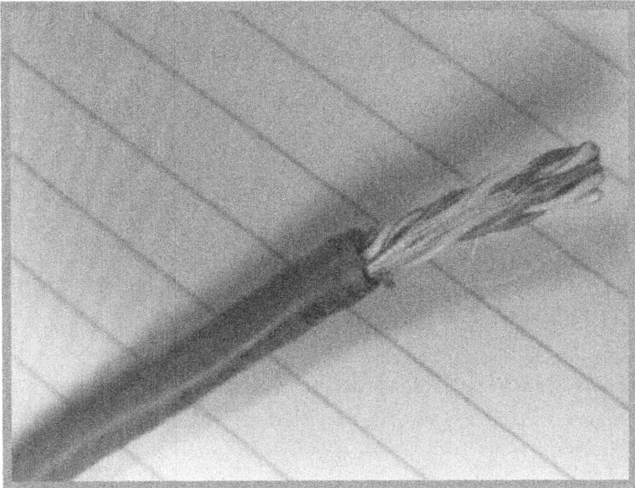

Figure 3.18: UTP cable

STP cables have four pairs of twisted wires that are shielded from EMI, and these wires are used to transmit electrical signals. The construction of STP cables contains an additional layer of metal foil or braiding to catch any EMI before it reaches the copper conductors and discharge it, hence adding a layer of protection. The added layer of metal foil or braiding reduces crosstalk and makes it suitable for environments with a lot of EMI. STP cables are commonly found within environments with high EMI, data centers, and industrial environments.

Figure 3.19 shows an STP cable:

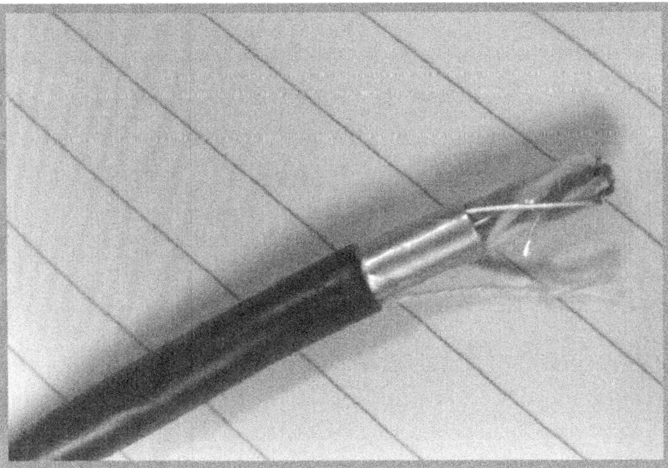

Figure 3.19: STP cable

Table 3.1 shows the different categories of twisted pair cables and their support speeds:

Type/Category	Speed	Frequency
Cat 5e (enhanced)	Up to 1 Gbps	100 MHz
Cat 6	Up to 10 Gbps (shorter distance)	250 MHz
Cat 6a (augmented)	Up to 10 Gbps (longer distance)	500 MHz
Cat 7	Up to 10 Gbps	600 MHz
Cat 8	Up to 25 Gbps or 40 Gbps	2000 MHz

Table 3.1 – Types of copper cables

Additionally, the **registered Jack 45** (**RJ45**) is an 8-pin connector that is used for terminating copper twisted-pair cables. *Figure 3.20* shows a copper twisted-pair cable with an RJ45 connector:

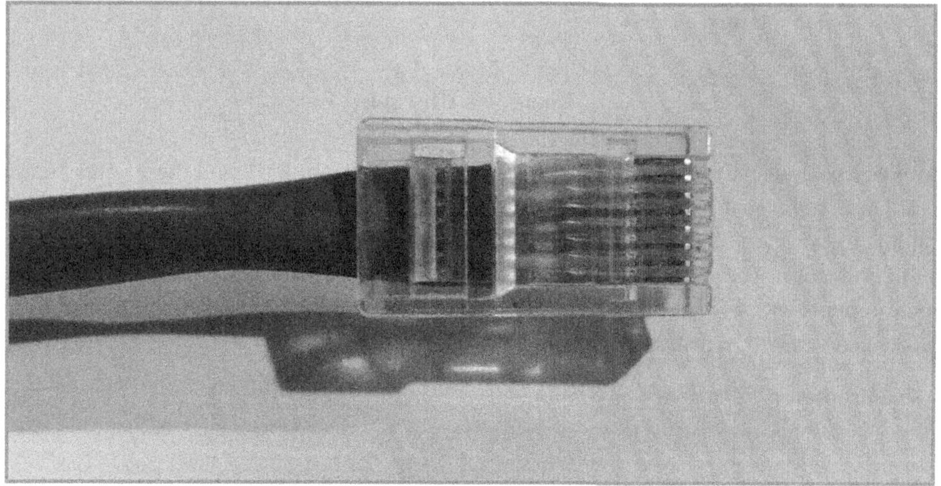

Figure 3.20: RJ45 connector

Identifying Interface and Cable Issues

Sometimes, networking devices can have faulty interfaces or damaged cables connected to them, which can cause issues that have the potential to affect the performance of a network segment. By understanding the potential causes, you will be able to identify and troubleshoot these issues:

- **Improper cable types**: Using the incorrect cable type, such as a straight-through or crossover cable, when connecting devices can create an issue. Therefore, it is important to remember that straight-through twisted-pair cables are used for connecting different devices, while crossover twisted-pair cables are used for connecting the same type of devices.

- **Exceeding cable length**: Many twisted-pair copper cables have a theoretical maximum length of 100 m, after which the electrical signal has the potential to experience attenuation, the loss of electrical signal over distance.
- **Bad/faulty cable**: Faulty network cables can cause issues such as runts, giants, and malformed packets.
- **Unseated cables**: Unseated or loose cables can cause errors.

Using the `show interfaces` command, you will be able to see whether an interface is encountering errors, collisions, or physical issues, as shown in *Figure 3.21*:

```
Switch#show interfaces gigabitethernet 0/1
GigabitEthernet0/1 is up, line protocol is up (connected)
  Hardware is Lance, address is 0004.9ad3.5a19 (bia 0004.9ad3.5a19)
 BW 1000000 Kbit, DLY 1000 usec,
     reliability 255/255, txload 1/255, rxload 1/255
  Encapsulation ARPA, loopback not set
  Keepalive set (10 sec)
  Full-duplex, 1000Mb/s
  input flow-control is off, output flow-control is off
  ARP type: ARPA, ARP Timeout 04:00:00
  Last input 00:00:08, output 00:00:05, output hang never
  Last clearing of "show interface" counters never
  Input queue: 0/75/0/0 (size/max/drops/flushes); Total output drops: 0
  Queueing strategy: fifo
  Output queue :0/40 (size/max)
  5 minute input rate 0 bits/sec, 0 packets/sec
  5 minute output rate 0 bits/sec, 0 packets/sec
     956 packets input, 193351 bytes, 0 no buffer
     Received 956 broadcasts, 0 runts, 0 giants, 0 throttles
     0 input errors, 0 CRC, 0 frame, 0 overrun, 0 ignored, 0 abort
     0 watchdog, 0 multicast, 0 pause input
     0 input packets with dribble condition detected
     2357 packets output, 263570 bytes, 0 underruns
     0 output errors, 0 collisions, 10 interface resets
     0 babbles, 0 late collision, 0 deferred
     0 lost carrier, 0 no carrier
     0 output buffer failures, 0 output buffers swapped out
```

Figure 3.21: Checking the interface status

The following is a brief description of each counter on an interface:

- **Input errors**: This is the total number of faulty packets that have entered the interface. The value is the sum of runts, giants, no buffers, CRCs, frames, overruns, and ignored counts on the interface.
- **Runts**: These packets are discarded because they are less than 64 bytes in size and are smaller than the minimum packet size.
- **Giants**: These packets are discarded because they exceed the maximum packet size as they are greater than 1,518 bytes in size.
- **Cyclic redundancy check** (**CRC**): CRC errors occur when the checksum within the frame trailer does not match the checksum received. The CRC value is stored within the **frame check sequence** (**FCS**).
- **Output errors**: These are a sum of the total errors that have prevented a packet from leaving the interface.
- **Collisions**: These are the number of messages that have been retransmitted due to a collision on the network.
- **Late collisions**: These collisions occur after 512 bits or 64 bytes of a frame have been transmitted.

> Note
>
> Both `txload` (transmitting) and `rxload` (receiving) values are given in *x*/255 format. A high *x* value in `txload` simply indicates the percentage of the interface's bandwidth that is currently being used to send traffic in real time. For `rxload`, the percentage indicates the amount of traffic being received on the interface. If `txload` and `rxload` are 255/255, this means the interface has 100% saturation for both inbound and outbound traffic.

If these counters are increasing, it's a sign that interface errors or network collisions are occurring. To resolve these issues, check the duplex and speed settings on the interfaces of the switch and the device it's connected to. Then, if the duplex and speed configurations are good, change the network cable and check whether the counters are still increasing. If changing the cable does not resolve the issue, then connect the network cable from the end device to another interface on the switch and monitor the new interface for any errors. Lastly, having a faulty network cable or NIC can generate a lot of errors and collisions, which then results in poor network performance, such as high latency and packet loss.

Mismatch Duplex

Duplex simply refers to the mode of communication that occurs between two networking devices, such as switches and routers. The duplex settings on the interface of a networking device determine how data is transmitted and received.

The following are the common duplex modes on Cisco devices:

- Half
- Full
- Auto (default)

Half-duplex allows only one device to communicate at a time. An example of half-duplex communication is using walkie-talkies, where one person can speak at a time while the other listens. Another example is on a computer network, where end devices are connected to a hub. Once again, only one device is able to use the medium to exchange messages.

Full-duplex allows bidirectional communication between one device and another, as when a computer is connected to a switch. Both devices can simultaneously send and receive messages.

Auto is the default mode on Cisco devices, such as switches, routers, and even firewalls. In auto-mode, both connected devices will auto-negotiate their preferred duplex modes and will either be half duplex or full duplex on both connected devices.

The interfaces on Cisco devices such as switches and routers have the following duplex modes:

- **Auto**: Enables auto duplex negotiation
- **Full**: Forces full-duplex mode
- **Half**: Forces half-duplex mode

By default, the interfaces on Cisco devices are set to use auto duplex mode. The idea of using auto is to allow two devices to negotiate how they want to exchange messages between each other (half-duplex or full-duplex). Ideally, if you connect two devices together with default configurations, they are supposed to negotiate their interfaces to both being full-duplex. There are times when the negotiation process does not work properly. For example, one device's interface may be operating at half-duplex and the other device is set to full-duplex. Additionally, if there are misconfigurations on the interface that do not allow both devices to operate using the same duplex mode, this will result in latency issues and collisions of packets on the network.

Figure 3.22 shows two switches with a mismatch in duplex settings:

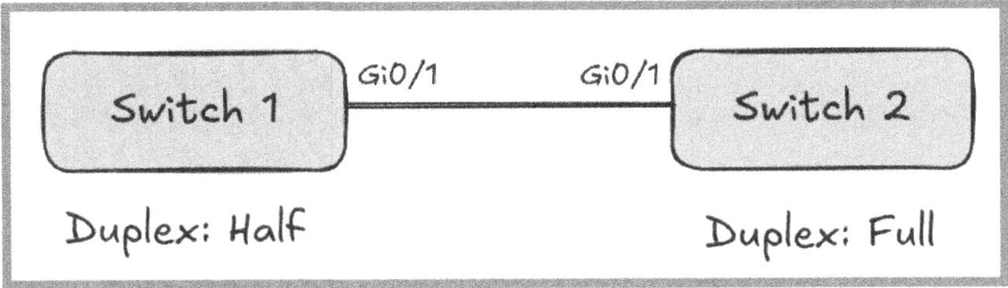

Figure 3.22: Duplex mismatch between switches

If you want to modify the duplex configurations on an interface, such as configuring the Gigabit Ethernet 0/1 interface on Switch 1 to operate in full duplex, then use the following commands:

1. Enter the interface mode of a switch and administratively shut down the interface:

```
Switch> enable
Switch# configure terminal
Switch(config)# interface gigabitEthernet 0/1
Switch(config-if)# shutdown
```

2. Use the `duplex` command followed by the duplex mode (`auto`, `full`, or `half`):

```
Switch(config-if)# duplex full
```

3. Using the `duplex ?` command enables you to see what options are available:

```
Switch(config-if)# duplex ?
  auto   Enable AUTO duplex configuration
  full   Force full duplex operation
  half   Force half-duplex operation
```

4. Next, re-enable the interface and exit interface mode:

```
Switch(config-if)# no shutdown
Switch(config-if)# exit
Switch(config)# exit
```

5. Lastly, to verify the duplex mode of an interface, use the `show interfaces status` command, as shown in *Figure 3.23*:

```
Switch1# show interfaces status
Port      Name               Status       Vlan  Duplex  Speed Type
Gig0/1                       connected    1     a-full  auto  10/100BaseTX
Gig0/2                       notconnect   1     auto    auto  10/100BaseTX
```

Figure 3.23: Duplex mode

6. Additionally, `show interfaces gigabitEthernet 0/1` allows you to verify the duplex mode on the interface, as shown in *Figure 3.24*:

```
Switch1# show interfaces gigabitEthernet 0/1
GigabitEthernet0/1 is up, line protocol is up (connected)
  Hardware is Lance, address is 0004.9a36.e919 (bia 0004.9a36.e919)
 BW 1000000 Kbit, DLY 1000 usec,
     reliability 255/255, txload 1/255, rxload 1/255
  Encapsulation ARPA, loopback not set
  Keepalive set (10 sec)
  Full-duplex, 1000Mb/s
  input flow-control is off, output flow-control is off
  ARP type: ARPA, ARP Timeout 04:00:00
  Last input 00:00:08, output 00:00:05, output hang never
  Last clearing of "show interface" counters never
  Input queue: 0/75/0/0 (size/max/drops/flushes); Total output drops: 0
  Queueing strategy: fifo
  Output queue :0/40 (size/max)
```

Figure 3.24: Duplex mode

As shown in *Figure 3.24*, the duplex mode is currently set as full-duplex on the interface.

Mismatch Speed

When two devices are set or configured to operate at different speeds on their connected interfaces, this causes errors and even link failures between both devices. Speed defines the maximum bandwidth supported on an interface of a device, whether the device is a computer, switch, router, or even a firewall. Simply put, the speed settings on an interface define the data transmission rate that is supported.

The following are common speed settings on modern Cisco devices:

- **100 Mbps**: Commonly referred to as Fast Ethernet
- **1,000 Mbps**: Commonly referred to as Gigabit Ethernet
- **10 Gbps**: Commonly referred to as 10 Gigabit Ethernet

The default speed setting on a Cisco device is set to auto, which enables the interface to detect the incoming signals from the other end of the cable and auto-negotiate the most suitable speed configurations.

Figure 3.25 shows a mismatch in speed between Switch 1 and Switch 2:

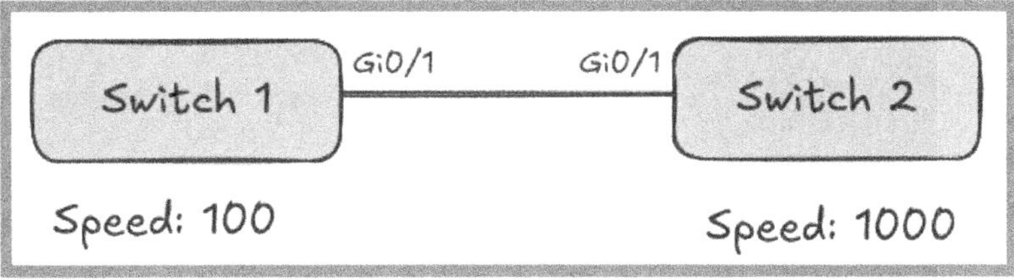

Figure 3.25: Speed mismatch

To enable the auto-negotiation features between both switches, use the following commands:

```
Switch> enable
Switch# configure terminal
Switch(config)# interface gigabitEthernet 0/1
Switch(config-if)# speed auto
Switch(config-if)# exit
```

To manually set the speed between both switches, use the following commands:

```
Switch> enable
Switch# configure terminal
Switch(config)# interface gigabitEthernet 0/1
Switch(config-if)# speed ?
  10     Force 10 Mbps operation
  100    Force 100 Mbps operation
  1000   Force 1000 Mbps operation
  auto   Enable AUTO speed configuration
```

Therefore, you can choose to set the speed to `1000` with the following commands:

```
Switch(config-if)# speed 1000
Switch(config-if)# exit
```

To verify the speed settings on an interface, use the following command:

```
Switch# show interfaces [interface-id] status
```

Figure 3.26 shows the speed configuration on the Gigabit Ethernet 0/1 interface:

```
Switch#show interfaces gigabitEthernet 0/1
GigabitEthernet0/1 is up, line protocol is up (connected)
  Hardware is Lance, address is 0004.9a36.e919 (bia 0004.9a36.e919)
 BW 1000000 Kbit, DLY 1000 usec,
     reliability 255/255, txload 1/255, rxload 1/255
  Encapsulation ARPA, loopback not set
  Keepalive set (10 sec)
  Full-duplex, 1000Mb/s
  input flow-control is off, output flow-control is off
  ARP type: ARPA, ARP Timeout 04:00:00
  Last input 00:00:08, output 00:00:05, output hang never
  Last clearing of "show interface" counters never
```

Figure 3.26: Checking speed settings

As shown in *Figure 3.26*, the speed is set to 1,000 Mbps.

Having completed this section, you have learned about the various interface and cabling issues that affect the performance of a network.

Summary

In this chapter, you learned about the various network topologies and architectures that are used within many organizations around the world. In addition, you have explored various WAN topologies and discovered how telcos interconnect the branch offices of an organization. Furthermore, you have learned about the fundamentals of cloud computing, cloud models, and common cloud services. Lastly, you explored the various physical interface and cabling issues that affect the performance of a network and how to identify the type of physical errors on the interface of a Cisco device.

This chapter will help in your journey toward preparing for the 200-301 CCNA v1.1 certification. In the next chapter, *Getting Started with Cisco IOS Devices*, you will learn how to set up a small Cisco network while gaining hands-on experience in configuring Cisco devices.

Additional Reading

- Cisco Campus LAN and wireless solution: `https://www.cisco.com/c/en/us/td/docs/solutions/CVD/Campus/cisco-campus-lan-wlan-design-guide.html`
- Cisco multi-tier architecture: `https://www.cisco.com/c/en/us/solutions/collateral/data-center-virtualization/application-centric-infrastructure/white-paper-c11-742214.html`
- Configuring VXLAN: `https://www.cisco.com/c/en/us/support/docs/switches/nexus-9000-series-switches/118978-config-vxlan-00.html`
- Troubleshoot Switch Port and Interface Problems: `https://www.cisco.com/c/en/us/support/docs/switches/catalyst-6500-series-switches/12027-53.html`

Exam Readiness Drill – Chapter Review Questions

Apart from mastering key concepts, strong test-taking skills under time pressure are essential for acing your certification exam. That's why developing these abilities early in your learning journey is critical.

Exam readiness drills, using the free online practice resources provided with this book, help you progressively improve your time management and test-taking skills while reinforcing the key concepts you've learned.

HOW TO GET STARTED

- Open the link or scan the QR code at the bottom of this page
- If you have unlocked the practice resources already, log in to your registered account. If you haven't, follow the instructions in *Chapter 19* and come back to this page.
- Once you log in, click the START button to start a quiz
- We recommend attempting a quiz multiple times till you're able to answer most of the questions correctly and well within the time limit.
- You can use the following practice template to help you plan your attempts:

Working On Accuracy		
Attempt	**Target**	**Time Limit**
Attempt 1	40% or more	Till the timer runs out
Attempt 2	60% or more	Till the timer runs out
Attempt 3	75% or more	Till the timer runs out
Working On Timing		
Attempt 4	75% or more	1 minute before time limit
Attempt 5	75% or more	2 minutes before time limit
Attempt 6	75% or more	3 minutes before time limit

The above drill is just an example. Design your drills based on your own goals and make the most out of the online quizzes accompanying this book.

First time accessing the online resources? 🔓

You'll need to unlock them through a one-time process. **Head to** *Chapter 19* **for instructions.**

Open Quiz	
`https://packt.link/ccnachap3` OR scan this QR code →	

4
IPv4 and IPv6 Addresses

As an aspiring network professional, it is essential to develop a solid foundation on why **IP version 4** (**IPv4**) and **IP version 6** (**IPv6**) are common components in modern networks. Understanding these address types, their structure, and how they are used in network management plays an important role when troubleshooting IP connectivity issues.

This chapter covers *Domain 1: Network Fundamentals, Objectives 1.6 Configure and verify IPv4 addressing and subnetting, 1.7 Describe private IPv4 addressing, 1.8 Configure and verify IPv6 addressing and prefix, 1.9 Describe IPv6 address types*, and *1.10 Verify IP parameters for Client OS* of the *200-301 CCNA v1.1 Certification* exam.

You will be able to identify the differences between IPv4 and IPv6 structures and formats and configure IPv6 addresses on Cisco IOS routers. Furthermore, you will be able to compare and contrast unicast, multicast, broadcast, and anycast addresses and gain a deeper understanding of how they affect the network transmission of packets from a sender to a destination host. Let's dive in!

Importance of IP Addresses

Internet Protocol (**IP**) is a Layer 3 network protocol of the **Open Systems Interconnection** (**OSI**) network model. IP addresses are the fundamental, logical addressing that is essential for network communication and identifying devices on a network architecture. The **Internet Assigned Numbers Authority** (**IANA**) is the standard organization that oversees the IP address allocation for the entire world. They are also responsible for managing the **domain name system** (**DNS**) root directories, **Autonomous System Number** (**ASN**) allocation space, and the protocol name and numbers registry.

At the time of writing this book, there are two address spaces that are managed and allocated by IANA. These are IPv4 and IPv6. On January 1, 1983, IPv4 was initially deployed on the internet and is still widely used in both public networks, such as the internet, and private networks within organizations. The deployment of IPv6 started in 1999 but officially surfaced on the internet in 2013.

IANA uses a hierarchical structure for distributing and allocating both IPv4 and IPv6 addresses. IANA distributions blocks of addresses to five **regional internet registries** (**RIRs**). The following are the five RIRs:

- **African Network Information Center** (**AFRINIC**): Supports the continent of Africa
- **Asia-Pacific Network Information Centre** (**APNIC**): Supports regions in Asia and the Pacific
- **American Registry for Internet Numbers** (**ARIN**): Supports regions in Canada, the USA, and parts of the Caribbean
- **Latin America and Caribbean Network Information Centre** (**LACNIC**): Supports regions in Latin America and parts of the Caribbean
- **Réseaux IP Européens Network Coordination Centre** (**RIPE NCC**): Supports Europe, the Middle East, and Central Asia

These RIRs are responsible for distributing addresses to **internet service providers** (**ISPs**). The ISPs are responsible for distributing addresses to their subscribers.

Figure 4.1 shows the hierarchical structure that is used for distributing addresses from IANA to users:

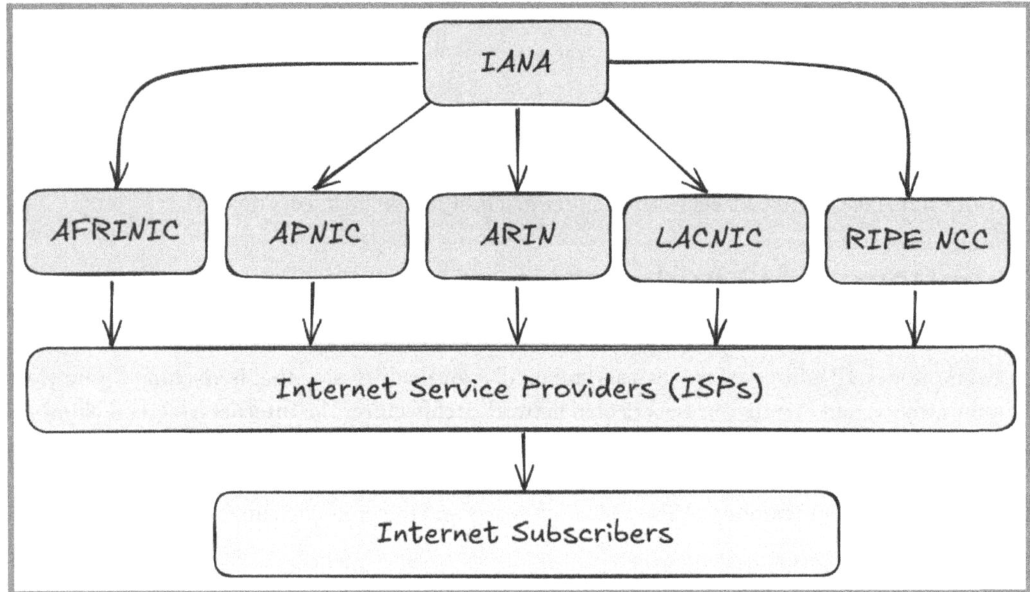

Figure 4.1: IP address delegation

Large and private organizations can register for an ASN, which is a unique identifier for an **autonomous system** (**AS**). An AS is a very large collection of internet routing network prefixes that are managed by a single organization, known as an operator. For instance, operators are typically ISPs that manage multiple publicly-routed networks. Each ISP is assigned a unique ASN that is used for exchanging network routes with other ASs using **Border Gateway Protocol** (**BGP**), an **Exterior Gateway Protocol** (**EGP**).

> **Note**
>
> To view each AS per country, please visit `https://ipinfo.io/countries`.

Figure 4.2 shows a representation of multiple ASNs interconnected via BGP:

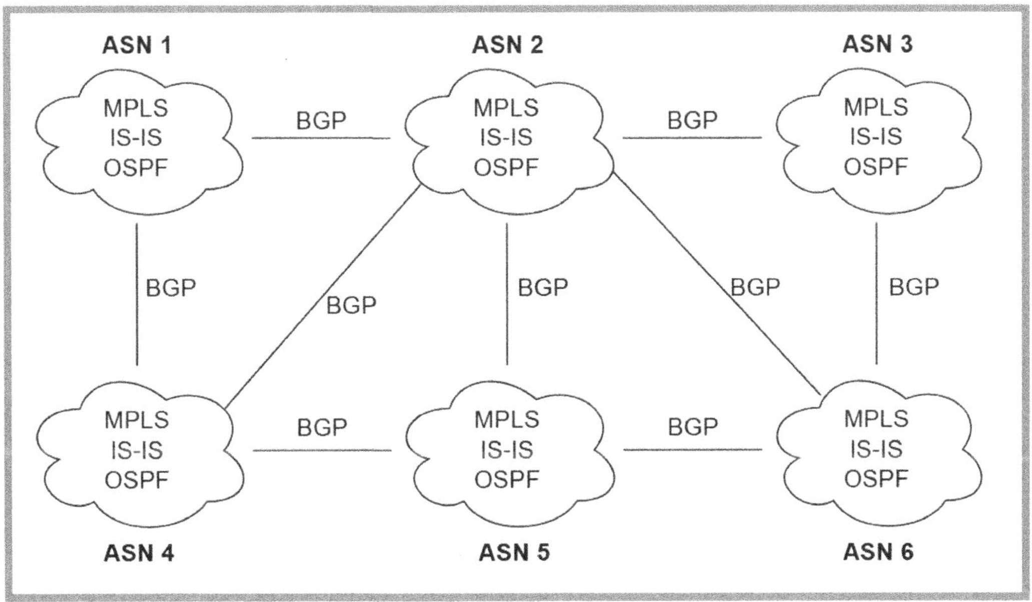

Figure 4.2: ASNs using BGP for exchanging routes

As shown in the preceding diagram, an AS usually establishes one or more redundant connections to other ASs and uses BGP to exchange routing information and updates. However, ASs commonly use one or more **Interior Gateway Routing Protocols** (**IGRPs**) such as **Open Shortest Path First** (**OSPF**), **Intermediate System to Intermediate System** (**IS-IS**), and **Enhanced Interior Gateway Routing Protocol** (**EIGRP**) within their network for routing traffic between their internal IP networks to their subscribers.

Fundamentals of IPv4

IPv4 addresses are 32-bit numbers that are commonly expressed in the dotted-decimal format as 4 octets separated by periods and the bits are 1s and 0s. Since an octet is 8 bits and there are 4 octets, this means 8 bits per octet x 4 octets = 32 bits.

IPv4 addresses are commonly written in a dotted-decimal format such as 172.16.1.1 or even 192.168.1.1. While the dotted-decimal format is easy to understand for humans, network devices and computers use electrical, light, and radio frequencies when communicating over a network. For instance, a 1 can represent a high electrical signal, while a 0 can represent a low electrical signal.

Therefore, part of the journey in learning about IPv4 addresses is understanding how to convert IPv4 addresses from the dotted-decimal to the dotted-binary format, and vice versa.

The following is an example of an IPv4 address in both dotted-decimal and dotted-binary format:

- **Dotted-decimal format**: 192.168.1.1
- **Dotted-binary format**: 11000000.10101000.00000001.00000001

As shown in the dotted-binary format, each octet has exactly eight bits. Whether the octet has all zeros or a few zeros, the zeros are not exempted from the address. In the next subsection, you will learn how to perform conversion and see why the zeros are not excluded.

Converting Binary to Decimal

You can start by taking a look at an IPv4 address in its binary format. You have already learned that an IPv4 address is made up of 32 bits, consisting of 1s and 0s. Take a look at an example of an IPv4 address that is written in the dotted-binary format:

```
11000000.10101000.00000001.10000001
```

All binary numbers are written in base-2 with a radix of 2. A radix is a unique number used in a positioning system, where the first position's value is 0. This may sound a bit confusing, but over the next few paragraphs, you will find the concept a bit clearer as you see it in action.

In mathematics, you learn that $A^0 = 1$, where A represents the radix or base. Now, use the radix of 2 as part of a positioning system, starting with 0 as the first position:

- $2^0 = 1$
- $2^1 = 2$
- $2^2 = 2 \times 2 = 4$
- $2^3 = 2 \times 2 \times 2 = 8$
- $2^4 = 2 \times 2 \times 2 \times 2 = 16$

- $2^5 = 2 \times 2 \times 2 \times 2 \times 2 = 32$
- $2^6 = 2 \times 2 \times 2 \times 2 \times 2 \times 2 = 64$
- $2^7 = 2 \times 2 \times 2 \times 2 \times 2 \times 2 \times 2 = 128$

When converting an IPv4 address, always convert one octet at a time and not the entire 32-bit address altogether to avoid any miscalculations. For this reason, the positioning system stops at the eighth position, which is 2^7. To further understand the positioning system using binary, *Table 4.1* shows the calculation for each bit within an octet:

Radix	2^7	2^6	2^5	2^4	2^3	2^2	2^1	2^0
Decimal	128	64	32	16	8	4	2	1

Table 4.1: Base 2 positioning system

When performing conversions, always remember the first position is always 2^0 and the eighth position is 2^7. The full binary format of each position can be expressed further, as follows:

- $2^0 = 00000001 = 1$
- $2^1 = 00000010 = 2$
- $2^2 = 00000100 = 4$
- $2^3 = 00001000 = 8$
- $2^4 = 00010000 = 16$
- $2^5 = 00100000 = 32$
- $2^6 = 01000000 = 64$
- $2^7 = 10000000 = 128$

Now, you can use our IPv4 address of `11000000.10101000.00000001.10000001` and convert it into a decimal number. To perform this exercise, use the following instructions:

1. Place the values of the first octet, `11000000`, within the table, as shown in *Table 4.2*:

Radix	2^7	2^6	2^5	2^4	2^3	2^2	2^1	2^0
Decimal	128	64	32	16	8	4	2	1
Binary	1	1	0	0	0	0	0	0

Table 4.2: Converting the first octet

When there's a binary number of `1`, the radix decimal value is ON. Therefore, in the preceding table, both the 2^7 and 2^6 positioning values are ON, which provides the following calculation:

```
27 + 26 = 128 + 64 = 192
```

1. You can now repeat the same procedure for the second octet, `10101000`, to determine its decimal value:

Radix	2^7	2^6	2^5	2^4	2^3	2^2	2^1	2^0
Decimal	128	64	32	16	8	4	2	1
Binary	1	0	1	0	1	0	0	0

Table 4.3: Converting the second octet

1. Using the same concept as the previous step, where `1 = ON` and `0 = OFF` for a radix, you will get the following calculation:

$2^7 + 2^5 + 2^3 = 128 + 32 + 8 = 168$

1. You can now convert the third octet, `00000001`, into decimal format by placing it into *Table 4.4*:

Radix	2^7	2^6	2^5	2^4	2^3	2^2	2^1	2^0
Decimal	128	64	32	16	8	4	2	1
Binary	0	0	0	0	0	0	0	1

Table 4.4: Converting the third octet

2. By converting `00000001` into decimal, you will get 2^0 `= 1.`
3. Next, convert the fourth octet by placing `10000001` into *Table 4.5*:

Radix	2^7	2^6	2^5	2^4	2^3	2^2	2^1	2^0
Decimal	128	64	32	16	8	4	2	1
Binary	1	0	0	0	0	0	0	1

Table 4.5: Converting the fourth octet

4. As shown in the preceding table, the following bit values are ON:

$2^7 + 2^0 = 128 + 1 = 129$

1. The last stage is simply placing all the decimal values together, as shown here:

```
11000000.10101000.00000001.10000001 = 192.168.1.129
```

What if all the bits within an octet are set to `1`? What will the decimal equivalency be? To perform this calculation, you will need to add the bit positioning values, as shown here:

$2^7 + 2^6 + 2^5 + 2^4 + 2^3 + 2^2 + 2^1 + 2^0$

To provide a further breakdown, you get the following value when adding all the bit positions:

```
128 + 64 + 32 + 16 + 8 + 4 + 2 + 1 = 255
```

This implies that an octet has a decimal range of `0-255`. A valid IPv4 address will never have an octet greater than `255`. Now that you have learned how to convert binary into decimal, take a look at converting decimal into binary.

Converting Decimal to Binary

You can get started by converting the IP address `172.19.43.67` into dotted-binary format. You are going to use an eight-step method that will guarantee the accuracy of the final result. In the previous section, *Converting Binary to Decimal*, you used a radix of 2 with different positioning ranging from 2^0 to 2^7. Within the eight-step process, you will be leveraging these values once again, but using a different approach: the method of subtraction.

To ensure the results are accurate, please adhere to the following rules:

- Convert only one octet at a time
- Start by subtracting the decimal value from the highest power of 2, which is 2^7 = `128`, while working your way down to the lowest power of 2, which is 2^0 = `1`
- If you can subtract a decimal value from a radix value, place `1` on the right
- If you are unable to subtract a decimal value from a radix value, place `0` to the right
- If you get `0`, attempt to subtract the decimal value from the next (lower) radix value

You can begin by converting the first octet, `172`, into binary format:

1. Is `172 - 128` (2^7) possible? Yes, giving you a remainder of `44`. Therefore, place `1` to the right.
2. Is `44 - 64` (2^6) possible? No; therefore, you carry `44` forward to be subtracted from the next power of 2 (2^5). Place `0` to the right.
3. Is `44 - 32` (2^5) possible? Yes, giving you a remainder of `12`. Place `1` to the right.
4. Is `12 - 16` (2^4) possible? No; therefore, carry `12` forward to be subtracted from the next power of 2 (2^3). Place `0` to the right.
5. Is `12 - 8` (2^3) possible? Yes, giving you a remainder of `4`. Place `1` to the right.
6. Is `4 - 4` (2^2) possible? Yes, giving a remainder of `0`. Place `1` to the right.

7. Is `0 - 2 (2`^{1}`)` possible? No; therefore, place `0` to the right.
8. Lastly, is `0 - 1 (2`^{0}`)` possible? No; therefore, your last value is `0` since this is the last power of `2` in the sequence.

The final answer in binary is taking all the ones and zeros starting from *step 1* and placing them in sequential order from *steps 1* to *8*. Therefore, the binary value of `172` is `10101100`.

The following is a visual representation of all the steps demonstrating the process you used to convert the decimal value of `172` into binary:

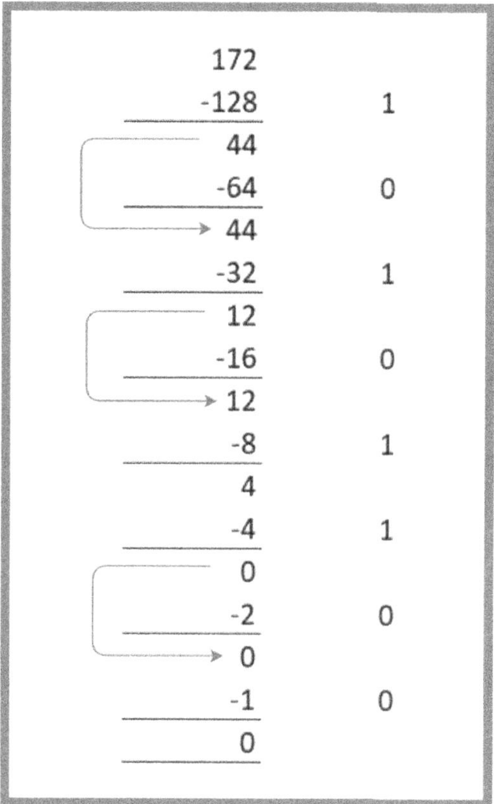

Figure 4.3: Calculation for converting the decimal value of 172 into binary

You can now convert the second octet, `19`, into binary using the same procedure:

1. Is `19 - 128 (2`^{7}`)` possible? No; therefore, you carry `19` forward to be subtracted from the next power of `2 (2`^{6}`)`. Place `0` to the right.
2. Is `19 - 64 (2`^{6}`)` possible? No; therefore, you carry `19` forward to be subtracted from the next power of `2 (2`^{5}`)`. Place `0` to the right.

3. Is 19 - 32 (2^5) possible? No; therefore, you carry 19 forward to be subtracted from the next power of 2 (2^4). Place 0 to the right.
4. Is 19 - 16 (2^4) possible? Yes, giving you a remainder of 3. Place 1 to the right.
5. Is 3 - 8 (2^3) possible? No; therefore, you carry 3 forward to be subtracted from the next power of 2 (2^2). Place 0 to the right.
6. Is 3 - 4 (2^2) possible? No; therefore, you carry 3 forward to be subtracted from the next power of 2 (21). Place 0 to the right.
7. Is 3 - 2 (2^1) possible? Yes, giving you a remainder of 1. Place 1 to the right.
8. Is 1 - 1 (2^0) possible? Yes, with a remainder of 0. Therefore, you get 1 to conclude the process.

Using the 1s and 0s from *steps 1* to *8*, the binary value of 19 is 00010011.

Figure 4.4 shows a visual representation of each step during the calculation process of converting 19 into a binary number:

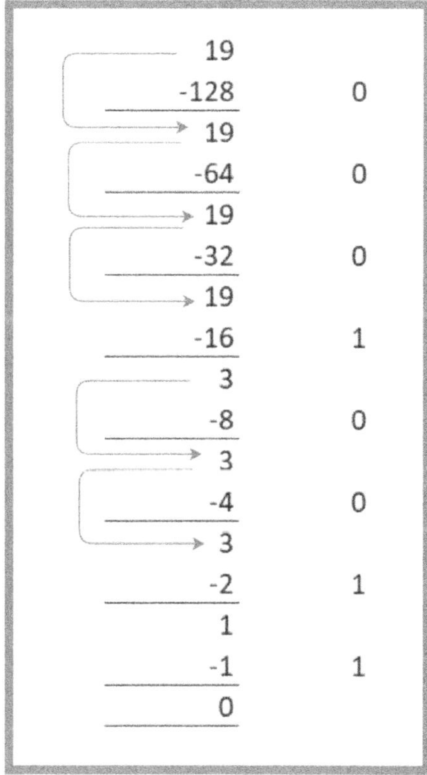

Figure 4.4: Converting 19 to binary

Next, you can convert the third octet, 43, from decimal to binary:

1. Is 43 - 128 (2^7) possible? No, so carry the 43 forward to be subtracted from the next lower power of 2. Place 0 to the right.
2. Next, is 43 - 64 (2^6) possible? No, so carry the 43 forward to be subtracted from the next lower power of 2. Place 0 to the right.
3. Next, is 43 - 32 (2^5) possible? Yes, with a remainder value of 11. Place 1 to the right.
4. Next, is 11 - 16 (2^4) possible? No, so carry the 11 forward to be subtracted from the next lower power of 2. Place 0 to the right.
5. Next, is 11 - 8 (2^3) possible? Yes, with a remainder value of 3. Place 1 to the right.
6. Next, is 3 - 4 (2^2) possible? No, so carry the 3 forward to be subtracted from the next lower power of 2. Place 0 to the right.
7. Next, is 3 - 2 (2^1) possible? Yes, with a remainder value of 1. Place 1 to the right.
8. Lastly, is 1 - 1 (2^0) possible? Yes, with a remainder value of 0. Place 1 to the right.

Using the 1s and 0s from *steps 1* to *8*, the binary value of 43 is 00101011.

Figure 4.5 shows a visual representation of each step during the calculation process of converting 43 into a binary number:

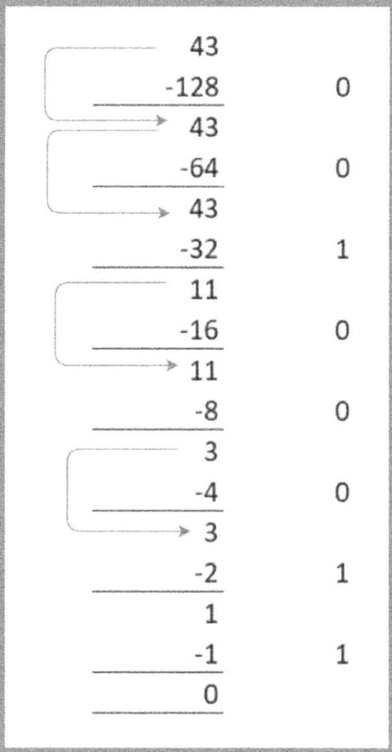

Figure 4.5: Converting 43 to binary

Next, you can convert the third octet, `67`, from decimal into binary:

1. Is `67 - 128 (2`^{7}`)` possible? No, so carry the `67` forward to be subtracted from the next lower power of `2`. Place `0` to the right.
2. Next, is `67 - 64 (2`^{6}`)` possible? Yes, with a remainder value of `3`. Place `1` to the right.
3. Next, is `3 - 32 (2`^{5}`)` possible? No, so carry the `3` forward to be subtracted from the next lower power of `2`. Place `0` to the right.
4. Next, is `3 - 16 (2`^{4}`)` possible? No, so carry the `3` forward to be subtracted from the next lower power of `2`. Place `0` to the right.
5. Next, is `3 - 8 (2`^{3}`)` possible? No, so carry the `3` forward to be subtracted from the next lower power of `2`. Place `0` to the right.
6. Next, is `3 - 4 (2`^{2}`)` possible? No, so carry the `3` forward to be subtracted from the next lower power of `2`. Place `0` to the right.
7. Next, is `3 - 2 (2`^{1}`)` possible? Yes, with a remainder value of `1`. Place `1` to the right.
8. Lastly, is `1 - 1 (2`^{0}`)` possible? Yes, with a remainder value of `0`. Place `1` to the right.

Using the 1s and 0s from *steps 1* to *8*, the binary value of `67` is `01000011`.

Figure 4.6 shows a visual representation of each step during the calculation process of converting `67` into a binary number:

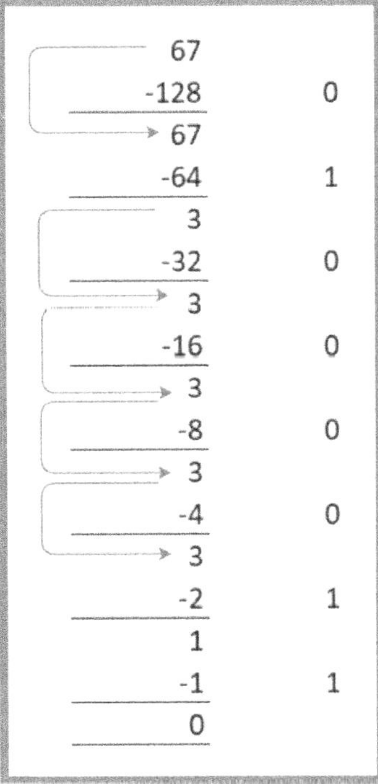

Figure 4.6: Converting 67 into binary

Lastly, put everything all together and view the binary notation of `172.19.43.67`:

	1st Octet	2nd Octet	3rd Octet	4th Octet
Decimal	172	19	43	67
Binary	10101100	00010011	00101011	01000011

Table 4.6: Binary and decimal notation

As shown in *Table 4.6*, the IPv4 address is `172.19.43.67 = 10101100.00010011.00101011.01000011`.

Understanding how to perform conversions between binary and decimal is an essential skill for all aspiring network professionals. This skill will help you better understand how to break down an IPv4 network block using subnetting techniques.

Next, you will learn about the various classes of IPv4 addresses.

IPv4 Address Classes

Who determines which IPv4 address can be assigned to internal devices on a private network, and which addresses can be assigned to devices that are directly connected to the internet? IANA created two address spaces and allocated specific ranges of addresses for private networks within organizations and address ranges for devices that are directly connected to the internet.

The following are the two address spaces:

- Public
- Private

Public addresses are unique over the internet, which means that each device that is directly connected to the internet is assigned a unique public IP address by its ISP.

Table 4.7 shows the ranges of public IPv4 addresses:

Class	Address Range	Networks	Usable Addresses per Network
A	1.0.0.0–126.0.0.0	128	16,777,214
B	128.0.0.0–191.255.0.0	16,384	65,534
C	192.0.0.0–233.255.255.0	2,097,152	254
D	224.0.0.–239.255.255.255	Used for multicast communication	
E	240.0.0.0–255.255.255.255	Reserved for future usage, research, and development	

Table 4.7: Public address ranges

As shown in *Table 4.7*, the public IPv4 address space is divided into five classes: A, B, C, D, and E. Classes A, B, and C are assigned to devices that are directly connected to the internet. Class D addresses are used for multicast network communication such as traffic from one sender to many recipients. Lastly, Class E is reserved for future usage, research, and development.

Unlike the public address space, which is routable on the internet, private IPv4 addresses are non-routable, specifically on the internet. To put it simply, if a device is assigned a private IPv4 address and is directly connected to the internet, it will not be able to communicate with any device on the internet that is assigned a public IPv4 address, and vice versa.

Table 4.8 shows the three classes of private IPv4 addresses, their address ranges, the number of networks per address class, and the number of assignable addresses per network for each address class:

Class	Address Range	No. of Networks	Assignable Addresses per Network
A	10.0.0.0–10.255.555.55	1	16,777,214
B	172.16.0.0–172.31.255.255	16	65,534
C	192.168.0.0–192.168.255.255	254	254

Table 4.8: Private address ranges

> **Note**
>
> The usage of private IPv4 addresses is covered in RFC 1918, which can be found at `https://datatracker.ietf.org/doc/html/rfc1918`.

For each class of IPv4 address, there is a default subnet mask that is coupled with it. *Table 4.9* shows the default subnet mask for each address class in IPv4:

Class	Address Range	Default Subnet Mask
A	10.0.0.0–10.255.255.255	255.0.0.0
B	172.16.0.0–172.31.255.255	255.255.0.0
C	192.168.0.0–192.168.255.255	255.255.255.0

Table 4.9: Default subnet mask

The subnet mask plays an important role for the following reasons:

- Helps network professionals determine the total IPv4 address in a network by enabling them to identify the network and host portions of the IP address
- Determines the total usable IPv4 addresses that are assignable on a network
- Helps a sender determine whether the recipient exists on the same IP network or a remote network
- Helps identify the network and host portions of an IP address

You will read more on the subnet mask and subnetting in the next chapter.

Since private IPv4 addresses are non-routable on the internet, this implies that they are only unique within an organization's private network. Therefore, multiple organizations can implement the same private IPv4 addressing scheme on their private networks without any issues.

As shown in *Figure 4.7*, the same private addresses can be used within an organization but those private addresses will not be permitted on the internet:

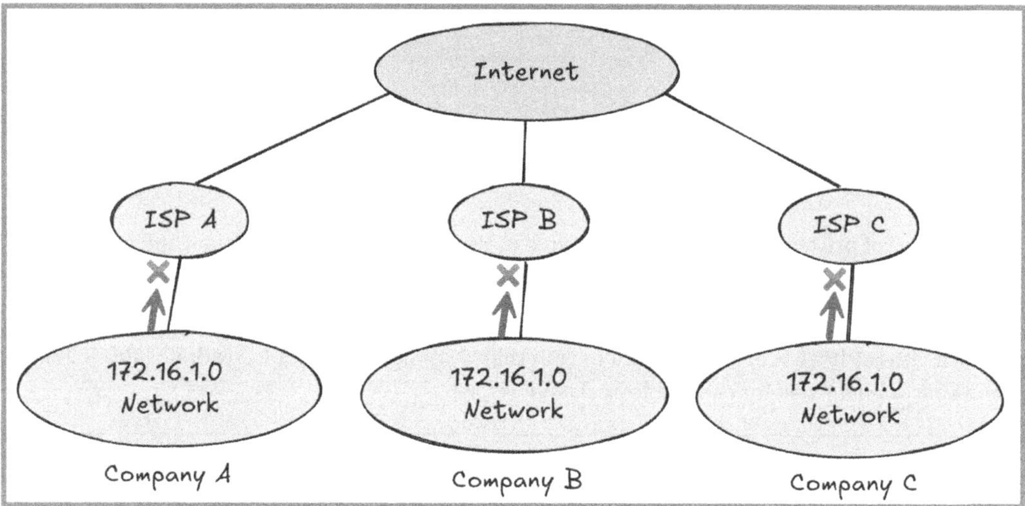

Figure 4.7: Non-routable addresses

Since private IPv4 addresses are non-routable, organizations will need to implement a router or firewall on their edge network and configure **Network Address Translation** (**NAT**), an IP service that translates the source private IPv4 address into the public IPv4 address for outbound traffic to the internet.

Figure 4.8 shows the placement of a NAT-enabled router on a network:

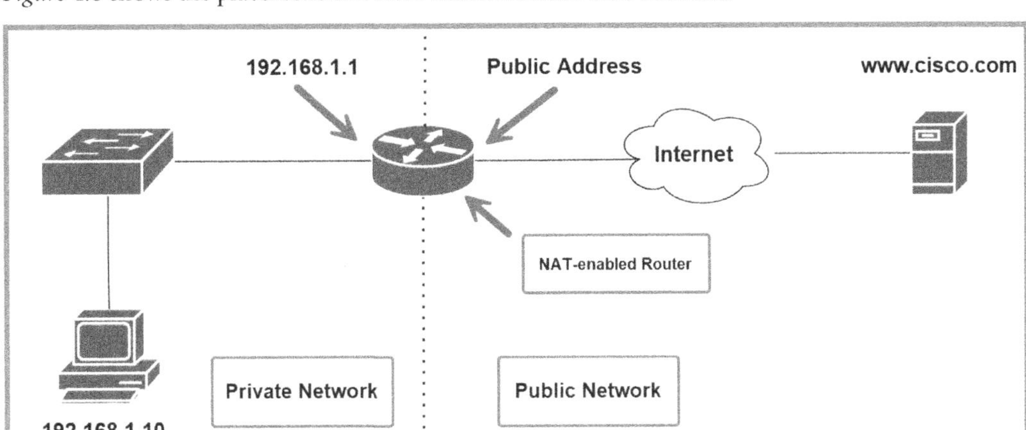

Figure 4.8: NAT-enabled router

Without NAT, internal devices such as a computer on a private network will not be permitted to communicate with external devices such as servers on the internet.

Types of IPv4 Addresses

In the world of IPv4, there are special addresses that are reserved and used for specific purposes, such as the following:

- Unicast
- Multicast
- Broadcast
- Loopback address
- Link-local

Unicast addresses are commonly used to identify a single and unique host device on a network such as a computer, server, or an **Internet of Things** (**IoT**) device. Unicast addresses are commonly used for one-to-one communication over a network.

Figure 4.9 shows a unicast communication between two devices:

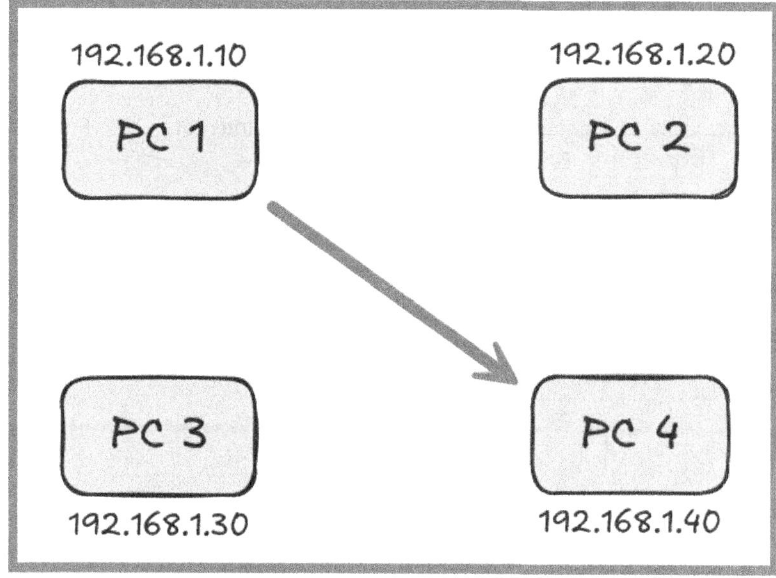

Figure 4.9: Unicast communication

A **multicast address** is used to identify a group of devices on a network. This type of address is commonly used for one-to-many communication, such that a sender transmits data to multiple recipients that all belong to a multicast group.

Figure 4.10 shows an example of a one-to-many communication:

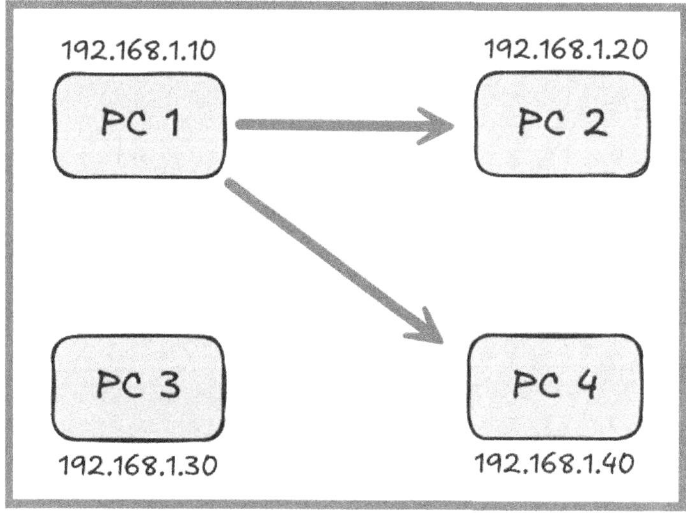

Figure 4.10: Multicast communication

A **broadcast address** enables a device to send data to all other hosts on the network. This type of address allows one-to-all communication within the same IP segment. For instance, if you want to send a packet to all live hosts on the same IP network as your computer, then sending a broadcast packet will ensure that it is delivered to all live hosts on the same IP network as the sender's device.

Figure 4.11 shows one-to-all communication:

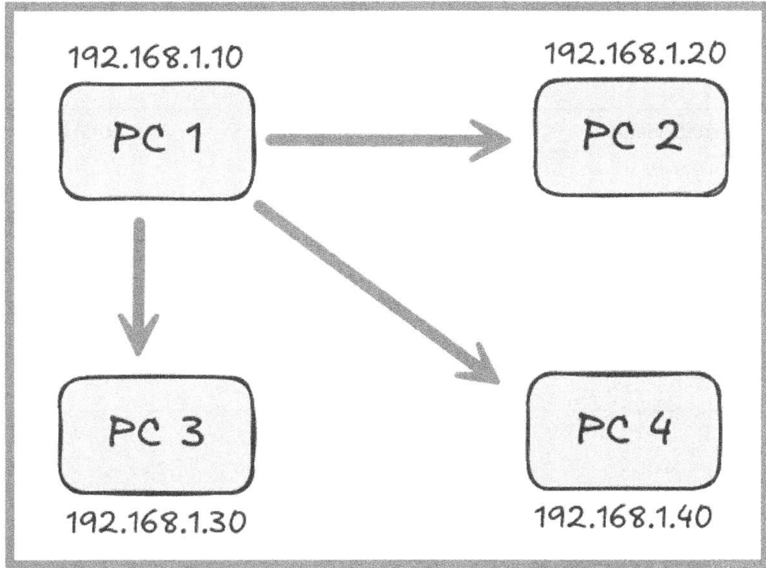

Figure 4.11: One-to-all communication

The **loopback address** is used by the operating system to test network applications on a local device. For instance, imagine if you install a web application server on your personal computer and place a basic web page in the web server directory. Then, using the web browser on the same host, you go to `http://127.0.0.1:80` to view the default web page. The application layer protocol is HTTP, the loopback address is `127.0.0.1`, and the sock/port number is `80`. In addition, the lookback address is commonly used for testing self-hosted network applications on a system and troubleshooting the TCP/IP network model on a device.

A **link-local address** is automatically assigned when a device is unable to obtain a dynamic IP address from a **Dynamic Host Configuration Protocol** (**DHCP**) server on the network. These addresses range from `169.254.0.0` to `169.254.255.255` with a default subnet mask of `255.255.0.0`.

> **Note**
>
> On Microsoft Windows, link-local addresses are commonly referred to as **Automatic Private IP Addressing** (**APIPA**).

Next, you will learn about the role and function of each field within an IPv4 header.

IPv4 Header

As an aspiring network professional, it is essential to understand the role and function of the various fields within an IPv4 header. Such information can be very useful in troubleshooting common networking issues.

Figure 4.10 shows the various fields within an IPv4 header:

<table>
<tr><td rowspan="2">Version</td><td rowspan="2">Internet Header Length</td><td colspan="2">Differentiated Services (DS)</td><td colspan="2" rowspan="2">Total Length</td></tr>
<tr><td>DSCP</td><td>ECN</td></tr>
<tr><td colspan="4">Identification</td><td>Flag</td><td>Fragment Offset</td></tr>
<tr><td colspan="2">Time to Live (TTL)</td><td colspan="2">Protocol</td><td colspan="2">Header Checksum</td></tr>
<tr><td colspan="6">Source IP Address</td></tr>
<tr><td colspan="6">Destination IP Address</td></tr>
<tr><td colspan="6">Options</td></tr>
</table>

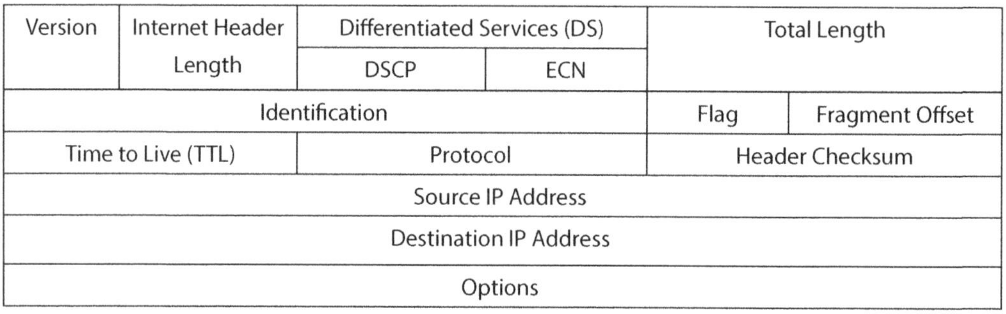

Figure 4.10: IPv4 header

The following are the roles and functions of each field within an IPv4 header:

- **Version**: A 4-bit field used to identify an IPv4 packet.
- **Internet Header Length** (**IHL**): A 4-bit field that indicates the end of the header and the beginning of the data section.
- **Differentiated Services** (**DS**): An 8-bit field used to identify the priority of the packet on the network. This was originally known as the **Type of Service** (**TOS**) field and contains the following sub-fields:
    - **Differentiated Service Code Point** (**DSCP**): This field identifies the classification and management of the packet on networks that use **quality of service** (**QoS**).
    - **Explicit Congestion Notification** (**ECN**): This field indicates network congestion without discarding packets.
- **Total Length**: A 16-bit field that is used to indicate the total size of the packet.
- **Identification**: A 16-bit field used for identifying a group of fragments that belongs to a single IP datagram.
- **Flag**: A 3-bit field used to control or identify whether the packet is part of a fragment group.

- **Fragment Offset**: A 13-bit field used to identify the sequencing position of a fragmented packet.
- **Time-to-Live (TTL)**: An 8-bit field that contains the TTL value, which determines the lifespan of the packet on a network and prevents routing loops. The TTL value decreases by 1 when it arrives at a router along the path from the sender to the receiver. When `TTL = 0`, the packet is discarded.
- **Protocol**: An 8-bit field used to identify the payload type within the packet.
- **Header Checksum**: A 16-bit field used for error checking of the packet.
- **Source IP Address**: A 32-bit field indicating the sender's IPv4 address.
- **Destination IP Address**: A 32-bit field indicating the intended recipient's IPv4 address.
- **Options**: This 32-bit field is not always used by the network layer.

A network protocol analyzer such as Wireshark enables you to inspect the fields and values of an IPv4 packet, as shown in *Figure 4.12*:

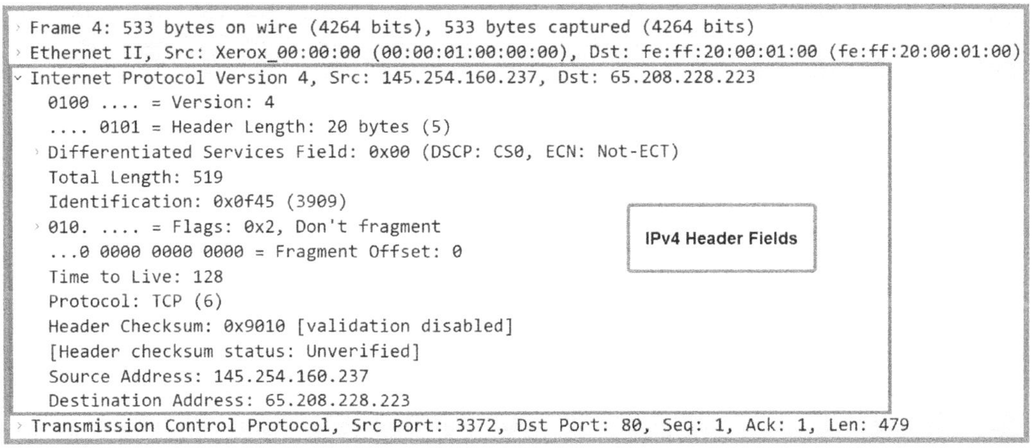

```
> Frame 4: 533 bytes on wire (4264 bits), 533 bytes captured (4264 bits)
> Ethernet II, Src: Xerox_00:00:00 (00:00:01:00:00:00), Dst: fe:ff:20:00:01:00 (fe:ff:20:00:01:00)
v Internet Protocol Version 4, Src: 145.254.160.237, Dst: 65.208.228.223
    0100 .... = Version: 4
    .... 0101 = Header Length: 20 bytes (5)
  > Differentiated Services Field: 0x00 (DSCP: CS0, ECN: Not-ECT)
    Total Length: 519
    Identification: 0x0f45 (3909)
  > 010. .... = Flags: 0x2, Don't fragment
    ...0 0000 0000 0000 = Fragment Offset: 0
    Time to Live: 128
    Protocol: TCP (6)
    Header Checksum: 0x9010 [validation disabled]
    [Header checksum status: Unverified]
    Source Address: 145.254.160.237
    Destination Address: 65.208.228.223
> Transmission Control Protocol, Src Port: 3372, Dst Port: 80, Seq: 1, Ack: 1, Len: 479
```

IPv4 Header Fields

Figure 4.12: IPv4 header using Wireshark

Having completed this section, you have learned the fundamentals of IPv4 addressing. Next, you will learn the fundamentals of IPv6 addressing.

Fundamentals of IPv6

The need for IPv6 is high on the internet today, with the creation of IoT devices that increase the rate of exhaustion of the public IPv4 address space. Nowadays, there are many data centers and cloud computing providers that offer virtual machines to their tenants. In addition, there are many more devices on the internet than there were over a decade ago. All of this contributes to the quick exhaustion of public IPv4 addresses from the various RIRs around the world.

Unlike the IPv4 address space, which has approximately 4.3 billion public addresses, IPv6 contains 128 bits that provide approximately 340 undecillion (3.4×10^{38}) IPv6 addresses in the world. Each IPv6 address has 8 hextets, each of which is made up of 16 bits. This implies **8 hextets x 16 bits per hextet = 128-bit address**.

Additionally, IPv6 is written using hexadecimal values and not decimals, as with IPv4. Hexadecimal values have the following range:

```
0 1 2 3 4 5 6 7 8 9 A B C D E F
```

Each hextet contains hexadecimal values between `0` and `F` and is written in base-16. A colon (`:`) is placed between each hextet in an IPv6 address. In addition, the least value of a hextet is `0` and the highest is `F`. A hextet ranges from `0000` to `FFFF`.

To get a better idea of IPv6 addressing, take a look at the following address:

```
2001:0DB8:0000:1111:0000:0000:0000:0200
```

The cool thing about writing an IPv6 address is that the alphabetical characters (A to F) are not case-sensitive. This means that regardless of whether you use a lowercase or uppercase character within the address, the device will accept it.

Additionally, it is recommended to write the shortened form of an IPv6 address. The leading zeros in a hextet can be removed as they have no value. Therefore, if an IPv6 address has a hextet of `0000`, you can use a single `0` to represent the entire hextet, as shown here:

```
2001:DB8:0:1111:0:0:0:200
```

Additionally, when there are two or more hextets with all zeros, you can substitute two or more hextets with a double colon (`::`), as shown here:

```
2001:DB8:0:1111::200
```

This is the shortest form of the original IPv6 address. Lastly, the double colon (`::`) can only be used once within an IPv6 address.

> **Note**
>
> The default subnet mask/network prefix of an IPv6 address is `/64`. This means the first half of an IPv6 address is known as the prefix, while the second half is referred to as the interface ID. In comparison to IPv4, the prefix is the network address while the interface ID is the host address.

IPv6 and IPv4 Coexistence

Natively, devices on an IPv4 network will not be able to communicate with devices on an IPv6 network. For coexistence and intercommunication between IPv4 and IPv6, the following technologies are implemented:

- Dual stacking
- Tunneling
- Translation

Dual stacking allows a single **network interface card** (**NIC**) to be configured with both IPv4 and IPv6 addresses. This allows the device to use the IPv4 address as the source address when communicating with devices on an IPv4 network and use the IPv6 address when communicating with devices on an IPv6 network.

This is possible because the internet layer of TCP/IP is responsible for encapsulating the IPv6 header onto the packet before passing it down to the network access layer of TCP/IP for transmission on the physical network.

Tunneling encapsulates an IPv6 packet within an IPv4 packet to allow the message to traverse over IPv4-only networks. This method is useful when an organization is connecting an isolated IPv6 network to an IPv4-only network infrastructure.

The following are some common types of tunneling:

- **6to4**: This method automatically creates a tunnel between an IPv6 network over an IPv4 network.
- **Teredo**: This method is commonly used for tunneling IPv6 over IPv4 networks that operate behind a NAT-enabled device.
- **Intra-Site Automatic Tunnel Addressing Protocol** (**ISATAP**): This protocol allows IPv6 host devices to communicate over an IPv4 internal network. It encapsulates IPv6 packets in IPv4 headers.

Translation is another method used for IPv6 and IPv4 coexistence. With translation, the Layer 3 device, such as a router, is responsible for translating/converting IPv6 packets into IPv4 packets, and vice versa, to enable communication between IPv6 and IPv4 networks.

The following are the two common types of translations:

- **NAT64**: Performs NAT from IPv6 to IPv4. This method enables IPv6-only devices to communicate with IPv4-only devices. Using NAT64 allows IPv6-only devices to communicate with IPv4-only devices by translating IPv6 packets into IPv4 packets, and vice versa. It typically requires a companion service such as **Domain Name System 64** (**DNS64**) to handle DNS translation, allowing IPv6-only clients to resolve IPv4 addresses.

- **DNS64**: This method works with NAT64 and translates the DNS queries from IPv6 devices to retrieve the IPv4 addresses of servers.

Without these technologies, IPv6 and IPv4 would not be able to coexist. Next, you will learn about the common types of IPv6 addresses.

IPv6 Address Types

Similar to IPv4, there are various types of IPv6 addresses with unique purposes on an IPv6 network. In this section, you will look at the following types of IPv6 address:

- Global unicast
- Loopback
- Link-local
- Unique local
- Anycast
- Multicast
- Modified EUI 64

Global unicast addresses are unique 128-bit addresses that are assignable on devices. This type of IPv6 address is globally routable on the internet and has the structure shown in *Figure 4.13*:

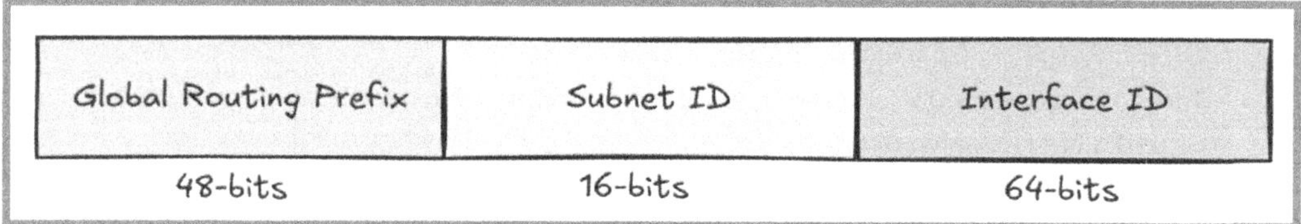

Figure 4.13: IPv6 structure

Since there are so many IPv6 addresses, there is no need for a private IPv6 address space like IPv4. Therefore, each global unicast IPv6 address is routable on the internet without the need for using NAT to translate a private address to a public routable address. Global unicast addresses belong to the `2000::/3` network block of addresses. An example of a global unicast address is `2001:0db8:85a3:0000:0000:8a2e:0370:7334`.

The **loopback address** has the same role and functionality as the IPv4 loopback address. It allows network professionals to test the functionality of TCP/IP on a host and enables the host operating systems to communicate with self-hosted services. The IPv6 loopback address is `::1`.

Figure 4.14 shows successful responses when pinging the IPv6 loopback address on a host:

```
C:\Users\glens> ping ::1

Pinging ::1 with 32 bytes of data:
Reply from ::1: time<1ms
Reply from ::1: time<1ms
Reply from ::1: time<1ms
Reply from ::1: time<1ms

Ping statistics for ::1:
    Packets: Sent = 4, Received = 4, Lost = 0 (0% loss),
Approximate round trip times in milli-seconds:
    Minimum = 0ms, Maximum = 0ms, Average = 0ms
```

Figure 4.14: Loopback address

The IPv6 **link-local address** is used for local communication within an IPv6 network. Devices that are connected to an IPv6 network are assigned two IPv6 addresses: a global unicast address for communicating with recipients on a remote network and a link-local address for communicating with hosts on the same local network as the sender.

All IPv6 link-local addresses begin with `fe80::/10` and are usually automatically assigned to an interface by the host device. However, IPv6 link-local addresses are not routable beyond the local subnet.

Figure 4.15 shows an IPv6 link-local address on an interface:

```
Ethernet adapter VMware Network Adapter VMnet8:

   Connection-specific DNS Suffix  . :
   Description . . . . . . . . . . . : VMware Virtual Ethernet Adapter for VMnet8
   Physical Address. . . . . . . . . : 00-50-56-
   DHCP Enabled. . . . . . . . . . . : No
   Autoconfiguration Enabled . . . . : Yes
   Link-local IPv6 Address . . . . . : fe80::3ff6:ea9c:              (Preferred)
   IPv4 Address. . . . . . . . . . . : 192.168.206.1(Preferred)
   Subnet Mask . . . . . . . . . . . : 255.255.255.0
```

Figure 4.15: Link-local address

Unique local addresses are used on private IPv6 networks only and these are not routable on the internet. The first 8 bits of a unique local address begin with `fc00::/7`.

Anycast addresses are assigned to multiple interfaces on different devices on a network. Therefore, when packets are sent to an anycast address, they are routed to the devices with the nearest interface. The routing decision is based on the routing protocol that is configured in the router on the network. Typically, anycast addresses are used in network architectures that focus on load balancing and redundancy.

Multicast addresses are used to identify a group of devices that are listening on a specific address. For instance, if a packet is sent to a multicast address, all devices that are listening on the multicast address will receive the packet. Multicast addresses start with `ff00::/8`. However, the `ff02::1` address is used for all nodes on a local network.

The modified **Extended Unique Identifier (EUI) 64** address is automatically created by a host device on an IPv6 network when a DHCPv6 server is not present but the network is configured to use **Stateless Address Autoconfiguration (SLAAC)**. A DHCP server usually provides the following addresses to clients:

- IP address
- Subnet mask
- Default gateway
- DNS server addresses

However, SLAAC is designed to help clients obtain the **global routing prefix** portion of an IPv6 global unicast address, which is the first 64 bits of the IPv6 address and not the interface ID portion. When a client obtains the global routing prefix only, it uses the EUI-64 process, which enables it to modify its 48-bit MAC address on the interface to create a 64-bit address to represent the interface ID portion of the IPv6 address.

To get a better understanding of the EUI-64 process, you can convert a 48-bit MAC address into an EUI-64-bit address and append it onto `2001:DB8:0:1111::/64`:

1. Firstly, split the 48-bit MAC address in half by separating the **organizational unique identifier (OUI)** portion, as shown in *Table 4.11*:

FC	99	47
11111100	10011001	01000111

75	CE	E0
01110101	11001110	11100000

Table 4.11: EUI-64 step 1

2. Next, insert the hexadecimal values of `FFFE` in the middle of the MAC address, as shown in *Table 4.12*:

FC	99	47	**FF**	**FE**	75	CE	E0
11111100	10011001	01000111	**11111111**	**11111110**	01110101	11001110	11100000

Table 4.12: EUI-64 step 2

> **Note**
> The `FFFE` insertion in EUI-64 addresses is a part of the process that modifies the 48-bit MAC address into a 64-bit interface identifier, as per the IEEE guidelines. It's not necessarily "reserved" in the traditional sense but is a specific requirement of the EUI-64 address format.

3. Next, flip the 7th bit within the first octet (8 bits), such that 0 becomes 1 and 1 becomes 0, as shown in *Table 4.13*:

11111110	10011001	01000111	**11111111**	**11111110**	01110101	11001110	11100000

Table 4.13: EUI-64 step 3

4. Next, convert the entire address from binary to hexadecimal, as shown in *Table 4.14*:

FC	99	47	**FF**	**FE**	75	CE	E0

Table 4.14: EUI-64 step 4

5. Lastly, append the EUI-64 address at the end of the global routing prefix (64-bit) portion of the IPv6 address: `2001:DB8:0:1111:FE99:47FF:FE75:CEE0`.

> **Note**
> To easily identify an EUI-64 address, the `FF:FE` values will always be in the middle of the interface ID portion of an IPv6 address.

Having completed this section, you have learned about common types of IPv6 addresses. Next, you will learn about the various fields found within an IPv6 header of a packet.

IPv6 Header

As an aspiring network professional, it is essential to understand the role and function of various fields within an IPv6 header. Such information can be very useful in troubleshooting common networking issues.

Table 4.15 shows an IPv6 header:

Version	Traffic Class	Flow Control
Payload Length	Next Header	Hop Limit
Source IP Address		
Destination IP Address		

Table 4.15: IPv6 header

The following are the roles and functions of each field within an IPv6 header:

- **Version**: A 4-bit field that identifies it's an IPv6 packet
- **Traffic Class**: An 8-bit field that has the same function as the DS field of an IPv4 packet, used to identify the priority of the packet on the network
- **Flow Control**: A 2-bit field, referred to as **Flow Label**, and used to inform the routers on the network to apply the same handling for IPv6 packets that have the same flow control label
- **Payload Length**: A 16-bit field used to identify the length of the payload (data)
- **Next Header**: An 8-bit field used to indicate the payload type
- **Hop Limit**: An 8-bit field used to specify the TTL value
- **Source IP Address**: A 128-bit field indicating the sender's IPv6 address
- **Destination IP Address**: A 128-bit field indicating the destination host's IPv6 address

Figure 4.16 shows an IPv6 header and its fields using Wireshark:

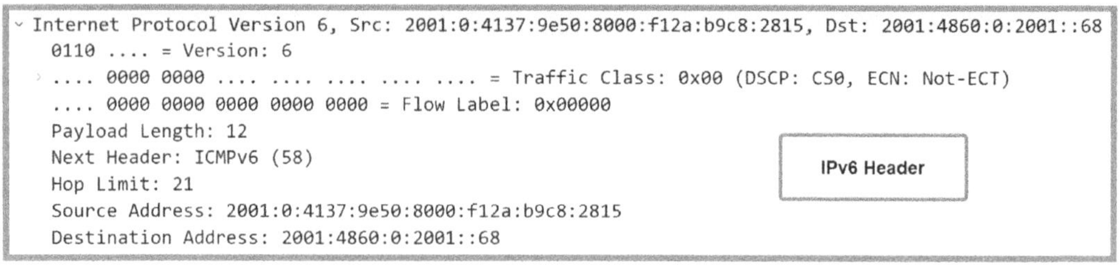

```
Internet Protocol Version 6, Src: 2001:0:4137:9e50:8000:f12a:b9c8:2815, Dst: 2001:4860:0:2001::68
  0110 .... = Version: 6
  .... 0000 0000 .... .... .... .... .... = Traffic Class: 0x00 (DSCP: CS0, ECN: Not-ECT)
  .... 0000 0000 0000 0000 0000 = Flow Label: 0x00000
  Payload Length: 12
  Next Header: ICMPv6 (58)
  Hop Limit: 21
  Source Address: 2001:0:4137:9e50:8000:f12a:b9c8:2815
  Destination Address: 2001:4860:0:2001::68
```

IPv6 Header

Figure 4.16: IPv6 header using Wireshark

As shown in *Figure 4.16*, there are fewer fields within an IPv6 header than in an IPv4 header.

Having completed this section, you have learned the fundamentals of IPv6 addresses. Next, you will learn how to verify IP addresses on client operating systems.

Verifying IP Parameters for Client OSs

As an aspiring network professional, it is essential to understand how to verify IP parameters on client operating systems such as Windows, Linux, and macOS. Verifying IP parameters helps network professionals ensure that the appropriate addresses are configured on the proper interface. It also helps with verifying connectivity between devices and assisting with troubleshooting networking issues. The process of verifying IP parameters checks for IP address, subnet mask, default gateway, and DNS server addresses on the appropriate interface of a client device.

Windows

To verify IP parameters on a Windows-based client device, open the Windows Command Prompt application, type the `ipconfig` or `ipconfig /all` command, and hit `Enter`, as shown in *Figure 4.17*:

```
C:\Users\glens> ipconfig

Windows IP Configuration


Ethernet adapter Ethernet 2:

   Connection-specific DNS Suffix  . :
   Link-local IPv6 Address . . . . . : fe80::b011:
   IPv4 Address. . . . . . . . . . . : 192.168.56.1
   Subnet Mask . . . . . . . . . . . : 255.255.255.0
   Default Gateway . . . . . . . . . :

Wireless LAN adapter Wi-Fi:

   Connection-specific DNS Suffix  . :
   Link-local IPv6 Address . . . . . : fe80::695e:
   IPv4 Address. . . . . . . . . . . : 172.16.17.65
   Subnet Mask . . . . . . . . . . . : 255.255.255.0
   Default Gateway . . . . . . . . . : 172.16.17.18
```

Figure 4.17: The ipconfig command

As shown in *Figure 4.17*, the `ipconfig` command displays all the local interfaces on the client and shows the assigned IP address, subnet mask, and default gateway addresses.

> **Note**
>
> It's important to ensure the clients on the same network segment are assigned an IP address within the same IP subnet range, the same subnet mask, and the default gateway address exists within the same subnet.

Figure 4.18 shows the output of the `ipconfig /all` command:

```
Wireless LAN adapter Wi-Fi:

   Connection-specific DNS Suffix  . :
   Description . . . . . . . . . . . : Realtek 8852BE Wireless LAN WiFi 6 PCI-E NIC
   Physical Address. . . . . . . . . :
   DHCP Enabled. . . . . . . . . . . : Yes
   Autoconfiguration Enabled . . . . : Yes
   Link-local IPv6 Address . . . . . : fe80::695e:                (Preferred)
   IPv4 Address. . . . . . . . . . . : 172.16.17.65(Preferred)
   Subnet Mask . . . . . . . . . . . : 255.255.255.0
   Lease Obtained. . . . . . . . . . : Saturday, August 10, 2024 7:50:06 PM
   Lease Expires . . . . . . . . . . : Wednesday, August 14, 2024 5:47:07 PM
   Default Gateway . . . . . . . . . : 172.16.17.18
   DHCP Server . . . . . . . . . . . : 172.16.17.18
   DHCPv6 IAID . . . . . . . . . . . : 168847416
   DHCPv6 Client DUID. . . . . . . . : 00-01-00-01-2C-AD-66-0A-08-BF-B8-6B-32-5B
   DNS Servers . . . . . . . . . . . : 2606:4700:4700::1113
                                       2606:4700:4700::1003
                                       1.1.1.3
                                       1.0.0.3
   NetBIOS over Tcpip. . . . . . . . : Enabled
```

Figure 4.18: Command output

As shown in the preceding screenshot, the `ipconfig /all` command provides more details about each interface. This command shows the network adapter type, IPv6 addresses, DHCP lease information, DHCP server address, DNS server address, and the MAC address of the interface.

Linux and macOS

To verify the IP parameters on a Linux-based and macOS client, open the Terminal application and execute the `ip address show` or `ifconfig` commands, as shown in *Figure 4.19*:

```
glen@linux:~$ ip addr
1: lo: <LOOPBACK,UP,LOWER_UP> mtu 65536 qdisc noqueue state UNKNOWN group default qlen 1000
    link/loopback 00:00:00:00:00:00 brd 00:00:00:00:00:00
    inet 127.0.0.1/8 scope host lo
       valid_lft forever preferred_lft forever
    inet6 ::1/128 scope host
       valid_lft forever preferred_lft forever
2: ens33: <BROADCAST,MULTICAST,UP,LOWER_UP> mtu 1500 qdisc fq_codel state UP group default qlen 1000
    link/ether 00:0c:29:bb:51:a5 brd ff:ff:ff:ff:ff:ff
    altname enp2s1
    inet 192.168.5.129/24 brd 192.168.5.255 scope global dynamic noprefixroute ens33
       valid_lft 1626sec preferred_lft 1626sec
    inet6 fe80::f05f:517f:c917:511b/64 scope link noprefixroute
       valid_lft forever preferred_lft forever
glen@linux:~$
```

Figure 4.19: Verifying interfaces

As shown in the preceding screenshot, the `ip address show` command enables network professionals to verify the interfaces and the assigned IPv4 and IPv6 addresses.

Additionally, the `ifconfig` command displays a list of interfaces and the addresses that are assigned, as shown in *Figure 4.20*:

```
glen@linux:~$ ifconfig
ens33: flags=4163<UP,BROADCAST,RUNNING,MULTICAST>  mtu 1500
        inet 192.168.5.129  netmask 255.255.255.0  broadcast 192.168.5.255
        inet6 fe80::f05f:517f:c917:511b  prefixlen 64  scopeid 0x20<link>
        ether 00:0c:29:bb:51:a5  txqueuelen 1000  (Ethernet)
        RX packets 337733  bytes 494266844 (494.2 MB)
        RX errors 114  dropped 134  overruns 0  frame 0
        TX packets 75584  bytes 4208843 (4.2 MB)
        TX errors 0  dropped 0 overruns 0  carrier 0  collisions 0
        device interrupt 19  base 0x2000

lo: flags=73<UP,LOOPBACK,RUNNING>  mtu 65536
        inet 127.0.0.1  netmask 255.0.0.0
        inet6 ::1  prefixlen 128  scopeid 0x10<host>
        loop  txqueuelen 1000  (Local Loopback)
        RX packets 782  bytes 68767 (68.7 KB)
        RX errors 0  dropped 0  overruns 0  frame 0
        TX packets 782  bytes 68767 (68.7 KB)
        TX errors 0  dropped 0 overruns 0  carrier 0  collisions 0
```

Figure 4.20: Verifying interface address

As shown in the preceding screenshot, the `ifconfig` command provides more, such as the transmitting and receiving load per interface.

Having completed this section, you have learned how to verify IP parameters on client operating systems such as Windows, Linux, and macOS. Next, you will learn how to configure IPv6 addresses on a Cisco IOS router.

Lab – Configuring IPv6 on a Cisco IOS Router

In this exercise, we will be using the topology shown in *Figure 4.21* with a computer that is directly connected to a Cisco IOS router:

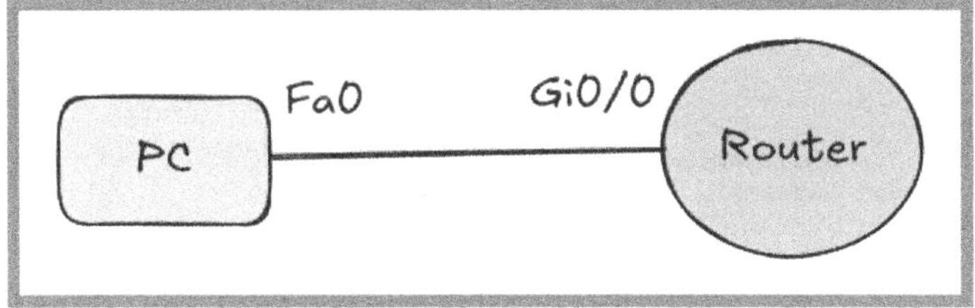

Figure 4.21: Lab topology

Table 4.16 shows the IP addressing scheme for the topology:

Device	Interface	IPv6 Address	Subnet Mask	Default Gateway
Router	GigabitEthernet 0/0	2001:DB8:1:1::1	/64	
	Link-Local	FE80::1		
PC	Fa0	2001:DB8:1:1::2	/64	2001:DB8:1:1::1

Table 4.16: Addressing table

To get started with configuring IPv6 addresses on the Cisco IOS device, please use the following instructions:

1. Download the lab file and open it with Cisco Packet Tracer from `https://packt.link/CCNArepoCh04`
2. *Figure 4.22* shows the lab file open in the Packet Tracer application:

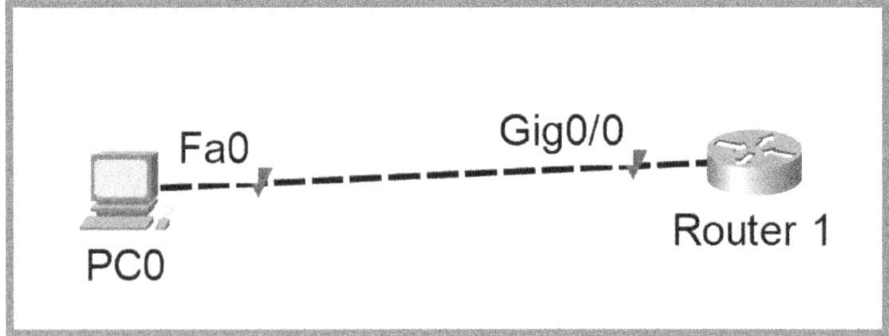

Figure 4.22: Lab topology in Packet Tracer

3. Next, click on `Router 1` and select the `CLI` tab to directly access the Cisco IOS, as shown in *Figure 4.23*:

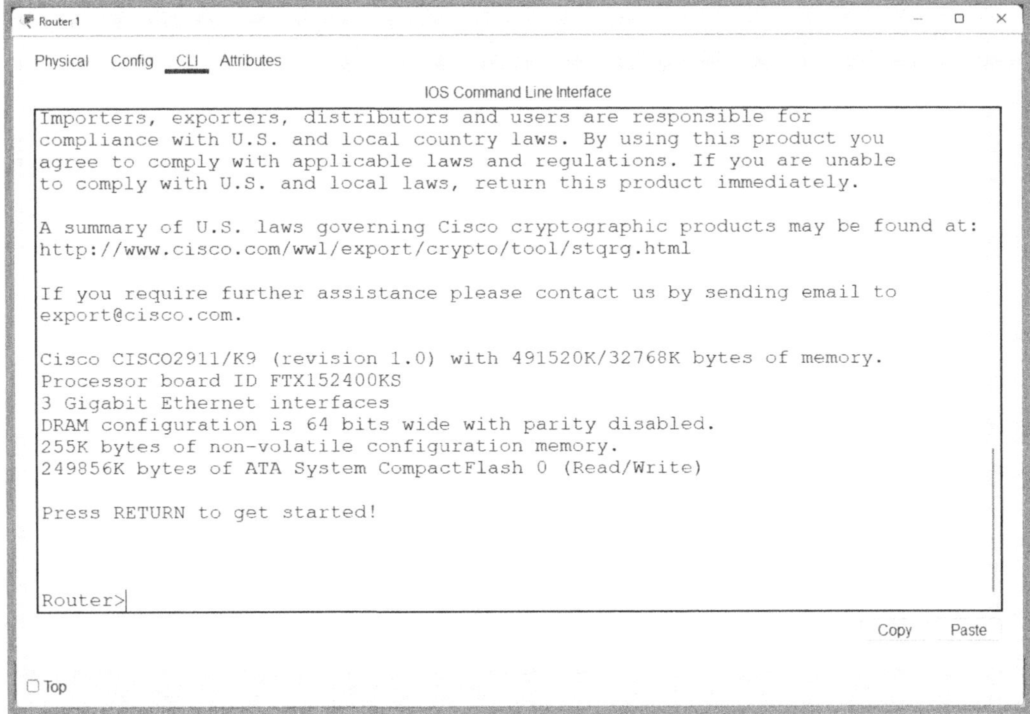

Figure 4.23: Router 1 CLI

4. Next, use the following commands to enter the global configuration mode and enable IPv6 routing:

```
Router> enable
Router# configure terminal
Router(config)# ipv6 unicast-routing
```

5. Next, access `interface gigabitEthernet 0/0` and configure the global unicast address on the interface with a static link-local address:

```
Router(config)# interface gigabitEthernet 0/0
Router(config-if)# description Connected to the PC
Router(config-if)# ipv6 address 2001:DB8:1:1::1/64
Router(config-if)# ipv6 address FE80::1 link-local
Router(config-if)# no shutdown
Router(config-if)# exit
Router(config)# exit
```

6. Next, use the `show ipv6 interface brief` command to verify the IPv6 addresses on each interface of the router:

```
Router# show ipv6 interface brief
GigabitEthernet0/0          [up/up]
    FE80::1
    2001:DB8:1:1::1
GigabitEthernet0/1          [administratively down/down]
    unassigned
GigabitEthernet0/2          [administratively down/down]
    unassigned
Vlan1                       [administratively down/down]
    unassigned
```

Figure 4.24: Output of the show ipv6 interface brief command

7. Use the `show ipv6 interface [interface-ID]` command to verify the IPv6 addresses of the interface:

```
Router# show ipv6 interface gigabitEthernet 0/0
GigabitEthernet0/0 is up, line protocol is up
  IPv6 is enabled, link-local address is FE80::1
  No Virtual link-local address(es):
  Global unicast address(es):
    2001:DB8:1:1::1, subnet is 2001:DB8:1:1::/64
  Joined group address(es):
    FF02::1
    FF02::2
    FF02::1:FF00:1
  MTU is 1500 bytes
```

Figure 4.25: Output of the show ipv6 interface command

8. Use the `show running-config` command to verify the configured IPv6 addresses on the interface:

```
Router# show running-config | section interface
interface GigabitEthernet0/0
 description Connected to the PC
 no ip address
 duplex auto
 speed auto
 ipv6 address FE80::1 link-local
 ipv6 address 2001:DB8:1:1::1/64
```

Figure 4.26: Output of the show running-config command

9. Save the configurations of the router using the `copy running-config startup-config` command, as shown in *Figure 4.27*:

```
Router# copy running-config startup-config
Destination filename [startup-config]?
Building configuration...
[OK]
```

Figure 4.27: Saving configurations

10. Check the end-to-end connectivity from the router to the PC by using the `ping [destination address]` command, as shown in *Figure 4.28*:

```
Router# ping 2001:DB8:1:1::2

Type escape sequence to abort.
Sending 5, 100-byte ICMP Echos to 2001:DB8:1:1::2, timeout is 2
seconds:
!!!!!
Success rate is 100 percent (5/5), round-trip min/avg/max = 0/0/0 ms
```

Figure 4.28: Ping results on Cisco IOS

11. As shown in the preceding screenshot, the router received exclamation marks (`!`), which means the ping messages were successfully sent and the router got five responses from the destination host.

Having completed this lab exercise, you have gained the skills of configuring IPv6 global unicast and link-local addresses on a Cisco IOS router. In addition, you have learned various troubleshooting commands.

Summary

Throughout this chapter, you have learned about the importance of IPv4 addressing and the various classes and types of addresses on a network. In addition, you have learned how to convert IPv4 addresses between binary and decimal format. Furthermore, you have learned about the various fields found within IPv4 and IPv6 headers and how they differ. You have also learned how to verify IP parameters on client operating systems and configure IPv6 addresses on a Cisco IOS router.

This chapter should be helpful in your journey toward learning how to implement and administer Cisco solutions and prepare for the *200-301 CCNA v1.1* certification. In the next chapter, you will gain hands-on skills as a network professional to break down network blocks into subnetworks using the technique of subnetting.

Additional Reading

- IANA IPv4 Address Space Registry: `https://www.iana.org/assignments/ipv4-address-space/ipv4-address-space.xhtml`
- IPv4 Addressing Configuration Guide: `https://www.cisco.com/c/en/us/td/docs/ios-xml/ios/ipaddr_ipv4/configuration/xe-3s/ipv4-xe-3s-book/configuring_ipv4_addresses.html`
- Pv6 Addressing and Basic Connectivity Configuration Guide: `https://www.cisco.com/c/en/us/td/docs/ios-xml/ios/ipv6_basic/configuration/xe-3s/ip6b-xe-3s-book/ip6-add-basic-conn-xe.html`
- Changing TCP/IP settings on Windows: `https://support.microsoft.com/en-us/windows/change-tcp-ip-settings-bd0a07af-15f5-cd6a-363f-ca2b6f391ace`
- Configuring network adapters on Linux: `https://ubuntu.com/server/docs/configuring-networks`
- Configuring addresses on macOS: `https://support.apple.com/en-ng/guide/mac-help/mchlp2718/mac`

Exam Readiness Drill – Chapter Review Questions

Apart from mastering key concepts, strong test-taking skills under time pressure are essential for acing your certification exam. That's why developing these abilities early in your learning journey is critical.

Exam readiness drills, using the free online practice resources provided with this book, help you progressively improve your time management and test-taking skills while reinforcing the key concepts you've learned.

HOW TO GET STARTED

- Open the link or scan the QR code at the bottom of this page
- If you have unlocked the practice resources already, log in to your registered account. If you haven't, follow the instructions in *Chapter 19* and come back to this page.
- Once you log in, click the START button to start a quiz
- We recommend attempting a quiz multiple times till you're able to answer most of the questions correctly and well within the time limit.
- You can use the following practice template to help you plan your attempts:

Working On Accuracy		
Attempt	**Target**	**Time Limit**
Attempt 1	40% or more	Till the timer runs out
Attempt 2	60% or more	Till the timer runs out
Attempt 3	75% or more	Till the timer runs out
Working On Timing		
Attempt 4	75% or more	1 minute before time limit
Attempt 5	75% or more	2 minutes before time limit
Attempt 6	75% or more	3 minutes before time limit

The above drill is just an example. Design your drills based on your own goals and make the most out of the online quizzes accompanying this book.

First time accessing the online resources? 🔓

You'll need to unlock them through a one-time process. **Head to** *Chapter 19* **for instructions.**

Open Quiz	
https://packt.link/ccnachap4	
OR scan this QR code →	

5

Practical Subnetting

In this chapter, you will learn about the role a subnet mask plays in the field of networking and how it helps networking professionals and devices determine whether the destination host is on the same IP network as the sender or a remote network. Furthermore, you will learn how to calculate the total number of IP addresses within a network and determine the usable range of addresses that can be assigned to the interface of a device. Additionally, you will learn how to plan and design an IPv4 addressing scheme for a multi-branch organization from start to end.

This chapter covers *Domain 1: Network Fundamentals*, specifically the *1.6 Configure and verify IPv4 addressing and subnetting* objectives of the *200-301 CCNA v1.1 Certification* exam.

In this chapter, you will learn about the following topics:

- Importance of a subnet mask
- Understanding network prefix
- Identifying the network ID
- Practical IPv4 subnetting

Let's dive in! By the end of this chapter, you will have gained hands-on skills, using a real-life exercise to design an IPv4 addressing scheme for an organization with multiple branch offices; here, you will learn how to perform subnetting.

Importance of a Subnet Mask

An IP address is not complete without being coupled with a subnet mask. The subnet mask has the following characteristics and responsibilities: IPv4 subnet masks are 32 bits in length, while IPv6 prefix lengths are /64 since it's not a traditional subnet mask like IPv4. Furthermore, an IPv4 subnet mask is used to identify both the network and host portions of an IP address. In addition, an IPv4 subnet mask is used to assist networking devices in determining the total number of networks, as well as the total usable IP addresses that exist on an IP network. Lastly, the IPv4 subnet mask is used to help a host device, such as a sender, determine whether a packet should be sent to the default gateway if the destination is beyond the local network.

As you learned in the previous chapter, *Chapter 4, IPv4 and IPv6 Addressing*, there are three main classes (*A*, *B*, and *C*) of assignable IPv4 addresses for both public and private networks. Similarly, there are three default subnet masks for each of these classes of IPv4 addresses.

Table 5.1 shows the default subnet masks:

Class	Default Subnet Mask
A	255.0.0.0
B	255.255.0.0
C	255.255.255.0

Table 5.1: Default subnet masks

If you are using a Class A IPv4 address, such as `10.1.2.3`, the default subnet mask will be `255.0.0.0`. If you are using a Class B IPv4 address, such as `172.15.5.6`, then the default subnet mask will be `255.255.0.0`, and so on. However, custom subnet masks are assigned in modern networks.

In modern networks, network professionals commonly assign custom subnet masks to systems on their network architecture. You will learn more about subnetting and creating custom subnet masks in the next few sections.

Understanding Network Prefix

You may have seen IPv4 addresses written in the format of `10.10.1.2/8` and wondered what `/8` is all about. This is known as the **network prefix**. The network prefix is another format that is commonly used in the networking industry to easily represent a subnet mask.

You are probably wondering how `/8` can represent the dotted-binary and dotted-decimal format of a subnet mask for an IPv4 address. To answer this question, take a look at *Table 5.2*, which shows the binary format of the subnet mask:

Class A- 255.0.0.0	11111111 00000000 00000000 00000000

Table 5.2: Class A subnet mask

When writing a subnet mask in binary, it is always written with a sequential series of 1s. There aren't any 0s between the 1s of a subnet mask; the 0s are placed after the continuous stream of 1s has ended. Looking at the previous example, there are eight 1s in the `255.0.0.0` subnet mask. Therefore, the network prefix can be written as `/8` to represent a default Class A subnet mask.

You can now determine the network prefix for a Class B subnet mask:

- **Dotted-decimal format**: `255.255.0.0`
- **Dotted-binary format**: `11111111.11111111.00000000.00000000`

In this example, there is a total of 16 1s in the subnet mask. Therefore, the network prefix can be denoted as `/16`.

Lastly, in calculating the network prefix for the default Class C subnet mask, you get the following:

- **Dotted-decimal format**: `255.255.255.0`
- **Dotted-binary format**: `11111111.11111111.11111111.00000000`

As expected, there are 24 1s within the default Class C subnet mask, and therefore you get a `/24` network prefix.

When attempting to determine the network prefix of a custom subnet mask, convert each octet of the custom subnet mask into binary. Your results should provide you with a continuous stream of 1s. Calculating the total number of 1s will give you the `/x` value, where `x` is the number of 1s in the subnet mask.

Imagine you need to determine the network prefix for the following:

- **IP address**: `192.1.2.3`
- **Subnet**: `255.255.224.0`

The following steps will help you quickly obtain the answer:

1. Convert the first octet of the subnet mask into binary. You will get `255 = 11111111`.
2. Convert the second octet into binary. You will also get `255 = 11111111`.
3. Converting the third octet, you will get `224 = 11100000`.
4. For the last octet, you will get `0 = 00000000`.
5. Putting the entire binary subnet together, you will get `11111111.11111111.11100000.00000000`. There are 19 1s in the `255.255.224.0` subnet mask, and the network prefix can be denoted as `/19` and the IP address as `192.1.2.3/19`.

Now that you have the skills to calculate the network prefix, take a deeper look at identifying the network ID.

Identifying the Network ID

Configuring IPv4 addresses and subnet masks on a router's interface is a simple task. However, if either the IPv4 address or subnet mask is incorrectly assigned on an interface of the device, the device will not be able to communicate with others.

To illustrate this theory, the following diagram shows a computer that is unable to communicate with the router:

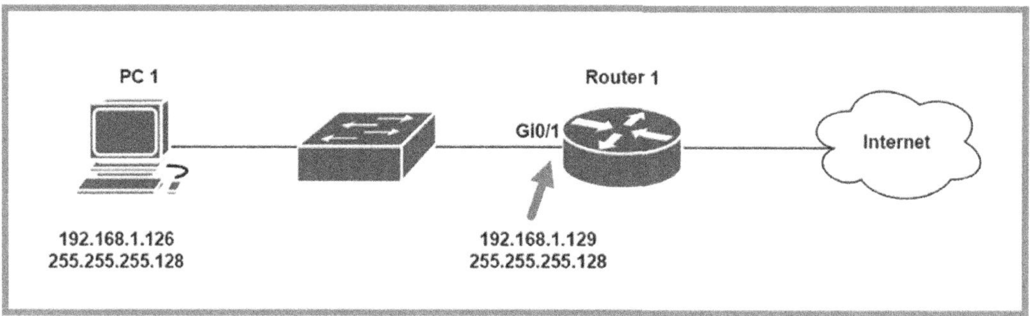

Figure 5.1: Small network

Considering all the devices are powered on and the appropriate cables are used for connecting each device to another, what could be the issue? As you will notice, the IPv4 addresses and subnet mask seem to be correct as the only difference between them is the IP address of the computer and the router. But is this really accurate? You can now determine if the PC and router both exist on the same logical Layer 3 network. Visually, both devices exist on the same physical network, but in the field of networking, they can belong to different IP networks based on their IP addresses and the subnet masks on their interfaces.

In this scenario, you can perform some calculations to determine if the PC is on the same IP network as the router, thus determining the network ID for each device. The network ID is simply the community address, similar to a neighborhood where each home shares the same community address with differing house or mailbox numbers.

To determine the network ID of a device, you need to perform a logical operation known as the `AND` operation between the IP address and subnet mask of the device.

The following are the Laws of `AND`:

- `0 AND 0 = 0`
- `0 AND 1 = 0`
- `1 AND 0 = 0`
- `1 AND 1 = 1`

You can determine whether two devices are on the same logical network as follows:

1. Convert the computer's IP address and subnet mask into the dotted-binary format using the Law of AND. When the IP address is AND against the subnet mask, the result is known as the network ID.
2. *Figure 5.2* shows the AND operation process for PC 1:

IP address	**11000000.10101000.00000001.01111110**
Subnet mask	**11111111.11111111.11111111.10000000**
Network ID	**11000000.10101000.00000001.00000000**

Figure 5.2: Network ID for PC1

3. Convert PC 1's network ID into decimal format, which indicates PC 1 belongs to the `192.168.1.0/25` network.
4. You can now perform the AND operation on the router's IP address and subnet mask. *Figure 5.3* shows the AND operation process for the router:

IP address	**11000000.10101000.00000001.10000001**
Subnet mask	**11111111.11111111.11111111.10000000**
Network ID	**11000000.10101000.00000001.10000000**

Figure 5.3: Network ID for the router

5. Converting the router's network ID into decimal format, you can determine that the router belongs to the `192.168.1.128/25` network.
6. Since the computer's and router's network IDs are not the same, it proves that both the devices are on different IP networks and will not be able to communicate with each other even though they are connected to the same physical network.

In this calculation, you have proved that the computer and the router are on different logical networks, and therefore will not be able to intercommunicate. To solve such issues, you need to assign the PC an IP address from the router's network or vice versa.

Now that you have the skills to determine the network ID and solve interconnectivity issues on a network, you can learn how to perform subnetting and calculate the ranges of addresses for a subnet.

Practical IPv4 Subnetting

Hearing the word "subnetting" can be a bit intimidating as it involves intermediate calculations using binary and decimal numbers. However, learning subnetting is unavoidable in your journey to becoming an aspiring network professional. You may be wondering what subnetting is and why you need to learn how to perform this task as a networking professional.

To get a better understanding of the answer to this question, you can look at a simple analogy. Imagine you are a network administrator at an organization with six networks, and each of these networks has no more than 50 devices that require IP addresses.

It would be easy to simply use a Class C network block, such as `192.168.0.0/24`, and assign it to the network, then choose another Class C address block to assign to the next network, and so on.

The following is a typical workable solution for assigning Class C network blocks to the six networks:

- **Network 1**: `192.168.1.0/24`
- **Network 2**: `192.168.2.0/24`
- **Network 3**: `192.168.3.0/24`
- **Network 4**: `192.168.4.0/24`
- **Network 5**: `192.168.5.0/24`
- **Network 6**: `192.168.6.0/24`

Using such an addressing scheme is workable, but it is definitely not efficient. Let's take a deeper look at why it is not appropriate. In this scenario, each network has 50 devices or less. First, determine the number of usable (assignable) IP addresses per Class C network block using the following formula:

1. Firstly, convert the IP address and subnet mask into binary format and draw a dotted line where the 1s end within the subnet mask, as shown in *Table 5.3*:

192.168.0.0	11000000 10101000 00000000	00000000
255.255.255.0	11111111 11111111 11111111	00000000

Table 5.3: Determining host bits

1. As shown in the preceding figure, the bits on the left side of the dotted line represent the network bits and the bits on the right side represent the host bits of the IP address. The network bits are the same for all hosts on the same IP network, while the host bits are unique for each host on the network.

2. Use the following formula to calculate the total number of IPv4 addresses within a network:

```
Total IPv4 addresses = 2^H
Where H is the number of host bits within the IP address.
```

3. Since there are eight host bits, substitute `H = 8` in the preceding formula:

```
Total IPv4 addresses = 2^H
                                        = 2^8
                                        = 2 x 2 x 2 x 2 x 2 x 2 x 2 x
2
                                        = 256
```

4. Based on the calculations, there are 256 total IPv4 addresses within any Class C network block when using the default subnet mask.

> **Note**
>
> On an IPv4 network, both the network ID and broadcast addresses cannot be assigned to a device's interface. Therefore, you subtract two from the total number of IP addresses to get the usable amount on a network.

5. Calculate the usable IPv4 addresses that can be assigned to host devices on a network by using the following formula:

```
Usable IP addresses = 2^H - 2
Where H is the number of host bits within an IP address
```

6. Since there are eight host bits in any of the Class C networks, you get the following results:

```
Usable IP addresses = 2^H - 2
                                        = 2^8 - 2
                                        - 256   2
                                        = 254 usable IP addresses
per Class C network
```

In effect, each network will have a wastage of approximately 204 IP addresses (254 – 50 hosts). Imagine if everyone assigned large address blocks to their network architecture without being concerned about the wastage of IPv4 addresses. On a larger scale, if **Internet Service Providers (ISPs)** distributed large network blocks to organizations that do not require more than just a few IPv4 addresses, the public IPv4 network blocks would have been exhausted decades ago.

This brings you back to understanding the reasons why you need to subnet. The benefits of subnetting include efficient distribution of IP addresses with the least wastage and the creation of more networks with smaller broadcast domains.

Why is having a large broadcast domain a bad thing? Imagine a network architecture within an organization that has approximately 300 devices, and client devices are generating unnecessary broadcast packets. All the other devices will be receiving those broadcast messages and processing them. The broadcast packets saturate the available network bandwidth, causing legitimate packets to be discarded/dropped from the network due to congestion.

A large broadcast domain contributes to high latency, in effect, slowing down the network performance. To put it simply, it is like rush hour in the morning or evening, when there are too many vehicles trying to access the roads at the same time within a city. This results in traffic congestion, and commuters experience a delay in reaching their destination in a timely manner.

By creating subnets, you can reduce the size of a Layer 3 broadcast domain. Using a Layer 3 switch or a router, these subnets can be interconnected, thus allowing users and devices to communicate efficiently.

Subnets can be determined by the following:

- The number of remote offices
- The number of business units within an organization
- The types of networks within the organization
- Applying network security best practices

To better understand subnetting, let's dive into some hands-on exercises.

Determining the Appropriate IPv4 Block

Figure 5.4 shows a visual representation of the network topology:

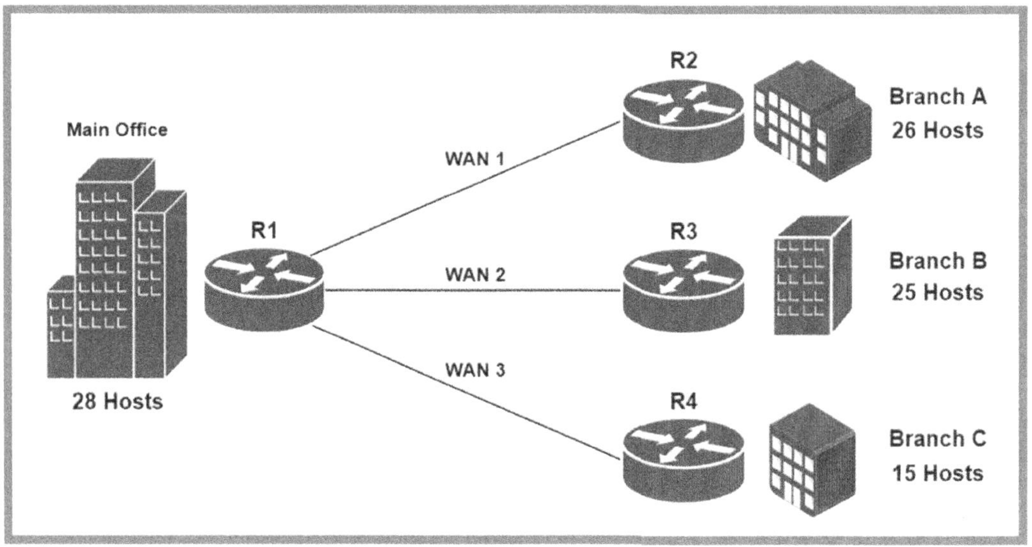

Figure 5.4: Network diagram

Scenario: You are a network professional at a company with four branch offices, including the head office. Each branch office has its own **local area network** (**LAN**) and an edge router that interconnects each branch office to the head office location using a hub-and-spoke topology.

Your objective is to design an IP scheme to ensure the least wastage and each branch location has its own IP subnet. To get started with this assignment, the following sections will guide you through how to create an efficient IP addressing scheme for the network topology.

To begin, determine which class of IPv4 addressing is most suitable for your network topology. As you may recall, there are three address classes: A, B, and C. Each class has a unique number of available IPv4 addresses based on their default subnet masks.

To determine the most suitable address class, use the following formula to determine the total number of IP addresses of each class:

```
Total number of IPv4 addresses = 2^H
Where H represents the number of host bits in an IP address.
```

In this step, you are using the subnet mask to determine the number of IP addresses available in a network. The 1s in the subnet masks identify the network portion of an IP address, while the 0s identify the host portion of an IP address.

Table 5.4 illustrates the default subnets for each class and their binary equivalents:

	1st Octet	2nd Octet	3rd Octet	4th Octet
Class A – 255.0.0.0	11111111	00000000	00000000	00000000
Class B – 255.255.0.0	11111111	11111111	00000000	00000000
Class C – 255.255.255.0	11111111	11111111	11111111	00000000

Table 5.4: Subnet masks

Use the formula 2^H to determine the total number of IPv4 addresses per class:

- Class A = 2^{24} = 16,777,216 total IP addresses
- Class B = 2^{16} = 65,536 total IP addresses
- Class C = 2^{8} = 256 total IP addresses

Furthermore, when assigning IPv4 addresses on a network, there are two addresses that cannot be assigned. These are the network ID and broadcast addresses. Therefore, to determine the number of usable/assignable IP addresses, you will need to subtract two addresses from the total number of IP addresses for a subnet.

To calculate the number of usable/assignable IP addresses, use the following formula:

Number of usable IP addresses = $2^{H} - 2$

The following are the number of usable/assignable IPv4 addresses for each class:

- Class A = 224 – 2 = 16,777,214 usable IP addresses
- Class B = 216 – 2 = 65,534 usable IP addresses
- Class C = 28 – 2 = 254 usable IP addresses

Next, you will need to identify the total number of networks within the topology and the size of each network:

- **Main office LAN**: 28 hosts
- **Branch A LAN**: 26 hosts
- **Branch B LAN**: 25 hosts
- **Branch C LAN**: 15 hosts
- **Wide Area Network (WAN) 1 (R1-R2)**: Two IPs are needed
- **WAN 2 (R2-R3)**: Two IPs are needed
- **WAN 3 (R3-R4)**: Two IPs are needed

Using a Class A network block is not suitable as there'll be over 16 million IP addresses being wasted. Using a Class B network block will result in approximately 65,000 addresses being wasted. This leaves you with using a Class C network block, as it's the smallest network block available, with 254 usable IP addresses.

> **Note**
>
> When creating subnets, keep in mind that each newly created subnetwork must be able to fit the largest network in your topology.

In the next step, you will learn how to leverage the subnet mask to determine the network and host portions (bits) of an IP address.

Creating New Subnets

When creating subnets, you will need to convert some host bits into new network bits. This process allows you to create new networks (subnets) while reducing the number of IPs per network.

To get started, use the Class C network block (`192.168.1.0/24`). Converting the address with the subnet mask will give what is shown in *Table 5.5*:

Network block	11000000 . 10101000 . 00000000 . 00000000
Subnet mask	11111111 . 11111111 . 11111111 . 00000000

Table 5.5: Network ID and default subnet mask

The 1s in the subnet mask tell you the network bits, while the 0s in the subnet mask indicate the host portion of the IP address.

As you can see, the network portion of the address is the first 24 bits, while the last 8 bits represent the host portion. Remember, all the hosts on the same subnet will have the same network bits for their IP address, while each host will have a unique bit value in the host portion.

Use the following formula to determine the number of networks:

```
Number of subnets = 2^N
Where N represents the number of hosts which you are going to convert
into new network bits.
```

As previously mentioned, where the 1s stop in the subnet mask (from left to right), the host bits begin. Start by converting one of the host bits, the 25th bit, into a network bit and determining the total number of new subnets that will be created:

Network block	11000000 . 10101000 . 00000000 . 00000000
Subnet mask	11111111 . 11111111 . 11111111 . 10000000

Table 5.6: Using one host bits

When converting a host bit into a network, the subnet bit is changed into a `1` to represent the network portion of the address.

To calculate the number of subnets, use the following formula:

```
Number of subnets = 2^N
                  = 2^1
                  = 2 subnets
```

Using one bit isn't sufficient as it only gives you two subnets. However, your goal is to create seven subnets, with each subnet having the capacity to support your largest network, which consists of 28 hosts.

Convert an additional host bit and perform calculations one more time:

Network block	11000000 . 10101000 . 00000000 . 00000000
Subnet mask	11111111 . 11111111 . 11111111 . 11000000

Table 5.7: Using two host bits

To calculate the number of subnets, use the following formula:

```
Number of subnets = 2^N
                                   = 2^2
                                   = 2 x 2
                                   = 4 subnets
```

Using two bits is not sufficient as it only gives you four subnets. However, your goal is to create 7, with each subnet having the capacity to support your largest network, which consists of 28 hosts.

Convert an additional host bit and perform our calculations one more time:

Network block	11000000 . 10101000 . 00000000 . 00000000
Subnet mask	11111111 . 11111111 . 11111111 . 11100000

Table 5.8: Using three host bits

To calculate the number of subnets, use the following formula:

```
Number of subnets = 2^N
                                   = 2^3
                                   = 2 x 2 x 2
                                   = 8 subnets
```

Using the three bits, you get eight subnets. Keep in mind that you really need seven subnets, but using two bits from the host portion was not sufficient. Therefore, you need to use the three bits and convert them into network bits. The additional 8th network can be reserved for further usage.

Having established that three host bits are converted into network bits, there are five host bits remaining in the address. You need to ensure these host bits are sufficient to create enough IPv4 addresses to fit our largest network in the topology.

Table 5.9 shows the remaining five host bits:

Network block	11000000 . 10101000 . 00000000 . 00000000
Subnet mask	11111111 . 11111111 . 11111111 . 11100000

Table 5.9: Remaining host bits

Therefore, you can use the following formula to determine the total number of IP addresses per network:

```
Total number of IP address = 2^H
                                                  = 2^5
                                                  = 2 x 2 x 2 x 2 x 2
                                                  = 32 total IP address
```

These 5 host bits give you a total of 32 IP addresses per subnet. However, you cannot assign two specific IPv4 addresses to any device: the network ID address and the broadcast address.

Therefore, you can use the following formula to calculate the number of usable/assignable IP addresses:

```
Number of usable IP address = 2^N - 2
                                                    = 2^5 - 2
                                                      = (2 x 2 x 2 x 2 x 2)
- 2
                                                      = 30 usable IP
addresses
```

This means that based on your calculations, you will be able to take three hosts from the address and create a total of eight subnets. Each of these 8 subnets will have 30 usable IP addresses. You now have a workable solution.

Lastly, when converting bits from the host portion, the subnet bits must also be changed from 0s to 1s. The 1s represent the network portion of the address. Since you took three host bits, you have a new subnet mask for each of the new subnets you are about to create. Therefore, the new subnet mask for each of the new eight networks is `255.255.255.224`, with a network prefix of `/27`.

> **Note**
>
> Keep in mind that each time you perform a subnetting process, the original network is broken down and each new network that's created will be smaller than the original. However, each subnet that's created is of equal size.

Before you begin creating the eight new subnetworks, please be sure to use the following guidelines:

- Do not modify the original network portion of the IP address (the first 24 bits)
- Do not modify the new host portion of the IP address (the last five host bits)
- Only modify the new network bits (the three host bits that you are converting into network bits)

When modifying the new network bits, simply change the 0s into 1s to create all the different possibilities. *Table 5.10* shows the calculations used to create the eight new subnets:

Subnet 1	11000000 . 10101000 . 00000000 . 00000000	192.168.0.0/27
Subnet 2	11000000 . 10101000 . 00000000 . 00100000	192.168.0.32/27
Subnet 3	11000000 . 10101000 . 00000000 . 01000000	192.168.0.64/27
Subnet 4	11000000 . 10101000 . 00000000 . 01100000	192.168.0.96/27
Subnet 5	11000000 . 10101000 . 00000000 . 10000000	192.168.0.128/27
Subnet 6	11000000 . 10101000 . 00000000 . 10100000	192.168.0.160/27
Subnet 7	11000000 . 10101000 . 00000000 . 11000000	192.168.0.192/27
Subnet 8	11000000 . 10101000 . 00000000 . 11100000	192.168.0.224/27

Table 5.10: Creating eight subnets

Always remember to start with the original network ID when performing subnetting. In your calculations, the first subnet is the `192.168.1.0/27` network. Each of your subnets is an increment of 32, and this value is derived from your formula, which is used to calculate the number of total IP addresses per network.

> **Note**
>
> At times, calculating the binary may be challenging. However, the subnets are equal in size. This means using the formula `2x` (*x* represents the number of bits) will provide you with the incremental value for each network ID.
>
> This technique will help you in calculating the new network IDs (subnets) quickly. Additionally, the last subnet (network ID) in your calculation always ends with the last portion of the new subnet mask.

Now that you have calculated all our network IDs (subnets), in the next step, you will learn how to calculate the network range for a subnet.

Assigning Subnets to Each Network

In this step, you will learn how to calculate the network ranges for each subnet, such as the first and last usable IP addresses with the broadcast address. To perform the calculations efficiently, please use the following guidelines:

- Calculate all subnets (network IDs) as your first task.
- To calculate the first usable IP address, use this formula: `Network-ID + 1`. In binary, the first bit from the right is set to `1`.
- To calculate the broadcast IP address, use this formula: `Next Network ID - 1`.
- In binary, all host bits are changed to 1s.
- To calculate the last usable IP address, use this formula: `Broadcast IP address - 1`. In binary, all host bits are 1s except for the last bit in the address.

Now, apply the guidelines, calculate the first subnet range, and assign it to the HQ LAN network, as shown in *Table 5.11*:

Subnet 1	11000000 . 10101000 . 00000000 . 00000000	192.168.0.0/27
First usable IP	11000000 . 10101000 . 00000000 . 00000001	192.168.0.1/27
Last usable IP	11000000 . 10101000 . 00000000 . 00011110	192.168.0.30/27
Broadcast	11000000 . 10101000 . 00000000 . 00011111	192.168.0.31/27

Table 5.11: Subnet 1 range

Calculate the second subnet and assign it to the Branch A LAN:

Subnet 2	11000000 . 10101000 . 00000000 . 00100000	192.168.0.32/27
First usable IP	11000000 . 10101000 . 00000000 . 00100001	192.168.0.33/27
Last usable IP	11000000 . 10101000 . 00000000 . 00111110	192.168.0.62/27
Broadcast	11000000 . 10101000 . 00000000 . 00111111	192.168.0.63/27

Table 5.12: Subnet 2 range

Calculate the third subnet and assign it to the Branch B LAN:

Subnet 3	11000000 . 10101000 . 00000000 . 01000000	192.168.0.64/27
First usable IP	11000000 . 10101000 . 00000000 . 01000001	192.168.0.65/27
Last usable IP	11000000 . 10101000 . 00000000 . 01011110	192.168.0.94/27
Broadcast	11000000 . 10101000 . 00000000 . 01011111	192.168.0.95/27

Table 5.13: Subnet 3 range

Calculate the fourth subnet and assign it to the Branch C LAN:

Subnet 4	11000000 . 10101000 . 00000000 . 01100000	192.168.0.96/27
First usable IP	11000000 . 10101000 . 00000000 . 01100001	192.168.0.97/27
Last usable IP	11000000 . 10101000 . 00000000 . 01111110	192.168.0.126/27
Broadcast	11000000 . 10101000 . 00000000 . 01111111	192.168.0.127/27

Table 5.14: Subnet 4 range

You can successfully assign the first four subnets to each of the LANs in each respective location. However, you still need to assign subnets to the WAN links that are connecting each branch router to the head office network.

Table 5.15 shows the remaining four subnets:

Subnet 5	11000000 . 10101000 . 00000000 . 10000000	192.168.0.128/27
Subnet 6	11000000 . 10101000 . 00000000 . 10100001	192.168.0.160/27
Subnet 7	11000000 . 10101000 . 00000000 . 11000000	192.168.0.192/27
Subnet 8	11000000 . 10101000 . 00000000 . 11100000	192.168.0.224/27

Table 5.15: Unallocated networks

You can take any four of the remaining subnets and assign them to each of the WAN links, but this will not be appropriate as each of the WAN links in the topology only requires two IP addresses on the router's interfaces, as follows:

- **WAN 1 (R1-R2)**: 2 IPs are needed
- **WAN 2 (R2-R3)**: 2 IPs are needed
- **WAN 3 (R3-R4)**: 2 IPs are needed

Taking any one of the subnets to assign to any of the WAN links will result in the following wastage:

```
Usable IP address per subnet = 2^H - 2
                                          = 2^5 - 2
                                          = (2 x 2 x 2 x 2 x 2)
- 2
                                          = 30 usable IP address
```

The following is what you will get when using only two IPs from a subnet for each WAN link:

```
30 address - 2 = 28 IP address will be wasted
```

You can use a slightly more advanced technique known as the **variable-length subnet mask** (**VLSM**) to break a subnet down into small subnetworks. Since you have four remaining subnets from the original calculations, reserve the following subnet for future usage, as shown in *Table 5.16*:

Subnet 5	11000000 . 10101000 . 00000000 . 10000000	192.168.0.128/27
Subnet 6	11000000 . 10101000 . 00000000 . 10100001	192.168.0.160/27
Subnet 7	11000000 . 10101000 . 00000000 . 11000000	192.168.0.192/27

Table 5.16: Reserve subnets

In the next step, you will cover how to use VLSM to break the eighth subnet, `192.168.1.224/27`, down into smaller networks to fit our WAN links.

Performing Variable-Length Subnet Masking

Performing VLSM calculations is simply subnetting a subnet. For each of the WAN links, you only require only two usable IP addresses on each link. To determine the number of host bits required to give you two usable IP addresses, use the following formula:

```
Number of usable IP addresses = 2^H - 2
Where H is the number of host bits taken from the right.
```

For a better visual, convert the eighth subnet into binary:

Network ID	11000000 . 10101000 . 00000000 . 11100000	192.168.0.224
Subnet mask	11111111 . 11111111 . 11111111 . 11100000	255.255.255.224

Table 5.17: Converting the eighth subnet into binary

As shown in the preceding figure, there are five host bits within the network ID. Using only one host bit, that is, the 32nd bit, in the formula to determine the total usable addresses will get you the following:

```
Number of usable IPv4 addresses = 2^H - 2
                                                    = 2^1 - 2
                                                    = 2 - 2
                                                    = 0 usable IP
addresses
```

If you use the 32nd bit as the host bit within the formula $2^H - 2$, the result is `0` usable IP addresses. Therefore, one host bit is not sufficient. Use an additional host bit:

```
Number of usable IPv4 addresses = 2^H - 2
                                                    = 2^2 - 2
                                                    = (2 x 2) - 2
                                                    = 4 - 2
                                                    = 2 unable IP
addresses
```

Now that you have a workable solution, ensure the last two bits, that is the 31st and 32nd bits, are always host bits in the `192.168.1.224` network ID, while the remaining hosts are converted into network bits. This is a bit of reverse engineering, where you will begin calculating the host address first, followed by the number of networks.

Furthermore, you now have three new network bits, which allows us to substitute them into the following formula:

```
Number of subnets = 2^N
                        = 2^3
                        = 2 x 2 x 2
                        = 8 subnets
```

Additionally, you can flip the new network bits in the subnet mask, as shown in *Table 5.18*:

Network ID	11000000 . 10101000 . 00000000 . 11100000	192.168.0.224
Subnet mask	11111111 . 11111111 . 11111111 . 11111100	255.255.255.252

Table 5.18: New subnet mask

Hence, each of the eight newly created subnets will have a new subnet mask of `255.255.255.252` or a network prefix of `/30`.

Calculate the total number of IP addresses per subnet and our network incremental value:

$$
\begin{aligned}
\text{Total number of IP address} &= 2^H \\
&= 2^2 \\
&= 2 \times 2 \\
&= 4 \text{ total IP addresses}
\end{aligned}
$$

Here, each number will have only two usable IP addresses, $2^H - 2 = (2 \times 2) - 2 = 2$.

Before you begin to create the new subnetworks from the `192.168.1.224/27` network block, please be sure to use the following guidelines:

- Do not modify the original network portion of the IP address (the first 27 bits)
- Do not modify the new host portion of the IP address (the last two host bits)
- Only modify the new network bits (the three host bits that you are converting into network bits)

When modifying the new network bits, you simply change the 0s into 1s to create all the different possibilities. *Table 5.19* shows the calculations to create the eight new subnets:

VLSM Subnet 1	11000000 . 10101000 . 00000000 . 11100000	192.168.0.224/30
VLSM Subnet 2	11000000 . 10101000 . 00000000 . 11100100	192.168.0.228/30
VLSM Subnet 3	11000000 . 10101000 . 00000000 . 11101000	192.168.0.232/30
VLSM Subnet 4	11000000 . 10101000 . 00000000 . 11101100	192.168.0.236/30
VLSM Subnet 5	11000000 . 10101000 . 00000000 . 11110000	192.168.0.240/30
VLSM Subnet 6	11000000 . 10101000 . 00000000 . 11110100	192.168.0.244/30
VLSM Subnet 7	11000000 . 10101000 . 00000000 . 11111000	192.168.0.248/30
VLSM Subnet 8	11000000 . 10101000 . 00000000 . 11111100	192.168.0.252/30

Table 5.19: Networks created via the VLSM network

Now, you have eight new networks that can be used for point-to-point WAN links. Calculate and assign the subnets accordingly.

Calculate the first subnet and assign it to WAN 1 (R1-R2):

Subnet 1	11000000 . 10101000 . 00000000 . 11100000	192.168.0.224/30
First usable IP	11000000 . 10101000 . 00000000 . 11100001	192.168.0.225/30
Last usable IP	11000000 . 10101000 . 00000000 . 11100010	192.168.0.226/30
Broadcast	11000000 . 10101000 . 00000000 . 11100011	192.168.0.227/30

Table 5.20: WAN 1 allocation

Calculate the second subnet and assign it to WAN 2 (R2-R3):

Subnet 2	11000000 . 10101000 . 00000000 . 11100100	192.168.0.228/30
First usable IP	11000000 . 10101000 . 00000000 . 11100101	192.168.0.229/30
Last usable IP	11000000 . 10101000 . 00000000 . 11100110	192.168.0.230/30
Broadcast	11000000 . 10101000 . 00000000 . 11100111	192.168.0.231/30

Table 5.21: WAN 2 allocation

Calculate the third subnet and assign it to WAN 3 (R3-R4):

Subnet 3	11000000 . 10101000 . 00000000 . 11101000	192.168.0.232/30
First usable IP	11000000 . 10101000 . 00000000 . 11101001	192.168.0.233/30
Last usable IP	11000000 . 10101000 . 00000000 . 11101010	192.168.0.234/30
Broadcast	11000000 . 10101000 . 00000000 . 11101011	192.168.0.235/30

Table 5.22: WAN 3 allocation

Having allocated the first three subnets of the `/30` networks, you are left with five additional networks, as shown in *Table 5.23*:

VLSM Subnet 4	11000000 . 10101000 . 00000000 . 11101100	192.168.0.236/30
VLSM Subnet 5	11000000 . 10101000 . 00000000 . 11110000	192.168.0.240/30
VLSM Subnet 6	11000000 . 10101000 . 00000000 . 11110100	192.168.0.244/30
VLSM Subnet 7	11000000 . 10101000 . 00000000 . 11111000	192.168.0.248/30
VLSM Subnet 8	11000000 . 10101000 . 00000000 . 11111100	192.168.0.252/30

Table 5.23: Additional WAN subnets

These remaining subnets can be reserved for future uses in the event the organization decides to create additional branch offices that require additional WAN links.

Having completed this section, you have learned how to use subnetting to create smaller IP subnetworks. Additionally, you have learned how to use VLSM to break a subnet down even further by subnetting a subnet.

Summary

In this chapter, you learned about the importance of subnetting and gained hands-on skills in calculating the network ID based on the IP address and subnet mask of a device. In addition, you learned how to perform various calculations to determine the number of IP addresses on a network and design an IP addressing scheme for an organization.

In the next chapter, *Chapter 6, Wireless Architectures and Virtualization*, you will learn about Cisco wireless architectures and network virtualization technologies.

Additional Reading

- *IPv4 Subnetting Reference Chart*: `https://learningnetwork.cisco.com/s/article/ipv4-subnetting-reference-chart`
- *Master IP Subnetting Forever from Networkers*: `https://learningnetwork.cisco.com/s/article/master-ip-subnetting-forever-from-networkers`
- *Understand Host and Subnet Quantities*: `https://www.cisco.com/c/en/us/support/docs/ip/routing-information-protocol-rip/13790-8.html`
- *Configure IP Addresses and Unique Subnets for New Users*: `https://www.cisco.com/c/en/us/support/docs/ip/routing-information-protocol-rip/13788-3.html`

Exam Readiness Drill – Chapter Review Questions

Apart from mastering key concepts, strong test-taking skills under time pressure are essential for acing your certification exam. That's why developing these abilities early in your learning journey is critical.

Exam readiness drills, using the free online practice resources provided with this book, help you progressively improve your time management and test-taking skills while reinforcing the key concepts you've learned.

HOW TO GET STARTED

- Open the link or scan the QR code at the bottom of this page
- If you have unlocked the practice resources already, log in to your registered account. If you haven't, follow the instructions in *Chapter 19* and come back to this page.
- Once you log in, click the START button to start a quiz
- We recommend attempting a quiz multiple times till you're able to answer most of the questions correctly and well within the time limit.
- You can use the following practice template to help you plan your attempts:

Working On Accuracy		
Attempt	**Target**	**Time Limit**
Attempt 1	40% or more	Till the timer runs out
Attempt 2	60% or more	Till the timer runs out
Attempt 3	75% or more	Till the timer runs out
Working On Timing		
Attempt 4	75% or more	1 minute before time limit
Attempt 5	75% or more	2 minutes before time limit
Attempt 6	75% or more	3 minutes before time limit

The above drill is just an example. Design your drills based on your own goals and make the most out of the online quizzes accompanying this book.

First time accessing the online resources? 🔓

You'll need to unlock them through a one-time process. **Head to** *Chapter 19* **for instructions**.

Open Quiz	
`https://packt.link/ccnachap5` OR scan this QR code →	

6
Wireless Architectures and Virtualization

Mobile devices are very common and organizations are improving their network architectures to support company-owned mobile devices that are provided to their employees. If wireless network architectures are unable to support the demand of wireless clients and **Internet of Things** (**IoT**) devices, users will experience poor network performance, which can result in lower levels of productivity. Hence, it is essential for aspiring network professionals to understand the fundamentals of network architectures and wireless technologies.

In addition to this, a lot of organizations around the world are using cloud computing technologies and service providers to improve the availability of their services and resources for their users and customers. The foundation of cloud computing begins with understanding the fundamentals of virtualization, and this technology has made its way into the field of networking. Therefore, it is important for both aspiring and seasoned network professionals to become familiar with virtualization technologies and their benefits.

In this chapter, you will learn about the importance of the role wireless networks play in many organizations. You will be able to compare various types of wireless networks and technologies and understand their usage. Furthermore, you will learn about common wireless standards and how they differ from each other. You will also discover common wireless components and their operations on small to medium-sized network architectures. Lastly, you will explore common virtualization concepts and technologies.

This chapter covers *Domain 1: Network Fundamentals*, objectives *1.11 Describe wireless principles* and *1.12 Explain virtualization fundamentals (server virtualization, containers, and VRFs)*, and *Domain 2: Network Access*, objective *2.6 Describe Cisco Wireless Architectures and AP modes* of the *200-301 CCNA v1.1 certification* exam.

In this chapter, you will read about the following topics:

- Wireless principles
- Wireless components
- Wireless operations
- Wireless channel management
- Virtualization fundamentals

Let's dive in!

Wireless Principles

Wireless Local Area Network (**WLAN**) is a common network architecture type that is usually implemented within **Small Office/Home Office** (**SOHO**) branch offices and organizations. Wireless networks or WLANs enable users with mobile devices such as smartphones and laptops to easily connect and access resources on a wired network.

Many organizations implement a robust WLAN infrastructure to support their employees with company-owned mobile devices such as laptops and ensure network-based applications are delivered efficiently between wired and wireless networks.

WLAN architectures provide several benefits to organizations. They reduce the costs associated with acquiring new equipment such as switches and routers to expand the network. They also reduce the complexity of reconfiguring a network to support the relocation of employees within the same building.

For instance, a user with a laptop can easily move from one office to another without the need to connect their device to a wired network. The laptop's wireless **Network Interface Card** (**NIC**) enables it to easily connect to a nearby access point to access resources on the wired network and the internet.

Types of Wireless Networks and Technologies

The **Institute of Electrical and Electronics Engineers** (**IEEE**) created and maintains the standards for wireless communication. It has also classified wireless networks into the following types:

- **Wireless Personal Area Network** (**WPAN**): This is a short-range low-powered wireless network with a range of up to 30 feet or approximately up to 9 meters from the transmitter.
- Common examples are **Bluetooth** and **ZigBee**, which are both based on the **IEEE 802.15 standard** and operate on the 2.4 GHz radio frequency. This standard enables users to establish a **Personal Area Network** (**PAN**) between devices to easily and quickly exchange data.

- **Wireless LAN (WLAN)**: WLANs usually provide coverage for medium-size wireless architectures such as up to 300 feet from an access point or wireless router. WLANs are most suitable for home offices, small to medium-sized businesses, and multi-floor office buildings.
- WLANs are based on the **IEEE 802.11 standard** and operate on the 2.4 GHz, 5 GHz, and 6 GHz radio frequencies.
- **Wireless Metropolitan Area Network (WMAN)**: WMANs are implemented by telecommunication providers with long-range transmitters to cover a large geographic area to cover a metropolitan area such as a city.
- **Wireless Wide Area Network (WWAN)**: WWANs use very long-range transmitters that cover a larger geographic area compared to WMANs. WWANs are used for nationwide and global communications.

While the preceding types of wireless networks are commonly used and operate on regulated radio frequencies, there are various wireless technologies that use unregulated frequencies for transmitting messages from one device to another.

The following are some common wireless technologies that operate on unlicensed frequencies:

- **Bluetooth**: Based on the **IEEE 802.15 standard** for WPAN, Bluetooth enables users to perform device-pairing up to 300 feet or 100 meters. Commonly, a person uses Bluetooth to pair their smartphone with their headphones or to their car entertainment system to leverage **Android Auto** or **Apple CarPlay**.
- However, Bluetooth is a short-range wireless technology. The following are the two types of Bluetooth technologies:
    - **Bluetooth Low Energy (BLE)**: This is a short-range implementation of Bluetooth that supports mesh and large wireless network topologies.
    - **Bluetooth Basic Rate/Enhanced Rate (BR/EDR)**: This type of Bluetooth supports point-to-point connections and is usually better for streaming audio.

> **Note**
>
> **Bluetooth range depends on the device class. Class 2 devices, which are most common, have a typical range of about 10 meters (33 feet). A 100-meter range is possible but is usually associated with Class 1 devices, which are less common.**

- **Worldwide Interoperability for Microwave Access** (**WiMAX**): Based on **IEEE 802.16** for WWAN, this supports high-speed internet access with a range of up to 30 miles or 50 kilometers. There are various factors that affect the range, such as the environment and line of sight between the sender and the destination. While theoretically possible, achieving a range of 30 miles typically requires ideal conditions and powerful transmitters. Real-world deployments often see significantly shorter ranges. Telecommunication providers strategically install WiMAX towers that transmit wireless signals over a large geographic area.
- **Cellular broadband**: Cellular technologies such as 4G and 5G are common examples of cellular broadband that are used for smartphones, tablets, and vehicles. Telecommunication providers install cell sites, which are cell towers that are interconnected and transmit the cellular network.
- The following are some common types of cellular networks:
  - **Global System for Mobile Communications** (**GSM**): This is a European standard that defines the protocols used for second-generation cellular networks by mobile devices.
  - **Code Division Multiple Access** (**CDMA**): This is a second- and third-generation communication standard that enables mobile devices to transmit voice and data between devices.
- **Satellite broadband**: Satellite broadband is commonly used for providing internet access in remote locations around the world. A subscriber uses a directional satellite dish on Earth that is aligned to a geostationary Earth orbit satellite.
- This type of technology is usually expensive and requires the directional satellite dish on the ground to have a direct line of sight to the geostationary Earth orbit satellite. Typically, weather conditions can affect the performance of the network.

Wireless 802.11 Standards

The IEEE creates and maintains wireless standards. These wireless standards define how radio frequencies are used for transmitting messages over a wireless connection between devices.

Table 6.1 shows some common IEEE 802.11 wireless standards:

IEEE Standard	Frequency	Bandwidth
802.11	2.4 GHz	Up to 2 Mbps
802.11b	2.4 GHz	Up to 11 Mbps
802.11a	5 GHz	Up to 54 Mbps
802.11g	2.4 GHz	Up to 54 Mbps
802.11n	2.4 GHz & 5 GHz	Ranges 150 - 600 Mbps
802.11ac	5 GHz	Ranges 450 Mbps - 1.3 Gbps
802.11ax (Wi-Fi 6)	2.4 GHz & 5 GHz	Up to 9.6 Gbps

Table 6.1: Wireless standards

The following are the highlights of each IEEE 802.11 standard:

- The IEEE 802.11 standard, being the original, was not implemented on any system. However, it was designed to provide up to 2 Mbps and define how radio frequencies are used for communication.
- The IEEE 802.11b standard was the first standard to be implemented. It operates on the 2.4 GHz spectrum, provides bandwidth up to 11 Mbps, and offers a long range for client devices.
- The IEEE 802.11a standard was implemented after IEEE 802.11b. It operates on the 5 GHz frequency and supports a bandwidth of up to 54 Mbps. However, it has a short coverage area.
- The IEEE 802.11g standard was implemented after IEEE 802.11a and supports a bandwidth of up to 54 Mbps with long-range coverage as it operates on the 2.4 GHz frequency. In addition to this, the IEEE 802.11g standard is backward compatible with IEEE 802.11b clients. The backward compatibility of IEEE 802.11g with IEEE 802.11b does not inherently reduce bandwidth. However, when both IEEE 802.11g and IEEE 802.11b devices operate on the same network, the overall network performance can degrade due to the slower data rates of IEEE 802.11b.
- The IEEE 802.11n standard, which supports a bandwidth of up to 600 Mbps, is backward compatible with IEEE 802.11a/b/g devices. The IEEE 802.11n standard introduced access points, wireless routers, and wireless clients to use multiple antennas by using the **Multiple-In Multiple-Out** (**MIMO**) technology.

> **Note**
> MIMO allows multiple antennas to operate as both the transmitter and receiver to improve the performance of communication on a wireless network.

- The IEEE 802.11ac standard operates on the 5 GHz frequency only and supports a bandwidth of up to 1.3 Gbps using MIMO. With IEEE 802.11ac, the access point can support up to eight antennas and is backward compatible with IEEE 802.11a/n devices.
- The IEEE 802.11ax standard, commonly known as Wi-Fi 6, was introduced in 2019 and operates on the 2.4 GHz and 5 GHz frequencies. This implementation of Wi-Fi supports higher data rates of up to 9.6 Gbps and handles multiple connected devices more efficiently than previous implementations of IEEE 802.11.
- With the previous versions of IEEE 802.11, the access point or wireless router was able to transmit messages only to one device at a time, using a round-robin approach. This means that if there are 10 laptops connected to the same access point and they are all downloading data from the wired network or internet, the access point will send some data to a laptop, then some data to another laptop, and so on while trying to distribute data to all devices as quickly as possible.
- With the implementation of Wi-Fi 6, compatible access points and clients are able to transmit data more efficiently. With Wi-Fi 6, the access point no longer uses a round-robin approach to send data to clients; it sends a continuous data stream to all clients at the same time.

Having completed this section, you have learned about the various types of wireless networks and technologies, and IEEE 802.11 wireless standards. Next, you will learn about common wireless components and their role in wireless networking.

Wireless Components

Wireless components enable mobile devices such as smartphones, laptops, and even **Internet of Things (IoT)** devices to connect and share resources on a wired network and with other wireless devices.

The following are some common wireless components:

- Wireless NIC
- Wireless home router
- Wireless access point
- Wireless antennas

Over the following sub-sections, you will learn about the role and function of each wireless component.

Wireless NIC

A **wireless NIC** enables a client device such as a laptop or a smart device to communicate over a wireless network. Wireless NICs are integrated into the motherboard of IoT devices and smartphones. However, laptops contain a wireless network adapter that is attached to the motherboard and connects to the antennas. For desktop computers, using a USB wireless adapter enables the device to communicate on a wireless network.

Figure 6.1 shows a USB wireless adapter:

Figure 6.1: USB wireless adapter

Wireless home routers are usually 3-in-1 devices as they contain the following components:

- **Access point**: Provides access to the IEEE 802.11 wireless network that's generated from the device.
- **Switch**: Most wireless routers provide 2–4 interfaces that operate on 10/100/1000 Mbps and provide switching operations for wired devices.
- **Router**: The router functionality operates as the default gateway for internal devices and is used for connecting different networks, such as interconnecting an Ethernet internal network to the internet.

Wireless Home Routers

Wireless home routers are not only implemented within home networks, but they are also commonly used within small businesses that require an inexpensive wireless architecture for their users. Wireless routers are typically an access point, router, and switch merged into an all-in-one device for home and small networks.

When a wireless router is powered on, it begins sending beacons that contain specific information about the wireless router, such as the following:

- **Service Set Identifier** (**SSID**): This is the name of the wireless network
- **Basic Service Set Identifier** (**BSSID**): The MAC address of the wireless router
- Wireless security standard, authentication method, and encryption algorithm

Wireless Access Points

Wireless access points are typically Layer 1 devices, as they are used for providing wireless connectivity for mobile devices to access the wired network of an organization. Similar to a wireless home router, when a wireless access point is powered on, it starts sending beacons to advertise its presence to any wireless clients within the vicinity.

The following are some common categories of wireless access points:

- Autonomous
- Controller-based

Autonomous access points are independently configured to make their own forward decisions and determine how they handle associations with wireless clients. Autonomous mode is great for small wireless architectures such as a home network or a small office location. However, as an organization grows, with more users and devices, so does the need to expand the wireless architecture with additional access points. A large wireless architecture with many access points can be centrally managed using a **Wireless LAN Controller** (**WLC**) on the network.

Controller-based access points are commonly referred to as **Lightweight Access Points** (**LAPs**) as they use the **Lightweight Access Point Protocol** (**LAPP**) for communicating with the WLC on the network. When a LAP is connected to a wireless architecture, it establishes a connection to the WLC and retrieves its configurations over the network, reducing the time and complexity of deploying new access points within an organization.

The diagram in *Figure 6.2* shows the on-premises deployment of a WLC:

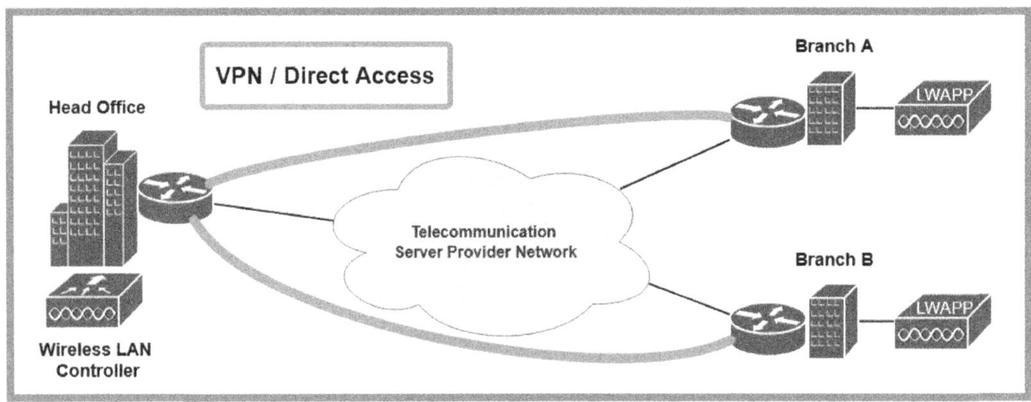

Figure 6.2: WLC deployment

As shown in the preceding diagram, the WLC appliance is implemented at the head office location of the organization and each access point is configured to communicate with the WLC over a **Virtual Private Network** (**VPN**) or using a **Wide Area Network** (**WAN**) circuit provided by the telecommunication provider.

Therefore, a network professional can access the WLC web interface to make modifications to the wireless network such as creating a new wireless network or changing the network name or password. Once the changes are completed, the configurations can be pushed to the access points, ensuring all devices' configurations are synchronized. Some organizations choose to deploy their WLC appliance within a data center to improve the availability of the device.

Additionally, Cisco offers a fully cloud-managed wireless solution known as Cisco Meraki. The Cisco Meraki solution uses a subscripted-based model and provides network professionals with a web portal for managing their Meraki devices.

> **Note**
>
> To learn more about Cisco Meraki, please see `https://meraki.cisco.com`.

Wireless Antennas

Wireless antennas are a mandatory component in wireless networking as they are connected to the wireless NIC and used for transmitting and receiving radio frequencies within the vicinity. For instance, mobile clients such as smartphones, laptops, and IoT devices usually have built-in wireless antennas that enable them to identify and connect to a nearby access point or wireless router.

Similar to mobile devices, access points and wireless home routers usually have multiple wireless antennas for transmitting a radio frequency signal and advertising its presence within the vicinity.

The following are some common types of wireless antennas:

- **Omnidirectional**: Radiates the wireless signal in all directions and it is commonly used for providing coverage in open spaces. These are commonly used on mobile devices, access points, and wireless routers.
- **Directional**: It focuses its signal in a specific direction and is commonly used for long-range communication using a point-to-point setup.

While wireless antennas are responsible for transmitting wireless signals, it is important to consider factors that affect the performance of a wireless network:

- **Line of sight**: While the radio frequency that is generated by a transmitter is wireless and penetrates through solid objects such as walls, the signal is still absorbed by these objects and becomes weaker as it travels further away from the transmitter.
- Ensuring a line of sight between the mobile client and antennas can be almost impossible in reality, but it provides optimal signal strength once the client is within the range of the access point.
- **Fresnel zone**: The Fresnel zone is the area between the direct line of sight of two antennas that affect the wireless signal quality and strength. Therefore, it is important for network professionals to consider strategic zones for deploying access points to ensure proper propagation of wireless signals while reducing any potential interference.
- **Environment**: If there are too many solid objects such as walls between transmitters, such as between the access point and the wireless client, the signal strength will become weak. Clients that receive weak signals from an access point usually experience poor network performance such as packet loss and high latency.

Having completed this section, you have learned about common wireless components and their functions. In the next section, you will learn about wireless operations and access point modes.

Wireless Operations

In this section, you will learn about the various wireless network topologies, the difference between **Basic Service Set** (**BSS**) and **Extended Service Set** (**ESS**), the components of a **Wireless LAN** (**WLAN**) frame, how **Carrier-Sense Multiple Access with Collision Avoidance** (**CSMA/CA**) prevents collisions on an IEEE 802.11 wireless network, the operations of a wireless client and an access point, and the importance of the **Control And Provisioning of Wireless Access Points** (**CAPWAP**) protocol.

Wireless Topology Modes

Learning about the fundamentals of wireless network topologies plays an important role in understanding communication over a Wi-Fi network and helps with planning future network upgrades.

The following are some common types of wireless topologies:

- Infrastructure mode
- Ad hoc mode
- Wireless mesh
- Wireless bridge

In **infrastructure mode**, there is always one access point or wireless router that operates as the centralized access point for all wireless clients of the network, as shown in *Figure 6.3*:

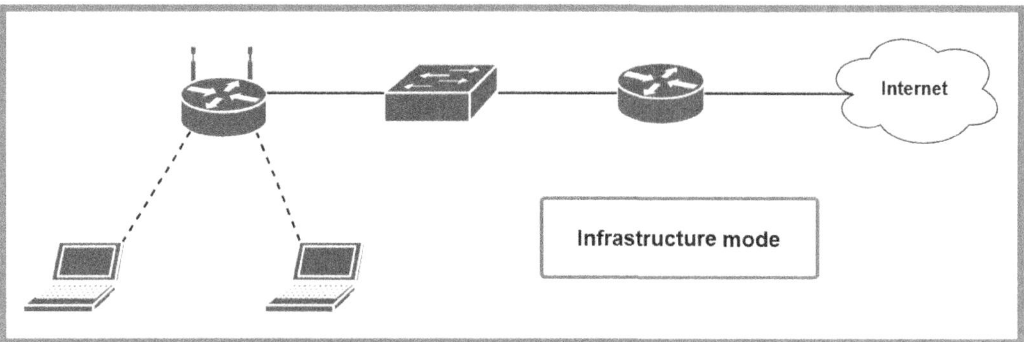

Figure 6.3: Infrastructure mode

This type of topology is most common within home networks and organizations as it provides centralized management of the wireless network, wireless network scalability for medium and large networks, and ensures that network professionals can set up roaming for wireless clients and advanced wireless security features.

In **ad hoc mode**, there's no Access Point or wireless router. The wireless clients communicate directly with each other without a centralized access point. Ad hoc mode provides direct peer-to-peer communication between clients and can be useful in situations when a temporary but small wireless network is needed. However, this type of wireless network topology does not support scalability and advanced wireless security features as compared to using infrastructure mode. Furthermore, each wireless client is responsible for managing its own wireless security.

The diagram in *Figure 6.4* shows an ad hoc wireless network:

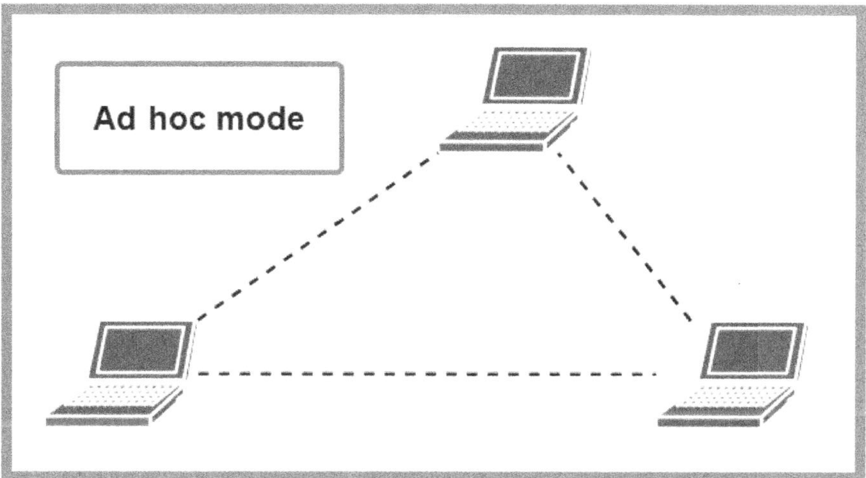

Figure 6.4: Ad hoc wireless network

The **wireless mesh** network topology enables multiple access points or wireless routers to establish a wireless link with each other for communication and extend the range of signal coverage in an area. This type of wireless topology provides extended coverage with redundant connections to all other access points and it is commonly implemented in outdoor deployments.

The diagram in *Figure 6.5* shows a wireless mesh network with four wireless routers or access points that are connected using mesh mode:

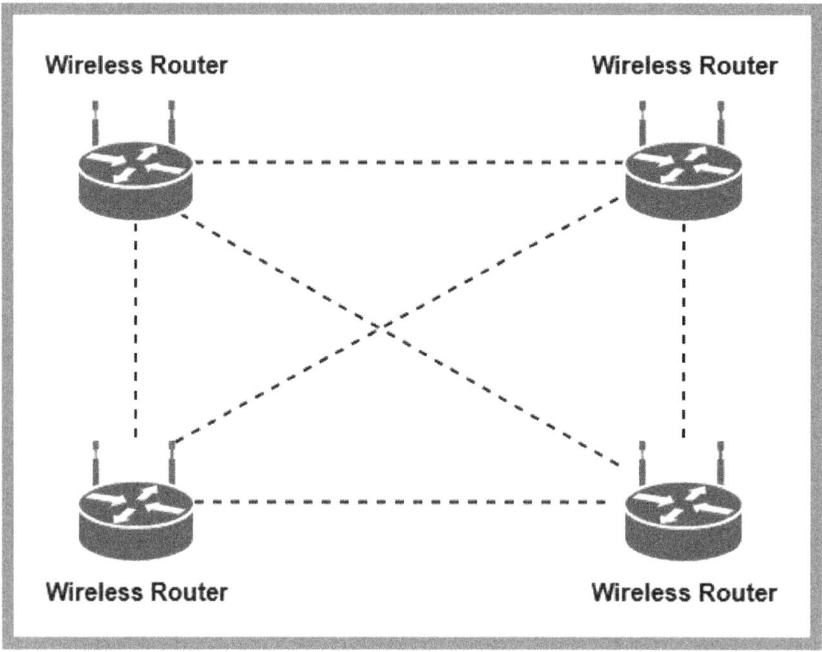

Figure 6.5: Wireless mesh network

Wireless bridge mode enables network professionals to connect two wired networks using wireless communication technologies. This type of topology is commonly used for connecting separate buildings and is usually implemented using a point-to-point or point-to-multipoint deployment model.

Figure 6.6 shows the wireless bridge topology:

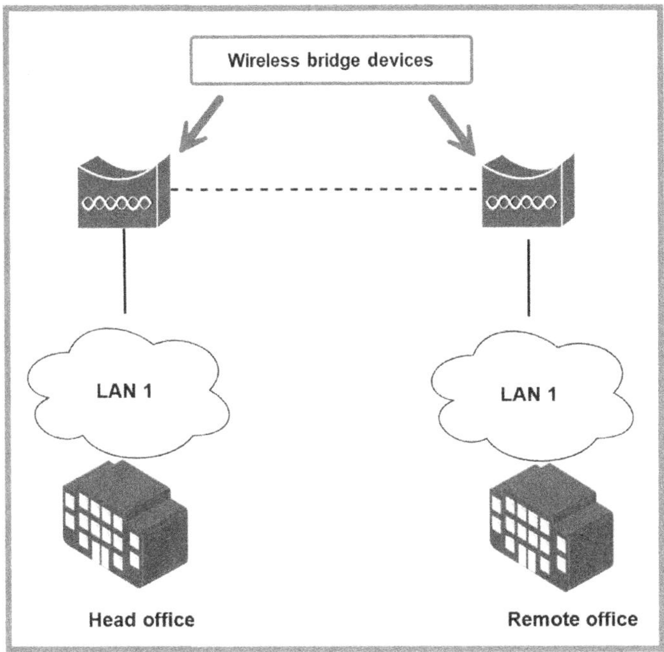

Figure 6.6: Wireless bridge topology

BSS and ESS

The **Basic Service Set** (**BSS**) consists of wireless clients known as **Stations** (**STAs**) that communicate with each other on a wireless network. There are two types of BSS in wireless networking:

- Infrastructure BSS
- Independent BSS

In an **infrastructure BSS**, the operation mode is the same as using **infrastructure mode** with a centralized access point or wireless router that manages the communication and security features of the wireless network topology. Clients communicate with each other through the centralized access point or wireless router on the network.

Figure 6.7 shows an infrastructure BSS:

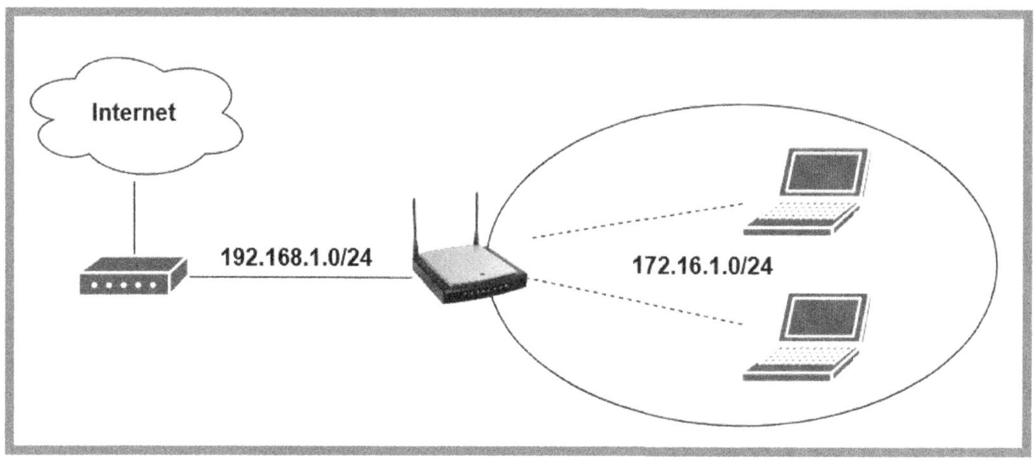

Figure 6.7: Infrastructure BSS

In an **independent BSS**, the stations communicate directly with each other without using a centralized access point or wireless router on the network. This is the same as using ad hoc mode in the wireless topology.

> **Note**
>
> Each BSS is identified by a **Basic Service Set Identifier** (**BSSID**), which is the 48-bit **Media Access Control** (**MAC**) address of the access point or wireless router.

In an **Extended Service Set** (**ESS**), there are two or more interconnected BSSes that appear to be a single BSS. In other words, there are two or more access points that are connected to the same wired network and both access points are configured to advertise the same **Service Set Identifier** (**SSID**) or network name.

The diagram in *Figure 6.8* shows an ESS:

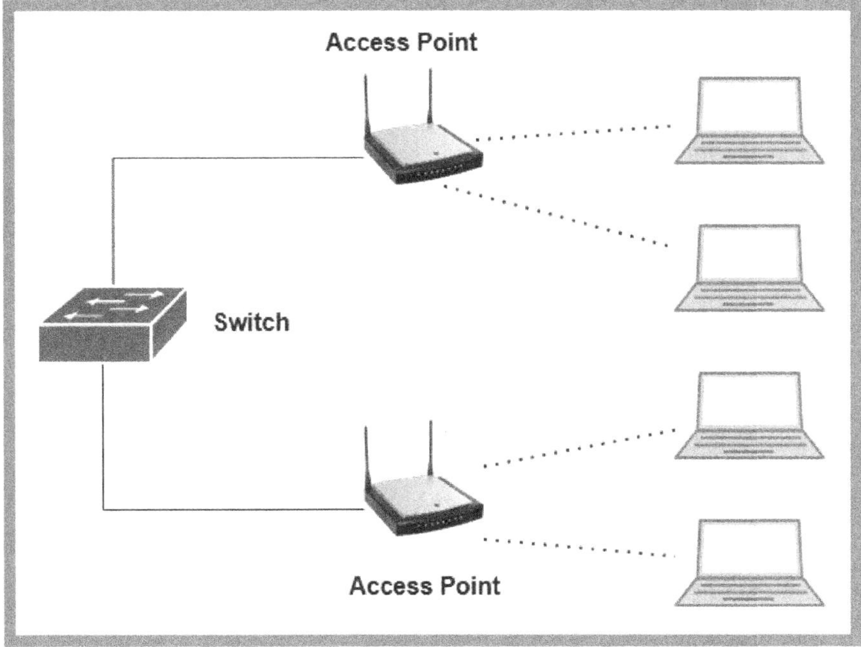

Figure 6.8: ESS operation

WLAN Frame

Like end devices and servers, wireless networks transmit WLAN frames between the wireless clients and the access point on the network. As an aspiring network professional, it is essential that you understand the structure and role of each field found within a WLAN frame.

Figure 6.10 shows the fields of a WLAN frame:

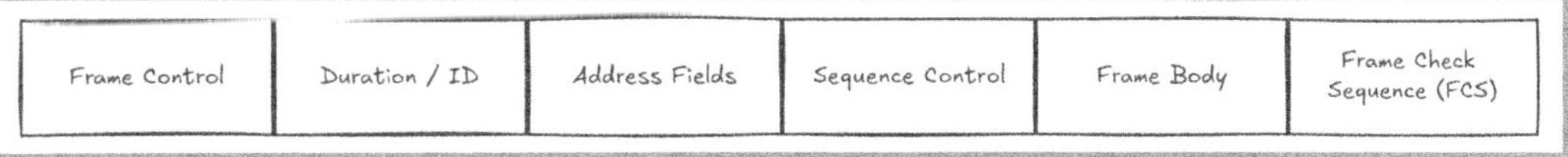

Figure 6.9: WLAN frame

The following is a description of each field found in a WLAN frame:

- **Frame control**: This is a two-byte field that specifies the type of frame and its function.
- **Duration/ID**: This is a two-byte field that indicates the amount of time the wireless channel will be occupied transmitting wireless frames on the network.
- **Address fields**: There are four six-byte address fields that contain the following:
    - **Source Address** (**SA**)
    - **Destination Address** (**DA**)
    - **Transmitting Station Address** (**TA**)
    - **Receiving Station Address** (**RA**)
- **Sequence control**: This is a two-byte field that contains the sequencing details of the message and helps with the reordering of fragments and removing duplicated frames on the receiving device.
- **Frame body**: This field can be up to 2,312 bytes in length to contain the data from the application-layer protocols.
- **Frame Check Sequence** (**FCS**): This is a four-byte field that contains the 32-bit **Cyclic Redundancy Check** (**CRC**) value that's used for integrity checking and error detection.

CSMA/CA

On IEEE 802.11 wireless networks prior to IEEE 802.11ax (Wi-Fi 6), all devices within a wireless network architecture used **Carrier Sense Multiple Access with Collision Avoidance** (**CSMA/CA**). CSMA/CA enables multiple client devices to access the same contention-based wireless network while reducing the risk of WLAN frame collisions. To put it simply, on IEEE 802.11 a/b/g/n/ac networks, multiple clients are unable to transmit WLAN frames at the same time through the access point or wireless router; only one device can transmit at a time.

With CSMA/CA, client devices such as laptops and IoT devices listen on the wireless medium to determine when it's idle, that is, no other device is transmitting. If the wireless medium is busy, the client device waits for a random period and re-checks again to determine that the medium is idle.

> Note
>
> The waiting period for wireless clients is known as the **Distributed Inter-Frame Space** (**DFIS**).

If the medium is idle, the client will send a **Ready to Send** (**RTS**) frame to the access point, indicating it wants to use the medium to send a message. The access point will respond to the client with a **Clear to Send** (**CTS**) frame, indicating that it can proceed. After the client receives the CTS frame, it will proceed to transmit the data and the recipient will provide ACK frames when the messages are successfully received.

Wireless Client and AP Association

When an access point or wireless router is powered on, it begins transmitting **beacons**, which are special WLAN frames that contain specific information about the BSS and wireless network. This enables wireless clients such as smartphones and laptops to scan the vicinity for any nearby wireless networks by listening for and analyzing any beacons.

When a client attempts to connect to a BSS or wireless network, it's prompted to enter authentication details such as the **Pre-Shared Key** (**PSK**) for small networks or using enterprise authentication for larger networks. Once the authentication process is successful, the client sends an **association request** to the access point. Then the access point responds and establishes a logical connection between itself and the client.

Once a client connects to a wireless network, the information is saved within a **Preferred Network List** (**PNL**). This is a convenient feature within computer and mobile operating systems. Therefore, when the wireless NIC is enabled on a device, the client sends **probes** for any wireless network that is saved in the PNL. Once a network is found, the client will attempt to automatically authenticate and establish an association with the access point.

CAPWAP Operation

When a **Lightweight Access Point** (**LAP**) is deployed on a network and is associated with a WLC appliance, a **Control and Provisioning of Wireless Access Points** (**CAPWAP**) tunnel is established between the WLC and LAP. The CAPWAP tunnel is a logical connection between the WLC appliance and LAP whether these devices are on the same network or not.

CAPWAP uses the following technologies:

- **Split MAC**: This type of architecture is commonly used on wireless architectures with a centralized controller such as a WLC appliance.
- **DTLS encryption**: CAPWAP uses **Datagram Transport Layer Security** (**DTLS**) for encrypting UDP-based applications and it's used for securing communication between the WLC appliance and the LAPs on the network.
- **FlexConnect**: FlexConnect is a Cisco proprietary feature for branch office access points that enables them to switch clients' traffic locally and perform local authentication on the access point when the CAPWAP tunnel is down or the WLC appliance is unavailable.

> **Note**
>
> CAPWAP uses UDP port `5246` for control and UDP port `5247` for data.

Having completed this section, you have learned about common wireless operations. In the next section, you will learn about wireless channel management.

Wireless Channel Management

Frequency channel saturation is an important factor all network professionals need to consider within their organization. Frequency channel saturation occurs when there are too many wireless devices and access points within the same vicinity that are using the same or overlapping IEEE 802.11 wireless channels.

The following are some common symptoms of frequency channel saturation:

- Poor wireless network performance
- High latency and packet loss
- Higher interference between wireless devices

Selecting the proper wireless channel on a BSS is crucial to the performance of the wireless network and the user experience of the wireless clients.

The following are some key factors to consider when choosing an appropriate channel:

- Try to choose a non-overlapping channel to reduce the level of interference. This may be almost impossible within a city when using the 2.4 GHz band.
- The physical placement of an access point or wireless router.
- Consider any potential sources of interference.
- When configuring the access points, enable automatic channel selection. This feature allows the access point to monitor the channels of nearby access points and automatically switch its own channel to one with less interference.

When using the 2.4 GHz band, there are 14 channels and each channel is 20-22 MHz wide and ranges from 2.400–2.435 GHz. This means that there are only three non-overlapping channels in the 2.4 GHz band – these are channels 1, 6, and 11.

The diagram in *Figure 6.10* shows each channel on the 2.4 GHz band and how they overlap:

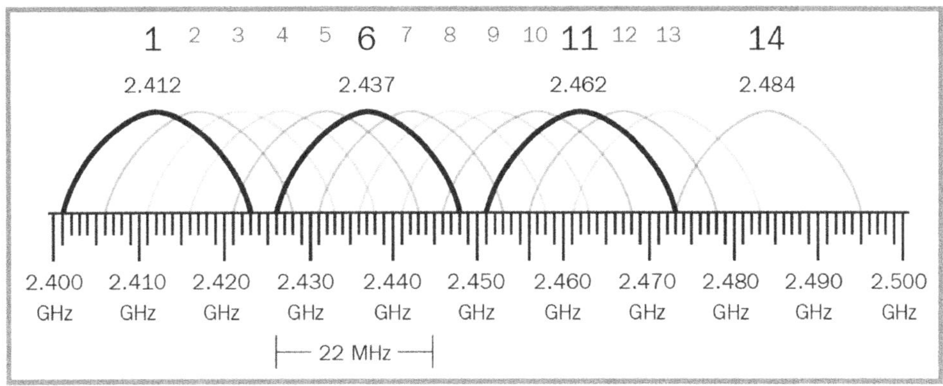

Figure 6.10: Channel overlapping

> **Note**
>
> Based on IEEE 802.11, channel 14 of the 2.4 GHz band is only permitted in Japan.

When using the 5 GHz band, there are a lot more non-overlapping channels as compared to the 2.4 GHz band. The 5 GHz frequency introduced far more channels than the older 2.4 GHz frequency. Additionally, the 5 GHz frequency leverages **channel bonding**, which allows two or more 5 GHz channels to combine and operate as a single but larger channel to support more bandwidth capacity. Keep in mind that channel bonding is more commonly associated with the 5 GHz band.

The following is a further breakdown of how channel bonding works. Each channel is 20 MHz in width. Using channel bonding, access points can combine 2 x 20 MHz channels to create a 40 MHz channel. Then, by using channel bonding again, combine 2 x 40 MHz channels to create an 80 MHz channel. Finally, combine 2 x 80 MHz channels using channel bonding to create a 160 MHz channel.

The benefit of using channel bonding is that it provides greater bandwidth capacity on a wireless network. Hence, it is more efficient to use the 5 GHz frequency within an organization when there's a large quantity of wireless devices.

Having completed this section, you have learned about the fundamentals of wireless architecture. In the next section, you will learn about virtualization.

Virtualization Fundamentals

In the early days, many organizations and IT professionals deployed a dedicated physical server for hosting an application. For instance, if an organization wanted to host an accounting application, the IT team would acquire a new server with robust hardware, install a licensed version of Windows Server, and install the account application on it.

If the organization wanted to host another application separate from the accounting application on the first server, the same process was repeated. This would result in multiple physical servers, increasing the need for physical storage space in the server room and an increase in expenditure to acquire new servers and maintain existing systems.

In addition to this, since physical servers usually have robust and server-grade hardware components, if a dedicated physical server were to host a single application, there's a strong possibility the hardware components would be under-utilized. This is commonly referred to as **server sprawl**.

Virtualization enables IT professionals to create virtual machines that contain the same hardware resources as a physical computer or server and run a full-fledged operating system. IT professionals can get started using a **hypervisor** to virtualize the operating system architecture on the physical hardware. This enables IT professionals to run multiple different operating systems at the same time within multiple virtual machines on the same physical hardware without issues. Imagine running two different flavors of Linux and two versions of Microsoft Windows server at the same time on the same physical server. In addition to this, virtualization enables IT professionals to efficiently leverage the available hardware resources and computing power on a physical system.

Type 1 Hypervisor

Type 1 hypervisors, commonly referred to as bare-metal hypervisors, are installed directly on hardware, that is, on the primary storage device, such as on a physical server. When the physical server is powered on, the hypervisor loads in memory and runs like an operating system, thus enabling IT professionals to manage the hypervisor via its web interface.

With a Type 1 hypervisor, IT professionals can create virtual machines with virtual hardware components that a typical server or computer will need. These would include the following:

- CPU
- Memory
- Storage
- Network adapters
- **Input/Output** (**I/O**) components

Once the virtual machine is created, IT professionals then install an operating system such as Windows, Linux, macOS, or even Android within the virtual environment. The operating system that is installed within a virtual machine is commonly referred to as the **guest operating system**.

Figure 6.11 shows the architecture of a Type 1 hypervisor:

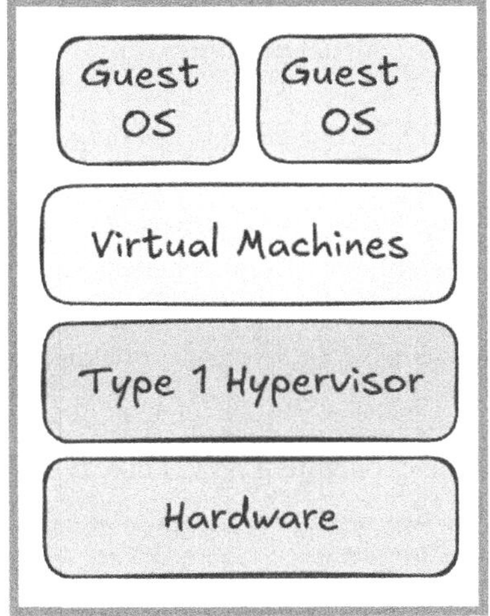

Figure 6.11: Type 1 hypervisor

The following are examples of free Type 1 hypervisors:

- Proxmox
- NCP-ng

The screenshot in *Figure 6.12* shows the web interface of VMware ESXi when it was free for users:

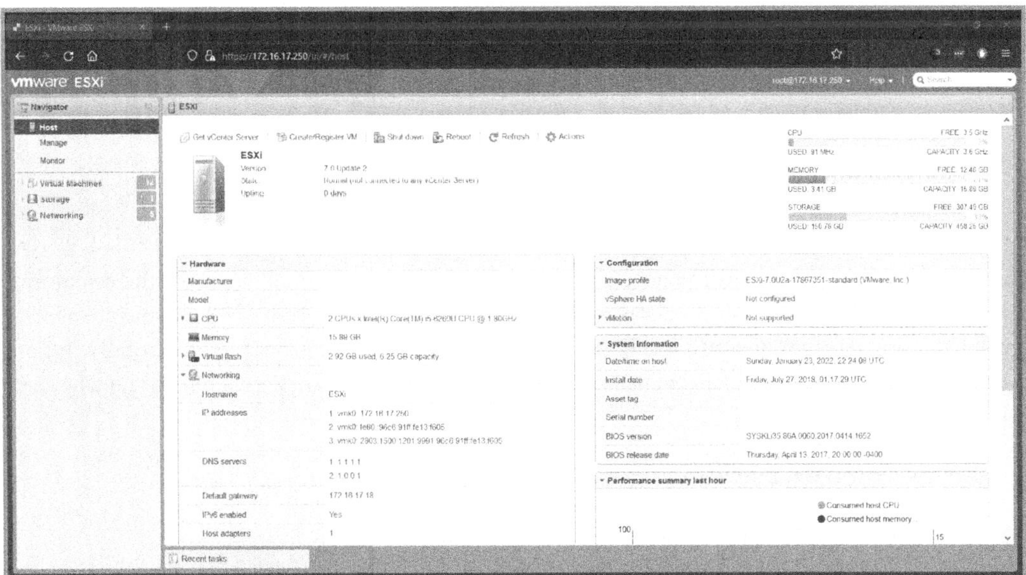

Figure 6.12: Type 1 hypervisor web interface

As shown in the preceding screenshot, Type 1 hypervisors enable users to monitor the utilization of computing resources on the server, create and modify virtual machines, and create virtual switches to perform virtual networking between virtual machines.

Type 2 Hypervisor

Type 2 hypervisors are installed on top of a host operating system. This type of hypervisor provides all the same essential functions and capabilities as a Type 1 hypervisor, but it is installed as an application on top of your existing operating system on a computer. Unlike a Type 1 hypervisor, which has more direct access to the hardware resources, a Type 2 hypervisor has access to the resources made available by the host operating system.

The diagram in *Figure 6.13* shows the deployment model of a Type 2 hypervisor:

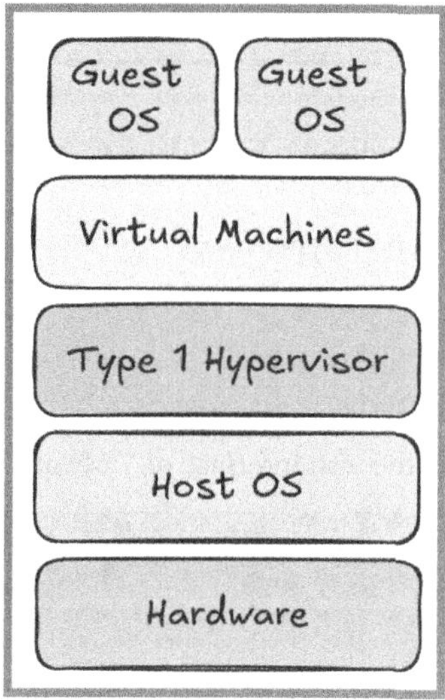

Figure 6.13: Type 2 hypervisor

The host operating system has full access to the physical hardware resources, while the remaining resources are shared with the hypervisor for the virtual machines. This type of hypervisor is beneficial if you have a single computer and would like to create virtual machines on it. If you install a Type 2 hypervisor on a laptop and create virtual machines, your virtual machines will be with you wherever you carry your laptop.

The following are free Type 2 hypervisors:

- VMware Workstation
- Oracle VM VirtualBox

The screenshot in *Figure 6.14* shows VMware Workstation as a Type 2 hypervisor:

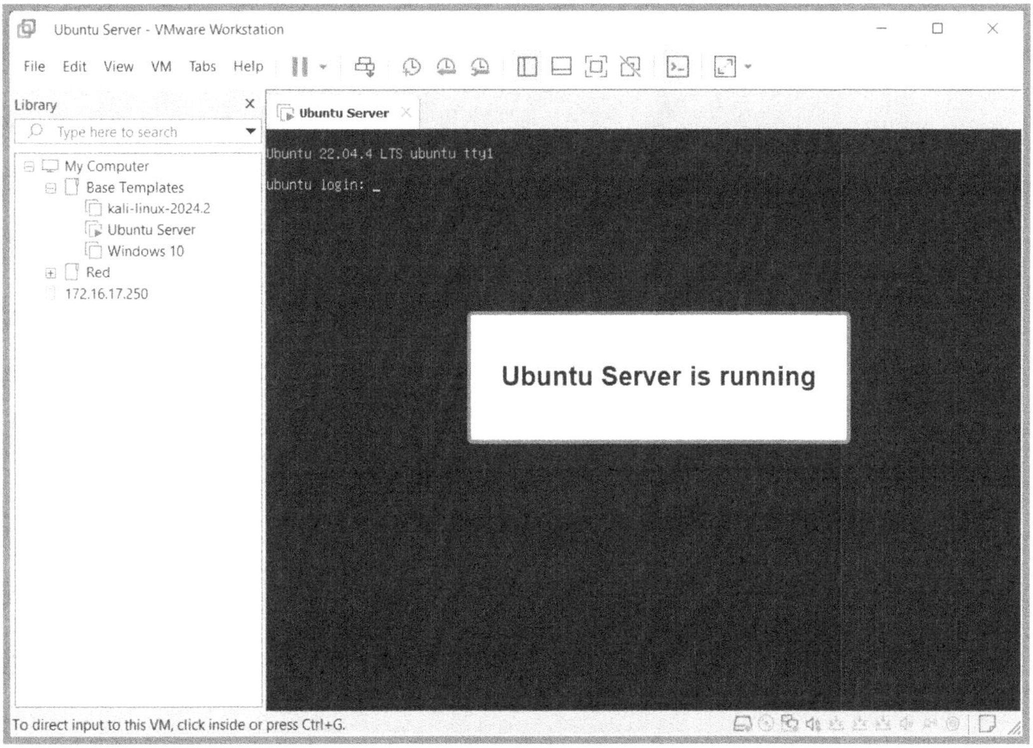

Figure 6.14: Type 2 hypervisor

Virtualization technologies have been around in the computing industry for over a decade. Within the last 10 years, there has been a growing need for professionals who can implement and support data center environments to create cloud computing technologies.

Containerization

Containerization enables IT professionals to virtualize applications and their software dependencies into an isolated container that runs on top of a host operating system. Unlike Type 1 and Type 2 hypervisors that virtualize an entire operating system, containerization enables us to run multiple, isolated containers at the same time while sharing the host operating system's kernel.

The concept of containerization focuses on enabling faster and more efficient startup of applications as compared to powering on a virtual machine with a guest operating system. In the networking industry, containerization enables network professionals to quickly deploy network services and applications and improve resource utilization.

The following are examples of container engines:

- Docker
- Kubernetes
- Containerd

Figure 6.15 shows the deployment of containerization:

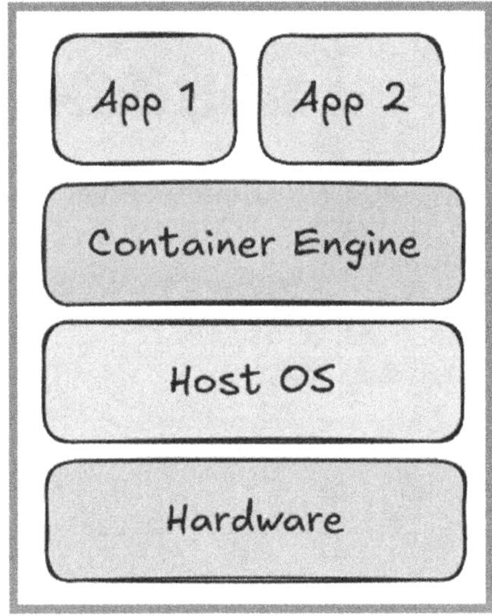

Figure 6.15: Containerization

As shown in *Figure 6.15*, a container engine is installed on the host operating system of a device. The container engine enables users to create, download, and manage containers on a computer.

Virtual Routing and Forwarding

Virtual Routing and Forwarding (**VRF**) is a virtualization technology within Cisco IOS routers that enables network professionals to create multiple instances of the routing table within the same router. Using VRF, network professionals can improve the functionality of a router and create multiple network paths without using multiple devices. Each RF instance uses its own routing table that is logically separated or independent of other VRF instances on the same device.

Figure 6.16 shows a VRF instance on a router:

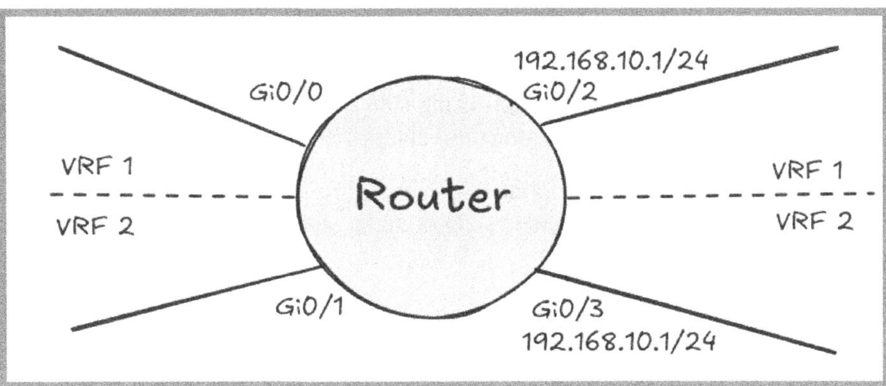

Figure 6.16: VRF router

As shown in *Figure 6.16*, there are two physical interfaces that are configured with IP addresses on the network. This is possible because VRF instances use isolated routing tables from other instances on the same device.

Summary

Having completed this chapter, you have learned about wireless networking concepts and architectures. You have also learned about the role and function of common wireless components and operations. Furthermore, you have learned the importance of wireless channel management and how it can affect the performance of a wireless network. Lastly, you have learned about the fundamentals of virtualization technologies, types of hypervisors, and how they are deployed to improve resource utilization on systems.

In the next *Chapter 7, Implementing VLANs and Interswitch Connectivity*, you will learn how to segment a physical network into virtually logical networks to improve network performance and security.

Additional Reading

- What is WiFi 6?: `https://www.cisco.com/c/en/us/products/wireless/what-is-wi-fi-6.html`
- Cisco wireless architectures: `https://www.cisco.com/en/US/docs/solutions/Enterprise/Mobility/emob30dg/TechArch.html`
- Introduction to VRFs: `https://learningnetwork.cisco.com/s/article/introduction-to-vrfs-part-1-ipv4-only-vrfs-x`
- Virtual Route Forwarding Design Guide: `https://www.cisco.com/c/en/us/td/docs/voice_ip_comm/cucme/vrf/design/guide/vrfDesignGuide.html`

Exam Readiness Drill – Chapter Review Questions

Apart from mastering key concepts, strong test-taking skills under time pressure are essential for acing your certification exam. That's why developing these abilities early in your learning journey is critical.

Exam readiness drills, using the free online practice resources provided with this book, help you progressively improve your time management and test-taking skills while reinforcing the key concepts you've learned.

HOW TO GET STARTED

- Open the link or scan the QR code at the bottom of this page
- If you have unlocked the practice resources already, log in to your registered account. If you haven't, follow the instructions in *Chapter 19* and come back to this page.
- Once you log in, click the START button to start a quiz
- We recommend attempting a quiz multiple times till you're able to answer most of the questions correctly and well within the time limit.
- You can use the following practice template to help you plan your attempts:

Working On Accuracy		
Attempt	**Target**	**Time Limit**
Attempt 1	40% or more	Till the timer runs out
Attempt 2	60% or more	Till the timer runs out
Attempt 3	75% or more	Till the timer runs out
Working On Timing		
Attempt 4	75% or more	1 minute before time limit
Attempt 5	75% or more	2 minutes before time limit
Attempt 6	75% or more	3 minutes before time limit

The above drill is just an example. Design your drills based on your own goals and make the most out of the online quizzes accompanying this book.

First time accessing the online resources? 🔓

You'll need to unlock them through a one-time process. **Head to** *Chapter 19* **for instructions.**

Open Quiz

https://packt.link/ccnachap6

OR scan this QR code →

7
Implementing VLANs and Interswitch Connectivity

Learning how to segment a physical network into smaller, logical networks provides many benefits within organizations, such as improved network performance and IT efficiency. Throughout this chapter, you will learn about the importance of segmenting a flat physical network into smaller broadcast domains to improve both network security and the efficiency of network performance using a Layer 2 technology known as a **virtual local area network** (**VLAN**).

You will also learn about the various types of VLANs and useable ranges within an organization, and how to implement and establish end-to-end connectivity between devices and different VLANs on a network.

This chapter covers *Domain 2: Network Access* and objectives *2.1 Configure and verify VLANs (normal range) spanning multiple switches* and *2.2 Configure and verify interswitch connectivity* of the *200-301 CCNA v1.1 Certification* exam.

In this chapter, you will learn about the following topics:

- Understanding VLANs
- Types of VLANs and their ranges
- Configuring and verifying VLANs
- Interswitch connectivity
- Configuring inter-VLAN routing

Time to dive in!

Understanding VLANs

VLANs enable network professionals to logically segment a physical Layer 2 network into multiple virtual networks, enabling small broadcast domains while improving network performance. Therefore, network professionals can group devices that belong to a specific group, such as all devices within the sales department, into a VLAN. If a user's device within the **Sales** VLAN generates a broadcast message, that message is limited to devices within the **Sales** VLAN and it is not propagated to other users on the same physical network.

The concept of VLANs is based on logical connections and segmentation rather than physical connections. VLANs are commonly used to segment traffic types such as voice, video, and data from each other, while also segmenting network-connected devices from each other.

For instance, the following diagram shows a multistorey building with many devices, all connected to the same physical network. If a device sends a broadcast message, all other devices will receive it, as shown in *Figure 7.1*:

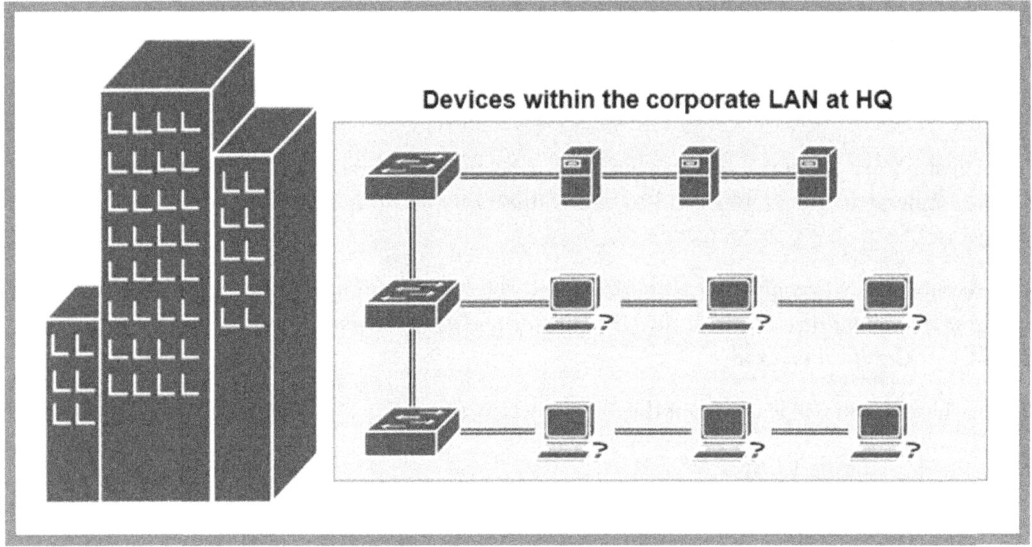

Figure 7.1: Single broadcast domain

By implementing VLANs, network professionals can create a VLAN for each business unit or organizational department within a building, such as the following:

- VLAN 10 – **Sales**
- VLAN 20 – **Human Resources** (**HR**)
- VLAN 30 – **Information Technology** (**IT**)

Once the VLANs are created on the network switches, network professionals can assign each interface of a switch to a specific VLAN. Therefore, end users on the same VLAN will be able to communicate with each other, regardless of the physical switch.

Figure 7.2 shows one physical network architecture with three VLANs, logically segmenting each business unit:

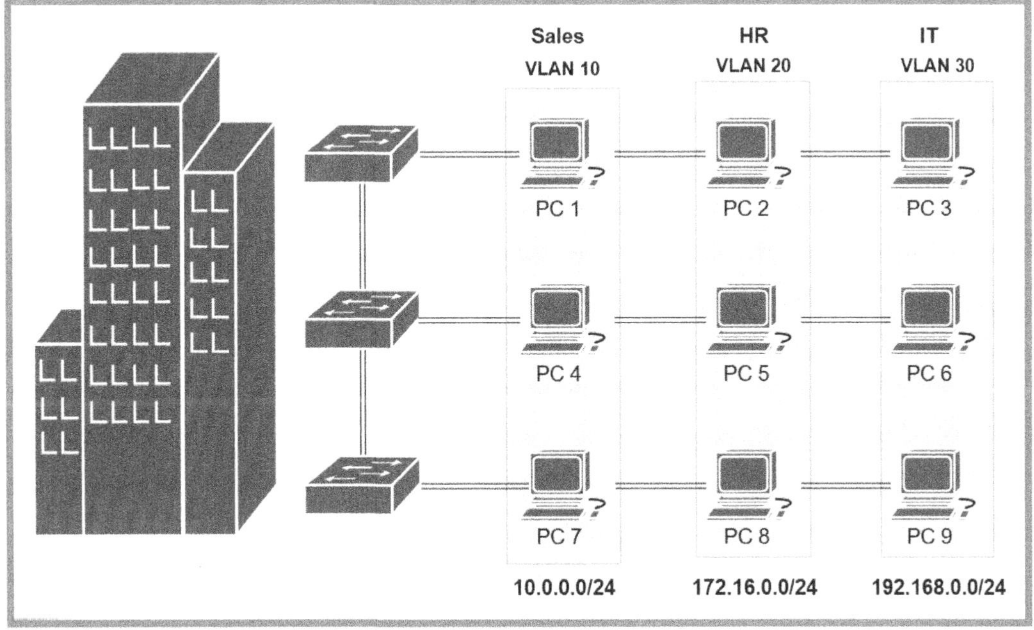

Figure 7.2: Network with VLANs

As shown in *Figure 7.2*, if **PC 1** sends a Layer 2 broadcast message, only **PC 4** and **PC 7** will receive it. Devices within **VLAN 20** (**HR**) and **VLAN 30** (**IT**) will be unaffected by the broadcast message from **PC 1**. This is one of the benefits of using VLANs within an organization. In addition, unicast, multicast, and broadcast network traffic are only sent to devices within the same logical segmentation.

A **broadcast domain** is a logical network segment that allows all connected devices to reach each other via the Data Link layer. The network topology in *Figure 7.3* shows the broadcast domains:

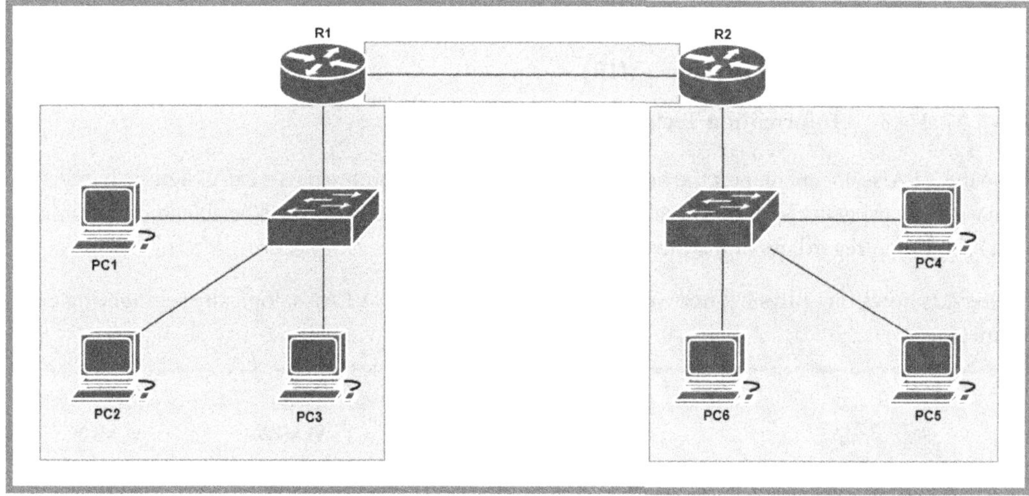

Figure 7.3: Broadcast domain

As shown in *Figure 7.3*, when an end device such as a PC sends a broadcast message, the switch that receives the message will perform a MAC address lookup to determine how it should forward the frame. Since Layer 2 broadcast messages have a destination MAC address of `FF-FF-FF-FF-FF-FF`, the switch will forward the message from all interfaces except the interface of the sender. Layer 2 broadcast messages will propagate the entire Layer 2 architecture but will stop at a Layer 3 device such as a router.

Reviewing *Figure 7.3*, when **PC1** sends a Layer 2 broadcast on the network, the switch will forward it to **PC2**, **PC3**, and **Router 1** (**R1**). **R1** will process the message, but will not forward it onward. Similarly, if **PC4** sends a broadcast on the network, the switch forwards the messages to **PC5**, **PC6**, and **Router 2** (**R2**). **R2** does not forward the Layer 2 broadcast to **R1**.

Benefits of Using VLANs

Each VLAN is assigned a unique IP subnet. Therefore, network professionals need to ensure that they have considered a hierarchical IP addressing scheme to support multiple VLANs and the future growth of the organization.

VLANs provide many benefits to network professionals, such as creating smaller broadcast domains by reducing the number of devices within a network segment. For instance, rather than all end devices operating on the IP and physical network segment, create multiple VLANs for each business unit and assign end devices to their corresponding VLANs. All devices within the sales department should be assigned to the **Sales** VLAN, and so on.

Since VLANs are used for creating small broadcast domains on a network, they reduce unnecessary traffic on the network and to other devices and improve the network's performance.

Devices within the same VLAN can communicate directly with each other. This improves network security. Therefore, if a threat actor compromises a segment of the network, a novice hacker may not be able to identify whether there are other devices on the same physical network that are separated into VLANs. Using a Layer 3 switch or a router, network professionals can implement inter-VLAN routing, which enables communication between different VLANs.

VLANs are commonly used to separate various traffic types from each other. For instance, a voice VLAN can be created for the purpose of transporting **Voice over IP** (**VoIP**) traffic over the same physical network. Another VLAN can be created and used to transport Video over IP traffic rather than purchasing new and dedicated devices to transport VoIP and Video over IP traffic.

Understanding Tagged Traffic

Apart from creating the VLANs on switches, network professionals must assign each switch interface to a specific VLAN. Once traffic enters a switch port, the frame is tagged with an `IEEE 802.1Q` tag, which enables the switch to identify one type of VLAN traffic from another. The interfaces that are assigned to a VLAN are commonly referred to as **access ports**, and only one VLAN can be assigned to an access port, with the exception of data VLANs and voice VLANs.

Figure 7.4 shows the interfaces of a switch and the VLAN assignment:

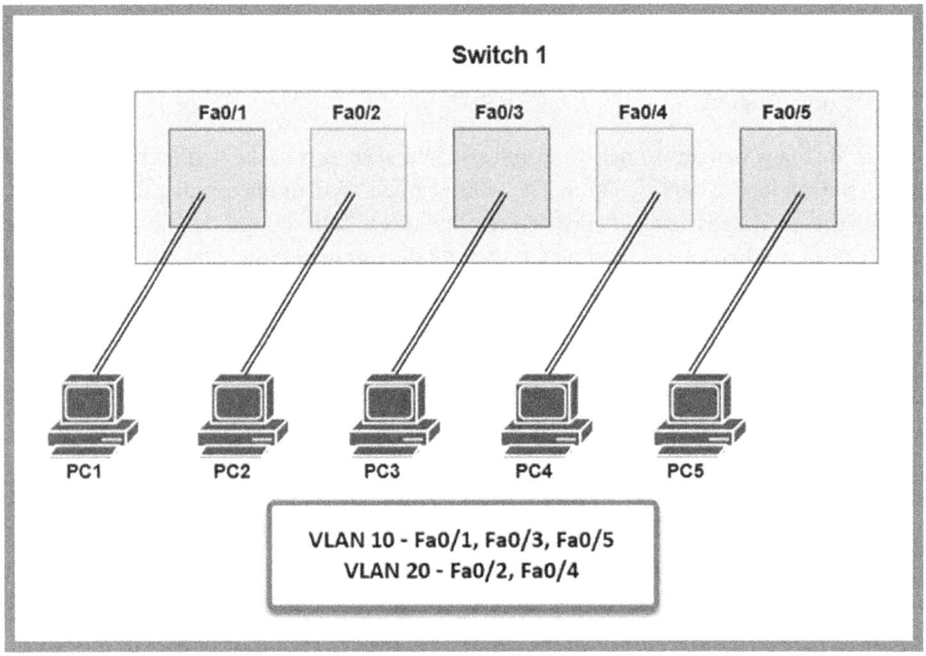

Figure 7.4: VLAN assignment

If **PC1** sends traffic to **FastEthernet port 1** (**Fa0/1**), the switch will insert an `IEEE 802.1Q` tag that contains VLAN 10 on all traffic entering that interface. Similarly, any traffic entering **FastEthernet port 2** (**Fa0/2**) will be tagged with VLAN 20.

Table 7.1 is a representation of an `802.1Q` tag within a frame:

Source MAC	Destination MAC	802.1Q tag	Type/length	Data	FCS

Table 7.1: Tagged frame

All traffic that enters a switch port becomes tagged traffic, and this helps the switch to determine which VLAN the traffic belongs to. However, before a switch forwards traffic out of an access port, it will remove the `IEEE 802.1Q` tag. Therefore, the switch will send an untagged frame to an end device, such as a computer that's connected to an access port.

Types of VLANs and Their Ranges

Network professionals commonly create and implement VLANs within their organizations for various reasons. The **default VLAN** on Cisco IOS switches is VLAN 1. By default, all switch ports are assigned to VLAN 1 unless the switch port is configured and assigned to another VLAN. Since all switch ports are assigned to VLAN 1 by default, this means all inbound Layer 2 traffic on the switch will be tagged with VLAN 1. In addition, the native VLAN is VLAN 1 by default, the management VLAN is VLAN 1 by default, and VLAN 1 cannot be deleted or removed from a Cisco IOS switch.

Figure 7.5 shows all interfaces on a Cisco IOS switch are assigned to VLAN 1 by default:

```
Switch# show vlan brief

VLAN Name                             Status    Ports
---- -------------------------------- --------- -------------------------------
1    default                          active    Fa0/1, Fa0/2, Fa0/3, Fa0/4
                                                Fa0/5, Fa0/6, Fa0/7, Fa0/8
                                                Fa0/9, Fa0/10, Fa0/11, Fa0/12
                                                Fa0/13, Fa0/14, Fa0/15, Fa0/16
                                                Fa0/17, Fa0/18, Fa0/19, Fa0/20
                                                Fa0/21, Fa0/22, Fa0/23, Fa0/24
                                                Gig0/1, Gig0/2
1002 fddi-default                     active
1003 token-ring-default               active
1004 fddinet-default                  active
1005 trnet-default                    active
```

Figure 7.5: Verifying VLAN and interface assignment

It's important to consider that VLAN 1 should not be used for security reasons. Since all ports are assigned to VLAN 1 by default, if a malware-infected device or a threat actor-owned device is connected to a switch, it'll be easy to directly connect to any other end device on the network.

Data VLANs are created and configured by network professionals to separate user-generated traffic. For instance, a network professional can create a unique VLAN for each business unit and assign the switch ports accordingly to each group of devices. In addition, it's recommended that voice and network management traffic be on separate VLANs; they should not be using the same data VLANs as user-generated traffic.

The **native VLAN** is used for transporting untagged traffic between switches over a **trunk port**. Within a network architecture, untagged traffic is usually switch-generated traffic that's used for network discovery, such as **Cisco Discovery Protocol** (**CDP**) and **Link Layer Discovery Protocol** (**LLDP**). Both CDP and LLDP are discovery protocols generated by switches and allow network professionals to identify neighbor devices and map a network topology. Since switch-generated traffic does not enter an access port to be tagged with a VLAN ID, it's classified as untagged traffic on the network.

A **trunk port** is configured on a switch to transport traffic from multiple VLANs from one switch to another, in contrast to an access port, which is assigned only one VLAN and therefore can only transport that VLAN's traffic and no other. To put it simply, the native VLAN is configured on the trunk port of a switch to transport untagged traffic between switches. Additionally, it's recommended to not use VLAN 1 as the native VLAN on the network.

The **management VLAN** is a type of data VLAN that's configured on a switch for network management purposes. For instance, network professionals commonly manage multiple networking devices each day, and most of the connections are done via remote access using **Secure Shell** (**SSH**), **Telnet**, **Hypertext Transfer Protocol Secure** (**HTTPS**), and even **Simple Network Management Protocol** (**SNMP**). However, it's recommended that a management VLAN other than VLAN 1 be created and used to manage a Cisco IOS switch.

The **voice VLAN** is a separate and dedicated VLAN used for transporting VoIP traffic within an organization. A dedicated voice VLAN helps provide bandwidth assurance for the quality of voice traffic and enables network professionals to configure a higher priority of transmission over other traffic types using **quality of service** (**QoS**) features. In addition, the voice VLAN improves the forwarding of voice traffic over a congested network and reduces the latency by less than 150 ms over a network.

VLAN Ranges

VLANs are identified by a numerical value based on the configurations you saw in the previous section. However, there are two different ranges of VLANs that are commonly used on medium to large networks. They are as follows:

- Normal range
- Extended range

Normal-range VLANs are VLAN IDs from 1 to 1005. VLANs 1002 to 1005 are reserved for various Layer 2 technologies, such as token ring and **Fiber Distributed Data Interface** (**FDDI**) technologies. Additionally, VLANs 1 and 1002–1005 are automatically created on Cisco IOS switches and cannot be deleted. Normal-range VLANs are stored in the `vlan.dat` file in flash memory and not in the `running-config` or the `startup-config` files. The `show flash:` command enables you to view the `vlan.dat` file. Lastly, if you are restoring a switch to its factory default, use the `delete vlan.dat` command to delete the VLAN database file.

The extended range consists of VLAN IDs from 1006 to 4094. Extended-range VLANs are not stored in the `vlan.dat` file, unlike the normal range, and the configurations are stored in the `running-config` file by default. Lastly, there are fewer VLAN features in the extended ranges than in the normal range.

Having completed this section, you have learned the fundamentals of VLAN ranges. In the next section, you will learn how to configure and verify VLANs on a Cisco IOS switch.

Configuring and Verifying VLANs

Understanding how to create and verify VLANs on a switch is part of being a network professional. To create, configure, and verify data VLANs on a Cisco IOS switch, please follow these instructions:

1. Create and name the VLAN:

```
Switch> enable
Switch# configure terminal
Switch(config)# vlan vlan-id
Switch(config-vlan)# name vlan-name
Switch(config-vlan)# exit
```

2. *Figure 7.6* shows an example of creating VLAN 10 on a Cisco IOS switch:

```
Switch> enable
Switch# configure terminal
Enter configuration commands, one per line.  End with CNTL/Z.
Switch(config)# vlan 10
Switch(config-vlan)# name Sales
Switch(config-vlan)# exit
Switch(config)#
```

Figure 7.6: Creating a VLAN

3. Assign the VLAN to a switch port on the Cisco IOS switch:

```
Switch(config)# interface interface-id
Switch(config-if)# switchport mode access
Switch(config-if)# switchport nonegotiate
Switch(config-if)# switchport access vlan vlan-id
Switch(config-if)# no shutdown
Switch(config-if)# exit
```

4. *Figure 7.7* shows an example of assigning an interface to a VLAN:

```
Switch(config)# interface fastEthernet 0/1
Switch(config-if)# switchport mode access
Switch(config-if)# switchport nonegotiate
Switch(config-if)# switchport access vlan 10
Switch(config-if)# no shutdown
Switch(config-if)# exit
```

Figure 7.7: Assigning an interface to a VLAN

5. The following summarizes the preceding commands:

   - `switchport mode access`: Statically sets the interface as an access port.
   - `switchport access vlan`: Statically assigns a VLAN to the interface.
   - `switchport nonegotiate`: Prevents the interface from generating **Dynamic Trunking Protocol** (**DTP**) frames. DTP enables connected switches to auto-negotiate whether their interfaces should operate as an **access** or **trunk** interface. However, it's recommended to disable DTP on Cisco IOS switches.

6. Use the `show vlan brief` command to verify the VLAN was created and an interface has been assigned to it, as shown in *Figure 7.8*:

```
Switch# show vlan brief

VLAN Name                             Status    Ports
---- -------------------------------- --------- -------------------------------
1    default                          active    Fa0/2, Fa0/3, Fa0/4, Fa0/5
                                                Fa0/6, Fa0/7, Fa0/8, Fa0/9
                                                Fa0/10, Fa0/11, Fa0/12, Fa0/13
                                                Fa0/14, Fa0/15, Fa0/16, Fa0/17
                                                Fa0/18, Fa0/19, Fa0/20, Fa0/21
                                                Fa0/22, Fa0/23, Fa0/24, Gig0/1
                                                Gig0/2
10   Sales                            active    Fa0/1
1002 fddi-default                     active
1003 token-ring-default               active
1004 fddinet-default                  active
1005 trnet-default                    active
Switch#
```

Figure 7.8: Verifying VLANs

7. To change the interface membership from VLAN to another, use the following commands:

```
Switch(config)# interface interface-id
Switch(config-if)# no switchport access vlan
Switch(config-if)# exit
```

8. As shown in *Figure 7.9*, the interface returns to the default VLAN:

```
Switch# show vlan brief

VLAN Name                             Status    Ports
---- -------------------------------- --------- -------------------------------
1    default                          active    Fa0/1, Fa0/2, Fa0/3, Fa0/4
                                                Fa0/5, Fa0/6, Fa0/7, Fa0/8
                                                Fa0/9, Fa0/10, Fa0/11, Fa0/12
                                                Fa0/13, Fa0/14, Fa0/15, Fa0/16
                                                Fa0/17, Fa0/18, Fa0/19, Fa0/20
                                                Fa0/21, Fa0/22, Fa0/23, Fa0/24
                                                Gig0/1, Gig0/2
10   Sales                            active
1002 fddi-default                     active
1003 token-ring-default               active
1004 fddinet-default                  active
1005 trnet-default                    active
```

Figure 7.9: Interface moves to default VLAN

9. Additionally, the `show interface interface-id switchport` command enables you to view information like the interface has been reset to VLAN 1, as shown in *Figure 7.10*:

```
Switch# show interface fastEthernet 0/1 switchport
Name: Fa0/1
Switchport: Enabled
Administrative Mode: static access
Operational Mode: down
Administrative Trunking Encapsulation: dot1q
Operational Trunking Encapsulation: native
Negotiation of Trunking: Off
Access Mode VLAN: 1 (default)
Trunking Native Mode VLAN: 1 (default)
Voice VLAN: none
```

Figure 7.10: Verifying the interface

10. As shown in *Figure 7.10*, the `show interface interface-id switchport` command provides the administrative mode of the interface. This helps network professionals to determine whether the interface is configured as an access or trunk port.

Configuring a Voice VLAN

Learning how to create and configure a voice VLAN on a Cisco IOS switch will be useful in your career as many organizations use a VoIP solution, and you may be tasked with creating and setting up the voice VLAN within your organization.

To create and assign a voice VLAN to interface on a Cisco IOS switch, please follow these steps:

1. Create and name the data and voice VLANs by using the following commands:

```
Switch> enable
Switch# configure terminal
Switch(config)# vlan 10
Switch(config-vlan)# name Sales
Switch(config-vlan)# exit
Switch(config)# vlan 50
Switch(config)# name Voice
Switch(config)# exit
```

2. To assign a voice VLAN on an interface, use the following commands:

```
Switch(config)# interface FastEthernet 0/1
Switch(config-if)# switchport mode access
Switch(config-if)# switchport access vlan 10
Switch(config-if)# mls qos trust cos
Switch(config-if)# switchport voice vlan 50
Switch(config-if)# exit
```

> **Note**
>
> By default, only one VLAN can be assigned to an access port, except when there is a voice VLAN configured in addition to the data VLAN.

3. Using the `show vlan brief` command enables you to verify that the interface is assigned to two VLANs at the same time, as shown in *Figure 7.11*:

```
Switch# show vlan brief

VLAN Name                             Status    Ports
---- -------------------------------- --------- -------------------------------
1    default                          active    Fa0/2, Fa0/3, Fa0/4, Fa0/5
                                                Fa0/6, Fa0/7, Fa0/8, Fa0/9
                                                Fa0/10, Fa0/11, Fa0/12, Fa0/13
                                                Fa0/14, Fa0/15, Fa0/16, Fa0/17
                                                Fa0/18, Fa0/19, Fa0/20, Fa0/21
                                                Fa0/22, Fa0/23, Fa0/24, Gig0/1
                                                Gig0/2
10   Sales                            active    Fa0/1
50   Voice                            active    Fa0/1
1002 fddi-default                     active
1003 token-ring-default               active
1004 fddinet-default                  active
1005 trnet-default                    active
```

Figure 7.11: Verifying VLANs

4. Additionally, the `show interface interface-id switchport` command enables you to further verify which VLAN is used for voice and data transmission, as shown in *Figure 7.12*:

```
Switch# show interface fastEthernet 0/1 switchport
Name: Fa0/1
Switchport: Enabled
Administrative Mode: static access
Operational Mode: down
Administrative Trunking Encapsulation: dot1q
Operational Trunking Encapsulation: native
Negotiation of Trunking: Off
Access Mode VLAN: 10 (Sales)
Trunking Native Mode VLAN: 1 (default)
Voice VLAN: 50
```

Figure 7.12: Verifying VLANs on an interface

Configuring a Management VLAN

Management VLANs enable network professionals to remotely manage Cisco IOS switches over a network. To create a management VLAN or a **switched virtual interface** (**SVI**), use the following commands:

```
Switch> enable
Switch# configure terminal
Switch(config)# vlan 80
Switch(config)# name Management
Switch(config-vlan)# exit
Switch(config)# interface vlan 80
Switch(config-if)# ip address 10.0.0.2 255.255.255.0
Switch(config-if)# no shutdown
Switch(config-if)# exit
```

The SVI enables network professionals to assign an IP address to the switch for remote management and administration of the device.

Deleting a VLAN

Before deleting a VLAN from a Cisco IOS switch, ensure that you have re-assigned all member interfaces to another VLAN. To put it simply, if you want to delete VLAN 20 on a switch, re-assign all VLAN 20 interfaces to another VLAN before deleting VLAN 20. If any interfaces are not re-assigned to another active VLAN, devices that are associated with the interfaces of the deleted VLAN will not be able to communicate with other devices on the same VLAN or other VLANs on the network. Those devices are assigned to a non-active VLAN.

The following are some common methods to remove VLANs from a Cisco IOS switch:

- To delete a VLAN from a switch, use the following command in global configuration mode:

  ```
  Switch(config)# no vlan vlan-id
  ```

- If you are restoring a Cisco IOS switch to factory settings, it's recommended to erase the `startup-config` file, then delete the entire VLAN database file, followed by reloading the switch by using the following commands in Privilege Exec mode:

  ```
  Switch# erase startup-config
  Switch# delete flash:vlan.dat
  Switch# reload
  ```

Having completed this section, you have learned how to create and verify VLANs on a Cisco IOS switch. In the next section, you will learn how to extend the VLANs from one switch to another using interswitch connectivity techniques.

Interswitch Connectivity

Implementing trunks can solve some major issues when spanning VLANs across multiple switches on a network. Trunks allow you to transport multiple lots of VLAN traffic simultaneously between switches, in contrast with access ports, which only allow a single VLAN.

To get a better understanding, take a look at *Figure 7.13*, where an access link is configured between the switches:

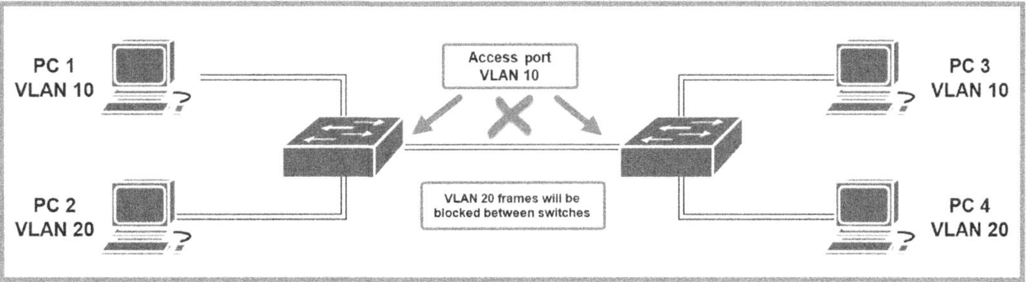

Figure 7.13: Access link between switches

In the topology shown in *Figure 7.13*, an access link is configured between the switches. However, **VLAN 10** is assigned on both physical interfaces. This will permit VLAN traffic and allow communication between **PC 1** and **PC 3** only, but **VLAN 20** traffic is not allowed between the switches. This is because the access ports were configured between the switches, which allowed only one VLAN.

> **Note**
>
> The link between one switch and another switch is known as a trunk. The link between a switch and a router is also known as a trunk.

Trunks transport multiple lots of VLAN traffic between switches. *Figure 7.14* shows the effect of converting the link between two switches into a trunk:

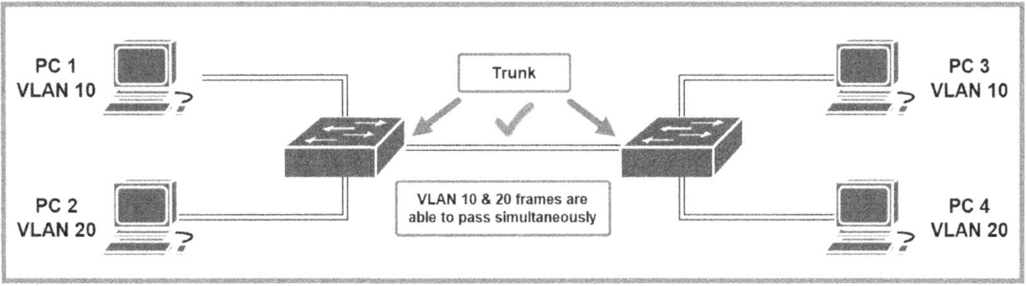

Figure 7.14: Trunk link between switches

As expected, both **VLAN 10** and **VLAN 20** traffic is allowed to flow bi-directionally, allowing device **PC 2** to exchange frames with **PC 4**.

To create a trunk interface, follow these instructions:

1. Create the data and native VLANs on both switches:

```
Switch(config)# vlan 10
Switch(config-vlan)# name Sales
Switch(config-vlan)# exit
Switch(config)# vlan 20
Switch(config-vlan)# name Accounting
Switch(config-vlan)# exit
Switch(config)# vlan 99
Switch(config-vlan)# name Native-VLAN
Switch(config-vlan)# exit
```

2. Configure the trunk port on both switches by assigning the data VLANs and the native VLANs using the following commands:

```
Switch(config)# interface gigabitEthernet 0/1
Switch(config-if)# switchport mode trunk
Switch(config-if)# switchport nonegotiate
Switch(config-if)# switchport trunk allowed vlan 10,20
Switch(config-if)# switchport trunk native vlan 99
Switch(config-if)# no shutdown
Switch(config-if)# exit
```

3. The following is a breakdown of the configurations used to create a trunk:

    - `switchport mode trunk`: Administratively set the interface to trunk mode
    - `switchport trunk allowed vlan`: Set the permitted list of VLANs on the trunk interface
    - `switchport trunk native vlan`: Assign the native VLAN onto the trunk interface

Note

To remove the allowed list of VLANs on a trunk interface, use the `no switchport trunk allowed vlan` command. To reset the native VLAN to its default, use the `no switchport trunk native vlan` command.

4. To verify whether the VLANs exist on the switch, use `show vlan brief`, as shown in *Figure 7.15*:

```
Switch# show vlan brief

VLAN Name                             Status    Ports
---- -------------------------------- --------- -------------------------------
1    default                          active    Fa0/1, Fa0/2, Fa0/3, Fa0/4
                                                Fa0/5, Fa0/6, Fa0/7, Fa0/8
                                                Fa0/9, Fa0/10, Fa0/11, Fa0/12
                                                Fa0/13, Fa0/14, Fa0/15, Fa0/16
                                                Fa0/17, Fa0/18, Fa0/19, Fa0/20
                                                Fa0/21, Fa0/22, Fa0/23, Fa0/24
                                                Gig0/2
10   Sales                            active
20   Accounting                       active
99   Native-VLAN                      active
1002 fddi-default                     active
1003 token-ring-default               active
1004 fddinet-default                  active
1005 trnet-default                    active
```

Figure 7.15: Verifying VLANs

5. If a VLAN does not exist on a switch, the switch will not be able to forward or transport frames on that VLAN. Therefore, it is recommended to create the VLANs on all switches within your network before configuring the access and trunk ports.
6. Use the `show interface trunk` command to verify the trunk ports, the permitted VLANs on each trunk port, and the native VLAN, as shown in *Figure 7.16*:

```
Switch# show interface trunk
Port        Mode         Encapsulation  Status        Native vlan
Gig0/1      on           802.1q         trunking      99

Port        Vlans allowed on trunk
Gig0/1      10,20

Port        Vlans allowed and active in management domain
Gig0/1      10,20

Port        Vlans in spanning tree forwarding state and not pruned
Gig0/1      10,20
```

Figure 7.16: Verifying trunk ports

7. Always ensure that both ends of the trunk link are configured with the same allowed VLANs and the native VLAN. If the native VLAN is not the same, the switch will report an error with the native VLAN.

8. The `show interface interface-if switchport` command shows the administrative and operational mode of the interface, the encapsulation type (`IEEE 802.1Q`), and the configured native and allowed VLANs on the interface:

```
Switch# show interface gigabitEthernet 0/1 switchport
Name: Gig0/1
Switchport: Enabled
Administrative Mode: trunk
Operational Mode: trunk
Administrative Trunking Encapsulation: dot1q
Operational Trunking Encapsulation: dot1q
Negotiation of Trunking: Off
Access Mode VLAN: 1 (default)
Trunking Native Mode VLAN: 99 (Native-VLAN)
Voice VLAN: none
Administrative private-vlan host-association: none
Administrative private-vlan mapping: none
Administrative private-vlan trunk native VLAN: none
Administrative private-vlan trunk encapsulation: dot1q
Administrative private-vlan trunk normal VLANs: none
Administrative private-vlan trunk private VLANs: none
Operational private-vlan: none
Trunking VLANs Enabled: 10,20
Pruning VLANs Enabled: 2-1001
Capture Mode Disabled
Capture VLANs Allowed: ALL
```

Figure 7.17: Verifying interface configurations

9. Lastly, to reset all trunking features on an interface, use the following commands:

```
Switch(config)# interface interface-id
Switch(config-if)# no switchport trunk allowed vlan
Switch(config-if)# no switchport trunk native vlan
Switch(config-if)# exit
```

Now that you have completed this section, you will learn about an auto-negotiation feature on Cisco IOS switch interfaces: DTP.

Dynamic Trunking Protocol

By default, Cisco IOS switches use DTP, a proprietary protocol that enables switches to automatically negotiate the trunking status with a directly connected switch. DTP enables network professionals to reduce the need and time for performing manual configurations on Cisco IOS switches to create trunk ports.

However, it's not recommended to use DTP due to a security flaw that enables a threat actor to force an interface into trunking mode to perform a **VLAN hopping** attack. This type of attack enables the malicious user to access multiple VLANs simultaneously from their laptop by connecting it directly to a switch port and injecting specially crafted DTP frames into the switch.

The following methods allow you to configure DTP on a switch:

- To disable DTP on an interface, use the following commands:

```
Switch(config)# interface interface-id
Switch(config-if)# switchport mode trunk
Switch(config-if)# switchport nonegotiate
```

- To re-enable DTP, use the following command within interface mode:

```
Switch(config)# interface interface-id
Switch(config-if)# switchport mode dynamic auto
```

Additionally, there are different interface modes on a Cisco IOS switch for setting the interface's operational mode. These are the following:

- `switchport mode access`: Puts the interface (access port) into permanent non-trunking mode and configures the link as a non-trunk link.
- `switchport mode dynamic auto`: Makes the interface able to convert the link to a trunk link. This is the default mode set on Cisco switches.
- `switchport mode dynamic desirable`: Makes the interface actively attempt to convert the link to a trunk link.
- `switchport mode trunk`: Puts the interface into permanent trunking mode and configures the neighboring link into a trunk link.

The `switchport nonegotiate` command prevents the interface from generating DTP frames. Without generating DTP frames, the interface will transition faster into a forwarding state as there is no need to negotiate trunking mode with a neighbor switch. Keep in mind that this command can only be applied to interfaces that are statically configured as an access or trunk port.

Note

The `show dtp interface interface-id` or `show dtp` command can be used to determine the current DTP mode on a switch port.

Table 7.2 provides all the possible outcomes when two switch interfaces are configured with DTP mode:

	Dynamic Auto	**Dynamic Desirable**	**Trunk**	**Access**
Dynamic Auto	Access	Trunk	Trunk	Access
Dynamic Desirable	Trunk	Trunk	Trunk	Access
Trunk	Trunk	Trunk	Trunk	Limited Connectivity
Access	Access	Access	Limited Connectivity	Access

Table 7.2: DTP negotiation chart

To get a better understanding, imagine there are two switches, A and B, connected using a cable. If both switches have default configurations, what is the type of link formed between them? Since the default interface mode on a Cisco IOS switch is `switchport mode dynamic auto`, according to the chart, the switches will automatically determine that their ports should be access ports. However, if switch A is configured as `switchport mode dynamic desirable` and switch B is using its default configuration, the result will be a trunk link between A and B.

Now that you have completed this section, you will take a deep dive into learning how a device on one VLAN is able to exchange messages with another located on a separate VLAN in the upcoming section.

Configuring Inter-VLAN Routing

Inter-VLAN routing enables devices on one VLAN to communicate with devices on another VLAN. To make this happen, you will need a Cisco IOS router with an available physical interface. Nowadays, a technique known as **router on a stick**, which enables you to create multiple sub-interfaces within a single physical interface on a router, is used.

Typically, each port on a router is connected to a unique IP network. Imagine there are five VLANs within your organization and each VLAN is assigned a unique IP subnet. Therefore, each subnet will require a default gateway to allow member devices to communicate with destination hosts on a remote network. Hence, a router is needed for each VLAN. Since there are five VLANs in the organization, five physical interfaces are needed on the router to support each IP subnet.

As network professionals create additional VLANs within their organization, more ports are needed and, eventually, more routers will be required to connect different IP subnets, and this becomes a problem.

Rather than connecting each VLAN from a switch to a unique physical interface on a router, network professionals can create sub-interfaces within a router's physical port. Each sub-interface will be configured to transport on a specific VLAN traffic and be assigned the default gateway IP address.

Figure 7.18 is a representation of sub-interfaces on a router:

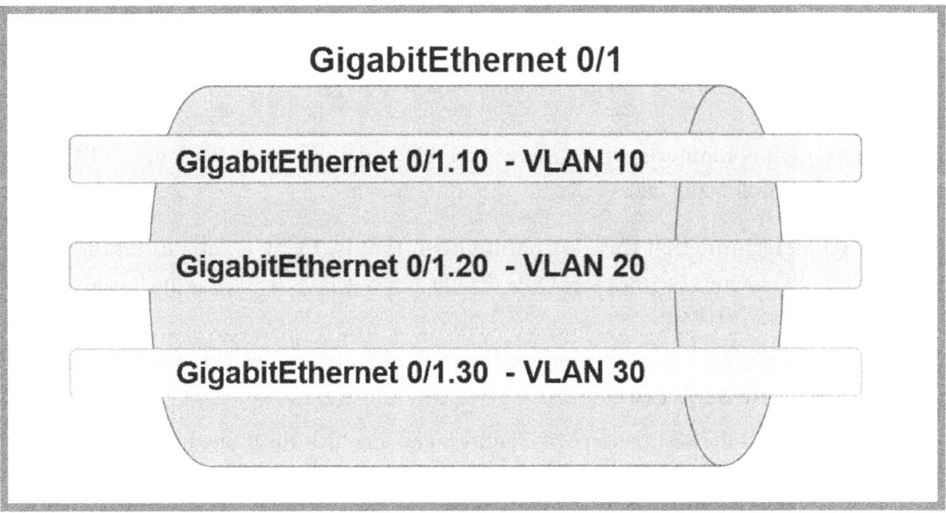

Figure 7.18: Sub-interfaces on a router

To get a better understanding of traffic flow between VLANs, examine *Figure 7.19*:

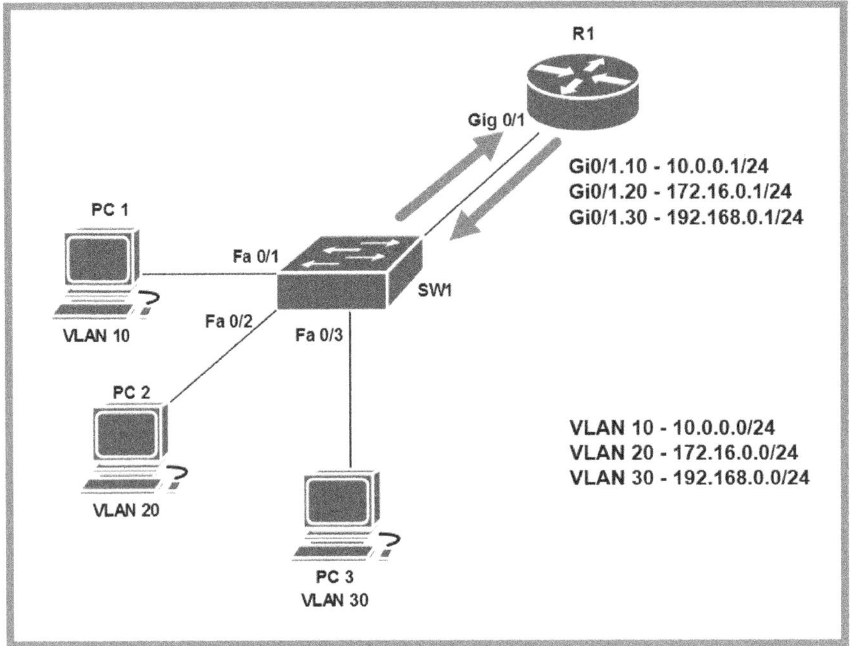

Figure 7.19: Inter-VLAN routing

In the topology, each computer is on a different VLAN and a different IP subnet. If **PC 1** sends a message to **PC 2**, the following takes place:

1. **PC 1** will determine that the destination host, that is, **PC 2**, is on a different IP subnet. Therefore, **PC 1** sends the message to its default gateway, `10.0.0.1`, which is located on **R1** GigabitEthernet 0/1.10.
2. The switch receives the incoming message from **PC 1** on FastEthernet 0/1 and inserts an `IEEE 802.1Q` tag with **VLAN 10**.
3. The switch checks the destination MAC address and forwards the frame from its trunk interface to the router.
4. The router receives the incoming message with VLAN ID 10 in its GigabitEthernet 0/1.10 sub-interface.
5. The router checks the destination's IP address for a suitable route in its routing table. The router notices the destination network is connected to its GigabitEthernet 0/1.20 sub-interface.
6. The router forwards the message from sub-interface GigabitEthernet 0/1.20 and the switch will receive it on its trunk.

7. The switch checks the destination MAC address and forwards the message from the FastEthernet 0/2 interface with the `IEEE 802.1Q` tag removed.

This technique allows you to create many sub-interfaces to support each VLAN within an enterprise network.

To set up inter-VLAN routing using the router-on-a-stick method, follow these instructions:

1. On the switch that is connected to the router, configure the trunk port:

```
Switch(config)# interface interface-id
Switch(config-if)# switchport mode trunk
Switch(config-if)# no shutdown
Switch(config-if)# exit
```

> **Note**
> Using the `switchport mode trunk` command only will permit all VLANs by default over the trunk port.

2. To configure a sub-interface on a router, use the following command to create a sub-interface:

```
Router(config)# interface GigabitEthernet 0/1.10
```

3. Associate the VLAN for this sub-interface:

```
Router(config-subif)# encapsulation dot1q 10
```

4. Assign the default gateway IP address onto the sub-interface:

```
Router(config-subif)# ip address 10.0.0.1 255.255.255.0
```

5. Exit the sub-interface mode using the `exit` command.
6. To enable all sub-interfaces within a physical port on the router, use the following commands:

```
Router(config)# interface GigabitEthernet 0/1
Router(config-if)# no shutdown
Router(config-if)# exit
```

> **Note**
> When you apply `no shutdown` to a physical interface, all member sub-interfaces are enabled automatically.

While the router-on-a-stick method is suitable for small to medium-sized networks, most medium-sized organizations use Layer 3 Cisco IOS switches with SVIs to interconnect different VLANs.

Inter-VLAN Routing Using a Layer 3 Switch

Network professionals can configure an SVI for each VLAN within their organization and assign the default gateway address to those SVIs. Therefore, whenever a host wants to forward traffic to a destination host on another VLAN, the sender will forward the message to the default gateway address that's assigned to the SVI belonging to the same VLAN as the sender.

Figure 7.20 shows inter-VLAN routing concepts using a Layer 3 switch:

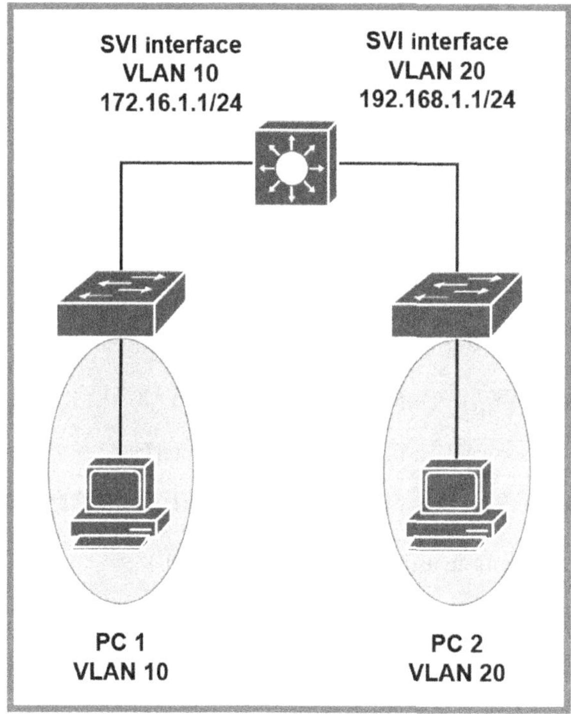

Figure 7.20: Inter-VLAN routing on a Layer 3 switch

As shown in *Figure 7.20*, **PC 1** will forward packets to the `172.16.1.1` interface, assigned on the SVI for **VLAN 10**. The switch will perform a route lookup and forward the message from the SVI for **VLAN 20**. The message will be sent to the Layer 2 switch, then to **PC 2** on the network.

To perform inter-VLAN routing using a Layer 3 switch, please follow these instructions:

1. Create the VLANs on the Layer 3 switch:

```
L3_Switch(config)# vlan 10
L3_Switch(config-vlan)# name Staff
L3_Switch(config-vlan)# exit
L3_Switch(config)# vlan 20
L3_Switch(config-vlan)# name Student
L3_Switch(config-vlan)# exit
L3_Switch(config)# vlan 99
L3_Switch(config-vlan)# name Native
L3_Switch(config-vlan)# exit
```

2. Create and configure the SVIs on the Layer 3 switch for each VLAN:

```
L3_Switch(config)# interface vlan 10
L3_Switch(config-if)# ip address 172.16.1.1 255.255.255.0
L3_Switch(config-if)# exit
L3_Switch(config)# interface vlan 20
L3_Switch(config-if)# ip address 192.168.1.1 255.255.255.0
L3_Switch(config-if)# exit
```

3. Configure the trunk port on the Layer 3 switch that connects to a Layer 2 switch:

```
L3_Switch(config)# interface gigabitEthernet 1/0/1
L3_Switch(config-if)# switchport mode trunk
L3_Switch(config-if)# switchport trunk native vlan 99
L3_Switch(config-if)# exit
```

4. Enable IP routing on the Layer 3 switch:

```
L3_Switch(config)# ip routing
```

5. Configure the VLANs on all other switches and the Layer 2 switches in the topology.
6. Configure a trunk port on the Layer 2 switch that's connected to the Layer 3 switch that's performing inter-VLAN routing using SVIs:

```
L2_Switch(config)# interface gi0/1
L2_Switch(config-if)# switchport mode trunk
L2_Switch(config-if)# switchport trunk native vlan 99
L2_Switch(config-if)# no shutdown
L2_Switch(config-if)# exit
```

Now that you have completed this section, take a hands-on approach and start implementing VLANs in the coming sections.

Lab: Creating and Verifying VLANs

It's time to get your hands dirty with some hands-on experience in implementing VLANs on a network. To get started, you will be using the Cisco Packet Tracer application, which allows you to simulate a Cisco environment.

Figure 7.21 shows the network topology that you will be working with for this exercise:

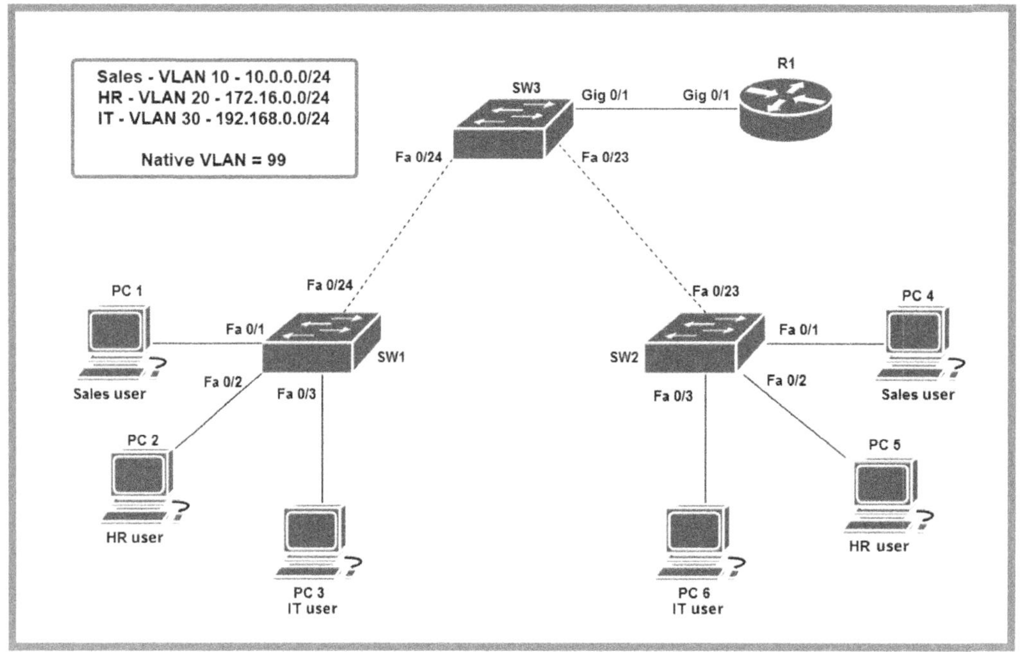

Figure 7.21: Lab topology

Before getting started with this exercise, please use the following guidelines:

1. Download the **Lab 7.1 – Creating and verifying VLANs** lab file from `https://packt.link/CCNArepoCh07`
2. Once you have finished downloading the lab file, ensure to open it using the Cisco Packet Tracer application.

To get started with this exercise, please use the following instructions to complete this lab:

1. On SW1, use the following commands to create each VLAN and assign a name:

```
SW1> enable
SW1# configure terminal
SW1(config)# vlan 10
SW1(config-vlan)# name Sales
SW1(config-vlan)# exit
SW1(config)# vlan 20
SW1(config-vlan)# name HR
SW1(config-vlan)# exit
SW1(config)# vlan 30
SW1(config-vlan)# name IT
SW1(config-vlan)# exit
SW1(config)# vlan 99
SW1(config-vlan)# name Native
SW1(config-vlan)# exit
```

2. Create the same VLANs on all other switches within the topology. If a VLAN does not exist on a switch, the missing VLAN traffic will not be allowed to pass. To perform this task on SW2, use the following configurations:

```
SW2> enable
SW2# configure terminal
SW2(config)# vlan 10
SW2(config-vlan)# name Sales
SW2(config-vlan)# exit
SW2(config)# vlan 20
SW2(config-vlan)# name HR
SW2(config-vlan)# exit
SW2(config)# vlan 30
SW2(config-vlan)# name IT
SW2(config-vlan)# exit
SW2(config)# vlan 99
SW2(config-vlan)# name Native
SW2(config-vlan)# exit+
```

3. To create the VLANs on `SW3`, please use the following configurations:

```
SW3> enable
SW3# configure terminal
SW3(config)# vlan 10
SW3(config-vlan)# name Sales
SW3(config-vlan)# exit
SW3(config)# vlan 20
SW3(config-vlan)# name HR
SW3(config-vlan)#exit
SW3(config)# vlan 30
SW3(config-vlan)# name IT
SW3(config-vlan)# exit
SW3(config)# vlan 99
SW3(config-vlan)# name Native
SW3(config-vlan)# exit
```

4. Use the `show vlan brief` command to verify that the VLANs have been created and named properly, as shown in *Figure 7.22*:

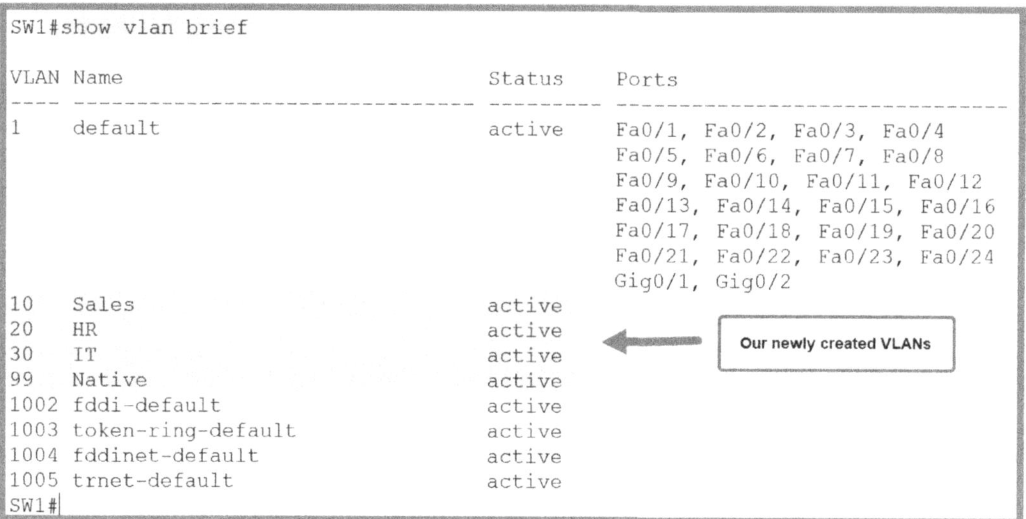

```
SW1#show vlan brief

VLAN Name                             Status    Ports
---- -------------------------------- --------- -------------------------------
1    default                          active    Fa0/1, Fa0/2, Fa0/3, Fa0/4
                                                Fa0/5, Fa0/6, Fa0/7, Fa0/8
                                                Fa0/9, Fa0/10, Fa0/11, Fa0/12
                                                Fa0/13, Fa0/14, Fa0/15, Fa0/16
                                                Fa0/17, Fa0/18, Fa0/19, Fa0/20
                                                Fa0/21, Fa0/22, Fa0/23, Fa0/24
                                                Gig0/1, Gig0/2
10   Sales                            active
20   HR                               active
30   IT                               active
99   Native                           active
1002 fddi-default                     active
1003 token-ring-default               active
1004 fddinet-default                  active
1005 trnet-default                    active
SW1#
```


Figure 7.22: Verifying VLANs

In *Figure 7.22*, all ports are assigned to VLAN 1 by default. In later configurations, you will re-assign ports according to your network topology.

5. You can now create access ports on SW1 and SW2, and then assign the ports to various VLANs. To set up the access points on SW1 and set the VLAN assignment configurations, please use the following configurations:

```
SW1(config)# interface FastEthernet 0/1
SW1(config-if)# switchport mode access
SW1(config-if)# switchport access vlan 10
SW1(config-if)# switchport nonegotiate
SW1(config-if)# no shutdown
SW1(config-if)# exit
SW1(config)# interface FastEthernet 0/2
SW1(config-if)# switchport mode access
SW1(config-if)# switchport access vlan 20
SW1(config-if)# switchport nonegotiate
SW1(config-if)# no shutdown
SW1(config-if)# exit
SW1(config)# interface FastEthernet 0/3
SW1(config-if)# switchport mode access
SW1(config-if)# switchport access vlan 30
SW1(config-if)# switchport nonegotiate
SW1(config-if)# no shutdown
SW1(config-if)# exit
```

6. To set up the access points and VLAN assignment on SW2, please use the following configurations:

```
SW2(config)# interface FastEthernet 0/1
SW2(config-if)# switchport mode access
SW2(config-if)# switchport access vlan 10
SW2(config-if)# switchport nonegotiate
SW2(config-if)# no shutdown
SW2(config-if)# exit
SW2(config)# interface FastEthernet 0/2
SW2(config-if)# switchport mode access
SW2(config-if)# switchport access vlan 20
SW2(config-if)# switchport nonegotiate
SW2(config-if)# no shutdown
SW2(config-if)# exit
SW2(config)# interface FastEthernet 0/3
SW2(config-if)# switchport mode access
SW2(config-if)# switchport access vlan 30
SW2(config-if)# switchport nonegotiate
SW2(config-if)# no shutdown
SW2(config-if)# exit
```

Since there are no end devices connected to SW3, there is no need to create access points on the switch.

7. Use the `show vlan brief` command to verify that the interfaces have been re-assigned on both `SW1` and `SW2`. *Figure 7.23* shows the results on `SW1`:

```
SW1#show vlan brief

VLAN Name                             Status    Ports
---- -------------------------------- --------- -------------------------------
1    default                          active    Fa0/4, Fa0/5, Fa0/6, Fa0/7
                                                Fa0/8, Fa0/9, Fa0/10, Fa0/11
                                                Fa0/12, Fa0/13, Fa0/14, Fa0/15
                                                Fa0/16, Fa0/17, Fa0/18, Fa0/19
                                                Fa0/20, Fa0/21, Fa0/22, Fa0/23
                                                Fa0/24, Gig0/1, Gig0/2
10   Sales                            active    Fa0/1
20   HR                               active    Fa0/2
30   IT                               active    Fa0/3
99   Native                           active
1002 fddi-default                     active
1003 token-ring-default               active
1004 fddinet-default                  active
1005 trnet-default                    active
SW1#
```

Figure 7.23: Interface assignments

8. Additionally, you can use the following commands to gain specific information about a VLAN:

   - Use the `show vlan id vlan-ID` to view details about a VLAN if you know the VLAN ID
   - Use the `show vlan name vlan-name` to view details about a VLAN if you know the name of the VLAN
   - The `show vlan summary` command provides a quick summary of all the VLANs on the switch

9. Use the `show interface interface-id switchport` command to view the administrative and operational status and the VLAN assignments on a specific interface, as shown in *Figure 7.24*:

```
SW1#show interfaces FastEthernet 0/1 switchport
Name: Fa0/1
Switchport: Enabled
Administrative Mode: static access
Operational Mode: static access
Administrative Trunking Encapsulation:
Operational Trunking Encapsulation: native
Negotiation of Trunking: Off
Access Mode VLAN: 10 (Sales)
Trunking Native Mode VLAN: 1 (default)
Voice VLAN: none
Administrative private-vlan host-association: none
Administrative private-vlan mapping: none
Administrative private-vlan trunk native VLAN: none
Administrative private-vlan trunk encapsulation: dot1q
Administrative private-vlan trunk normal VLANs: none
Administrative private-vlan trunk private VLANs: none
Operational private-vlan: none
Trunking VLANs Enabled: All
Pruning VLANs Enabled: 2-1001
Capture Mode Disabled
Capture VLANs Allowed: ALL
```

Figure 7.24: Verifying the interface status

Additionally, the `show running-config` command will provide you with the configurations listed under each interface.

Now that you have implemented VLANs on all switches and assigned the interfaces accordingly, you can implement trunk ports for transporting VLAN 10, 20, 30, and 99 traffic between the switches in your topology.

Lab: Setting up Interswitch Connectivity

In this section, you will continue from the previous lab exercise, so be sure to complete the previous exercise before proceeding with this one. To get an idea of the objective, you will be configuring the trunk links shown in *Figure 7.25*:

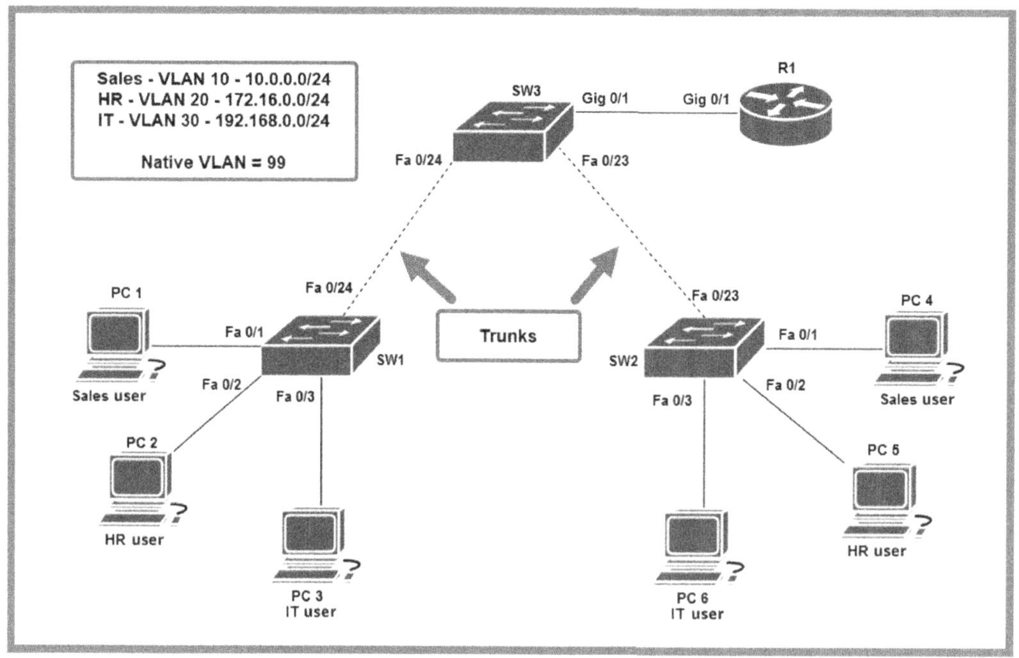

Figure 7.25: Trunk interfaces

To get started creating and configuring trunk interfaces, use the following configurations:

1. Configure the trunk interface on `SW1` using the following configurations:

```
SW1# enable
SW1# configure terminal
SW1(config)# line console 0
SW1(config-line)# logging synchronous
SW1(config-line)# exit
SW1(config)# interface FastEthernet 0/24
SW1(config-if)# switchport mode trunk
SW1(config-if)# switchport trunk allowed vlan 10,20,30
SW1(config-if)# switchport trunk native vlan 99
SW1(config-if)# switchport nonegotiate
SW1(config-if)# no shutdown
SW1(config-if)# exit
```

After changing the native VLAN from 1 to 99, you will see a syslog message similar to the one shown here:

```
%CDP-4-NATIVE_VLAN_MISMATCH: Native VLAN mismatch discovered on
FastEthernet0/24 (1), with SW3 FastEthernet0/24 (99)
```

This message is generated because the native VLANs must match in switches that are sharing a trunk. Currently, you have set the native VLAN to `99` on `SW1`, but the native VLAN remains at the default of `1` on `SW3` because it has not been configured to use VLAN 99 as the native VLAN yet. The `logging synchronous` command will prevent this message from breaking into your command line while you work.

2. Configure the trunk interface on `SW2` using the following configurations:

```
SW2# enable
SW2# configure terminal
SW2(config)# line console 0
SW2(config-line)# logging synchronous
SW2(config-line)# exit
SW2(config)# interface FastEthernet 0/23
SW2(config-if)# switchport mode trunk
SW2(config-if)# switchport trunk allowed vlan 10,20,30
SW2(config-if)# switchport trunk native vlan 99
SW2(config-if)# switchport nonegotiate
SW2(config-if)# no shutdown
SW2(config-if)# exit
```

3. Configure the trunk interfaces on `SW3` to share VLANs with both `SW1` and `SW2` using the following configurations:

```
SW3# enable
SW3# configure terminal
SW3(config)# line console 0
SW3(config-line)# logging synchronous
SW3(config-line)# exit
SW3(config)#interface range FastEthernet 0/23 - FastEthernet 0/24
SW3(config-if)#switchport mode trunk
SW3(config-if)#switchport trunk allowed vlan 10,20,30
SW3(config-if)#switchport trunk native vlan 99
SW3(config-if)#switchport nonegotiate
SW3(config-if)#no shutdown
SW3(config-if)#exit
```

The native VLAN mismatch log messages should stop as all trunk interfaces are now using native VLAN ID `99`.

4. Use the `show interfaces trunk` command on each switch to verify that each trunk has the same allowed list of VLANs and native VLANs, as shown in *Figure 7.26*:

```
SW3#show interfaces trunk
Port        Mode         Encapsulation  Status        Native vlan
Fa0/23      on           802.1q         trunking      99
Fa0/24      on           802.1q         trunking      99

Port        Vlans allowed on trunk
Fa0/23      10,20,30
Fa0/24      10,20,30

Port        Vlans allowed and active in management domain
Fa0/23      10,20,30
Fa0/24      10,20,30

Port        Vlans in spanning tree forwarding state and not pruned
Fa0/23      10,20,30
Fa0/24      10,20,30
```

Figure 7.26: Verifying trunk interfaces

Ensure that the `switchport trunk allowed vlan` command contains all the VLANs that are required to allow interswitch connectivity. If a VLAN's traffic is not able to go across to other switches, check the following:

- Check whether the VLAN has been created on all switches using the `show vlan brief` command
- Check whether the VLAN is allowed on the trunk interfaces on all switches using the `show interfaces trunk` command
- Check the administrative and operational status of interfaces using the `show interfaces interface-ID switchport` command
- Check the physical connections between devices on the topology

Additionally, use the `show running-config` command to check the configurations applied to each interface, as shown in *Figure 7.27*:

```
!
interface FastEthernet0/23
 switchport trunk native vlan 99
 switchport trunk allowed vlan 10,20,30
 switchport mode trunk
 switchport nonegotiate
!
interface FastEthernet0/24
 switchport trunk native vlan 99
 switchport trunk allowed vlan 10,20,30
 switchport mode trunk
 switchport nonegotiate
!
```

Figure 7.27: Configurations on trunk interfaces

To complete the lab, use the IP configurations shown in *Table 7.3* for each PC in the topology:

	Hostname	IP Address	Subnet Mask	Default Gateway
VLAN 10- Sales	**PC 1**	10.0.0.10	255.255.255.0	10.0.0.1
VLAN 20- HR	**PC 2**	172.16.0.10	255.255.255.0	172.16.0.1
VLAN 30- IT	**PC 3**	192.168.0.10	255.255.255.0	192.168.0.1
VLAN 10- Sales	**PC 4**	10.0.0.11	255.255.255.0	10.0.0.1
VLAN 20- HR	**PC 5**	172.16.0.11	255.255.255.0	172.16.0.1
VLAN 30- IT	**PC 6**	192.168.0.11	255.255.255.0	192.168.0.1

Table 7.3: IP addressing scheme for PCs in the topology

Once you're finished assigning the IP addresses, open **Command Prompt** on each PC and attempt to test connectivity to another device on the same VLAN.

Figure 7.28 shows **PC 1** has connectivity to **PC 4**:

```
C:\>ping 10.0.0.11

Pinging 10.0.0.11 with 32 bytes of data:

Reply from 10.0.0.11: bytes=32 time<1ms TTL=128
Reply from 10.0.0.11: bytes=32 time<1ms TTL=128
Reply from 10.0.0.11: bytes=32 time<1ms TTL=128
Reply from 10.0.0.11: bytes=32 time=1ms TTL=128

Ping statistics for 10.0.0.11:
    Packets: Sent = 4, Received = 4, Lost = 0 (0% loss),
Approximate round trip times in milli-seconds:
    Minimum = 0ms, Maximum = 1ms, Average = 0ms
```

Figure 7.28: Ping results between PC 1 and PC 4

If you recall, you can only communicate with devices on the same VLAN as your device and, therefore, **PC 1** will not be able to reach devices on VLAN 20 and 30. To enable two or more VLANs to exchange messages, you will need the help of a router. In the next section, you will learn how to configure the Cisco IOS router to perform **inter-VLAN routing**.

Lab: Setting up Inter-VLAN Routing

In this section, you will continue from the previous lab exercise, so be sure to complete it before proceeding to follow the steps here. To get an idea of the goal of this exercise, you will be configuring inter-VLAN routing using the router-on-a-stick method, as shown in *Figure 7.29*:

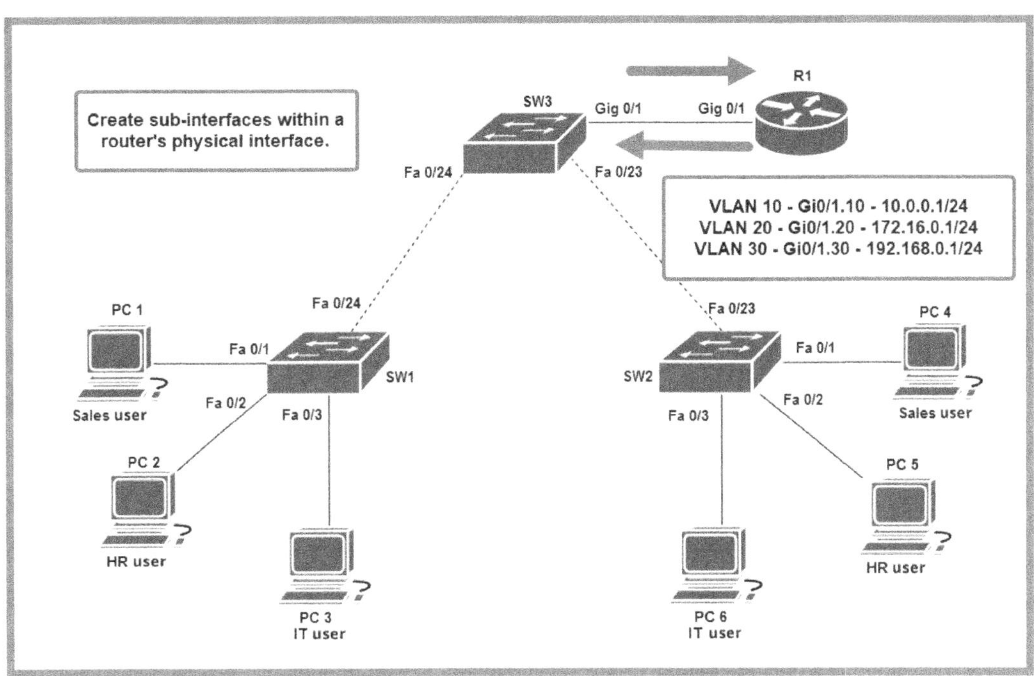

Figure 7.29: Inter-VLAN routing topology

To get started with configuring inter-VLAN routing, please follow these steps:

1. Create a trunk interface on `SW3` that is connecting to the router:

```
SW3(config)#interface GigabitEthernet 0/1
SW3(config-if)#switchport mode trunk
SW3(config-if)#no shutdown
SW3(config-if)#exit
```

2. For this trunk port on the switch, you are not required to use either the `switchport trunk allowed vlan` or `switchport trunk native vlan` command on the interface.
3. Create a sub-interface on the router to carry traffic to and from VLAN 10:

```
R1(config)#interface GigabitEthernet 0/1.10
R1(config-subif)#encapsulation dot1q 10
R1(config-subif)#ip address 10.0.0.1 255.255.255.0
R1(config-subif)#exit
```

4. Create a sub-interface on the router to carry traffic to and from VLAN 20:

```
R1(config)#interface GigabitEthernet 0/1.20
R1(config-subif)#encapsulation dot1q 20
R1(config-subif)#ip address 172.16.0.1 255.255.255.0
R1(config-subif)#exit
```

5. Create a sub-interface on the router to carry traffic to and from VLAN 30:

```
R1(config)#interface GigabitEthernet 0/1.30
R1(config-subif)#encapsulation dot1q 30
R1(config-subif)#ip address 192.168.0.1 255.255.255.0
R1(config-subif)#exit
```

6. Activate the physical interface to enable all sub-interfaces:

```
R1(config)#interface GigabitEthernet 0/1
R1(config-if)#no shutdown
R1(config-if)#exit
```

When configuring a sub-interface to transport a specific VLAN traffic, ensure `encapsulation dot1q` VLAN ID is set correctly. If not, the sub-interface may not accept or transmit tagged traffic properly.

Now that the environment is fully configured and ready, you can test the connectivity between VLANs. Try to ping between VLANs from one PC to another.

Figure 7.30 shows the connectivity between **PC 1** (VLAN 10) and **PC 2** (VLAN 20):

```
C:\>ping 172.16.0.10

Pinging 172.16.0.10 with 32 bytes of data:

Reply from 172.16.0.10: bytes=32 time<1ms TTL=127
Reply from 172.16.0.10: bytes=32 time=13ms TTL=127
Reply from 172.16.0.10: bytes=32 time<1ms TTL=127
Reply from 172.16.0.10: bytes=32 time=3ms TTL=127

Ping statistics for 172.16.0.10:
    Packets: Sent = 4, Received = 4, Lost = 0 (0% loss),
Approximate round trip times in milli-seconds:
    Minimum = 0ms, Maximum = 13ms, Average = 4ms
```

Figure 7.30: Connectivity between PC 1 and PC 2

Additionally, you can perform a traceroute between **PC 1** and **PC 2** to see the path the packet is using, as in *Figure 7.31*:

```
C:\>tracert 172.16.0.10

Tracing route to 172.16.0.10 over a maximum of 30 hops:

  1   0 ms     3 ms     1 ms     10.0.0.1
  2   0 ms     12 ms    11 ms    172.16.0.10

Trace complete.
```

Figure 7.31: Traceroute between PC 1 and PC 2

As you can see, **PC 1** sends its packet to its default gateway, `10.0.0.1`, which is sub-interface GigabitEthernet 0/1.10 on the router. Then, the router forwards the packet to the intended destination, **PC 2** - `172.16.0.10`.

Lastly, use the following points as guidelines for troubleshooting VLANs and trunk interfaces:

- Check IP addressing on all devices
- Verify VLAN assignment on switch ports
- Check for native VLAN mismatch
- Check for allowed VLANs on the trunk interface
- Check for trunk mode mismatch
- Use the `show ip interface brief` command to verify the IP addresses on each sub-interface
- Use the `show interface trunk` command to verify port, mode, allowed, and native VLANs
- Use the `show interface interface-ID switchport` command to check the administrative and operating mode of an interface
- Use the `show interface sub-interface-ID` command on the router to verify the encapsulation mode and VLAN ID on the sub-interface
- Use the `show running-config` command to verify the configurations applied to interfaces

Having completed this section, you have learned all about VLANs, trunking, inter-VLAN routing, and much more.

Summary

Having completed this chapter, you have learned the importance of segmenting a network using VLANs to improve both network performance and security. You've learned how to create and verify VLANs on Cisco switches and set up interswitch connectivity to extend VLANs over multiple switches within a network. In addition, you have gained the hands-on skills required to implement inter-VLAN routing using a Layer 3 switch and the router-on-a-stick method. You've learned about DTP and its role in auto-negotiating interface roles on access or trunk ports. You now have the hands-on experience to create and assign VLANs, configure both access and trunk ports, and perform inter-VLAN routing on a Cisco network.

In the next chapter, *Chapter 8, EtherChannels and Layer 2 Discovery Protocols*, you will learn how to perform link aggregation and use discovery protocols to map a network topology.

Additional Reading

Configuring VLANs: `https://www.cisco.com/c/en/us/td/docs/switches/datacenter/sw/5_x/nx-os/layer2/configuration/guide/Cisco_Nexus_7000_Series_NX-OS_Layer_2_Switching_Configuration_Guide_Release_5-x_chapter4.html`

Exam Readiness Drill – Chapter Review Questions

Apart from mastering key concepts, strong test-taking skills under time pressure are essential for acing your certification exam. That's why developing these abilities early in your learning journey is critical.

Exam readiness drills, using the free online practice resources provided with this book, help you progressively improve your time management and test-taking skills while reinforcing the key concepts you've learned.

HOW TO GET STARTED

- Open the link or scan the QR code at the bottom of this page
- If you have unlocked the practice resources already, log in to your registered account. If you haven't, follow the instructions in *Chapter 19* and come back to this page.
- Once you log in, click the START button to start a quiz
- We recommend attempting a quiz multiple times till you're able to answer most of the questions correctly and well within the time limit.
- You can use the following practice template to help you plan your attempts:

Working On Accuracy		
Attempt	**Target**	**Time Limit**
Attempt 1	40% or more	Till the timer runs out
Attempt 2	60% or more	Till the timer runs out
Attempt 3	75% or more	Till the timer runs out
Working On Timing		
Attempt 4	75% or more	1 minute before time limit
Attempt 5	75% or more	2 minutes before time limit
Attempt 6	75% or more	3 minutes before time limit

The above drill is just an example. Design your drills based on your own goals and make the most out of the online quizzes accompanying this book.

First time accessing the online resources? 🔓

You'll need to unlock them through a one-time process. **Head to** *Chapter 19* **for instructions.**

Open Quiz `https://packt.link/ccnachap7` OR scan this QR code →	

8

EtherChannels and Layer 2 Discovery Protocols

Link aggregation is usually implemented between the access layer and distribution layer switches within a branch office to combine the bandwidth of multiple physical interfaces into a single, logically bundled port to support more bandwidth. EtherChannel is a LAG technology on Cisco IOS switches, and it is essential to gain a solid understanding of how to set up both Layer 2 and Layer 3 EtherChannels on a Cisco network. In addition to this, you will learn about the fundamentals of Layer 2 discovery protocols and how network professionals leverage them to map a network topology.

This chapter covers *Domain 2: Network Access*, objectives *2.3 Configure and verify Layer 2 discovery protocols (Cisco Discovery Protocol and LLDP)* and *2.4 Configure and verify (Layer 2/Layer 3) EtherChannel (LACP)* of the *200-301 CCNA v1.1 certification* exam.

In this chapter, you will read about the following topics:

- Understanding EtherChannels
- Layer 2 discovery protocols

Let's dive in!

Understanding EtherChannels

As an aspiring network professional, you will one day be assigned a task to interconnect two switches together using multiple physical connections between them. You might think that using multiple physical connections between the two switches would provide more bandwidth and that they would load balance the traffic, but this does not occur. A Layer 2 technology known as **Spanning Tree Protocol** (**STP**) prevents loops on a switched network. STP identifies redundant connections that have the potential to create a Layer 2 loop and logically blocks the redundant path. It therefore ensures a loop-free network and path between a sender and destination on the network architecture.

This means that if you are using two physical connections between two switches, only one connection will be active while the other is logically blocked by STP to prevent a Layer 2 loop on the network. Hence, STP defeats the purpose of link aggregation to provide more bandwidth between the two switches in the scenario.

Figure 8.1 shows a visual representation of the connection:

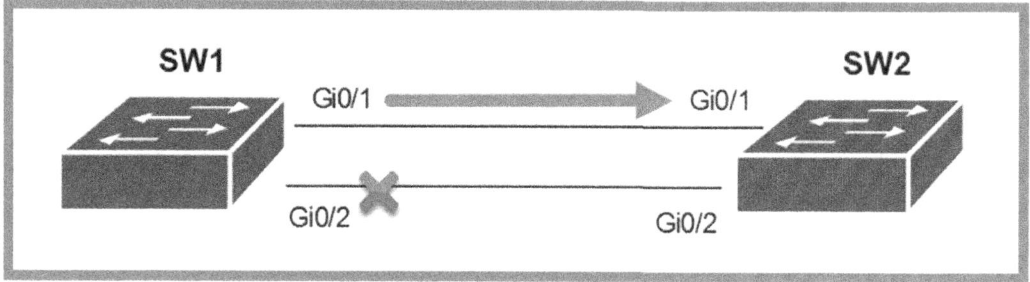

Figure 8.1: Two switches connected to each other

As shown in *Figure 8.1*, STP has logically blocked the Gigabit Ethernet 0/2 interface on SW1. Therefore, the total bandwidth between SW1 and SW2 is 1 Gbps.

Using link aggregation technology such as EtherChannel enables network professionals to group multiple physical interfaces of a switch into one single logical interface. EtherChannels simply allow increased bandwidth by using the shared bandwidth across the interfaces that are bundled as a port group and redundancy between switches, providing load sharing and fault tolerance on the network.

> **Note**
>
> In the Cisco world, physical link aggregation is known as **EtherChannel**. With other vendors, this technology is known as a **link aggregation group** (**LAG**).

EtherChannel provides many benefits to an organization. Rather than configuring individual interfaces, configurations can be applied directly on the EtherChannel interface rather than on each physical port. In addition to this, implementing EtherChannels on a network can assist with load balancing and the link aggregation of traffic between switches. EtherChannels use the existing physical interfaces on a switch and, therefore, you do not need to install additional modules.

There are some things, however, that you need to keep in mind while creating EtherChannels between switches. The interface type must match between switches. For example, if switch A is using Gigabit Ethernet interfaces, then switch B must use them too, with the same number of physical interfaces on both switches. If switch A uses four physical interfaces, then switch B must use four physical interfaces as well. Additionally, both duplex and speed must match on all physical interfaces that are being used to create the EtherChannel, and the allowed VLANs and native VLANs must match on the interfaces. To put it simply, everything must match to ensure the EtherChannel is established.

Figure 8.2 shows what happens when two switches attempt to establish an EtherChannel when all configurations match:

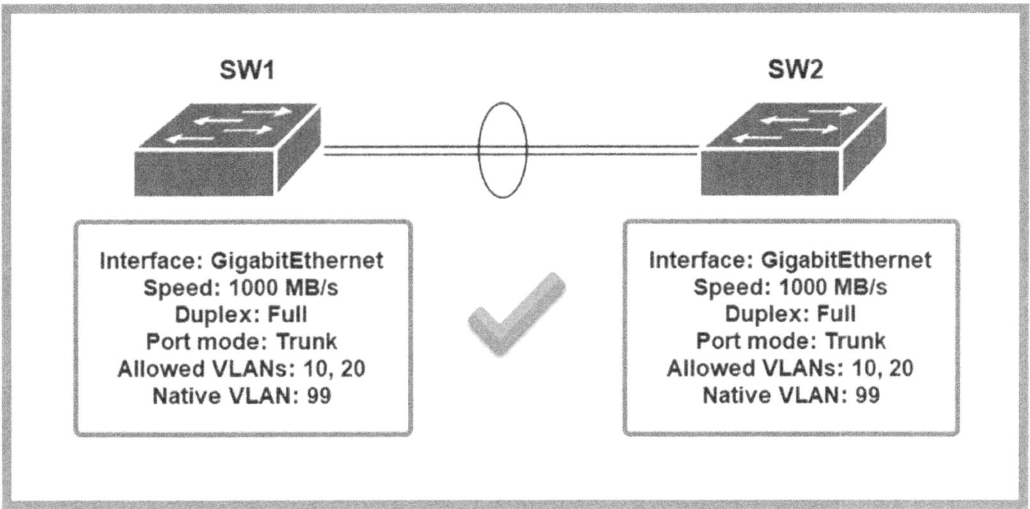

Figure 8.2: EtherChannel

However, if there is a mismatch in the configurations on either switch, the EtherChannel will not be established. *Figure 8.3* shows a misconfiguration on one device that prevents the formation of the EtherChannel:

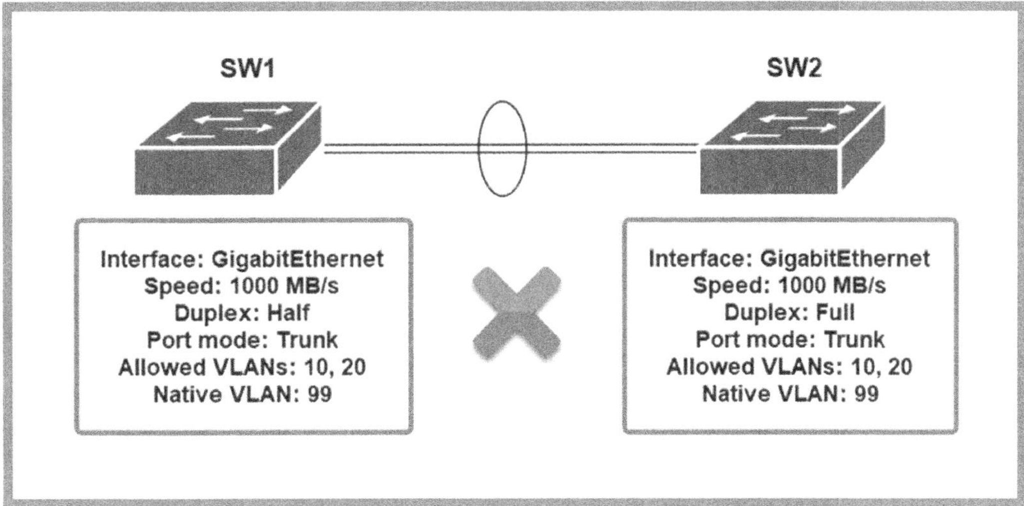

Figure 8.3: Misconfiguration preventing the formation of the EtherChannel

The following are the two auto-negotiation protocols for establishing EtherChannels on Cisco IOS devices:

- **Port Aggregation Protocol** (**PAgP**)
- **Link Aggregation Control Protocol** (**LACP**)

PAgP is a Cisco proprietary protocol for auto-negotiating EtherChannel links between Cisco IOS switches. When PAgP identifies a matching group of physical ports, it groups the ports into an EtherChannel, then it is added to STP as a single logical interface.

Once PAgP establishes an EtherChannel, it sends PAgP packets every 30 seconds and checks for consistency on the configurations between the two switches. It simply ensures that all physical ports in the EtherChannel group are using the same type of interfaces and configurations.

The following are the various PAgP configuration modes:

- **On**: Forces the interface to operate as an EtherChannel without using PAgP
- **Desirable**: The interface actively seeks to become an EtherChannel by sending PAgP messages to other interfaces of a neighboring or directly connected switch
- **Auto**: Sets the interface in a passive state and responds to any PAgP messages it receives but does not actively initiate the EtherChannel negotiation

When using PAgP, an EtherChannel will only form when using the conditions shown in *Table 8.1*:

Switch A	**Switch B**	**EtherChannel Status**
On	On	Yes
On	Desirable/Auto	No
Desirable	Desirable	Yes
Desirable	Auto	Yes
Auto	Desirable	Yes
Auto	Auto	No

Table 8.1: PAGP conditions

LACP, on the other hand, is an open standard defined by **IEEE 802.3ad**, an open standard that allows any vendor of switches to implement LACP in their product to support the auto-negotiation of EtherChannels. LACP has become the standard when creating EtherChannels. LACP uses the newer **IEEE 802.1AX** standard, which supports LACP on switches with features that enable EtherChannels for both **local area networks** (**LANs**) and **metropolitan area networks** (**MANs**).

LACP uses the following modes:

- **On**: Sets the interface to become an EtherChannel without using LACP or negotiating
- **Active**: Actively seeks whether the other device wants to form an EtherChannel
- **Passive**: Passively waits for the other device to negotiate creating an EtherChannel

When using LACP, an EtherChannel will only form when using the conditions shown in *Table 8.2*:

Switch A	Switch B	EtherChannel Status
On	On	Yes
On	Active/Passive	No
Active	Active	Yes
Active	Passive	Yes
Passive	Active	Yes
Passive	Passive	No

Table 8.2: LACP conditions

Now that you have gained an understanding of EtherChannel and its functions on a network, you can dive into a hands-on lab on configuring EtherChannels on a Cisco network.

Lab: Configuring a Layer 2 EtherChannel

In this exercise, you will learn how to establish Layer 2 EtherChannels using LACP with Cisco IOS switches using Cisco Packet Tracer.

Figure 8.4 shows the network topology that you will be using for the exercise:

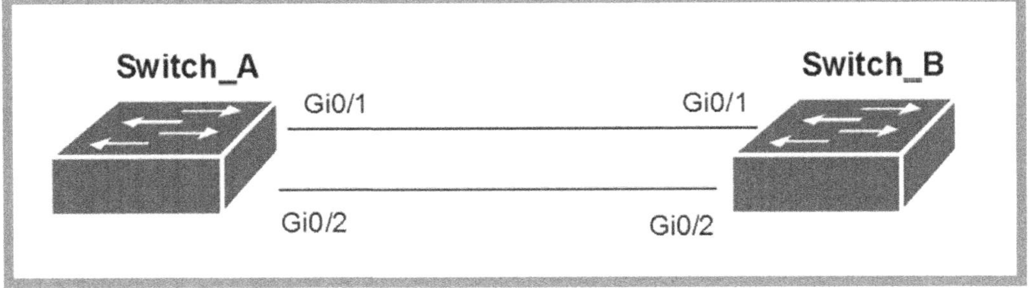

Figure 8.4: EtherChannel lab topology

Before getting started with this exercise, please go through the following guidelines:

1. Download the `Lab 8.1 - EtherChannel using LACP` lab file from `https://packt.link/CCNArepoCh08`
2. Once you have finished downloading the lab file, open it using the Cisco Packet Tracer application on your computer.

You can now get started with this exercise:

1. On `Switch_A`, perform an administrative shutdown on the `GigabitEthernet 0/1` and `GigabitEthernet 0/2` interfaces by using the following commands:

```
Switch_A> enable
Switch_A# configure terminal
Switch_A(config)# interface range gigabitEthernet 0/1 -
gigabitEthernet 0/2
Switch_A(config-if-range)# shutdown
Switch_A(config-if-range)# exit
```

2. This will prevent any layer 2 loops from forming, resulting in the interfaces going into an `err-disable` state.

> **Note**
>
> If an interface is in an `err-disable` state and you want to restore the interface to a connected status, you should apply the `shutdown` command on the interface to enable its administrative shutdown. Then, wait a few seconds before applying the `no shutdown` command to restore the interface to a connected state.

3. On `Switch_A`, use the following commands to initiate negotiation using LACP on both the `GigabitEthernet 0/1` and `GigabitEthernet 0/2` interfaces:

```
Switch_A(config)# interface range gigabitEthernet 0/1 -
gigabitEthernet 0/2
Switch_A(config-if-range)# channel-group 1 mode active
Switch_A(config-if-range)# no shutdown
Switch_A(config-if-range)# exit
```

4. On `Switch_A`, access the newly created channel group (EtherChannel) and configure it as an IEEE 802.1Q trunk:

```
Switch_A(config)# interface port-channel 1
Switch_A(config-if)# switchport mode trunk
Switch_A(config-if)# exit
```

5. On `Switch_B`, repeat *steps 1–3*, as shown here:

```
Switch_B> enable
Switch_B # configure terminal
Switch_B (config)# interface range gigabitEthernet 0/1 -
gigabitEthernet 0/2
Switch_B (config-if-range)# shutdown
Switch_B (config-if-range)# channel-group 1 mode active
Switch_B (config-if-range)# no shutdown
Switch_B (config-if-range)# exit
Switch_B (config)# interface port-channel 1
Switch_B (config-if)# switchport mode trunk
Switch_B (config-if)# exit
```

6. To verify EtherChannels on the Cisco switches, use the `show etherchannel summary` command, as shown in *Figure 8.5*:

```
Switch_A# show etherchannel summary
Flags:  D - down        P - in port-channel
        I - stand-alone s - suspended
        H - Hot-standby (LACP only)
        R - Layer3      S - Layer2
        U - in use      f - failed to allocate aggregator
        u - unsuitable for bundling
        w - waiting to be aggregated
        d - default port


Number of channel-groups in use: 1
Number of aggregators:           1

Group  Port-channel  Protocol    Ports
------+-------------+-----------+------------------------------

1      Po1(SU)           LACP   Gig0/1(P) Gig0/2(P)
Switch_A#
```

Figure 8.5: The show etherchannel summary output

As shown in the preceding screenshot, there is one port group that is using LACP to negotiate the EtherChannel status and that is operating as a layer 2 EtherChannel. The members of the port group are `GigabitEthernet 0/1` and `GigabitEthernet 0/2`.

7. Lastly, use the `show etherchannel port-channel` command for more details about EtherChannels on the switch:

```
Switch_A# show etherchannel port-channel
                Channel-group listing:
                ----------------------

Group: 1
----------
                Port-channels in the group:
                ---------------------------

Port-channel: Po1    (Primary Aggregator)
------------

Age of the Port-channel   = 00d:00h:17m:13s
Logical slot/port   = 2/1       Number of ports = 2
GC                  = 0x00000000      HotStandBy port = null
Port state          = Port-channel
Protocol            =   LACP
Port Security       = Disabled

Ports in the Port-channel:

Index   Load   Port     EC state        No of bits
------+------+------+------------------+-----------
  0     00     Gig0/1   Active             0
  0     00     Gig0/2   Active             0
Time since last port bundled:    00d:00h:09m:01s    Gig0/2
```

Figure 8.6: The show etherchannel port-channel output

Having completed this section, you have gained the skills to implement and troubleshoot Layer 2 EtherChannel technologies in a Cisco environment.

Lab: Configuring a Layer 3 EtherChannel

In this exercise, you will learn how to establish Layer 3 EtherChannels using LACP with Cisco IOS switches using Cisco Packet Tracer.

Figure 8.7 shows the network topology that you will be using for this exercise:

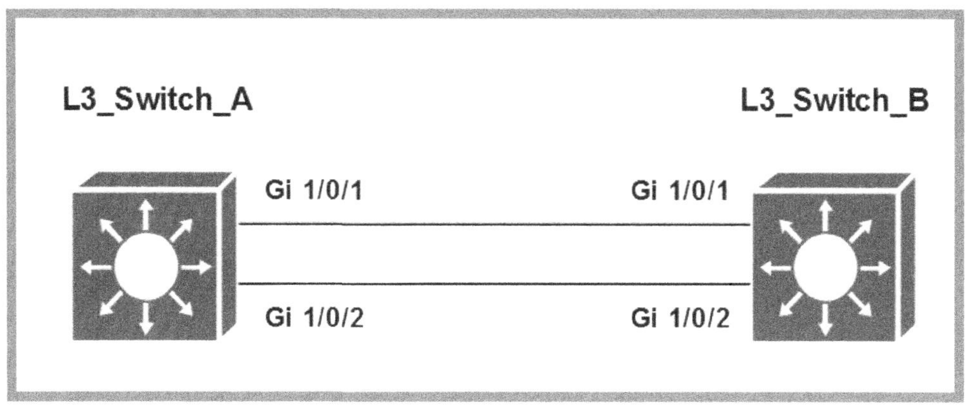

Figure 8.7: Layer 3 EtherChannel topology

Before getting started with this exercise, please go through the following guidelines:

1. 1. Download the `Lab 8.2 - L3 EtherChannel using LACP` lab file from `https://packt.link/CCNArepoChapter8`
2. 2. Once you have finished downloading the lab file, open it using the Cisco Packet Tracer application on your computer.

You can now get started with this exercise:

1. On `L3_Switch_A`, create a port channel and configure it as a routed port that is a Layer 3 interface with an IP address. Use the following commands:

```
L3_Switch_A> enable
L3_Switch_A# configure terminal
L3_Switch_A(config)# interface port-channel 1
L3_Switch_A(config-if)# no switchport
L3_Switch_A(config-if)# ip address 172.16.1.10 255.255.255.0
L3_Switch_A(config-if)# exit
```

2. Next, on `L3_Switch_A`, configure the member interfaces as routed ports and use LACP to auto-negotiate the EtherChannel status:

```
L3_Switch_A(config)# interface range gigabitEthernet 1/0/1 -
gigabitEthernet 1/0/2
L3_Switch_A(config-if-range)# no switchport
L3_Switch_A(config-if-range)# channel-group 1 mode active
L3_Switch_A(config-if-range)# exit
```

3. On `L3_Switch_B`, create a port channel and configure it as a routed port that is a layer 3
4. nterface with an IP address. Use the following commands:

```
L3_Switch_B> enable
L3_Switch_B# configure terminal
L3_Switch_B(config)# interface port-channel 1
L3_Switch_B(config-if)# no switchport
L3_Switch_B(config-if)# ip address 172.16.1.11 255.255.255.0
L3_Switch_B(config-if)# exit
```

5. Next, on `L3_Switch_B`, configure the member interfaces as routed ports and use LACP to auto-negotiate the EtherChannel status:

```
L3_Switch_B(config)# interface range gigabitEthernet 1/0/1 -
gigabitEthernet 1/0/2
L3_Switch_B(config-if-range)# no switchport
L3_Switch_B(config-if-range)# channel-group 1 mode active
L3_Switch_B(config-if-range)# exit
```

6. Next, to verify the status of the EtherChannel, the auto-negotiation protocol, and to check whether it is a layer 3 EtherChannel, use the `show etherchannel` command, as shown in *Figure 8.8*:

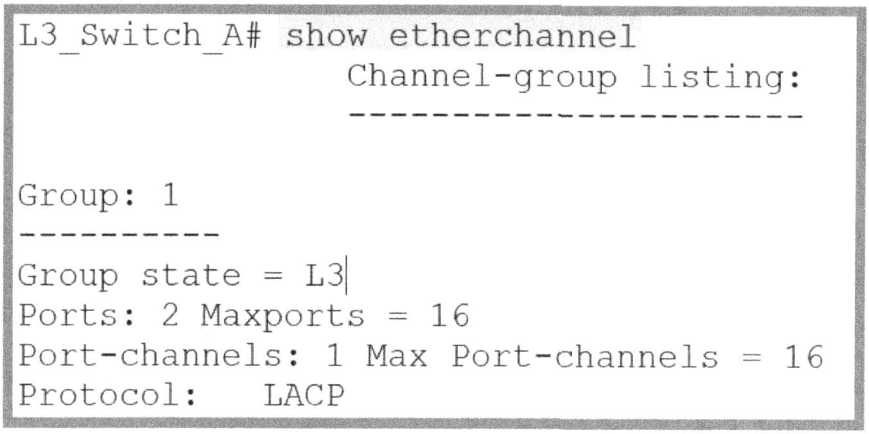

```
L3_Switch_A# show etherchannel
                Channel-group listing:
                ----------------------

Group: 1
----------
Group state = L3
Ports: 2 Maxports = 16
Port-channels: 1 Max Port-channels = 16
Protocol:   LACP
```

Figure 8.8: Verifying EtherChannel protocol and type

7. Lastly, use the `show etherchannel summary` command for more details about the EtherChannels on the switch, as shown in *Figure 8.9*:

```
L3_Switch_A# show etherchannel summary
Flags:  D - down        P - in port-channel
        I - stand-alone s - suspended
        H - Hot-standby (LACP only)
        R - Layer3      S - Layer2
        U - in use      f - failed to allocate aggregator
        u - unsuitable for bundling
        w - waiting to be aggregated
        d - default port


Number of channel-groups in use: 1
Number of aggregators:           1

Group  Port-channel  Protocol    Ports
------+-------------+-----------+-----------------------

1      Po1(RU)           LACP   Gig1/0/1(P) Gig1/0/2(P)
```

Figure 8.9: Verifying EtherChannel status

Having completed this section, you have learned about the fundamentals of EtherChannels and how to implement and troubleshoot them. In the next section, you will learn how Layer 2 discovery protocols help network professionals in mapping a network topology.

Layer 2 Discovery Protocols

In this section, you will learn how network professionals leverage Layer 2 discovery protocols to map their network topology and identify directly connected devices. In addition to this, you will explore the type of information exchanged between switches and how you can use the information to determine the role of a device and the interfaces used for connecting to a neighbor device.

Cisco Discovery Protocol

Cisco Discovery Protocol (**CDP**) is a Cisco proprietary protocol that operates at Layer 2, the data link layer. CDP is used to assist Cisco devices in learning about their directly connected neighbors, such as other switches and routers. CDP is enabled by default on Cisco switches and routers.

A CDP message contains the following:

- Cisco IOS version
- Device model and type
- Connected interfaces for both the local and remote device
- Hostnames

Such information helps network devices to better understand what is directly connected to them and helps network professionals with troubleshooting network-related issues.

To globally enable CDP on a Cisco IOS switch, use the following command:

```
Switch(config)# cdp run
```

To globally turn off CDP on a Cisco IOS switch, use the following command:

```
Switch(config)# no cdp run
```

Additionally, CDP can be enabled on an individual interface using the following command:

```
Switch(config)# interface fastEthernet 0/1
Switch(config-if)#cdp enable
```

Since CDP messages contain important and identifiable information about devices on a network, it is a security concern. If a malicious user were to intercept and capture those CDP messages, the malicious user would be able to determine the various types of devices, their operating system versions, and how they are interconnected. Therefore, it is recommended to disable CDP on interfaces that are connected to end devices, and those that are connected to the internet. In addition to this, CDP messages should only be exchanged between switches and routers that are authorized on the organization's network.

The `show cdp neighbors` command provides you with the characteristics and roles of directly connected devices. *Figure 8.10* shows various devices connected to SW3:

```
SW3#show cdp neighbors
Capability Codes: R - Router, T - Trans Bridge, B - Source Route Bridge
                  S - Switch, H - Host, I - IGMP, r - Repeater, P - Phone
Device ID     Local Intrfce    Holdtme    Capability    Platform     Port ID
R1            Gig 0/1           157            R        C2900        Gig 0/1
SW1           Fas 0/24          157            S        2960         Fas 0/24
SW2           Fas 0/23          157            S        2960         Fas 0/23
R1            Gig 0/1           157            R        C2900        Gig 0/1.10
R1            Gig 0/1           157            R        C2900        Gig 0/1.20
R1            Gig 0/1           157            R        C2900        Gig 0/1.30
SW3#
```

Figure 8.10: CDP neighbors

Figure 8.10 shows you some switches and routers that are connected, their functions, platform or model numbers, and local and remote ports that are being used. Such information is useful when you are remotely accessing a device via its IP address and you're not too sure about the network topology. Additionally, this information helps you map a network without seeing a network diagram.

The `show cdp neighbors detail` command provides you with more information about directly connected devices and their IP addresses, as shown in *Figure 8.11*:

```
Device ID: R1
Entry address(es):
  IP address : 10.0.0.1
Platform: cisco C2900, Capabilities: Router
Interface: GigabitEthernet0/1, Port ID (outgoing port): GigabitEthernet0/1.10
Holdtime: 167

Version :
Cisco IOS Software, C2900 Software (C2900-UNIVERSALK9-M), Version 15.1(4)M4, RELEASE
(fc2)
Technical Support: http://www.cisco.com/techsupport
Copyright (c) 1986-2012 by Cisco Systems, Inc.
Compiled Thurs 5-Jan-12 15:41 by pt_team

advertisement version: 2
Duplex: full
```

Figure 8.11: CDP provides the IP addresses of connected devices

The following are some additional characteristics of CDP:

- CDP messages are sent every 60 seconds.
- The default hold-down timer is 180 seconds. If a CDP message is not received within this time, the neighbor device is removed from the CDP cache/database.
- The `show cdp interface interface-ID` command can be used to determine the CDP timers on an interface.

One of the common limitations of using CDP within a network is the fact that it only works on Cisco devices. In a lot of enterprise networks, there is a mixture of Cisco and non-Cisco devices, and this is a major shortcoming of CDP. In the next section, you will learn about another Layer 2 discovery protocol that helps network professionals efficiently discover connected switches and routers on a network, but also works with both Cisco and non-Cisco devices.

Link Layer Discovery Protocol

Link Layer Discovery Protocol (**LLDP**) is another discovery protocol that operates over Layer 2. LLDP is supported on both Cisco and non-Cisco devices, thus surpassing the shortcomings of being a proprietary protocol such as CDP. For this reason, LLDP is the industry standard of discovery protocols on enterprise networks.

> **Note**
>
> LLDP is defined by **IEEE 802.1AB**, which makes it interoperable on other vendor devices. LLDP is not turned on by default on Cisco devices.

To configure LLDP on a Cisco IOS device, use the following steps:

1. To turn on LLDP globally, execute the `lldp run` command in global configuration mode:

```
Switch> enable
Switch# configure terminal
Switch(config)# lldp run
```

2. Configure the interfaces you want to use with LLDP:

```
Switch(config)# interface FastEthernet 0/24
Switch(config-if)# lldp receive
Switch(config-if)# lldp transmit
```

3. To verify the LLDP status on a Cisco IOS switch, use the `show lldp` command, as shown in *Figure 8.12*:

```
SW3#show lldp

Global LLDP Information:
    Status: ACTIVE
    LLDP advertisements are sent every 30 seconds
    LLDP hold time advertised is 120 seconds
    LLDP interface reinitialisation delay is 2 seconds
SW3#
```

Figure 8.12: LLDP status output

4. To view all connected devices, use the `show lldp neighbors` command, shown in *Figure 8.13*:

```
SW3#show lldp neighbors
Capability codes:
    (R) Router, (B) Bridge, (T) Telephone, (C) DOCSIS Cable Device
    (W) WLAN Access Point, (P) Repeater, (S) Station, (O) Other
Device ID           Local Intf     Hold-time  Capability      Port ID
SW1                 Fa0/24         120        B               Fa0/24
R1                  Gig0/1         120        R               Gig

Total entries displayed: 2
```

Figure 8.13: LLDP connected neighbors

5. Additionally, to get further details and the IP addresses of connected LLDP neighbors, use the `show lldp neighbors detail` command, as shown in *Figure 8.14*:

```
SW3#show lldp neighbors detail
------------------------------------------------
Chassis id: 0003.E411.4818
Port id: Fa0/24
Port Description: FastEthernet0/24
System Name: SW1
System Description:
Cisco IOS Software, C2960 Software (C2960-LANBASE-M),
SOFTWARE (fc1)
Copyright (c) 1986-2005 by Cisco Systems, Inc.
Compiled Wed 12-Oct-05 22:05 by pt_team
Time remaining: 90 seconds
System Capabilities: B
Enabled Capabilities: B
Management Addresses   not advertised
Auto Negotiation - supported, enabled
Physical media capabilities:
    100baseT(FD)
    100baseT(HD)
    1000baseT(HD)
Media Attachment Unit type: 10
Vlan ID: 1
```

Figure 8.14: LLDP neighbor with IP address

Gathering the information from either the CDP or LLDP output, you will now be able to build an up-to-date network diagram easily. Having completed this section, you have learned about the fundamentals of Layer 2 discovery protocols, and how to configure and use them to map a network topology.

Summary

In this chapter, you have explored the benefits of using link aggregation technology such as EtherChannels to logically bundle multiple physical interfaces of a switch. You have also learned how to configure and verify Layer 2 and Layer 3 EtherChannels between Cisco switches. Additionally, you have learned how network professionals use Layer 2 discovery protocols to help identify connected devices within their network topology. Furthermore, you have learned about the differences between CDP and LLDP while gaining better insights into their use cases and gained hands-on skills in configuring both CDP and LLDP on a Cisco network.

In the next chapter, *Understanding and Configuring Spanning Tree*, you will learn how to configure and troubleshoot STP on a Cisco network.

Additional Reading

- *Configuring Cisco Discovery Protocol*: `https://www.cisco.com/c/en/us/support/docs/network-management/discovery-protocol-cdp/43485-cdponios43485.html`
- *Configure Link Layer Discovery Protocol*: `https://www.cisco.com/c/en/us/support/docs/smb/switches/cisco-small-business-300-series-managed-switches/smb5578-configure-link-layer-discovery-protocol-lldp-port-settings-o.html`

Exam Readiness Drill – Chapter Review Questions

Apart from mastering key concepts, strong test-taking skills under time pressure are essential for acing your certification exam. That's why developing these abilities early in your learning journey is critical.

Exam readiness drills, using the free online practice resources provided with this book, help you progressively improve your time management and test-taking skills while reinforcing the key concepts you've learned.

HOW TO GET STARTED

- Open the link or scan the QR code at the bottom of this page
- If you have unlocked the practice resources already, log in to your registered account. If you haven't, follow the instructions in *Chapter 19* and come back to this page.
- Once you log in, click the START button to start a quiz
- We recommend attempting a quiz multiple times till you're able to answer most of the questions correctly and well within the time limit.
- You can use the following practice template to help you plan your attempts:

Working On Accuracy		
Attempt	Target	Time Limit
Attempt 1	40% or more	Till the timer runs out
Attempt 2	60% or more	Till the timer runs out
Attempt 3	75% or more	Till the timer runs out
Working On Timing		
Attempt 4	75% or more	1 minute before time limit
Attempt 5	75% or more	2 minutes before time limit
Attempt 6	75% or more	3 minutes before time limit

The above drill is just an example. Design your drills based on your own goals and make the most out of the online quizzes accompanying this book.

First time accessing the online resources? 🔓

You'll need to unlock them through a one-time process. **Head to** *Chapter 19* **for instructions.**

Open Quiz	
https://packt.link/ccnachap8 OR scan this QR code →	

9
Understanding and Configuring Spanning Tree

When extending your layer 2 network and ensuring all devices are connected, it is important to implement physical redundancy. This is to ensure that there are multiple paths available between hosts on a network in the event that a network switch or link goes down. In this chapter, you will learn how redundancy can create a broadcast storm and deteriorate network stability. You'll also learn how to configure layer 2 loop prevention protocols to ensure that there are no loops on your switch network.

This chapter covers *Domain 2: Network Access*, objective *2.5 Interpret basic operations of Rapid PVST+ Spanning Tree Protocol* of the *200-301 CCNA v1.1 certification* exam.

In this chapter, the following topics will be covered:

- Understanding Spanning Tree
- Spanning Tree standards
- Port roles and states
- Determining the root bridge
- Configuring and troubleshooting Spanning Tree Protocol labs

You can now begin learning about these topics.

Understanding Spanning Tree

A major topic in the CCNA certification is understanding how **Spanning Tree Protocol** (**STP**) works on a layer 2 network architecture. In all sizes of networks, from small businesses to large enterprises with multiple branch sites, there are many interconnected switches to provide connectivity to end devices. In *Chapter 2*, Network Architectures and Physical Infrastructure, you read about the Cisco hierarchical three-tier design, which contains core, distribution, and access layers.

To recap, *Figure 9.1* shows the Cisco three-tier switch model:

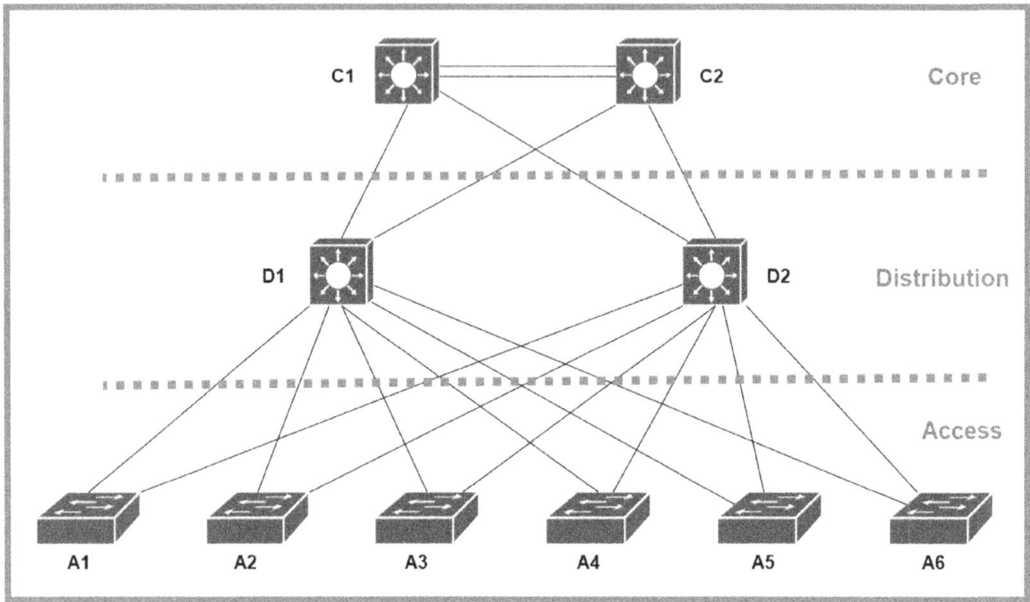

Figure 9.1: Cisco's three-tier model

Cisco recommends that this model be implemented in networks of any size, as it provides the following benefits:

- Supports scalability
- Allows EtherChannel connections between devices
- Provides redundancy and fault tolerance

Scalability allows us to simply add more access-layer switches and connect the newly added switches to the distribution layer to support growth as an organization may be expanding its physical infrastructure. Additionally, as you learned in the previous chapter, EtherChannel plays a vital role in networks, as it is used to combine physical interfaces into a single logical interface and therefore carries more bandwidth between switches. Lastly, redundancy is very important in a network of any size. Without redundancy, should a switch or link go down, an area of the network will be unavailable without any alternative paths.

We can focus a little more now on how redundancy is both a good and bad thing in a network. It is a bit of a double-edged sword. While we know that redundancy is good to ensure multiple paths and switches are available, how can redundancy be a bad thing within a network? To get a better understanding of how redundancy can cripple a network, take a look at *Figure 9.2*:

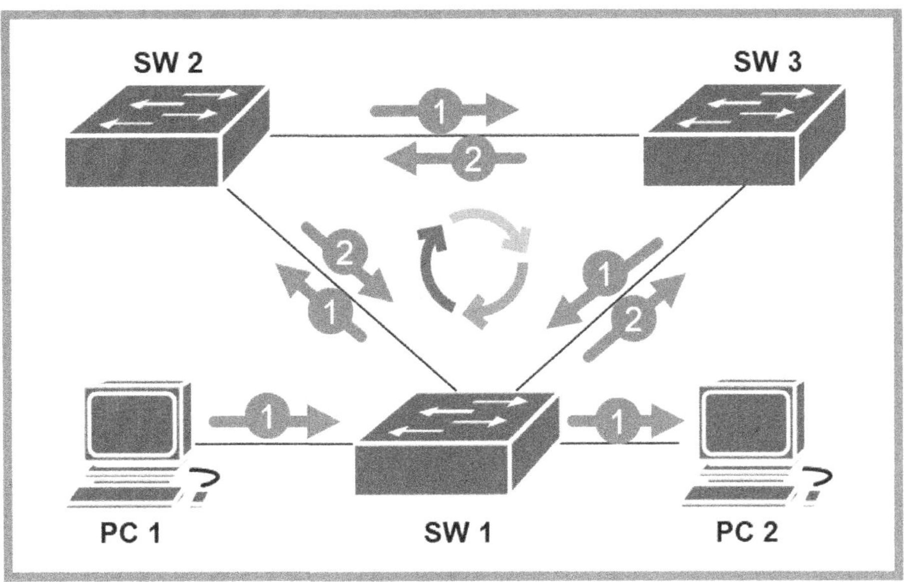

Figure 9.2: Layer 2 loops

If **PC 1** sends a broadcast message on the network, the following is the effect without Spanning Tree:

1. **PC 1** sends a broadcast message, with destination MAC address **FF-FF-FF-FF-FF-FF**, to **SW 1**.
2. **SW 1** will see the destination MAC address of the frame is a broadcast and forward it out of all other ports. This means the message is sent to **SW 2**, **SW 3**, and **PC 2**.
3. When **PC 2** receives the message, it will process it.
4. When **SW 2** receives the broadcast, it will forward it to **SW 3**.
5. **SW 3** will forward the message it received from **SW 2** to **SW 1**.
6. **SW 3** will forward the message it received from **SW 1** to **SW 2**.
7. **SW 1** will forward the message it received from **SW 3** to **PC 1**, **PC 2**, and **SW 2**, thus creating a never-ending layer 2 loop on the network.

The overall effect of **PC 1** generating a single broadcast message will be a never-ending re-generation of broadcast messages between the switches that are continuously being created and looping between devices. This will create a broadcast storm on the network, and therefore will eventually cripple the layer 2 network infrastructure.

STP is a layer 2 loop prevention protocol that is defined by IEEE 802.1D. STP automatically creates one logical active path between all devices on a layer 2 network while logically blocking a redundancy path to prevent loops from occurring on the network.

Figure 9.3 shows Spanning Tree blocking a redundant path to ensure there are no loops:

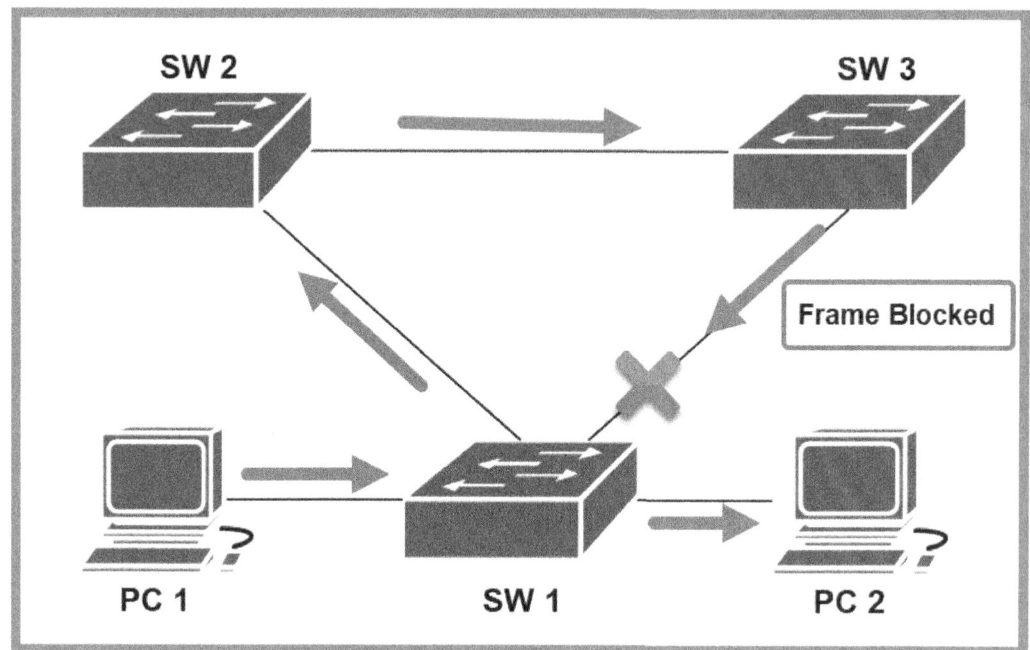

Figure 9.3: Redundant path blocked

In *Figure 9.3*, if **PC 1** sends a broadcast message, STP has already placed its logically blocking mechanism to prevent the re-generation of the broadcast message from propagating the network. If the active path goes down, what will Spanning Tree do? Spanning Tree will automatically detect the failure on the network within a few seconds and convert a logically blocked path into the active state to allow devices to reach each other while ensuring there are no loops.

Bridge Protocol Data Unit

How does Spanning Tree know when a path is down? By default, Spanning Tree is enabled on Cisco IOS switches, and every two seconds, each Cisco switch exchanges a special frame known as a Bridge Protocol Data Unit (BPDU). The following is the composition of each BPDU frame sent by a Cisco IOS switch:

- **Bridge ID**: Each switch contains a priority value that is used to elect a root bridge. The default bridge ID on all Cisco switches is set to `32768`. This value can be modified in increments of `4096` and supports a range from `0` to `61440`. The benefit of adjusting the priority is the lower the value, the more likely the switch is to be elected as the root bridge on the network.

- Extended system ID: This value is the same as the VLAN ID for the Spanning Tree instance. On a Cisco IOS switch, there is a separate Spanning Tree instance for each VLAN existing on the device. This means if there are six VLANs on the network, then there are six instances of Spanning Tree.
- MAC address: Each switch has its own unique MAC address that it uses for communication with other devices on the network. To view the MAC address of a switch, use the show version command, as shown in *Figure 9.4*:

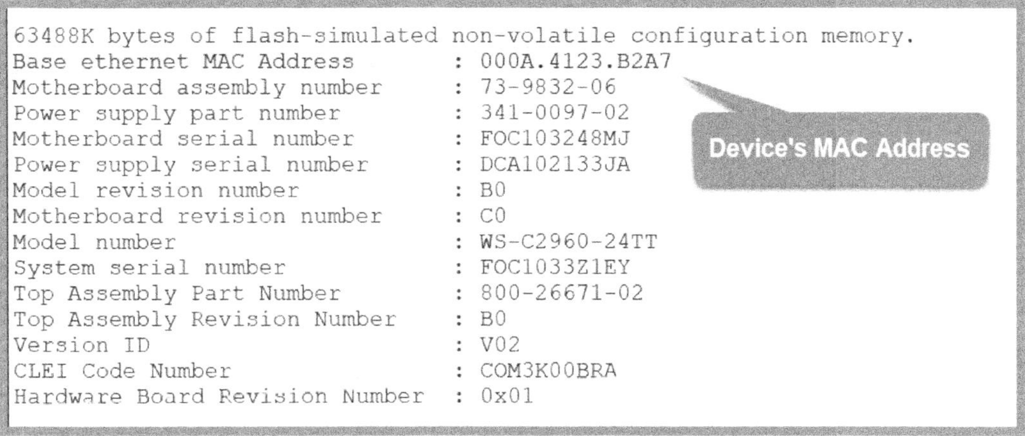

Figure 9.4: MAC address of a Cisco IOS switch

Figure 9.5 shows a graphical representation of a BPDU frame, such as the size of the bridge priority as a 4-bit field, the extended system ID as a 12-bit field, and the MAC address being a 48-bit field:

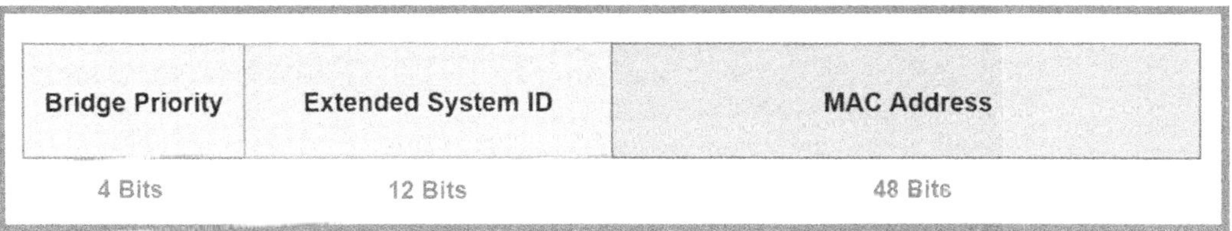

Figure 9.5: BPDU frame

The information contained within the BPDU message helps the switches to determine (elect) a root bridge on the network. Now that you have learned the fundamentals of Spanning Tree, you can take a look at how Spanning Tree makes its choices on a network in the following section.

Root Bridge and Secondary Root Bridge

In many organizations, there are managers for almost every department. The purpose of a manager is to simply guide and support employees in their daily duties. The organization usually hires a manager to ensure their business unit/department is able to meet the business objectives and goals on a daily basis.

Similarly, on a network, a special switch has to be elected to inform all other switches of the paths to leave as active to ensure there is only one logical path between any devices on the network, while all other paths are to be logically blocked to prevent any layer 2 loops. This special switch is known as the root bridge.

The root bridge is determined by the switch with the lowest priority on the network. All Cisco IOS switches have a default priority of `32768`. In a situation where all switches have the same priority value, the switch with the lowest MAC address is elected as the root bridge on the network. Once a root bridge has been elected, all other switches on the network will now point toward the root bridge, as it serves as the **central reference point** for all traffic.

Using the show spanning-tree command, network professionals can view the STP details and operations on a switch, as shown in *Figure 9.6*:

```
D2#show spanning-tree
VLAN0001
  Spanning tree enabled protocol ieee
  Root ID    Priority    4097
             Address     00D0.FFA3.AC10
             Cost        19
             Port        7(FastEthernet0/7)
             Hello Time  2 sec  Max Age 20 sec  Forward Delay 15 sec

  Bridge ID  Priority    32769  (priority 32768 sys-id-ext 1)
             Address     0001.9671.BEDE
             Hello Time  2 sec  Max Age 20 sec  Forward Delay 15 sec
             Aging Time  20

Interface        Role Sts Cost      Prio.Nbr Type
---------------- ---- --- --------- -------- --------------------------
Fa0/2            Desg FWD 19        128.2    P2p
Fa0/5            Desg FWD 19        128.5    P2p
Fa0/7            Root FWD 19        128.7    P2p
Fa0/6            Desg FWD 19        128.6    P2p
```

Figure 9.6: Spanning Tree operation

On each switch, you will always see both the root bridge information, as shown in the upper section of *Figure 9.6*, and the local switch's information in the `Bridge ID` section, as seen in the middle of *Figure 9.6*. Each switch on the network will always point toward the root bridge and has the root ID details in their Spanning Tree instance for the VLAN.

From *Figure 9.6*, the following can be determined about the root bridge:

- The Spanning Tree instance is for VLAN 1
- This switch is running the default Spanning Tree mode, **Per-VLAN Spanning Tree Plus** (PVST+)
- The root ID for the root bridge is `4097`
- The root bridge MAC address is `00D0.FFA3.AC10`
- The cost is `19`, therefore the local switch is using a FastEthernet interface as the root port
- The `Hello Time` value is `2` seconds (default)

Additionally, the following can be determined about the local switch (`D2`):

- The `Priority` value of `D2` is `32768` (default value).
- The extended system ID (VLAN) is `1`.
- The bridge ID = priority + extended system ID, which is 32,768 + 1 = 32,769. Keep in mind that the bridge ID is not the priority value.
- The MAC address of `D2` is `0001.9671.BEDE`.

Furthermore, each type of interface on a Cisco IOS switch has a cost value associated with it. They are as follows:

- 10 Mbps = 100
- 100 Mbps = 19
- 1 Gbps = 4

Spanning Tree also uses the accumulative cost that's associated with interfaces that point toward the root bridge in choosing the closest path.

Spanning Tree will automatically elect a switch to be the root bridge, but this is not a good thing. In a bad situation, Spanning Tree may elect an access-layer switch that has no redundant power supply. Access-layer switches are used to connect end devices to a network. These can be regularly moved (disconnected). Therefore, it is recommended that a switch in the core layer be configured as the root bridge.

One major concern is if the root bridge goes down, Spanning Tree will automatically elect another switch to take up the role of being the new root bridge on the network. As a network professional, it's not recommended to allow the auto-election process to select a root bridge. Rather, you can manually configure a specific switch to be the secondary root bridge in the event that the primary root bridge goes offline.

Creating a secondary root bridge can be done by simply assigning a priority value that's higher than the root bridge, that is, at least one increment of `4096` higher than the priority of the root bridge. This would enable the secondary root bridge to become the primary root bridge if the designated root bridge should become unavailable.

Additionally, if there are multiple VLANs on the network, there must be a root bridge for each VLAN. At times, you may think it's wise that one core switch be the root bridge for all the VLANs, but in reality, it should not. If a single core switch is the root bridge for all VLANs, that's an extra load and resources that the core switch has to exert in performance. What if you load balance the VLANs between multiple core switches?

Figure 9.7 shows two core switches load balancing the function of a root bridge between multiple VLANs on a network:

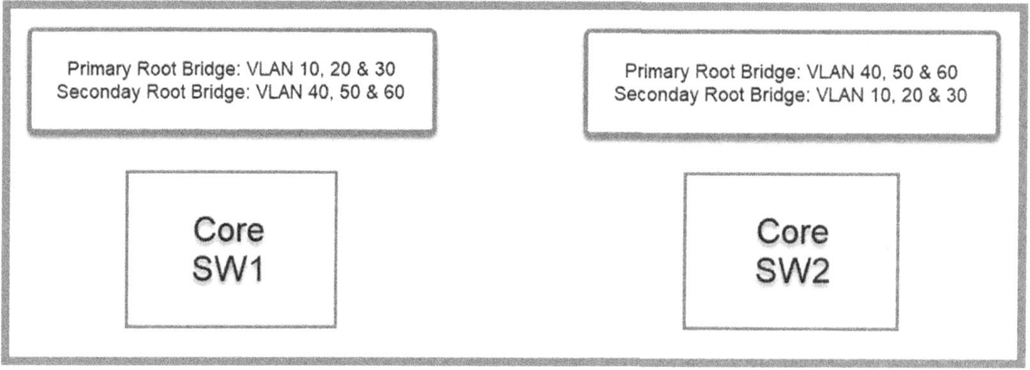

Figure 9.7: Spanning Tree load balancing

Should **Core SW1** go down, **Core SW2** will take the role of the root bridge for VLANs 10, 20, and 30, in addition to VLANs 40, 50, and 60, and vice versa if **Core SW2** goes down as well.

Both the **primary root bridge** and the **secondary root bridge** can be configured to automatically adjust their bridge priority value to be the lowest on the network at all times. Using different commands on each switch makes this option available to you.

To configure the primary root bridge, use the following command:

```
C1(config)#spanning-tree vlan 1 root primary
```

To configure the secondary root bridge, use the following command:

```
C2(config)#spanning-tree vlan 1 root secondary
```

The preceding commands remove the need to specify the priority value, and instead, the VLAN-ID is needed.

Spanning Tree Standards

STP is an open source layer 2 loop prevention mechanism that is enabled on switches by default. STP is defined by **IEEE 802.1D**. However, Cisco does not implement the IEEE 802.1D version of Spanning Tree on their devices.

PVST+

Cisco has taken the IEEE 802.1D standard and created an improved proprietary version known as **PVST+** that is enabled on all Cisco IOS switches by default. Unlike STP (IEEE 802.1D), Cisco PVST+ creates a unique instance of each VLAN existing on the network, hence the name **Per-VLAN Spanning Tree Plus**.

Both STP and PVST+ have the following port roles:

- Blocking
- Listening
- Learning
- Forwarding

> **Note**
> Cisco allows PVST+ to interoperate with other vendors that run the IEEE 802.1D STP.

Networks that run STP and PVST+ usually take about 30-50 seconds to converge and allow traffic to flow on the network. However, sometimes, after devices have booted up following a power outage, or if modifications are being made on the network, waiting 50 seconds for traffic to start flowing can be too long.

> **Note**
> **Multiple Spanning Tree Protocol** (**MSTP**), defined by **IEEE 802.1s**, is an open source protocol that is designed to use a single instance of Spanning Tree to manage all the VLANs on a network.

Rapid PVST+

There's a much faster version of STP, known as **Rapid Spanning Tree Protocol** (**RSTP**), and it is defined by **IEEE 802.1w**. It has the ability to converge the entire networking in approximately two seconds, which is much quicker than the IEEE 802.1D standard. Cisco took the improved RSTP (IEEE 802.1w) standard and made their proprietary version, known as **Rapid PVST+**.

To enable Rapid PVST+ on a Cisco network, use the following command in global configuration mode on all Cisco IOS switches:

```
Switch(config)# spanning-tree mode rapid-pvst
```

Rapid PVST+ supports the following port roles:

- Discarding
- Learning
- Forwarding

Keep in mind that Rapid PVST+ has three port states – discarding, learning, and forwarding. Blocking is merged into the discarding state and is not eliminated entirely.

Portfast

This feature allows the port to directly go into a forwarding state without having to move through the learning and listening states. Portfast should be configured on **edge ports** only.

> **Note**
> Edge ports are those interfaces that are not connected to another switch.

Edge ports (Portfast) should not receive BPDUs on their interfaces. The BPDU guard feature should be used with Portfast to prevent BPDUs from entering an edge port. If a BPDU is received on an edge port with the BPDU guard enabled, the port will switch into an `err-disabled` state (logically shuts down).

In the *Lab: Implementing Rapid PVST+ on a Cisco Network* section, you will discover how to configure both Portfast and a BPDU guard.

Security Mechanisms

A root guard is a security mechanism within a Cisco IOS switch that prevents a designated interface of a switch from becoming a root port during the STP election process. When this feature is enabled on an interface, if the port receives a BPDU with a lower bridge ID value, the interface is placed in the `root-inconsistent` state until the interface is no longer receiving BPDUs with a lower bridge ID or priority. This ensures the current root bridge remains unchanged. Typically, a root guard is configured on edge ports that are usually connected to end devices, routers, and firewalls on the network.

The following commands can be used to configure a root guard on a Cisco IOS switch:

```
Switch# configure terminal
Switch(config)# interface <interface-id>
Switch(config-if)# spanning-tree guard root
```

A loop guard is another security mechanism found on Cisco IOS switches that prevents loops on an interface that should not be receiving BPDUs such as edge ports. If this feature is configured on a switch interface and the port does not receive any BPDU from the designated interface of a neighbor switch for a certain time interval, the interface will transition to a `loop inconsistent` state and logically block the interface to prevent a possible loop. This security mechanism is commonly configured on interfaces that may be attached to a misconfigured switch that has the potential of creating a layer 2 loop by not sending BPDUs on the network.

The following commands are used to configure a loop guard on a Cisco IOS switch:

```
Switch# configure terminal
Switch(config)# interface <interface-id>
Switch(config-if)# spanning-tree loopguard default
```

A BPDU filter enables Cisco IOS switches to suppress a BPDU transmission on an interface. For instance, if network professionals enable a BPDU filter on a switch interface, that interface will not be able to send or receive any BPDU messages. This means that the BPDU filter has the potential to turn off Rapid PVST+ on that interface. This security feature is commonly used on interfaces that are connected to end devices such as edge ports.

The following commands are used to configure a BPDU filter on a Cisco IOS switch:

```
Switch# configure terminal
Switch(config)# interface <interface-id>
Switch(config-if)# spanning-tree bpdufilter enable
```

A BPDU guard is a security mechanism that's usually coupled with the **edge port** configurations, which prevents unexpected inbound BPDU messages from inadvertently affecting the STP process on a switch. When an interface, such as an edge port, is configured with a BPDU guard and a BPDU message arrives on the interface, the switch will change the state of the interface to `err-disabled`.

The following command is used to configure a BPDU guard on a Cisco IOS switch:

```
Switch# configure terminal
Switch(config)# interface <interface-id>
Switch(config-if)# spanning-tree bpduguard enable
```

Port Roles and States

In this section, you will learn about the various port roles and states as an interface transitions into forwarding or blocking traffic.

The following are the port roles used in Spanning Tree:

- **Root ports**: These are the ports that are closest to the root bridge. If you recall, each switch always points toward the root bridge at the end of the election process. This means each switch has a root port that points back to the root bridge on the network. Root ports are never on the root bridge itself.
- **Designated ports**: These are what are known as non-root ports, which forward traffic between devices on the network.
- **Alternate or backup ports**: These are interfaces that are in a logically blocked state that is caused by STP to prevent any layer 2 loops on redundant paths.

To view the port roles and state of each interface on a Cisco IOS switch, use the `show spanning-tree` command. *Figure 9.8* shows both the roles and states of each interface:

```
Interface          Role Sts Cost       Prio.Nbr Type
------------------ ---- --- ---------  -------- -------
Fa0/2              Desg FWD 19         128.2    P2p
Fa0/3              Desg FWD 19         128.3    P2p
Fa0/4              Desg FWD 19         128.4    P2p
Fa0/1              Desg FWD 19         128.1    P2p
Fa0/8              Desg FWD 19         128.8    P2p
Fa0/5              Desg FWD 19         128.5    P2p
Fa0/7              Root FWD 19         128.7    P2p
Fa0/6              Desg FWD 19         128.6    P2p
```

Figure 9.8: Port roles and states

When a switch boots up, its interfaces do not go directly into a forwarding state to allow traffic to flow immediately. Rather, the switch goes through a few phases. The following is the order in which an interface transitions from the time a switch boots up:

1. **Blocking**: In this state, user data is not passed onto the network. However, BPDUs are still received on the port.
2. **Listening**: This state processes BPDUs but neither forwards user traffic onto the network.
3. **Learning**: This state processes BPDUs and learns MAC addresses but does not forward frames.

4. **Forwarding**: This is the normal operating state of a switch's interface. It can send and receive users' data and process BPDUs.
5. **Disabled**: This state is administratively shut down by the device administrator.

Now that you have learned about the various port roles and states, you can learn how to identify the root bridge and each port role on a network topology.

Determining the Root Bridge and Port Roles

An important skill as an upcoming network professional is the ability to look at a Spanning Tree topology and identify the root bridge and all the port roles. In this section, you will discover the process of how easily this can be done by using the information from the previous sections and a few additional guidelines.

The following is a rule of thumb to help identify the roles of each port in Spanning Tree:

1. Identify the root bridge.
2. Identify the root ports.
3. Identify the designated ports.
4. Identify the alternate ports.

To get started, study the network topology with Spanning Tree shown in *Figure 9.9*:

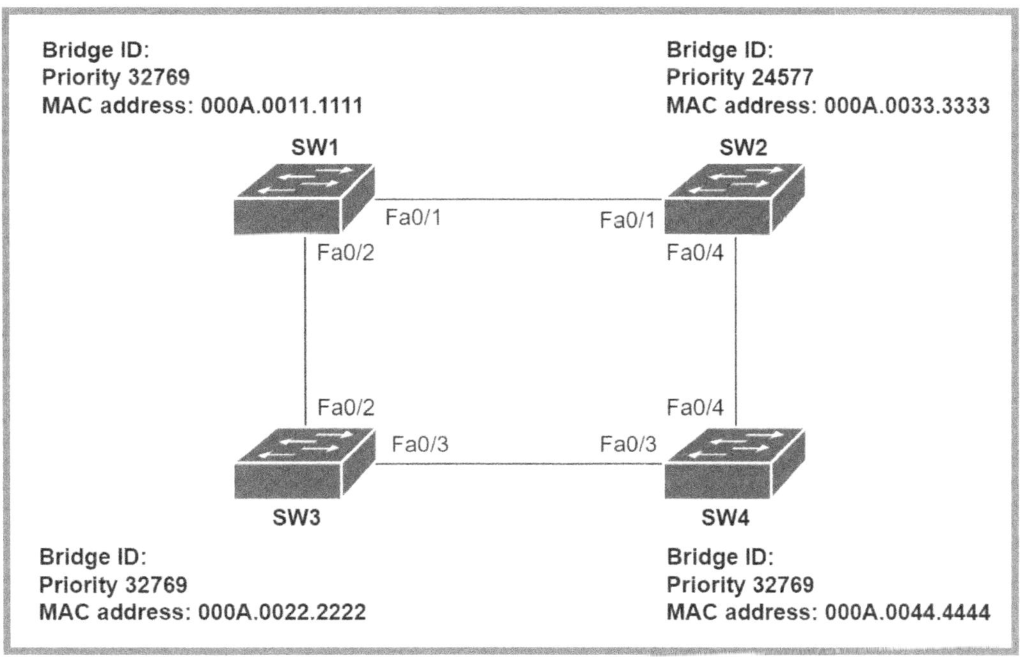

Figure 9.9: Spanning Tree topology

Using all you have learned thus far, including the guidelines and the network topology, you can now determine all the port roles and understand why each port has a specific role as well. The following steps describe how to determine what is taking place in STP:

1. Firstly, identify the root bridge. From the topology, we can see that **SW2** has the lowest bridge ID and therefore will take the role of root bridge in the network.
2. Identify all the root ports on the network. Root ports are those that are closest to the root bridge. From the topology, the **SW1** `FastEthernet 0/1` and **SW4** `FastEthernet 0/4` interfaces are the closest and directly connected to the root bridge. Therefore, these are root ports.
3. Does **SW3** have any root ports? Yes, it does. There are two paths from **SW3** to the root bridge. These are **SW3** to **SW2** and **SW3** to **SW4**. These paths are of equal cost (interface value). Therefore, you need to take a look at which device has a lower bridge ID between **SW1** and **SW4**. Looking closely, you can see that **SW1** has a lower bridge ID because the MAC address portion of the bridge ID is lower than that of **SW4**. This means the preferred path from **SW3** to the root bridge is via **SW1**. Therefore, **SW3** FastEthernet 0/2 will also be a root port.
4. Now that you have labeled all the root ports, you can assign designated ports. All ports on the root bridge are always designated ports.
5. Since the preferred path from **SW3** to the root bridge is via **SW1**, FastEthernet 0/2 on **SW1** will also be a designated port.
6. Lastly, one of the interfaces between **SW3** and **SW4** has to be an alternate port to prevent a layer 2 loop on the network. The question is how to determine which interface should be the alternate and which should be a designated port. You can take a look at their bridge IDs. Since **SW3** has a lower bridge ID than **SW4**, **SW3** FastEthernet 0/3 will be a designated port and **SW4** FastEthernet 0/3 will be the alternate port.

Figure 9.10 shows the complete port labels of each switch in your network topology:

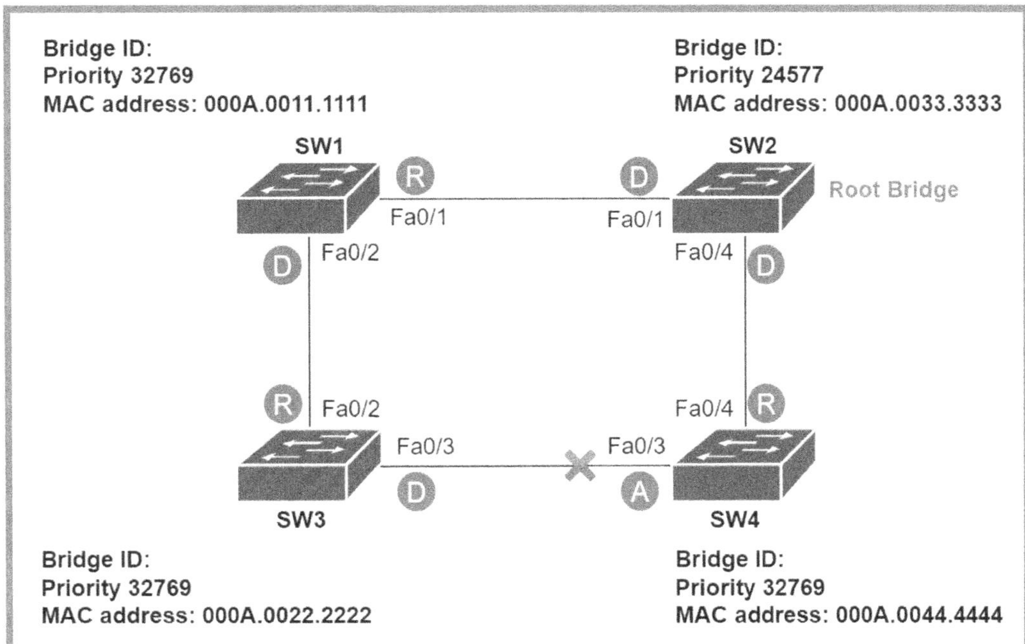

Figure 9.10: Port labels

Identifying and understanding how Spanning Tree works is important when working with networks as well as for the CCNA examination. Having completed this section, you have gained the skills to identify the roles and functions of each port in a Spanning Tree topology. In the next section, you will gain hands-on experience in implementing Spanning Tree in a Cisco environment.

Lab: Discovering the Root Bridge

It's time to get hands-on experience with how to discover the root bridge on a Cisco switch network. The network topology shown in *Figure 9.11* will be used during this exercise:

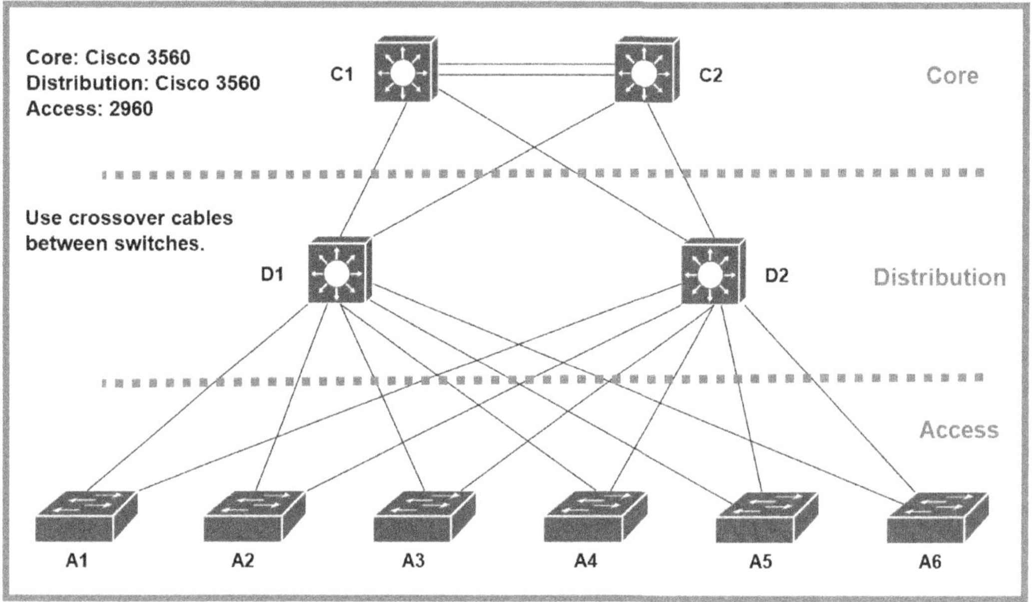

Figure 9.11: Discovering the root bridge on a Cisco network

To follow along, download the pre-built Packet Tracer template from: `http://packt.link/CCNArepoCh09`

One of the first tasks you may have as a network professional is to discover which switch within your network has the role of being the root bridge. To ensure you can successfully perform this task, please use the following instructions:

1. In an enterprise network, it's preferred and recommended that the core switch becomes the root bridge, but this is not always the expected result in many networks. Use the `show spanning-tree` command as shown in *Figure 9.12* to verify the status:

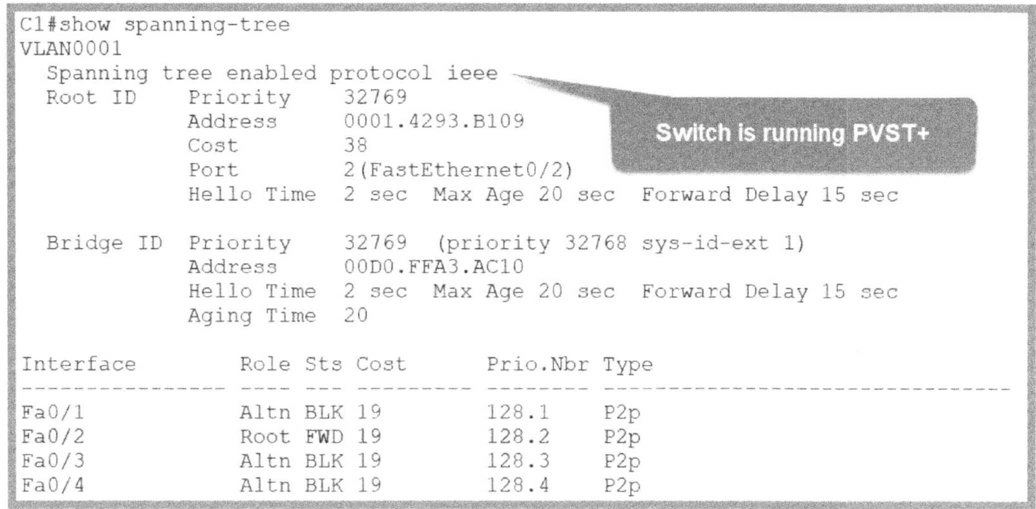

```
C1#show spanning-tree
VLAN0001
  Spanning tree enabled protocol ieee
  Root ID    Priority    32769
             Address     0001.4293.B109
             Cost        38
             Port        2(FastEthernet0/2)
             Hello Time  2 sec  Max Age 20 sec  Forward Delay 15 sec

  Bridge ID  Priority    32769  (priority 32768 sys-id-ext 1)
             Address     00D0.FFA3.AC10
             Hello Time  2 sec  Max Age 20 sec  Forward Delay 15 sec
             Aging Time  20

Interface        Role Sts Cost      Prio.Nbr Type
---------------- ---- --- --------- -------- --------------------------------
Fa0/1            Altn BLK 19        128.1    P2p
Fa0/2            Root FWD 19        128.2    P2p
Fa0/3            Altn BLK 19        128.3    P2p
Fa0/4            Altn BLK 19        128.4    P2p
```


Figure 9.12: Spanning Tree status on C1

The output shows the Spanning Tree instance for VLAN 1. Here, you can see that **C1** is running PVST+ by default, as highlighted in the snippet. Additionally, you can see the root ID information about the root bridge and **C1**'s bridge ID information.

Notice that the root ID details do not match that of **C1**'s bridge information. This is an indication that **C1** is not the root bridge. Remember, the **root ports** are always closest to the **root bridge**. Notice that **C1** has a root port, `FastEthernet 0/2`. You can use this information to help to find the root bridge.

2. Next, use the show cdp neighbors command to identify and trace the type of device that is connected to **C1** on its `FastEthernet 0/2` interface:

```
C1#show cdp neighbors
Capability Codes: R - Router, T - Trans Bridge, B - Source Route Bridge
                  S - Switch, H - Host, I - IGMP, r - Repeater, P - Phone
Device ID    Local Intrfce   Holdtme    Capability   Platform    Port ID
C2           Fas 0/3          179                    3560        Fas 0/3
C2           Fas 0/4          179                    3560        Fas 0/4
D1           Fas 0/1          131                    3560        Fas 0/7
D2           Fas 0/2          145                    3560        Fas 0/7
C1#
```

Figure 9.13: Discovering connected devices on C1

You can see that there's another switch (the 3560 model) connected to **C1**'s `FastEthernet 0/2` interface. You can now log on to **D2** and check whether it is the root bridge.

3. On **D2**, you can execute the show spanning-tree command to verify whether it is the root bridge:

```
D2#show spanning-tree
VLAN0001
  Spanning tree enabled protocol ieee
  Root ID    Priority    32769
             Address     0001.4293.B109
             Cost        19
             Port        3(FastEthernet0/3)
             Hello Time  2 sec  Max Age 20 sec  Forward Delay 15 sec

  Bridge ID  Priority    32769  (priority 32768 sys-id-ext 1)
             Address     0001.9671.BEDE
             Hello Time  2 sec  Max Age 20 sec  Forward Delay 15 sec
             Aging Time  20

Interface        Role Sts Cost      Prio.Nbr Type
---------------- ---- --- --------- -------- --------------------------
Fa0/7            Desg FWD 19        128.7    P2p
Fa0/1            Desg FWD 19        128.1    P2p
Fa0/2            Desg FWD 19        128.2    P2p
Fa0/3            Root FWD 19        128.3    P2p
Fa0/4            Desg FWD 19        128.4    P2p
```

Figure 9.14: Spanning Tree status on D2

The results indicate that **D2** is not the root bridge but it also has a root port, `FastEthernet 0/3`, which points to the root bridge.

Once again, you can use the show cdp neighbors command to identify what is connected to **D2**'s `FastEthernet 0/3` interface.

```
D2#show cdp neighbors
Capability Codes: R - Router, T - Trans Bridge, B - Source Route Bridge
                  S - Switch, H - Host, I - IGMP, r - Repeater, P - Phone
Device ID    Local Intrfce   Holdtme    Capability   Platform    Port ID
A2           Fas 0/2          146            S        2960        Fas 0/2
C2           Fas 0/8          146                     3560        Fas 0/2
A1           Fas 0/1          146            S        2960        Fas 0/2
A3           Fas 0/3          146            S        2960        Fas 0/2
A4           Fas 0/4          146            S        2960        Fas 0/2
```

Figure 9.15: Discovering connected devices on D2

You can see that there's another switch (the 2960 model) connected to **D1**'s `FastEthernet 0/3` interface. You can now log on to **D2** and check whether it's the root bridge.

4. On **A3**, you can execute the show spanning-tree command once more to verify whether it is the root bridge:

```
A3#show spanning-tree
VLAN0001
  Spanning tree enabled protocol ieee
  Root ID     Priority     32769
              Address      0001.4293.B109
              This bridge is the root
              Hello Time   2 sec   Max Age 20 sec   Forward Delay 15 sec

  Bridge ID   Priority     32769   (priority 32768 sys-id-ext 1)
              Address      0001.4293.B109
              Hello Time   2 sec   Max Age 20 sec   Forward Delay 15 sec
              Aging Time   20

Interface        Role Sts Cost      Prio.Nbr Type
---------------- ---- --- --------- -------- -------------------------
Fa0/1            Desg FWD 19        128.1    P2p
Fa0/2            Desg FWD 19        128.2    P2p
```

Figure 9.16: Spanning Tree status on A3

At this point, you have hit a pot of gold here on finding the root bridge in your topology. The first indicator that identifies the root bridge is the sentence that says, `This bridge is the root`. If you cross-reference each show spanning-tree output from all other switches in the topology, you will see that they all have the root ID that matches that of **A3**'s bridge ID details.

> **Note**
>
> Furthermore, all ports on the root bridge always have the role of being designated ports with their operating statuses as forwarding.

Throughout this lab exercise, you have seen that each switch on the topology has been using its default configurations with the exception of its hostname. Each switch has a bridge priority of 32768 and an extended system ID of 1 (for VLAN 1).

In *Figure 9.17*, the highlighted links are those made active by the root bridge, while the others are those that are logically blocked to prevent any layer 2 loops on the network:

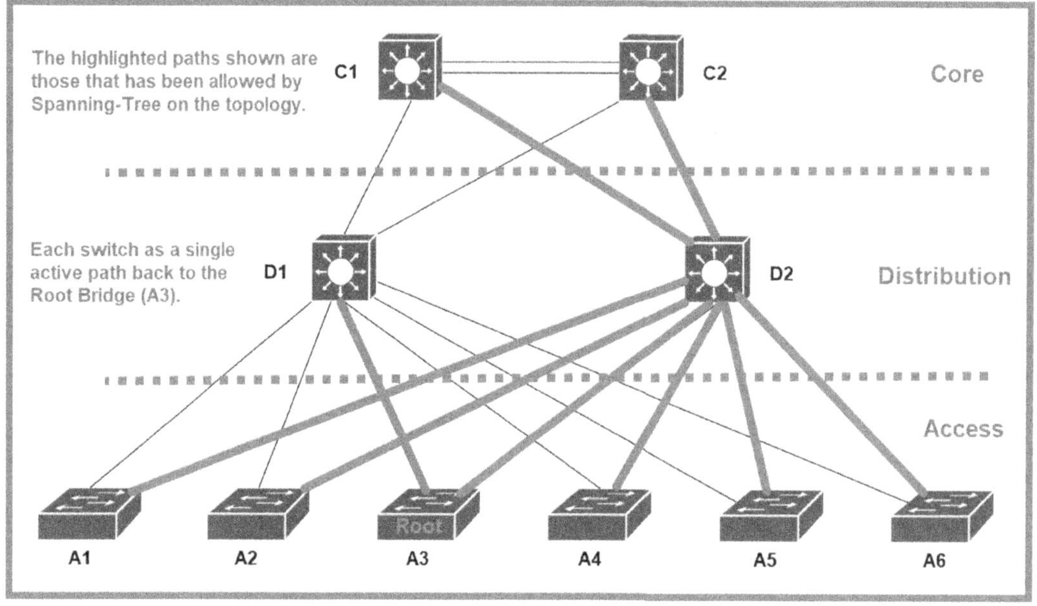

Figure 9.17: Active paths

Additionally, if you recall, the root bridge is the central reference point for all traffic on the switch network. As you have discovered, the root bridge in our network is at the access layer. The access-layer switches are not as robust and resilient as the core switches in a network with their redundant power supplies and support for hot-swappable components. Therefore, it's recommended to configure one of the core switches as the root bridge.

The intention of this exercise was to provide you with hands-on experience of discovering the root bridge on a network using one of the most important commands when learning Spanning Tree, the `show spanning-tree` command. The `show cdp neighbors` command has also been very helpful in the process.

In the next lab, you will continue using the existing topology and gain hands-on experience in configuring STP in a Cisco environment.

Lab: Implementing Rapid PVST+ on a Cisco Network

In the previous lab, you saw that the Spanning Tree election process automatically selects an access-layer (**A3**) switch as the root bridge. In this lab, you will learn how to manipulate the election process by configuring the preferred root bridge with the lowest priority in the lab topology.

To get started with this exercise, please use the following instructions:

1. By default, the Cisco IOS switch is running PVST+. You can first configure Rapid PVST+ to ensure convergence on your network. Execute the `spanning-tree mode rapid-pvst` command in global configuration mode on *all switches* on the network. The following is a demonstration on one of the core switches:

```
C1(config)# spanning-tree mode rapid-pvst
```

2. After enabling Rapid PVST+ on all switches, use the `show spanning-tree` command on each device to verify whether the new operating standard has been changed to Rapid PVST+. *Figure 9.18* shows how to identify that Rapid PVST+ is enabled:

```
C1#show spanning-tree
VLAN0001
  Spanning tree enabled protocol rstp
  Root ID     Priority    32769
              Address     0001.4293.B109
              Cost        38
              Port        2(FastEthernet0/2)
              Hello Time  2 sec  Max Age 20 sec  Forward Delay 15 sec

  Bridge ID   Priority    32769  (priority 32768 sys-id-ext 1)
              Address     00D0.FFA3.AC10
              Hello Time  2 sec  Max Age 20 sec  Forward Delay 15 sec
              Aging Time  20
```


Figure 9.18: Rapid PVST+ status

Cisco IOS has a very unusual way of telling you that Rapid PVST+ is running – in the output, it says `RSTP (Rapid Spanning Tree Protocol)`, but in reality, it is truly Rapid PVST+ that is running on the device, as shown in the preceding snippet, because Cisco runs only their proprietary version of the IEEE 802.1w.

3. To make **C1** the root bridge on the network, you need to adjust its bridge priority to be lower than all other switches on the topology. The bridge priority ranges from `0` to `61440` in increments of `4096`. We can use the following command to set a bridge priority of `4096` for VLAN 1 on our **C1** switch:

```
C1(config)# spanning-tree vlan 1 priority 4096
```

4. You can use the `show spanning-tree` command to verify that **C1** is the root bridge on the network:

```
C1#show spanning-tree
VLAN0001
  Spanning tree enabled protocol rstp
  Root ID     Priority    4097
              Address     00D0.FFA3.AC10
              This bridge is the root
              Hello Time  2 sec  Max Age 20 sec  Forward Delay 15 sec

  Bridge ID   Priority    4097  (priority 4096 sys-id-ext 1)
              Address     00D0.FFA3.AC10
              Hello Time  2 sec  Max Age 20 sec  Forward Delay 15 sec
              Aging Time  20

Interface        Role Sts Cost      Prio.Nbr Type
---------------- ---- --- --------- -------- ---------------------------
Fa0/3            Desg FWD 19        128.3    P2p
Fa0/1            Desg FWD 19        128.1    P2p
Fa0/2            Desg FWD 19        128.2    P2p
Fa0/4            Desg FWD 19        128.4    P2p
```

Figure 9.19: Root bridge status on C1

As expected, **C1** has now become the root bridge for VLAN 1 on the network and is running Rapid PVST+.

5. Additionally, you can create a secondary root bridge such that in the event **C1** goes offline, the secondary root bridge can take the role of being the primary root bridge for VLAN 1. To set **C2** as the secondary root bridge, use the following command:

```
C2(config)# spanning-tree vlan 1 priority 8192
```

To create the secondary root bridge, ensure the priority value is one increment of `4096` higher than the primary root bridge priority value.

> **Note**
>
> The Cisco IOS will not allow you to set any value that is not an increment of `4096`.

6. Lastly, check switch `A3` to verify the change has also taken place:

```
A3#show spanning-tree
VLAN0001
  Spanning tree enabled protocol rstp
  Root ID    Priority    4097
             Address     00D0.FFA3.AC10                C1 Details
             Cost        38
             Port        1(FastEthernet0/1)
             Hello Time  2 sec  Max Age 20 sec  Forward Delay 15 sec

  Bridge ID  Priority    32769  (priority 32768 sys-id-ext 1)
             Address     0001.4293.B109
             Hello Time  2 sec  Max Age 20 sec  Forward Delay 15 sec
             Aging Time  20

Interface        Role Sts Cost      Prio.Nbr Type
---------------- ---- --- --------- -------- --------------------------------
Fa0/1            Root FWD 19        128.1    P2p
Fa0/2            Desg FWD 19        128.2    P2p
```

Figure 9.20: Switch A3 points to C1 as the new root bridge

As expected, switch **A3** contains the details of the new root bridge, **C1**, within the Spanning Tree of VLAN 1 and has a root port that points toward **C1** on the topology.

In *Figure 9.21*, the highlighted links are those made active by the root bridge on the network, while the others are those that are logically blocked to prevent any layer 2 loops on the network:

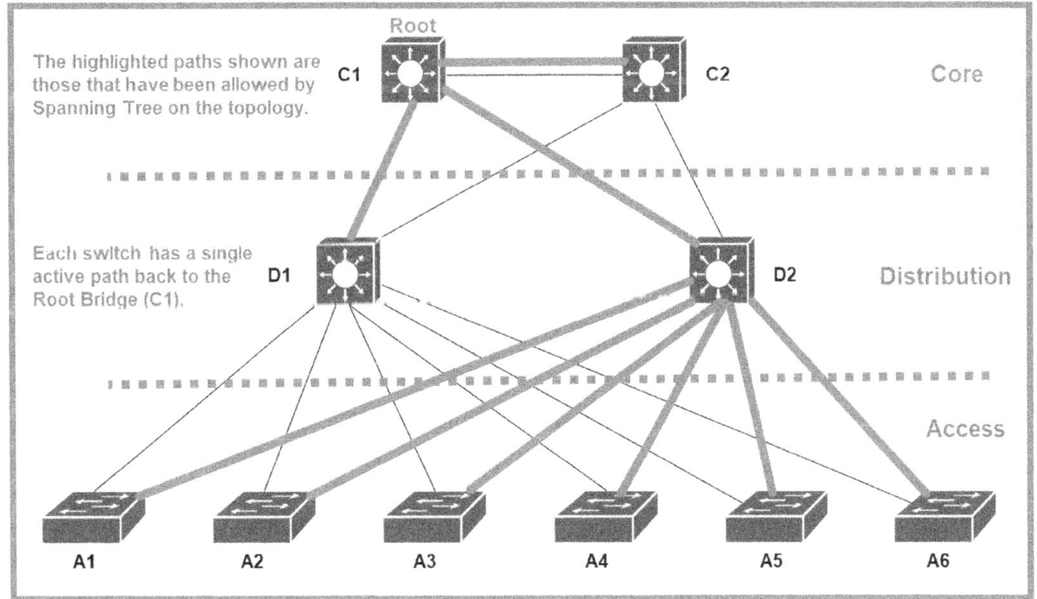

Figure 9.21: Active paths

As you can see, the entire logical topology has changed with the configuration of the new root bridge and there is only one logical path, therefore preventing any layer 2 loops on the network.

Having completed this exercise, you have gained the skills to configure and implement Rapid PVST+ on a Cisco network. In the next lab, you will continue using this existing topology where you will gain hands-on experience in configuring Portfast on a Cisco switch.

Lab: Configuring Portfast and a BPDU Guard

As you learned earlier, **Portfast** is a feature that allows an interface to transition into a **forwarding** state without going through both the **learning** and **listening** states. This feature is available when running Rapid PVST+ on a Cisco switch.

In this lab, you will learn how to configure an interface with Portfast and implement a BPDU guard to prevent any unwanted BPDU messages from entering the interface.

> **Note**
>
> These configurations should only be applied on edge ports. Edge ports are those ports that are not connected to another switch, such as end devices, routers, firewalls, and printers.

To complete this exercise, please use the following instructions:

1. Imagine a PC is connected to a switch such as **A1** on `FastEthernet 0/3`. You can implement Portfast by ensuring the interface is first configured as an access port:

   ```
   A1(config)#interface FastEthernet 0/3
   A1(config-if)#switchport mode access
   A1(config-if)#switchport nonegotiate
   ```

2. To enable the Portfast feature on the interface, use the following command:

   ```
   A1(config-if)#spanning-tree portfast
   ```

3. Once Portfast has been enabled, enable a BPDU guard to prevent BPDUs from entering the port:

   ```
   A1(config-if)#spanning-tree bpduguard enable
   ```

Figure 9.22 shows the expected sequence and outcomes of completing the previous steps:

```
A1(config)#interface FastEthernet 0/3
A1(config-if)#switchport mode access
A1(config-if)#switchport nonegotiate
A1(config-if)#spanning-tree portfast
%Warning: portfast should only be enabled on ports connected to a single
host. Connecting hubs, concentrators, switches, bridges, etc... to this
interface  when portfast is enabled, can cause temporary bridging loops.
Use with CAUTION

%Portfast has been configured on FastEthernet0/3 but will only
have effect when the interface is in a non-trunking mode.
A1(config-if)#spanning-tree bpduguard enable
A1(config-if)#exit
```

Figure 9.22: Configuring Portfast and a BPDU guard

4. Lastly, you can use the show running-config command to verify the configuration of the interface, as shown in *Figure 9.23*:

```
A1#show running-config
Building configuration...

Current configuration : 1186 bytes
!
version 12.2
no service timestamps log datetime msec
no service timestamps debug datetime msec
no service password-encryption
!
hostname A1
!
spanning-tree mode rapid-pvst
spanning-tree extend system-id
!
interface FastEthernet0/3
 switchport mode access
 switchport nonegotiate
 spanning-tree portfast
 spanning-tree bpduguard enable
!
```

Figure 9.23: running-config file

Having completed this exercise, you have acquired the skills to implement the Portfast and BPDU guard features on all edge ports within a Cisco environment.

Summary

Throughout the course of this chapter, you have learned the importance of discovering physical issues that may cause errors and collisions on a network. Having learned about speed and duplex configurations and how they affect traffic flow, you now have the essential skills to perform troubleshooting at layer 1 of the OSI reference model.

Additionally, you took a deep dive to learn how redundancy can be good but also bad and may create a layer 2 loop in the switch network. Most importantly, you read about the importance of understanding Spanning Tree and how it works to help prevent physical redundancy from taking down our enterprise network. Having completed this chapter, you have gained the skills to determine port roles in a Spanning Tree topology, configure both primary and secondary root bridges, and lastly, implement Portfast with a BPDU guard.

In the next chapter, *Chapter 10, Interpreting Routing Components*, you will learn how routers make their forwarding decisions.

Exam Readiness Drill – Chapter Review Questions

Apart from mastering key concepts, strong test-taking skills under time pressure are essential for acing your certification exam. That's why developing these abilities early in your learning journey is critical.

Exam readiness drills, using the free online practice resources provided with this book, help you progressively improve your time management and test-taking skills while reinforcing the key concepts you've learned.

HOW TO GET STARTED

- Open the link or scan the QR code at the bottom of this page
- If you have unlocked the practice resources already, log in to your registered account. If you haven't, follow the instructions in *Chapter 19* and come back to this page.
- Once you log in, click the START button to start a quiz
- We recommend attempting a quiz multiple times till you're able to answer most of the questions correctly and well within the time limit.
- You can use the following practice template to help you plan your attempts:

Working On Accuracy		
Attempt	Target	Time Limit
Attempt 1	40% or more	Till the timer runs out
Attempt 2	60% or more	Till the timer runs out
Attempt 3	75% or more	Till the timer runs out
Working On Timing		
Attempt 4	75% or more	1 minute before time limit
Attempt 5	75% or more	2 minutes before time limit
Attempt 6	75% or more	3 minutes before time limit

The above drill is just an example. Design your drills based on your own goals and make the most out of the online quizzes accompanying this book.

First time accessing the online resources? 🔓

You'll need to unlock them through a one-time process. **Head to** *Chapter 19* **for instructions.**

Open Quiz

`https://packt.link/ccnachap9`

OR scan this QR code →

10

Interpreting Routing Components

Understanding the fundamentals of IP routing on a Cisco router is an important skill each network professional must possess. If you are unable to configure routers to forward packets to remote networks, then it becomes challenging for internal users to access resources on remote IP networks. Routers help devices communicate with other systems on the internet and remote networks, access resources online, and share information with each other.

Upon completing this chapter, you will understand the process that Cisco IOS routers use to make their forwarding decisions. Additionally, you will have gained the essential skills of identifying and describing each component within the **routing table** of a router and will be able to predict the forwarding decision of each device in a Cisco environment.

This chapter covers *Domain 3, IP Connectivity*, objectives *3.1 Interpret the components of routing table* and *3.2 Determine how a router makes a forwarding decision by default*, of the *200-301 CCNA v1.1* certification exam.

In this chapter, you will learn about the following topics:

- Understanding IP routing
- Components of the routing table
- Forwarding decisions
- Routing metrics

Let's dive in!

Understanding IP Routing

Routers play an important role in networks each day. Without them, you won't be able to connect to other networks and the internet. An important question is how a router makes its decision to forward packets toward the intended destination. In this section, you will take a deep dive into learning and understanding how Cisco routers function to interconnect remote and foreign networks, allowing you to connect with remote devices and applications located within a data center or even another location somewhere on the internet.

One of the key things you may have noticed with Cisco IOS switches is that a new Cisco switch with default configurations will allow you to connect end devices to its physical interfaces and it will forward traffic (frames) without the need for additional configurations on the device. However, this is not the same with a Cisco IOS router.

The Cisco IOS router with default configurations or factory settings does not do anything such as forward traffic (packets) between its interfaces. To enable a router to perform routing operations, a network professional such as yourself has to tell the router how traffic should flow between its interfaces. In other words, without configuring the Cisco router, it will simply do nothing on a network while it is powered on.

A router has the capability to inspect the Layer 3 header of an IP packet and make a decision on how to proceed in forwarding the packet. When a packet enters an interface on a router (the inbound interface), it is de-encapsulated by removing the Layer 2 header information such as the source and destination MAC addresses. However, the router takes a look at the destination IPv4 or IPv6 address and checks its routing table for a suitable route.

The routing table is dynamically updated when a local interface on the router is assigned an IP address and it is enabled. The router also has the capability of running dynamic routing protocols that allow other routers on the network to exchange routes. A **route** is simply a path to reach a destination network. Without any routes, a router will not be able to forward packets to their destinations.

Lab: Exploring IP Routing

To gain a better understanding of how routers work, the topology shown in *Figure 10.1* represents an organization's network consisting of the headquarters and three remote offices. The organization uses a **Metro Ethernet** (**MetroE**) WAN to interconnect its branches to the **headquarters** (**HQ**); the WAN service is managed by a local **internet service provider** (**ISP**).

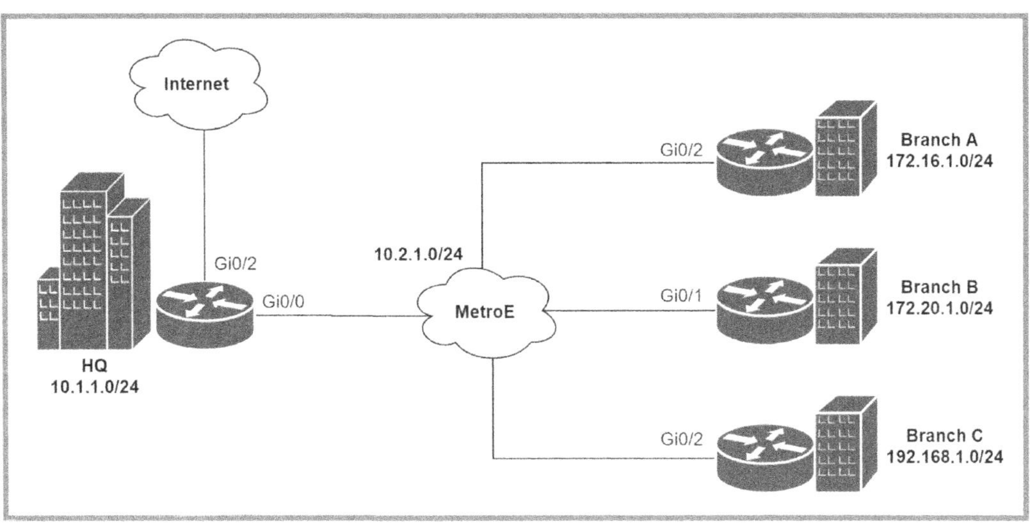

Figure 10.1: Simply network topology

> **Note**
>
> A metropolitan-area Ethernet or MetroE connection is a type of layer 2 WAN service that is commonly provided by ISPs using Ethernet standards.

Imagine a PC on the Branch A network (`172.16.1.0/24`) that wants to connect to another PC in HQ that is located on the `10.1.1.0/24` network. What path or route will the traffic take? To answer this question and fully understand what takes place behind the scenes, take a look at *Figure 10.2*, which shows a low-level view of the topology:

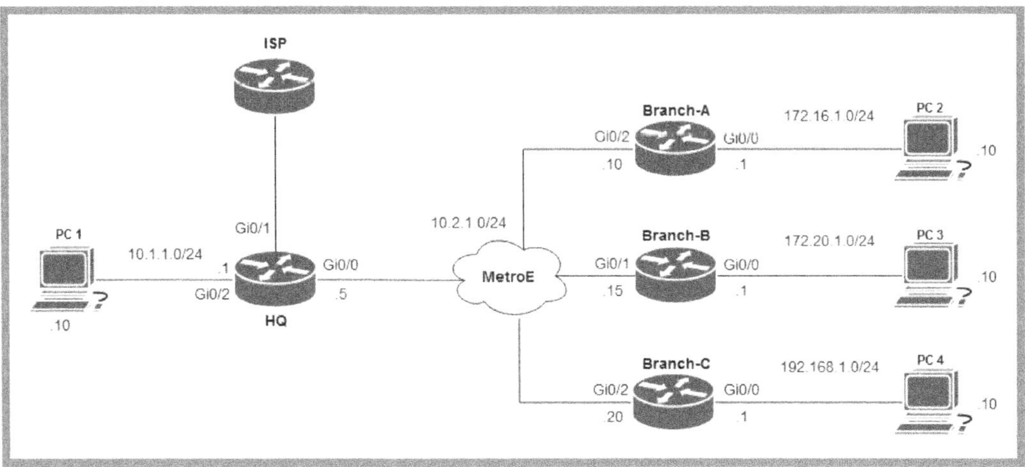

Figure 10.2: Low-level topology

To follow along with this exercise, please download and open the preceding topology within Cisco Packet Tracer, using the following link: `https://packt.link/CCNArepoCh10`

The following steps will help you understand IP routing better:

1. See whether PC 2 on the Branch A network is able to ping PC 1 on the HQ network. But first, verify the IP address on PC 2 by using the `ipconfig` command:

```
C:\>ipconfig

FastEthernet0 Connection:(default port)

   Link-local IPv6 Address.........: FE80::202:4AFF:FE61:7DD5
   IP Address......................: 172.16.1.10
   Subnet Mask.....................: 255.255.255.0
   Default Gateway.................: 172.16.1.1
```

Figure 10.3: PC 2 IP address

2. Being a good network professional, it is recommended to check network connectivity between PC 2 and its default gateway, the Branch-A router:

```
C:\>ping 172.16.1.1

Pinging 172.16.1.1 with 32 bytes of data:

Reply from 172.16.1.1: bytes=32 time=1ms TTL=255
Reply from 172.16.1.1: bytes=32 time<1ms TTL=255
Reply from 172.16.1.1: bytes=32 time<1ms TTL=255
Reply from 172.16.1.1: bytes=32 time<1ms TTL=255

Ping statistics for 172.16.1.1:
    Packets: Sent = 4, Received = 4, Lost = 0 (0% loss),
Approximate round trip times in milli-seconds:
    Minimum = 0ms, Maximum = 1ms, Average = 0ms
```

Figure 10.4: Connectivity test to the Branch A router

3. From *Figure 10.4*, it can be determined that four **ICMP echo request** messages were sent from PC 2 to the Branch-A router. The router has responded to each message with an **ICMP echo reply**. This means that PC 2 has end-to-end connectivity to its default gateway, the Branch-A router.

4. Check whether PC 2 has connectivity to PC 1. Ping PC 1 from PC 2 as shown in *Figure 10.5*:

```
C:\>ping 10.1.1.10

Pinging 10.1.1.10 with 32 bytes of data:

Reply from 172.16.1.1: Destination host unreachable.
Reply from 172.16.1.1: Destination host unreachable.
Reply from 172.16.1.1: Destination host unreachable.
Reply from 172.16.1.1: Destination host unreachable.

Ping statistics for 10.1.1.10:
    Packets: Sent = 4, Received = 0, Lost = 4 (100% loss),
```

Figure 10.5: Connectivity failure between PC 2 and PC 1

5. This time, the results are different. Whenever the response is `Destination host [or network] unreachable`, it means the device you are testing connectivity from does not know how to reach the destination host or network. In the previous step, PC 2 was able to reach its default gateway.
6. Attempt to perform some basic troubleshooting to further investigate and learn why there's no end-to-end connectivity. Use the `traceroute` tool in Microsoft Windows to check the path the packet will take from PC 2 to PC 1:

```
C:\>tracert 10.1.1.10

Tracing route to 10.1.1.10 over a maximum of 30 hops:

  1    1 ms      1 ms      0 ms      172.16.1.1
  2    0 ms      *         0 ms      172.16.1.1
  3    *         0 ms      *         Request timed out.
```

Figure 10.6: Performing traceroute

7. The `traceroute` utility uses the **Internet Control Message Protocol** (**ICMP**) to send ICMP echo requests to a destination host device, adjusting the **time to live** (**TTL**) value of each packet it sends to the destination. The purpose of this tool is to check the path between two devices and also check for latency issues between hops. A hop is each Layer 3 device the packet has to pass to reach its destination.

Note

On Microsoft Windows systems, the `tracert` command is used within Command Prompt while Linux and Cisco devices use the `traceroute` command.

8. The `traceroute` output shows that `Request timed out` messages start to appear at 172.16.1.1 (Branch-A router). At this point, network professionals would begin troubleshooting to better understand why they are experiencing a connectivity problem.

9. Head over to the Branch-A router and check its routing table using the `show ip route` command in Privileged EXEC mode:

```
Gateway of last resort is not set

     10.0.0.0/8 is variably subnetted, 2 subnets, 2 masks
C       10.2.1.0/24 is directly connected, GigabitEthernet0/2
L       10.2.1.10/32 is directly connected, GigabitEthernet0/2
     172.16.0.0/16 is variably subnetted, 2 subnets, 2 masks
C       172.16.1.0/24 is directly connected, GigabitEthernet0/0
L       172.16.1.1/32 is directly connected, GigabitEthernet0/0
```

Figure 10.7: Routing table of the Branch-A router

10. The Cisco IOS router only contains destination routes within its routing table. In *Figure 10.7*, there is no destination network of 10.1.1.0/24 in any of the rows (entries). If a route is not present here, it simply means the router does not know how to forward the packet to the 10.1.1.0/24 network and will send an ICMP message back to PC 2, indicating that it does not have a valid route to the destination, hence the response was `Destination host unreachable`.

Furthermore, the Branch-A router only knows about two unique networks: the 10.2.1.0/24 network that is used for the MetroE WAN connection on the `GigabitEthernet0/2` interface and the 172.16.1.0/24 network that is connected to `GigabitEthernet0/0` for the LAN interface. However, the Branch-A router does not know about the other three LANs: the Branch-B, Branch-C, and HQ locations.

If the Branch-A router had known about all networks within the topology, the expected route would be pointing toward the HQ router at the IP address 10.2.1.5. Routers are not concerned about the entire path a packet will take to reach a destination host or network. All a router is concerned about is handing off the packet to the next hop, which is another router that will forward the packet toward its destination. Keep in mind that this process is repeated until the packet is delivered.

> **Note**
>
> Cisco routers read their routing table from top to bottom each time they check for a suitable or available route.

The following is a breakdown of the actions carried out by a router when it receives an IP packet:

1. When a router receives an IP packet on one of its interfaces, it checks the destination IP address with the Layer 3 header of the packet.
2. It then uses the destination IP address and checks its routing table for an available route (path).
3. If a suitable route is found, it sends the packet to the next hop via the exit interface.
4. If a route is not found, the router checks for a gateway of last resort to forward the packet.
5. If neither route is found, the router replies to the sender with a `Destination host [network] not found` message.

Now that you have completed this section, you have learned how Cisco IOS routers determine a suitable path to forward a packet. In the next section, you will learn about each component within the routing table in detail.

Components of the Routing Table

To further understand how routers make forwarding decisions between networks, it's important to understand each component of the routing table within a Cisco IOS router. In this section, you will learn about the essential components that are part of the routing table, such as the following:

- Routing protocol codes
- Prefix
- Network mask
- Next hop
- Administrative distance
- Metric
- Gateway of last resort

Let's dive in!

Routing Protocol Codes

When you execute the `show ip route` command on a Cisco router, the very first thing you will see is a concise list of codes. This list is formally referred to as routing protocol codes. Each code is used to help you identify how a route has been learned and added to the routing table.

Figure 10.8 shows the routing protocol codes of a Cisco IOS router:

```
Branch-A#show ip route
Codes: L - local, C - connected, S - static, R - RIP, M - mobile, B - BGP
       D - EIGRP, EX - EIGRP external, O - OSPF, IA - OSPF inter area
       N1 - OSPF NSSA external type 1, N2 - OSPF NSSA external type 2
       E1 - OSPF external type 1, E2 - OSPF external type 2, E - EGP
       i - IS-IS, L1 - IS-IS level-1, L2 - IS-IS level-2, ia - IS-IS inter area
       * - candidate default, U - per-user static route, o - ODR
       P - periodic downloaded static route
```

Figure 10.8: Routing protocol codes

The following is a brief description of the essential codes as a CCNA student:

- `C` – This code indicates that the route is **directly connected** to the router. To put it simply, when you can configure an IP address on a router's interface and enable the port, the router then automatically inserts a directly connected route to that network within its routing table.
- `L` – This code indicates that the route is a **local route**. A local route is one that points not to a network like the others but to a specific host device on a network. By default, local routes are commonly inserted into the routing table when you configure an IP address on an active interface on a router. If you look closely at a routing table, you will notice the IP address on a local route is the same as the address on the interface. Additionally, you can configure a local route that points to a device on a remote network.
- `S` – This code indicates that the route has been manually configured and inserted in the routing table; this is known as a **static route**. Static routes are administratively configured and do not change unless they are modified by the network professional.
- `R` – This routing code indicates that the router has learned about a remote network via a dynamic routing protocol known as **Routing Information Protocol** (**RIP**). RIP is an old routing protocol that allows routers to simultaneously exchange routing information and update their routing tables automatically. RIP is used within an internal network.
- `B` – This code indicates that the router has learned about a remote network via the **Border Gateway Protocol** (**BGP**). BGP is known as an **Exterior Gateway Protocol** (**EGP**) and is commonly used on the internet between ISPs to exchange public networks.
- `D` – This routing code indicates that the route has been learned by the **Enhanced Interior Gateway Routing Protocol** (**EIGRP**).

- `EX` – This code indicates that an external route such as the route to the internet has been learned via EIGRP.
- `O` – This code indicates that the route has been learned by the **Open Shortest Path First** (**OSPF**) routing protocol.
- `*` – This code indicates that the route is a **default route** that usually points to the internet. This code is commonly coupled with other routing codes, as you will discover in the next chapter.

Figure 10.9 shows the current routing table of the Branch-A router:

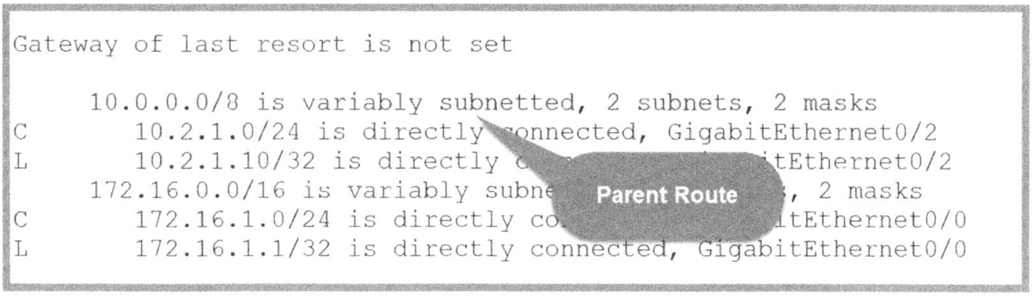

```
Gateway of last resort is not set

     10.0.0.0/8 is variably subnetted, 2 subnets, 2 masks
C       10.2.1.0/24 is directly connected, GigabitEthernet0/2
L       10.2.1.10/32 is directly                    tEthernet0/2
     172.16.0.0/16 is variably subne   Parent Route  , 2 masks
C       172.16.1.0/24 is directly co                tEthernet0/0
L       172.16.1.1/32 is directly connected, GigabitEthernet0/0
```

Figure 10.9: Parent route

Within the routing table, you will commonly see routes installed without an actual path or way to reach the destination network. The highlighted route is known as a parent route. The **parent route** is usually indicated by a classful network ID. In the preceding screenshot, the parent route contains a destination network of 10.0.0.0./8 with two child routes for the destination networks: 10.2.1.0/24 and 10.2.1.10/32.

Take a look at *Figure 10.10*, which shows examples of child routes on the Branch-A router:

```
Gateway of last resort is not set

     10.0.0.0/8 is variably subnetted, 2 subnets, 2 masks
C       10.2.1.0/24 is directly connected, GigabitEthernet0/2
L       10.2.1.10/32 is directly connected, GigabitEthernet0/2
     172.16.0.0/16 is variably subnetted, 2 subnets, 2 masks
C       172.16.1.0/24 is directly connected, GigabitEthernet0/0
L       172.16.1.1/32 is directly connected, GigabitEthernet0/0
```

Figure 10.10: Child routes

Looking closely, only child routes contain the routing protocol codes, not parent routes. A feature of Cisco IOS is that it places each route in numerical order within the routing table, which makes it easy for both network professionals and the router to perform route lookups.

Figure 10.11 shows an example of routes learned via the OSPF routing protocol:

```
Branch-A#show ip route

Gateway of last resort is 10.2.1.5 to network 0.0.0.0

      2.0.0.0/8 is variably subnetted, 2 subnets, 2 masks
C        2.2.2.0/24 is directly connected, Loopback0
L        2.2.2.2/32 is directly connected, Loopback0
      10.0.0.0/8 is variably subnetted, 3 subnets, 2 masks
O        10.1.1.0/24 [110/2] via 10.2.1.5, 00:01:21, GigabitEthernet0/2
C        10.2.1.0/24 is directly connected, GigabitEthernet0/2
L        10.2.1.10/32 is directly connected, GigabitEthernet0/2
      172.16.0.0/16 is variabl                        2 masks
C        172.16.1.0/24 is dir                         thernet0/0
L        172.16.1.1/32 is d                          Ethernet0/0
      172.20.0.0/24 is s  netted, 1 subnets
O        172.20.1.0/24 [110/2] via 10.2.1.15, 00:01:21, GigabitEthernet0/2
O     192.168.1.0/24 [110/2] via 10.2.1.20, 00:01:11, GigabitEthernet0/2
O*E2 0.0.0.0/0 [110/1] via 10.2.1.5, 00:01:21, GigabitEthernet0/2
```

Dynamically learnt routes

Figure 10.11: Dynamically learned routes

A dynamically learned route always contains extra parameters within the route as compared to both the local and directly connected routes. Over the next few sections, you will take a look at these additional components and their functions.

Prefix and Network Mask

An important component of the routing table and specifically part of a route is the prefix. The prefix is identified as the destination network ID. When the route is looking for a suitable route, it checks the prefix of each installed route in its routing table for a suitable match.

Figure 10.12 shows the prefix within the routing table:

```
Gateway of last resort is 10.2.1.5 to network 0.0.0.0

      2.0.0.0/8 is variably subnetted, 2 subnets, 2 masks
C        2.2.2.0/24 is directly connected, Loopback0
L        2.2.2.2/32 is directly connected, Loopback0
      10.0.0.0/8 is variably subnetted, 3 subnets, 2 masks
O        10.1.1.0/24 [110/2] via 10.2.1.5, 00:05:16, GigabitEthernet0/2
C        10.2.1.0/24 is directly connected, GigabitEthernet0/2
L        10.2.1.10/32 is directly connected, GigabitEthernet0/2
      172.16.0.0/16 is variably subnetted, 2 subnets, 2 masks
C        172.16.1.0/24 is directly connected, GigabitEthernet0/0
L        172.16.1.1/32 is directly connected, GigabitEthernet0/0
      172.20.0.0/24 is subnetted, 1 subnets
O        172.20.1.0/24 [110/2] via 10.2.1.15, 00:05:16, GigabitEthernet0/2
O*E2  0.0.0.0/0 [110/1] via 10.2.1.5, 00:05:16, GigabitEthernet0/2
```

Prefix

Figure 10.12: Prefix

For every prefix within the routing table, there is an associated network mask in */x* format. In the following snippet, the highlighted area within each route shows the network mask after the prefix:

```
Gateway of last resort is 10.2.1.5 to network 0.0.0.0

      2.0.0.0/8 is variably subnetted, 2 subnets, 2 masks
C        2.2.2.0/24 is directly connected, Loopback0
L        2.2.2.2/32 is directly connected, Loopback0
      10.0.0.0/8 is variably subnetted, 3 subnets, 2 masks
O        10.1.1.0/24 [110/2] via 10.2.1.5, 00:05:16, GigabitEthernet0/2
C        10.2.1.0/24 is directly connected, GigabitEthernet0/2
L        10.2.1.10/32 is directly connected, GigabitEthernet0/2
      172.16.0.0/16 is variably subnetted, 2 subnets, 2 masks
C        172.16.1.0/24 is directly connected, GigabitEthernet0/0
L        172.16.1.1/32 is directly connected, GigabitEthernet0/0
      172.20.0.0/24 is subnetted, 1 subnets
O        172.20.1.0/24 [110/2] via 10.2.1.15, 00:05:16, GigabitEthernet0/2
O*E2  0.0.0.0/0 [110/1] via 10.2.1.5, 00:05:16, GigabitEthernet0/2
```

Network Mask

Figure 10.13: Network mask

The network mask in the routing table represents the subnet mask for each prefix (network ID). If you recall, in *Chapter 4, IPv4 and IPv6 Addressing*, and *Chapter 5, Practical Subnetting*, the subnet masks were represented in binary and played various important roles on a network.

Next Hop

When a remote route is inserted into the routing table, the next hop is usually associated with reaching the destination network. To get a better understanding, look at *Figure 10.14*:

```
Gateway of last resort is 10.2.1.5 to network 0.0.0.0

      2.0.0.0/8 is variably subnetted, 2 subnets, 2 masks
C        2.2.2.0/24 is directly connected, Loopback0
L        2.2.2.2/32 is directly connected, Loopback0
      10.0.0.0/8 is variably subnetted, 3 subnets, 2 masks
O        10.1.1.0/24 [110/2] via 10.2.1.5, 00:07:45, GigabitEthernet0/2
C        10.2.1.0/24 is directly connected, GigabitEthernet0/2
L        10.2.1.10/32 is directly connected, Gi              /2
      172.16.0.0/16 is variably subnetted, 2 su
C        172.16.1.0/24 is directly connected,                 0
L        172.16.1.1/32 is directly connecte  , GigabitEthernet0/0
      172.20.0.0/24 is subnetted, 1 subnets
O        172.20.1.0/24 [110/2] via 10.2.1.15, 00:07:45, GigabitEthernet0/2
O     192.168.1.0/24 [110/2] via 10.2.1.20, 00:07:45, GigabitEthernet0/2
O*E2  0.0.0.0/0 [110/1] via 10.2.1.5, 00:07:45, GigabitEthernet0/2
```

Next-Hop

Figure 10.14: Next hop

In *Figure 10.14*, you can identify a total of four remote networks learned via the OSFP routing protocol. Take a look at the route for the 10.1.1.0/24 network. In our topology, you can see this network is located on the HQ LAN, and the only way a branch router is able to forward a packet to that network is for the packet to be sent to the HQ router on the 10.2.1.5 address.

Break down the route and the topology a bit further. Once again, you can dissect the following route:

```
O        10.1.1.0/24 [110/2] via 10.2.1.5, 00:07:45, GigabitEthernet0/2
```

The following can be determined from the preceding network route:

- The route was learned via the OSPF routing protocol.
- The destination network is 10.1.1.0/24.
- The only way to reach the destination network (10.1.1.0/24) is through 10.2.1.5, which is known as the next hop in the routing table.
- The timer indicates how long the route has been added to the routing table.
- The interface (`GigabitEthernet0/2`) represents the exit interface. The exit interface is simply the exit door from the Branch-A router that leads toward 10.2.1.5.

In the next chapter, you will learn that not all configured routes have a next hop, as some use only an exit interface while others use a next hop or even both at times.

Administrative Distance

Each day, in a city, many commuters travel to and from a destination. In today's world, there is also more than one mode of transportation available, depending on your geographic location. You are familiar with using common public transportation services. However, during certain hours of the day and night, transportation may be a bit of a challenge.

Today, citizens can even simply request a taxi from a taxi service. Unlike traditional public transportation services, a private taxi can take an alternate and faster route to ensure that their customers (passengers) arrive at their destinations on time. You are probably wondering how a taxi service and choosing a better route explains **administrative distance** (**AD**) in a computer network.

AD is simply the **trustworthiness** of a route or path. A Cisco IOS router can support multiple routing protocols running at the same time. Each routing protocol has its own algorithm that is used to make a decision in choosing the best path or route to forward packets to a destination.

Take a look at the topology in *Figure 10.15*:

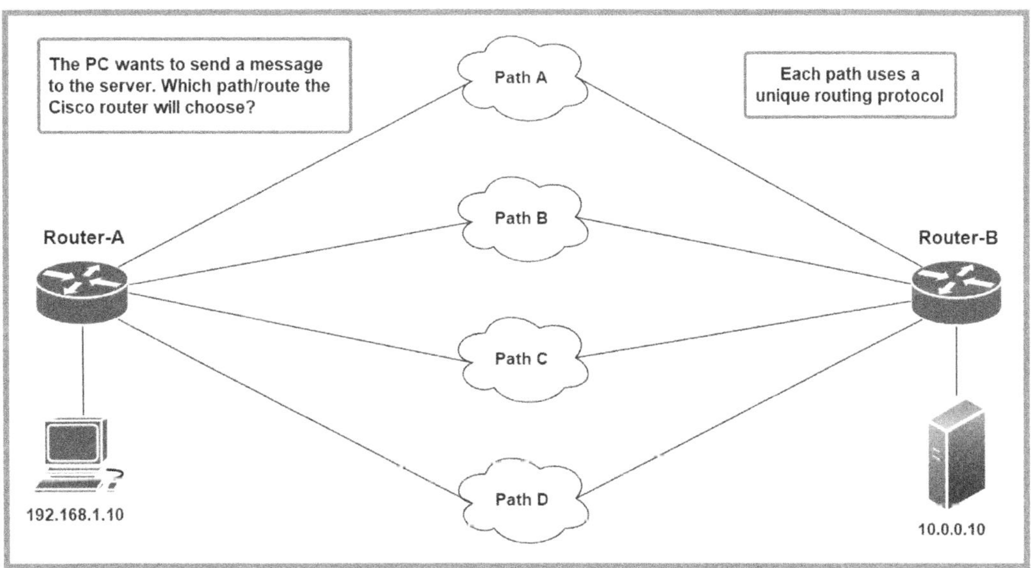

Figure 10.15: AD topology

In *Figure 10.15*, imagine the PC wants to send a message to the server. The following are the steps taken by the PC and the router when forwarding a packet:

1. The PC will check the destination's IP address and determine whether 10.0.0.10 belongs on the same IP network as the PC. Since it's a different network, the PC will proceed to send the message to its default gateway. Additionally, the PC will set the destination MAC address as that of the default gateway, Router-A. This is how end devices send messages to the default gateway that is intending to leave the network.

> **Note**
> The default gateway is a device such as a router that has a path to the internet or a foreign network that does not belong to the organization.

2. When the router receives the incoming packet from the PC, it will de-encapsulate it and check the destination IP address. In this scenario, the destination IP address is 10.0.0.10.
3. The router will then check its routing table for a suitable route (path) to forward the packet.

At this point, the router is connected to four routes to reach the server: Path A, Path B, Path C, and Path D. Assume each path has a unique routing protocol:

- RIP configured on Path A
- OSPF configured on Path B
- EIGRP configured on Path C
- Static route configured on Path D

What would the router do? Cisco has set the default AD for each routing protocol and source of a route within their Cisco IOS for all their devices. *Table 10.1* shows the ADs for each routing protocol and the source of a route:

Routing Protocol	Administrative Distance
Connected	0
Static	1
External BGP (eBGP)	20
EIGRP	90
OSPF	110
RIP	120
Internal BGP (iBGP)	200

Table 10.1: AD table

Back to the scenario, from *Table 10.1*, the route with the lowest AD will be the most preferred route to the destination network (the static route via Path D) because it has an AD of 1, which is the lowest of the other routing protocols and paths.

Another important question is how can you determine the AD of a route. As an aspiring networking professional, the simplest method is learning the table provided. Additionally, for each route the routers have installed within its routing table, the router inserts the AD value after the prefix and network mask, as shown in *Figure 10.16*:

```
Gateway of last resort is 10.2.1.5 to network 0.0.0.0

     2.0.0.0/8 is variably subne                2 masks
C       2.2.2.0/24 is directly                 ck0
L       2.2.2.2/32 is directl                 ack0
     10.0.0.0/8 is variabl  subnetted, 3 subnets, 2 masks
O       10.1.1.0/24 [110/2] via 10.2.1.5, 00:05:16, GigabitEthernet0/2
C       10.2.1.0/24 is directly connected, GigabitEthernet0/2
L       10.2.1.10/32 is directly connected, GigabitEthernet0/2
     172.16.0.0/16 is variably subnetted, 2 subnets, 2 masks
C       172.16.1.0/24 is directly connected, GigabitEthernet0/0
L       172.16.1.1/32 is directly connected, GigabitEthernet0/0
     172.20.0.0/24 is subnetted, 1 subnets
O       172.20.1.0/24 [110/2] via 10.2.1.15, 00:05:16, GigabitEthernet0/2
O*E2 0.0.0.0/0 [110/1] via 10.2.1.5, 00:05:16, GigabitEthernet0/2
```


Figure 10.16: AD in the routing table

Imagine if the routing table of a Cisco IOS router does not contain any routing protocol code. How, then, would a network professional determine the source of the route? By simply looking at the AD value next to each prefix and cross-referencing the table in *Table 10.1*, you can quickly determine the routing protocol, and vice versa.

If you look closely at the preceding routing table, you see that directly connected (`C`) routes do not contain any ADs. It is simply implied that the AD value is 0, where 0 is the most trustworthy route as it is physically connected to the router.

Routing Metric

What if the router is using only one routing protocol, such as OSPF, and there are multiple paths to the same destination network? What will the router do? The router will check the metric value for each possible route and will only install the route that has the lowest metric.

> **Note**
>
> The metric is also referred to as the cost of a route. Each routing protocol uses its own algorithm to calculate the best possible path to a destination network and assigns a numerical value (metric) to each available path.

Figure 10.17 shows a routing table containing various routes and their metric value:

```
Gateway of last resort is 10.2.1.5 to network 0.0.0.0

     2.0.0.0/8 is variably subnet          , 2 masks
C       2.2.2.0/24 is directly c          ack0
L       2.2.2.2/32 is directly             back0
     10.0.0.0/8 is variably  ubnetted, 3 subnets, 2 masks
O       10.1.1.0/24 [110/2] via 10.2.1.5, 00:05:16, GigabitEthernet0/2
C       10.2.1.0/24 is directly connected, GigabitEthernet0/2
L       10.2.1.10/32 is directly connected, GigabitEthernet0/2
     172.16.0.0/16 is variably subnetted, 2 subnets, 2 masks
C       172.16.1.0/24 is directly connected, GigabitEthernet0/0
L       172.16.1.1/32 is directly connected, GigabitEthernet0/0
     172.20.0.0/24 is subnetted, 1 subnets
O       172.20.1.0/24 [110/2] via 10.2.1.15, 00:05:16, GigabitEthernet0/2
O*E2 0.0.0.0/0 [110/1] via 10.2.1.5, 00:05:16, GigabitEthernet0/2
```


Figure 10.17: Routing table showing metric value

As mentioned, each routing protocol uses a different method of calculating the metric (cost) to reach a destination network. Here, you can take a brief look at the metrics used by each IGP. The following is a brief list of dynamic routing protocols.

RIP

RIP is one of the first generation of routing protocols that allowed routers to automatically learn about new networks and update with a routing table if a change was made on the network topology. The downside of RIP is that it uses a metric of **hop count** and supports a maximum hop count of only 15. This means that between a sender and a destination network, there must exist 15 or fewer routers. If there are more than 15 hops from the sender and the destination, the 15th hop router will discard the packet and the sender of the message will receive a `Destination host unreachable` response from the router.

If you recall, an IP packet contains a TTL field that contains a numerical value that decreases as it passes each hop (router or Layer 3 device) along the way to its destination. This is a loop-prevention mechanism to ensure that a packet does not live forever on a computer network.

> **Note**
>
> RIP is a distance-vector routing protocol. However, RIP is no longer a path in the CCNA 200-301 examination objectives.

Lastly, RIP uses the **Bellman-Ford** algorithm, which calculates the hop count between a local router and the destination networks. It will use the route with the lowest number of hops (metric) and install it within the routing table.

OSPF

The OSPF routing protocol uses the **shortest path first** (**SPF**) algorithm, which was created by Edsger Dijkstra and was designed to use the **cumulative bandwidth** to calculate the metrics for a route (path) to a destination network. With OSPF, it doesn't matter how many hops a packet has to pass before reaching its destination but rather the fastest route to reach there.

EIGRP

EIGRP was a proprietary Cisco protocol until 2013. It uses the **diffusing update algorithm** (**DUAL**) to calculate the best and most cost-effective path. Unlike the other dynamic routing protocols, EIGRP is considered a hybrid routing protocol as it not only calculates the best loop-free path to a destination network but also a backup loop-free path, such that in the event the main path goes down, EIGRP can almost immediately place the backup loop-free path into the routing table.

> **Note**
>
> EIGRP is no longer part of the 200-301 CCNA examination objectives.

DUAL uses the following to calculate the metric for network routes:

- `Bandwidth`
- `Delay`
- `TX Load`
- `RX Load`
- `Reliability`

These are known as EIGRP metric weights and are represented by a `K` value. By default, EIGRP only uses the `Bandwidth` and `Delay` values during its metric calculations. The other metrics (`TX Load`, `RX Load`, and `Reliability`) are turned off by default.

Gateway of Last Resort

The last component of the routing table, and one that has a lot of importance, is the gateway of last resort. This is the default gateway that is inserted within the routing table of a Cisco router. Cisco routers also need to be configured with a default gateway that points to the internet. Without a gateway of last resort, Cisco routers will not be able to forward traffic from the internal LANs to the internet.

The gateway of last resort is either statically configured by a network professional on the Cisco router or it can be distributed via a dynamic routing protocol such as OSPF.

Figure 10.18 shows that a Cisco route has a gateway of last resort within its routing table:

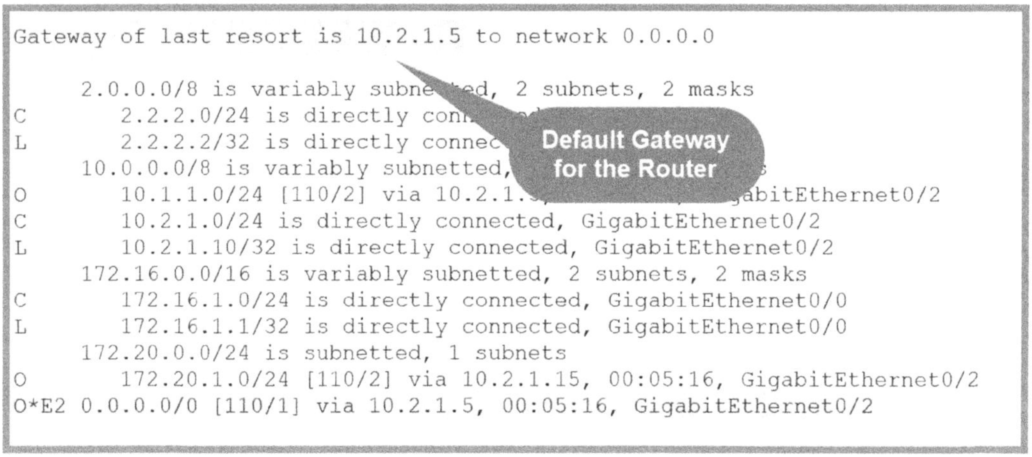

```
Gateway of last resort is 10.2.1.5 to network 0.0.0.0

      2.0.0.0/8 is variably subne   ed, 2 subnets, 2 masks
C        2.2.2.0/24 is directly con
L        2.2.2.2/32 is directly connec
      10.0.0.0/8 is variably subnetted,
O        10.1.1.0/24 [110/2] via 10.2.1.                 abitEthernet0/2
C        10.2.1.0/24 is directly connected, GigabitEthernet0/2
L        10.2.1.10/32 is directly connected, GigabitEthernet0/2
      172.16.0.0/16 is variably subnetted, 2 subnets, 2 masks
C        172.16.1.0/24 is directly connected, GigabitEthernet0/0
L        172.16.1.1/32 is directly connected, GigabitEthernet0/0
      172.20.0.0/24 is subnetted, 1 subnets
O        172.20.1.0/24 [110/2] via 10.2.1.15, 00:05:16, GigabitEthernet0/2
O*E2 0.0.0.0/0 [110/1] via 10.2.1.5, 00:05:16, GigabitEthernet0/2
```


Figure 10.18: Gateway of last resort

In *Figure 10.18*, the gateway of last resort is 10.2.1.5. Additionally, the last route in the routing table contains a default route that is learned via OSPF and also has a next hop of 10.2.1.5. As an upcoming network professional, default routes are always placed at the bottom of the routing table.

> **Note**
>
> A default route is one that is configured to point toward any network that does not exist within a routing table. Cisco routers do not contain every network that exists on the internet; if they did, the routing table would be extra large. The default route is designed to send traffic to a device that leads to the internet; this device is known as the gateway of last resort.

The reason for such placement is that when a router performs a lookup, it always starts at the top of the list and works its way down. If there are no available routes to forward the packet, the default route is used to forward the packet. However, if a router does not have an available route or a default route, the router sends a `Destination unreachable` message back to the sender.

Having completed this section, you have gained the essential skills to predict the decisions that a Cisco router will make when populating routes within its routing table and its forwarding decisions to ensure that the packets always take the most trusted and cost-efficient path to their destinations.

Summary

In this chapter, you learned about the strategies that Cisco IOS routers use to forward packets to their intended destinations. You looked at the routing table and broke down each component to give you a much greater understanding of their purpose and responsibility on the router. You learned how to predict the forwarding decision of a Cisco router if multiple routing protocols are giving a route to the same destination network and if the same routing protocol has multiple paths to the same network, and how to predict the outcomes if there are multiple paths with the same cost (metric).

In the next chapter, *Chapter 11, Understanding Static and Dynamic Routing*, you will take a deep dive into learning how to set up both static and dynamic routing protocols to ensure IP connectivity between multiple networks in a Cisco environment.

Additional Reading

- Route selection: `https://www.cisco.com/c/en/us/support/docs/ip/enhanced-interior-gateway-routing-protocol-eigrp/8651-21.html`
- Understanding the routing table: `https://www.ciscopress.com/articles/article.asp?p=2180210&seqNum=12`

Exam Readiness Drill – Chapter Review Questions

Apart from mastering key concepts, strong test-taking skills under time pressure are essential for acing your certification exam. That's why developing these abilities early in your learning journey is critical.

Exam readiness drills, using the free online practice resources provided with this book, help you progressively improve your time management and test-taking skills while reinforcing the key concepts you've learned.

HOW TO GET STARTED

- Open the link or scan the QR code at the bottom of this page
- If you have unlocked the practice resources already, log in to your registered account. If you haven't, follow the instructions in *Chapter 19* and come back to this page.
- Once you log in, click the START button to start a quiz
- We recommend attempting a quiz multiple times till you're able to answer most of the questions correctly and well within the time limit.
- You can use the following practice template to help you plan your attempts:

Working On Accuracy		
Attempt	Target	Time Limit
Attempt 1	40% or more	Till the timer runs out
Attempt 2	60% or more	Till the timer runs out
Attempt 3	75% or more	Till the timer runs out
Working On Timing		
Attempt 4	75% or more	1 minute before time limit
Attempt 5	75% or more	2 minutes before time limit
Attempt 6	75% or more	3 minutes before time limit

The above drill is just an example. Design your drills based on your own goals and make the most out of the online quizzes accompanying this book.

First time accessing the online resources? 🔓

You'll need to unlock them through a one-time process. **Head to** *Chapter 19* **for instructions.**

Open Quiz

`https://packt.link/ccnachap10`

OR scan this QR code →

11 Understanding Static and Dynamic Routing

Routers are computers too and they help organizations interconnect different IP networks together. Without them, you would not be able to communicate or exchange messages with a device or user on another IP network. These devices are smart and help forward packets to their intended destinations. Routers determine the best path to forward packets to their destinations rather than you having to make a decision each time a device wants to exchange a message across a network.

In this chapter, you will learn about static routing, the types of static routes that can be implemented on a network, and their use cases. Furthermore, you will learn how to configure dynamic routing protocols and perform static routing on Cisco IOS routers. Throughout this chapter, you will learn the differences and use cases of both dynamic and static routing while gaining the real-world, hands-on experiences needed to perform IP routing for a small to medium-sized network.

This chapter covers *Domain 3: IP Connectivity*, objectives *3.3 Configure and verify IPv4 and IPv6 static routing*, *3.4 Configure and verify single area OSPFv2*, and *3.5 Describe the purpose, functions, and concepts of first hop redundancy protocols* of the *200-301 CCNA v1.1 certification* exam.

In this chapter, you will learn about the following topics:

- Understanding static routing
- Configuring static routing
- Understanding dynamic routing
- Configuring dynamic routing protocols
- Understanding First Hop Redundancy Protocol
- Implementing **Hot Standby Router Protocol** (**HSRP**)

Let's dive In!

Understanding Static Routing

Why do Cisco routers not automatically forward traffic like Cisco IOS switches do? Each interface on a Cisco router must be on a unique IP network. Without configuring an IP address on any of the router's interfaces, the router will not know what to do with messages attempting to enter an interface without an IP assignment. Put simply, when you unbox a new Cisco IOS router and insert it into your network, it does not do anything by default.

When you configure an IP address on a Cisco IOS router's interfaces, the router inserts two routes within its routing table. Take a look at the topology in *Figure 11.1* to get a better understanding:

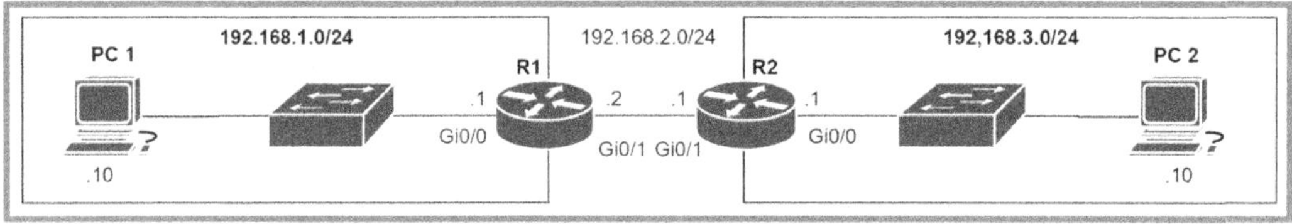

Figure 11.1: Simple network topology

Within the network topology, there are a total of three networks: `192.168.1.0/24`, `192.168.2.0/24`, and `192.168.3.0/24`. You might think that these routers would automatically know about all the networks and update their routing table automatically without user intervention, but this does not happen.

Take a look at R1's routing table after you have configured the IP addresses on the `GigabitEthernet0/0` and `GigabitEthernet0/1` interfaces:

```
R1#show ip route

Gateway of last resort is not set

     192.168.1.0/24 is variably subnetted, 2 subnets, 2 masks
C       192.168.1.0/24 is directly connected, GigabitEthernet0/0
L       192.168.1.1/32 is directly connected, GigabitEthernet0/0
     192.168.2.0/24 is variably subnetted, 2 subnets, 2 masks
C       192.168.2.0/24 is directly connected, GigabitEthernet0/1
L       192.168.2.2/32 is directly connected, GigabitEthernet0/1

R1#
```

Figure 11.2: Routing table

R1 only knows about its directly connected networks: `192.168.1.0/24` and `192.168.2.0/24`. Therefore, if PC 1 tries to send a message to the `192.168.3.0/24` network, R1 will respond with a `Destination host unreachable` message. By default, routers only know about directly connected networks. All other networks are considered to be remote. Static routing allows you to manually implement a static route that tells R1 how to reach the `192.168.3.0/24` network.

How do you create a static route? Firstly, look at the topology; it is important to first ask yourself how a packet reaches the `192.168.3.0/24` network if is currently on R1. It definitely has to be sent to R2, but more specifically, it has to be sent to R2's `GigabitEthernet0/1` interface via the `192.168.2.1` IP address. If you were to write a statement, you would get the following:

```
Traffic with a destination of 192.168.3.0 that has a subnet mask of
255.255.255.0, forward it to 192.168.2.1 as the next-hop
```

To create a static route on R1 from the preceding statement, you will get the following command:

```
ip route 192.168.3.0 255.255.255.0 192.168.2.1
```

Whenever you are creating a static route, start with the destination network followed by its subnet mask, and lastly, specify the next-hop IP address. Additionally, instead of specifying the next hop, you can specify the exit interface of R1, `GigabitEthernet0/1`. Keep in mind that R2 will also need a route to return traffic to the `192.168.1.0/24` network.

Implementing static routes has both pros and cons. You will take a look at the benefits and downsides of using static routing in an enterprise network in the next section.

Do You Need Static Routing?

As a network grows, additional static routes are created. Therefore, the number of static routes increases as the network topology grows. Additionally, if there is a change in the network topology, whether a new network is created, removed, or modified, the network engineer has to manually adjust the static route configurations on each device to support the change on the network. Static routes are good enough for small and simple network topologies, but for a large enterprise topology that has many IP subnets with remote sites (offices/networks), static routing can become complex.

However, there are advantages to using static routing on a network. When a network administrator installs a static route within the routing table of a router, it is manually configured and inserted. This provides improved security as compared to using dynamic routing protocols that can modify the routing table automatically. Imagine that a hacker injects unsolicited dynamic routes within an enterprise routing domain and causes all the organization's routers to forward traffic destined for the internet through the hacker's computer. With static routes, the router has to be manually adjusted.

Static routing uses fewer computing resources on the router than dynamic routing protocols do. With dynamic routing protocols, algorithms have to calculate the best path by using various metrics to determine the best path. With static routing, there is no algorithm. The router simply checks the routing table for a best-match route; once a suitable route is found, the router simply stops searching and executes the static route.

When it comes to predicting the next hop, it is easy with static routing as the path does not change. However with dynamic routing protocols, if there is a change in the network topology, the next-hop address may change based on the dynamic routing protocol algorithm recalculating the best path to the destination, but keep in mind that this is not an immediate account of the protocol itself.

What are the best situations to use static routes? The following are the best situations when static routes could be used in your network environment:

- When you want the router to always choose a specific path when forwarding packets to a destination network
- When a default route is needed for forwarding packets to the internet
- When a backup route is needed for forwarding packets to a destination when the primary route is no longer available

In the following sections, you will discover and learn about the various types of static routes and their use case scenarios.

Types of Static Routes

There are many types of static routes and each one is used in a different scenario on a network. In this section, you will learn about the characteristics of each type of static route and look at ways to implement each on a Cisco network.

Network Routes

Static network routes are those that are commonly used when configuring static routing. These routes are created to tell the router how to forward packets that are destined for a remote network. To put it simply, static network routes are used to specify a destination network.

To configure an IPv4 static route, use the following syntax:

```
Router(config)# ip route destination-network-address subnet-mask
[next-hop-IP-address | exit-interface]
```

To configure an IPv6 static route, use the following syntax:

```
Router(config)# ipv6 unicast-routing
Router(config)# ipv6 route ipv6-prefix/ipv6-mask [next-hop-ipv6-
address | exit-interface]
```

In the next section, you will take a look at next-hop static routes.

Next-Hop Static Routes

Next-hop static routes do the same as the previously described **network routes**, but **next-hop** is used to specify which IP address the local router forwards the packet to.

To configure an IPv4 next-hop static route, use the following syntax:

```
Router(config)# ip route destination-network-address subnet-mask next-hop-IP-address
```

The following is an example of an IPv4 static route using a next hop:

```
Branch-A(config)# ip route 10.1.1.0 255.255.255.0 10.2.1.5
```

To configure an IPv6 next-hop static route, use the following syntax:

```
Router(config)# ipv6 unicast-routing
Router(config)# ipv6 route ipv6-prefix/ipv6-mask next-hop ipv6 address
```

The following is an example of an IPv6 next-hop static route:

```
HQ(config)# ipv6 route 2001:ABCD:1234:2::/64 2001:ABCD:1234:5::10
```

The benefit of using a next hop is that the route specifies an IP address. Remember that static routes do not change without user intervention. Therefore, the router will always use the next-hop IP address.

In the next section, you will take a look at directly connected static routes.

Directly Connected Static Routes

A directly connected static route has the same functionality as the network route, but rather than specifying a next hop, you use the exit interface of the local router when configuring this route.

To configure an IPv4 directly connected static route, use the following syntax:

```
Router(config)# ip route destination-network-address subnet-mask exit-interface
```

The following is an example of an IPv4 directly connected static route:

```
Branch-A(config)#ip route 10.1.1.0 255.255.255.0 gigabitethernet 0/2
```

To configure an IPv6 directly connected static route, use the following syntax:

```
Router(config)# ipv6 unicast-routing
Router(config)# ipv6 route ipv6-prefix/ipv6-mask exit-interface
```

The exit interface is the outbound interface that the router will use for sending the packet to the destination. When using this type of static route, the router is not concerned about the device on the other end to catch this packet. It simply shoots the packet out a doorway (exit interface) and does not care about the device on the other end that receives it.

In the next section, you will take a look at configuring a fully specified static route.

Fully Specified Static Routes

A fully specified static route is created when both the exit interface of the local router and the next-hop IP address of the next router receive the packet.

To configure an IPv4 fully specified static route, use the following syntax:

```
Router(config)# ip route destination-network-address subnet-mask exit-interface next-hop IP address
```

The following is an example of an IPv4 fully specified static route:

```
Branch-A(config)# ip route 10.1.1.0 255.255.255.0 gigabitethernet 0/2 192.168.2.1
```

To configure an IPv6 fully specified static route, use the following syntax:

```
Router(config)# ipv6 unicast-routing
Router(config)# ipv6 route ipv6-prefix/ipv6-mask exit-interface next-hop Link-Local IPv6 address
```

The fully specified static route ensures that all parameters are manually configured on the local router. Next, you will learn why default routes are needed on a network.

Default Route

What if the router receives a packet that has a destination address that is located on the internet? What will the router do then? As you have realized by now, if a router does not have a route within its routing table, it will reply to the sender with either a `Destination host unreachable` or `Destination network unreachable` message. On the internet, there are hundreds or even thousands of public networks, and it would be inefficient to install all those public networks within the routing table of your router. At such a point, your router not knowing how to reach or forward packets to the internet is a major issue.

To solve this problem, you can use a special type of static route known as a **default route**. The default static route specifies the exit point to use when the routing table does not contain a path for the destination network. A default static route is useful when a router has only one exit point to another router, such as when the router connects to a central router or service provider. In other words, the default route is used to forward traffic to another router that may know what to do with a packet. Practically speaking, default routes are used to forward traffic to the internet.

To configure an IPv4 default route, use the following syntax:

```
Router(config)# ip route 0.0.0.0 0.0.0.0 <next-hop-IP-address | exit-
interface>
```

In the preceding syntax, the destination network ID and subnet mask are all zeros (0s). This implies that any network that does not exist within the routing table uses this route.

The following is an example of an IPv4 default route that uses `10.2.1.5` as the next hop:

```
Branch-A(config)# ip route 0.0.0.0 0.0.0.0 10.2.1.5
```

To configure an IPv6 default route, use the following syntax:

```
Router(config)# ipv6 unicast-routing
Router(config)# ipv6 route ::/0 <next-hop-IPv6-address | exit-
interface>
```

The following is an example of an IPv6 default route:

```
Branch-A(config)# ipv6 route ::/0 2001:ABCD:1234:5::5
```

Why use `::/0` as the IPv6 destination network? If you recall, the double-colon (`::`) shows that two or more hextets are zeros (0s). In this instance, the double-colon (`::`) shows that all hextets are 0s with a subnet mask of `0`, as well.

Host Routes

Host routes are either in the form of IPv4 or IPv6 addresses in the routing table. They can be installed automatically in the routing table, configured as a static host route, or obtained automatically through other methods. Host routes are used to route traffic to a specific host.

Figure 11.3 shows host routes automatically installed in the routing table:

```
R3#show ip route
Codes: L - local, C - connected, S - static, R - RIP, M - mobile, B - BGP
       D - EIGRP, EX - EIGRP external, O - OSPF, IA - OSPF inter area
       N1 - OSPF NSSA external type 1, N2 - OSPF NSSA external type 2
       E1 - OSPF external type 1, E2 - OSPF external type 2, E - EGP
       i - IS-IS, L1 - IS-IS level-1, L2 - IS-IS level-2, ia - IS-IS inter area
       * - candidate default, U - per-user static route, o - ODR
       P - periodic downloaded static route

Gateway of last resort is not

     172.31.0.0/16 is vari                    ets, 5 masks
S       172.31.0.0/24 i    ectly connected, Serial0/0/1
S       172.31.1.0/25   directly connected, Serial0/0/1
C       172.31.1.1  /26 is directly connected, GigabitEthernet0/0
L       172.31.1.129/32 is directly connected, GigabitEthernet0/0
S       172.31.1.192/30 is directly connected, Serial0/0/1
C       172.31.1.196/30 is directly connected, Serial0/0/1
L       172.31.1.198/32 is directly connected, Serial0/0/1
```

Host Route

Figure 11.3: Host routes

A host route is a static route that simply specifies a host rather than a network. This type of static route allows you to create individual static routes that specify how to reach a specific host on a network.

To configure an IPv4 host route, use the following syntax:

```
Router(config)# ip route destination-ipv4-address 255.255.255.255
<next-hop-IP-address | exit-interface>
```

To configure an IPv6 host route, use the following syntax:

```
Router(config)# ipv6 unicast-routing
Router(config)# ipv6 route destination-ipv6-global-unicat-address/128
<next-hop-IP-address | exit-interface>
```

When configuring a host route, ensure all bits are 1s within the subnet mask to imply that all the bits in the destination IPv4 addresses match. For an IPv4 host route, the subnet mask is `255.255.255.255`, and for IPv6, it's `/128`.

Floating Route

Imagine your organization is using two **internet service providers** (**ISPs**), ISP A and ISP B, for internet connectivity redundancy. ISP A serves as the primary link, while ISP B is the backup in the event the connection to ISP A goes down.

Figure 11.4 shows a simple network topology:

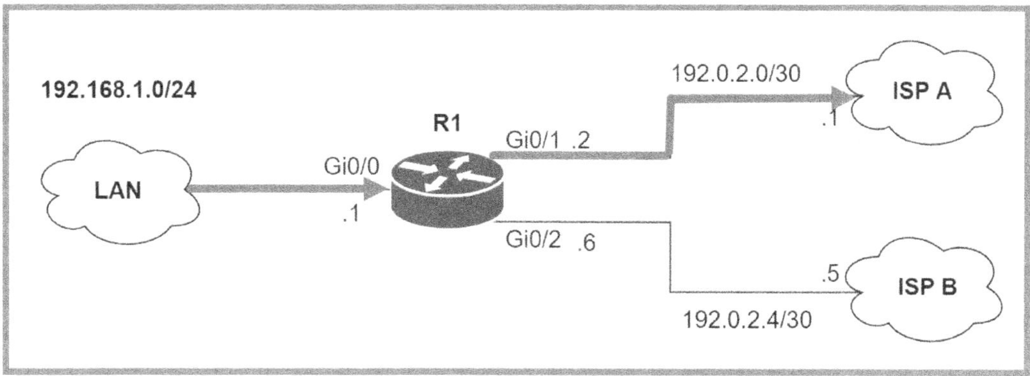

Figure 11.4: Redundant internet connections

All traffic from the internal LAN will use ISP A as the preferred route. The following is the configuration used on R1 to ensure packets are sent to ISP A:

```
R1config)# ip route 0.0.0.0 0.0.0.0 192.0.2.1
```

A floating static route is a route that has an administrative distance greater than the administrative distance of another static route or dynamic route. Floating static routes are used when providing a backup path to a primary link. After configuring a floating static route, it is not installed within the routing table. It is only when the primary route from the routing table is removed that the floating static route is implemented by the router as the new primary route.

To create a floating route on R1, use the following command:

```
R1config)# ip route 0.0.0.0 0.0.0.0 192.0.2.1 2
```

Notice that at the end of the next hop, there is a numerical value. The Cisco IOS allows you to specify an **administrative distance** (**AD**) value for the route. This allows you to create backup routes for dynamic routes that are no longer available.

Figure 11.5 shows the path that packets will take if ISP A goes down:

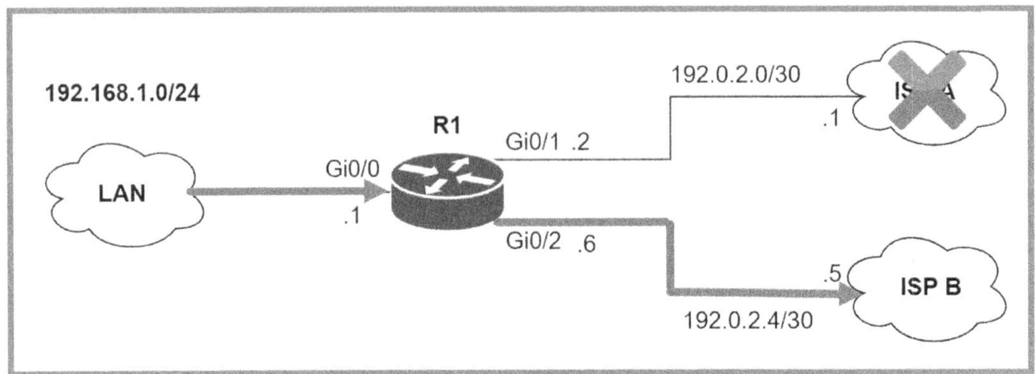

Figure 11.5: Backup route

The original route will be removed from the routing table and the floating route will be installed and will become the primary route/path to reach the internet.

To configure an IPv4 floating route, use the following syntax:

```
Router(config)# ip route destination-network-address subnet-mask
[next-hop IP address | exit-interface] administrative-distance-value
```

To configure an IPv6 floating route, use the following syntax:

```
Router(config)# ipv6 unicast-routing
Router(config)# ipv6 route ipv6-prefix/ipv6-mask [next-hop ip address
| exit-interface] administrative-distance-value
```

Having completed this section, you have learned about the various types of static routes and how to implement them. The following sections will take you through a few hands-on labs that will help you develop your static routing skills as a professional.

Lab: Configuring Static Routing Using IPv4

It's time to get your hands on some practical experience, implementing static routes, to gain connectivity between remote networks. In this exercise, the network topology shown in *Figure 11.6* will be used:

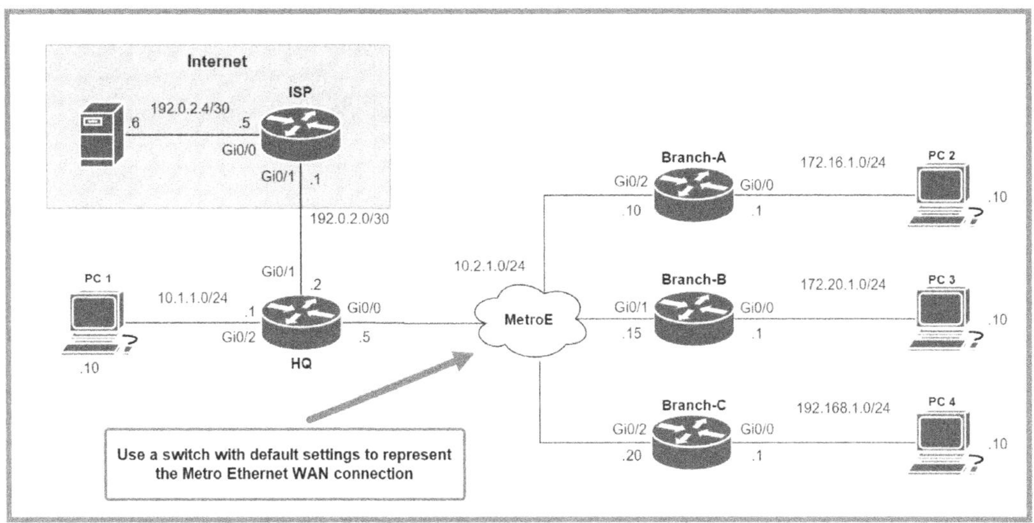

Figure 11.6: IPv4 static routing lab topology

To follow along with this exercise, please download the pre-built Packet Tracer template from `https://packt.link/CCNArepoCh11`.

Having opened the pre-built template within the Cisco Packet Tracer, use the following instructions to implement static routes:

1. Firstly, as a good network professional, it is wise to verify the IP configurations on your devices. On each PC, open Command Prompt and execute the `ipconfig` command to verify that the correct IP address, subnet mask, and default gateway are assigned.

> **Note**
>
> If you are using a physical lab with a Linux operating system, use the `ifconfig` command to validate your IP address configurations.

2. On each router, use the `show ip interface brief` command to verify that the appropriate IP address is assigned on the correct interfaces and that the interfaces are in an `Up/Up` status.

3. Test the connectivity between each PC and its default gateway. On PC 1, ping the HQ router, as shown in *Figure 11.7*:

```
C:\>ping 10.1.1.1

Pinging 10.1.1.1 with 32 bytes of data:

Reply from 10.1.1.1: bytes=32 time<1ms TTL=255
Reply from 10.1.1.1: bytes=32 time<1ms TTL=255
Reply from 10.1.1.1: bytes=32 time<1ms TTL=255
Reply from 10.1.1.1: bytes=32 time<1ms TTL=255

Ping statistics for 10.1.1.1:
    Packets: Sent = 4, Received = 4, Lost = 0 (0% loss),
Approximate round trip times in milli-seconds:
    Minimum = 0ms, Maximum = 0ms, Average = 0ms
```

Figure 11.7: Default gateway connectivity test

The HQ router responds to the ICMP messages sent from PC 1. These responses verify connectivity between PC 1 and its default gateway.

4. Next, attempt to test the connectivity between remote networks. Ping from PC 1 to PC 2, as shown in *Figure 11.8*:

```
C:\>ping 172.16.1.10

Pinging 172.16.1.10 with 32 bytes of data:

Reply from 10.1.1.1: Destination host unreachable.
Reply from 10.1.1.1: Destination host unreachable.
Reply from 10.1.1.1: Destination host unreachable.
Reply from 10.1.1.1: Destination host unreachable.

Ping statistics for 172.16.1.10:
    Packets: Sent = 4, Received = 0, Lost = 4 (100% loss),
```

Figure 11.8: Connectivity test from PC 1 to PC 2

The default gateway, HQ router, has responded with the `Destination host unreachable` message, indicating it does not have a route to reach the `172.16.1.10` host in its routing table.

5. Next, use the `show ip route` command on each router to determine which network routers are installed in their routing table and which are not. The snippet in *Figure 11.9* shows the routing table of the HQ router:

```
Gateway of last resort is not set

     10.0.0.0/8 is variably subnetted, 4 subnets, 2 masks
C       10.1.1.0/24 is directly connected, GigabitEthernet0/2
L       10.1.1.1/32 is directly connected, GigabitEthernet0/2
C       10.2.1.0/24 is directly connected, GigabitEthernet0/0
L       10.2.1.5/32 is directly connected, GigabitEthernet0/0
```

Figure 11.9: Routing table of the HQ router

You will have noticed that each router only knows about its directly connected networks. Your job is to ensure that each router knows how to reach all other networks.

6. You can begin by configuring the HQ router with static routes to reach the Branch-B, Branch-C, and HQ networks. Ensure that you enter the following commands in the `global configuration` mode:

   ```
   HQ(config)# ip route 172.16.1.0 255.255.255.0 10.2.1.10
   HQ(config)# ip route 172.20.1.0 255.255.255.0 10.2.1.15
   HQ(config)# ip route 192.168.1.0 255.255.255.0 10.2.1.20
   ```

   These configurations will install a static route for each branch network in the topology.

Note

To remove a static route, use the `no` command followed by the entire static route, such as `no ip route 172.16.1.0 255.255.255.0 10.2.1.10`.

7. Use `the show ip route` command to verify that the routing table has been updated, as shown in *Figure 11.10*:

```
     10.0.0.0/8 is variably subnetted, 4 subnets, 2 masks
C       10.1.1.0/24 is directly connected, GigabitEthernet0/2
L       10.1.1.1/32 is directly connected, GigabitEthernet0/2
C       10.2.1.0/24 is directly connected, GigabitEthernet0/0
L       10.2.1.5/32 is directly connected, GigabitEthernet0/0
     172.16.0.0/24 is subnetted, 1 subnets
S       172.16.1.0/24 [1/0] via 10.2.1.10
     172.20.0.0/24 is subnetted, 1 subnets
S       172.20.1.0/24 [1/0] via 10.2.1.15
S    192.168.1.0/24 [1/0] via 10.2.1.20
```

Figure 11.10: Updated routing table on the HQ router

You have now installed static routes on the HQ routing table for each remote branch network.

8. You can now attempt to ping between PC 1 and PC 2 again to verify whether you have end-to-end connectivity:

```
C:\>ping 172.16.1.10

Pinging 172.16.1.10 with 32 bytes of data:

Request timed out.
Request timed out.
Request timed out.
Request timed out.

Ping statistics for 172.16.1.10:
    Packets: Sent = 4, Received = 0, Lost = 4 (100% loss),
```

PC is not receiving any ICMP Echo Replies

Figure 11.11: Request timed out messages

The responses have changed, and now you are getting `Request timed out` responses. What does this mean? These responses are provided when the target device (PC 2) has disabled ICMP responses, a firewall or security appliance is blocking ICMP messages, or when the target does not have a route back to the sender (PC 1). In this situation, a firewall or ICMP has not been blocked anywhere. Therefore, it's the third reason.

9. Check the routing table on the Branch-A router to verify whether it has a route back to the HQ network, as shown in *Figure 11.12*:

```
Gateway of last resort is not set

     10.0.0.0/8 is variably subnetted, 2 subnets, 2 masks
C       10.2.1.0/24 is directly connected, GigabitEthernet0/2
L       10.2.1.10/32 is directly connected, GigabitEthernet0/2
     172.16.0.0/16 is variably subnetted, 2 subnets, 2 masks
C       172.16.1.0/24 is directly connected, GigabitEthernet0/0
L       172.16.1.1/32 is directly connected, GigabitEthernet0/0
```

Figure 11.12: Routing table of the Branch-A router

As suspected, the Branch-A router does not have a router back to the `10.1.1.0/24` network or the other remote networks.

10. Use the following commands to configure the Branch-A router with static routes to all other remote branch networks within the topology:

```
Branch-A(config)# ip route 10.1.1.0 255.255.255.0 10.2.1.5
Branch-A(config)# ip route 172.20.1.0 255.255.255.0 10.2.1.15
Branch-A(config)# ip route 192.168.1.0 255.255.255.0 10.2.1.20
```

11. Check the routing table of the Branch-A router and verify whether the new routes are in place, as shown in *Figure 11.13*:

```
     10.0.0.0/8 is variably subnetted, 3 subnets, 2 masks
S       10.1.1.0/24 [1/0] via 10.2.1.5
C       10.2.1.0/24 is directly connected, GigabitEthernet0/2
L       10.2.1.10/32 is directly connected, GigabitEthernet0/2
     172.16.0.0/16 is variably subnetted, 2 subnets, 2 masks
C       172.16.1.0/24 is directly connected, GigabitEthernet0/0
L       172.16.1.1/32 is directly connected, GigabitEthernet0/0
     172.20.0.0/24 is subnetted, 1 subnets
S       172.20.1.0/24 [1/0] via 10.2.1.15
S    192.168.1.0/24 [1/0] via 10.2.1.20
```

Figure 11.13: Static routes on the Branch-A router

Now that the Branch-A router has a route (path) back to the HQ network (`10.1.1.0/24`) via `10.2.1.5`, test the end-to-end connectivity once more.

12. Test the connectivity from PC 1 to PC 2 to verify that the routing is working properly between the HQ and Branch-A routers:

```
C:\>ping 172.16.1.10

Pinging 172.16.1.10 with 32 bytes of data:

Reply from 172.16.1.10: bytes=32 time<1ms TTL=126
Reply from 172.16.1.10: bytes=32 time<1ms TTL=126
Reply from 172.16.1.10: bytes=32 time=1ms TTL=126
Reply from 172.16.1.10: bytes=32 time=4ms TTL=126

Ping statistics for 172.16.1.10:
    Packets: Sent = 4, Received = 4, Lost = 0 (0% loss),
Approximate round trip times in milli-seconds:
    Minimum = 0ms, Maximum = 4ms, Average = 1ms
```

Figure 11.14: Connectivity test

Additionally, you can perform a traceroute to validate the path that the packet takes between PC 1 and PC 2:

```
C:\>tracert 172.16.1.10

Tracing route to 172.16.1.10 over a maximum of 30 hops:

  1   0 ms      0 ms      0 ms      10.1.1.1
  2   0 ms      1 ms      0 ms      10.2.1.10
  3   0 ms      0 ms      0 ms      172.16.1.10

Trace complete.
```

Figure 11.15: Traceroute showing the path

The first hop is the default gateway for PC 1, the second hop is the next hop for the address for the `172.16.1.0/24` network as seen within the routing table of the HQ router, and the third hop is the actual destination host.

13. Do not forget to configure static routes on the Branch-B router using the following commands:

```
Branch-B(config)# ip route 10.1.1.0 255.255.255.0 10.2.1.5
Branch-B(config)# ip route 172.16.1.0 255.255.255.0 10.2.1.10
Branch-B(config)# ip route 192.168.1.0 255.255.255.0 10.2.1.20
```

14. Use the following commands to configure static routes on the Branch-C router:

```
Branch-C(config)# ip route 10.1.1.0 255.255.255.0 10.2.1.5
Branch-C(config)# ip route 172.16.1.0 255.255.255.0 10.2.1.10
Branch-C(config)# ip route 172.20.1.0 255.255.255.0 10.2.1.15
```

15. Lastly, use `ping` to validate end-to-end connectivity between all devices on the topology.

Having completed this lab, you have gained the hands-on skills to implement static routing and perform troubleshooting techniques in a Cisco environment.

Lab: Configuring an IPv4 Default Route

In this lab, you will learn how to implement a default route that points to the internet. Please keep in mind that this lab is simply an extension of the *Configuring Static Routing Using IPv4* lab. If you recall, a default route is a route that points to a foreign network that does not belong to your organization, such as the internet. It's simply your path (route) to the internet.

To get started with configuring a default route, use the following instructions:

1. Use the following command on the Branch-A router to create a default route that points to the HQ router, as that is where the internet link is located:

```
Branch-A(config)# ip route 0.0.0.0 0.0.0.0 10.2.1.5
```

2. Check the routing table of the Branch-A router to validate that the default route has been installed and the gateway of last resort has been set:

```
Branch-A#show ip route

Gateway of last resort is 10.2.1.5 to network 0.0.0.0

     10.0.0.0/8 is variably subnetted, 3 subnets, 2 masks
S       10.1.1.0/24 [1/0] via 10.2.1.5
C       10.2.1.0/24 is directly connected, GigabitEthernet0/2
L       10.2.1.10/32 is directly connected, GigabitEthernet0/2
     172.16.0.0/16 is variably subnetted, 2 subnets, 2 masks
C       172.16.1.0/24 is directly connected, GigabitEthernet0/0
L       172.16.1.1/32 is directly connected, GigabitEthernet0/0
     172.20.0.0/24 is subnetted, 1 subnets
S       172.20.1.0/24 [1/0] via 10.2.1.15
S    192.168.1.0/24 [1/0] via 10.2.1.20
S*   0.0.0.0/0 [1/0] via 10.2.1.5
```

Figure 11.16: Default route

Configuring the default route on Branch-A will enable the router to forward any packets whose destination network is not found within the routing table to the default gateway (the gateway of last resort). For instance, if the Branch-A router receives a packet for `8.8.8.8`, the router will check its routing table using a top-down approach. If a destination route is not found, then it will use the default route and forward the packet to `10.2.1.5`.

Furthermore, since the default route does not have an exit interface, the router will perform a **recursive lookup** within the routing table to determine which network `10.2.1.5` belongs to. The recursive lookup is when the router performs a route lookup a second time to determine which interface is associated with the next-hop address. According to the routing table, the router will forward the packet out of the `GigabitEthernet0/2` interface since `10.2.1.5` belongs to the `10.2.1.0/24` subnet.

3. Repeat *Steps 1* and *2* on the Branch-B and Branch-C routers as well to configure a default route.

4. Configure the HQ router as the stub router that has the actual internet connection. On the HQ router, you can configure a default route that points to the internet gateway address, `192.0.2.1`, on the ISP router:

   ```
   HQ(config)# ip route 0.0.0.0 0.0.0.0 192.0.2.1
   ```

> **Note**
> In a real environment, the ISP will provide you with the public IP address to configure on your stub router's interface and the internet gateway address.

   At this point, all routers have a default route that points toward the internet or ISP network. To kick it up a notch, you can use the following additional configurations to simulate the internet:

   I. Ensure the ISP router and the server are configured with the IP scheme as shown in the topology.

   II. Ensure that the server is able to ping the ISP router, and vice versa.

   III. Configure a default route on the ISP router to point toward the HQ router:

   ```
   ISP(config)# ip route 0.0.0.0 0.0.0.0 192.0.2.2
   ```

   The purpose of this step is to allow the PCs to reach the public server on the internet within our lab.

5. Test the connectivity from any PC to the server that is on the internet. *Figure 11.17* shows the results from PC 2 on your network:

```
C:\>ping 192.0.2.6

Pinging 192.0.2.6 with 32 bytes of data:

Reply from 192.0.2.6: bytes=32 time<1ms TTL=125
Reply from 192.0.2.6: bytes=32 time=11ms TTL=125
Reply from 192.0.2.6: bytes=32 time=12ms TTL=125
Reply from 192.0.2.6: bytes=32 time=12ms TTL=125

Ping statistics for 192.0.2.6:
    Packets: Sent = 4, Received = 4, Lost = 0 (0% loss),
Approximate round trip times in milli-seconds:
    Minimum = 0ms, Maximum = 12ms, Average = 8ms
```

Figure 11.17: Connectivity test to the server

6. Perform a traceroute from PC 2 to the server:

```
C:\>tracert 192.0.2.6

Tracing route to 192.0.2.6 over a maximum of 30 hops:

  1   0 ms      0 ms      0 ms      172.16.1.1
  2   0 ms      1 ms      0 ms      10.2.1.5
  3   0 ms      0 ms      11 ms     192.0.2.1
  4   11 ms     0 ms      14 ms     192.0.2.6

Trace complete.
```

Figure 11.18: Traceroute test

As you can see, the traceroute shows the path the packet took from PC 2 to the server. Furthermore, looking at the routing table of any router, the network `192.0.2.4/30` does not exist, as shown in *Figure 11.19*:

```
Branch-A#show ip route

Gateway of last resort is 10.2.1.5 to network 0.0.0.0

     10.0.0.0/8 is variably subnetted, 3 subnets, 2 masks
S       10.1.1.0/24 [1/0] via 10.2.1.5
C       10.2.1.0/24 is directly connected, GigabitEthernet0/2
L       10.2.1.10/32 is directly connected, GigabitEthernet0/2
     172.16.0.0/16 is variably subnetted, 2 subnets, 2 masks
C       172.16.1.0/24 is directly connected, GigabitEthernet0/0
L       172.16.1.1/32 is directly connected, GigabitEthernet0/0
     172.20.0.0/24 is subnetted, 1 subnets
S       172.20.1.0/24 [1/0] via 10.2.1.15
S    192.168.1.0/24 [1/0] via 10.2.1.20
S*   0.0.0.0/0 [1/0] via 10.2.1.5
```

Figure 11.19: Routing table of the Branch-A router

The Branch-A router used the default route, the gateway of last resort, to forward the packet to another device that may have a path or route to the destination host.

> **Note**
>
> For each branch router, rather than installing a static route for each remote network, you can simply install a single default route to the main office such as the HQ router. This will ensure that the routing table within reach remote branch router is kept small and concise. Additionally, the HQ router should contain static routes to each remote branch network. To put it simply, whenever a branch officer has to send a message to another branch or remote network, the message will always be sent to the HQ router. In the next lab exercise, you will apply this method.

Having completed this lab, you have gained hands-on skills and experience in configuring and implementing a default route on an IPv4 network.

Lab: Configuring Static Routing Using IPv6

In this lab, you will learn how to configure both IPv6 static and default routes in a Cisco environment. You are not required to rebuild a new topology for this exercise. IPv6 supports dual-stacking, which allows you to configure both an IPv4 and IPv6 address on the same interface. Therefore, you can simply continue working from the previous lab on this one.

Figure 11.20 shows the IPv6 topology you will be using to complete this hands-on exercise:

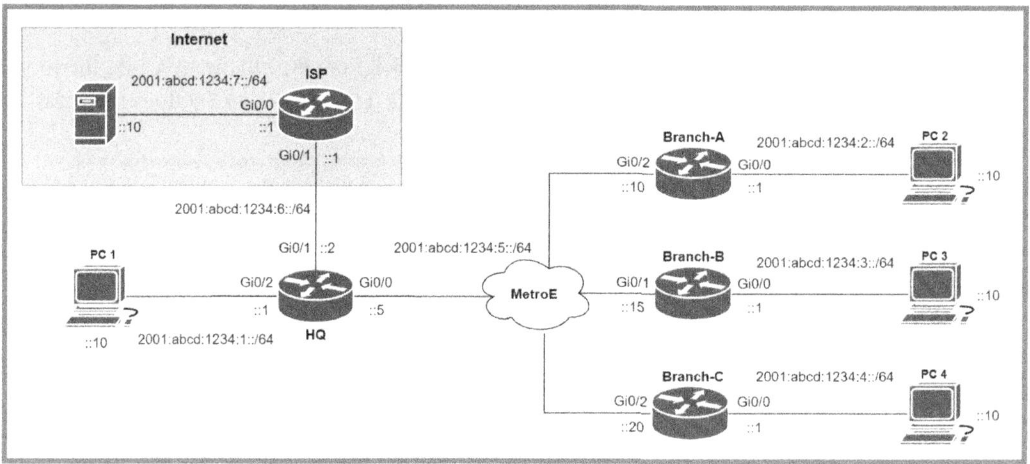

Figure 11.20: IPv6 routing lab topology

Before you begin, ensure you download and open the pre-built lab template within Cisco Packet Tracer from `https://packt.link/CCNArepoCh11`.

To get started with implementing IPv6 static routes, use the following instructions:

1. Enter `global configuration mode` on each router and execute the `ipv6 unicast-routing` command to enable IPv6 routing.
2. Firstly, install IPv6 static routes to each branch network on the HQ router, as shown:

```
HQ(config)# ipv6 route 2001:ABCD:1234:2::/64
2001:ABCD:1234:5::10
HQ(config)# ipv6 route 2001:ABCD:1234:3::/64
2001:ABCD:1234:5::15
HQ(config)# ipv6 route 2001:ABCD:1234:4::/64
2001:ABCD:1234:5::20
```

3. On each branch router, install only an IPv6 default route that points to HQ as its IPv6 gateway of last resort. Use the following commands to achieve this task:

```
Branch-A(config)# ipv6 route ::/0 2001:ABCD:1234:5::5
Branch-B(config)# ipv6 route ::/0 2001:ABCD:1234:5::5
Branch-C(config)# ipv6 route ::/0 2001:ABCD:1234:5::5
```

   At this point, each PC can reach another on a remote network and all traffic passes through the HQ router.

4. Install a default route on the HQ router to point toward the internet:

```
HQ(config)# ipv6 route ::/0 2001:abcd:1234:6::1
```

   To ensure you are able to simulate the internet within the lab environment, you also need to install a default route on the ISP router to point back to the HQ router, as shown here:

```
ISP(config)# ipv6 route ::/0 2001:abcd:1234:6::2
```

5. Verify end-to-end connectivity from one PC to another. *Figure 11.21* shows the ping results between PC 2 and PC 4:

```
C:\>ping 2001:abcd:1234:4::10

Pinging 2001:abcd:1234:4::10 with 32 bytes of data:

Reply from 2001:ABCD:1234:4::10: bytes=32 time<1ms TTL=125
Reply from 2001:ABCD:1234:4::10: bytes=32 time=10ms TTL=125
Reply from 2001:ABCD:1234:4::10: bytes=32 time=10ms TTL=125
Reply from 2001:ABCD:1234:4::10: bytes=32 time=11ms TTL=125

Ping statistics for 2001:ABCD:1234:4::10:
    Packets: Sent = 4, Received = 4, Lost = 0 (0% loss),
Approximate round trip times in milli-seconds:
    Minimum = 0ms, Maximum = 11ms, Average = 7ms
```

Figure 11.21: Connectivity between PC 2 and PC 4

   Figure 11.22 shows the path the packet took from PC 2 and PC 4:

```
C:\>tracert 2001:abcd:1234:4::10

Tracing route to 2001:abcd:1234:4::10 over a maximum of 30 hops:

  1    0 ms      0 ms      0 ms      2001:ABCD:1234:2::1
  2    0 ms      0 ms      0 ms      2001:ABCD:1234:5::5
  3    0 ms      10 ms     10 ms     2001:ABCD:1234:5::20
  4    12 ms     12 ms     10 ms     2001:ABCD:1234:4::10

Trace complete.
```

Figure 11.22: Traceroute between PC 2 and PC 4

As expected, all traffic passes through the HQ router as the configuration uses the default route on each branch router.

6. Using the `show ipv6 route` command, you can validate the IPv4 routing table of each router. *Figure 11.23* shows the routing table of the Branch-A router:

```
Branch-A#show ipv6 route
IPv6 Routing Table - 6 entries
Codes: C - Connected, L - Local, S - Static, R - RIP, B - BGP
       U - Per-user Static route, M - MIPv6
       I1 - ISIS L1, I2 - ISIS L2, IA - ISIS interarea, IS - ISIS summary
       O - OSPF intra, OI - OSPF inter, OE1 - OSPF ext 1, OE2 - OSPF ext 2
       ON1 - OSPF NSSA ext 1, ON2 - OSPF NSSA ext 2
       D - EIGRP, EX - EIGRP external
S   ::/0 [1/0]
     via 2001:ABCD:1234:5::5
C   2001:ABCD:1234:2::/64 [0/0]
     via GigabitEthernet0/0, directly connected
L   2001:ABCD:1234:2::1/128 [0/0]
     via GigabitEthernet0/0, receive
C   2001:ABCD:1234:5::/64 [0/0]
     via GigabitEthernet0/2, directly connected
L   2001:ABCD:1234:5::10/128 [0/0]
     via GigabitEthernet0/2, receive
L   FF00::/8 [0/0]
     via Null0, receive
```

Figure 11.23: Branch-A IPv6 routing table

7. Lastly, you can use the `show ipv6 interface brief` command to verify the IPv6 address on each router's interface. *Figure 11.24* shows both the IPv6 Link-Local and global unicast addresses on the HQ router:

```
HQ#show ipv6 interface brief
GigabitEthernet0/0          [up/up]
    FE80::1
    2001:ABCD:1234:5::5
GigabitEthernet0/1          [up/up]
    FE80::2
    2001:ABCD:1234:6::2
GigabitEthernet0/2          [up/up]
    FE80::1
    2001:ABCD:1234:1::1
Vlan1                       [administratively down/down]
    unassigned
```

Figure 11.24: IPv6 interfaces on the HQ router

Finally, you will be able to test the connectivity between each branch network and the simulated internet with the server.

Having completed this lab, you have gained the hands-on skills to implement IPv6 static routes within a Cisco networking environment. In the next section, you will take a deep dive, learning how to configure your Cisco routers to automatically learn routes and update their routing table using the dynamic routing protocol.

Understanding Dynamic Routing

Imagine you are the network engineer for a very large organization that has a lot of subnets spanning multiple remote offices that are all interconnected by routers. Manually implementing static routes to each network can be a very daunting task. Imagine if there is a failure on the network; routers will not automatically discover a new path and reroute network traffic. Furthermore, as the network engineer, your job gets tougher when there are issues on the network as static routing becomes more difficult to troubleshoot as the network expands.

To save the day, there are dynamic routing protocols. What exactly are dynamic routing protocols? They are layer 3 routing protocols that can be configured on a router to automatically discover remote networks, maintain and update routing tables, calculate the best path to a destination network, and, in the event that a route or path is no longer available, find a new path and install it in the routing table automatically.

There are various types of dynamic routing protocols. *Figure 11.25* provides a breakdown:

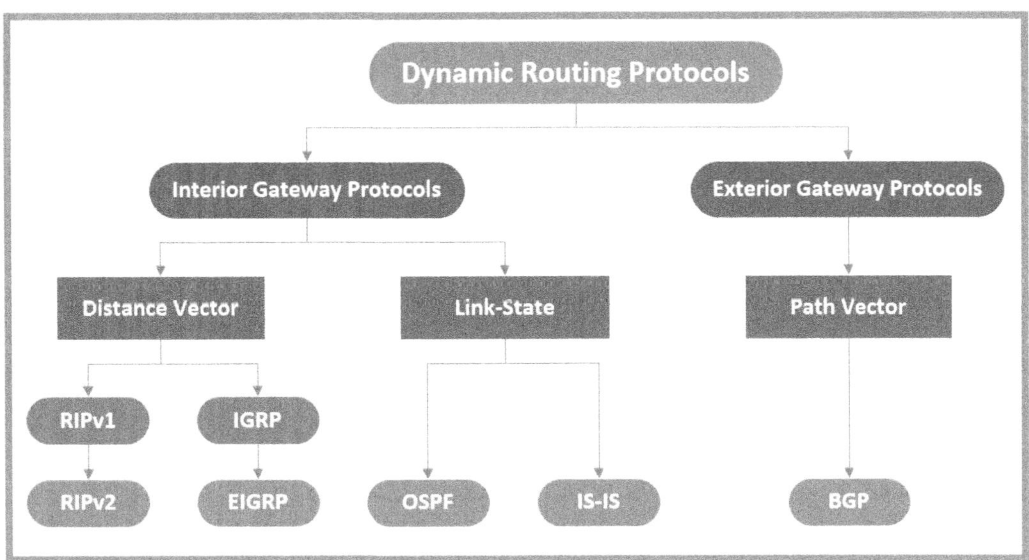

Figure 11.25: Dynamic routing protocols

There are various categories and sub-categories of dynamic routing protocols that are grouped based on their characteristics as a routing protocol and how they function.

Types of Dynamic Routing Protocol

There are two main categories of dynamic routing protocol – **interior gateway protocols** (**IGPs**) and **exterior gateway protocols** (**EGPs**). IGPs are used within a private network owned by an organization. If IGPs are used on private networks, where do you think EGPs are used? They are mostly used on the internet, a public network.

There is currently one EGP and its name is **Border Gateway Protocol** (**BGP**). BGP is used to exchange routing information between **autonomous systems** (**ASs**) on the internet. An AS is defined as an organization that manages a lot of public networks, a simple example being an ISP. Imagine ISP_A has to inform other ISPs around the world about the networks that ISP_A owns and how to reach them. Each ISP shares routing information via the BGP routing protocol on the internet.

Figure 11.26 shows a simple representation of BGP interconnecting via **autonomous system numbers** (**ASNs**):

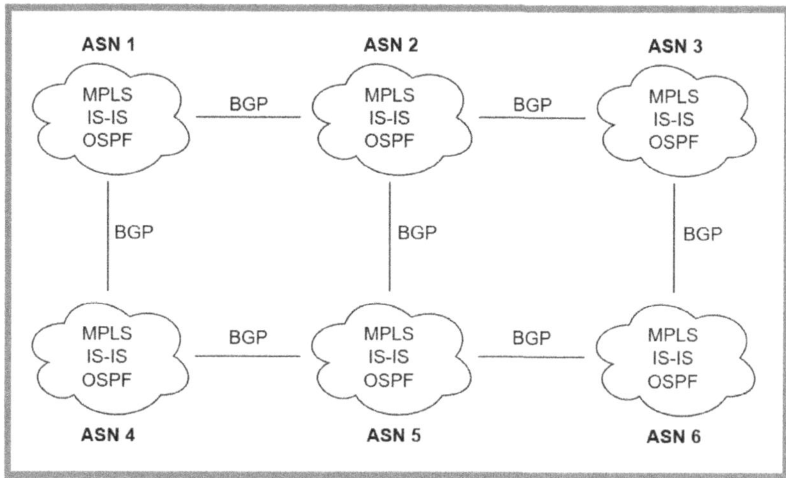

Figure 11.26: BGP being used between various ASNs

BGP is a very slow converging dynamic routing protocol, and hence, is mostly used on the internet.

> **Note**
>
> BGP is no longer covered in the *200-301 CCNA* exam objectives and has moved to the **Cisco Certified Network Professional** (**CCNP**) Enterprise certification level. However, it's worth mentioning in this section.

Each ISP has a unique ASN that allows it to establish a BGP adjacency with another ASN to exchange BGP routes. BGP is unlike the other routing protocols, as it chooses the best route based on its path.

Figure 11.27 shows a BGP routing table of a public BGP router:

```
route-views>show bgp
BGP table version is [illegible], local router ID is [illegible]
Status codes: s suppressed, d damped, h history, * valid, > best, i - internal,
              r RIB-failure, S Stale, m multipath, b backup-path, f RT-Filter,
              x best-external, a additional-path, c RIB-compressed,
Origin codes: i - IGP, e - EGP, ? - incomplete
RPKI validation codes: V valid, I invalid, N Not found

     Network          Next Hop            Metric LocPrf Weight Path
Nr>  0.0.0.0          162.251.163.2                          0 53767 3257 i
V*   1.0.0.0/24       202.93.8.242                           0 24441 13335 i
V*                    212.66.96.126                          0 20912 13335 i
V*                    91.218.184.60                          0 49788 13335 i
V*                    37.139.139.17            0             0 57866 13335 i
V*                    140.192.8.16                           0 54728 20130 6939 13335 i
V*                    194.85.40.15             0             0 3267 13335 i
```

Figure 11.27: BGP routing table

Figure 11.27 shows the destination networks (on the left), their next hop, and their paths. The path provides the ASN values. Therefore, to reach the `1.0.0.0/24` network from this router, the packet has to be sent to AS `24441` via `202.93.8.242`, then to AS `13335`, and so on.

> **Note**
>
> The **BGP Lookup Glass project** is a global initiative among ISPs that allows anyone to access BGP-enabled routers via Telnet to learn more about the BGP routing protocol. Simply use the search term `bgp looking glass` within your web browser to find publicly accessible BGP routers.

One of the oldest IGP dynamic routing protocols is the **Routing Information Protocol** (**RIP**). RIP is defined as a distance vector routing protocol. Distance vector routing protocols are only concerned with the distance and direction of the destination network. RIP uses the **Bellman-Ford** algorithm, which uses **hop count** as its metric to calculate the distance between the router and the destination network.

> **Note**
>
> RIP has a maximum hop count of 15. For a network that has more than 15 hops, RIP will not be suitable. Additionally, RIP does not support **Variable Length Subnet Masking** (**VLSM**).

The path with the least number of hops (routers) will be elected as the best route and will be installed in the routing table. Furthermore, being a distance vector protocol, RIP will forward the packet to the next hop (neighbor), and so on, by each hop along the path until the packet is delivered.

> **Note**
>
> RIP was covered in the previous versions of CCNA. It is no longer part of the *200-301 CCNA* examination objectives and is beyond the scope of this book.

The **Enhanced Interior Gateway Routing Protocol** (**EIGRP**) is another distance vector routing protocol and was a Cisco-proprietary routing protocol until March 2013 when Cisco announced it open to the network community and vendors for implementation. EIGRP uses the **diffusing update algorithm** (**DUAL**) to calculate the best path to a destination network.

DUAL uses the following factors when calculating a suitable route:

- Bandwidth (`BW`)
- Delay (`DLY`)
- Transmitting load (`txload`)
- Receiving load (`rxload`)
- `reliability`

However, EIGRP uses `BW` and `DLY` by default. The other factors are off by default. *Figure 11.28* shows the values used by DUAL for its calculation:

```
Branch-A#show interfaces gigabitEthernet 0/2
GigabitEthernet0/2 is up, line protocol is up (connected)
  Hardware is CN Gigabit Ethernet, address is 0000.0c41.b003
  Description: WAN interface to HQ
  Internet address is 10.2.1.10/24
  MTU 1500 bytes, BW 1000000 Kbit, DLY 100 usec,
     reliability 255/255, txload 1/255, rxload 1/255
  Encapsulation ARPA, loopback not set
  Keepalive set (10 sec)
  Full-duplex, 100Mb/s, media type is RJ45
```

Figure 11.28: Interface details

The advantage EIGRP has over other dynamic routing protocols is its ability to calculate a backup loop-free path during its phase of learning networks and calculate its primary loop-free path to a destination network.

> **Note**
>
> EIGRP is no longer covered in the *200-301 CCNA* exam objectives and has been moved to the *CCNP* Enterprise certification level. However, it is worth mentioning in this section.

A loop-free path is one that does not have a layer 3 routing loop on a network. This is very useful when a route is unavailable. EIGRP can almost immediately insert the backup loop-free path within the routing table to ensure connectivity.

Open Shortest Path First

One of the most popular link-state routing protocols is **Open Shortest Path First version 2 (OSPFv2)**. Defined by RFC 1247, OSPFv2 was introduced to the networking industry back in 1991 and has since been widely adopted and implemented in many organizations.

The following are the benefits of using OSPF:

- **Open source** – Being open source allows an organization with mixed vendor equipment to implement OSPF to exchange routing information between the various manufacturers of routers.
- **Scalability** – OSPF can be implemented into a network of any size. Additionally, it can be configured in a hierarchical system where OSPF-enabled routers can be grouped into areas.
- **Secure** – The OSPF routing protocol supports both **Message Digest 5 (MD5)** and **Secure Hash Algorithm (SHA)** for authentication. This allows two OSPF-enabled routers to authenticate with each other before exchanging OSPF routing details such as network information.
- **Efficiency** – Unlike older dynamic routing protocols, OSPF will only send an update if a change occurs on a network rather than sending periodic updates at specific intervals.
- **Classless** – The OSPF routing protocol supports the use of custom subnet masks and VLSM.

The OSPF routing protocol is made up of various components that enable the protocol to have a clear idea or representation of the entire network topology when it has to tell the router how to forward a packet.

The following are the OSPF components:

- **Adjacency table** – Before OSPF exchanges routing information with a neighbor router on the network, they both need to establish an OSPF **adjacency** with each other. The adjacency is simply like a mutual handshake indicating an agreement that both are willing to share network routes. This adjacency table contains a list of all the neighbor routers that have established an adjacency with a local router. This table is sometimes referred to as the **neighbor table**. The `show ip ospf neighbor` command allows you to view the adjacency table.
- **Link-state database** – The **link-state database (LSDB)** simply contains a list of information about all the OSPF-enabled routers on the network. The LSDB is also used to create the network topology table that OSPF uses to determine the cost of the best path or route to a destination network. The `show ip ospf database` command will allow you to view the contents of the LSDB.
- **Forwarding database** – This is simply the routing table. After the OSPF algorithm, **Shortest Path First (SPF)** calculates all the paths to all the destination networks. It will install the best path (route) within the router's routing table. By using the `show ip route` command, you will be able to view the forwarding database.

In the following section, you will take a deeper dive to further understand the operations of OSPF as a link-state routing protocol.

OSPF Operations

OSPF-enabled routers ensure their OSPF database has up-to-date information about the entire network topology. This allows OSPF to choose the best path at all times. However, to ensure everything works smoothly, OSPF uses the following sequence of operations between all enabled routers on the network:

1. OSPF will attempt to establish **neighbor adjacencies** with other OSPF-enabled routers on the network. When OSPF is enabled on a router's interface, it sends a **hello packet** every 10 seconds like a pulse out of its interface. The hello packet is simply a way to let a neighbor router know it wants to establish an adjacency.
2. After establishing OSPF adjacencies, the routers will begin to exchange **link-state advertisements (LSAs)** with their neighbors on the network. LSAs are special OSPF packets that contain information about the cost and state of the directly connected networks on each neighbor router. When an OSPF-enabled router receives an LSA, it will send that same LSA to all other directly connected neighbors. This process is repeated until all routers within the network receive all the LSAs.
3. All OSPF-enabled routers will use the information contained with the LSAs to build the LSDB. This allows OSPF to virtually see the entire network topology, interface costs, and their states.
4. After the LSDB is built, OSPF executes the **SPF algorithm** to calculate the best path between networks.
5. The SPF algorithm then installs the best path to each network within the forwarding database, also known as the routing table. However, keep in mind that if there is a route with a lower AD than OSPF that already exists within the routing table, the OSPF route will not be installed since the AD takes priority.

The OSPFv2 routing protocol uses the following layer 2 and layer 3 addresses to exchange information:

- Destination multicast MAC address: `01-00-5E-00-00-05` or `01-00-5E-00-00-06`
- IPv4 multicast address: `224.0.0.5` or `224.0.0.6`

In the next section, you will look at the various types of OSPF messages exchanged between routers on a network.

OSPF Messages

Enabling the OSPF routing protocol on a router's interface is quite simple. As a network professional, you need to understand the technical details that happen in the background of OSPF. The OSPF protocol uses various OSPF packet types to send information to a neighbor router. The following are the OSPF packet types and their descriptions:

- **Type 1** – These are the OSPF **hello packets** that are used to create and maintain the neighbor adjacencies.
- **Type 2** – These are known as **database descriptor** (**DBD**) packets. These packets are used to ensure each OSPF-enabled router's LSDB is exactly the same.
- **Type 3** – This type of packet is known as a **link-state request** (**LSR**) packet. OSPF-enabled routers use this packet to request further information about any entry in the DBD by simply sending an LSR.
- **Type 4** – This packet is known as the **link-state update** (**LSU**). These packets are used by OSPF to respond to LSRs and new routing information.
- **Type 5** – This type of packet is the **link-state acknowledgment** (**LSA**). These are sent when an LSU is received from another router.

In the next section, you will learn about the importance of the OSPF hello packet.

OSPF Hello and Dead Timers

To create and maintain an OSPF adjacency with a neighbor router, hello packets are sent every 10 seconds by default to the IPv4 multicast address of `224.0.0.5` and the IPv6 address of `FF02::5`. Sending hello packets constantly creates a pulse that tells a router its neighbor is alive and does not remove any network from the routing table that belongs to the neighbor router. However, on slower networks, such as those that are defined as non-broadcast multiple access networks, OSPF uses a default hello timer of **30 seconds**.

What would happen if an OSPF-enabled router does not receive a hello packet from one of its neighbors within 10 seconds? The neighbor router will be considered down and will be removed from the routing table and its directly connected networks and associated routes. However, OSPF has a default **Dead timer** of **40 seconds** by default, and 120 seconds for non-broadcast multiple access networks. The `Dead` timer is simply a period that an OSPF-enabled router waits to receive a hello packet from its neighbor before declaring the neighbor device is down.

The hello timer must match between neighbors for an OSPF adjacency to be formed. *Figure 11.29* shows two routers – R1 is using the default OSPF `Hello` timer of 10 seconds on its `GigabitEthernet0/1` interface and R2 is using 11 seconds:

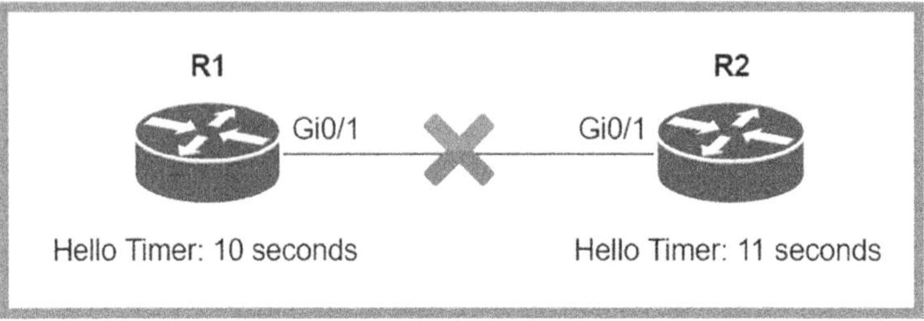

Figure 11.29: Hello timer mismatch

By using the `show ip ospf interface` command, you can verify the `Hello` and `Dead` timers on the interface:

```
R2#show ip ospf interface gigabitEthernet 0/1

GigabitEthernet0/1 is up, line protocol is up
  Internet address is 192.168.1.1/30, Area 0
  Process ID 1, Router ID 192.168.1.1, Network Type BROADCAST, Cost: 1
  Transmit Delay is 1 sec, State WAITING, Priority 1
  No designated router on this network
  No backup designated router on this network
  Timer intervals configured, Hello 11, Dead 40, Wait 40, Retransmit 5
    Hello due in 00:00:08
  Index 1/1, flood queue length 0
  Next 0x0(0)/0x0(0)
```

Figure 11.30: Checking interface timers

Figure 11.30 shows that the OSPF `Hello` timer has been adjusted to 11 seconds on the interface. OSPF allows you to modify the `Hello` and `Dead` timers on each interface on a router. To adjust the `Hello` and `Dead` timers, use the following commands:

```
R2(config)# interface gigabitEthernet 0/1
R2(config-if)# ip ospf hello-interval time-in-seconds
R2(config-if)# ip ospf dead-interval time-in-seconds
```

Keep in mind that the `Dead` timer is always four times the `Hello` timer. In the next section, you will take a look at the various OSPF interface states and their descriptions.

OSPF Interface States

Before OSPF establishes an adjacency with a neighbor, the OSPF-enabled interface on a router has to transition between various operational states. These states are used when creating neighbor adjacencies, exchanging routing details, calculating the best path to a destination network, and ensuring that all routers converge.

The following is the sequence an interface progresses as it reaches convergence:

1. **Down** – In this state, the router sends hello packets but doesn't receive any hello packets from any neighboring router.
2. **Init** – Hello packets are received from a neighboring router.
3. **Two-way** – This state indicates there is two-way communication between two routers.
4. **ExStart** – This state indicates the link is a point-to-point network and the router negotiates which will send the DBD.
5. **Exchange** – This state is where routers are exchanging DBD packets on the network.
6. **Loading** – Within this state, LSR and LSU packets are exchanged between routers to gain more information about routes. The SPF algorithm processes all the routes to calculate the best path to destination networks.
7. **Full** – This state indicates all the routers have converged and know about all the networks, interface costs, and routers.

To verify the OSPF interface states, use the `show ip ospf neighbor` command, as shown in *Figure 11.31*:

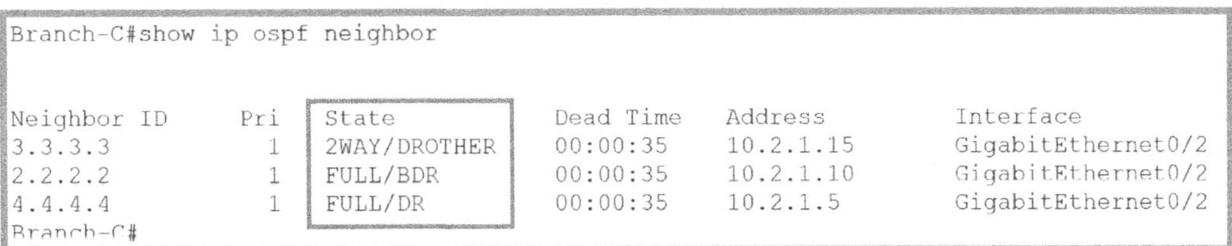

```
Branch-C#show ip ospf neighbor


Neighbor ID     Pri   State           Dead Time   Address         Interface
3.3.3.3           1   2WAY/DROTHER    00:00:35    10.2.1.15       GigabitEthernet0/2
2.2.2.2           1   FULL/BDR        00:00:35    10.2.1.10       GigabitEthernet0/2
4.4.4.4           1   FULL/DR         00:00:35    10.2.1.5        GigabitEthernet0/2
Branch-C#
```

Figure 11.31: Verifying OSPF interface states

In the next section, you will learn how OSPF uses the interface bandwidth to choose its best path.

OSPF Interface Cost

OSPF is a link-state routing protocol, meaning it uses cumulative bandwidth as its metric to determine the most cost-efficient path to a destination network. OSPF uses the following formula to calculate its path cost:

```
Cost = reference bandwidth / interface bandwidth
```

Firstly, you will need to determine the default reference bandwidth on a router. This can be done by using the `show ip ospf` command, as shown in *Figure 11.32*:

```
Number of areas transit capable is 0
External flood list length 0
IETF NSF helper support enabled
Cisco NSF helper support enabled
Reference bandwidth unit is 100 mbps
   Area BACKBONE(0)
       Number of interfaces in this area is 2
       Area has no authentication
       SPF algorithm last executed 00:00:42.221 ago
       SPF algorithm executed 3 times
       Area ranges are
       Number of LSA 3. Checksum Sum 0x018A6A
       Number of opaque link LSA 0. Checksum Sum 0x000000
       Number of DCbitless LSA 0
       Number of indication LSA 0
       Number of DoNotAge LSA 0
       Flood list length 0
```

Figure 11.32: Reference bandwidth

As shown in the preceding snippet, the default reference bandwidth is set to `100`. Next, you can use the `show interfaces` command to obtain the bandwidth value on an interface, as shown in *Figure 11.33*:

```
Branch-A#show interfaces GigabitEthernet 0/2
GigabitEthernet0/2 is up, line protocol is up
  Hardware is iGbE, address is 0ce5.e030.2302 (bia 0ce5.e030.2302)
  Description: Connected to WAN
  Internet address is 10.2.1.10/24
  MTU 1500 bytes, BW 1000000 Kbit/sec, DLY 10 usec,
     reliability 255/255, txload 1/255, rxload 1/255
  Encapsulation ARPA, loopback not set
```

Figure 11.33: Interface bandwidth

Now, you can substitute your values in the formula:

```
Cost = 100 / 1000000
```

The result rounds off to `1`. You can verify the cost of an OSPF-enabled interface, as shown in *Figure 11.34*:

```
Branch-A#show ip ospf interface GigabitEthernet 0/2
GigabitEthernet0/2 is up, line protocol is up
  Internet Address 10.2.1.10/24, Area 0, Attached via Network Statement
  Process ID 1, Router ID 2.2.2.2, Network Type BROADCAST, Cost: 1
  Topology-MTID    Cost    Disabled    Shutdown      Topology Name
        0           1         no          no            Base
  Transmit Delay is 1 sec, State BDR, Priority 1
  Designated Router (ID) 4.4.4.4, Interface address 10.2.1.5
  Backup Designated router (ID) 2.2.2.2, Interface address 10.2.1.10
  Timer intervals configured, Hello 10, Dead 40, Wait 40, Retransmit 5
```

Figure 11.34: OSPF cost

As expected, the OSPF cost on this interface is `1`. OSPF calculates the cost of each interface on all the routers between all networks, then uses the path that has the overall lowest cost as the best path to a destination network.

Interface costs can be manually adjusted simply by using the following commands:

```
R2(config)# interface gigabitEthernet 0/1
R2(config-if)# ip ospf cost value-in-kilobits
```

In the next section, you will cover the concepts of the **designated router** (**DR**) and **backup designated router** (**BDR**).

Designated Router

As mentioned previously, each OSPF-enabled router establishes an adjacency with its neighbors before it can share network routes. Once the adjacencies have been established, hello packets are continuously exchanged between neighbors. What if a router has multiple adjacencies on the same interface?

Take a look at *Figure 11.35* where each router has an adjacency with every other router:

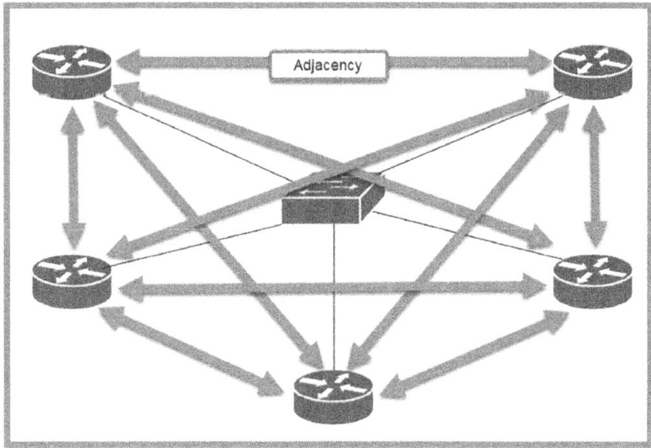

Figure 11.35: OSPF adjacencies

In *Figure 11.35*, all routers share a single multi-access network via the switch. In such situations, each router will be sending hello packets to all other routers, and if there is a topology change, the routers will flood updates to all routers as well.

> **Note**
>
> To calculate the number of adjacencies on a multiaccess network, use the formula $N(N - 1)/2$, where N is the number of routers.

Having so many adjacencies causes extensive flooding of LSAs across the network; creating so many OSPF adjacencies is unnecessary. To help solve this issue, OSPF assigns a DR and a BDR on the network.

All other routers that are not DRs or BDRs become a `DROTHER`. Each `DROTHER` will create an adjacency to the DR and the BDR only. Each router will send its hello packet to both the DR and BDR. When the DR receives the packet from another router, the DR will send the packet to all other routers that require the message. Therefore, a `DROTHER` will have two adjacencies only: one adjacency to the DR and another to the BDR. This reduces the number of unnecessary adjacencies and flooding of link-state messages across the network.

Router ID

A router ID is required by each router to participate in an OSPF domain. Router IDs can be assigned manually or automatically by the router. The router ID is used to uniquely identify a router and participate in the DR and BDR election process.

The router ID is identified in the following order of precedence:

1. The router ID is manually configured via the `router ospf` mode.
2. An IPv4 loopback interface is configured; the IPv4 address of this interface is then used as the router ID.
3. The highest active configured IPv4 address on any interface is used as the router ID.

Figure 11.36 shows both how to configure the router ID using the loopback interface on the router and how to manually configure it within the `router ospf` mode:

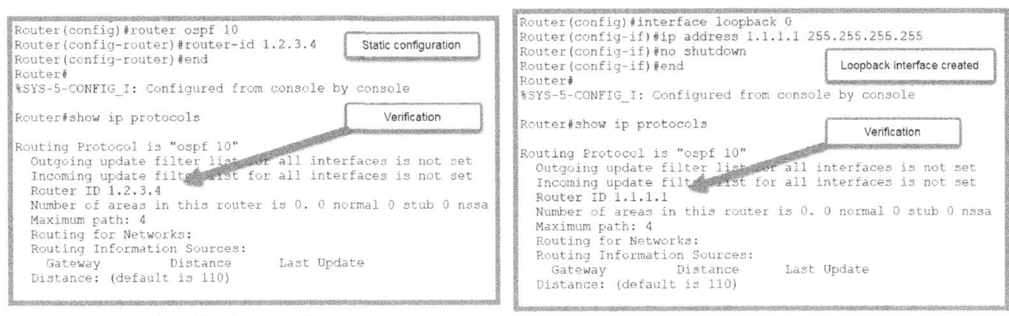

Figure 11.36: Router ID configuration

To reset the router ID, use the `clear ip ospf process` command within privilege mode.

The router ID plays a key role during the DR and BDR election process. In the next section, you can take a look at how OSPF makes its choice in electing a DR on the network.

DR and BDR Election Process

In this section, you will read about the OSPF DR and BDR election process in detail. Imagine there are five OSPF-enabled routers, all sharing a single broadcast network. Each router has been manually configured with a unique 32-bit router ID, as shown in *Figure 11.37*:

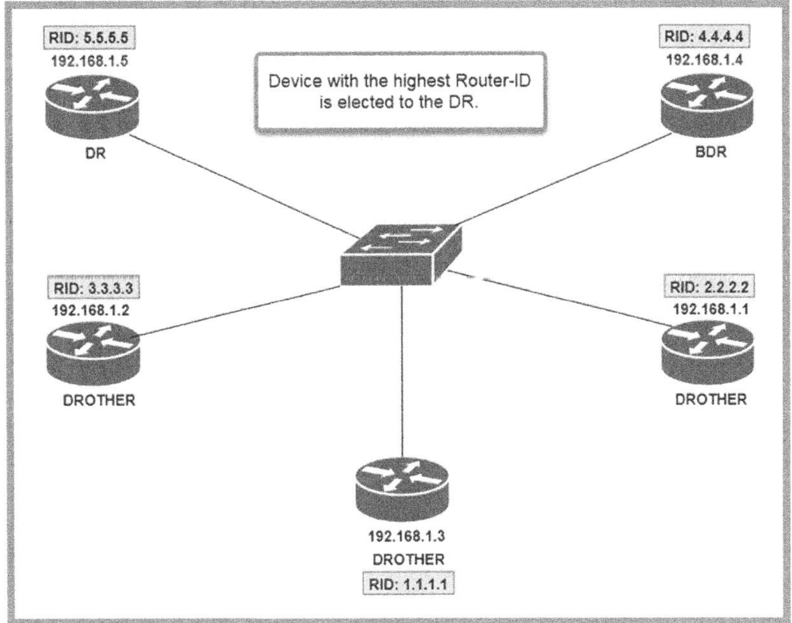

Figure 11.37: DR and BRD election process part 1

The router with the highest router ID is elected as the DR, the router with the second highest router ID is elected as the BDR, and all other routers become DROTHER.

Now, what if the DR goes down? The BDR will become the new DR within the network while the DROTHER with the highest router ID will now become the new BDR, as shown in *Figure 11.38*:

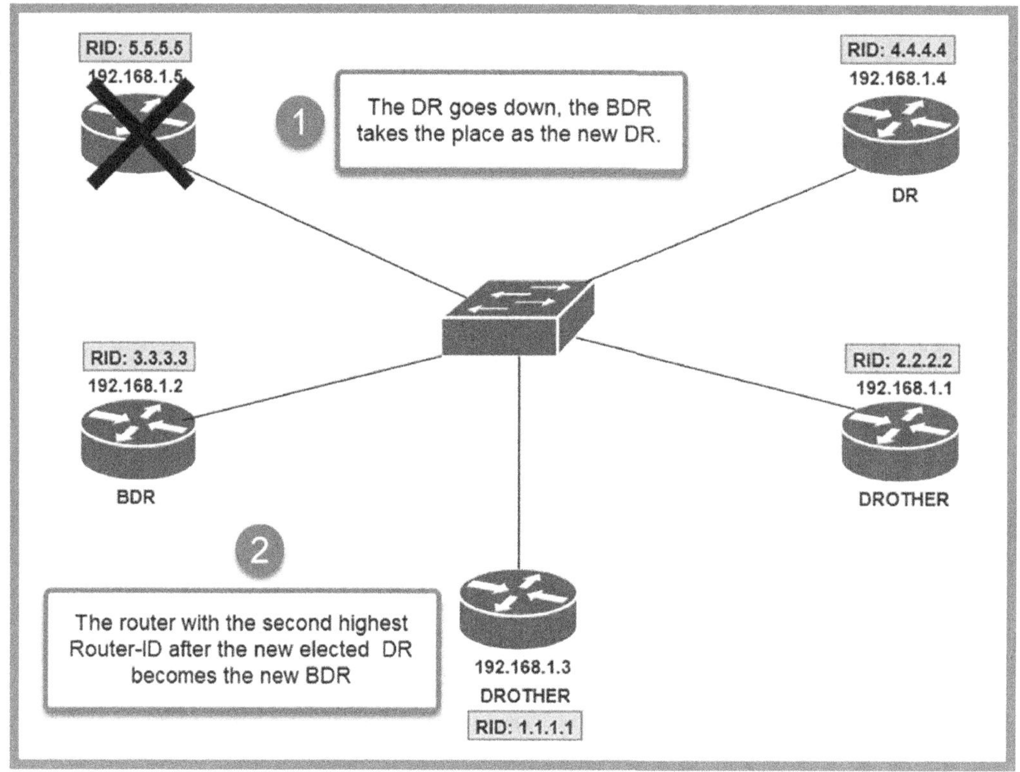

Figure 11.38: DR and BRD election process part 2

What if the original DR comes back online, does it regain the role of DR on the network? The answer is no, it becomes a DROTHER simply because the election process has ended. *Figure 11.39* shows the effect of this situation:

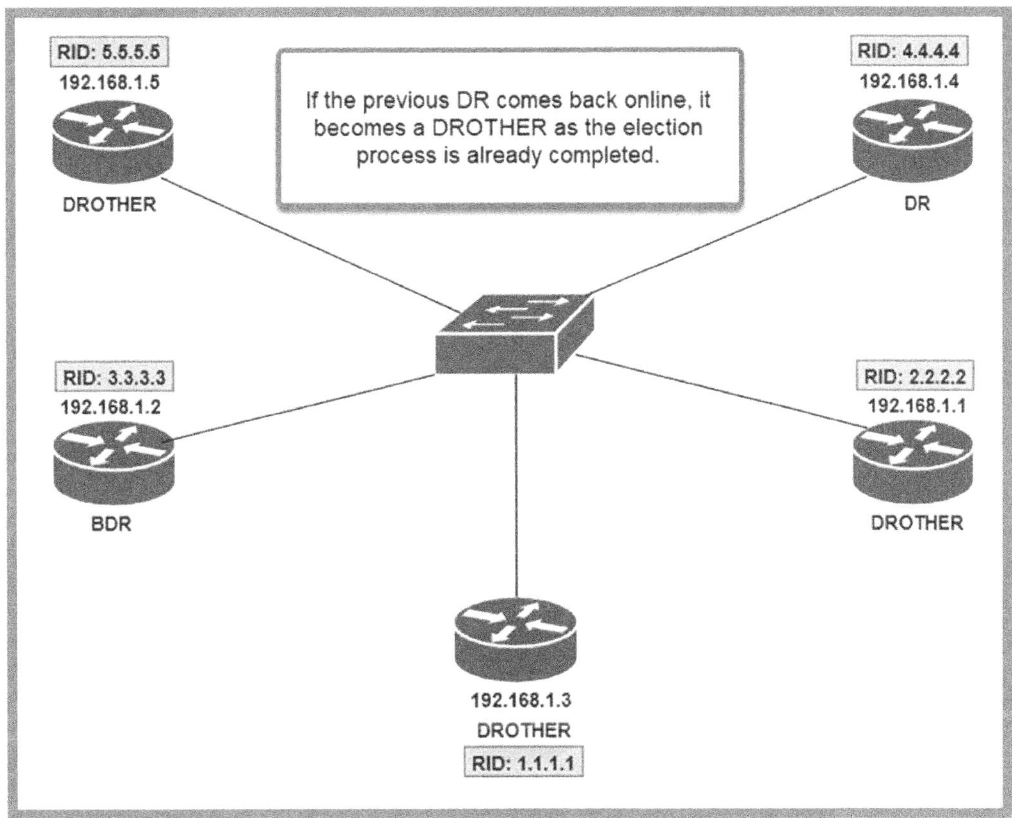

Figure 11.39: DR and BRD election process part 3

In another situation, if a new router with a higher router ID than the DR is inserted within the network, would the new router with the higher router ID become the new DR? As with the previous scenario, since the election process has ended, the new router will be a DROTHER, as shown in *Figure 11.40*:

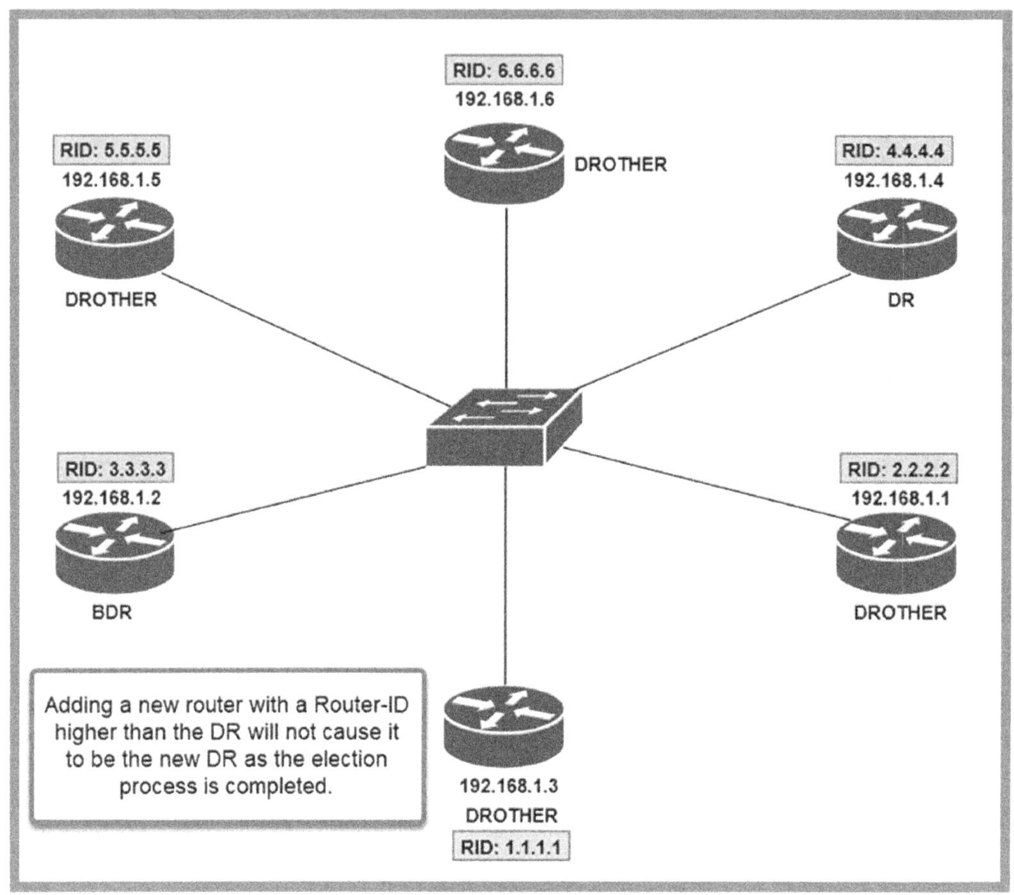

Figure 11.40: DR and BRD election process part 4

Having completed this section, you have gained the essential skills to predict the election of a DR and BDR on a multiaccess network. In the next section, you will learn how to configure OSPFv2 on a Cisco IOS router.

OSPFv2 Commands

Imagine you have to enable the OSPF routing protocol to share routing information on the network topology shown in *Figure 11.41*:

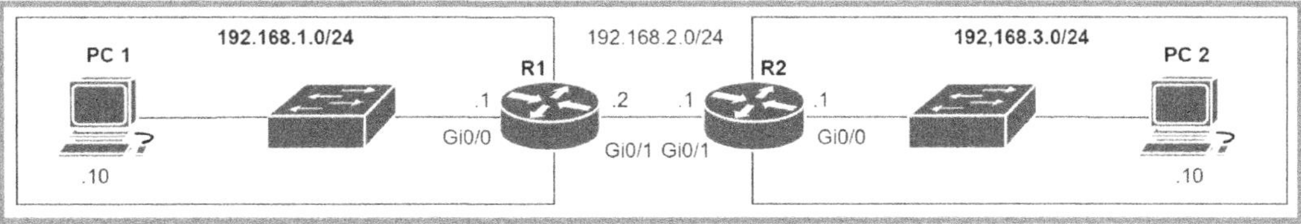

Figure 11.41: Simple network

You can begin by looking to enable OSPF on R1. You will first need to access the `router ospf` mode by using the following syntax:

```
R1(config)# router ospf process-id
```

Here, `process-id` is a numerical value that ranges from `1-65535` and does not have to be the same on other OSPF-enabled routers on the network.

When configuring a dynamic routing protocol, you only advertise your directly connected networks. On R1, there are two directly connected networks: `192.168.1.0/24` and `192.168.2.0/24`. To advertise these two networks, you can use the following syntax:

```
R1(config-router)# network network-ID wildcard-mask area area-id
```

When using the `network` command to advertise a network, OSPF does not allow you to specify a subnet mask but, rather, uses a wildcard mask. A wildcard mask is simply the inverse of a subnet mask. Say you have to represent the subnet mask `255.255.255.0` as a wildcard. You can then use the calculations shown in *Figure 11.42*:

Broadcast Address	255	255	255	255
Subnet Mask	− 255	255	255	0
Wildcard Mask	0	0	0	255

Figure 11.42: Wildcard mask calculations

The broadcast IP address `255.255.255.255` is used at all times with the subnet mask of the network ID. As shown in *Figure 11.42*, the subnet mask is subtracted from the broadcast IP address and the result is the wildcard mask.

Therefore, to advertise the directly connected networks on R1, use the following command:

```
R1(config-router)# network 192.168.1.0 0.0.0.255 area 0
R1(config-router)# network 192.168.2.0 0.0.0.255 area 0
```

Additionally, you can enable OSPF on a specific interface by using the following commands:

```
R1(config-router)# network 192.168.1.1 0.0.0.0 area 0
R1(config-router)# network 192.168.2.2 0.0.0.0 area 0
```

The preceding sets of commands imply that OSPF will only be enabled on interfaces that match the IP addresses `192.168.1.2` and `192.168.2.1`. Therefore, OSPF will not be enabled on an interface with the IP address `192.168.1.129/25`.

Once OSPF has been enabled on a router interface, it is recommended to prevent OSPF messages from entering and leaving interfaces that are not connected to another OSPF neighbor router. Such interfaces include those that are connected to the internet and the LAN interfaces that have switches and end users.

To prevent OSPF messages from entering and leaving an interface, use the following command:

```
R1(config-router)# passive-interface GigabitEthernet 0/0
```

Please keep in mind that this command also prevents OSPF hello packets from being sent and received on the interface and, therefore, prevents OSPF adjacency from forming on this interface.

To manually configure the router ID on R1, use the `router-id` command, as shown here:

```
R1(config-router)# router-id 1.1.1.1
```

To adjust the global reference bandwidth on OSPF, use the following syntax:

```
R1(config-router)# auto-cost reference-bandwidth ?
  <1-4294967>  The reference bandwidth in terms of Mbits per second
```

On Cisco 2911 routers, the default reference bandwidth is set as `100` Mbps. To change the default to 1 Gbps (`1000` Mbps), use the following command within the `router ospf` mode:

```
R1(config-router)# auto-cost reference-bandwidth 1000
```

This configuration must be applied to all other OSPF-enabled routers on the network to ensure OSPF makes accurate calculations to determine the best path and routes.

Now that you have learned about the essential commands needed to implement OSPF on a network, you can dive into a hands-on lab in the next section.

Lab: Configuring OSPFv2

In this hands-on lab, you will learn how to implement the OSPF routing protocol to automatically populate the routing table on each Cisco router and calculate the best path to each remote network. The topology shown in *Figure 11.43* will be used in this exercise:

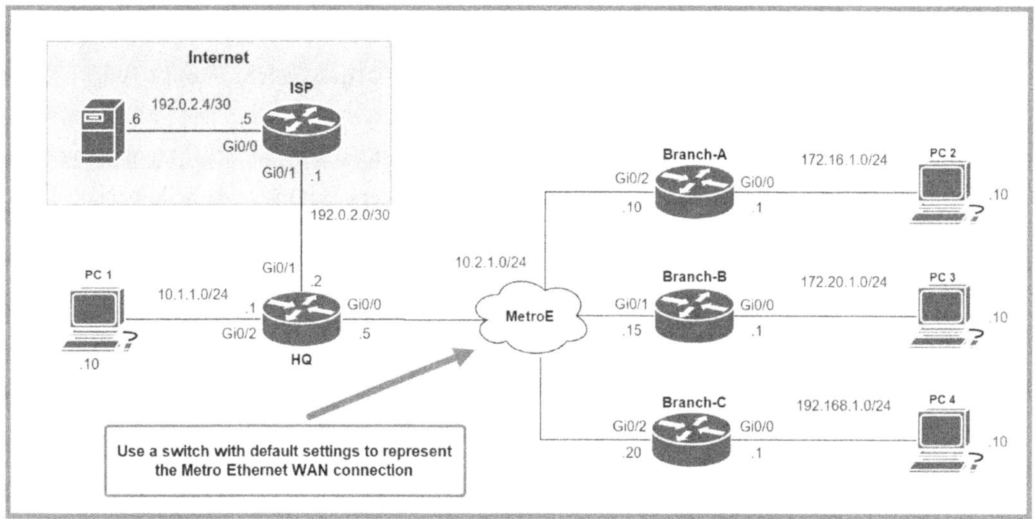

Figure 11.43: IPv4 OSPF routing lab topology

Before getting started, ensure you have downloaded a copy of the pre-built lab template from `https://packt.link/CCNArepoCh11`.

To get started with configuring OSPF in your topology, use the following instructions:

1. Begin by configuring the HQ router to use OSPF to automatically learn remote networks. To begin, enter the router's OSPF mode using the process ID of `1`:

```
HQ(config)# router ospf 1
```

2. Manually set the `router-ID` value as `4.4.4.4`:

```
HQ(config-router)# router-id 4.4.4.4
```

3. Disable LSAs or OSPF packets from leaving all interfaces as a security measure:

```
HQ(config-router)# passive-interface default
```

4. Use the `network` command to advertise the networks that are directly connected to `HQ` and use the default `area` value of `0`:

```
HQ(config-router)# network 10.1.1.0 0.0.0.255 area 0
HQ(config-router)# network 10.2.1.0 0.0.0.255 area 0
```

5. Allow OSPF packets/LSAs to only be sent out of interfaces that have another OSPF-enabled router:

```
HQ(config-router)# no passive-interface GigabitEthernet 0/0
HQ(config-router)# exit
```

   If the `passive-interface` command is applied to the WAN interface, it will not be able to form an adjacency with the other OSPF-enabled routers as it prevents hello packets from entering and leaving the interface. Now that you have configured OSPF on the `HQ` router, you can do the same for the other branch routers.

6. Use the following commands on the `Branch-A` router to enable the OSPF routing protocol:

```
Branch-A(config)# router ospf 1
Branch-A(config-router)# router-id 2.2.2.2
Branch-A(config-router)# passive-interface default
Branch-A(config-router)# network 172.16.1.0 0.0.0.255 area 0
Branch-A(config-router)# network 10.2.1.0 0.0.0.255 area 0
Branch-A(config-router)# no passive-interface GigabitEthernet
0/2
Branch-A(config-router)# exit
```

7. Use the following commands to configure the `Branch-B` router:

```
Branch-B(config)# router ospf 1
Branch-B(config-router)# router-id 3.3.3.3
Branch-B(config-router)# passive-interface default
Branch-B(config-router)# network 172.20.1.0 0.0.0.255 area 0
Branch-B(config-router)# network 10.2.1.0 0.0.0.255 area 0
Branch-B(config-router)# no passive-interface GigabitEthernet
0/1
Branch-B(config-router)# exit
```

8. Let's not forget about the `Branch-C` router. Use the following configurations to enable OSPF:

```
Branch-C(config)# router ospf 1
Branch-C(config-router)# router-id 1.1.1.1
Branch-C(config-router)# passive-interface default
Branch-C(config-router)# network 192.168.1.0 0.0.0.255 area 0
Branch-C(config-router)# network 10.2.1.0 0.0.0.255 area 0
Branch-C(config-router)# no passive-interface GigabitEthernet
0/2
Branch-C(config-router)# exit
```

   At this point, each branch network is able to intercommunicate. However, you cannot forget about setting up a default route to the internet.

9. To configure a default route on HQ that points toward the internet, use the following commands:

```
HQ(config)# ip route 0.0.0.0 0.0.0.0 192.0.2.1
```

10. Use OSPF to automatically propagate the default route to all other OSPF-enabled routers from HQ:

```
HQ(config)# router ospf 1
HQ(config-router)# default-information originate
HQ(config-router)# exit
```

   By using the `default-information originate` command, the default route will automatically be distributed to all other OSPF-enabled routers. This saves you time from manually configuring a default route on each router within your topology and network.

11. To simulate your internet connection properly, create a default route from the ISP router back to HQ:

```
ISP(config)# ip route 0.0.0.0 0.0.0.0 192.0.2.2
```

Having completed this lab, you have gained the hands-on skills to deploy the OSPF routing protocol in a real-world network environment using Cisco routers. In the next section, you will take a look at understanding how to perform troubleshooting when using the OSPF routing protocol.

Validating OSPF Configurations

As a network professional, you need to always verify the configurations on your devices. You can start by taking a look at the routing table and ensuring that each router has routes to all remote networks and a route that points to the internet.

Figure 11.44 shows the routing table of the Branch-A router:

```
Branch-A#show ip route
Gateway of last resort is 10.2.1.5 to network 0.0.0.0

     10.0.0.0/8 is variably subnetted, 3 subnets, 2 masks
O       10.1.1.0/24 [110/2] via 10.2.1.5, 00:37:01, GigabitEthernet0/2
C       10.2.1.0/24 is directly connected, GigabitEthernet0/2
L       10.2.1.10/32 is directly connected, GigabitEthernet0/2
     172.16.0.0/16 is variably subnetted, 2 subnets, 2 masks
C       172.16.1.0/24 is directly connected, GigabitEthernet0/0
L       172.16.1.1/32 is directly connected, GigabitEthernet0/0
     172.20.0.0/24 is subnetted, 1 subnets
O       172.20.1.0/24 [110/2] via 10.2.1.15, 00:33:19, GigabitEthernet0/2
O    192.168.1.0/24 [110/2] via 10.2.1.20, 00:32:11, GigabitEthernet0/2
O*E2 0.0.0.0/0 [110/1] via 10.2.1.5, 00:30:01, GigabitEthernet0/2
```

Figure 11.44: Branch-A routing table

In *Figure 11.44*, you can see that all remote networks are learned and populated within the routing table via the OSPF routing protocol. The remote networks are those that are not directly connected to the Branch-A router. Furthermore, the last route is the default route from the HQ router that you propagate using the `default-information originate` command. Hence, the Branch-A router has a gateway of last resort that has been set automatically via OSPF.

Another important troubleshooting command you must know is the `show ip protocols` command. Whenever you have a dynamic routing protocol such as OSPF, EIGRP, and RIP, the `show ip protocols` command will always prevent details about the current running protocols on the local router.

Take a look at *Figure 11.45*:

```
Branch-A#show ip protocols

Routing Protocol is "ospf 1"        <-- Process-ID
  Outgoing update filter list for all interfaces is not set
  Incoming update filter list for all interfaces is not set
  Router ID 2.2.2.2
  Number of areas in this router is 1. 1 normal 0 stub 0 nssa
  Maximum path: 4
  Routing for Networks:
    172.16.1.0 0.0.0.255 area 0
    10.2.1.0 0.0.0.255 area 0
```

Figure 11.45: OSPF process ID

From the output, you can determine the following about the routing protocol:

- The OSPF routing protocol is currently enabled on the `Branch-A` router.
- OSPF is currently using the `process-ID` value of `1`. Please note, the `process-ID` value does not need to match between OSPF-enabled routers.
- The router ID was manually configured as `2.2.2.2`.
- If there are multiple routes to the same network that have the same cost value (metric), OSPF will load-balance up to a total of four paths.
- The `Branch-A` router is advertising it has networks `10.2.1.0/24` and `172.16.1.0/24`.

Take a look at the remaining portions of the `show ip protocols` output, shown in *Figure 11.46*:

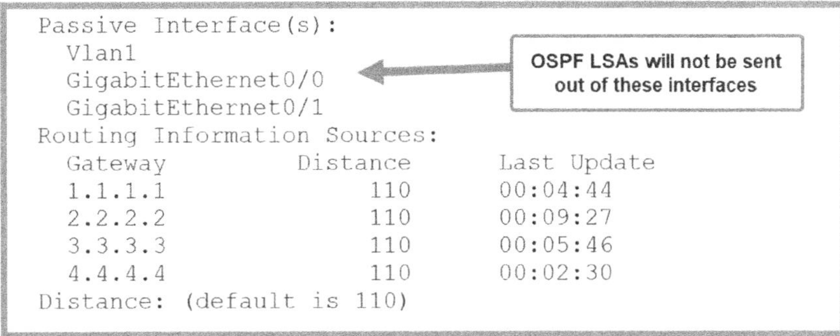

```
Passive Interface(s):
  Vlan1
  GigabitEthernet0/0
  GigabitEthernet0/1
Routing Information Sources:
  Gateway          Distance        Last Update
  1.1.1.1               110        00:04:44
  2.2.2.2               110        00:09:27
  3.3.3.3               110        00:05:46
  4.4.4.4               110        00:02:30
Distance: (default is 110)
```


Figure 11.46: Analyzing the routing protocol

You can further determine the following based on *Figure 11.46*:

- The interfaces listed under `Passive Interface(s)` will not send or receive any OSPF messages
- The local router is sharing routes with additional OSPF-enabled routers, their AD, and their `Last Update` timer

The `show ip ospf neighbor` command provides you with details about OSPF-enabled neighbor devices:

```
Branch-A#show ip ospf neighbor


Neighbor ID     Pri   State           Dead Time   Address         Interface
4.4.4.4           1   FULL/DR         00:00:34    10.2.1.5        GigabitEthernet0/2
3.3.3.3           1   FULL/BDR        00:00:38    10.2.1.15       GigabitEthernet0/2
1.1.1.1           1   2WAY/DROTHER    00:00:31    10.2.1.20       GigabitEthernet0/2
Branch-A#
```

Figure 11.47: OSPF neighbors

The following is a breakdown of each column from the `show ip ospf neighbor` output:

- The `Neighbor ID` columns contain a list of OSPF neighbors that have an adjacency with the local router. This value is the router ID.
- The `Pri` column contains the priority value for each neighbor adjacency.
- The `State` column contains the link status for each OSPF neighbor adjacency.
- The `Dead Time` column is used to indicate when a hello packet was last received from each neighbor. This timer always counts down and refreshes whenever the local router receives a hello packet.
- The `Address` column contains the actual IP address assigned on the neighbor's interface.
- The `Interface` column displays the local interface used to create an adjacency with the neighbor router.

The `show ip ospf interface` command can be used to verify the following details about OSPF:

- The OSPF process ID associated with the OSPF-enabled interface on the router
- The OSPF router ID value
- The DR and its IP address
- The BDR and its IP address
- The OSPF `Hello` and `Dead` timer values on the interface
- The number of OSPF adjacencies that exist on this interface

Figure 11.48 shows the output of using the `show ip ospf interface` command for `Branch-A`:

```
Branch-A#show ip ospf interface GigabitEthernet 0/2

GigabitEthernet0/2 is up, line protocol is up
  Internet address is 10.2.1.10/24, Area 0
  Process ID 1, Router ID 2.2.2.2, Network Type BROADCAST, Cost: 1
  Transmit Delay is 1 sec, State DROTHER, Priority 1
  Designated Router (ID) 4.4.4.4, Interface address 10.2.1.5
  Backup Designated Router (ID) 3.3.3.3, Interface address 10.2.1.15
  Timer intervals configured, Hello 10, Dead 40, Wait 40, Retransmit 5
    Hello due in 00:00:09
  Index 2/2, flood queue length 0
  Next 0x0(0)/0x0(0)
  Last flood scan length is 1, maximum is 1
  Last flood scan time is 0 msec, maximum is 0 msec
  Neighbor Count is 3, Adjacent neighbor count is 2
    Adjacent with neighbor 4.4.4.4  (Designated Router)
    Adjacent with neighbor 3.3.3.3  (Backup Designated Router)
  Suppress hello for 0 neighbor(s)
Branch-A#
```

Figure 11.48: Verifying OSPF interface details

Another useful command to check the interfaces of a router that is participating in OSPF is the `show ip ospf interface brief` command. The link will provide you with details about an interface. Take a look at *Figure 11.49*, which was taken from the `Branch-A` router:

```
Branch-A#show ip ospf interface brief
Interface    PID   Area            IP Address/Mask    Cost  State Nbrs F/C
Gi0/2        1     0               10.2.1.10/24       1     BDR   3/3
Gi0/0        1     0               172.16.1.1/24      1     DR    0/0
Branch-A#
```

Figure 11.49: OSPF interfaces

The first row indicates that `GigabitEthernet0/2` is participating in the OSPF instance that's associated with the OSPF process ID value of `1` and the interface belongs to OSPF area `0`, the backbone area. Additionally, the IP address and subnet mask provided for the interface are shown with the OSPF `Cost` value and the OSPF state of the interface.

Lastly, you must not forget to test end-to-end connectivity on the lab network. *Figure 11.50* shows a ping test from the `Branch-A` LAN interface (`172.16.1.1`) to the server at `192.0.2.6`:

```
Branch-A#ping 192.0.2.6 source 172.16.1.1
Type escape sequence to abort.
Sending 5, 100-byte ICMP Echos to 192.0.2.6, timeout is 2 seconds:
Packet sent with a source address of 172.16.1.1
!!!!!
Success rate is 100 percent (5/5), round-trip min/avg/max = 9/14/23 ms
Branch-A#
```

Figure 11.50: Connectivity test

The syntax used in *Figure 11.50* will only work on the actual Cisco IOS images and devices. It allows you to specify a source IP address, such that you can use the source IP address from an interface on the router that is attempting to connect between remote networks.

Now that you have completed this section, you have gained the knowledge and hands-on skills to describe, configure, troubleshoot, and validate OSPF and its configurations in a Cisco environment.

Understanding First-Hop Redundancy

Within your organization, each device is configured to use a specific IP address as its default gateway to the internet. What if that IP address or device goes offline? How will your client devices reach the internet?

Figure 11.51 shows how a default gateway goes down, preventing clients from reaching the internet:

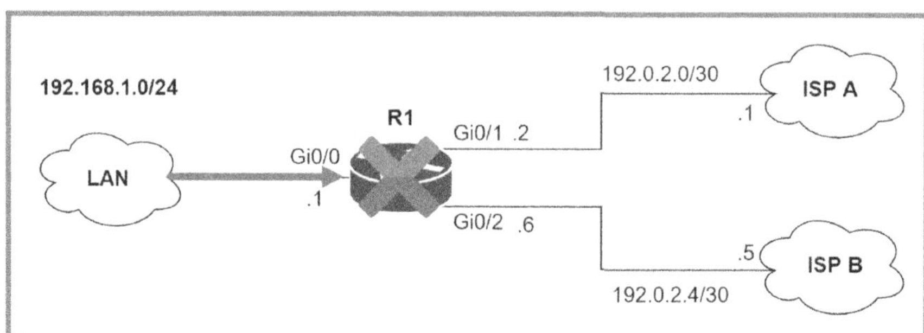

Figure 11.51: Default gateway goes offline

You may be thinking that you can replace the router with another and apply the same configurations to it and the internet connectivity will be restored. This is a workable solution, but it is not too efficient, because it requires many interventions and is a reactive solution.

How can you implement redundancy for the default gateway to ensure continuous connectivity if the main router fails? What if there is another device that will act as the new default gateway without changing the default gateway's IP address on any of the clients? This is possible with a Cisco IOS router.

The technology known as **First Hop Redundancy Protocol** (**FHRP**) allows you to use two Cisco IOS routers to create a single virtual router that has a virtual IP address and virtual MAC address. The virtual IP address and virtual MAC address will be shared between the two physical routers. Additionally, the virtual IP address will act as the default gateway for the clients. Therefore, one physical router will have the role of the active router, which will route traffic back and forth to the internet, and the other physical router will be the standby router. In the event the active router goes offline, the standby router will assume the role of the new active router with the virtual IP address.

Figure 11.52 shows R1 as the active router:

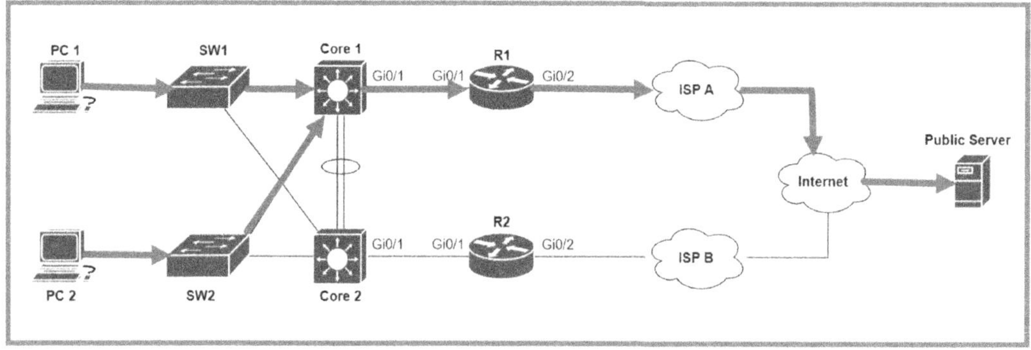

Figure 11.52: Active router

In the event that R1 goes down in the network topology, the standby router (R2) will take up the role of the active router on the network. This causes very little service interruption as the failover happens. *Figure 11.53* shows the traffic flow when the R2 becomes the new active router on the network:

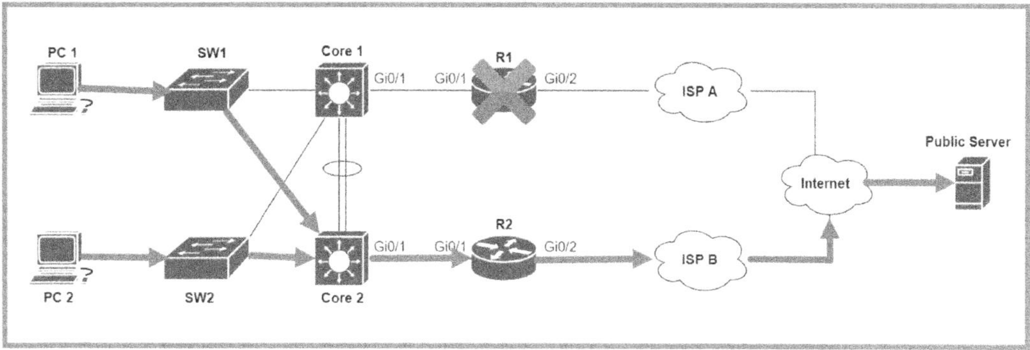

Figure 11.53: New active router

Using FHRP is a better solution as it's proactive and does not require the intervention of the network professional. There are a few FHRPs in the industry: in the next section, you will learn their characteristics.

Various FHRPs

The following subsection will briefly outline the characteristics of each FHRP that can be implemented in a network to ensure internal host devices are always able to reach their default gateway.

Hot Standby Router Protocol

The **Hot Standby Router Protocol** (**HSRP**) is a Cisco-proprietary FHRP that allows two or more Cisco IOS routers to be grouped into a cluster to create a virtual router. The virtual router will have a virtual IP address that will be shared between all physical routers that are part of the HSRP group.

The following are the two states of an HSRP router:

- **Active** – The active router is one that is actively forwarding packets as the default gateway
- **Standby** – In the event the active router goes offline, the standby router will assume the role of being the new active router and traffic will be routed through the new active router

Table 11.1 outlines the differences between HSRP version 1 and version 2:

HSRP Version 1	**HSRP Version 2**
Enabled by default on Cisco IOS 15	Not enabled by default
Supports group numbers between `0` and `255`	Supports group numbers between `0` and `4095`
Uses multicast address of `224.0.0.2`	Uses multicast address of `224.0.0.102`
Uses virtual MAC address range `0000.0C07.AC00` to `0000.0C07.ACFF`	Uses virtual MAC address range `0000.0C9F.F000` to `0000.0C9F.FFFF` for IPv4 and `0005.73A0.0000` through `0005.73A0.0FFF` for IPv6 addresses
Does not support authentication	Uses MD5 for authentication

Table 11.1: HSRP versions

When configuring HSRP, the router with the highest IPv4 address will be selected as the active router within the group while all others will be standby routers. Additionally, the default HSRP priority is `100` on all routers; the router with the highest HSRP priority value will be elected as the active router. The `preempt` command enables preemption and forces an HSRP re-election process; this should be done to ensure a specific router becomes the active router.

> **Note**
> By default, preemption is disabled in HSRP.

Since preemption is disabled, the router that boots up first will take the role of the active router. HSRP uses hello packets that are sent every three seconds by default. If a standby router does not receive a hello packet from the active router after 10 seconds, it will assume that the active router is down and take the role of the new active router.

Furthermore, there is an HSRP for IPv6 networks. This version of HSRP has the same functionality as its IPv4 version.

Virtual Router Redundancy Protocol

The **Virtual Router Redundancy Protocol** (**VRRP**), currently at version 2, is a vendor-neutral FHRP that also supports two or more physical routers being grouped together to create a virtual router on an IPv4 network. VRRPv2 allows multiple routers to join the VRRP group and share the same virtual IP address to provide default gateway redundancy on an enterprise network.

> **Note**
> Preemption is enabled by default in VRRP.

VRRP uses the following two router states:

- **Master** – The master router is the one that currently has the responsibility of acting as the default gateway and forwarding packets back and forth between networks
- **Backup** – The backup router takes the role of master only in the event of the actual master router going offline

Additionally, VRRPv3 supports first-hop redundancy on an IPv6 network environment and is a bit more scalable as compared to VRRPv2.

Gateway Load Balancing Protocol

The **Gateway Load Balancing Protocol** (**GLBP**) is a bit different from the previously mentioned FHRPs. GLBP allows load-balancing between the routers that are part of the GLBP group. To put it simply, if you have two physical routers within a GLBP group, traffic that is sent to the default gateway IP address will be load-balanced between all the routers using a round-robin technique.

> **Note**
> GLBP is another Cisco-proprietary FHRP. Preemption is disabled by default on GLBP.

GLBP ensures that one router does not handle all the load and constraint of being the default gateway, it allows the other routers to share the load as well. GLBP uses the following router statuses:

- **Active** – Similar to HSRP, the active router is the one that has the current role as the default gateway
- **Standby** – The standby router provides the failover in the event the active router goes down

Lastly, GLBP for IPv6 supports the implementation within an IPv6 environment.

Lab: Implementing HSRP

In this hands-on lab, you will learn how to implement HSRP as the preferred FHRP in a Cisco environment to ensure the default gateway is always available. The topology shown in *Figure 11.54* will be used for this exercise:

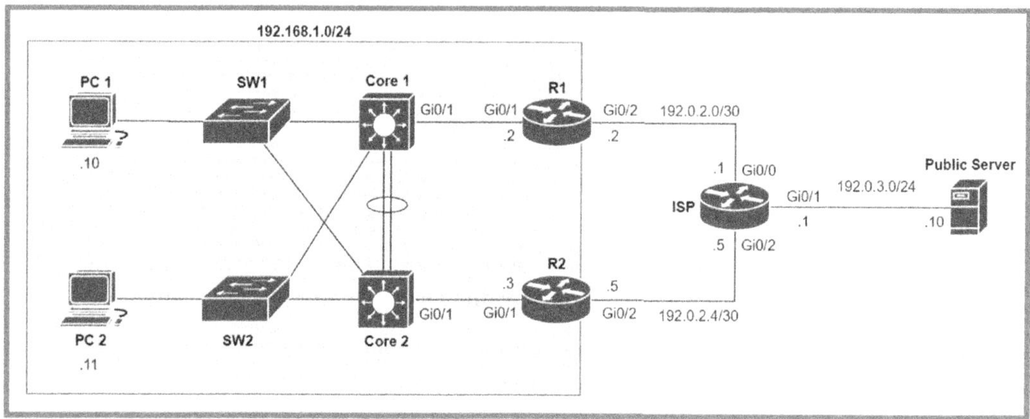

Figure 11.54: HSRP lab topology

To follow along, ensure you download the pre-built lab template from `https://packt.link/CCNArepoCh11`.

Now that your lab is ready, follow the given instructions to create a virtual router using HSRP:

1. Ensure R1 and R2 have the following default routes within their routing tables:

```
R1(config)# ip route 0.0.0.0 0.0.0.0 192.0.2.1
R2(config)# ip route 0.0.0.0 0.0.0.0 192.0.2.5
```

2. On R1, enable HSRP version 2 on the LAN interface on the router using the following commands:

```
R1(config)# interface GigabitEthernet 0/1
R1(config-if)# standby version 2
```

3. Create the virtual IP address that will be used as the default gateway for clients on the network:

```
R1(config-if)# standby 1 ip 192.168.1.1
```

4. Set the HSRP priority number to be greater than 100 to ensure this router becomes the active (desired) router by using the following command:

```
R1(config-if)# standby 1 priority 150
```

5. Configure this router to preempt the standby router:

```
R1(config-if)# standby 1 preempt
R1(config-if)# exit
```

Now that you have configured R1 as the active router, head over to R2 as it requires configuration to be the standby router within the HSRP group. The standby router will take the place of the active router in the event that R1 goes down or offline.

6. To configure R2 as the standby router, use the following commands:

```
R2(config)# interface GigabitEthernet 0/1
R2(config-if)# standby version 2
```

7. Configure the virtual IP address of the default gateway:

```
R2(config-if)# standby 1 ip 192.168.1.1
R2(config-if)# exit
```

8. Configure the following default routes on the ISP router to ensure that the internet side of the lab is working:

```
ISP(config)# ip route 0.0.0.0 0.0.0.0 192.0.2.2
ISP(config)# ip route 0.0.0.0 0.0.0.0 192.0.2.6 2
```

Now that you have finished with the configuration aspect of this lab, you can validate and troubleshoot the configurations on your lab environment.

Use the following steps to perform troubleshooting on HSRP:

1. One of the most important troubleshooting commands for HSRP is the `show standby` command. The output of this command provides you with vital information about the HSRP status on the local router, such as the following:

   - The HSRP router's state, whether active or standby
   - The virtual IP address and MAC address for the virtual router
   - The `Hello` and `Hold down` timers on the interface
   - Whether preempt has been configured on the interface or not
   - Whether the local router is the active or standby router
   - The IP address of the standby router
   - The HSRP priority value

2. *Figure 11.55* shows the output of the `show standby` command on R1 in our lab:

```
R1#show standby
GigabitEthernet0/1 - Group 1 (version 2)
  State is Active
    15 state changes, last state change 00:21:43
  Virtual IP address is 192.168.1.1
  Active virtual MAC address is 0000.0C9F.F001
    Local virtual MAC address is 0000.0C9F.F001 (v2 default)
  Hello time 3 sec, hold time 10 sec
    Next hello sent in 0.638 secs
  Preemption enabled
  Active router is local
  Standby router is 192.168.1.3, priority 100 (expires in 9 sec)
  Priority 150 (configured 150)
  Group name is hsrp-Gig0/1-1 (default)
R1#
```

Figure 11.55: HSRP status on R1

3. Take a look at the `show standby` output on R2. You will notice the state of R2 is set to `Standby` and the active router in the group is `192.168.1.1`, which is R1's IP address:

```
R2#show standby
GigabitEthernet0/1 - Group 1 (version 2)
  State is Standby
    13 state changes, last state change 00:22:03
  Virtual IP address is 192.168.1.1
  Active virtual MAC address is 0000.0C9F.F001
    Local virtual MAC address is 0000.0C9F.F001 (v2 default)
  Hello time 3 sec, hold time 10 sec
    Next hello sent in 1.031 secs
  Preemption disabled
  Active router is 192.168.1.2, priority 150 (expires in 8 sec)
    MAC address is 0000.0C9F.F001
  Standby router is local
  Priority 100 (default 100)
  Group name is hsrp-Gig0/1-1 (default)
R2#
```

Figure 11.56: HSRP status on R2

4. Furthermore, to see a summary of the HSRP status on either router, use the `show standby brief` command:

```
R1#show standby brief
                     P indicates configured to preempt.
                     |
Interface   Grp  Pri P State   Active          Standby         Virtual IP
Gig0/1      1    150 P Active  local           192.168.1.3     192.168.1.1
R1#
```

Figure 11.57: HSRP status summary

5. The `show standby brief` output provides you with the local interface configured with HSRP, the HSRP group number, the HSRP priority value, the interface state, the HRSP router state, the standby router, and the virtual IP address of the virtual router.
6. For the final connectivity test, perform a traceroute from PC 1 (`192.168.1.10`) to the public server at `192.0.3.10`:

```
C:\>tracert 192.0.3.10

Tracing route to 192.0.3.10 over a maximum of 30 hops:

  1    1 ms       0 ms       0 ms       192.168.1.2
  2    0 ms       0 ms       1 ms       192.0.2.1
  3    1 ms       0 ms       0 ms       192.0.3.10

Trace complete.
```

Figure 11.58: Traceroute connectivity test

7. According to the output shown in *Figure 11.58*, the packet took the path via R1 as the active router within the HSRP group as expected.
8. Create a network failure by shutting down both the `GigabitEthernet0/1` and `GigabitEthernet0/2` interfaces on R1 only. This will create the effect of R1 going offline on the network. After a few seconds, perform another traceroute test from PC 1 to the server once more.
9. *Figure 11.59* shows the new traceroute results when R1 has gone offline:

```
C:\>tracert 192.0.3.10

Tracing route to 192.0.3.10 over a maximum of 30 hops:

  1    1 ms       0 ms       0 ms       192.168.1.3
  2    0 ms       0 ms       0 ms       192.0.2.5
  3    0 ms       0 ms       1 ms       192.0.3.10

Trace complete.
```

Figure 11.59: New traceroute results

10. R2 has assumed the role of being the active router within the HSRP group and the packets are now taking a new path via R2 (`192.168.1.3`) to reach the public server. The default gateway configured on the client devices remained as `192.168.1.1`.

Having completed this section, you have gained the hands-on experience to configure first-hop redundancy using HSRP to create a virtual router to ensure internal devices on the corporate LAN are able to access the internet.

Summary

During the course of this chapter, you have taken a deep dive into discussing and demonstrating how to establish IP connectivity between remote networks using Cisco routers. Having completed this chapter on IP connectivity, you have gained the skills to set up both static and dynamic routing on an enterprise network to ensure there's end-to-end connectivity. Furthermore, you've learned how to propagate a default router through a Cisco environment that allows users to reach the internet from their client device.

Covering the different types of static routes and understanding their use cases is important for both the certification exam and applying the skills in the real world. Understanding how OSFP works will enable you to predict the potential route/path that a router will use for sending a packet toward its destination. In addition, having covered the role and function of various FHRPs, you have learned how industry professionals implement redundancy in their gateways.

In the next chapter, *Configuring Network Address Translation (NAT)*, you will take a deep dive into learning how to implement various types of NAT on a Cisco router.

Additional Reading

- Understanding static routing: `https://www.cisco.com/c/en/us/td/docs/switches/datacenter/sw/5_x/nx-os/unicast/configuration/guide/l3_cli_nxos/l3_route.html`
- RIP routing: `https://www.cisco.com/c/en/us/td/docs/ios-xml/ios/iproute_rip/configuration/15-mt/irr-15-mt-book/irr-cfg-info-prot.html`
- EIGRP routing: `https://www.cisco.com/c/en/us/td/docs/ios-xml/ios/iproute_eigrp/configuration/15-mt/ire-15-mt-book/ire-enhanced-igrp.html`
- OSPF routing: `https://www.cisco.com/c/en/us/td/docs/ios-xml/ios/iproute_ospf/configuration/xe-16/iro-xe-16-book/iro-cfg.html`
- Understanding HSRP: `https://www.cisco.com/c/en/us/td/docs/switches/lan/catalyst3750x_3560x/software/release/12-2_55_se/configuration/guide/3750xscg/swhsrp.html`

Exam Readiness Drill – Chapter Review Questions

Apart from mastering key concepts, strong test-taking skills under time pressure are essential for acing your certification exam. That's why developing these abilities early in your learning journey is critical.

Exam readiness drills, using the free online practice resources provided with this book, help you progressively improve your time management and test-taking skills while reinforcing the key concepts you've learned.

HOW TO GET STARTED

- Open the link or scan the QR code at the bottom of this page
- If you have unlocked the practice resources already, log in to your registered account. If you haven't, follow the instructions in *Chapter 19* and come back to this page.
- Once you log in, click the START button to start a quiz
- We recommend attempting a quiz multiple times till you're able to answer most of the questions correctly and well within the time limit.
- You can use the following practice template to help you plan your attempts:

Working On Accuracy		
Attempt	**Target**	**Time Limit**
Attempt 1	40% or more	Till the timer runs out
Attempt 2	60% or more	Till the timer runs out
Attempt 3	75% or more	Till the timer runs out
Working On Timing		
Attempt 4	75% or more	1 minute before time limit
Attempt 5	75% or more	2 minutes before time limit
Attempt 6	75% or more	3 minutes before time limit

The above drill is just an example. Design your drills based on your own goals and make the most out of the online quizzes accompanying this book.

First time accessing the online resources? 🔓

You'll need to unlock them through a one-time process. **Head to** *Chapter 19* **for instructions.**

Open Quiz https://packt.link/ccnachap11 OR scan this QR code →	

12
Network Address Translation

By now, you have learned about some amazing technologies and have gained a lot of hands-on skills. One of the most important parts of learning about networking is establishing connectivity between different IP networks. However, connecting a private IP network to a public network such as the internet will not work as simply as expected. Private networks (as defined by RFC 1918 addresses) are non-routable on the internet. So how do devices on a private network access the internet?

Network address translation (**NAT**) creates the magic between private and public networks. By completing this chapter, you will learn about the various types of NAT and how to implement static NAT, dynamic NAT, and **port address translation** (**PAT**) on a Cisco network. Finally, you will learn how to implement NAT to ensure you have internet connectivity on an enterprise network.

This chapter covers *Domain 4: IP Services*, objective *4.1 Configure and verify inside source NAT using static and pools* of the *200-301 CCNA v1.1* certification exam.

In this chapter, you will learn about the following topics:

- Understanding NAT
- Types of NAT
- Configuring PAT
- Configuring static NAT with port forwarding
- Implementing dynamic NAT

Let's dive in!

Challenges of Using IPv4 on the Internet

One of the common issues that exist with IPv4 addresses is that there aren't enough public IPv4 addresses to assign for each unique device that is connected to the internet, whether these devices are on private networks within organizations or directly connected to the internet. As you learned in *Chapter 4, IPv4 and IPv6 Addressing*, each device that is directly connected to the internet must be assigned a unique IP address. Furthermore, there are 232 public IPv4 addresses, which is 4,294,967,296 public IPv4 addresses that are routable on the internet. This number seems to be a lot, but in reality, most of these devices have already been assigned on the internet and the remainder is reserved by various organizations for special uses.

In our world today, there are more than 4 billion devices that are connected to the internet. How is it possible to have more devices online but not enough public IPv4 addresses? The answer lies in private IPv4 addresses. RFC 1918 defines three classes of IPv4 addresses that are assignable on private networks and are not routable on the internet.

Table 12.1 shows the private IPv4 address classes:

Class	Network Address Block	Address Ranges
A	10.0.0.0/8	10.0.0.0–10.255.255.255
B	172.16.0.0/12	172.16.0.0–172.31.255.255
C	192.168.0.0/24	192.168.0.0–192.168.255.255

Table 12.1: Private IPv4 address classes

Each class needs to be unique between organizations and private networks. To put it simply, each organization can use any class of private IPv4 addresses as they see fit or desire. Each class provides a range of usable IPv4 addresses per network, ranging from 254 to over 16 million usable addresses. RFC 1918 addresses allow an organization of any size to assign these addresses to a unique device without needing to assign a public IPv4 address to each device. Therefore, these addresses are strictly for use on private computer networks only.

The **Internet Assigned Numbers Authority** (**IANA**) has defined these specific IPv4 classes as private and non-routable addresses on the internet. **Internet service providers** (**ISPs**) have implemented security mechanisms such as **access control lists** (**ACLs**) to prevent RFC 1918 addresses from entering the ISP network and the internet.

Another important concern, since the RFC 1918 addresses are non-routable on the internet, is regarding how a device with a private IPv4 address can communicate and access resources on the internet. In the next section, you will read about how devices that are on a private network are able to communicate on the internet.

What Is NAT?

Devices that are assigned a private IPv4 address will not be able to or not be allowed to communicate with devices on the internet. Look at a real-world scenario now – imagine your computer or a smart device is assigned a private IPv4 address such as `10.11.12.13` on your network, and it's able to communicate with other devices that belong on the same IP network but not with devices on the internet. The major question now is, how is that possible?

This is where NAT comes into the picture and helps make our lives a bit easier in networking. NAT allows a router to **translate** a private address into a public address. Take a look at *Figure 12.1* to get a clear idea of how NAT really works:

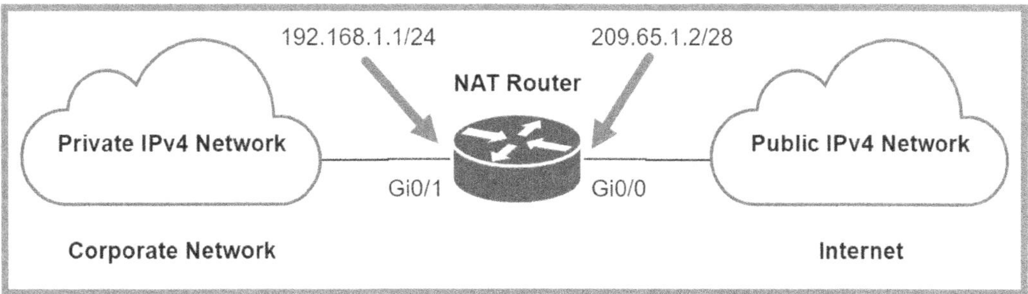

Figure 12.1: NAT topology

In *Figure 12.1*, there are two networks: a corporate network and the internet, and in between both is a NAT router. Imagine there is a device on the corporate network, PC 1, with an IP address of 192.168.1.10. PC 1 wants to send a message to a device on the internet. Let's say it's a Cisco web server at 23.10.104.199. The following are the actions taken by the router:

1. PC 1 sends the message to its default gateway, the router in our topology.
2. When the packet is received by the router, the Layer 3 header is inspected to determine the destination IP address.
3. Since the destination address is a public IP address, the router will translate the source IP address from 192.168.1.10 to the router's public IP address of 209.65.1.2. This process is known as NAT.
4. After the NAT process is completed, the router forwards the packet to its destination, 23.10.104.199.

If another device on the corporate network wishes to communicate with another device on the internet, the process is repeated. Devices on the internet do not see the corporate, private network. They only see the internet IP address of 209.65.1.2. Therefore, returning traffic will be sent to the 209.65.1.2 address, and the router will reverse the translation process and forward the message back to PC 1.

Such a feature of NAT allows you to conserve the IPv4 public address space, allowing you to assign a single public IPv4 address per organization and per owner of a private network. A simple example is the modem at your home. It has a single public IPv4 address assigned to its internet-facing interface (port) and on the internal side of your home network, you are using a private address scheme with many devices being translated through that single public IP address. This allows organizations with hundreds of devices on their private network to use a single public IPv4 address via NAT on their internet router or modem.

Note

The primary benefit of using NAT is to conserve the public IPv4 address space.

There are many advantages of using NAT on a network. A common benefit is that it enables network professionals to conserve the public IPv4 address space. In addition to this, NAT allows the flexibility of using pools of addresses such as public IPv4 addresses for load-balancing traffic to the internet. This feature ensures the reliability of connections to public networks, such as the internet. From a security perspective, NAT masks/hides users and devices that are using RFC 1918 addressing schemes behind a single public IPv4 address. In other words, NAT prevents users and devices that are located on the internet from seeing into your private network; those users and systems on the internet will only see your public IP address.

NAT allows network administrators to maintain consistency for their internal network addressing standards. This allows all internal devices to use RFC 1918 addresses without having to be assigned a public IPv4 address to access the internet. The NAT router will handle the translations of addresses between the internal and public networks.

While the advantages seem plenty, you must also understand that NAT has some disadvantages. One of the major disadvantages of using NAT is related to degrading network performance on various types of network traffic such as **voice over IP** (**VoIP**). As traffic passes through a NAT-enabled router, there is some delay as the router must perform the address translation process. As each packet enters the router, the router has to inspect the Layer 3 header of each packet to determine whether to perform NAT or not before forwarding the packet to its destination.

Another important disadvantage to note is that end-to-end addressing is lost with NAT. As a packet passes through NAT-enabled routers, the source IP address of the packet is changed, which makes it harder to trace the actual source or sender of a packet. Additionally, **virtual private network** (**VPN**) technologies such as **IP security** (**IPsec**) do not work well with NAT at all. Since NAT modifies the Layer 3 header of packets, it causes a major problem for IPsec VPNs to establish a secure tunnel between remote branches.

NAT Terminologies

In the world of Cisco and NAT, there are a few terminologies that are used to help you identify whether an IPv4 address is on a private network or a public network. In this section, you will learn about the various NAT terminologies.

Inspect *Figure 12.2* to better understand NAT operations:

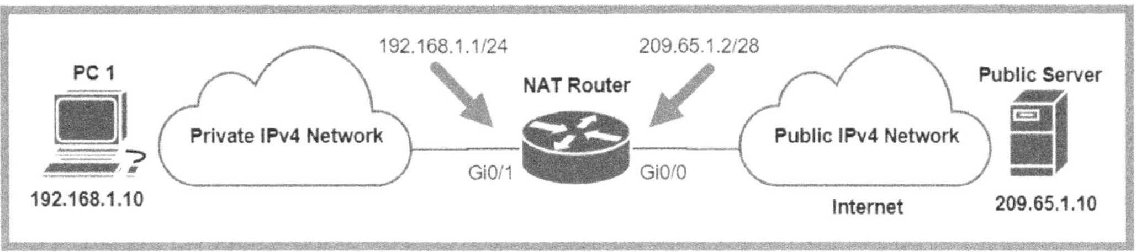

Figure 12.2: Simple NAT operations

In the preceding network topology, there are two types of networks: the private network, which is typically the corporate network owned by an organization, and the public network, known as the internet. By default, the Cisco IOS router does not know which type of network PC 1 or the server belongs to. All that the router knows is that there are two different IPv4 networks and its job is to route traffic between them. Looking at the topology, you can simply say that PC 1 is on a private network with a private IPv4 address class that is non-routable on the internet, while the public server has a public IPv4 address and is on the internet.

The main question now is that when the router must perform NAT operations by translating the private IPv4 address into a public address, how does the router know which side of the network each IP address belongs to? To get a better understanding, you must first identify the **inside** and **outside addresses**.

The inside address is the IP address that is to be translated by the router. In the previous topology, we can identify the inside address as any address on the private or internal network. The outside address is quite simple to identify, as it's the address of the destination device. Once again, if the PC is attempting to communicate with the server, the outside address is 209.65.1.10. However, as simple as it is, the router does not see as plainly as we do. Furthermore, NAT uses **local** and **global** to tell the router additional details about the addresses that are to be translated. The local address is any IP address that is on the inside network while the global address is any address on the public side of the network.

To get a better understanding, take a look at *Figure 12.3*:

Source Address	Destination Address
Inside Local	*Outside Local*
192.168.1.10	209.65.1.10

PC 1 wants to send a message to the server

PC 1

192.168.1.10

Private IPv4 Network

192.168.1.1/24

Gi0/1

209.65.1.2/28

Gi0/0

Public IPv4 Network

Internet

Public Server

209.65.1.10

Figure 12.3: NAT process part 1

In *Figure 12.3*, imagine that PC 1 wants to send a packet to the public server. When NAT is enabled on the Cisco IOS router, it sees the inside local address as 192.168.1; the outside local address is the destination device, which is 209.65.1.10. These addresses are before the NAT process.

Figure 12.4 shows the results after the addresses have been translated by NAT:

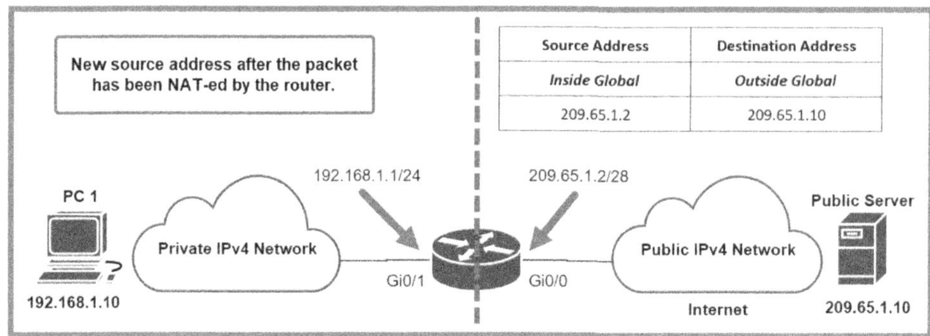

Source Address	Destination Address
Inside Global	*Outside Global*
209.65.1.2	209.65.1.10

Figure 12.4: NAT process part 2

When the packet enters the router, the process of NAT takes place. The router takes a look at the source and destination address, and if the destination address belongs to the global network, the router performs NAT on the inside local address, converting it to the inside global address. In other words, NAT translates the private IPv4 address of the PC to the public IPv4 address on the router's interface.

> **Note**
>
> The outside local and outside global addresses are usually the same IP address. These addresses are those that belong to the destination device.

In the next section, you will read about the various types of NAT, their use cases, and how to configure each on a Cisco IOS router.

Types of NAT

There are many flavors or types of NAT. Each type has its advantages, disadvantages, and real-world use cases. In this section, you will learn about the characteristics, operations, and how to configure each type of NAT on a Cisco IOS router.

Static NAT

Static NAT uses a one-to-one mapping of the inside local address with the inside global address. This type of NAT mapping does not change; as the name implies, the mapping remains constant. This is very useful when you want to allow external users on the internet to access a device such as a web server that sits on your internal, private network in your organization.

Imagine your organization has a web server located on a private network and you are tasked with allowing users from the internet access to the server. To complete this task, you can create a one-to-one static mapping between the web server's private IP address (inside local) with the public IP address on the router (inside global). This will allow anyone on the internet to simply enter the public IP address (inside global) on their web browser, and when the router receives traffic, it will simply forward it to the inside local address, which is the server.

Figure 12.5 shows that PC 2 can access the internal web server via static NAT:

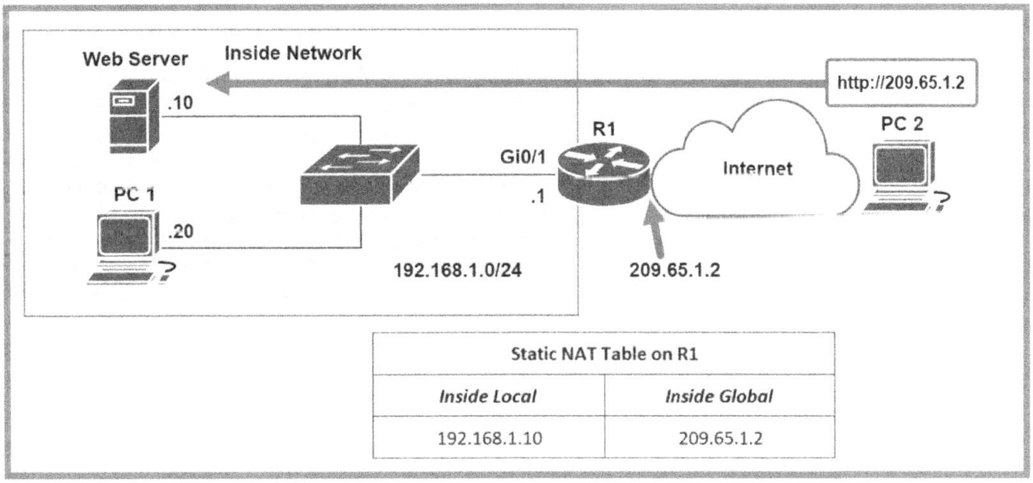

Static NAT Table on R1	
Inside Local	*Inside Global*
192.168.1.10	209.65.1.2

Figure 12.5: Static NAT

The devices on the internet, such as PC 2, will not see the inside local address of the server, only the inside global address. Additionally, devices on the internet will not be aware that the router is performing NAT in the background.

To configure static NAT on a Cisco IOS router, use the following instructions:

1. Configure the inside interface on the router. This interface is connected to the inside network:

```
Router(config)# interface interface-ID
Router(config-if)# ip nat inside
Router(config-if)# exit
```

2. Configure the outside interface. This interface is connected to the outside network:

```
Router(config)# interface interface-ID
Router(config-if)# ip nat outside
Router(config-if)# exit
```

3. Create the map between the inside local address and the inside global address:

```
Router(config)# ip nat inside source static inside-local-ip
inside-global-ip
```

In the next section, you will take a look at using a pool of public IP addresses in dynamic NAT.

Dynamic NAT

Dynamic NAT uses a pool of inside global addresses that are automatically translated on a first-come, first-served basis by the NAT-enabled router. Unlike static NAT, which manually creates a static mapping between an inside local address and an inside global address, dynamic NAT allows you to allocate a range of available addresses via a NAT pool.

Imagine your company has a range of public IPv4 addresses allocated to your organization by the local ISP, and you want to allow a small IP subnet of end devices to use any address with the allocated range when communicating to the outside network. Dynamic NAT simply allows you to create an ACL to specify which IP subnets are allowed to use the range (pool) of public IP addresses.

Figure 12.6 shows a router that is configured with a range of public IPv4 addresses:

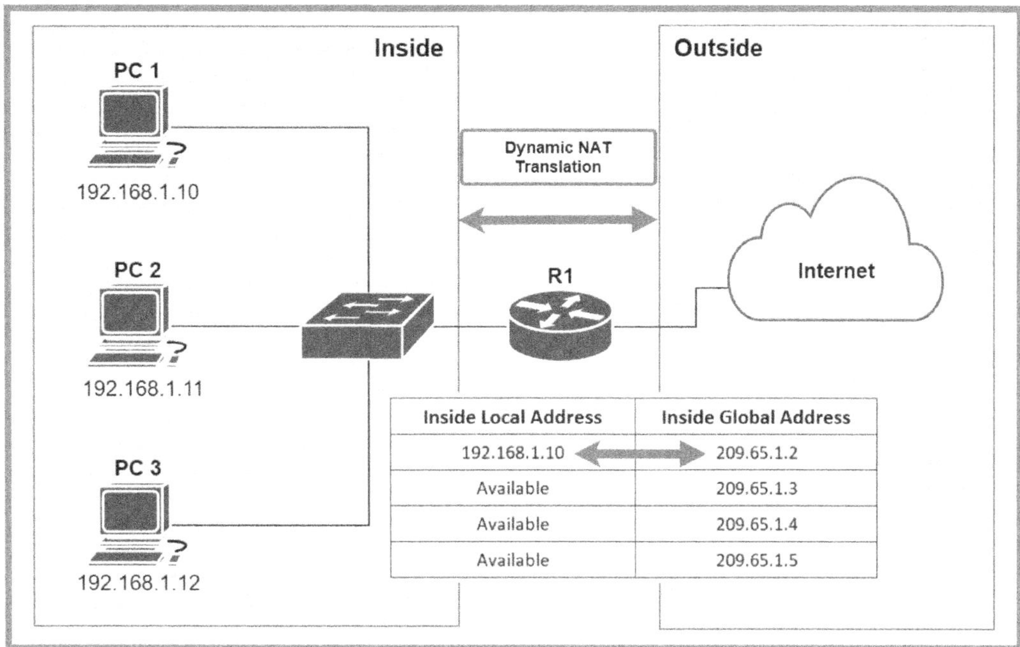

Inside Local Address	Inside Global Address
192.168.1.10	209.65.1.2
Available	209.65.1.3
Available	209.65.1.4
Available	209.65.1.5

Figure 12.6: Dynamic NAT

The outside interface of the router is configured with a NAT pool of addresses ranging from 209.65.1.2 to 209.65.1.5. These addresses are allocated for use by the inside network. When PC 1 wants to communicate on the outside network, the router checks the NAT pool for an available IPv4 address and translates the inside local address to an available inside global address. In this situation, the inside local address is 192.168.1.10, which will then be translated to 209.65.1.2. If another device such as PC 2 (192.168.1.11) wants to communicate on the internet (outside network), the process is repeated. This time, the router will use the next available from the pool, which is 209.65.1.3.

The disadvantage of dynamic NAT is that since each address in the pool can be mapped to only one inside local address, the number of addresses in the pool is limited. Therefore, if more devices on the inside network are attempting to simultaneously communicate on the outside network, the pool of available addresses will become exhausted.

When dynamic mapping occurs, it is only temporary for the duration of the session between the inside device and the destination device. The router monitors for inactivity in dynamic NAT. When it detects that dynamic NAT is no longer being used, it will make the inside global address available for future translations.

> **Note**
> The `clear ip nat translation *` command will allow you to clear all NATs on the router.

If you are implementing dynamic NAT within your network, ensure that there are enough public IP addresses to satisfy the number of simultaneous sessions that will be generated by the inside network.

To configure dynamic NAT on a Cisco IOS router, use the following instructions:

1. Configure the inside interface on the router. This interface is connected to the inside network:

   ```
   Router(config)# interface interface-ID
   Router(config-if)# ip nat inside
   Router(config-if)# exit
   ```

2. Configure the outside interface. This interface is connected to the outside network:

   ```
   Router(config)# interface interface-ID
   Router(config-if)# ip nat outside
   Router(config-if)# exit
   ```

3. Create a pool of global inside addresses to use with dynamic NAT:

   ```
   Router(config)# ip nat pool pool-name start-ip end-ip [netmask
   subnet-mask | prefix-length prefix-length]
   ```

4. Create an ACL to allow the addresses that are to be translated:

   ```
   Router(config)# ip access-list standard access-list-name
   Router(config-std-nacl)# permit network-ID wildcard-mask
   Router(config-std-nacl)# exit
   ```

5. Merge the dynamic NAT pool of addresses with the ACL of addresses for translation:

   ```
   Router(config)# ip nat inside source list access-list-name pool
   pool-name
   ```

In the next section, you will take a look at the third type of NAT, which is PAT.

PAT

PAT, also known as **NAT overload**, is a bit different from both static and dynamic NAT. PAT allows a router to translate multiple private IPv4 addresses into a single public address. This type of NAT is commonly used within home users' networks. The ISP usually assigns a single public IP address to the internet modem/router. The modem is configured with PAT (NAT overload) that translates any number of private addresses on the inside network to the single public address assigned on the modem/router interface on the outside network.

If you recall from previous chapters, when a device wants to initiate a connection with another device, the sender generates either a TCP/UDP source port or destination port based on the application layer protocol/service. PAT takes advantage and keeps track of the port numbers being used for each session and IP address. Within each session, the sender always generates a unique source port with its source IP address, and this ensures that the IP-to-port combination is kept unique; hence, PAT tracks these unique sessions to identify specific NAT translations.

> **Note**
> PAT also ensures that devices always use unique TCP ports for sessions with web servers on the internet.

To get a better understanding of how PAT works, take a look at *Figure 12.7*. There are two devices on the inside network, PC 1 and PC 2, which want to communicate with the web servers on the internet:

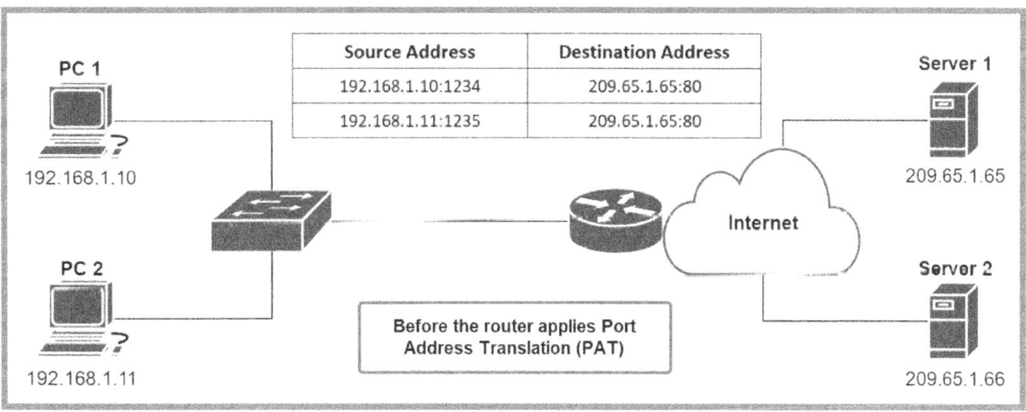

Figure 12.7: PAT operations

Each device on the inside network sends its message containing the source IP address, source port, destination IP address, and destination port to the router. When the router receives the messages, on its inside interface, it will inspect the destination device. Since the destination devices are located on the outside network, the router performs PAT. The router translates the inside local address to the inside global address while keeping track of the port number, as shown in *Figure 12.8*:

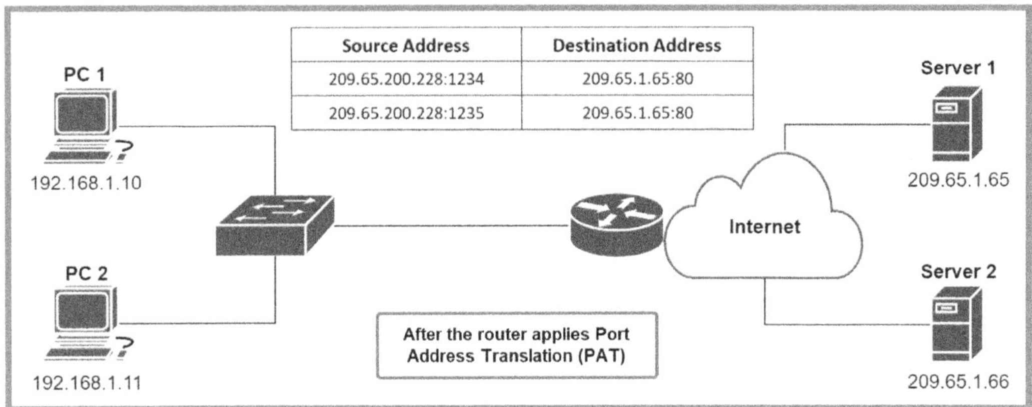

Figure 12.8: PAT operations

When the message leaves the router's outside interface, it will contain the new source IP address of 209.65.200.228. Devices on the internet such as the web servers in *Figure 12.8* will see the sender as 209.65.200.228, and not the devices on the inside network (PC 1 and PC 2).

During sessions between the inside and outside networks, PAT tries to maintain the original port numbers that are being used. However, if a source port number is already being used by another inside device, PAT will attempt to use the next available port number and keep track of the session and translation mapping.

There are two methods to configure PAT (NAT overload) on a Cisco IOS router. The first method is configuring PAT to use a pool of inside global addresses. This method is useful in situations where all port numbers are using a single public IP address. PAT then moves to the next available public IP address within the pool and begins allocating port numbers.

To configure PAT with a pool of addresses, use the following instructions:

1. Configure the inside interface on the router. This interface is connected to the inside network:

```
Router(config)# interface interface-ID
Router(config-if)# ip nat inside
Router(config-if)# exit
```

2. Configure the outside interface. This interface is connected to the outside network:

```
Router(config)# interface interface-ID
Router(config-if)# ip nat outside
Router(config-if)# exit
```

3. Create a pool of global inside addresses to use with NAT overload:

```
Router(config)# ip nat pool pool-name start-ip end-ip [netmask
subnet-mask | prefix-length prefix-length]
```

4. Create an ACL to allow the addresses that are to be translated:

```
Router(config)# ip access-list standard access-list-name
Router(config-std-nacl)# permit network-ID wildcard-mask
Router(config-std-nacl)# exit
```

5. Merge the dynamic NAT pool of addresses with the ACL of addresses for translation using the `overload` keyword:

```
Router(config)# ip nat inside source list access-list-name pool
pool-name overload
```

The second method of configuring PAT allows you to translate all inside addresses to a single public IP address. This method is useful when you have only a single public IP address and multiple inside devices that require connectivity to the internet.

To configure PAT to use a single inside global address, use the following instructions:

1. Configure the inside interface on the router. This interface is connected to the inside network:

```
Router(config)# interface interface-ID
Router(config-if)# ip nat inside
Router(config-if)# exit
```

2. Configure the outside interface. This interface is connected to the outside network:

```
Router(config)# interface interface-ID
Router(config-if)# ip nat outside
Router(config-if)# exit
```

3. Create a pool of global inside addresses to use with NAT overload:

```
Router(config)# ip nat pool pool-name start-ip end-ip [netmask
subnet-mask | prefix-length prefix-length]
```

4. Create an ACL to allow the addresses that are to be translated:

```
Router(config)# ip access-list standard access-list-name
Router(config-std-nacl)# permit network-ID wildcard-mask
Router(config-std-nacl)# exit
```

5. Merge the dynamic NAT pool of addresses with the interface on the router that has the inside global address:

```
Router(config)# ip nat inside source list access-list-name
interface interface-ID overload
```

Lastly, you can use NAT to perform port forwarding on a Cisco router.

To configure port forwarding on a Cisco IOS router, use the following instructions:

1. Configure the inside interface on the router. This interface is connected to the inside network:

```
Router(config)# interface interface-ID
Router(config-if)# ip nat inside
Router(config-if)# exit
```

2. Configure the outside interface. This interface is connected to the outside network:

```
Router(config)# interface interface-ID
Router(config-if)# ip nat outside
Router(config-if)# exit
```

3. Create the map between the inside local address and the inside global address:

```
Router(config)# ip nat inside source static inside-local-ip
local-port inside-global-ip global-port
```

Having completed this section, you have learned how to configure various types of NAT on a Cisco IOS router. In the next section, you will gain hands-on experience in implementing each type of NAT in a Cisco environment.

Lab: Implementing NAT Overload (PAT)

In this hands-on lab, you will learn how to implement PAT or what Cisco defines as NAT overload. *Figure 12.9* shows an organization network (left) that is connected to the internet via the ISP router:

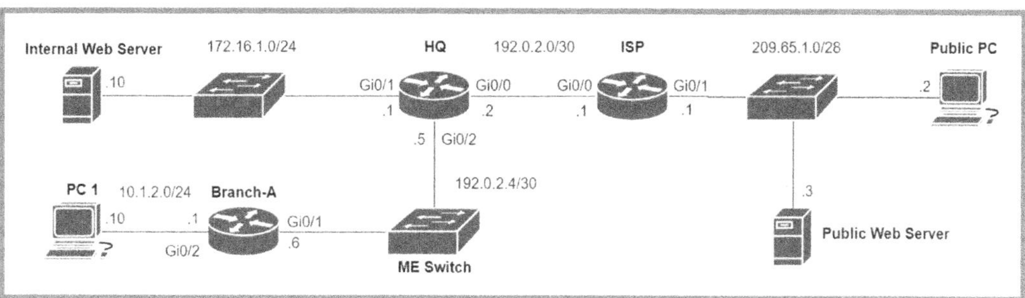

Figure 12.9: NAT overload topology

The objective of this lab is to configure the HQ router with NAT overload to all devices on the corporate network such as translating the PC 1 private IP address (10.1.2.10/24) to a public IP address when it's attempting to connect to the public web server (209.65.1.3/28).

To get started with this exercise, ensure you download and open the pre-built lab file from `https://packt.link/CCNArepoCh12first`.

Now that your lab environment is ready, use the following instructions to configure NAT overload:

1. Configure the inside interfaces on the HQ router for NAT:

```
HQ(config)# interface GigabitEthernet 0/1
HQ(config-if)# ip nat inside
HQ(config-if)# exit
HQ(config)# interface GigabitEthernet 0/2
HQ(config-if)# ip nat inside
HQ(config-if)# exit
```

2. Configure the outside interface on the HQ router for NAT:

```
HQ(config)# interface GigabitEthernet 0/0
HQ(config-if)# ip nat outside
HQ(config-if)# exit
```

3. Create an ACL with a wildcard mask on the HQ router to only allow the private addresses to be translated via NAT:

```
HQ(config)# ip access-list standard NAT-LIST
HQ(config-std-nacl)# permit 172.16.1.0 0.0.0.255
HQ(config-std-nacl)# permit 10.1.2.0 0.0.0.255
HQ(config-std-nacl)# exit
```

   We've used a named ACL called `NAT-LIST` to help us understand the purpose of the ACL on the router.

4. Merge `NAT-LIST` to the interface with the public IP address (192.0.2.2):

```
HQ(config)# ip nat inside source list NAT-LIST interface
gigabitEthernet 0/0 overload
```

5. On PC 1, open the web browser, enter the IP address of the public web server, and hit `Enter`:

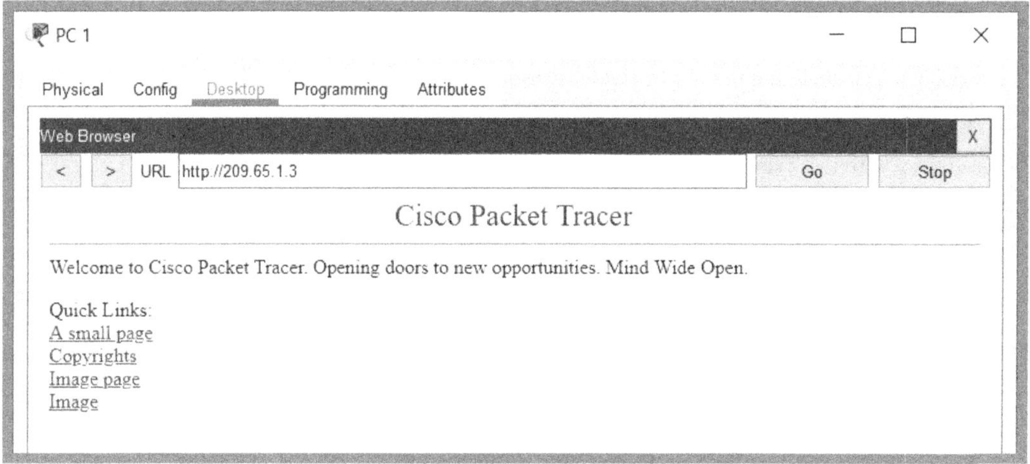

Figure 12.10: Web page

   This is a good sign that PC 1 has connectivity to the public web server.

6. On HQ, use the `show ip nat translations` command to validate that the private IP addresses are being translated to the public IP address using NAT overload or PAT:

```
HQ#show ip nat translations
Pro  Inside global      Inside local       Outside local      Outside global
tcp 192.0.2.2:1025     10.1.2.10:1025     209.65.1.3:80      209.65.1.3:80
```

Figure 12.11: PAT

As shown in *Figure 12.11*, the NAT is using TCP as expected since the application layer protocol between the sender's web browser and the destination web server is using HTTP. The inside global address is the public IPv4 address that's configured on the outside interface on the HQ router, that is, 192.0.2.2. In addition, the sender device is using a source port of `1025` with the inside local address as 10.1.2.10. Both the outside local and outside global addresses belong to the public web server, 209.65.1.3, with a destination port of `80`.

7. On HQ, use the `show ip nat statistics` command to verify the NAT interfaces and pool, as shown in *Figure 12.12*:

```
HQ#show ip nat statistics
Total translations: 1 (0 static, 1 dynamic, 1 extended)
Outside Interfaces: GigabitEthernet0/0
Inside Interfaces: GigabitEthernet0/1 , GigabitEthernet0/2
Hits: 9  Misses: 1
Expired translations: 0
Dynamic mappings:
```

Figure 12.12: NAT statistics

The output provides you with information about which interfaces are used as inside and outside interfaces on the router for NAT, the number of translations that have occurred, and whether there is any dynamic mapping.

Since the lab is translating private IPv4 addresses to a single public IPv4 address via the GigabitEthernet 0/0 interface, there are no dynamic mappings in the output. Additionally, the total translations indicate whether the router is using static NAT, dynamic NAT, or extended (NAT overload or PAT).

Having completed this lab, you have acquired the hands-on skills to implement and validate NAT overload (PAT) configurations in a Cisco environment. In the next lab, you will learn how to configure static NAT to perform port-forwarding to an internal web server within a private, corporate network.

Lab: Implementing Static NAT with Port Forwarding

In this lab, you will learn how to implement static NAT on an organization's router to forward traffic that is originating from the internet to an internal private server. To complete this exercise, you will be continuing from where you left off from the previous lab. To put it simply, this exercise is an extension of the previous lab and you will be using the topology shown in *Figure 12.13*:

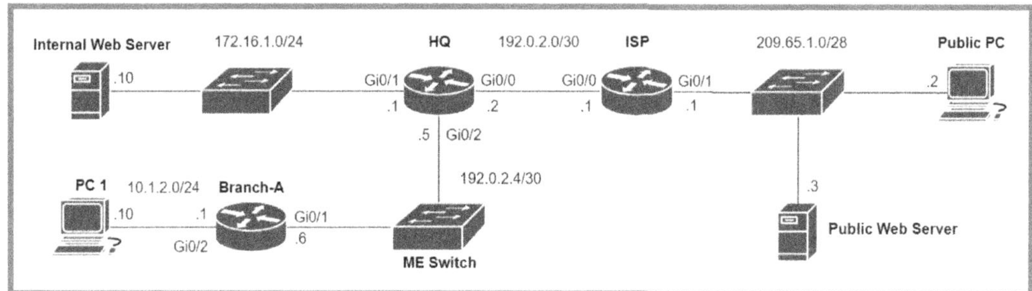

Figure 12.13: Static NAT with port forwarding topology

The objective of this lab is to allow users (public PC) on the internet to access the internal web server on the private corporate network via NAT. Therefore, when the public PC enters the public IP address of the HQ router within the web browser, the HQ router will translate and forward the traffic to only the internal web server.

To get started with implementing static NAT with port forwarding, use the following instructions:

1. Configure the inside interface on the HQ router that points to the internal web server:

```
HQ(config)# interface GigabitEthernet 0/1
HQ(config-if)# ip nat inside
HQ(config-if)# exit
```

2. Configure the outside interface on the HQ router for NAT:

```
HQ(config)# interface GigabitEthernet 0/0
HQ(config-if)# ip nat outside
HQ(config-if)# exit
```

3. Configure the static translation between the inside global address and the inside local address of the internal web server. Furthermore, since it's a web server, use the default service port `80`:

```
HQ(config)# ip nat inside source static tcp 172.16.1.10 80
190.0.2.2 80
```

   This static mapping will allow any device that is on the internet side of the topology to access the internal web server by simply using the public IP address of the HQ router, 192.0.2.2, with a destination port of `80`.

4. On HQ, use the `show ip nat translations` command to verify the static NAT map:

```
HQ#show ip nat translations
Pro  Inside global      Inside local       Outside local      Outside global
tcp 190.0.2.2:80        172.16.1.10:80     ---                ---
```

Figure 12.14: Static NAT mapping

Whenever you create a static NAT mapping on a Cisco IOS router, both the inside global and inside local mapping are shown within the `show ip nat translations` output. Keep in mind that if the port numbers were not specific during the previous step, they will not appear in the preceding snippet.

5. On PC 2 (public PC), open the web browser, enter the public IP address of the HQ router, and hit `Enter` to verify whether you have connectivity:

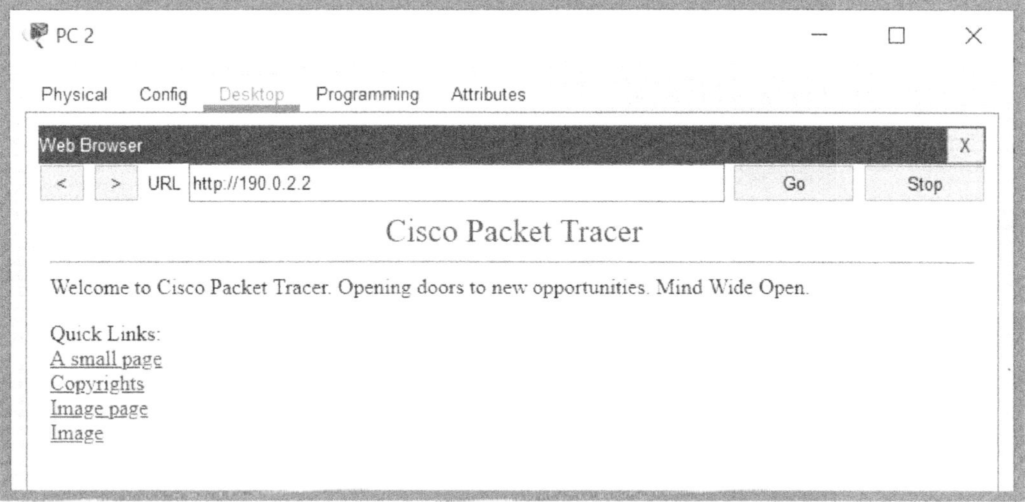

Figure 12.15: Connectivity test via web browser

Figure 12.15 validates that there is connectivity to the internal web server on the private corporate network from the internet side of the topology.

6. On HQ, use the `show ip nat translations` command to validate that the static NAT is working with port forwarding, as shown in *Figure 12.16*:

```
HQ#show ip nat translations
Pro  Inside global      Inside local       Outside local      Outside global
tcp 190.0.2.2:80        172.16.1.10:80     ---                ---
tcp 190.0.2.2:80        172.16.1.10:80     209.65.1.2:1029    209.65.1.2:1029
```

Figure 12.16: Static NAT on HQ

As shown in the snippet, NAT is working as expected. The traffic is originating from PC 2 (public PC) with an IP address of 209.65.1.2 and the HQ router is performing static NAT with port forwarding to the internal web server at 172.16.1.10:80. The public PC is seeing the internal web server as 190.0.2.2 but HQ translates and forwards the traffic to the private IP address, 172.16.1.10.

7. On HQ, use the `show ip nat statistics` command, as shown in *Figure 12.17*:

```
HQ#show ip nat statistics
Total translations: 2 (1 static, 1 dynamic, 2 extended)
Outside Interfaces: GigabitEthernet0/0
Inside Interfaces: GigabitEthernet0/1 , GigabitEthernet0/2
Hits: 57  Misses: 175
Expired translations: 10
Dynamic mappings:
HQ#
```

Figure 12.17: NAT statistics

From the output, you can determine there is a static NAT mapping on the HQ router with two port translations that have taken place. Furthermore, the NAT outside and inside interfaces are displayed, and this information helps us determine whether any misconfigurations exist on a translated interface.

Having completed this lab, you have gained the hands-on skills to configure a Cisco IOS router to perform static NAT with port forwarding. This exercise also demonstrates how to allow users on the internet to access internal servers on a corporate network, specifically, via a service port such as port `80` for the HTTP server in your lab. In the next lab, you will learn how to implement dynamic NAT in a Cisco environment.

Lab: Implementing Dynamic NAT

In this lab, you will learn how to implement dynamic NAT with a pool of IP addresses. The following network topology shows an organization network (left) that is connected to the internet via the ISP router:

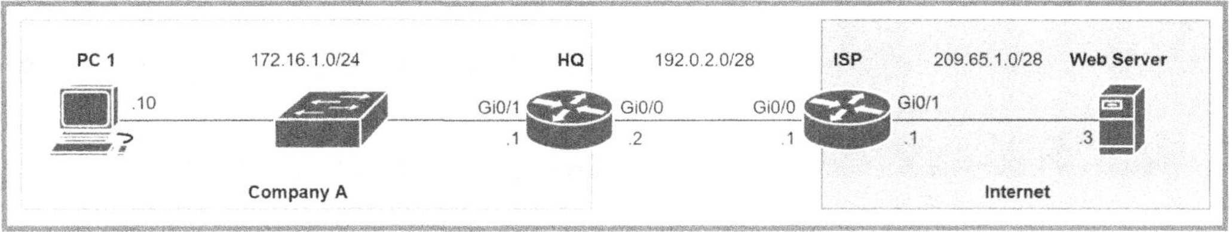

Figure 12.18: Dynamic NAT topology

To get started with this exercise, ensure you download and open the pre-built lab file from `https://packt.link/CCNArepoCh12third`.

Now that your lab environment is ready, use the following instructions to configure Dynamic NAT:

1. Configure the inside interface on the HQ router for NAT:

```
HQ(config)# interface GigabitEthernet 0/1
HQ(config-if)# ip nat inside
HQ(config-if)# exit
```

2. Configure the outside interface on the HQ router for NAT:

```
HQ(config)# interface GigabitEthernet 0/0
HQ(config-if)# ip nat outside
HQ(config-if)# exit
```

3. Create a NAT pool to specify the range of usable public IP addresses; begin with the starting IP address as 190.0.2.2 and the ending IP address as 192.0.2.5, and a network mask of 255.255.255.240:

```
HQ(config)# ip nat pool NAT-IPAdd 192.0.2.2 192.0.2.5 netmask
255.255.255.240
```

4. Create an ACL with a wildcard mask on the HQ router to only allow the private addresses to be translated via NAT. Use the ACL name `NAT-List`:

```
HQ(config)# ip access-list standard NAT-List
HQ(config-std-nacl)# permit 172.16.1.0 0.0.0.255
HQ(config-std-nacl)# exit
```

5. Merge `NAT-List` with the NAT IP pool (`NAT-IPAdd`) to create the dynamic mapping:

```
HQ(config)# ip nat inside source list NAT-List pool NAT-IPAdd
```

6. On PC 1, open the web browser, enter the IP address of the web server, and hit `Enter`:

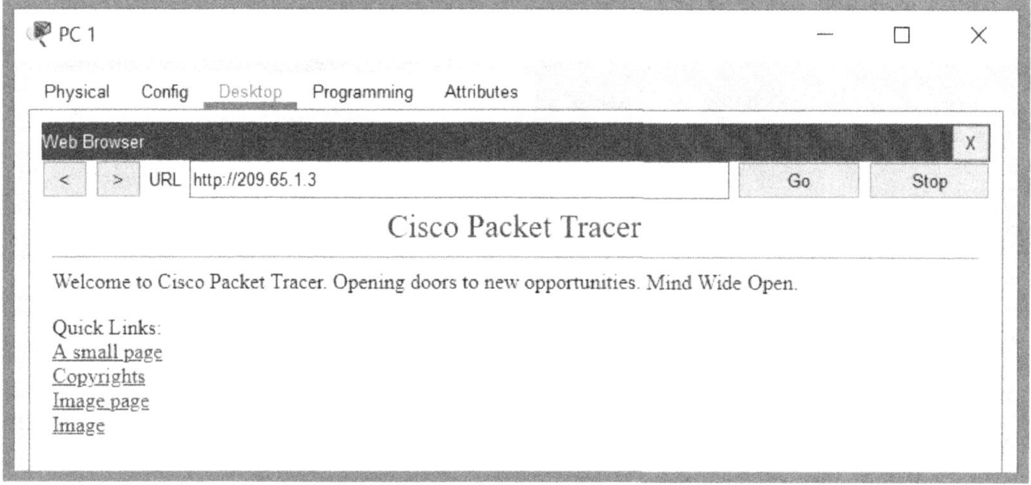

Figure 12.19: Web server

7. On HQ, use `show ip nat translations` to verify whether dynamic NAT is working, as shown in *Figure 12.20*:

```
HQ#show ip nat translations
Pro  Inside global      Inside local        Outside local       Outside global
tcp 192.0.2.2:1026      172.16.1.10:1026    209.65.1.3:80       209.65.1.3:80
tcp 192.0.2.2:1027      172.16.1.10:1027    209.65.1.3:80       209.65.1.3:80
tcp 192.0.2.2:1028      172.16.1.10:1028    209.65.1.3:80       209.65.1.3:80
tcp 192.0.2.2:1029      172.16.1.10:1029    209.65.1.3:80       209.65.1.3:80
```

Figure 12.20: Dynamic NAT

The output proves that dynamic NAT is working as expected. If another client device on the company side of the network establishes a connection to the web server, another public IP address will be used from the NAT pool and will reflect in the translation window.

8. On HQ, use the `show ip nat statistics` command to validate dynamic NAT configurations:

```
HQ#show ip nat statistics
Total translations: 4 (0 static, 4 dynamic, 4 extended)
Outside Interfaces: GigabitEthernet0/0
Inside Interfaces: GigabitEthernet0/1
Hits: 28  Misses: 4
Expired translations: 0
Dynamic mappings:
-- Inside Source
access-list NAT-List pool NAT-IPAdd refCount 4
 pool NAT-IPAdd: netmask 255.255.255.240
       start 192.0.2.2 end 192.0.2.5
       type generic, total addresses 4 , allocated 1 (25%), misses 0
```

Figure 12.21: Dynamic NAT statistics

The output shows the name of the dynamic NAT pool, the IP ranges and subnet mask, the number of IP addresses that are being used at the point in time (allocated), and inside and outside NAT interfaces.

Having completed this lab, you have gained the essential skills to configure dynamic NAT in a Cisco environment.

Summary

In this chapter, you learned about the important role that NAT plays in almost all private networks of all sizes. You also looked at the characteristics and functions of each type of NAT with their use cases. By completing this chapter, you have gained both the theoretical knowledge and understanding of the operations of NAT on an enterprise network and have obtained the hands-on skills to implement static NAT, dynamic NAT, and PAT on a Cisco network.

By completing each lab exercise in this chapter, you have gained the experience, knowledge, and real-world skills necessary for implementing NAT as an IP service within an enterprise environment. Without NAT, devices with private IPv4 addresses won't be able to communicate with devices on the public network such as the internet.

In the next chapter, *Implementing Network Services and IP Operations*, you will take a deep dive into learning how to implement **Network Time Protocol** (**NTP**), **Dynamic Host Configuration Protocol** (**DHCP**), and other IP services in a Cisco environment.

Additional Reading

- NAT: `https://www.cisco.com/c/en/us/support/docs/ip/network-address-translation-nat/13772-12.html`
- Configuring NAT: `https://www.cisco.com/c/en/us/td/docs/ios-xml/ios/ipaddr_nat/configuration/15-mt/nat-15-mt-book/iadnat-addr-consv.html`

Exam Readiness Drill – Chapter Review Questions

Apart from mastering key concepts, strong test-taking skills under time pressure are essential for acing your certification exam. That's why developing these abilities early in your learning journey is critical.

Exam readiness drills, using the free online practice resources provided with this book, help you progressively improve your time management and test-taking skills while reinforcing the key concepts you've learned.

HOW TO GET STARTED

- Open the link or scan the QR code at the bottom of this page
- If you have unlocked the practice resources already, log in to your registered account. If you haven't, follow the instructions in *Chapter 19* and come back to this page.
- Once you log in, click the START button to start a quiz
- We recommend attempting a quiz multiple times till you're able to answer most of the questions correctly and well within the time limit.
- You can use the following practice template to help you plan your attempts:

Working On Accuracy		
Attempt	Target	Time Limit
Attempt 1	40% or more	Till the timer runs out
Attempt 2	60% or more	Till the timer runs out
Attempt 3	75% or more	Till the timer runs out
Working On Timing		
Attempt 4	75% or more	1 minute before time limit
Attempt 5	75% or more	2 minutes before time limit
Attempt 6	75% or more	3 minutes before time limit

The above drill is just an example. Design your drills based on your own goals and make the most out of the online quizzes accompanying this book.

First time accessing the online resources?

You'll need to unlock them through a one-time process. **Head to** *Chapter 19* **for instructions.**

Open Quiz	
https://packt.link/ccnachap12 OR scan this QR code →	

13

Network Services and IP Operations

The Cisco IOS operating system is full of features that you have yet to explore. The operating system contains a wide variety of network services that are designed to provide scalability and flexibility on a network; these features are commonly referred to as IP services. IP services are the essential services that all networks use, such as the **Dynamic Host Configuration Protocol** (**DHCP**), used to assist with the automatic assignment of IP addresses to client devices; a **domain name system** (**DNS**) to resolve hostnames to IP addresses; and even network monitoring and management protocols to provide accountability and visibility on a network.

Throughout the course of this chapter, you will learn how to implement the **Network Time Protocol** (**NTP**) to ensure all devices' clocks are synchronized so that proper timekeeping is maintained on a network, implement DHCP on a Cisco device to distribute IP configurations to end devices and allow network connectivity, understand the importance of DNS for a network and the vital role it plays on the internet, and configure the **Simple Network Management Protocol** (**SNMP**) and syslog to assist in network management. Lastly, you will learn about the importance of using **quality of service** (**QoS**) to improve network performance.

This chapter covers *Domain 4: IP Services*, specifically the *4.2 Configure and verify NTP operating in a client and server mode*, *4.3 Explain the role of DHCP and DNS within the network*, *4.4 Explain the function of SNMP in network operations*, *4.5 Describe the use of syslog features including facilities and levels*, *4.6 Configure and verify DHCP client and relay*, and *4.7 Explain the forwarding per-hop behavior (PHB) for QoS, such as classification, marking, queuing, congestion, policing, and shaping* objectives of the 200-301 CCNA v1.1 Certification exam.

In this chapter, you will cover the following topics:

- Understanding NTP
- Understanding DHCP
- Exploring DNS
- Understanding SNMP
- Working with syslog
- QoS traffic classification

Let's dive in!

Understanding NTP

Time plays such an important role in our daily lives. From helping you measure how long it takes you to arrive at a destination or event to calculating how quickly you perform in sports such as track and field in the Olympic games, time is simply the measurement between past, present, and future events.

Time is also used to help you keep an account of an event. Timestamps are used on electronic devices, surveillance systems, and computer and networking devices to provide accountability for actions and events that occur on a system. In an enterprise network, it is critical to ensure that proper timekeeping is maintained throughout the organization.

Why is timekeeping a critical factor in a network? Ensuring that all devices are configured with accurate time is important when logging and managing events on an enterprise network. Events occur frequently on networks. Throughout the labs that you have completed in this book, you will have noticed the Cisco devices generating log messages on the console. These messages usually contain details about the events that have occurred, and these messages are known as **syslog** messages.

> **Note**
>
> The topic of syslog and its purpose will be covered in more detail later in this chapter, in *Working with syslog*.

Log messages are generated all the time for various purposes, such as for checking when an interface status has changed, for checking security-related events, and even for troubleshooting network issues. Time helps us coordinate and gain a better picture of the sequences that occur on a network. Therefore, it is important to ensure that all devices within an organization have accurate configurations on the system clocks. Cisco IOS devices have an internal clock known as the system clock, which the device uses as its primary source of timekeeping. The system clock begins ticking (working) when the device boots up.

> **Note**
>
> By default, the system clock does not automatically set the current time and date.

There are two methods that you can use to configure timekeeping on a Cisco IOS device:

- Manually configuring the clock on the Cisco device
- Using NTP to automatically synchronize the Cisco device's clock with an NTP server

The manual method involves using the `clock set` command, followed by the time and date, in Privileged mode. The following is an example of the syntax for configuring time manually:

```
Switch# clock set hh:mm:ss month day year
```

The issue you face when configuring time manually on a network is that it's a very time-consuming process and, most importantly, the time may not be in sync with other devices on the network. As mentioned previously, accurate timekeeping is very important on a network, as timestamps are inserted within event logs, such as syslog messages generated by devices. If the time is not accurate when tracking the sequences of log messages for an event, there may be inconsistencies, which would result in inaccurate log events between devices.

To view the system clock on a Cisco IOS device, use the `show clock` command, as shown in *Figure 13.1*:

```
R1#show clock
*15:03:22.694 UTC Tue Apr 28 2020
R1#
```

Figure 13.1: System clock on a Cisco router

As a network grows, it becomes even harder to maintain accurate timekeeping on devices. Using NTP helps you synchronize time through an entire network of any size easily and efficiently. Cisco IOS devices such as routers and switches can synchronize their local system clocks with NTP servers as their source of time, enabling the routers and switches to become NTP clients on a network.

> **Note**
>
> NTP uses UDP port `123` by default.

NTP uses a hierarchical system to manage the time sources through a network and the internet. Each level within the hierarchy is referred to as a **stratum**. A stratum is used to measure the distance between an authoritative source and the NTP clients.

> **Note**
>
> An authoritative source is a device that is manually configured to provide time and has the most accurate time on the network. The authoritative source is at the top of the hierarchy at all times and is located at the stratum-0 level of the NTP hierarchical structure.

Figure 13.2 shows the NTP stratum hierarchical structure:

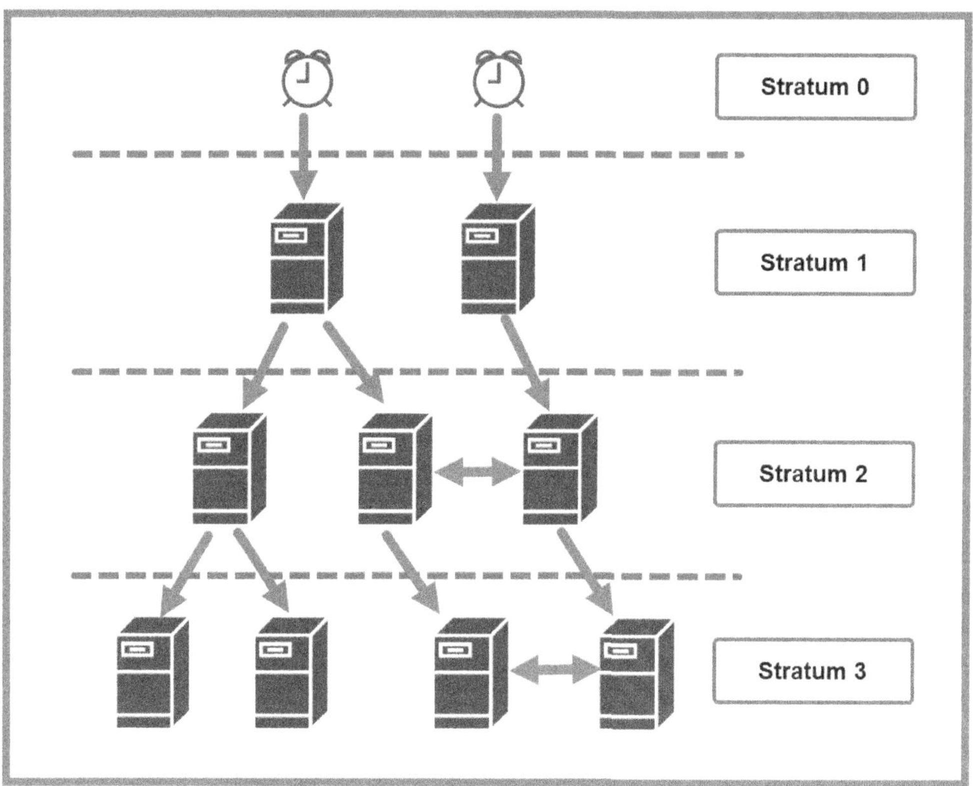

Figure 13.2: Stratum hierarchy

The authoritative sources are the devices with the most accurate time and are located at the stratum-0 layer. Stratum-0 devices are very precise in timekeeping, and it is assumed that they have no delays or inaccuracies in time management. Stratum-1 devices are those that synchronize their local time clocks with the authoritative system servers at stratum 0. Stratum-2 devices are those that synchronize their time clocks with the NTP servers at the upper layer, that is, stratum 1. When a device has a lower stratum number, it is an indication the NTP client is closer to the authoritative source of time. A higher stratum number indicates that the NTP client is further away. The maximum number of hops within NTP is 15.

> **Note**
>
> Stratum levels range from 0-15.

Any device that exists on a stratum-16 layer is considered to be unsynchronized with NTP. In the next section, you will learn how to configure Cisco devices as both NTP servers and NTP clients.

Lab: Configuring NTP

In this hands-on lab, you will learn how to implement NTP throughout a Cisco environment to ensure that time is synchronized between Cisco switches and routers. For this lab, you will be using the network topology shown in *Figure 13.3*:

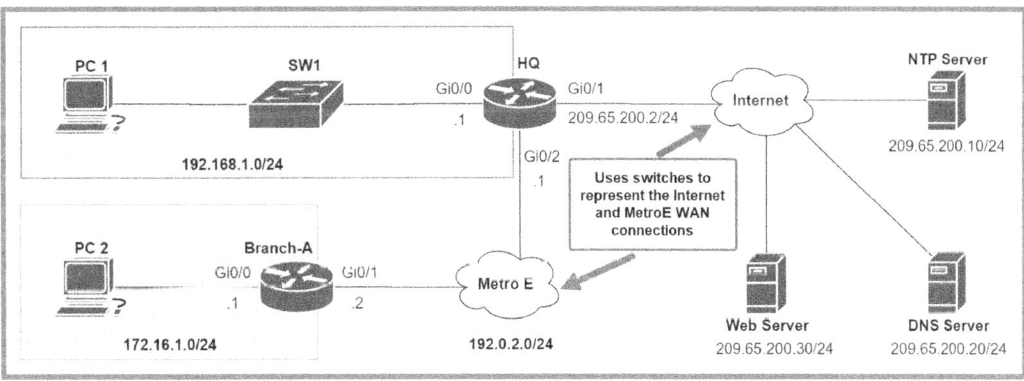

Figure 13.3: IP Service lab topology

To get started with this exercise, download and open the pre-built lab file from `https://packt.link/CCNArepoCh13first`.

Now that your Cisco lab is ready, use the following instructions to implement NTP:

1. Firstly, configure the NTP server with the current time. Click on the NTP server, choose the `Services` tab, and click on `NTP`, as shown in *Figure 13.4*:

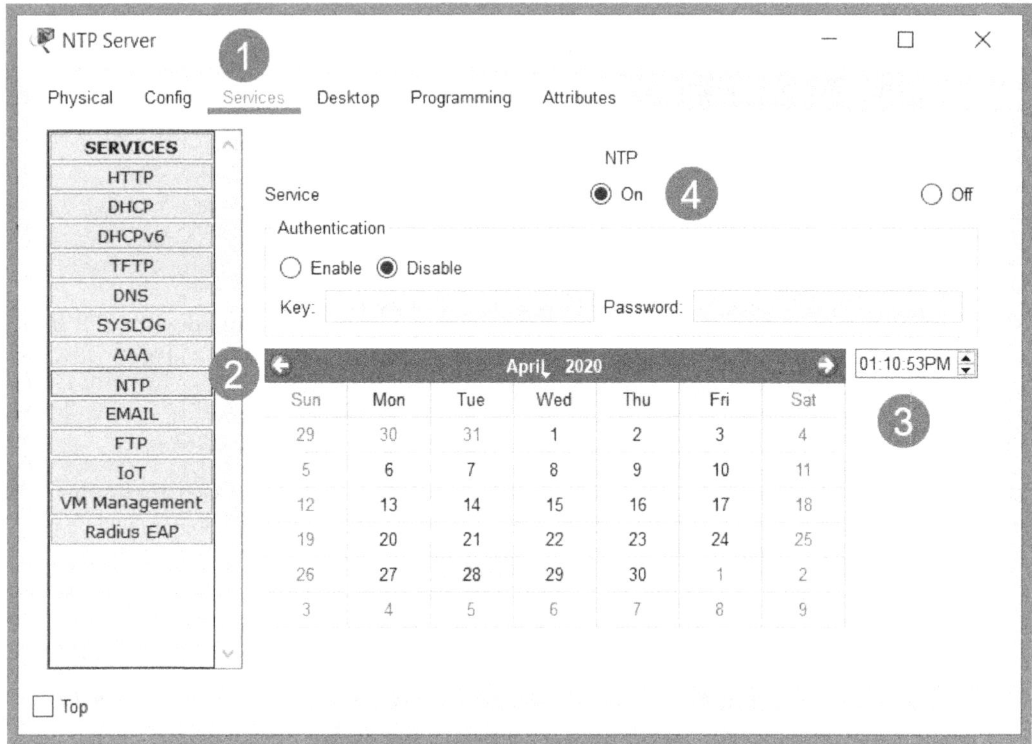

Figure 13.4: NTP Server configuration

Ensure the NTP service is `On` and that the time is accurately configured.

2. Configure the HQ router to be an NTP client and synchronize with the NTP server by using the following commands in `global config` mode:

```
HQ(config)# ntp server 209.65.200.10
```

Sometimes, there is a long delay for an NTP client to synchronize with an NTP server.

3. Use the `show ntp status` command to check whether the NTP client and server have been synchronized:

```
HQ#show ntp status
Clock is synchronized, stratum 2, reference is 209.65.200.10
nominal freq is 250.0000 Hz, actual freq is 249.9990 Hz, precision is 2**24
reference time is E22B2084.000003CA (13:26:28.970 UTC Tue Apr 28 2020)
clock offset is 0.00 msec, root delay is 0.00  msec
root dispersion is 10.89 msec, peer dispersion is 0.12 msec.
loopfilter state is 'CTRL' (Normal Controlled Loop), drift is - 0.000001193
s/s system poll interval is 4, last update was 13 sec ago.
HQ#
```

Figure 13.5: NTP synchronization

The output verifies that the HQ router (the NTP client) is synchronized with NTP server 209.65.200.10 and that the router is operating as a stratum-2 device. This indicates that the NTP server is a stratum-1 device.

4. Use the `show ntp associations` command to validate any NTP associations on the HQ router, as shown in *Figure 13.6*:

```
HQ#show ntp associations

address          ref clock       st   when     poll     reach  delay          offset
*~209.65.200.10 127.127.1.1      1    13       16       377    0.00           0.00
 * sys.peer, # selected, + candidate, - outlyer, x falseticker, ~ configured
HQ#
```

Figure 13.6: NTP associations

The output verifies that the HQ router is configured and peered with device 209.65.200.10 as a stratum-1 NTP server. The `sys.peer (*)` code can take some time to appear next to the IP address.

5. Use the `show clock` command to verify that the time is now accurate and the same as the NTP server, as shown in *Figure 13.7*:

```
HQ#show clock
13:29:12.19 UTC Tue Apr 28 2020
HQ#
```

Figure 13.7: System clock

6. Make the HQ router an NTP server for the HQ LAN and Branch-A LAN networks. To perform this task, use the `ntp master <stratum-number>` command, or you can simply use the `ntp master` command and the router will automatically increment the stratum number by one from the NTP server:

```
HQ(config)# ntp master
```

7. Use the `show ntp associations` command once more to verify that the HQ router is now an NTP server:

```
HQ#show ntp associations

address          ref clock       st   when     poll    reach  delay        offset
*~209.65.200.10 127.127.1.1     1    4        16      377    0.00         0.00
 ~127.127.1.1    .LOCL.          7    8        64      377    0.00         0.00
 * sys.peer, # selected, + candidate, - outlyer, x falseticker, ~ configured
HQ#
```

Figure 13.8: Verifying the HQ router is an NTP server

The second line indicates that the HQ router is operating as an NTP server because it is represented by a loopback IP address (link-local) and the reference clock is set to local.

8. Next, configure the `Branch-A` router as an NTP client and use HQ for time synchronization:

```
Branch-A(config)# ntp server 192.0.2.1
```

The `show ntp associations` command verifies that the Branch-A router is synchronized with HQ as the NTP server:

```
Branch-A#show ntp associations

address          ref clock       st   when     poll    reach  delay        offset
*~192.0.2.1      209.65.200.10   2    13       32      377    0.00         0.00
 * sys.peer, # selected, + candidate, - outlyer, x falseticker, ~ configured
Branch-A#
```

Figure 13.9: NTP associations on the Branch-A router

9. Before you can configure the switch within the HQ LAN as an NTP client, you need to configure a **switch virtual interface** (**SVI**) using the following commands:

```
SW1(config)# interface vlan 1
SW1(config-if)# ip address 192.168.1.2 255.255.255.0
SW1(config-if)# no shutdown
SW1(config-if)# exit
```

10. Configure the default gateway on the switch as shown:

```
SW1(config)# ip default-gateway 192.168.1.1
```

11. Use the `ntp server` command to configure the switch as an NTP client:

```
SW1(config)# ntp server 192.168.1.1
```

12. Use the `show ntp associations` command to verify that the switch is associated with HQ:

```
SW1#show ntp associations

address         ref clock       st   when     poll    reach  delay          offset
*~192.168.1.1   209.65.200.10   2    32       32      377    0.00           0.00
 * sys.peer, # selected, + candidate, - outlyer, x falseticker, ~ configured
SW1#
```

Figure 13.10: NTP association on the switch

By completing this lab, you have gained the hands-on skills needed to implement both NTP clients and NTP servers on a Cisco network. In the next section, you will learn about the importance of DHCP as an IP service on an enterprise network.

Understanding DHCP

On any computer network, there are many end devices, network intermediary devices, and even servers. Each device requires an IP address to exchange messages and share resources. A network administrator usually assigns static IP addresses to devices, such as switches, routers, firewalls, and servers, that provide a service or resource to the network. When a device is assigned a static IP address, it provides the convenience for network administrators to remotely access and manage the device, as the address will never change.

Since a network is mostly made up of computers and other end devices that often change physical locations, it is not wise to always assign static IP addresses to such devices. When a device with a static IP address is moved to another location, whether physical or logical, the IP scheme at the new location may not be the same as the IP configurations on the device itself. Therefore, the network administrator will be required to reconfigure the device with the appropriate IP configurations to match the new location on the network.

As a network grows, it becomes challenging and a bit time-consuming to manually configure static IP addresses on new devices as users move between locations. Additionally, static IP address configurations are also vulnerable. The administrator could misconfigure the device with a duplicate IP address that is assigned to another device or even an incorrect subnet mask.

The DHCP server can be implemented on a local network to automatically provide IP addresses, such as host addresses, subnet masks, default gateways, and DNS server addresses, to clients on the network. Having a DHCP server on a network simplifies and automates the task of assigning IP configurations to end devices efficiently.

A Cisco IOS router has many network services. A network administrator can configure a Cisco IOS router to provide DHCP services on a network. The DHCP server feature within the Cisco IOS allows the router to also provide DHCP services to clients on a network. This feature is useful for branch offices and other small offices, as a dedicated DHCP server is not required, and the Cisco IOS router is capable of providing DHCP services to the local network.

DHCP Operations

Whenever a client is connected to a network, whether it's a wired or wireless connection, most clients automatically search for an active DHCP server that will assign or lease an IP address and other IP configurations to the client. The IP addresses that are provided by the DHCP server are always leased for a period of time.

To get a better idea of DHCP operations, take a look at the following DHCP process:

1. When a client connects to a network, it starts looking for a local DHCP server. It creates a **DHCP discover** message and sends it as a broadcast on the network, as shown in *Figure 13.11*:

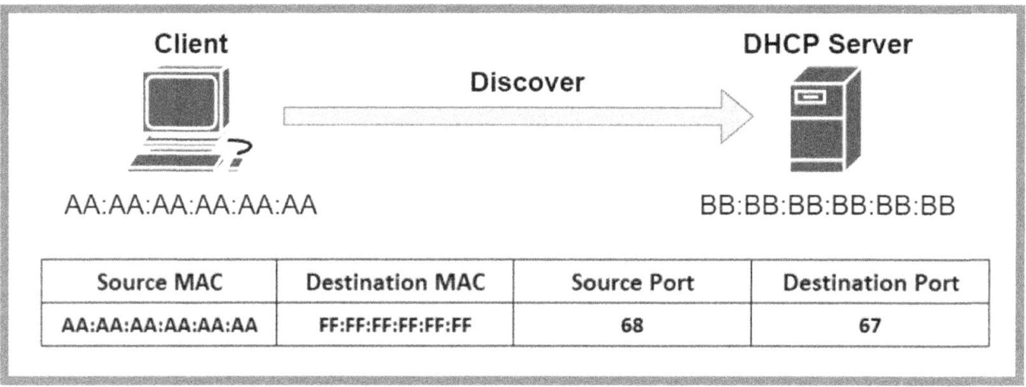

Source MAC	Destination MAC	Source Port	Destination Port
AA:AA:AA:AA:AA:AA	FF:FF:FF:FF:FF:FF	68	67

Figure 13.11: DHCP discover

The DHCP discover packet uses the client's source MAC address, a source UDP port of `68`, and a destination UDP port of `67`. The destination MAC address for the broadcast is `FF:FF:FF:FF:FF:FF`. The DHCP client uses UDP port `68`, while the DHCP server uses UDP port `67`. The source IP address is left blank, while the destination IP address is `255.255.255.255`.

2. When the DHCP server receives the DHCP discover message, it will respond with a **DHCP offer** message. At this phase, the DHCP server uses the source MAC address from the DHCP discover message to create a lease for an available IP address for the client. The DHCP server sends the information in the DHCP offer message back to the client, as shown in *Figure 13.12*:

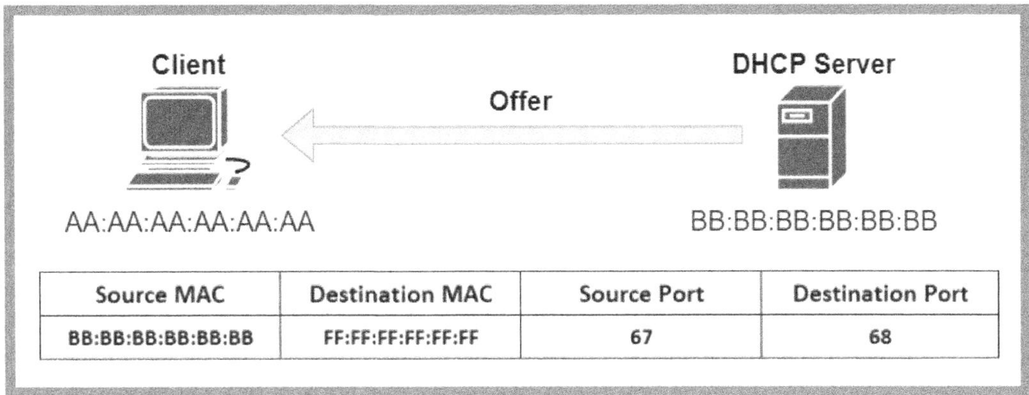

Figure 13.12: DHCP offer

The DHCP server responds with a broadcast and sets the destination MAC address as the layer 2 broadcast, `FF:FF:FF:FF:FF:FF`.

3. When the client receives the DHCP offer from the server, a **DHCP request** message is sent back to the DHCP server as a form of acceptance for the IP configurations the client has received, as shown in *Figure 13.13*:

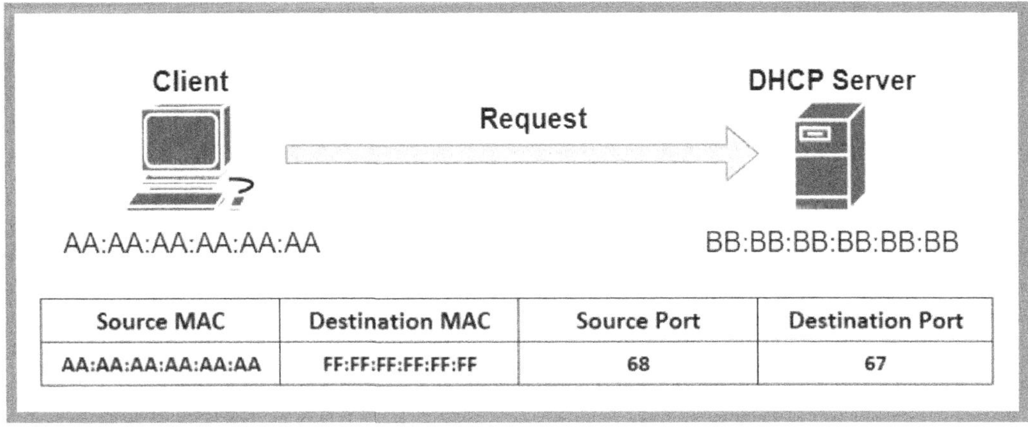

Figure 13.13: DHCP request

The DHCP request message is sent as a broadcast to the server.

4. When the DHCP server receives the DHCP request from the client, the server verifies that the lease information is not being used already by sending an ICMP ping message to the IP address it has assigned to the new client. The DHCP server responds with a **DHCP acknowledgment** to complete the DHCP process, as shown in *Figure 13.14*:

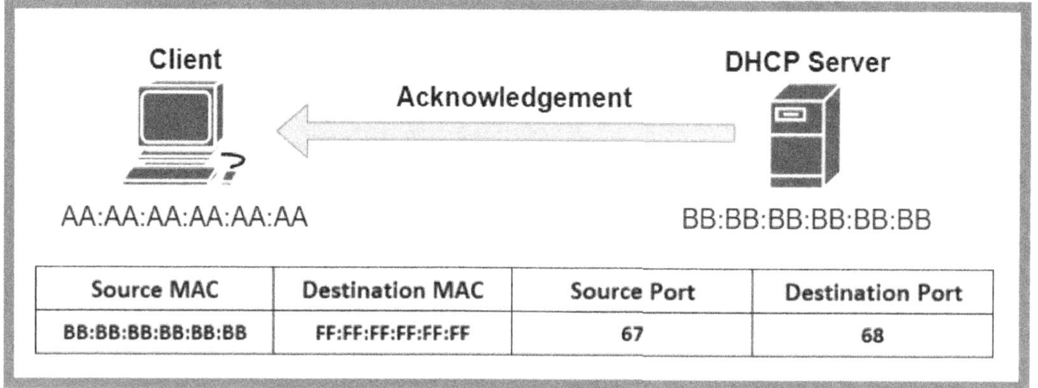

Figure 13.14: DHCP acknowledgment

The DHCP acknowledgment message is also sent as a broadcast to the client on the network.

The lease provided to the DHCP client is valid for a period of time. If a client wants to continue using the IP address assigned by the DHCP server, the client sends a **DHCP request** (unicast) message to the DHCP server, requesting the lease to be renewed.

> **Note**
> For renewal of leases, both the DHCP request and DHCP acknowledgment messages are sent as unicast messages.

The DHCP server will verify whether the lease information is available and return a DHCP acknowledgment (unicast) message and the client will continue using the current IP address once it's available. Keep in mind that the client does not wait until a lease has expired to request a renewal. The client does this renewal process prior to the expiration.

Cisco's DHCP configurations

Configuring the DHCP service on a Cisco IOS device is quite simple. Use the upcoming steps as a guideline when configuring DHCP on a Cisco router.

To exclude addresses, you will need to create a DHCP pool of addresses. The Cisco IOS router begins distributing IP addresses automatically. It's recommended to create an exclusion pool or range of addresses that you do not want the DHCP server to distribute on the network. Such addresses may include those that are statically assigned to devices and any reservations.

The following steps are used for creating an exclusion list:

1. To exclude a single address, use the `ip dhcp excluded-address` **`ip-address`** command.
2. To exclude a range of addresses, use the `ip dhcp excluded-address` **`start-address end-address`** command.

When creating a DHCP pool, it contains all the IP configurations that will be sent to DHCP clients on the network such as IP address, subnet mask, default gateway, DNS server, and so on.

The following steps are used for creating a DHCP pool:

1. To create a DHCP pool, use the `ip dhcp pool` **`pool-name`** command. Once you've created a pool, you will enter the DHCP configuration mode for the pool.
2. Use the `network` **`network-ID subnet-mask`** command to define the address pool.
3. The `default-router` **`ip-address`** command is used to specify the default gateway address.
4. The `dns-server` **`ip-address`** command is used to define the DNS servers.
5. The `domain-name` **`domain`** command is used to define the domain name on the network.

> **Note**
> To disable DHCP services on a Cisco IOS router, use the `no service dhcp` command in global configuration mode. To enable DHCP services, use the `service dhcp` command.

Multiple pools can be created on the same DHCP server or Cisco IOS device to facilitate an organization with multiple networks and a single DHCP server.

> **Note**
> A Cisco device interface can be configured as a DHCP client by using the `ip address dhcp` command.

In the next section, you will learn about the concepts and benefits of using DHCP relay on a Cisco network.

DHCP Relay

In many organizations with large and complex networks, the servers are usually logically located within a data center or a different subnet. These servers usually provide network services and host applications for the entire organization's users and devices. Such services include DHCP, DNS, file-hosting services, and so on. When a client wants to access these network services, the client device sends a broadcast message, hoping to locate the relevant server.

Imagine a client is connected to a network. It broadcasts a DHCP discover message to locate a DHCP server because it needs an IP address. If the DHCP server is not on the same subnet as the DHCP client, the router will prevent the DHCP discover message from propagating below the local subnet. This causes an issue because the client will not receive the IP address and other IP configurations needed to communicate with other devices on the network.

Figure 13.15 shows a DHCP server located on another subnet:

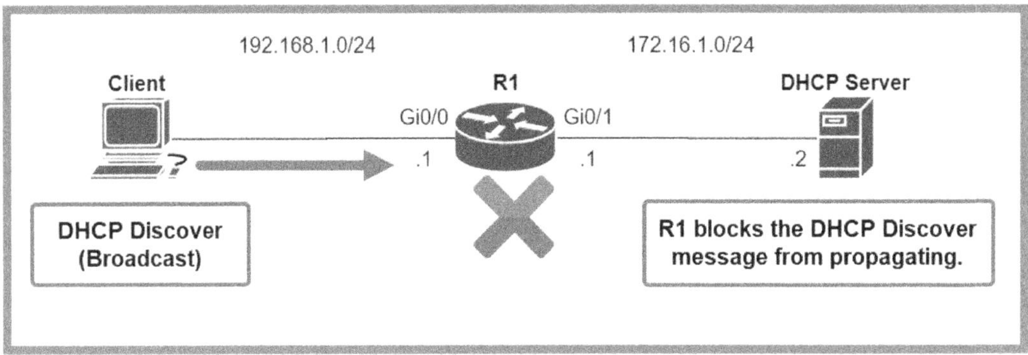

Figure 13.15: Router does not forward broadcast messages

Since a DHCP discover message is sent as a broadcast, routers (layer 3 devices) block any broadcast messages from propagating by default. However, the Cisco IOS has a solution to allow the forwarding of DHCP discover and DHCP request messages to a DHCP server on a different subnet.

The `ip helper-address` command can be applied on the interface of the router that receives DHCP discover and DHCP request messages. Therefore, you can use the following commands to configure the router to forward DHCP broadcast messages:

```
R1(config)# interface GigabitEthernet 0/0
R1(config-if)# ip helper-address 172.16.1.2
R1(config-if)# exit
```

Figure 13.16 shows the effect of applying the `ip helper-address` command:

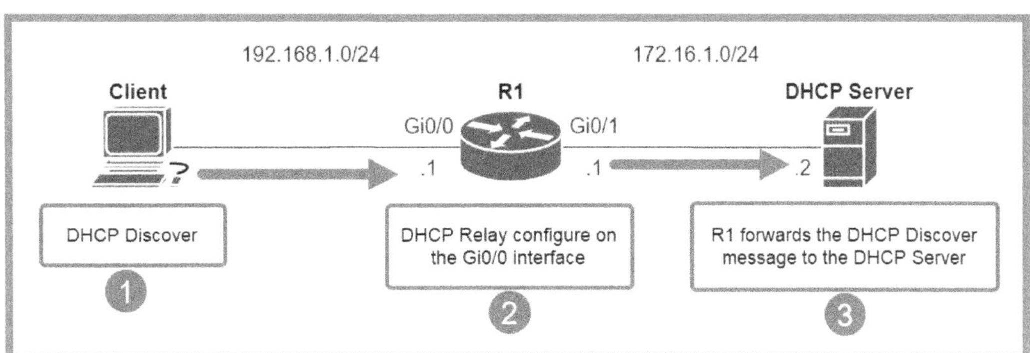

Figure 13.16: DHCP propagation

`ip helper-address` should always be applied on the interface that is connected to or facing the DHCP clients on the network. In the next section, you will learn how to configure DHCP services and DHCP relay on a Cisco IOS router.

Lab: Configuring DHCP and DHCP Relay

In this lab, you will learn how to configure DHCP services in a Cisco environment. Please keep in mind that this lab is simply an extension of the previous lab on NTP services and will use the same network topology, as shown in *Figure 13.17*:

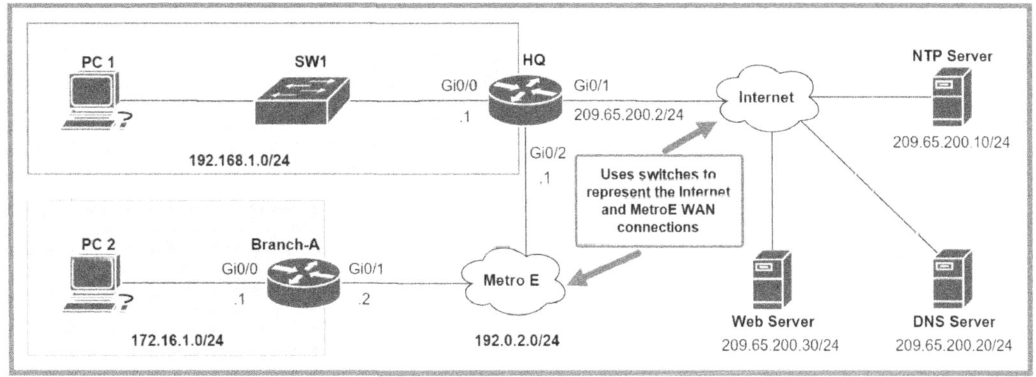

Figure 13.17: DHCP lab

The pre-built lab template can be downloaded from `https://packt.link/CCNArepoCh13second`.

To get started, use the following instructions to implement DHCP on the topology:

1. Exclude the addresses that you do not want to assign to client devices by the DHCP server:

```
HQ(config)# ip dhcp excluded-address 192.168.1.1 192.168.1.10
HQ(config)# ip dhcp excluded-address 172.16.1.1 172.16.1.10
```

   You have excluded the first 10 addresses of each private network: `192.168.1.0/24` and `172.16.1.0/24`.

2. Create a DHCP pool for the HQ LAN network on the HQ router:

```
HQ(config)# ip dhcp pool HQ-LAN
HQ(dhcp-config)# network 192.168.1.0 255.255.255.0
HQ(dhcp-config)# default-router 192.168.1.1
HQ(dhcp-config)# dns-server 209.65.200.20
HQ(dhcp-config)# exit
```

   For each DHCP pool, you configure the range of addresses by using the `network` command to be distributed via the server. The `default-router` command is used to specify the default gateway for DHCP clients, and the DNS server information will be used in the next lab.

3. Create another DHCP pool for the Branch-A LAN network on the HQ router:

```
HQ(config)# ip dhcp pool Branch-A-LAN
HQ(dhcp-config)# network 172.16.1.0 255.255.255.0
HQ(dhcp-config)# default-router 172.16.1.1
HQ(dhcp-config)# dns-server 209.65.200.20
HQ(dhcp-config)#exit
```

4. Configure the Branch-A router as a DHCP relay to the HQ router:

```
Branch-A(config)# interface GigabitEthernet 0/0
Branch-A(config-if)# ip helper-address 192.0.2.1
Branch-A(config-if)# exit
```

   `ip helper-address` is always configured on the LAN side of the router with the IP address of the DHCP server.

5. On the Branch-A router, use the `show ip interface` command to verify that the DHCP helper address is configured:

```
Branch-A#show ip interface gigabitEthernet 0/0
GigabitEthernet0/0 is up, line protocol is up (connected)
  Internet address is 172.16.1.1/24
  Broadcast address is 255.255.255.255
  Address determined by setup command
  MTU is 1500 bytes
  Helper address is 192.0.2.1
  Directed broadcast forwarding is disabled
```

Figure 13.18 – Helper address

6. Click on `PC 1` and `PC 2`, select the `Desktop` tab, click on `IP Configuration`, and set it to `DHCP`, as shown in *Figure 13.19*:

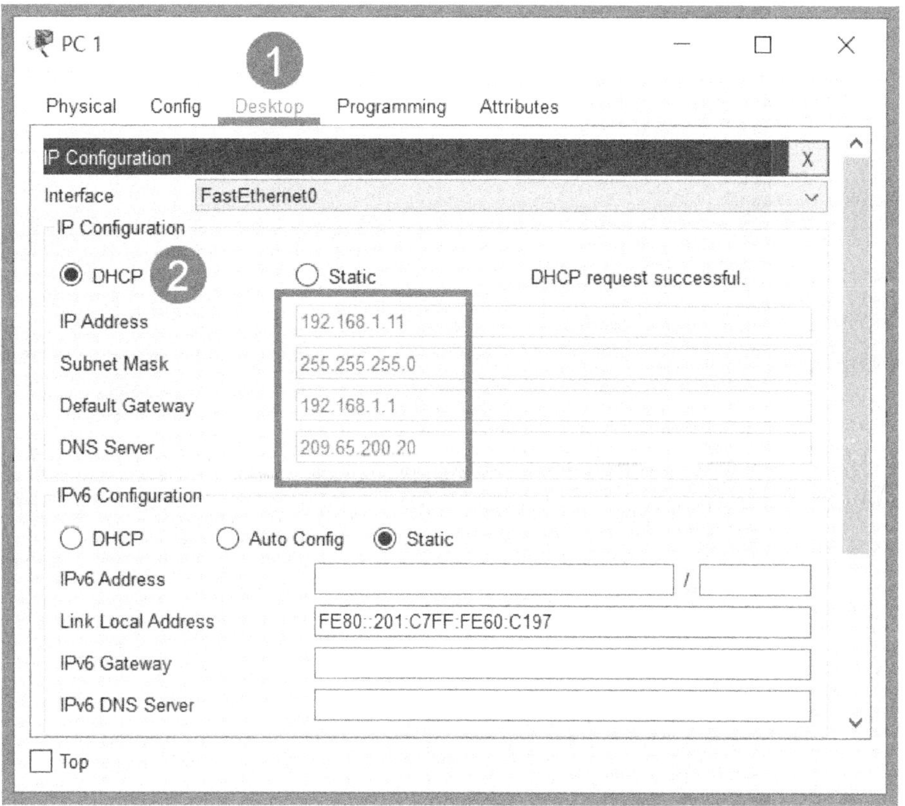

Figure 13.19: IP addressing

After a while, each DHCP client – PC 1 and PC 2 – will receive their IP configurations from the DHCP server, the HQ router.

7. On the HQ router, the `show ip dhcp binding` command shows the number of client devices that are using an IP address from the DHCP server, the client's MAC address, lease time, and type:

```
HQ#show ip dhcp binding
IP address        Client-ID/              Lease expiration        Type
                  Hardware address
192.168.1.11      0001.C760.C197           --                     Automatic
172.16.1.11       00E0.B0E8.1A13           --                     Automatic
HQ#
```

Figure 13.20: DHCP binding table

8. Lastly, the `show ip dhcp pool` command provides details about statistics within each DHCP pool on the Cisco IOS router:

```
HQ#show ip dhcp pool

Pool HQ-LAN :
 Utilization mark (high/low)    : 100 / 0
 Subnet size (first/next)       : 0 / 0
 Total addresses                : 254
 Leased addresses               : 1
 Excluded addresses             : 2
 Pending event                  : none

 1 subnet is currently in the pool
 Current index        IP address range                    Leased/Excluded/Total
 192.168.1.1          192.168.1.1      - 192.168.1.254     1     / 2      / 254
```

Figure 13.21: DHCP pool

Having completed this lab, you have gained the hands-on skills needed to use a Cisco IOS router as a DHCP server and a DHCP relay on a network. In the next section, we will take a look at DNS as a network service.

Exploring the Domain Name System (DNS)

Imagine you want to research additional information about the CCNA certification. The best place to start researching would be Cisco's website at www.cisco.com. Therefore, you open your favorite web browser and simply enter the URL into the address bar and hit *Enter*. After a few seconds, the Cisco website appears and you can continue your research. Everything seems to work like magic, but have you ever wondered how your computer determines the IP address for the web server that is hosting Cisco's website?

As mentioned in *Chapter 4, IPv4 and IPv6 Addressing*, each device that is connected and exchanging messages on a computer-based network must be assigned a unique IPv4 or IPv6 address. The same is also applied to all devices on the internet, such as web and mail exchange servers. If a web server is identified by its IP address, why does it have a website URL address such as www.cisco.com?

To help you understand the situation a bit better, imagine having to remember all the IP addresses of each website you want to visit on the internet. That would be very challenging as IP addresses may change or be re-assigned to another device on a network. You cannot connect to a server or device on the internet if you do not know the IPv4 or IPv6 address.

To solve this issue, the **DNS** network service protocol was created with the primary purpose of resolving hostnames to IP addresses. It's a lot easier to remember a **uniform resource locator** (**URL**) or domain name of a website. With the convenience of using DNS, IT professionals can easily purchase a domain name and point it to a web server or device. This allows anyone who knows the domain name, such as www.cisco.com, to visit the Cisco website easily using a computer or smart device with a standard web browser.

Before the days of DNS, each computer had a file known as the `hosts` file. The `hosts` file would contain hostname to IP address mapping. Whenever a user wanted to visit a website, the user would enter the hostname and the computer would query the local `hosts` file in search of an available map that would inform the computer of the IP address to reach the hostname. However, if the `hosts` file did not have an available entry for the hostname, the computer would not know how to reach the server. Users had to ensure the `hosts` file was frequently updated to contain the most up-to-date records.

To view the `hosts` file on a Windows operating system, go to `C:\Windows\System32\drivers\etc\hosts`. *Figure 13.22* shows the contents within the `hosts` file on a Windows 10 operating system:

```
hosts - Notepad
File Edit Format View Help
# Copyright (c) 1993-2009 Microsoft Corp.
#
# This is a sample HOSTS file used by Microsoft TCP/IP for Windows.
#
# This file contains the mappings of IP addresses to host names. Each
# entry should be kept on an individual line. The IP address should
# be placed in the first column followed by the corresponding host name.
# The IP address and the host name should be separated by at least one
# space.
#
# Additionally, comments (such as these) may be inserted on individual
# lines or following the machine name denoted by a '#' symbol.
#
# For example:
#
#      102.54.94.97     rhino.acme.com          # source server
#       38.25.63.10     x.acme.com              # x client host

# localhost name resolution is handled within DNS itself.
#       127.0.0.1       localhost
#       ::1             localhost

Ln 1, Col 1    100%    Windows (CRLF)    UTF-8
```

Figure 13.22: hosts file

Frequently updating the `hosts` file was not a good strategy as the internet is always growing, with new devices coming online all the time with new and unique hostnames. The creation of DNS servers then came about, with each server being the root of its domain and containing all the DNS records for a specific **top-level domain** (**TLD**). A TLD is a domain that has the root (.) and ends with a name such as `.com`, `.net`, `.org`, `.xyz`, and so on. A domain name is a domain that contains a name with a TLD, as in cisco.com. A **fully qualified domain name** (**FQDN**) contains an additional extension, a hostname, and a domain, as in www.cisco.com. The FQDN specifies the exact location or device. For example, cisco.com is simply a domain name that may contain many devices, but specifying an FQDN such as www.cisco.com simply says you are trying to connect to a device with the hostname *www* that belongs within the cisco.com domain.

DNS Root Servers

As previously mentioned, there are various root DNS servers that contain the DNS records for each object that belongs to the parent domain. As shown in *Figure 13.23*, the `.com` root server contains all the DNS records for cisco.com and its sub-domains, such as `community.cisco.com`:

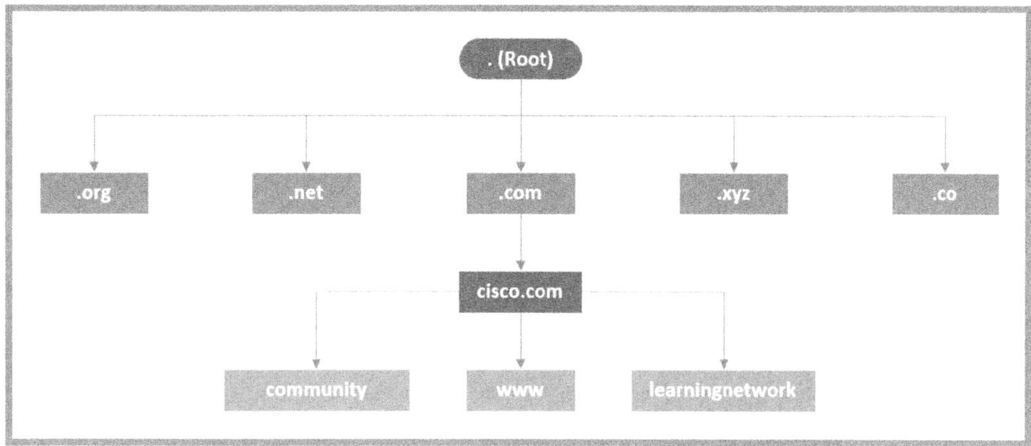

Figure 13.23: DNS hierarchy

Whenever a device wants to look up the IP address for a hostname, it will send a DNS query to its configured DNS server. Once the record is found, the DNS server will send a DNS reply with the IP address for the hostname back to the computer. The computer will use the IP address to reach the hostname or device.

Figure 13.24 shows the DNS process when a user enters a URL within the web browser:

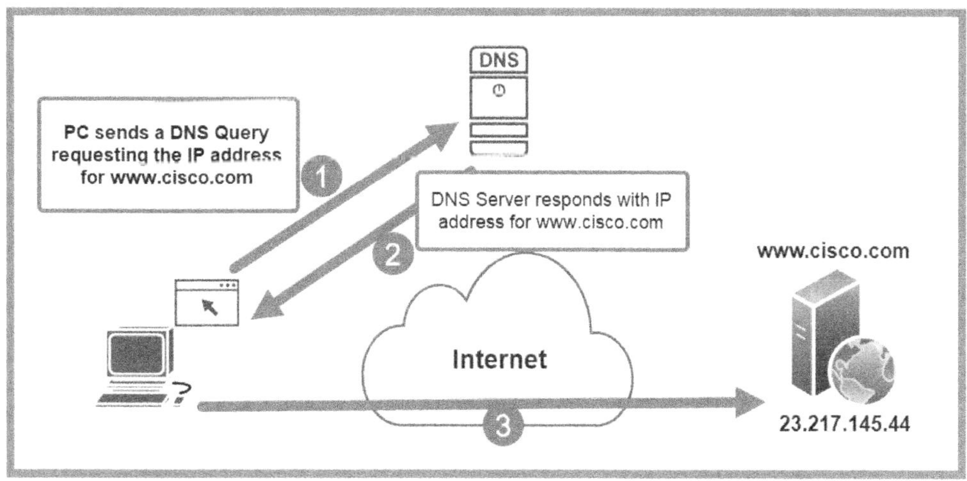

Figure 13.24: DNS process

There are many free public and reliable DNS servers on the internet. The following are some recommended servers, as they provide speed and security:

- Cloudflare DNS: https://1.1.1.1/
- Cisco OpenDNS: https://www.opendns.com/
- Google DNS: https://developers.google.com/speed/public-dns

What if your DNS server does not have the record for a specific hostname or domain name? What will it do? DNS servers often exchange information with each other to ensure that their records are always up to date. If a DNS server does not have a record, it can respond, informing the client that it does not have a record, or simply ask another DNS server for the information and then relay the response back to the client.

DNS Record Types

There are many DNS record types that are used on a DNS server. The following are their descriptions:

- **A** – Resolves a hostname to an IPv4 address.
- **AAAA** – Resolves a hostname to an IPv6 address.
- **MX** – Maps the domain to mail exchange (email) servers.
- **NS** – Points to the domain's name servers.
- **CNAME** – Allows you to create an Alias name for the domain.
- **SOA** – Used to specify the authority for the domain.
- **SVR** – Specifies the service records.
- **PTR** – Maps an IP address to a hostname.
- **RP** – Specifies the responsible person for a domain.
- **HINFO** – Specifies host information.
- **TXT** – Allows you to add text as a DNS record.

Therefore, if a computer wants to determine the IPv4 address for Cisco's website, www.cisco.com, the computer will need to send a DNS query requesting the A record from the DNS server. The `nslookup` utility on both Microsoft Windows and Linux operating systems is used to troubleshoot DNS issues on the client side of the network.

Lab: Configuring DNS

In this lab, you will learn how to configure DNS services in a Cisco environment. Please keep in mind that this lab is simply an extension of the previous lab on NTP and DHCP services and will be using the same network topology, as shown in *Figure 13.25*:

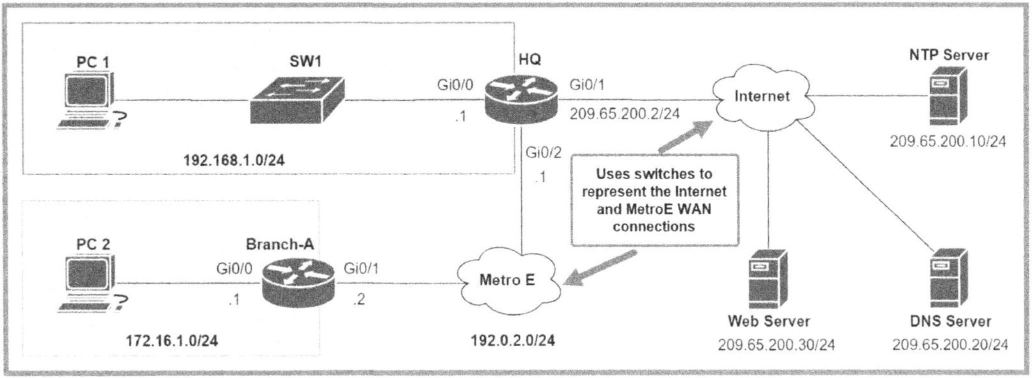

Figure 13.25: DNS lab

To get started, use the following instructions to implement DNS on the topology:

1. Firstly, you need to create and configure your DNS server within Cisco Packet Tracer. Click on the DNS server, select the `Services` tab, and click on `DNS`, as shown in *Figure 13.26*:

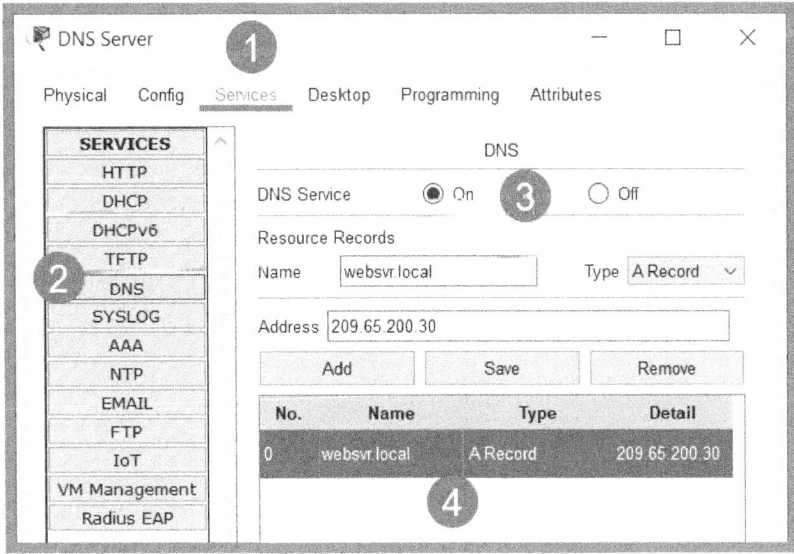

Figure 13.26: DNS server

Ensure that `DNS Service` is set to `On`. Create a new `Resource Record: websvr.local`, `Type: A` instance and IP address as the web server on the network `209.65.200.30`, and click `Add` to save the DNS record.

2. Since you have already configured each client to use the DNS server `209.65.200.20` via DHCP, you can move on to the next step.
3. On PC 1 and PC 2, click on `Desktop` and open the `Web Browser` application. Enter the web address of the web server, http://websvr.local, and click on `Go`:

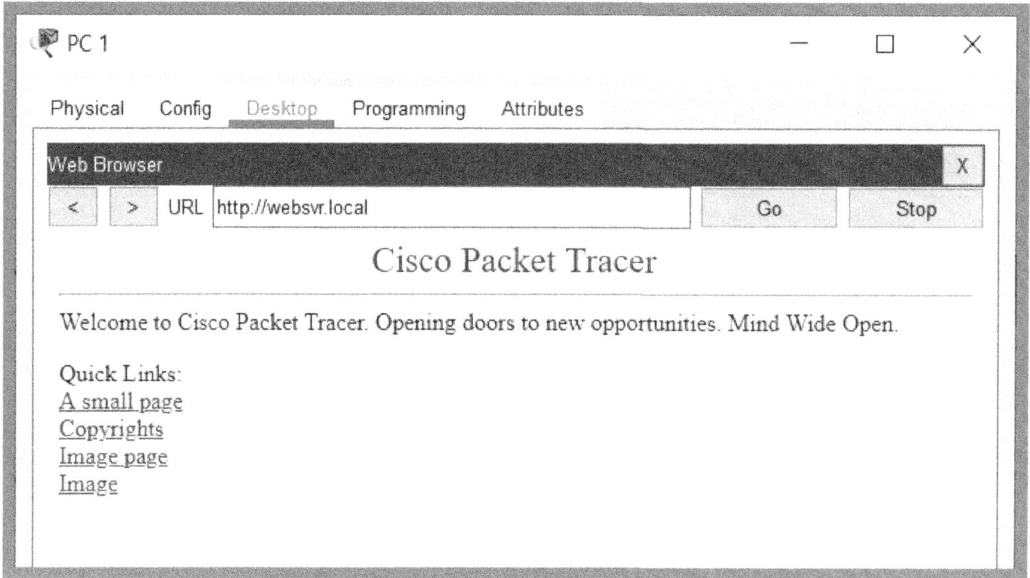

Figure 13.27: Web page

The output shows that PC 1 is able to reach the web server via the hostname `websvr.local`. This is validation that the DNS server is able to resolve the hostname `websvr.local` to its IP address in the background.

4. On PC 1, open the `Command Prompt` application. Use the `nslookup` utility to verify the DNS configurations on the local machine:

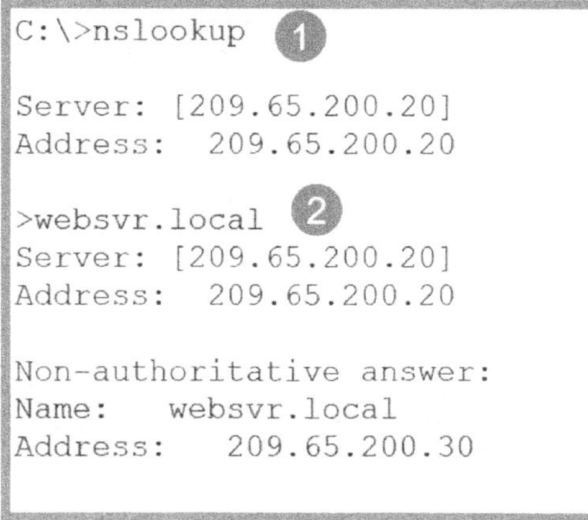

```
C:\>nslookup

Server: [209.65.200.20]
Address:  209.65.200.20

>websvr.local
Server: [209.65.200.20]
Address:  209.65.200.20

Non-authoritative answer:
Name:   websvr.local
Address:   209.65.200.30
```

Figure 13.28: DNS validation

After entering the `nslookup` command, the system provides you with the DNS settings it is currently using, 209.65.200.20, as its DNS server. Next, using the hostname `websvr.local`, the system queries the DNS server (209.65.200.20) to retrieve the DNS **A Record** value to the hostname. The DNS server (209.65.200.20) was able to resolve the hostname `websvr.local` to the IP address 209.65.200.30. Additionally, if you attempt to ping the domain name `websvr.local`, the DNS server will resolve the IP address and will respond.

Having completed this lab, you have gained the skills needed to configure and understand the concepts of DNS on a Cisco enterprise network.

Working with Syslog

When events occur on a network, networking devices, such as routers, switches, and firewalls, generate log messages with details about the event for the purpose of notifying the administrator. These log messages can contain details about critical and non-critical events. Network professionals use a wide range of tools and options for managing these log messages, such as storing, displaying, interpreting, and normalizing. This helps network professionals focus on the most important log messages to determine event timelines.

Syslog is both a protocol and a standard for accessing, creating, and managing log messages on a computer or network device. Syslog defines how log messages are generated, formatted, shown on a console, and sent over a network.

> **Note**
> Syslog uses UDP port `514` to send event messages across a network to a centralized syslog server for management.

Implementing proper log management on a network has several benefits, such as helping network professionals to improve both monitoring and troubleshooting. In addition, you can configure devices to send log messages of a certain severity level to a centralized syslog server on the network. As a network professional, you can specify the destination for forwarding syslog messages, such as a server.

By default, Cisco devices log their system messages to the console line. However, a device can be configured to log its messages to an internal buffer within the device itself, on a **virtual terminal** (**VTY**) line, and even to a syslog server on the network. It is recommended that a centralized log server be set up on the network to capture log messages from all network devices. This strategy will allow you to view all the correlated logs in a sequential order. It thus allows you to see a timeline of events throughout the network using a single dashboard interface on the server.

Syslog Severity Levels

Each syslog message contains a severity level and a facility. *Table 13.1* shows all the severity levels and their descriptions:

Severity Name	**Severity Level**	**Description**
Emergency	0	System is unusable
Alert	1	Immediate action is needed
Critical	2	Critical condition
Error	3	Error condition
Warning	4	Warning condition
Notification	5	Normal but significant condition
Information	6	Information message
Debugging	7	Debugging message

Table 13.1: Syslog severity levels

A simple way to remember the syslog severity levels is to take each initial letter from every level and create a phase. The following phrase is a bit goofy but an awesome way to remember each severity level: **E***very* **A***wesome* **C***isco* **E***ngineer* **W***ill* **N***eed* **I***ce-cream* **D***aily*.

The following is the default Syslog message format on Cisco IOS devices:

```
seq no: timestamp: %facility-severity-MNEMONIC: description
```

The following is a breakdown of each part of the syslog message format:

- `seq no` represents the sequence number assigned to each log message. To enable the sequence number, use the `service sequence-numbers` command in global configuration mode.
- The `timestamp` part includes the date and time of the event. To enable the timestamp, use the `service timestamps` command in global configuration mode.
- The `facility` part represents what the log message is referring to.
- The `severity` part provides a severity code in the range 0–7 that describes how important the alarm is.
- The `MNEMONIC` part is simply text that is used to describe the alarm.
- The `description` part contains a brief description of the event or alarm.

The following is an example of a syslog message generated by a Cisco IOS router:

```
*Apr 28, 15:53:58.5353: %LINEPROTO-5-UPDOWN: Line protocol on
Interface GigabitEthernet0/1, changed state to up
```

You can see the timestamp is April 28 at `15:53:58.5353`, the facility is `LINEPROTO`, the severity level is `5`, the mnemonic is `UPDOWN`, and the description is `Line protocol on Interface GigabitEthernet0/1, changed state to up`.

> **Note**
>
> To force the log messages to display date and time, use the `service timestamps log datetime` command in global configuration mode.

When it comes to acquiring a logging server, there are many free and commercial products from reputation vendors that allow you to simply download and install them on your operating system. For example, **Solarwinds** has its Kiwi Syslog Server (`www.kiwisyslog.com`) as a commercial product, while **PRTG** (www.paessler.com) is able to function as a free syslog server.

In the next section, you will learn how to implement Syslog on a Cisco network.

Lab: Configuring Syslog

In this lab, you will learn how to configure Cisco IOS devices to use syslog and forward log messages to a centralized log management server on a network. *Figure 13.29* shows the topology you will be using for this exercise. Please note that it is the same as in the previous labs, but with the addition of a Syslog server on the 192.168.1.0/24 network with a static IP address of 192.168.1.5:

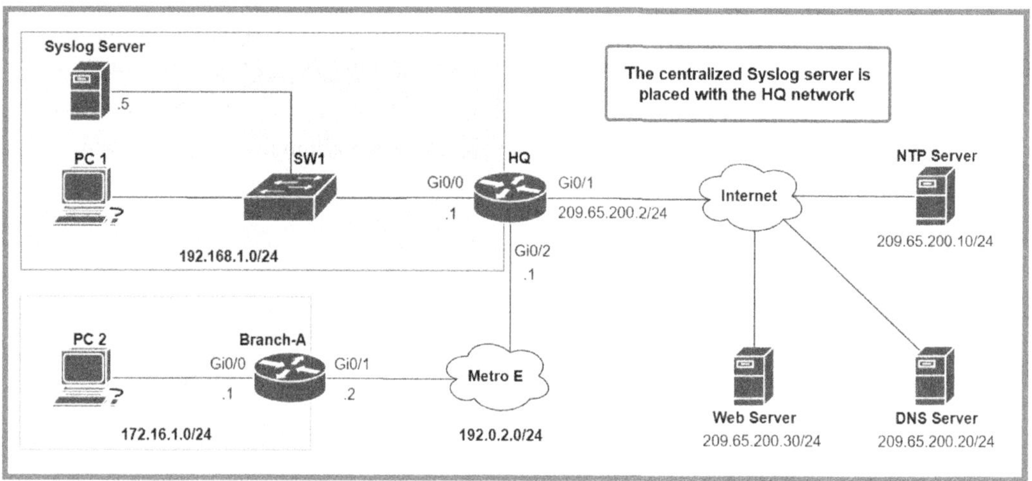

Figure 13.29: Syslog topology

To get started with this exercise, ensure you download and open the pre-built lab file from `https://packt.link/CCNArepoCh13third`.

Now that you are lab-ready, use the following instructions to configure syslog on your network topology:

1. Firstly, you will configure the new server to accept syslog messages. Click on the new server (`192.168.1.5`), select the `Services` tab, and then click on `Syslog`, as shown in *Figure 13.30*:

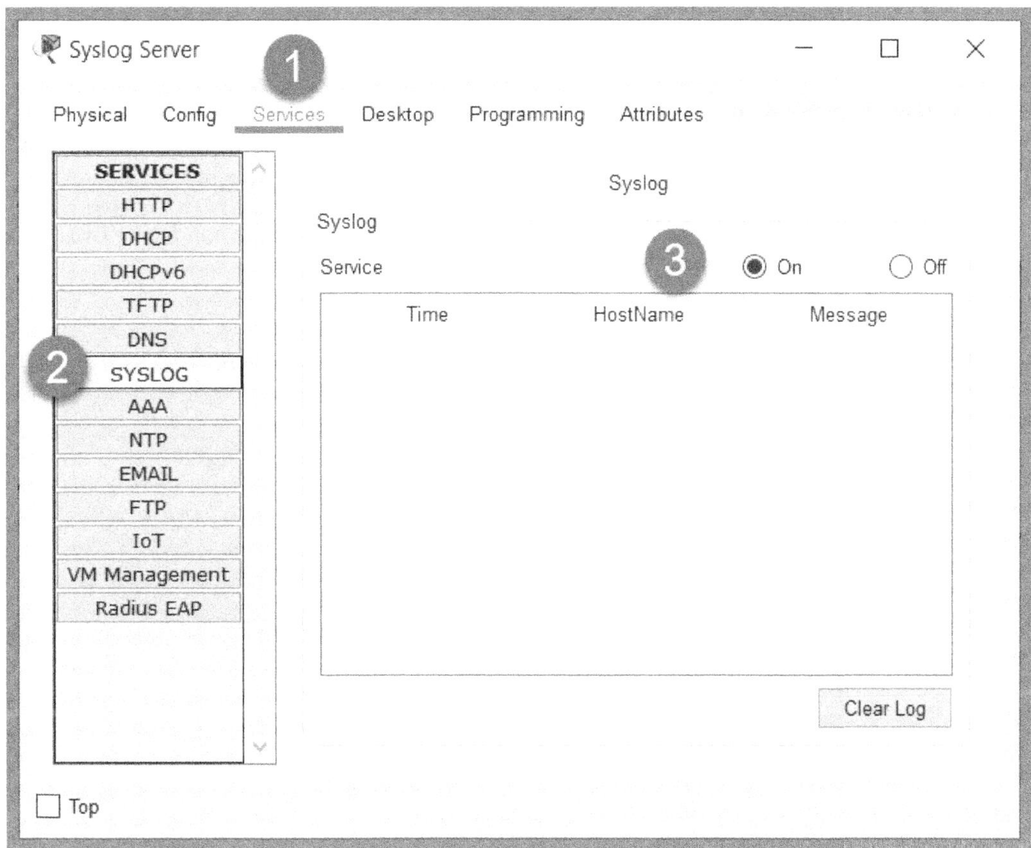

Figure 13.30: Syslog Server

Ensure the syslog service is set to `On`.

2. Configure the Branch-A router to send syslog messages to the syslog server:

```
Branch-A(config)# logging 192.168.1.5
```

3. Configure the Branch-A router to send all syslog messages to the syslog server by specifying the eighth severity level, `debugging`:

```
Branch-A(config)# logging trap debugging
```

When you specify a severity level, the router will send all severity level messages that range from severity level 0 to the severity level you specify. By specifying `debugging`, the router will send all syslog severity messages from level 0 to level 8, as `debugging` is severity level 8.

4. Enable timestamps with milliseconds on log messages by using the following commands:

```
Branch-A(config)# service timestamps log datetime msec
```

5. On the Branch-A router, either disconnect and reconnect the LAN cable or administratively shut down the LAN interface to generate some syslog messages on the device.
6. Configure the HQ router to send syslog messages to the syslog server.
7. Head on over to the syslog server and check the syslog service, as shown in *Figure 13.31*:

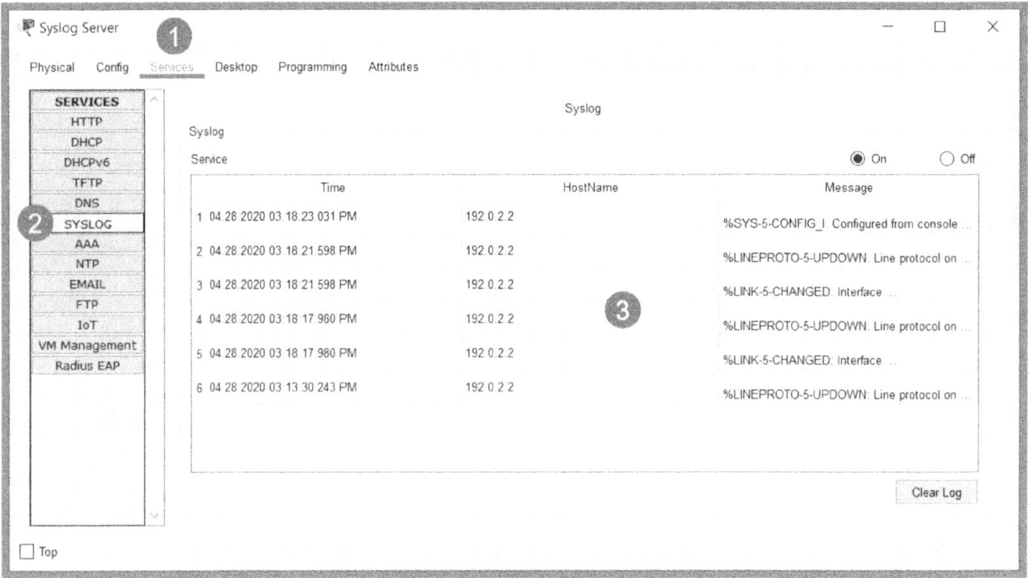

Figure 13.31: Syslog messages

The syslog messages that appear here were those generated by the Branch-A router.

8. Use the `show logging` command to verify the default logging service settings on the router.

```
Branch-A#show logging
Syslog logging: enabled (0 messages dropped, 0 messages rate-limited,
          0 flushes, 0 overruns, xml disabled, filtering disabled)

No Active Message Discriminator.


No Inactive Message Discriminator.


    Console logging: level debugging, 10 messages logged, xml disabled,
          filtering disabled
    Monitor logging: level debugging, 10 messages logged, xml disabled,
          filtering disabled
    Buffer logging:  disabled, xml disabled,
          filtering disabled
```

Figure 13.32: Logging service

As shown in *Figure 13.32*, you can determine the local router's syslog configuration and which severity syslog messages were logged.

Having completed this lab, you have gained the hands-on skills to implement syslog on Cisco IOS devices.

Understanding SNMP

The **Simple Network Management Protocol** (**SNMP**) was designed to enable IT administrators to easily manage network and end devices, such as workstations, servers, switches, routers, and security appliances, on an IP-based network. SNMP provides the functionality to allow device administrators to monitor, manage, and troubleshoot network performance.

SNMP is made up of three components: the SNMP manager, the SNMP agent, and the **Management Information Base** (**MIB**). These three components all work together to create a **network management system** (**NMS**).

The **SNMP manager** is an application that is installed and running on the administrator's computer. The SNMP manager is responsible for collecting information from the SNMP agents using SNMP GET messages; the manager is able to make modifications to the network device's configuration by using SNMP SET messages.

The SNMP agent and MIB exist on the actual networking device, such as a switch or router. The SNMP agent is the component that communicates with the SNMP manager across the network. The user interacts with the SNMP manager, which then relays the information to the SNMP agent. The SNMP agent either gathers information and sends it back to the SNMP manager or executes a set of instructions.

The MIB is like a database that contains data about the network device and its operational state. Such information is available only to users who are authenticated via SNMP on the local device. To put it simply, the SNMP agent must be configured on a network device, and then the user opens an SNMP manager application on their computer and specifies the IP address of the target device and user credentials, such as a community string. If the credentials are valid, the SNMP manager will authenticate to the SNMP agent on the network device, allowing the user to interact, gather information, and make adjustments on the device.

> **Note**
>
> SNMP operates on UDP port `161`. However, SNMP agents send SNMP trap messages to the SNMP manager on UDP port `162`.

Figure 13.33 shows the overall flow of messages on the NMS:

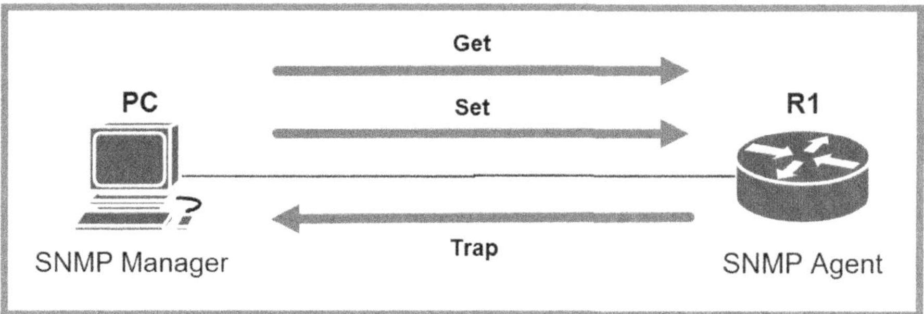

Figure 13.33: SNMP messages

The SNMP **Get** request is used to gather or query the device for information, and the SNMP **Set** request is used to modify the configuration on the device via the SNMP agent.

Figure 13.34 shows an SNMP manager interface:

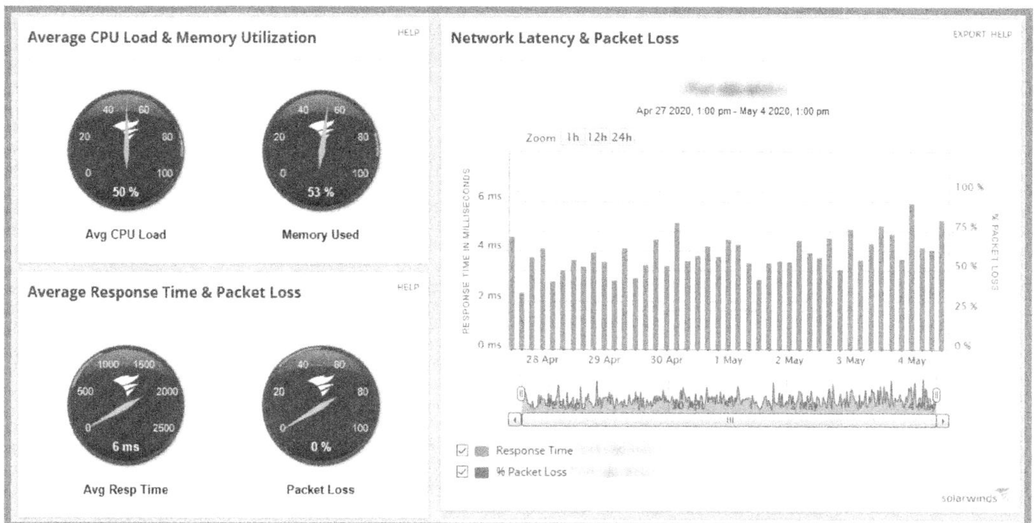

Figure 13.34: SNMP manager

Figure 13.34 shows some information about a switch on an enterprise network. To gather this information, the SNMP manager (Solarwinds) has sent an SNMP GET message to retrieve the information for us. Once the information is gathered, it is presented on the SNMP manager's **graphical user interface** (**GUI**). The SNMP protocol was able to gather details such as CPU and memory load, latency, and packet loss statistics. Without using the command line, the SNMP manager is able to show us the days and times when network latency was higher than usual. Such information can be used to generate reports, create network baselines, and determine any network performance issues.

SNMP traps are continuously exchanged between the SNMP manager and the SNMP agent to gather information about the network device. The downside of the SNMP polling mechanism is the delay of time between the occurrence of an event on a network device and the time the SNMP manager takes to notice it. Some organizations configure their SNMP polling intervals to 10 minutes, which allows the NMS to detect an event/issue within 10 minutes of the occurrence. However, this interval may be too long when it comes to detecting a failure on a critical network. Such polling intervals can be adjusted to better fit the organization's response time to network issues. Keep in mind that too many polling messages may flood the available bandwidth on the network.

SNMP Versions

There are several versions of SNMP:

- **SNMPv1** – SNMPv1 does not provide any form of authentication, privileges, or encryption between the SNMP manager and the SNMP agent.
- **SNMPv2c** – SNMPv2c uses community strings: public and private for administrative tasks. The public string is used for read-only tasks, while the private string is used for read-write actions. However, SNMPv2c does not provide any authentication or encryption.
- **SNMPv3** – SNMPv3 comes with improved security to provide authentication for users and user groups. SNMPv3 uses **Message Digest 5** (**MD5**) or **Secure Hashing Algorithm** (**SHA**) during the authentication phase and **Data Encryption Standard** (**DES**) or **Advanced Encryption Standard** (**AES**) for data encryption.

As mentioned, SNMPv1 and SNMPv2c use community strings for access to MIB on a network or computer device. The following are two types of community strings used in SNMP:

- **Read-only (ro)** – This string allows you to access the MIB on the network devices but does not allow you to make modifications on the device, hence read-only.
- **Read-write (rw)** – This allows you to both read and write to all objects within the MIB on the device.

Management Information Base

The **management information base** (**MIB**) is a database that contains all the **object IDs** (**OIDs**) for each component on the network device. To put it simply, for the SNMP manager to interact with an interface of a router, for example, to gather network statistics from the interface, an OID must exist for that specific task on the router.

OIDs are represented as variables within the MIB. The MIB is designed as a hierarchical tree structure containing many child sub-sections, known as branches. *Figure 13.35* shows the MIB OIDs:

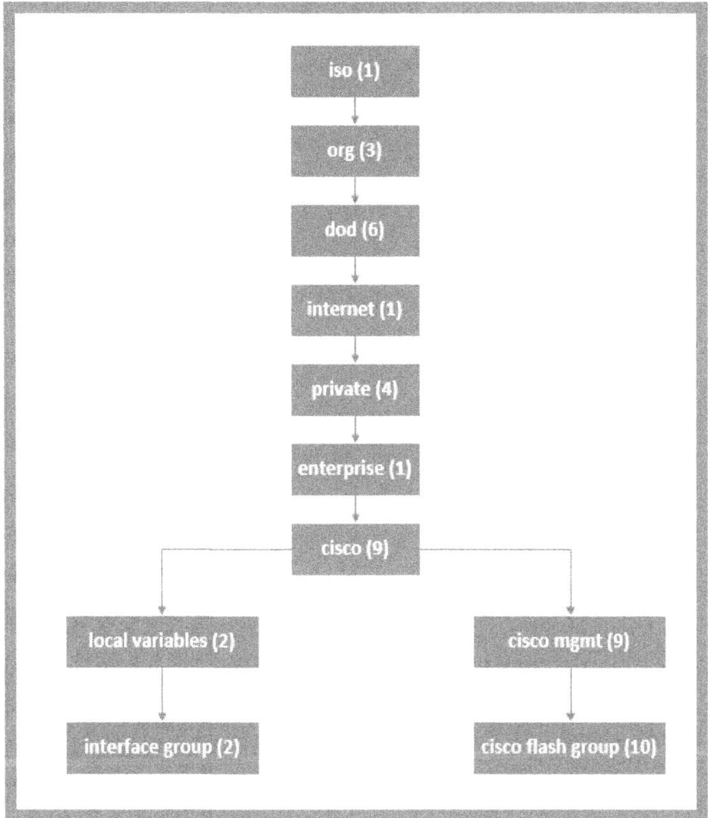

Figure 13.35: MIB

The SNMP manager uses the OID values from the MIB to gather information or make a change to an object on the SNMP agent device.

> **Note**
>
> The **Cisco SNMP Object Navigator** is a free online tool to help you translate OIDs into their respective object names and details.

In the following exercise, you will learn how to configure SNMP on the Cisco devices.

Lab: Configuring SNMP

In this lab, you will learn how to configure the SNMP service in a Cisco environment. Please keep in mind that this lab is an extension of the previous lab on DNS services and will be using the same network topology, as shown in *Figure 13.36*:

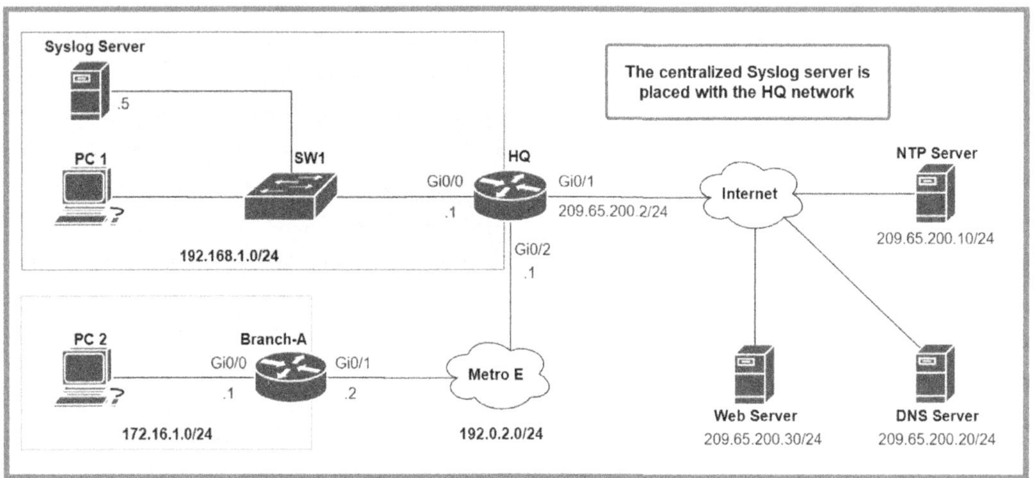

Figure 13.36: SNMP lab topology

The objective of this lab is to enable SNMP on both the HQ and Branch-A routers. Once SNMP is enabled, you can use PC 1 as the SNMP manager to retrieve device information and make configurations to the `running-config` file on the router.

Use the following link to download a pre-built template of the lab topology: `https://packt.link/CCNArepoCh13fourth`.

To configure SNMP on the Cisco IOS router, use the following instructions:

1. On the Branch-A router, configure the community string (`public`) and the access level for read-only (`ro`) using the following commands:

```
Branch-A(config)# snmp-server community public ro
```

2. Next, configure a community string (`private`) with an access level for read-write (`rw`) on the Branch-A router:

```
Branch-A(config)# snmp-server community private rw
```

Read-write will allow the SNMP manager to use the `private` community string to make modifications to the configurations of the device.

1. Apply steps 1 and 2 on the HQ router:

```
HQ(config)# snmp-server community public ro
HQ(config)# snmp-server community private rw
```

2. Head on over to PC 2, open the `Desktop` tab, and select `MIB Browser`, as shown in *Figure 13.37*:

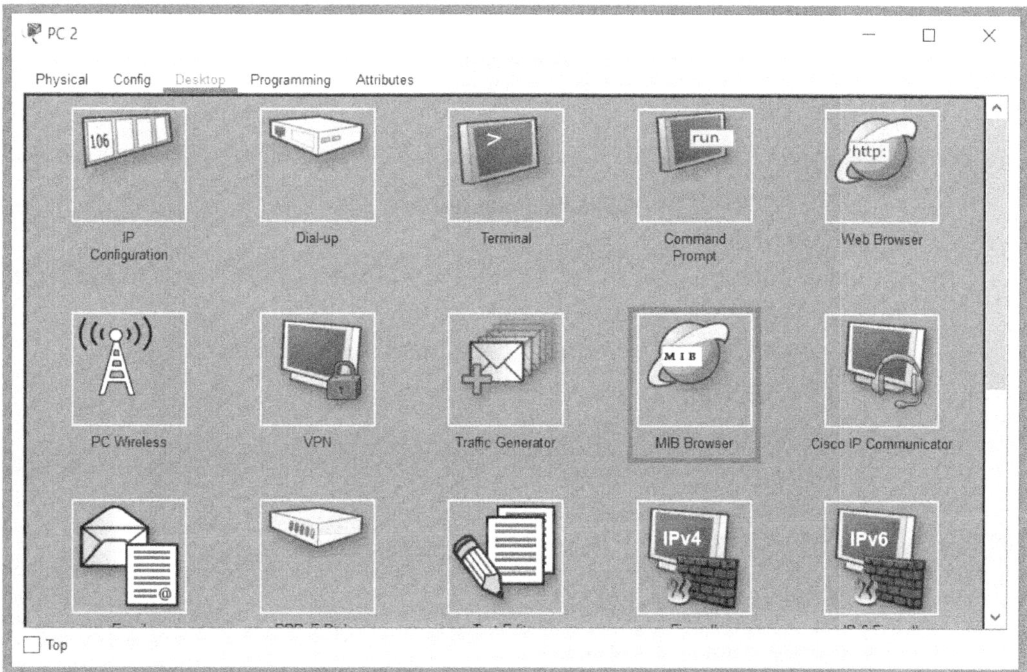

Figure 13.37: PC 2 Desktop interface

3. Click the `Advanced` button, as shown in *Figure 13.38*:

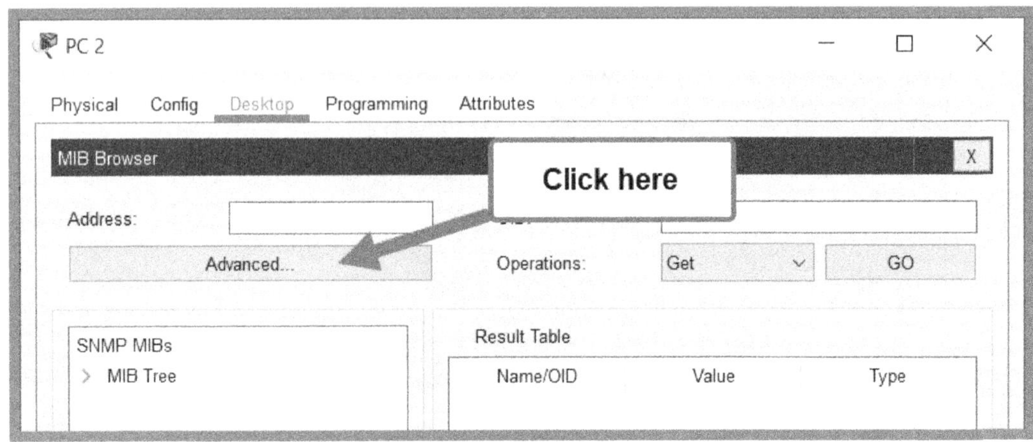

Figure 13.38: MIB Browser

4. A new window will appear. Set `Read Community` to `public`, `Write Community` to `private`, and `SNMP Version` to `v3`, and click `OK`:

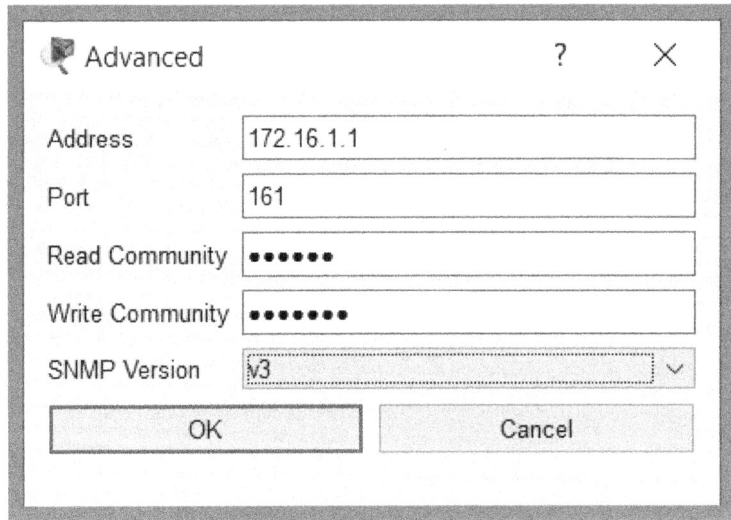

Figure 13.39: SNMP browser settings

5. On the left panel, expand the MIB tree structure to `.iso > org > dod > internet > mgmt > mib-2 > system > sysUpTime`, set `Operations` to `Get`, and click on `GO`:

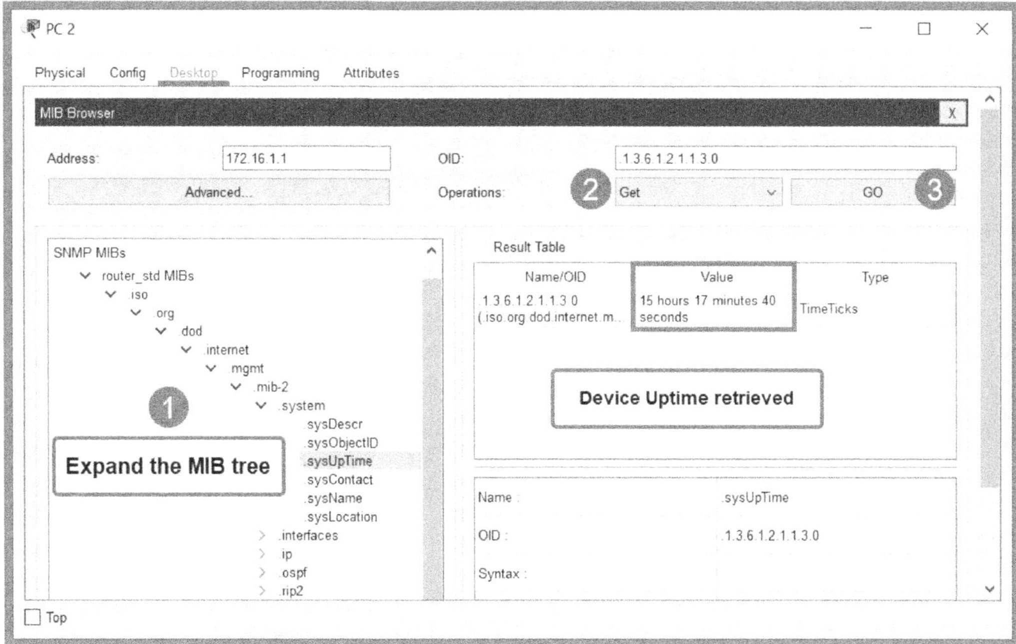

Figure 13.40: Device uptime

The SNMP manager on PC 2 was able to retrieve (GET) the device's uptime from the SNMP agent on the router.

6. To make a modification to the device's configuration, you can use the SNMP SET operation. To change the device's hostname to Branch-A-RTR, navigate to the `sysName` branch, use the `Set` operation, set `Data Type` to `OctetString`, and set `Value` to `Branch-A-RTR`, as shown in *Figure 13.41*:

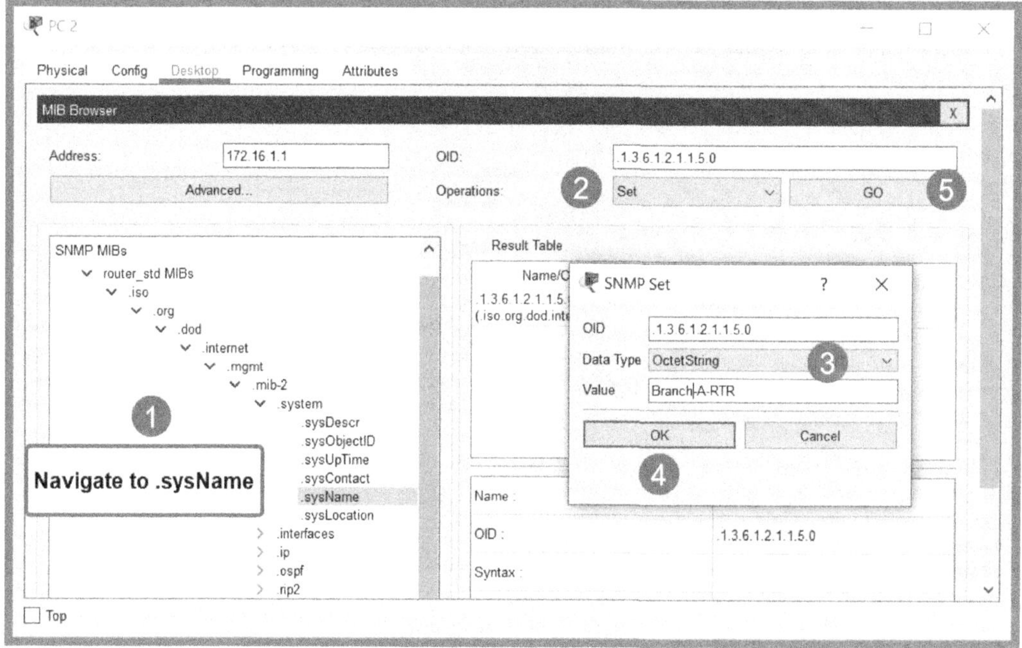

Figure 13.41: SNMP SET operation

Once you click on GO, the MIB manager will use the SNMP SET message to inform the SNMP agent on the router to make the adjustment on the device.

Having completed this lab, you have learned how to enable SNMP on Cisco IOS devices and have seen the operations of SNMP on a Cisco network. In the next section, we will take a look at understanding the key role QoS plays in an enterprise network.

QoS Traffic Classification

Imagine you are the network engineer for a very large organization with a lot of users and many network applications. Every day, users are simultaneously accessing both internal resources on the network, such as locally hosted applications and external resources. There are tons of traffic types that are traveling along the network each day. What should you do if users begin experiencing an unacceptable user experience on the corporate network, such as very slow response times?

Every day, there are thousands and even millions of packets that are generated by devices and sent with messages to other devices as a form of digital communication. Sometimes, when there is too much traffic on the network that exceeds the bandwidth between a sender and a destination, network congestion occurs. Similarly, the roads of a city do not widen automatically, and if there are too many vehicles using the roads and if they do not exit quickly enough, traffic starts accumulating and results in congestion. Therefore, each person will take longer to reach their destination.

On a network, some of these traffic types include voice and video transmission for online and virtual collaboration with other members of staff, while other traffic types might use the **User Datagram Protocol** (**UDP**) as their transport layer protocol, which does not guarantee the delivery of a message. By using QoS tools on a network, professionals can classify and prioritize network traffic types such as voice and video over non-time-sensitive traffic, such as web browsing and email.

While devices such as computers, servers, and IP phones are sending traffic to the network switch and routers, they do not consider whether the networking devices are able to transmit messages as fast as they are being received. Switches and routers are used to interconnect devices and provide users with access to network resources. They sit at the core of all exchange points on an enterprise network. This means that they accept thousands of packets per minute on their physical interfaces, process each incoming message, and forward them through an outgoing interface toward their destination. All networking devices have a buffer of limited size that temporarily stores incoming messages (queue) until the device is able to process and forward them. When a device, such as a router, receives too many incoming messages and the buffer is full, new incoming messages may be discarded until the router is able to process the exiting messages and free the buffer memory.

> **Note**
>
> The queuing of traffic increases delays on a network, so network congestion causes delays.

This is not good for a network that has critical applications that generate time-sensitive traffic such as voice and video. Imagine your organization has a **voice over IP** (**VoIP**) solution and during each phone call with another employee or external party, for the duration of the call, there is an unacceptable experience, such as not hearing what the other person is saying, hearing static, or experiencing delays. Voice and video traffic use UDP as their preferred transport layer protocol because UDP creates a lot less overhead on the network and it's much faster than the **Transport Control Protocol** (**TCP**).

However, the disadvantage of using UDP, especially for voice and video traffic types, is that it is connection-less and lacks the guaranteed delivery of packets from the sender to the destination. Therefore, voice and video traffic has a higher possibility of being discarded or dropped on a network if congestion occurs along the path. Using QoS tools, a network engineer can configure network devices to prioritize certain traffic types over others to ensure that users receive an acceptable experience on the network.

> **Note**
> A network device will only implement QoS when it experiences some form of congestion.

QoS Terminology

Throughout your journey in the field of networking, you will encounter many technologies and terminologies. In this section, you will learn about the terminology that is used to describe certain characteristics of a network and how it helps you define network transmission quality:

- **Bandwidth** – Bandwidth refers to the amount of bits that can be transmitted in a second. This is commonly measured as **bits per second** (**bps**). On newer network devices, there are higher-capacity interfaces such as Gigabit Ethernet ports, which can support up to one gigabit per second of traffic.
- **Congestion** – As mentioned earlier, congestion causes delays on a network. Congestion occurs when there is a lot more traffic on a network than it can handle. The buffer within network devices becomes overwhelmed when there is a lot of incoming traffic filling up the buffer memory faster than the network device can process and forward to an outgoing interface. Network devices at the congestion points on a network may experience packet loss, delays, and reduced performance.
- **Delay** – Delay is also referred to as latency. This is the time it takes a packet to travel between a source and a destination. A network with high latency will result in users experiencing slower response times to network-based applications that are hosted on a local server. The objective is to ensure that a network has a very low response time between any sender and destination.
- **Jitter** – Jitter is the variation of delay of incoming packets. On a stable network, the latency of a continuous stream of packets received from a single source will be the same. However, network congestion, improper queuing, and interface errors (collisions) affect the latency between each packet being received on a device.
- **Packet loss** – As mentioned previously, when the internal buffer of a network device is full, new incoming packets are discarded or dropped from the network. This results in packet loss. Having too much packet loss on a network makes it difficult to transmit a message between a source and a destination. If the message uses the **Transmission Control Protocol** (**TCP**), the sender will re-transmit the dropped packet until the destination sends an acknowledgment, which is unlike the case with UDP, where the sender will not re-transmit the message.

Traffic Type Characteristics

More users are moving their business applications to the cloud, employees are working remotely, and academic institutions are using the internet and other technologies to deliver their classes to a global audience and go beyond geographic borders. Voice and video traffic has increased a lot over the years and is continuing to surpass data traffic such as web browsing.

Voice traffic is quite predictable and smooth-flowing. However, voice traffic is highly susceptible to packet loss and delays over a network. Since voice traffic uses UDP, if a packet is lost, the sender does not re-transmit the message. Therefore, voice traffic should be configured with a higher priority than all other traffic on the network. Voice traffic can tolerate some levels of packet loss, latency (delay), and jitter before it becomes noticeable to the receiver.

Voice traffic should use the following recommendations:

- The delay or latency should not exceed 150 **milliseconds** (**ms**)
- Jitter should not exceed 30 ms
- Packet loss should not exceed 1%
- Voice traffic requires a minimum of 30 kbps of bandwidth

Unlike voice traffic, video traffic uses a lot of extra bandwidth and without any QoS mechanism to prioritize the traffic type, the quality of the video stream degrades. From the user's point of view, the video will begin to appear blurry and jagged, and the audio may not be in sync with the picture. Video traffic is known to be inconsistent, unpredictable, and less resilient to packet loss as compared to voice traffic. With video traffic, packets may be received at a 20-ms time interval, which then may change to 40 ms due to network congestion, high CPU utilization on an intermediary networking device, or the retransmission of a packet, before returning again to 20 ms. Additionally, video packets are not all of the same size, creating inconsistency when transporting small and large video packets along a network.

Put simply, video traffic uses UDP as its transport layer protocol, making it very vulnerable to packet loss and delays on a network. Additionally, video traffic uses a lot of network bandwidth and its message size varies from packet to packet.

- Video traffic should use the following recommendations:
- The latency should not exceed 400 ms
- Jitter should not exceed 50 ms
- Packet loss should not be more than 1%
- Video traffic requires a minimum of 384 kbps of bandwidth

Another traffic type is data. There are many applications and network resources that do not have tolerance for packet loss during transmission and hence use TCP as the preferred transport layer protocol. During a TCP stream, if any packet is lost during the transmission, the sender will re-transmit the message to the destination. There are certain traffic types such as web browsing that use the **Hypertext Transfer Protocol** (**HTTP**) and **HTTP Secure** (**HTTPS**) protocols. These protocols sometimes occupy a lot of bandwidth on a network and do not leave room for other time-sensitive protocols. If TCP traffic takes up all the bandwidth on a network, the UDP traffic will have a higher chance of being discarded or dropped.

Although some data traffic types may be mission-critical to the organization to improve the **quality of experience** (**QoE**), a network administrator can simply configure the QoS tools to prioritize certain data traffic types on the network.

QoS Queuing Algorithms

One method that a Cisco device uses to queue incoming traffic is **first-in, first-out** (**FIFO**). This technique is quite simple. It operates on a first come, first served basis. When packets enter the interface of a network device, they are placed in a queue while the device processes each message, one at a time, and then forwards the message out of an exit interface to their destination. With FIFO, the packets are processed in the order they arrive. No packet is prioritized over another as there is only a single queue and all packets are treated equally. Packets will be processed and sent out in the same way they arrived on the device, hence the name first-in, first-out.

Another algorithm is **weighted fair queuing** (**WFQ**). WFG ensures that fair bandwidth allocation is given to all traffic on the network. This algorithm uses the concept of applying weights (priority) to identify and classify network traffic into what it calls conversations or flows. Once the traffic has been classified, WFQ automatically determines the amount of bandwidth that should be allocated to each flow over the other flows.

> **Note**
>
> The **type of service** (**ToS**) field within an IP packet can be used to classify traffic types.

The downside of using WFQ is that it does not support encryption tunneling, simply because that security feature would modify the packet content information that is required by WFQ for its classification mechanism.

The **class-based weighted fair queuing** (**CBWFQ**) algorithm simply is an extension of WFQ. With CBWFQ, traffic classes can be defined based on various matching criteria such as network protocols, **access control lists** (**ACLs**), and even the input interfaces on network devices. Once a match is found, a FIFO queue is reserved for each class, and the traffic that belongs to each class is then sent to the queue. For each class of traffic, you can assign various characteristics such as bandwidth, maximum packet limit, and even weights. During times of congestion, the allocated bandwidth is delivered to the class.

The **low-latency queuing** (**LLQ**) algorithm adds very strict priority queuing to CBWFQ. Priority queuing enables traffic types such as voice traffic to be sent before packets that are in other queues. With LLQ, there is a reduction in jitter during voice conservations on a network. With LLQ, traffic types that are vulnerable to delay are sent before all other packets in other queues.

QoS Tools

When it comes to choosing the appropriate QoS policy for a network, you must first understand the following three QoS policy models: best-effort, integrated services, and differentiated services.

Using **best-effort** as a policy model simply provides no guarantee or reassurance for the delivery of a message on a network. A simple analogy to help explain this model is the local postal service. When you send a letter using the standard postal service, your letter is treated the same as all other letters within the postal company. There is no prioritization. When the letter is delivered to the intended recipient, there isn't any notification that the letter has been delivered successfully. In both private and public networks, best-effort is the predominant method being used on the internet today and will continue for most general purposes.

The best-effort model has advantages such as being very scalable, no QoS mechanisms being required, and being readily available to be deployed on a network.

There are some disadvantages of using the best-effort model, such as the fact that it does not provide any guarantee of delivery for messages, packets may arrive out of order and not all at once, and there is no prioritization applied to mission-critical applications or time-sensitive traffic types.

Since best-effort is not implemented by QoS, it's not administratively configured by the network administrator. Keep in mind that, when using this model, all messages are treated exactly the same. This means voice traffic will be treated the same as web browsing traffic; no prioritization is applied.

Another QoS model is **integrated services** (**IntServ**). IntServ supports real-time traffic types, such as remote video, online conferencing, and virtual reality applications. This model was designed to support multiple QoS requirements. This model has the ability to provide end-to-end QoS between a source and destination, unlike the other models. Such a feature is usually required by real-time applications to manage packet streams of traffic. This is known as **microflows**.

IntServ uses a connection-oriented technique that allows each unique or individual communication to specify its requested resources on the network. These resources may include bandwidth, delay, and even packet loss metrics to ensure the delivery of each microflow. To ensure each network device between the source and destination is made aware of the required resources, IntServ uses the **Resource Reservation Protocol** (**RSVP**) to inform the networking devices of the needs of a microflow. However, if the resources are not available on the path, the sending application does not forward any data along the path.

The advantages of using IntServ are that it provides end-to-end admission control of resources and that individual communication has its own per-request policy admission control along the network. The disadvantages of IntServ are that it's very resource intensive and that the flow-based approach is not scalable in large networks.

The third policy model is known as **differentiated services** (**DiffServ**). DiffServ uses a simple and scalable mechanism to classify and manage traffic types using QoS. This model is able to provide low latency for mission-critical and time-sensitive traffic types, such as voice and video, while using the best-effort approach for non-critical traffic types, such as web browsing and email. One major advantage that DiffServ has over IntServ is that it can provide *almost-guaranteed* QoS to packet streams while remaining scalable.

DiffServ does not provide the end-to-end QoS feature; however, being scalable on large implementations has its advantages. When a sender forwards its traffic to a router, the router will classify the traffic flow in a class and provide the appropriate QoS policy for the class.

QoS Implementation Methods

In this section, you will discover how QoS mechanisms are applied to traffic types.

Classification

QoS tools are applied on a device's interface, and this enables the router or switch to match the fields in a packet (message) and make a choice to take some QoS action. After the device has classified packets, they are placed in a waiting queue for the outgoing interface. The queuing tool will then schedule which packet should be taken forward from the waiting queue. This is based on the priority that is given to the packet (message).

Figure 13.42 shows the classification process:

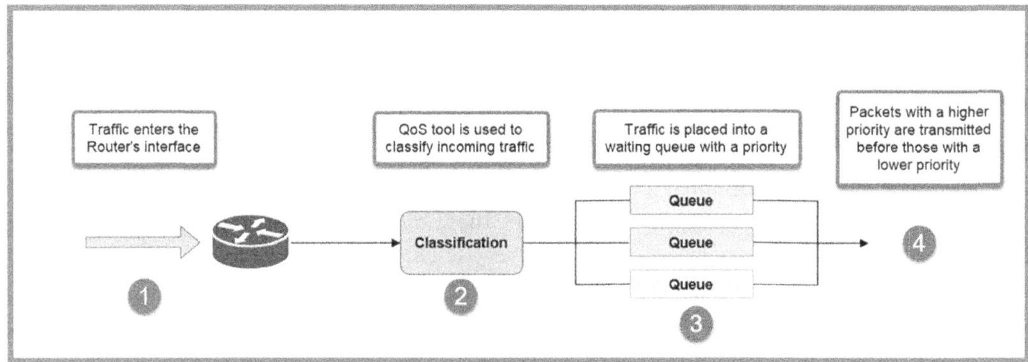

Figure 13.42: Traffic type classification

Marking

Marking is the process where the QoS tool changes one or more header fields in a packet, setting a value in the header. Within an IP packet, there are certain header fields that are designed to be marked by a QoS tool. When the marked packet is passed along to other networking devices, classification is much easier.

> **Note**
>
> The **differentiated services code point** (**DSCP**)field is a 6-bit field within an IP packet that is used for QoS marking.

Figure 13.43 shows the DSCP field within an IP packet using Wireshark:

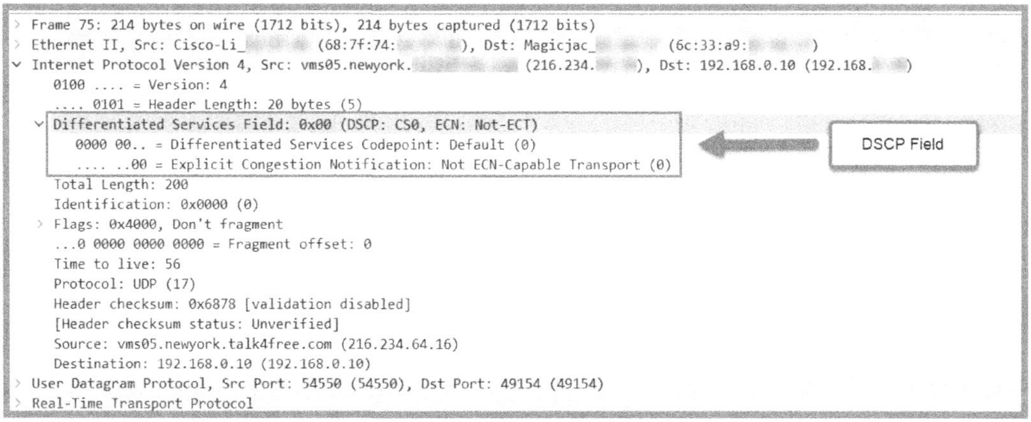

```
> Frame 75: 214 bytes on wire (1712 bits), 214 bytes captured (1712 bits)
> Ethernet II, Src: Cisco-Li_ (68:7f:74: ), Dst: Magicjac_ (6c:33:a9: )
v Internet Protocol Version 4, Src: vms05.newyork. (216.234. ), Dst: 192.168.0.10 (192.168. )
    0100 .... = Version: 4
    .... 0101 = Header Length: 20 bytes (5)
  v Differentiated Services Field: 0x00 (DSCP: CS0, ECN: Not-ECT)
      0000 00.. = Differentiated Services Codepoint: Default (0)
      .... ..00 = Explicit Congestion Notification: Not ECN-Capable Transport (0)
    Total Length: 200
    Identification: 0x0000 (0)
  > Flags: 0x4000, Don't fragment
    ...0 0000 0000 0000 = Fragment offset: 0
    Time to live: 56
    Protocol: UDP (17)
    Header checksum: 0x6878 [validation disabled]
    [Header checksum status: Unverified]
    Source: vms05.newyork.talk4free.com (216.234.64.16)
    Destination: 192.168.0.10 (192.168.0.10)
> User Datagram Protocol, Src Port: 54550 (54550), Dst Port: 49154 (49154)
> Real-Time Transport Protocol
```

DSCP Field

Figure 13.43: DSCP field

Cisco has created a tool known as **Network-Based Application Recognition** (**NBAR**), which is used to match packets (traffic) for classification.

Queuing

Queuing refers to the QoS process used for managing the queues that hold packets while they wait their turn to exit an interface on a network device such as a switch or router. All network devices place packets in a queue while they make a decision to forward a packet out of an exit interface to its destination.

In using a queuing system, the traffic must first be classified to be placed in a particular queue, if there are multiple queues present. Additionally, a scheduler is used to determine which packet is to be sent when the interface of the device becomes available.

Cisco devices use a scheduler algorithm known as round-robin. This algorithm cycles through each queue, taking either one message or a number of bytes per queue. In other words, the algorithm takes a few messages from the first queue, then a few from the second queue, and so on, and then it starts back at queue 1 until the algorithm acquires enough messages to create a total number of bytes to send to an exit interface.

The router uses the CBWFQ tool to ensure a minimum amount of bandwidth for each class of traffic. The network engineer will configure the weights as a percentage of bandwidth per traffic class for the interface.

Policing and Shaping

These QoS tools are typically used on the WAN edge of a typical enterprise network. Both of these tools note each packet as it passes and measures the number of bits per second over time. The policing tool is responsible for discarding packets, while the shaping tool is responsible for holding/keeping packets in the queue. These tools are designed to keep the bitrate below a certain speed.

Congestion

Congestion avoidance is used to reduce the overall packet loss by preemptively discarding some packets in a TCP connection.

Having completed this section, you have gained essential knowledge and understanding of the operations of QoS and its importance for a network.

Summary

In this chapter, you have covered a wide array of IP services that are vital to improving the efficiency of an enterprise network. In this chapter, you have learned about the importance of proper timekeeping and how to implement NTP to ensure that devices' system clocks are synchronized. Furthermore, you saw the benefits of implementing DHCP on a network to automatically distribute IP addresses to end devices and DNS to help resolve hostnames to IP addresses easily.

You also saw how network management protocols such as SNMP can be used to help network engineers easily monitor and manage network devices, and you saw how syslog can be used to improve log management using a centralized logging server. Lastly, you have learned about the difference that QoS can make on a network.

In the next chapter, *Chapter 14, Exploring Network Security*, you will learn about the essentials of protecting your network from cyber threats and improving the security posture of your organization.

Additional Reading

The following links are recommended for additional reading:

- Configuring NTP: `https://www.cisco.com/c/en/us/td/docs/switches/datacenter/sw/5_x/nx-os/system_management/configuration/guide/sm_nx_os_cg/sm_3ntp.html`
- Configuring DHCP: `https://www.cisco.com/c/en/us/td/docs/ios-xml/ios/ipaddr_dhcp/configuration/xe-3se/3850/dhcp-xe-3se-3850-book/config-dhcp-server.html`
- Configuring DNS: `https://www.cisco.com/c/en/us/support/docs/ip/domain-name-system-dns/24182-reversedns.html`
- Configuring syslog: `https://www.cisco.com/c/en/us/td/docs/routers/access/wireless/software/guide/SysMsgLogging.html`
- Configuring SNMP: `https://www.cisco.com/c/en/us/td/docs/ios-xml/ios/snmp/configuration/xe-16/snmp-xe-16-book/nm-snmp-cfg-snmp-support.html`
- Configuring QoS: `https://www.cisco.com/c/en/us/td/docs/routers/access/800M/software/800MSCG/QoS.html`

Exam Readiness Drill – Chapter Review Questions

Apart from mastering key concepts, strong test-taking skills under time pressure are essential for acing your certification exam. That's why developing these abilities early in your learning journey is critical.

Exam readiness drills, using the free online practice resources provided with this book, help you progressively improve your time management and test-taking skills while reinforcing the key concepts you've learned.

HOW TO GET STARTED

- Open the link or scan the QR code at the bottom of this page
- If you have unlocked the practice resources already, log in to your registered account. If you haven't, follow the instructions in *Chapter 19* and come back to this page.
- Once you log in, click the START button to start a quiz
- We recommend attempting a quiz multiple times till you're able to answer most of the questions correctly and well within the time limit.
- You can use the following practice template to help you plan your attempts:

Working On Accuracy		
Attempt	Target	Time Limit
Attempt 1	40% or more	Till the timer runs out
Attempt 2	60% or more	Till the timer runs out
Attempt 3	75% or more	Till the timer runs out
Working On Timing		
Attempt 4	75% or more	1 minute before time limit
Attempt 5	75% or more	2 minutes before time limit
Attempt 6	75% or more	3 minutes before time limit

The above drill is just an example. Design your drills based on your own goals and make the most out of the online quizzes accompanying this book.

First time accessing the online resources? 🔓

You'll need to unlock them through a one-time process. **Head to** *Chapter 19* **for instructions.**

Open Quiz

https://packt.link/ccnachap13

OR scan this QR code →

14
Exploring Network Security

Designing and implementing a network without security in mind is like leaving all the windows and doors of your house open while you go to the mall. An unauthorized visitor can access your personal space and remove your valuables, simply because all points of entry are open. The same concept applies to a network. Security is one of the most important factors a network engineer should remember when designing any size and type of network.

In this chapter, you will look at how to identify various threat actions and attacks, understand the need for security on an enterprise network, and learn how to develop a security program to improve user awareness and training.

This chapter covers *Domain 5: Security Fundamentals*, objectives *5.1 Define key security concepts (threats, vulnerabilities, exploits, and mitigation techniques)*, *5.2 Describe security program elements (user awareness, training, and physical access control)*, *5.4 Describe security password policies elements, such as management, complexity, and password alternatives (multifactor authentication, certificates, and biometrics)*, and *5.8 Compare authentication, authorization, and accounting concepts* of the *200-301 CCNA v1.1 certification* exam.

In this chapter, you will learn about the following topics:

- Security concepts (threats, vulnerabilities, and exploits)
- **Authentication, authorization, and accounting** (**AAA**)
- Elements of a security program
- Password management

Let's dive in!

Security Concepts

As a network professional, your primary responsibility is ensuring all devices have end-to-end connectivity. However, with the rise of cyber threats and attacks, organizations now need to ensure their assets are well protected from cybercriminals who try to compromise systems and networks. An essential component of every size and type of network is security. Without network security, your network is left vulnerable to all types of threats and attacks from hackers and other threat actors.

When designing a security network, it is important to first identify all assets within the organization. An **asset** is simply anything that is valuable to an organization. Assets are usually broken down into three categories.

Tangible assets are physical items within the organization, such as furniture, computers, servers, network devices, and components. These assets usually store data about the organization and sometimes contain system logs, which are valuable during an incident. **Intangible assets** are items that are non-physical, including intellectual property, procedures, data, and anything that is digital that has value to the organization. Another type of asset, that some businesses do not consider, is **people**. People are employees, customers, and even suppliers. An organization also needs to protect its human resources from cyber-attacks and threats.

Many organizations in various industries sell a product or service to their customers. Such organizations keep a record of their customer information, such as name, location, and contact details. This type of data is referred to as **personally identifiable information** (**PII**). Such data must be secured and kept away from hackers.

Nowadays, hackers aren't just launching disruptive attacks to prevent users from accessing a resource. They are creating more sophisticated attacks to steal money and other financial assets, for example, cryptocurrencies such as Bitcoin. Hackers have realized that they can make money by simply stealing your data and selling it on the dark web or holding it hostage and persuading you to pay a ransom to retrieve it.

The need for information security is always rising, as is the need for security professionals in all industries to help organizations protect their assets from hackers and other threats. The foundation of information security is three main pillars: **confidentiality, integrity, and availability** (**CIA**). These three pillars form what is commonly referred to as the CIA triad within the field of information security.

CIA Triad

As mentioned previously, data is the most important asset for an organization. The way data is managed is crucial to its security. Data itself exists in three states. These are the following:

- **Data at rest**: Data at rest refers to any data that is stored on a medium or device. This can be data that is stored on a **hard disk drive** (**HDD**), online storage such as AWS S3 buckets, or even an off-site storage location. Data at rest is simply data that is not currently being used by an application or a user.

- **Data in use**: Data in use is defined as any data that is currently being accessed/used by an application or a user. A simple example of data in use is opening a PDF file on your hard disk and reading its contents.
- **Data in motion**: Data in motion is simply data that is traveling along a network or being accessed remotely by an application or a user. An example of data in motion is a user copying a file from the local/remote file server onto their local computer. While the application is currently accessing the PDF file, the state changes from **data at rest** to **data in use**. As security professionals, our task is to protect all forms and states of data within an organization. Applying CIA will help us achieve information security.

Confidentiality ensures that only authorized people have access to view a system or data. In the real world, a person can simply keep a secret from another, thus keeping the information private from those who are not authorized for disclosure. In the computing world, you can apply cryptography, such as applying encryption to any data to keep it private. During symmetric encryption, an encryption algorithm and a secret key are used to perform the encryption process. The secret key is used to encrypt and decrypt the message. The secret key should always be kept private and safe. If the key is lost or stolen, the data is compromised.

Confidentiality plays an important role in ensuring hackers and other threat actors do not gain access to an organization's data. The Microsoft Windows 10 operating system contains a data encryption application known as BitLocker. This application allows a user to create an encrypted storage container to store data while at rest. If a hacker is able to access the Windows 10 system, they will not be able to access the contents of the BitLocker container as long as it's locked and the secret key is safe. However, if the attacker has the secret key and access to the BitLocker contents, they can retrieve the contents and therefore the data is compromised.

> **Note**
>
> To get more information about BitLocker on Windows 10, please use the following link: `https://docs.microsoft.com/en-us/windows/security/information-protection/bitlocker/bitlocker-overview`.

Integrity plays the role of ensuring data is not modified between a source and a destination. In the digital world, when a device receives a message, it needs to validate whether the message was modified during transmission from the source to the destination. Hackers and other malicious threats can intercept messages as they are passing along a network and modify the message before sending it off to the destination. Hackers use this technique for various purposes, such as spoofing, pretending to be someone or something else on a network, or attempting to trick an unsuspecting person into falling victim to a cyber-attack.

> **Note**
>
> The network access or link layer of the **Transmission Control Protocol/Internet Protocol** (**TCP/IP**) inserts a **cyclic redundancy check** (**CRC**) value into each message before sending it on a network. This CRC value is not cryptographic but is simple error-detecting code used to detect accidental changes to raw data. It does not provide cryptographic security properties such as collision resistance or confidentiality.

Integrity plays an important role in information security, ensuring a receiver is able to detect whether a message was compromised.

The role of availability is a simple but challenging one. **Availability** simply means ensuring a system or resource is always available to those who have access to it. During a cyber-attack, an organization's resources, such as data, applications, network devices, and even systems, may become unreachable and unusable. If a system or resource is unusable by legitimate and authorized people, an organization may not be able to continue working at optimal performance.

An example of disrupting availability is a **denial of service** (**DoS**) attack. A DoS attack is designed to exhaust all the available computing power of a target system, thus making it unavailable to legitimate users. Such an attack can be applied to a scenario with an online web server; if an attacker launches a DoS attack on the web server, the web application will process all the incoming HTTP/HTTPS web request messages and eventually become overwhelmed with the high volume of messages originating from the attacker. Therefore, when legitimate users on the internet are attempting to retrieve the web pages from the server, the server may not respond to the users. Thus, availability has been compromised.

Figure 14.1 shows the CIA triad in a triangular format:

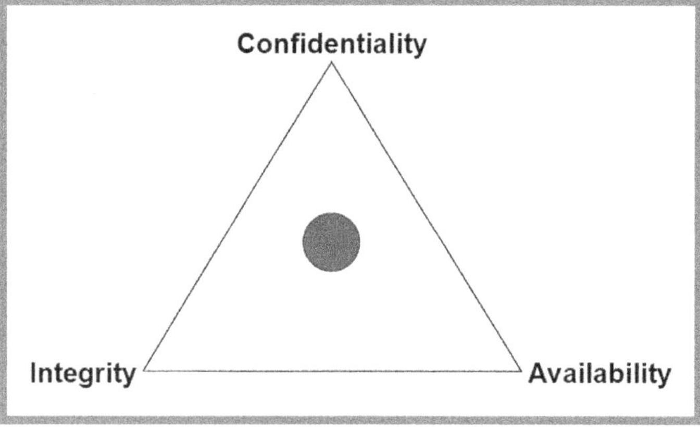

Figure 14.1: CIA triad

One of the objectives of information security is to ensure that all three pillars are applied as equally as possible within an organization. To represent this, the circle is positioned very close to the center of the triangle. Maintaining this balance is somewhat difficult as some organizations focus more on confidentiality; this means the ball in the preceding diagram is placed closer to the **Confidentiality** pillar while moving away from **Integrity** and **Availability**. This means data will be more secure, but access to the data will be more difficult (availability) and there'll be less checking for any modifications to data (integrity).

If an organization makes its data and resources easily accessible, that is, focusing on availability more than the other pillars, there will be fewer security controls in place to ensure the data is kept private to authorized persons only (confidentiality) and less checking for any unauthorized changes to the data (integrity).

As a security professional, it's important to understand threats, exploits, vulnerabilities, and attacks to better safeguard the assets of an organization. In the following sections, these terminologies will be covered in detail.

Threats

In the world of **information technology** (**IT**), as more devices and people are connecting to the internet, more threats are being faced each day. A threat is defined as anything with the motivation to cause harm or damage to a person, system, or network. In today's world, many organizations are going online to expand their customer reach and support for their products and services. Many organizations are no longer using traditional brick-and-mortar operations, but now opt for the internet as a tool and resource to support their customers and expand their IT operations.

Almost all modern-day businesses have an internet connection, and this creates a huge risk as it's a connection for an attacker or malware to access the organization's internal network. During your career as a network professional, you'll see many organizations investing to ensure their network infrastructure is scalable and resilient and has redundancy to ensure all devices have end-to-end connectivity. However, one of the most important factors is not always acknowledged, and it is security. Designing a network to perform at optimal capacity is excellent, but without security, your entire network infrastructure is left vulnerable to both internal and external threats.

Threats exist in many forms. A hacker may attempt to retrieve a victim's username and password for their online accounts, gain unauthorized access into a system by exploiting a security vulnerability on a computer, and even crack the passphrase for the wireless network in your organization.

Assets

As a security professional, it's important to secure the organization's assets. Tangible assets are physical objects, such as computers, servers, and furniture. This type of asset needs to be protected just as much as everything else. Tangible assets are vulnerable to physical damage and even theft. Imagine a small business has a customer service team that assists customers with conducting transactions on a daily basis. Say each customer service representative is assigned a laptop at their desk to perform their duties and complete tasks. If each laptop is not physically secured using a Kensington cable, a "customer" with bad intent may simply pick up a laptop while the employee is not looking and walk away.

Some companies may look at the incident as physical theft, but a cybersecurity professional will determine it as both physical and data theft. Within the laptop is storage media such as an HDD, and there may be important and confidential data stored within it. A malicious user could simply retrieve the data from the HDD and sell it on the dark web.

The most valuable asset to any organization is data. Hackers are continuously developing new strategies and techniques to gain access to systems and networks to steal data. Our job as network professionals is not only to create an efficient network but also to create a secure network design to prevent various cyber threats. Creating a secure network design extends to all areas where an organization stores its data. These will include all the local area networks and even the cloud.

The cloud is an important location that many professionals do not consider to be very vulnerable. With cloud computing getting cheaper as time passes, more organizations are migrating their physical infrastructure to a cloud service provider. There are many companies that have almost all their data and other assets, such as servers and applications, on the cloud; however, the cloud is just as vulnerable as a physical network. Attention must be given to applying the same level of security to your cloud platform as you would for your physical network.

Lastly, let's not forget about our people, such as employees, customers, and suppliers. The human element also needs to be protected from cyber-attacks and threats such as social engineering. Hackers use social engineering, a type of psychological manipulation, to trick their potential victims into revealing sensitive information or performing an action that can lead to compromising a system or network.

Threat Actors

Threat actors are usually someone or something responsible for a security event or incident. Threat actors can be categorized based on their characteristics and the motivation behind their malicious actions.

One type of threat actor is **script kiddies**. A script kiddie isn't necessarily a child or young person, or a beginner who wants to learn how to hack systems and networks; they can also be someone who is a novice within the cybersecurity realm who uses instructions and tutorials provided by real, malicious hackers to conduct their actions. This type of hacker does not fully understand the technical details of the actual cyber-attack or the tools being used. However, by simply following instructions to launch an attack, they can have the same effect as the malicious hacker who created it and cripple a system or network.

Hacktivist is another type of hacker, who is both an activist and a hacker. This person uses their technical skills to perform malicious actions to serve a social or political agenda. Some actions of a hacktivist are defacing political and government websites, coordinating DoS attacks against an organization's network resources, and leaking confidential data such as documents on various online sites.

Hackers who work in groups using the most elite tools and resources that money can buy are commonly referred to as **organized crime groups**. Within these groups, each hacker is an expert within their own field and is assigned a unique role and function such that one person may be responsible for developing an exploit kit while another performs extensive reconnaissance on the target. This type of hacking group is well funded and has the best hacking tools.

Each nation usually has its own team of hackers. They are referred to as **state-sponsored hackers**. This group of hackers is well funded and provided with the best tools and resources the government can buy. These types of hackers are usually hired to protect the nation's security and even perform cyber-attacks on other nations. There are many movies that explain such types of hacking groups, one of which is *Snowden (2016)*, which explores how various nations prepare for cyber warfare.

> **Note**
>
> To learn more about cyber warfare, check out the book *Cyber Warfare – Truth, Tactics, and Strategies* by Packt Publishing at the following link: `https://www.packtpub.com/en-us/product/cyber-warfare-truth-tactics-and-strategies-9781839214486`.

There are many organizations that think all cyber threats originate from the internet. Sometimes an **insider threat** can occur and remain undetected because the organization is busy looking at the internet only and not within their own corporate network for internal threats and attacks. An insider is simply someone who shares information about the organization they work for with unauthorized parties. This person has intentions such as learning the ins and outs of the network, understanding the security controls, and infiltrating the organization from within.

With the number of cyber-attacks rising, organizations are investing in cybersecurity solutions and people to help safeguard their networks and assets. In every network and system, there are vulnerabilities that are known and those that have not been discovered yet. Organizations hire a special type of hacker known as a **white hat hacker**, commonly also referred to as an **ethical hacker**. These are the good guys who use their skill set to help organizations discover vulnerabilities within their own infrastructure before the bad guys find and exploit them. White hat hackers obtain legal permission before their engagement in a penetration test exercise. The security assessment performed by the white hat hacker is a real-world simulation of the targeted systems and network, using the same tools and techniques as a real malicious hacker to discover and exploit security vulnerabilities and gain access to the organization.

Black hat hackers use their skill set to perform malicious and unethical actions on computers and networks for personal gain. These are the types of hackers that your organization and assets need to be well protected and fortified against. The **gray hat hacker** simply sits between the white hat and black hat hackers. This type of hacker commits crimes and performs malicious actions. However, they can use their skill set for both good and bad things.

Vulnerabilities

One question that students frequently ask at the beginning of their cybersecurity journey is, how are hackers able to break into a system or network? The simple answer is hackers and other threat actors look for vulnerabilities in a target system. A vulnerability is a security weakness or flaw that could simply be exploited or taken advantage of by a threat. Vulnerabilities exist within everything; there is an ongoing race between security researchers and hackers for who will discover a security flaw first, and this race will continue over time. Security researchers are always looking for new vulnerabilities to help software and product vendors fix and close security weaknesses, while hackers look to exploit and gain access to a victim's system or network.

> Note
>
> **Nessus** is one of the most popular vulnerability assessment tools within the cybersecurity industry. Further information on Nessus can be found at https://www.tenable.com/products/nessus.

A vulnerability can exist in the form of a weakness or flaw in a configuration, security policy, or even something technological in nature. As you have learned thus far, TCP/IP is the language all devices speak when connected to an Ethernet network. You may think the TCP/IP protocol suite is designed with security in mind, but in reality, it is not.

Many vulnerabilities exist within the various protocols of TCP/IP. Some of these protocols are **Internet Protocol** (**IP**), **Internet Control Message Protocol** (**ICMP**), **Hypertext Transfer Protocol** (**HTTP**), and even **Simple Network Management Protocol** (**SNMP**). Attackers can take advantage of various weaknesses within these protocols and capture sensitive information while network traffic is traveling along a network.

Network components such as routers, switches, and firewalls can contain security vulnerabilities within their operating system and features. Hackers are always looking for a way inside your network and devices, and your network components provide an easy way in if they are not updated and secured properly.

Figure 14.2 shows Nmap with the EternalBlue vulnerability on a Windows system:

```
Host script results:
| smb-vuln-ms17-010:
|   VULNERABLE:
|   Remote Code Execution vulnerability in Microsoft SMBv1 servers (ms17-010)
|     State: VULNERABLE
|     IDs:  CVE:CVE-2017-0143
|     Risk factor: HIGH
|       A critical remote code execution vulnerability exists in Microsoft SMBv1
|        servers (ms17-010).
|
|     Disclosure date: 2017-03-14
|     References:
|       https://technet.microsoft.com/en-us/library/security/ms17-010.aspx
|       https://blogs.technet.microsoft.com/msrc/2017/05/12/customer-guidance-for-wannacrypt-attacks/
|_      https://cve.mitre.org/cgi-bin/cvename.cgi?name=CVE-2017-0143
```

Figure 14.2: EternalBlue

Additionally, some enterprise network devices, such as routers and switches, support network security functions to help prevent various malicious threats and attacks on your network. Sometimes, a misconfiguration on a router can allow an attacker remote access to the management pane of the device.

Each device requires firmware or an operating system to work and perform functions. Operating system vendors are always searching for vulnerabilities within their products so that they can quickly release updates and security patches to fix any issues for their customers. Many organizations do not update their computers' operating systems for many months, which increases the risk of being compromised. Imagine if a new threat came about and the operating system vendor released a security patch to fix the issues, but organizations ignored the updates and patches by the vendor. Their systems would then be vulnerable to the threat until security patching occurs on their network. Remember, hackers are always looking for ways into your systems, and operating system vendors release updates very frequently to help protect you.

Many configuration vulnerabilities exist on a network. This type of security weakness exists within user account management, misconfigured network services, and default configurations on devices. When logging in to a system, your user credentials may be sent across the network via an unsecured protocol.

Figure 14.3 shows a Windows user credential captured as it was sent to the Active Directory server on the network:

```
[+] Listening for events...
[*] [LLMNR]  Poisoned answer sent to 10.10.10.14 for name Windows10
[*] [NBT-NS] Poisoned answer sent to 10.10.10.14 for name WINSVR16 (service: Workstation/Redirector)
[*] [NBT-NS] Poisoned answer sent to 10.10.10.14 for name WINSVR16 (service: File Server)
[*] [NBT-NS] Poisoned answer sent to 10.10.10.14 for name PENTESTLAB (service: Domain Master Browser)
[SMBv2] NTLMv2-SSP Client   : 10.10.10.14
[SMBv2] NTLMv2-SSP Username : PENTESTLAB\bob
[SMBv2] NTLMv2-SSP Hash     : bob::PENTESTLAB:83443f84b4d7914d:AF19E4539E28BE7228CFFEE89E1B0AD5:0101000
000000000C0653150DE09D2016969F12C91967196000000000200080053004D004200330001001E00570049004E002D00500052
004800340039003200520051004100460056000400140053004D00420033002E006C006F00630061006C0003003400570049004
E002D00500052004800340039003200520051004100460056002E0053004D00420033002E006C006F00630061006C0005001400
53004D00420033002E006C006F00630061006C0007000800C0653150DE09D201060004000200000008003000300000000000000
0000000002000004E6B1037D98FAC9C5B50794EB17A0F93686B2154EACC40F6B09AA029269AA7BA0A001000000000000000000
0000000000000000000900200063006900660073002F00310030002E00310030002E00310030002E0031003600000000000000000
00000000000
[*] Skipping previously captured hash for PENTESTLAB\bob
[*] Skipping previously captured hash for PENTESTLAB\bob
```

Figure 14.3: User account details

In *Figure 14.3*, you can see that the user Bob enters his username and password on a Windows 10 system to authenticate himself. However, in this scenario, the Active Directory server (Windows Server) is using the default directory query protocol, **Lightweight Directory Access Protocol** (**LDAP**). LDAP does not encrypt user information by default. Only the user's password is hashed using NTLMv2 and sent across the network. In *Figure 14.3*, the captured password hash will enable the attacker to perform offline password-based attacks to retrieve the victim's password. This is an example of an unsecured user account and protocols on a network.

Configuration vulnerabilities also exist when an administrator configures weak or unsecured passwords for user accounts. Such a vulnerability enables a hacker to easily compromise user accounts on a system and quickly gain access. Another vulnerability is using default configurations on a system or network device. Default configurations are settings that are applied on a device at the point it leaves the manufacturer. They allow you to easily get the device up and working quickly without having to spend too much time trying to figure out how to get it working. Default configurations often contain many weaknesses, such as no security features and remote access being enabled for all. It's important to ensure default configurations are never to be used on systems and devices on a production network.

Human Vulnerabilities

One major vulnerability many often overlook when designing a secure network design is the human factor. Humans are also vulnerable to various online and offline cyber-attacks, such as being a victim of a social engineering attack. Social engineering is simply where an attacker is able to manipulate a person to reveal sensitive information or perform a task.

> **Note**
>
> Social engineering is usually not technical in nature. This means a computer is not required to perform various types of social engineering attacks on a victim. The attack usually exploits the trust and social behavior of the victim.

Phishing is a form of social engineering that is done using a computer. The attacker creates and sends a fake email to a potential victim. The email is crafted to look and sound as if it came from a legitimate source, such as a financial institution. The message usually contains some instructions and a malicious link embedded within the message. The instructions could say, `Your user account has been hacked. Click the following link to reset it.` If the user believes this message and clicks the link, malware could be downloaded and infect the system and the remainder of the network. Or, the user may visit a compromised site where the attacker is able to capture the victim's username and password.

Another type of social engineering is spear phishing. In a **spear-phishing** attack, the attacker makes a fake message or email look legitimate and believable. This type of attack is usually focused on a specific group of persons. An example of a spear-phishing attack is where an attacker crafts an email that seems like it originates from **Bank X** and sends it to a large number of people. People with accounts with **Bank X** will have a higher possibility of falling victim to the scam and clicking any malicious links or following any instructions contained in the message. A person who does not have an account with **Bank X** will simply block, delete, or ignore the message.

Whaling is a type of phishing attack that focuses on high-profile people within an organization, such as a CEO or even a director. The objective of the attack is to compromise a high-profile person's account and use the account to conduct transactions. Imagine if the CEO's email account is compromised; the attacker sends emails to the accounting department requesting confidential financial details about the organization. People within the accounting department will see the email originating from the CEO and trust that it's the actual CEO requesting the information. In such an attack, trust is being exploited between the employee and the CEO.

Social engineering attacks can be done over a telephone conversation, and this is known as **vishing**. In vishing, the attacker calls the potential victim while pretending to be someone with authority or a person the victim may trust. During the conversation, the attacker may also try to build or improve the trust between them and the victim and take advantage of that trust. In vishing attacks, the attacker may pretend to be calling from the victim's bank and request the victim's online banking user credentials or their credit card number and pin.

Social engineering can also be done using **Short Message Service** (**SMS**). This form of attack is known as **smishing**. This is when an attacker attempts to perform a social engineering attack using the text messaging service on mobile phones.

Sometimes, an attacker may take a more aggressive approach to get victims to visit a compromised website. Hackers are able to compromise vulnerable **Domain Name System** (**DNS**) servers and can modify the DNS records, such as changing the A record for a hostname to point to a compromised website rather than the legitimate IP address. This means any device requesting the IP address of a certain website will be redirected to a malicious website. This type of social engineering is known as **pharming**.

It's important to build a fortress around and within your organization to protect it from both internal and external cyber-attacks and threats. Sometimes, when an attacker realizes they are unable to compromise the target's network, they may attempt to perform a waterhole attack. In a **waterhole attack**, the attacker will attempt to compromise a site or location the employees of the target organization commonly visit, such as a local coffee shop during lunchtime or after work. Compromising the coffee shop's Wi-Fi network means that on any device connected to the network, a payload will be downloaded and the mobile device will be infected. If an employee's mobile device gets infected, and they then connect to the corporate network on that device, the organization becomes compromised. This is the effect of a waterhole attack. However, anyone else who connects to the network is also infected.

Password Vulnerabilities and Management

To prove your identity to a system, you must provide a valid username and password. People often create simple and easy-to-remember passwords for their online accounts. While it's simple for the user to remember, it's a security vulnerability as a hacker can easily gain access to the victim's account. Creating a secure and complex password is important and prevents hackers and other threat actors from compromising a user account and gaining access to sensitive information.

To create secure and complex passwords, use the following guidelines:

- Passwords should be at least 8 characters in length
- Ensure the password includes a combination of uppercase and lowercase letters, numbers, special characters, and symbols
- Ensure the password is not being used on another account you may own
- Passwords should not be simple words found in a dictionary, as they can be easily guessed
- Passwords should not contain any personal details, such as birthday, relatives' names, or any special numbers
- Passwords should be changed frequently to prevent any unknown compromise of user accounts
- Passwords should not be written down in any location around your workspace

Using a password manager can help create, store, and manage secure passwords. There are many free password managers available on the internet.

Figure 14.4 shows a secure password generated by a password manager:

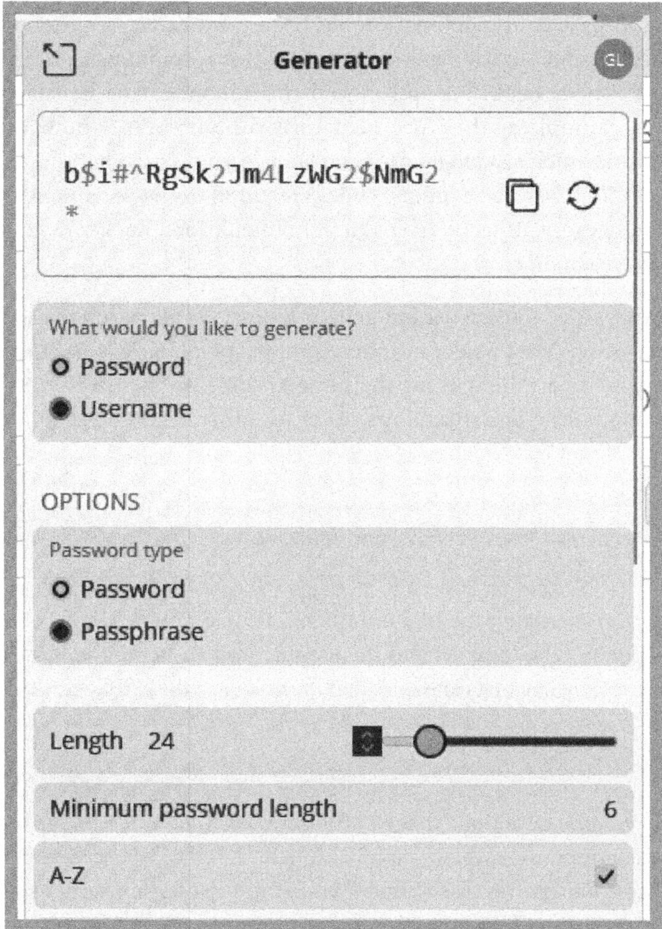

Figure 14.4: Secure password

Secure passwords are still breakable by a hacker who has a lot of time and computing power. You use a username to provide your identity to a system and a password to authenticate yourself. This is only one form of authentication onto a system; if a hacker is able to retrieve your password, they can gain access to your accounts, systems, and networks. Using **multifactor authentication** (**MFA**), where the user has to provide multiple factors to prove their identity, adds an extra layer of security to your user accounts.

After a username and password combination has been validated by a system, it might request a second form of authentication to validate your identity. This is sometimes referred to as **two-factor authentication** (2FA). An authenticator app on your smartphone can be associated with a supported website. Cisco is an example as their user accounts support 2FA, which allows you to add a third-party authenticator such as Google Authenticator to your Cisco user account. Each time you attempt to log in to a Cisco website, a unique code is required from the authenticator app. This code changes approximately every 30 seconds, making it difficult for a hacker to guess the sequence of codes being generated each time.

Rather than using passwords, you can use biometrics. Biometrics allow you to use a part of your body to authenticate to a system. Most new smartphones support biometric authentication, which allows a person to unlock their smartphone using their fingerprint. On Microsoft Windows 11, **Windows Hello** is a facial recognition system that allows a user to authenticate and sign in on a computer.

> **Note**
>
> Other forms of biometrics are voice, iris, and retina scans.

Digital certificates are an alternative method to authenticate to a system. Digital certificates are granted by a **certificate authority** (CA) that verifies the identity and authenticity of the requester. The CA functions as a trusted third party that can verify that the holder of the certificate is who they claim to be.

Exploits

Exploits are malicious code or actions that an attacker uses to take advantage of a vulnerability on a system. Within each operating system, application, and device, there are known and unknown vulnerabilities. Once a hacker has discovered a vulnerability on their target system, the next step is to acquire an exploit that will leverage the security flaw. One popular website to find exploits is **Exploit Database** (www.exploit-db.com). This website is maintained by Offensive Security, who are the creators of the popular Kali Linux penetration testing Linux distribution. The purpose of such a website is information sharing for other cybersecurity professionals, such as penetration testers who require exploits during their jobs.

> **Note**
>
> An easy method to understand how threats, vulnerabilities, and exploits all fit together is to consider the following sentence: a threat uses an exploit to take advantage of a vulnerability on a system.

Figure 14.5 shows the search results for the EternalBlue (ms17-010) vulnerability on Exploit Database:

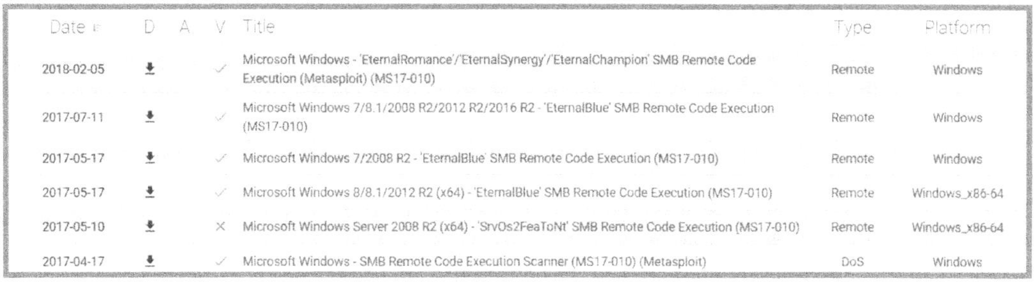

Date	D	A	V	Title	Type	Platform
2018-02-05	⬇		✓	Microsoft Windows - 'EternalRomance'/'EternalSynergy'/'EternalChampion' SMB Remote Code Execution (Metasploit) (MS17-010)	Remote	Windows
2017-07-11	⬇		✓	Microsoft Windows 7/8.1/2008 R2/2012 R2/2016 R2 - 'EternalBlue' SMB Remote Code Execution (MS17-010)	Remote	Windows
2017-05-17	⬇		✓	Microsoft Windows 7/2008 R2 - 'EternalBlue' SMB Remote Code Execution (MS17-010)	Remote	Windows
2017-05-17	⬇		✓	Microsoft Windows 8/8.1/2012 R2 (x64) - 'EternalBlue' SMB Remote Code Execution (MS17-010)	Remote	Windows_x86-64
2017-05-10	⬇		×	Microsoft Windows Server 2008 R2 (x64) - 'SrvOs2FeaToNt' SMB Remote Code Execution (MS17-010)	Remote	Windows_x86-64
2017-04-17	⬇		✓	Microsoft Windows - SMB Remote Code Execution Scanner (MS17-010) (Metasploit)	DoS	Windows

Figure 14.5: Search results for EternalBlue

Additionally, the attacker or the penetration tester can use an exploitation development framework such as Metasploit to create a custom payload and deliver it to the target. Metasploit allows a cybersecurity professional to build custom payloads to leverage the weaknesses found in applications and operating systems; however, an attacker can do the same as well.

Note

If you want to learn more about Metasploit, please use the following link: `https://www.offensive-security.com/metasploit-unleashed/`.

Once an attacker has gained access to a system, they will be able to escalate their user privileges on the victim system and even pivot the attack through the compromised system to all other internal devices on the network.

Attacks

In this section, you will learn about various types of cyber-attacks and how they can cause harm to systems and networks.

Malware

Malware is code that is designed to perform malicious actions on a system. The term malware is taken from the words malicious software, which has the capabilities to exfiltrate data, make a system unusable, or even delete important files on the local disk. There are many types of malware on the internet, and each day, security researchers and cybersecurity professionals discover new threats.

One type of malware that is well known is the computer **virus**. A computer virus is similar to a human virus. Computer viruses are malicious code that is designed to reproduce itself on an infected system and cause additional damage on the system. Computer viruses are not self-executable, which means a user has to download a virus on their system and manually execute it in order for the payload to be unleashed on the victim's system.

> **Note**
>
> There are other types of viruses, such as a boot sector virus, a program virus, a macro virus, and even a firmware virus.

Another type of malware is a **worm**. A worm is self-replicating malware that automatically propagates itself on a network to compromise additional vulnerable systems. Once a system is infected with a worm, it automatically attempts to spread to other vulnerable systems on the network. A worm is designed to exhaust the computing resources on a system, making the infected system work very slowly or unusable by the user.

Hackers also create **crypto-malware** and **ransomware**. These types of malware are designed to infect a system, encrypt all the victim's data, and request a ransom be paid to release the hostage (data). Once a system is infected with ransomware, all data is encrypted except the operating system files. The hacker then displays text onscreen demanding that you pay the ransom by providing your credit card number, Bitcoin, or another cryptocurrency. It is never recommended to pay the ransom as there is no guarantee or assurance that the hacker will keep their word and provide you with the decryption key. It's important to regularly back up your data such that in the event systems are not recoverable, the systems can be wiped and data can be restored.

A **trojan horse** is a type of malware that disguises itself to look like a legitimate program or application but contains a malicious payload. Once an unsuspecting user executes a trojan horse, the malicious payload executes in the background and the system is compromised. This type of malware is typically used to trick a user into installing it, and the payload opens a backdoor to the victim's system. Once a backdoor is opened on the victim's system, the hacker can gain access. Trojan horses sometimes take the form of fake anti-virus software, games, and even applications. A **remote access trojan** (**RAT**) is another type of trojan horse. A RAT simply allows the hacker to gain remote access and control over the victim's system. The attacker is able to modify configurations, enable the microphone to record audio and the webcam to record video, perform actions, exfiltrate data, and so on.

A **rootkit** is a type of malware that infects the kernel of an operating system. Once a rootkit infects the kernel, it gains root-level access to the system. The term **rootkit** derives from the Linux world, as the highest-level user account on a Linux system is the **root** account. The root account is able to perform unrestricted tasks and actions on a system. Similarly, a rootkit is able to control the kernel and therefore is able to perform administrative actions on a compromised system. Since rootkits infect the kernel, this area in the operating system is usually inaccessible by anti-virus programs. However, some anti-virus programs allow you to perform a **boot system scan**, which is done before an operating system is loaded in memory. This type of scan is able to detect rootkits.

Adware is a type of malware that displays advertisements in the form of popups on your desktop and within your browser. Adware is usually distributed by software from the internet. During the installation of software, adware may be installed in the background and will only appear after the installation process has completed.

Spyware is a type of malware that spies on the victim's activities without consent. This information is sent back to the hacker. A user's activity may seem a bit harmless in terms of cybersecurity but it can actually be worth a lot of money to various organizations.

Reconnaissance

The first phase in hacking is information gathering, or reconnaissance. During this phase, the attacker attempts to gather as much information as possible about the target before exploiting any weaknesses. The attacker usually attempts to discover any operating systems, open ports on systems, vulnerabilities, and even running services on the target. Such information can be gathered using **open source intelligence** (**OSINT**) techniques such as performing various online searches using Google hacking and checking the target's website, WHOIS databases, and even DNS records.

> Note
>
> **Nmap** is one of the best network scanners to detect open ports and profile operating systems, service versions, and much more.

Furthermore, an attacker can use vulnerability scanners to detect open ports and vulnerabilities within an operating system and applications. Some well-known vulnerability scanners in the industry are Nessus, SAINT, and Core Impact.

> Note
>
> To learn more about how to perform ethical hacking and penetration testing techniques, check out my book *The Ultimate Kali Linux Book, Third Edition*, at https://www.amazon.com/Ultimate-Kali-Linux-Book-cutting-edge/dp/1835085806/.

Once vulnerabilities are found, the attacker can then use exploitation tools such as Metasploit, sqlmap, Core Impact, and even **Social-Engineer Toolkit** (**SET**) to gain access to a vulnerable system.

Spoofing

Spoofing is a technique that an attacker uses to fake their identity on a network. In technical terms, when a device such as a computer sends a message to another device, the sender inserts its source IP address within the layer 3 header of the packet. This information is needed to identify the source and sender of the message. Attackers are able to spoof both their MAC address and IP address, simply to fake their identity when launching any attack.

Figure 14.6 shows an attacker sending a message to a target with a spoof IP address:

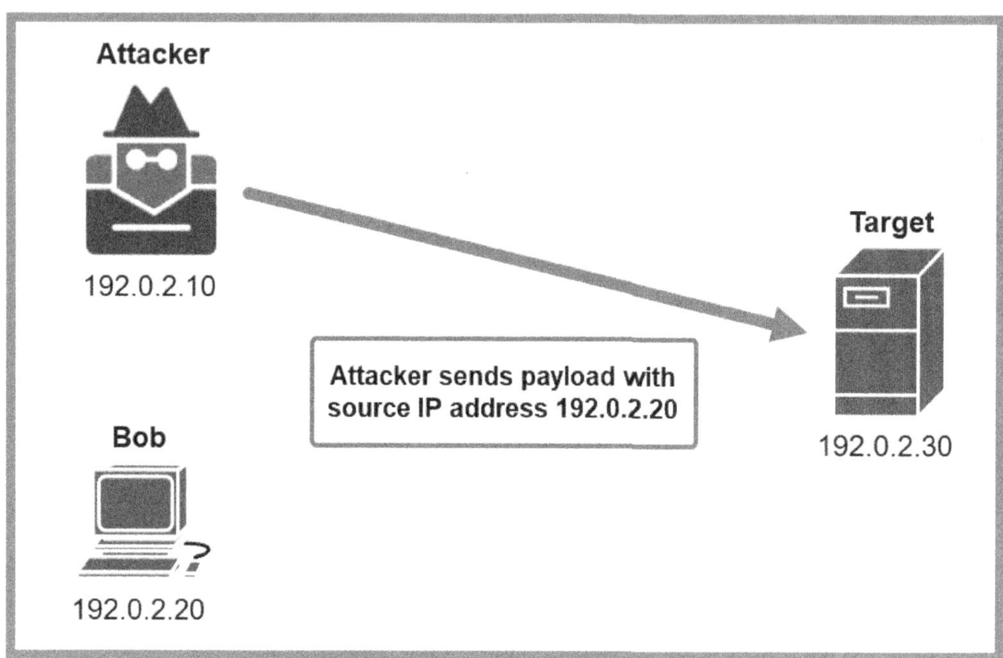

Figure 14.6: Spoofing attack

As you can see in *Figure 14.6*, the attacker uses Bob's IP address as the source IP address. Therefore, when the victim checks the source of the traffic, it shows the attack came from Bob's computer.

Denial of Service

Sometimes, gaining access to or stealing data from a victim's system isn't the goal. Some hackers simply want to disrupt a service and prevent legitimate users from accessing resources. This type of attack is known as DoS. A DoS attack is typically launched from a single source against a target such as a web server. The attacker sends a continuous stream (flood) of unsolicited messages to the target. The target device has to process all messages it is receiving from both the attacker and legitimate users on the network. Since a DoS attack sends hundreds and even thousands of messages per minute, the target will eventually become overwhelmed by processing each message.

Figure 14.7 shows an attacker launching a TCP SYN flood attack on a server:

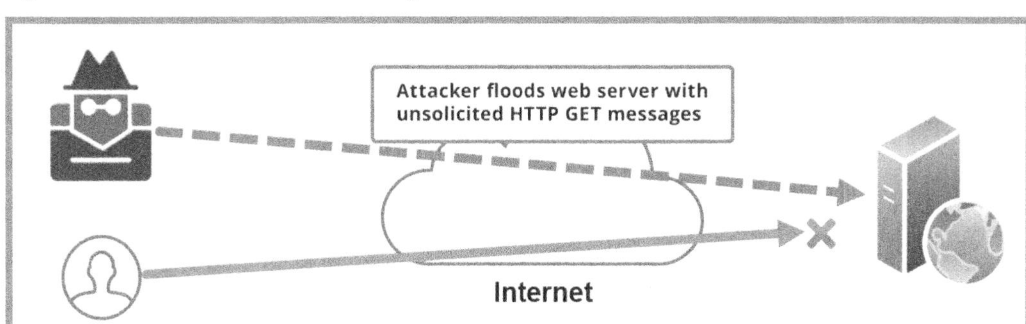

Figure 14.7: HTTP DoS attack

If the target is overwhelmed, it won't be able to respond to legitimate user requests and hence legitimate users are denied access to the resources/services. Since a DoS attack is usually from a single source, it's easy to block the attack as it happens. When a DoS attack is launched from multiple geographic locations, the attack is amplified and becomes difficult to block as there are multiple sources of the attack. This is known as a **distributed denial of service** (**DDoS**).

Another type of DoS attack is a reflective attack. In a reflective attack, the attacker spoofs the IP address of the target device. The attacker then sends a flood of unsolicited request messages to a server on the network or internet. The server will respond to each request and the responses will be sent to the actual target and not the attacker.

Figure 14.8 shows an example of a reflective attack:

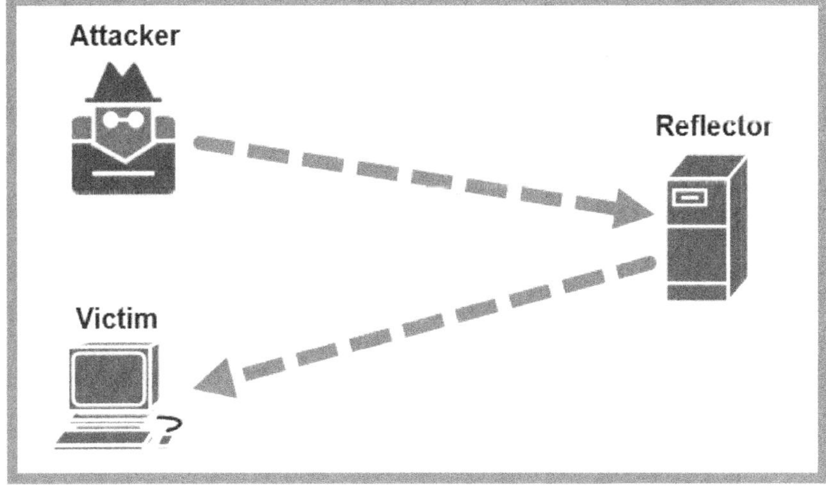

Figure 14.8: DoS reflective attack

On the target system, the logs will indicate the attack is originating from the server and not the attacker's machine.

In an amplification attack, the attacker sends spoofed request messages to multiple servers on the internet. Each server will then respond to each message. Therefore, the victim's machine will receive a flood of messages from multiple servers.

Figure 14.9 shows an example of an amplification attack:

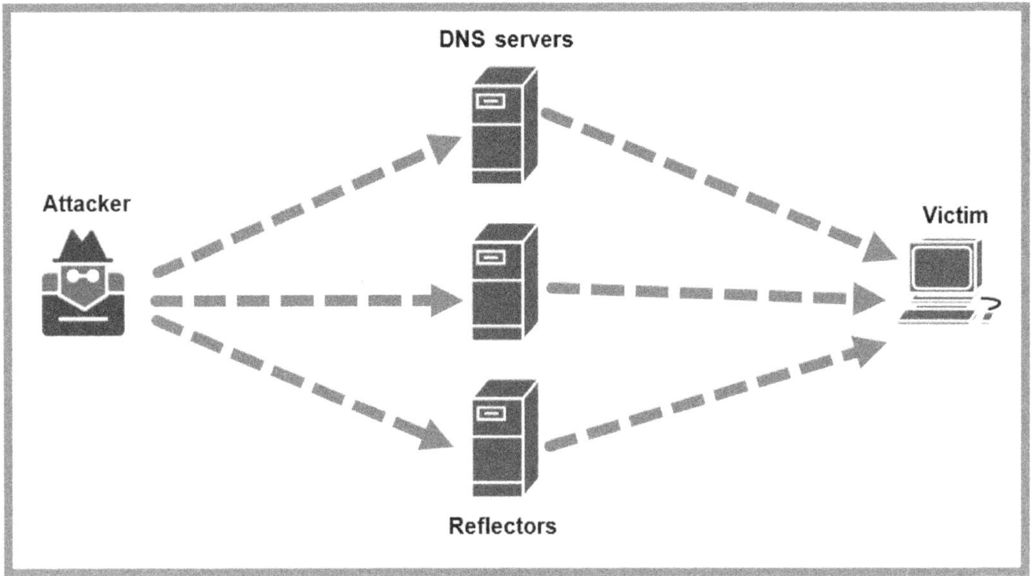

Figure 14.9: Amplification attack

The attacker spoofs the victim's IP address and sends request messages to multiple servers (reflectors). When each server receives each request, they will process and send a reply. However, the reply message is sent to the victim instead.

Man in the Middle (MiTM)

In a **Man-in-the-Middle** (**MiTM**) attack, the attacker sits between the source and the destination of the network traffic. This allows an attacker to intercept and capture all data that is flowing between a victim's machines and its destination. This type of attack is usually done on an internet network such as one within an organization to capture any sensitive data and user credentials that are passed along the network.

For this attack to work properly, the attacker's machine must be connected to the local area network. It learns both the IP address and MAC addresses associated with the victim's machine and the default gateway. The attacker then sends gratuitous **Address Resolution Protocol** (**ARP**) messages to the victim's machine informing it that the attacker machine is the default gateway. Therefore, any traffic with a destination to the internet will now be sent to the attacker's machine. The attacker's machine also sends gratuitous ARP messages to the default gateway, tricking the router into believing the attacker's machine is the victim's device.

Figure 14.10 shows the effect of an MiTM attack on a network:

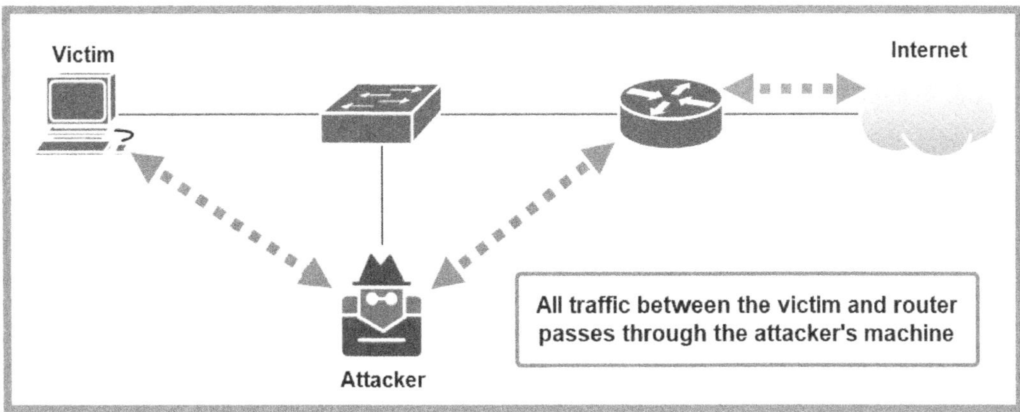

Figure 14.10: MiTM attack

All traffic between the victim's machine and the internet will flow through the attacker's machine. This type of attack takes advantage of a vulnerability within ARP. ARP was not designed with security in mind to prevent such types of attacks. However, Cisco IOS switches support many security features to prevent such an attack. In later chapters, you will learn how to implement layer 2 security on an enterprise network.

Buffer Overflow

Operating system and software developers create a special area in memory to temporarily store data while the application is running. This area is known as a buffer. A buffer is limited to the amount of data an application can store at any time. Software developers continually test their software or applications to ensure data is being processed accurately and efficiently.

There are times when application/software developers do not properly test their applications and sometimes a buffer overflow vulnerability may exist. In a buffer overflow, excess data that is being stored within a buffer spills over into reserved areas of memory that are not allocated for code execution. If an attacker is able to determine an application is vulnerable to such a security weakness, malicious code can be injected into the buffer, causing it to overflow. The spilled code/data is the malicious code sent by the attacker. This code will then be executed in the reserved area of memory.

Attackers can create custom payloads to create backdoors on the victim's system and even set up a reverse shell/connection from the victim's machine back to the attacker.

Authentication, Authorization, and Accounting (AAA)

Implementing AAA within a network is very important to ensure authorized people are able to access a system or network, the appropriate privileges or user rights are granted to the user, and each action performed by the user is accounted for. Imagine your organization has multiple network devices, such as switches, routers, and firewalls, at various remote branches and at the headquarters location. Your team of IT professionals each has a unique role and is responsible for ensuring the IT infrastructure of the organization is well maintained and operating efficiently. Since each IT professional may be required to log in to various network devices, a user account containing the appropriate privileges is required for each person.

Creating individual user accounts for each user per device is a tedious and redundant task. Imagine a user has to change their password; this means the password for the user account has to be manually changed on each individual device that the user can use for access. What if a user makes an unauthorized change to a device's configuration, causing a network outage; how can you determine when the change was made? Who made the change? On which device(s) was the change made by the user? Using AAA can help us better manage user accounts and their privileges and log all actions performed by a user for accountability and record keeping.

The issue with a system such as a computer or device is it cannot recognize a trusted user in the same way as humans. A simple example is that you can identify a family member such as a sibling by simply looking at their face, and once you recognize the person, trust is established. However, a system does not have that human trait and thinking. Therefore, a computer identifies a human user by simply checking their user account details, such as a username (identity) and password combination. To log in to a computer, you must provide a valid username and password. If the computer determines that the user credentials are valid, the user is authenticated to the system and access is granted. **Authentication** is the process in which a system verifies whether the account holder is able to use the account. Without authentication, anyone can access a system and will be able to perform any tasks, both good and bad in nature.

To authenticate to a system, a user will need credentials to prove their identity. The following are some examples of user credentials:

- **Something the user knows**: This is a password, pin, or even a passphrase
- **Something the user has**: This can be a physical security token or a smart card
- **Something you are**: This is something such as your fingerprint or iris and retina patterns

After a user has been authenticated on a system, they are unable to perform any tasks or actions until the authorization phase is complete. **Authorization** is the process through which an authenticated user is granted or assigned privileges to access and modify resources on the system or network. To put it simply, authorization simply determines what a user can and cannot do on a system. Within an organization, there are many groups of users with various roles and responsibilities, such as people within an IT department. Each person may not have the same role and task, therefore each person should be granted only the privileges to complete the tasks based on their job description and no more.

Once a user has been granted the necessary privileges, logs are generated as a record of all the actions performed by the user while they are logged in to the system. This is known as **accounting**. Having logs for each user's action on a network can help determine who performed an action, which device was affected, and the time and date the action was completed.

Within an enterprise organization, an AAA server is usually deployed at a centralized location on the network. This server is used to centrally manage all user accounts, assign privileges, and log all user actions.

Figure 14.11 shows an AAA server on a network:

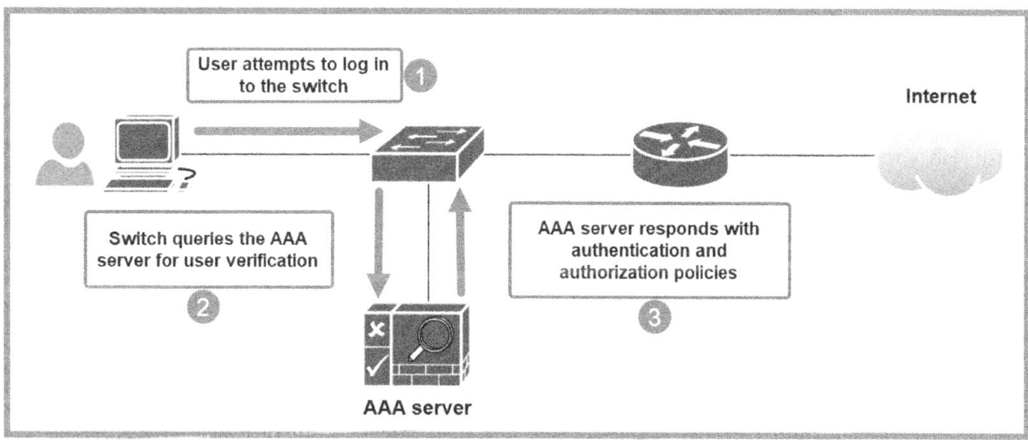

Figure 14.11: AAA server

In *Figure 14.11*, the network administrator wants to log in to the switch to make a configuration change. The switch prompts the user to provide a username and password. The user credentials are then sent to the AAA server to verify the identity of the user. The AAA server confirms the user's identity and applies privileges to what the user can do while they are logged in. The information is sent back to the switch and the user is granted access. While the user is logged in, all actions are logged on the AAA server for accountability.

There are currently two AAA servers. These are the following:

- **Remote Authentication Dial-In User Service** (**RADIUS**)
- **Terminal Access Controller Access-Control System Plus** (**TACACS+**)

RADIUS is an AAA service that supports multi-vendor environments and uses UDP port `1812` for authentication and UDP port `1813` for accounting. However, the communication between an AAA client and a RADIUS server is not completely encrypted. RADIUS encrypts only the password that is exchanged between the client and the server.

> Note
> In the Cisco world, the Cisco **Identity Services Engine** (**ISE**) security appliance is used as an AAA server.

TACACS+ is a Cisco-proprietary AAA service that is similar to RADIUS but provides more flexibility. TACACS+ separates each AAA function into its own secure, encrypted communication between an AAA client and a TACACS+ server over TCP port `49`.

Lab: Implementing AAA

In this lab, you will learn how to implement AAA within a Cisco environment between a Cisco 2911 router and an AAA server using the TACACS+ protocol. For this lab, you will be using the topology within Cisco Packet Tracer, shown in *Figure 14.12*:

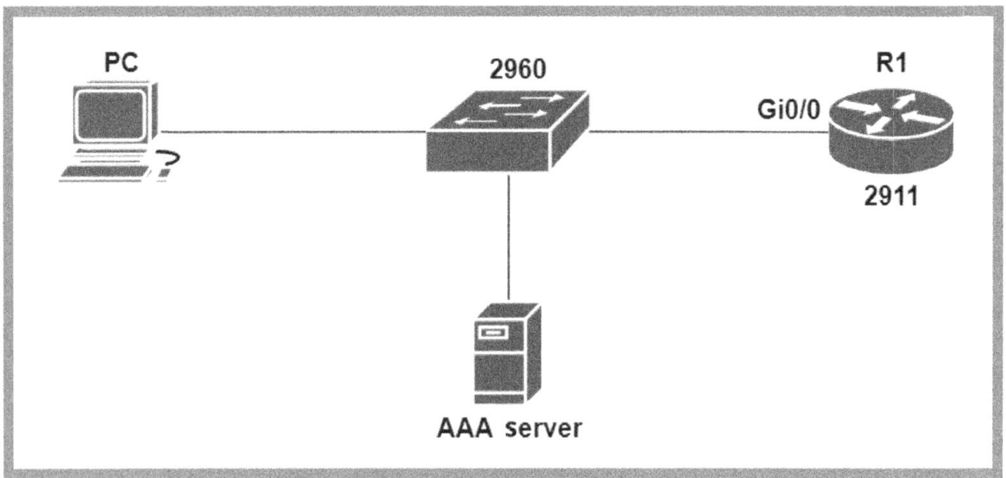

Figure 14.12: AAA lab topology

The topology in *Figure 14.12* uses the addressing scheme shown in *Table 14.1*:

Device	IP Address	Subnet Mask	Gateway
PC	192.168.1.10	255.255.255.0	192.168.1.1
Router	192.168.1.1	255.255.255.0	
Server	192.168.1.5	255.255.255.0	192.168.1.1

Table 14.1: IP scheme

To follow along with this exercise, please download the pre-built lab file from `https://packt.link/CCNArepoCh14`

Now that your lab is ready, use the following instructions to implement AAA:

1. On the server, enable the AAA service, configure the client information (`Client Name`: `R1`, `Client IP`: `192.168.1.1`, `Secret`: `aaa-secret`, and `ServerType`: `Tacacs`), and configure a user account for remote access from the PC to the router:

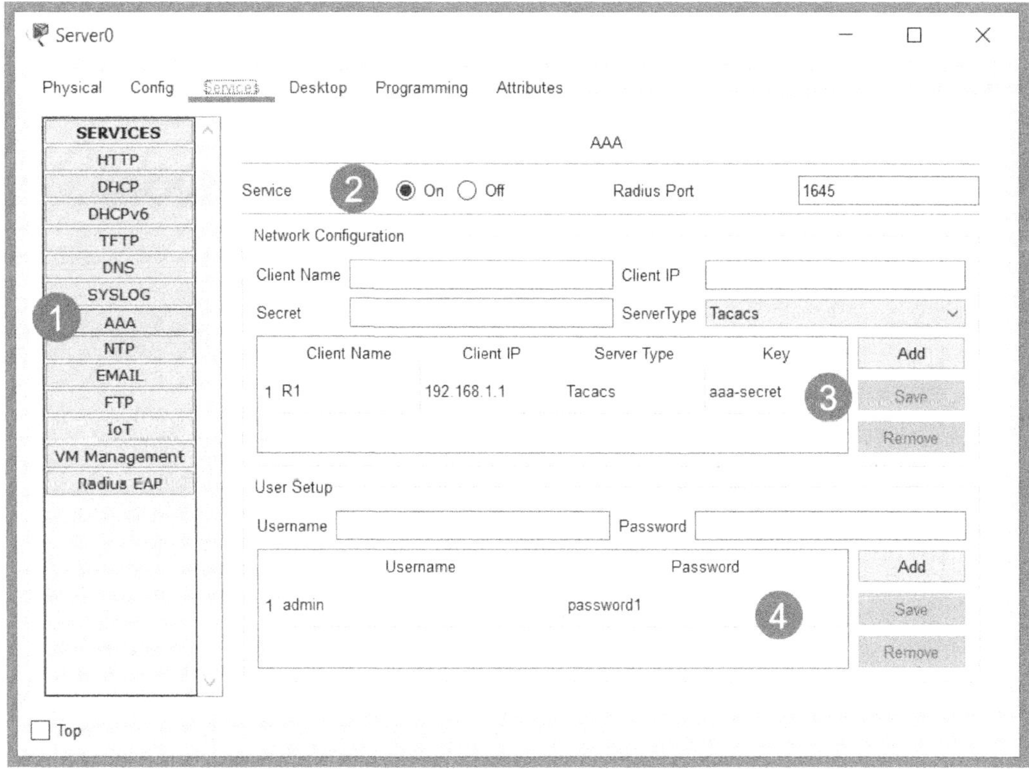

Figure 14.13: AAA server configurations

2. Enable the new AAA features on the router using the following commands:

```
R1(config)# aaa new-model
```

3. Specify the TACACS server and the secret key on the router:

```
R1(config)# tacacs-server host 192.168.1.5 key aaa-secret
```

4. Create an AAA method list (`AAA-Login`) for authentication (`login`) using the server group (`group`) using TACACS+:

```
R1(config)# aaa authentication login AAA-Login group tacacs+
```

5. Apply the method list (`AAA-Login`) to the VTY lines on the router:

```
R1(config)# line vty 0 15
R1(config-line)# login authentication AAA-Login
R1(config-line)# exit
```

6. On the PC, click the `Desktop` tab, open the Telnet/SSH client, and connect to the router using Telnet, as shown in *Figure 14.14*:

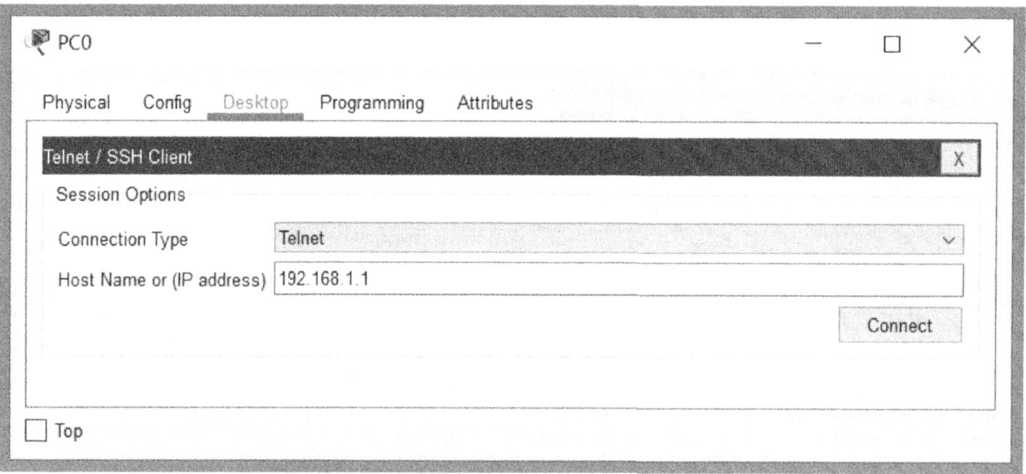

Figure 14.14: Telnet/SSH client

7. Once you're logged in, enter the user credential to test the AAA service between the router and the AAA server, as shown in *Figure 14.15*:

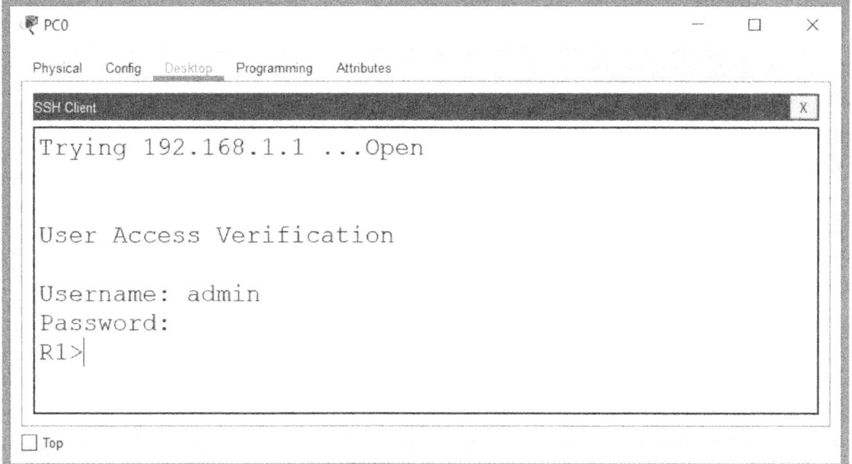

Figure 14.15: AAA service

As shown in *Figure 14.15*, the AAA service works between the router and the AAA server. Having completed this lab, you have gained the essential skills for deploying AAA on a Cisco network for authentication using Telnet.

Elements of a Security Program

Many times, when designing a security network, you will forget to train all users within the organization on cybersecurity awareness. Not all corporate users are able to identify threats and attacks or understand what procedures should be followed if their computer is infected with a virus. Therefore, it is important to design a proper security program to suit all users within the organization.

User awareness is a key factor in any security program. It teaches a user about the need for confidentiality to keep data safe and secure from unauthorized people. Users should be taught about potential threats and attacks and procedures on how to report a security incident within the organization.

Continual **user training** is important, where each user is made aware of any updates to the security training program and to ensure they are familiar with the security policies and procedures within the organization.

Physical access control should be made mandatory in restricted areas of the organization, such as access to data centers, network closets, and any other areas where unauthorized people are not allowed to enter.

Summary

During the course of this chapter, you learned about the importance of information security and the need to protect all assets within an organization. For instance, the CIA triad helps information security, cybersecurity, and network security professionals to better understand the types of security controls that are needed to protect their assets while learning how they affect the security posture of an organization. In addition to this, you covered the differences between common types of threat actors and their motivations behind cyber-attacks.

Furthermore, you explored common human-based vulnerabilities and discovered why threat actors are improving their social engineering techniques and procedures with the intent to steal sensitive data and gain unauthorized access to a system. Lastly, you learned about the various types of network-based attacks and how these attacks can compromise the CIA of critical assets within an organization.

In the next chapter, *Chapter 15, Configuring Device Access Controls and VPNs*, you will learn how to secure your network devices and about **virtual private networks** (**VPNs**).

Additional Reading

The following links are recommended for additional reading:

- Type of malware: `https://www.cisco.com/c/en/us/products/security/advanced-malware-protection/what-is-malware.html`
- Configuring AAA: `https://www.cisco.com/c/en/us/td/docs/routers/connectedgrid/cgr1000/1_0/software/configuration/guide/security/security_Book/sec_aaa_cgr1000.html`
- Wireshark user's guide: `https://www.wireshark.org/docs/wsug_html/`

Exam Readiness Drill – Chapter Review Questions

Apart from mastering key concepts, strong test-taking skills under time pressure are essential for acing your certification exam. That's why developing these abilities early in your learning journey is critical.

Exam readiness drills, using the free online practice resources provided with this book, help you progressively improve your time management and test-taking skills while reinforcing the key concepts you've learned.

HOW TO GET STARTED

- Open the link or scan the QR code at the bottom of this page
- If you have unlocked the practice resources already, log in to your registered account. If you haven't, follow the instructions in *Chapter 19* and come back to this page.
- Once you log in, click the START button to start a quiz
- We recommend attempting a quiz multiple times till you're able to answer most of the questions correctly and well within the time limit.
- You can use the following practice template to help you plan your attempts:

Working On Accuracy		
Attempt	Target	Time Limit
Attempt 1	40% or more	Till the timer runs out
Attempt 2	60% or more	Till the timer runs out
Attempt 3	75% or more	Till the timer runs out
Working On Timing		
Attempt 4	75% or more	1 minute before time limit
Attempt 5	75% or more	2 minutes before time limit
Attempt 6	75% or more	3 minutes before time limit

The above drill is just an example. Design your drills based on your own goals and make the most out of the online quizzes accompanying this book.

First time accessing the online resources?

You'll need to unlock them through a one-time process. **Head to** *Chapter 19* **for instructions**.

Open Quiz

https://packt.link/ccnachap14

OR scan this QR code →

15
Device Access Controls and VPNs

It is important within the field of information technology to ensure that secure configurations are always applied to your devices. Secure configurations help make sure that unauthorized people are not granted access to a device due to device misconfigurations. Quite often, hackers can gain access to companies' perimeter devices, such as routers and firewalls, simply by guessing the password, and many times, device administrators use default configurations and default user accounts. Sometimes, administrative access is not securely configured, and attackers are able to access and perform malicious actions. Ensuring secure access to your networking devices should be a top priority for all IT professionals.

In this chapter, you will learn how to secure your networking devices to prevent unauthorized access by implementing secure configuration best practices. Furthermore, you will discover and learn about the importance of using **virtual private networks** (**VPNs**) to establish secure communication between remote offices and remote workers.

This chapter covers *Domain 5: Security Fundamentals*, objectives *5.3 Configure and verify device access control using local passwords*, *5.5. Describe IPsec remote access and site-to-site VPNs*, and *5.6 Configure and verify access control lists* of the *200-301 CCNA v1.1 Certification* exam.

In this chapter, you will cover the following topics:

- Securing Cisco IOS devices
- Securing remote access management
- Local password management on Cisco devices
- VPNs

Let's dive in!

Device Access Control

Aspiring network professionals are usually excited to configure networking devices to forward traffic efficiently either on a local network or between subnets. It is always a fascinating experience to design an efficient and robust network for your organization or customer. However, your networking devices have important and confidential information, such as the device's configurations, routing protocol and network routers, MAC addresses, and even syslog information, stored in them. If an attacker or an unauthorized person can successfully access your network devices, they can perform a lot of malicious actions, such as re-configuring your network routes to forward traffic to another path, accessing the Cisco IOS image and device's configurations, and adjusting spanning tree paths.

In this section, you will focus on securing physical, remote, and administrative access to your Cisco devices.

Securing Console Access

When you acquire a new Cisco IOS device, a console cable is usually provided in the box. This cable allows you to connect your computer to the console port of a Cisco device for the purpose of device management. By default, there is no security applied to this interface. Anyone who has physical access to your network devices and a console cable will be able to access your Cisco switches, routers, firewalls, and even the **access points** (**APs**), allowing that person to make unauthorized changes to the components. Securing the console port on all Cisco devices is mandatory to ensure that unauthorized people are not able to physically access a device.

Lab: Securing the Console Port

In this hands-on lab, you will learn how to secure and enable authenticated access to the console port of a Cisco IOS router. For this lab, you will be using the network topology within Cisco Packet Tracer, shown in *Figure 15.1*:

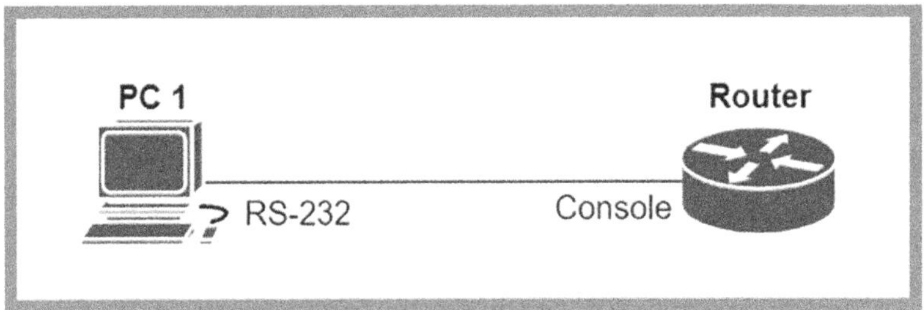

Figure 15.1: Console port lab topology

To follow along with this exercise, please download the pre-built lab template from `https://packt.link/CCNArepoCh15first`.

Now that your Cisco lab is ready, use the following instructions to learn about the default configurations on the console port and how to secure physical access:

1. Click on `PC 1`, select the `Desktop` tab, and click on `Terminal`, as shown in *Figure 15.2*:

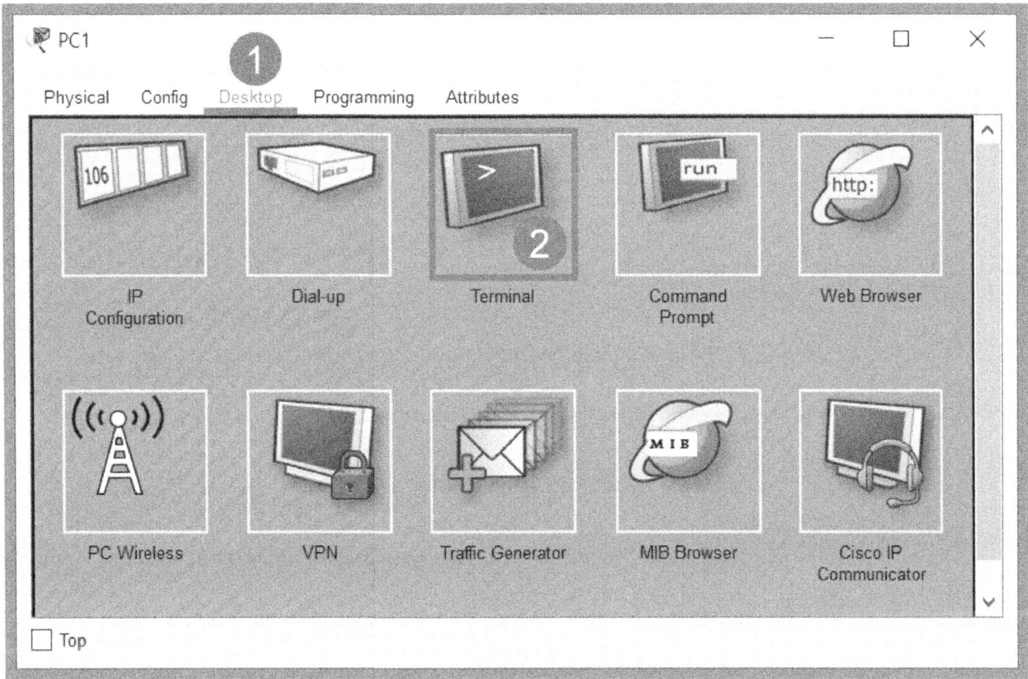

Figure 15.2: Access terminal in Cisco Packet Tracer

In a production environment, you will need to use a terminal emulation application, such as Putty, SecureCRT, or TeraTerm, to interface with a Cisco device over a console connection.

2. Ensure the following parameters are set on the Terminal application and click OK to establish a session, as shown in *Figure 15.3*:

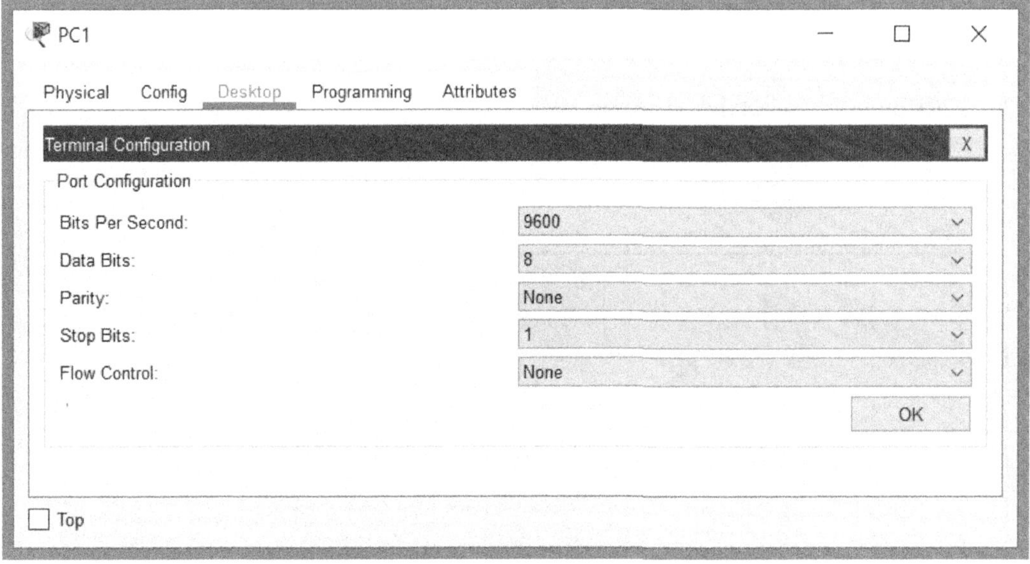

Figure 15.3: Terminal settings

3. The initial system configuration dialog will appear; type no and hit Enter twice, as shown in *Figure 15.4*:

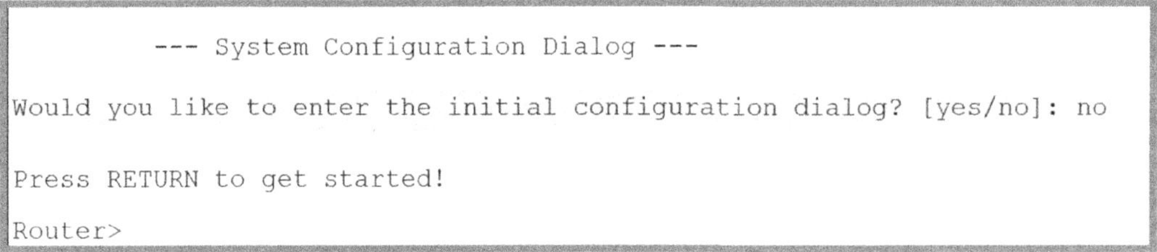

Figure 15.4: Terminal connection

Notice that you have gained access to User Exec mode on the router without being prompted to enter a username or password to authenticate yourself to the device. This is the default setting on the console port; there is no authentication.

4. Use the `show users` command to verify the method currently being used to access the router:

```
Router>show users
    Line       User       Host(s)              Idle       Location
*  0 con 0                idle                 00:00:00

  Interface    User               Mode         Idle      Peer Address
Router>
```

Figure 15.5: Verify access

The asterisk (`*`) indicates the method currently being used to gain access to the device. To put it simply, you have currently accessed the router via its console interface.

5. In `User Exec` mode, the user has least privileges and limited access to Cisco commands. To view the privilege level of the current user, use the `show privilege` command, as shown in *Figure 15.6*:

```
Router>show privilege
Current privilege level is 1
Router>
```

Figure 15.6: Privilege level in User Exec mode

Privilege levels range from 1 to 15. A user with privilege level 1 access will not be able to perform many actions as compared with a user with privilege 15, who has full administrative rights to perform any action on the device.

6. Access `Privilege Exec` mode using the `enable` command, then use the `show running-config` command to verify the configurations on the console line:

```
!
line con 0
!
line aux 0
!
line vty 0 4
 login
!
```

Figure 15.7: Checking configurations

As shown, there are no configurations on the console port. Therefore, anyone can access the device via this interface.

7. Apply a password and enable authentication on the console port, as shown in *Figure 15.8*:

```
Router#configure terminal
Enter configuration commands, one per line.  End with CNTL/Z.
Router(config)#line console 0
Router(config-line)#password consolepass
Router(config-line)#login
Router(config-line)#exit
```

Figure 15.8: Securing the console port

The `line console 0` command was used to access `Console line` mode, the `password` command was used to set the password, and the `login` command was used to enable user authentication on the console port. Without the `login` command, any unauthenticated user will be able to access the device.

8. Re-establishing a console connection between PC 1 and the router, Cisco IOS will provide an authentication prompt as shown here; the password configured under the console line is `consolepass`:

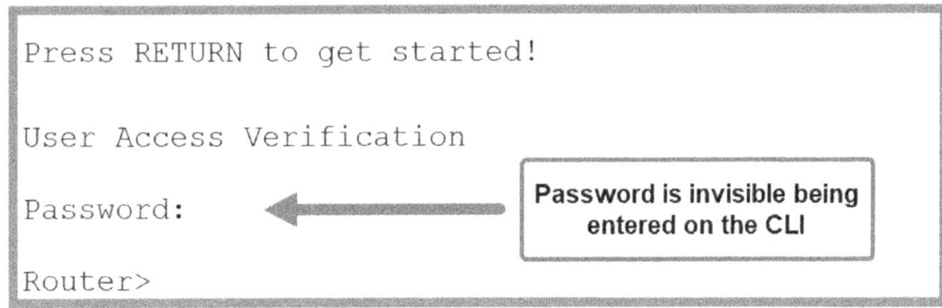
Press RETURN to get started!

User Access Verification

Password:

Router>

Figure 15.9: Verifying console authentication

9. Lastly, you can use the `show running-config` command to verify that the configurations have been updated under the console port, as shown in *Figure 15.10*:

```
Router#show running-config | section line
line con 0
 password consolepass
 login
```

Figure 15.10: Verifying console configurations

In this lab, you have gained the skills to both secure and verify physical access to a Cisco IOS device via its console port.

Securing the AUX Line

Older Cisco devices, such as routers, had support for an **auxiliary** (**AUX**) port. This interface was used to connect to a modem, which allows a user to remotely access a Cisco router over a **command-line interface** (**CLI**) session. By default, the AUX port is not secure and allows unauthenticated access.

Lab: Securing the AUX Port

In this hands-on lab, you will learn how to secure and enable authenticated access to the AUX port of a Cisco IOS router. For this lab, you will be using the network topology provided in Cisco Packet Tracer, as shown in *Figure 15.11*:

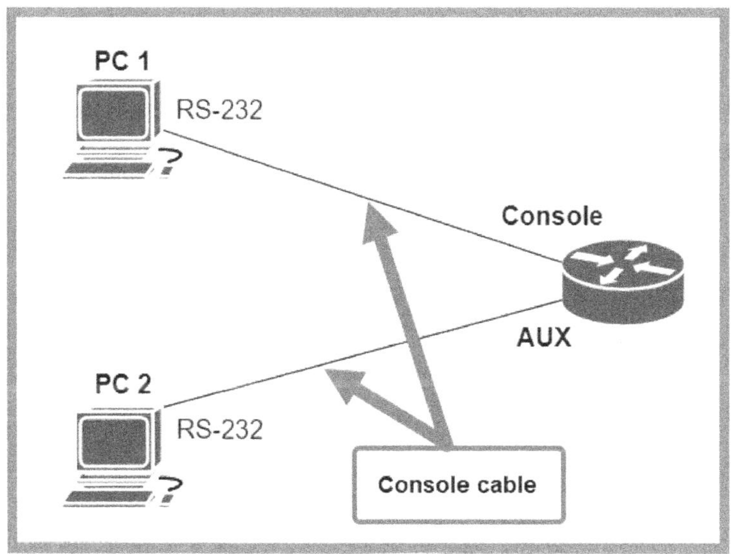

Figure 15.11: AUX line topology

To follow along with this exercise, please download the pre-built lab template from `https://packt.link/CCNArepoCh15second`.

Now that your Cisco lab is ready, use the following instructions to understand the default configurations on the AUX port and how to secure physical access to it:

1. On PC 2, open a `Terminal` connection to the router via its AUX port. Press `Enter` a couple of times to see the CLI prompt.
2. Use the `show users` command to verify the method and interface used to access the router:

```
Router>show users
    Line       User       Host(s)              Idle       Location
   0 con 0                idle                 00:00:12
*  1 aux 0                idle                 00:00:00

  Interface    User               Mode         Idle     Peer Address
Router>
```

Figure 15.12: AUX connection

   As shown, the router indicates the current connection is via the AUX port. Additionally, you gain unauthenticated access to `User Exec` mode. This means there is no security applied to the AUX port by default.

3. Let's use the `enable` command to go into `Privilege Exec` mode to verify the configurations under the AUX line:

```
Router>enable
% No password set.
Router>
```

Figure 15.13: Restriction to Privilege Exec mode

   By default, access is restricted to `Privilege Exec` mode via the AUX port only if there is no password configured on `Privilege Exec` mode.

4. To secure the AUX port, use the console port on PC 1 to access the router via Terminal.
5. Use the following commands to access the AUX port, configure a password, and enable authentication:

```
Router(config)# line aux 0
Router(config-line)# password auxpass
Router(config-line)# login
Router(config-line)# exit
```

6. Re-establishing an AUX session between PC 2 and the router, a user authentication prompt is present:

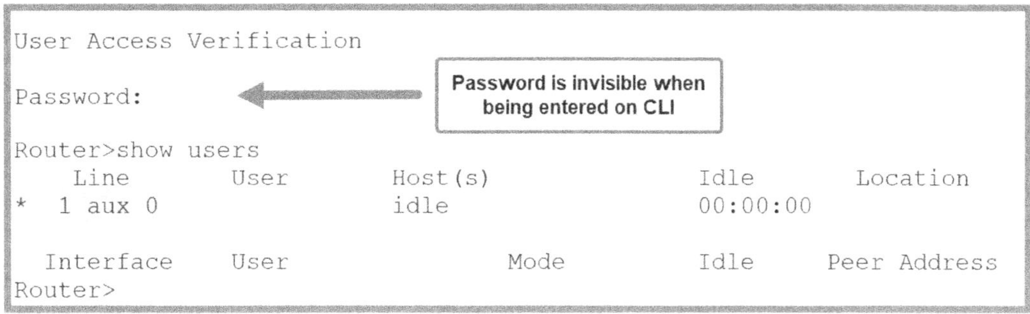

Figure 15.14: Verifying AUX authentication

7. Lastly, use the `show running-config` command to verify whether the configurations are present under the AUX line, as shown in *Figure 15.15*:

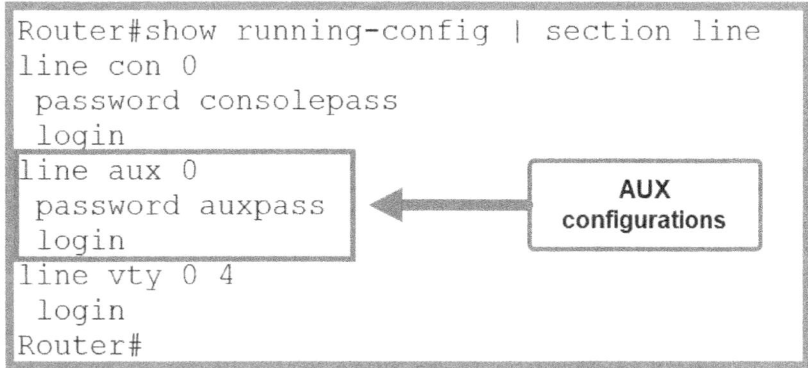

Figure 15.15: AUX configurations

In this lab, you have gained the skills needed to both secure and verify access to a Cisco IOS device via its AUX interface.

VTY Line Access

On a Cisco IOS router or switch, there are 16 **virtual terminal** (**VTY**) lines, ranging from 0 to 15. These VTY lines allow a network engineer to remotely connect to the device for management. Often, as a network engineer, you will not have physical access to the network components, as they may be deployed at a remote location such as another branch office or a customer's site. Furthermore, these VTY lines also support outgoing connections to other Cisco devices.

Telnet is a network protocol that allows you to establish a remote terminal session between a client and a server. On Cisco devices, there is a built-in Telnet server that allows network engineers to remotely connect to and perform remote administration on the device. However, Telnet is an unsecured protocol and transfers all data in plaintext. Due to this security vulnerability within the protocol, it is highly recommended to not use Telnet for anything, as an attacker can capture the data between the client and server.

> **Note**
>
> Telnet operates on port `23` by default.

Since Telnet contains this vulnerability, **Secure Shell** (**SSH**) is the preferred protocol for remote terminal access on a network. SSH provides data encryption of all messages between client and server. Additionally, a user must provide their identity, such as a username and password, to be authenticated to the SSH server. This feature adds improved security as compared to Telnet.

> **Note**
>
> SSH operates on port `22` by default.

Lab: Configuring Telnet on a Cisco Router

In this hands-on lab, you will learn how to configure Telnet access on a Cisco IOS router. For this lab, you will be using the network topology shown in *Figure 15.16*:

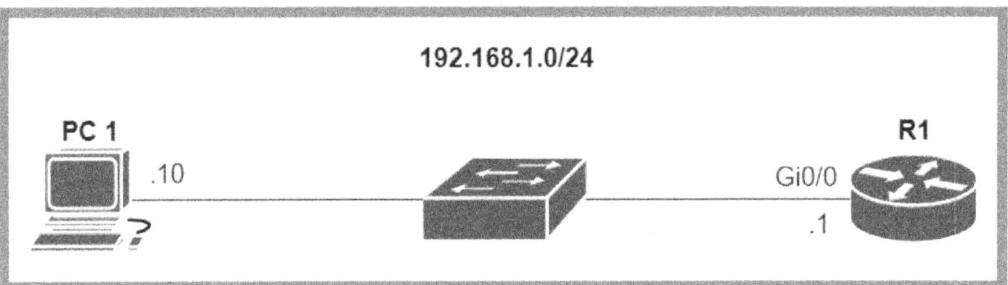

Figure 15.16: Telnet lab topology

To follow along with this exercise, please download the pre-built lab template from `https://packt.link/CCNArepoCh15third`.

Now that your Cisco lab is ready, use the following instructions to configure Telnet for remote access from the PC to the router:

1. Access the console of the router and use the `show running-config` command to verify the Telnet settings on the VTY lines:

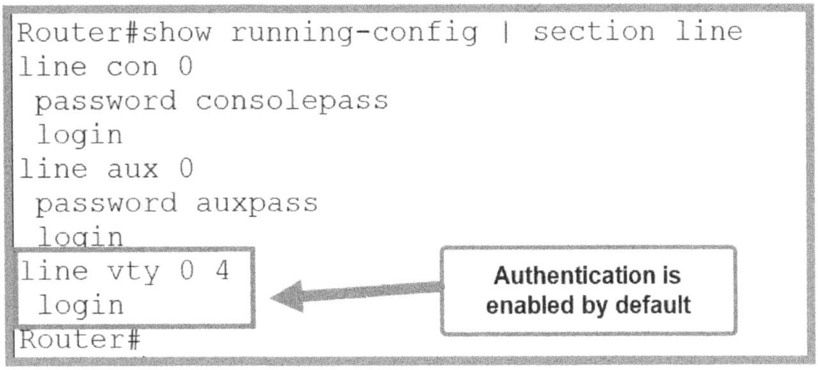

```
Router#show running-config | section line
line con 0
 password consolepass
 login
line aux 0
 password auxpass
 login
line vty 0 4
 login
Router#
```


Figure 15.17: VTY default configuration

On VTY lines 0–4, Telnet is enabled by default, and authentication is also enabled. However, if you try to access the router remotely using Telnet, the connection will automatically terminate simply because there is no password set on the VTY lines.

2. To configure Telnet on all 16 VTY lines on the router, use the following configurations:

```
Router(config)# line vty 0 15
Router(config-line)# password telnetpass
Router(config-line)# login
Router(config-line)# exit
```

The `login` command is not required in this instance as it's already there from the default configurations; however, it's good practice to still enable authentication on the VTY lines.

3. Use the `show running-config` command once more to verify that the configurations are present under the VTY lines, as shown in *Figure 15.18*:

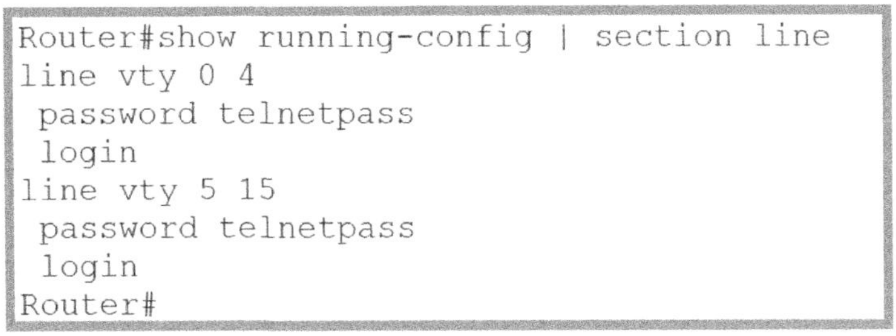

```
Router#show running-config | section line
line vty 0 4
 password telnetpass
 login
line vty 5 15
 password telnetpass
 login
Router#
```

Figure 15.18: Verifying Telnet configurations

4. To test the Telnet connection, open `Telnet / SSH Client` on the `Desktop` tab of `PC 1`:

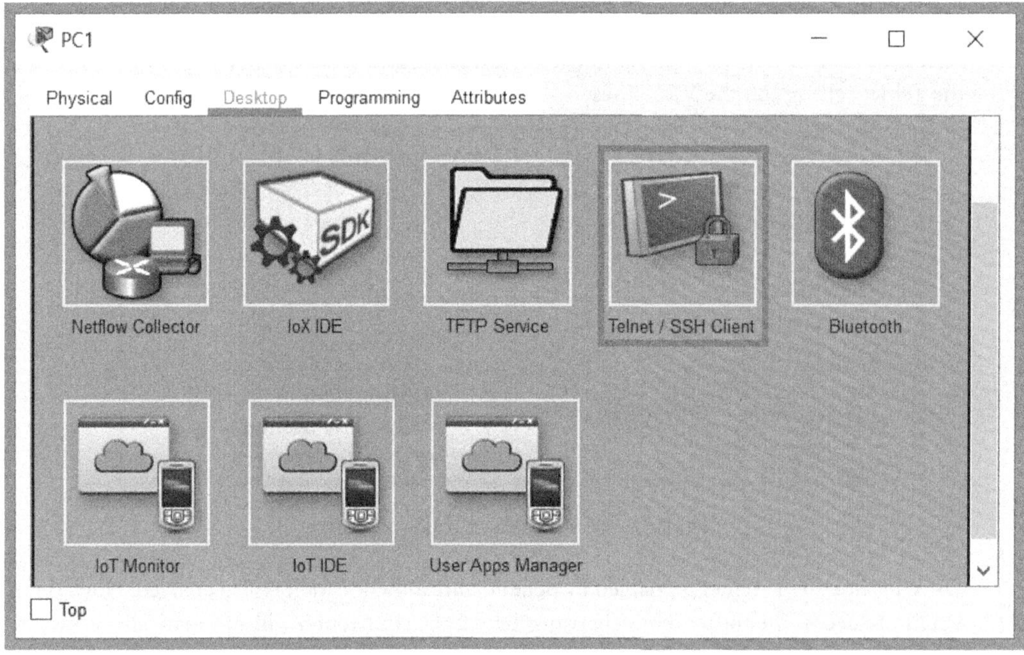

Figure 15.19: Telnet / SSH Client

5. Change `Connection Type` to `Telnet`, set the router's IP address, and click `Connect`:

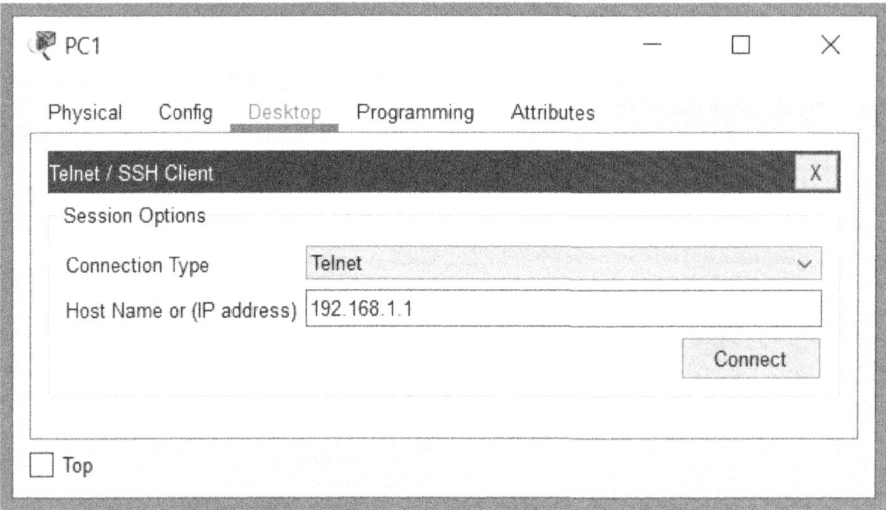

Figure 15.20: Telnet client settings

6. You'll be prompted for a password; use the Telnet password you've assigned under the VTY lines:

```
PC1
Physical  Config  Desktop  Programming  Attributes
SSH Client
Trying 192.168.1.1 ...Open


User Access Verification

Password:
Router>show users
    Line       User       Host(s)              Idle       Location
   0 con 0                idle                 00:02:56
*390 vty 0                idle                 00:00:00 192.168.1.10

  Interface    User               Mode         Idle     Peer Address
Router>
Top
```

Figure 15.21: Telnet connection

Since the authentication prompt was present, this is an indication that Telnet was enabled on the router. Additionally, the `show users` command verified that the current connection to the router is via the VTY line from `192.168.1.10` (PC 1).

Having completed this lab, you have gained the hands-on experience needed to enable Telnet on a Cisco IOS device. In the next lab, you will learn how to configure SSH for remote access.

Lab: Enabling SSH on a Cisco IOS Device

In this hands-on lab, you will learn how to configure SSH access on a Cisco IOS router. For this lab, you will be using the network topology shown in *Figure 15.22*:

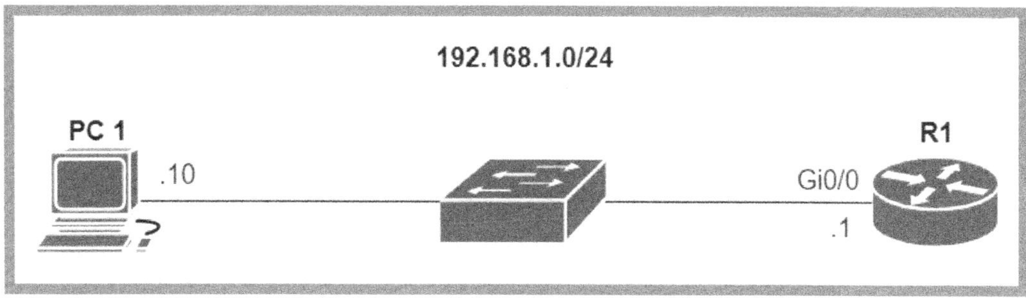

Figure 15.22: SSH lab topology

Please note that this lab is simply an extension of the previous exercise. You are not required to rebuild the network. Now that your Cisco lab is ready, use the following instructions to configure SSH for remote access from the PC to the router:

1. Change the default hostname on the router:

   ```
   Router(config)# hostname R1
   ```

2. Join the device to a domain:

   ```
   R1(config)# ip domain-name ccnalab.local
   ```

3. Create a local user account for the SSH user:

   ```
   R1(config)# username user1 secret sshpass
   ```

4. Generate RSA encryption keys and set the key size to `1024`:

   ```
   R1(config)# crypto key generate rsa general-keys modulus 1024
   ```

5. Enable `ssh version 2` for improved security:

   ```
   R1(config)# ip ssh version 2
   ```

   By default, SSHv1 is enabled.

6. Configure VTY lines 0–15 to only accept SSH connections (disables Telnet):

   ```
   R1(config)# line vty 0 15
   R1(config-line)# transport input ssh
   ```

7. Configure the VTY lines to query the local user database for authentication:

   ```
   R1(config-line)# login local
   ```

8. Since Telnet is disabled and the local database will be used for user authentication, remove the password under the VTY lines:

   ```
   R1(config-line)# no password
   ```

9. Configure an inactivity timeout for idle sessions on the VTY lines; let's use two minutes:

   ```
   R1(config-line)# exec-timeout 2
   ```

10. To test SSH, head on over to `PC 1` and open `Telnet / SSH Client`.

11. Set `Connection Type` to `SSH`, specify the IP address of the router, and use the username from the user account, as shown in *Figure 15.23*:

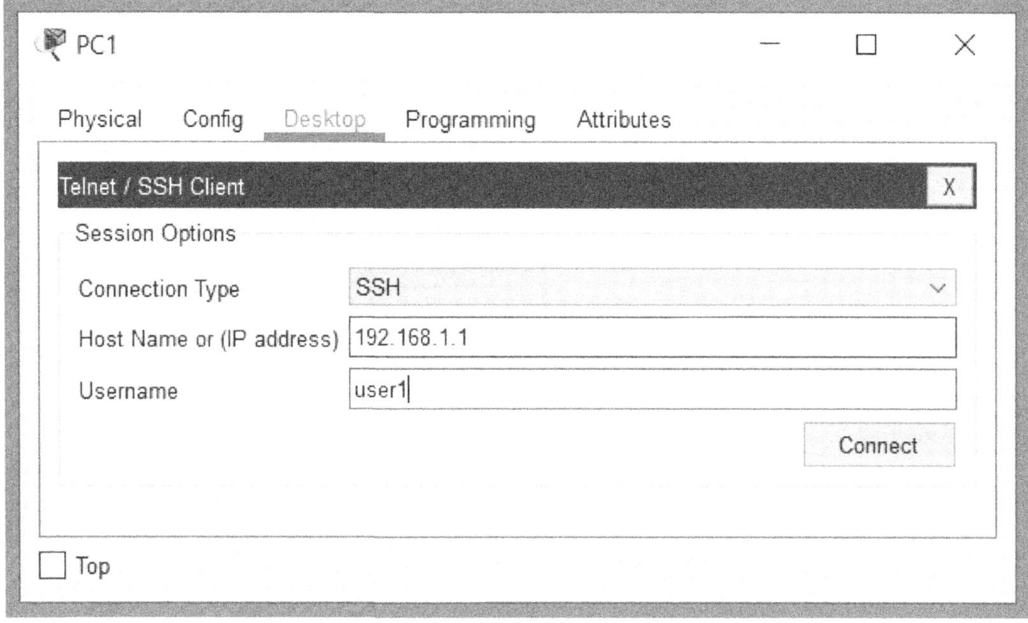

Figure 15.23: SSH client configurations

12. You will receive an authentication prompt asking for a password (the username will be taken from the previous step); simply enter the password for the account and hit `Enter`:

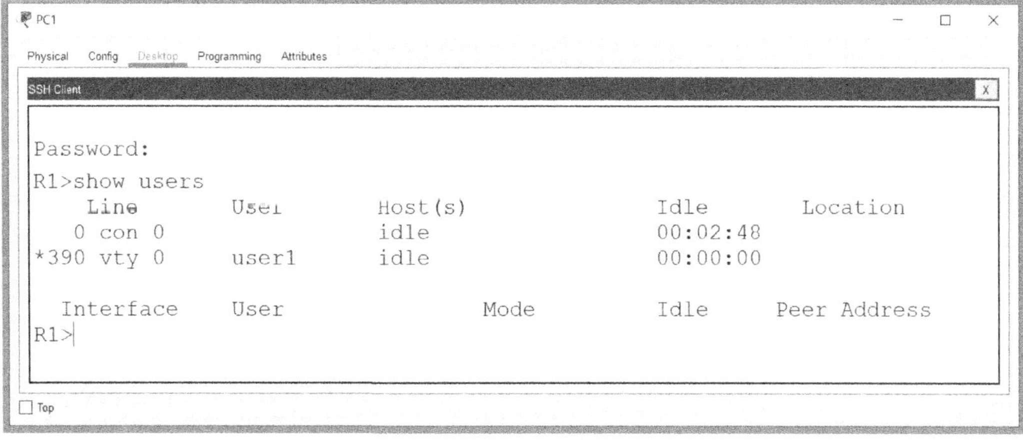

Figure 15.24: SSH session

As shown in the preceding snippet, you are connected to the router on VTY line 0 with the account `user1`.

13. Additionally, the `show ip ssh` command verifies the SSH version, the authentication time value, and the number of authentications retries, as shown in *Figure 15.25*:

```
R1#show ip ssh
SSH Enabled - version 2.0
Authentication timeout: 120 secs; Authentication retries: 3
R1#
R1#show ssh
Connection      Version Mode Encryption  Hmac State             Username
389             1.99    IN   aes128-cbc    hmac-sha1   Session Started         user1
389             1.99    OUT  aes128-cbc    hmac-sha1   Session Started   user1
%No SSHv1 server connections running.
R1#
```

Figure 15.25: Verifying SSH details

Furthermore, `show ssh` verifies the current SSH sessions and users. The `ip ssh time-out seconds` command allows you to modify the default SSH timeout values, and the `ip ssh authentication-retries number` command allows you to change the authentication retry value.

> **Note**
>
> The `login block-for` **`seconds`** `attempts` **`tries`** `within` **`seconds`** command is used to disable user login after a specified number of failed authentication attempts within a specific time interval.

By completing this lab, you have gained hands-on experience in configuring and enabling SSH for remote access on a Cisco IOS router.

Securing Privilege Exec

By now, you will have noticed that once someone is able to access `Privilege Exec` mode, they will be able to gather sensitive and confidential information about the network and the device. Furthermore, a user can escalate their privilege to `Global Config` mode, where the user can apply configurations and make modifications to the device. This creates a security risk.

> **Note**
>
> The `secure boot-image` command prevents a user from either purposely or accidentally deleting the Cisco IOS image and the `secure boot-config` command is used to protect the running configurations.

Cisco IOS has many built-in security features, which enable you to prevent unauthorized access to the operating system. One such feature that helps you prevent unauthorized access to `Privilege Exec` mode specifically is using the `enable password` **<mypassword>** command to restrict access to `Privilege Exec` mode.

> **Note**
>
> The `auto secure` command is used to initialize the Cisco IOS lockdown feature on the device.

The following is an example of using the `enable password` command with a password of `cisco123`:

```
R1(config)# enable password cisco123
```

Once this configuration is applied, each time a user moves from `User Exec` mode to `Privilege Exec` mode, Cisco IOS will prompt the user to authenticate before proceeding. The downside of using the `enable password` command is that it does not provide any encryption of the actual password. If a user is able to access the `running-config` or `startup-config` files, the password is visible in plaintext, as shown in *Figure 15.26*:

```
R1#show running-config
Building configuration...

Current configuration : 998 bytes
!
version 15.1
no service timestamps log datetime msec
no service timestamps debug datetime msec
no service password-encryption
!
hostname R1
!
!
!
enable password cisco123
!
```

Password is in plaintext

Figure 15.26: Password in plaintext

Due to this security vulnerability, Cisco has implemented a secure version of the `enable password` command. This improved method uses the `enable secret` command, which encrypts the password by default using the **Message Digest 5** (**MD5**) hashing algorithm.

The following is an example of securing access to `Privilege Exec` mode using the `enable secret` command followed by the password `cisco456`:

```
R1(config)# enable secret cisco456
```

Figure 15.27 shows the password has been encrypted within the `running-config` file:

```
R1#show running-config
Building configuration...

Current configuration : 1045 bytes
!
hostname R1
!
!
!
enable secret 5 $1$mERr$nU5A2OzzVK4SUlSP717zP.
enable password cisco123
!
```

Password is encrypted

Figure 15.27: Enabling the secret

Cisco uses a numerical value to indicate the type of password stored within `running-config` and `startup-config`. The following are the password types on Cisco IOS devices:

- **enable password**: The password is in plaintext – Type 0 encoding.
- **enable secret**: The MD5 algorithm is used to encrypt the password – Type 5 encoding. MD5 is a hashing algorithm that's used to help users and systems to verify the integrity of a message. Hashing algorithms such as MD5 provide a one-way function, such as creating a hash value of a message that's known as a digest.

Since the device is configured with both `enable password` and `enable secret`, which password will be accepted by Cisco IOS? The simple answer is that it will always be the stronger password, which is the one applied using the `enable secret` command. Since the stronger password will be used by the device, `enable password` is now obsolete and should be removed. Using the `Global Config` command, `no enable password` will remove `enable password` from the device's `running-config` file, as shown in *Figure 15.28*:

```
R1(config)#no enable password
R1(config)#
R1(config)#do show running-config
Building configuration...

Current configuration : 1020 bytes
!
version 15.1
no service password-encryption
!
hostname R1
!
!
!
enable secret 5 $1$mERr$nU5A2OzzVK4SU1SP717zP.
!
!
```

The "*enable password*" removed.

Figure 15.28: Removing enable password

Over the years, security researchers and hackers were able to compromise the MD5 hashing algorithm. This means attackers were able to reverse the MD5 hash value of the password and retrieve the actual password. In light of this security vulnerability, Cisco implemented a more secure hashing algorithm known as **SCRYPT**.

Figure 15.29 shows the command to create a secure password using SCRYPT on a Cisco IOS device:

```
Router(config)#enable algorithm-type ?
  md5      Encode the password using the MD5 algorithm
  scrypt   Encode the password using the SCRYPT hashing algorithm       1
  sha256   Encode the password using the PBKDF2 hashing algorithm

Router(config)#enable algorithm-type scrypt ?
  secret   Assign the privileged level secret (MAX of 25 characters)   2

Router(config)#enable algorithm-type scrypt secret ?                   3
  LINE    The UNENCRYPTED (cleartext) 'enable' secret
  level   Set exec level password

Router(config)#enable algorithm-type scrypt secret level9password      4
Router(config)#
```

Figure 15.29: Enabling SCRYPT on Cisco devices

SCRYPT is more secure than MD5 and therefore uses Type 9 encoding with the SHA256 hashing algorithm. *Figure 15.30* shows that the SCRYPT hash is a lot longer than the `enable secret` MD5 hash:

```
Router#show running-config
Building configuration...

Current configuration : 3228 bytes
!
! Last configuration change at 15:27:08 UTC Tue May 26 2020
!
version 15.7
service timestamps debug datetime msec
service timestamps log datetime msec
no service password-encryption
!
hostname Router
!
boot-start-marker
boot-end-marker
!
!
enable secret 9 $9$h5kKO0lYugj8L9$jHWp1AnEkO8zVCPzu2.DOKPI8O6LRxSxpLCGe01w5EA
!
```

Figure 15.30: Type 9 encoding

When configuring access to `Privilege Exec` mode, ensure that you use the most secure method available on the device. Some devices may not support SCRYPT; in such cases, `enable secret` will be the more secure option as compared to `enable password`, which does not provide any encryption.

Encrypting All Plaintext Passwords

Some modes on Cisco IOS, such as `line console 0`, `line AUX 0`, and the VTY lines, do not support secure password configuration. Within these modes, the `password` command allows us to create and set a password in plaintext. From discussions in the previous sections of this chapter, you have learned that the `password` command does not encrypt passwords stored within the device's configuration.

Figure 15.31 shows that passwords are stored when the `password` command is used:

```
R1#show running-config | section line
line con 0
 password consolepass
 login
line aux 0
 password auxpass
 login
line vty 0 4
 exec-timeout 2 0
 login local
 transport input ssh
```

Passwords are in plaintext

Figure 15.31: Plaintext passwords

Additionally, within Cisco IOS, there are other modes and configurations that require a password to be configured but that only support the `password` command. A simple example is configuring **point-to-point** (**PPP**) using the **password authentication protocol** (**PAP**) on a **wide area network** (**WAN**). The Cisco IOS configurations require a password to be sent across the WAN link to authenticate both routers before establishing the WAN connection. In PAP authentication, the `password` command is available. This means the password is stored in plaintext on the router.

On a Cisco IOS device, the `service password-encryption` command is applied in `Global Config` mode and its purpose is to automatically encrypt existing and new plaintext passwords in the `running-config` file. Once this command is applied on a device, all passwords that are configured in plaintext will automatically be encrypted. The following is an example of using the command on a Cisco IOS router:

```
R1(config)# service password-encryption
```

Figure 15.32 shows the password under the console and AUX lines, which are now encrypted:

```
R1#show running-config | section line
line con 0
 password 7 082243401A160912020A1F17
 login
line aux 0
 password 7 0820595619181604
 login
R1#
```

Passwords are encrypted

Figure 15.32: service password-encryption

Type 7 password encoding is not a strong form of encryption. This type of encryption can be easily broken by an attacker. However, this is the only way to encrypt plaintext passwords on a Cisco IOS device at this time.

Virtual Private Networks

Imagine you have started a business that provides products and services to customers. You begin by opening a single physical location and hiring staff to help run your company and ensure the day-to-day transactions are conducted efficiently. After some time, you realize that the business needs to expand to provide more support and services to customers located in another country and decide that another branch office is better suited to meet the demands of the new location. However, one concern is how the employees at the new remote location will access the resources at the main building in your home country.

There are a few solutions to this issue. One is to replicate the IT infrastructure of the home location at the new remote branch, but this would be costly, as the new branch only requires a few employees, and having a dedicated IT team is not necessary. Another solution is to set up a WAN via your local **internet service provider** (**ISP**) to extend your local area network from your main office over to the remote branch. Having a dedicated WAN connection will ensure that both offices will be able to interconnect and share network resources. However, the downside of having a WAN service is the subscription fees payable to the service provider. The cost of a dedicated WAN service may not be within your budget, and perhaps an alternative solution may be required.

Another solution is to create a VPN between the two offices. A VPN creates an encrypted tunnel between two or more devices over an unsecured network such as the internet. This means all traffic that is sent through the VPN tunnel will be encrypted and kept confidential from hackers on a network and the internet.

The following are the benefits of using a VPN:

- Using a VPN will save you money as it's free. However, commercial VPN solutions usually come with a cost.
- VPNs provide security for all traffic that is sent across the VPN tunnel.
- It supports scalability, so more remote sites and users can connect to the corporate network securely.

Since many organizations already have a firewall at their network perimeter, most firewalls already have support for VPN capabilities built into their operating system. Therefore, you do not need to purchase additional components or devices. Since a VPN encrypts all traffic sent across its tunnel, you don't have to worry if a hacker is intercepting and reading your data. Data encryption provides an extra layer of security as the traffic passes through the internet. Additionally, VPNs use authentication protocols to ensure your data is protected from unauthorized access while it is being sent to the destination. VPNs allow two or more branch networks and users to establish a secure connection over the internet to the corporate network.

Since VPNs use the internet, it is very simple to add new remote workers without having to expand the infrastructure of the service. To put it simply, once a user has access to the internet, they can access the corporate network using a VPN connection.

In the next section, you will learn about a type of VPN that allows you to connect remote branch networks together over the network.

Site-to-Site VPN

One challenge many organizations experience is ensuring that all their remote branch offices are always connected to their corporate HQ location, because most resources, such as application servers, are centralized and stored at the main office. There are many types of WAN solutions from various ISPs, such as **Metro Ethernet** (**MetroE**) and **Multiprotocol Label Switching** (**MPLS**) solutions. However, these solutions are subscription-based services and a customer may not have the required budget or may be looking for an alternative solution.

> **Note**
>
> An ISP can use MPLS to create layer 2 or layer 3 virtual paths between sites. On a layer 2 MPLS VPN, the ISP is not responsible for the routing of the customer's traffic; instead, the ISP implements a **virtual private LAN service** (**VPLS**) to emulate Ethernet over the MPLS network. On a layer 3 MPLS VPN, the customer and the ISP routers are peered, and the customer's routers are redistributed via the MPLS network to the customer's remote sites.

A simple solution is to create a site-to-site VPN between the HQ location and the branch office. Since both locations would already have an internet connection, there is no need to purchase any additional services from your local ISP. However, each location will require a VPN concentrator device for both establishing and terminating the VPN tunnel. A VPN concentrator is a router or firewall that can establish a VPN connection between itself and a VPN client or another VPN concentrator.

Figure 15.33 shows two branch networks interconnected using a site-to-site VPN:

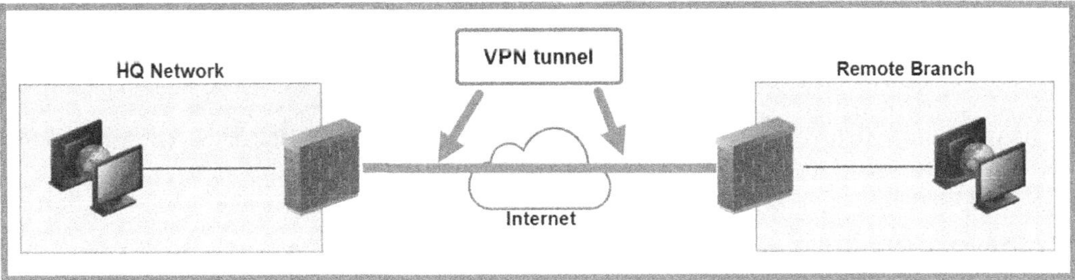

Figure 15.33: Site-to-site VPN

As shown in *Figure 15.33*, the VPN tunnel is established between the two firewalls only. Therefore, traffic between the remote branch and HQ networks will be sent across the VPN tunnel and all data will be encrypted by the firewalls. Keep in mind that not all traffic within each LAN will be encrypted, only the traffic that passes through the VPN tunnel.

Such a VPN allows organizations to reduce their expenditure on connecting remote sites and using their existing infrastructure and devices. Additionally, a site-to-site VPN can be used as a redundant connection between branch offices.

Remote Access VPNs

There are many employees who work remotely. Such people may need to access resources on the corporate network, and coming into the office to do so might not be convenient. A simple solution is to deploy a remote access VPN that allows remote workers to establish a VPN tunnel between their devices, such as computers, and the corporate network over the internet.

Figure 15.34 shows a VPN tunnel between a remote worker's PC and the corporate network:

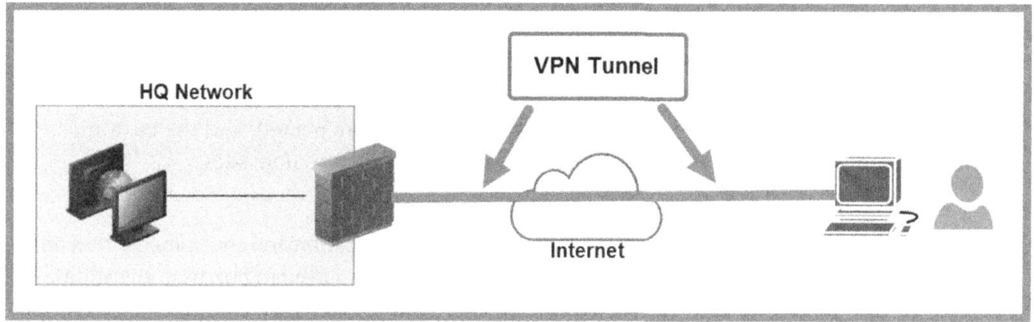

Figure 15.34: Remote access VPN

With a remote access VPN, a VPN client such as **Cisco AnyConnect Secure Mobility Client** must be installed on the remote worker's device. When the remote worker needs to access a resource on the HQ network, the VPN client is used to establish a secure tunnel between the device and the VPN concentrator, such as a firewall or router at the corporate site.

The firewall administrator can configure the remote access VPN for users in one of the following modes:

- Full tunnel
- Split tunnel

In **full tunnel** mode, all traffic that has to go out to the internet from the client's PC will be sent across the VPN tunnel to the VPN concentrator, and then it will be sent out to the internet. All returning traffic will take the same path back to the client's PC.

In **split tunnel** mode, only traffic with a destination of the corporate network will be encrypted and sent across the VPN tunnel. Traffic that has a destination of the internet will not be sent via the VPN tunnel but rather directly out to the internet from the user's PC. This mode creates less overhead on the VPN tunnel and reduces the CPU and RAM consumption on the VPN concentrator.

Another type of VPN connection is by using a **clientless VPN**. With a clientless VPN, there is no need to install a VPN client on the user's machine. However, the connection is encrypted and secure between a client's web browser using SS/TLS encryption over HTTPS. Keep in mind that only traffic between the web browser and the VPN concentrator is encrypted; all other traffic is not.

IPsec

Internet Protocol Security (**IPsec**) is a framework that defines how VPNs can be secured over an IP-based network. The following are the benefits of using an IPsec VPN:

- Confidentiality
- Integrity
- Origin authentication
- Anti-replay

Confidentiality ensures that all data sent across the IPsec VPN tunnel is encrypted with an encryption algorithm such as **Data Encryption Standard** (**DES**), **Triple DES** (**3DES**), or **Advanced Encryption Standard** (**AES**). Data encryption prevents eavesdropping while data is being transmitted.

> **Note**
>
> IPsec contains two protocols: **Authentication Header** (**AH**) and **Encapsulating Security Protocol** (**ESP**). The difference between these two protocols is that AH only authenticates layer 3 packets, while ESP encrypts layer 3 packets. Keep in mind that these protocols are not commonly used together.

Integrity ensures that no data sent across the IPsec VPN tunnel is altered or modified. On an IPsec VPN, hashing algorithms such as MD5 and SHA are used to detect any alteration of messages over the IPsec tunnel.

Authentication on an IPsec VPN ensures that each user is identified correctly and that messages do not originate from persons unknown. In IPsec, **Internet Key Exchange** (**IKE**) is used to authenticate users and VPN clients. IKE uses various methods to validate and authenticate users, such as digital certificates (RSA), **pre-shared keys** (**PSKs**), and usernames and passwords.

Anti-replay prevents a user from capturing and attempting to perform a replay attack on an IPsec VPN tunnel.

Diffie-Hellman (**DH**) is an algorithm used to securely distribute public keys over an unsecured network. The public keys are part of a key pair: a private key and a public key used for data encryption and decryption. There are various DH groups, such as DH1, DH2, DH 4, DH 14, DH15, DH 16, DH19, DH20, DH21, and DH24.

In the next section, you will learn how to configure a site-to-site VPN using IPsec on a Cisco environment.

Lab: Configuring a Site-to-Site VPN

In this hands-on lab, you will learn how to configure and implement a site-to-site IPsec VPN using Cisco IOS routers. For this lab, you will be using the following topology within Cisco Packet Tracer, as shown in *Figure 15.35*:

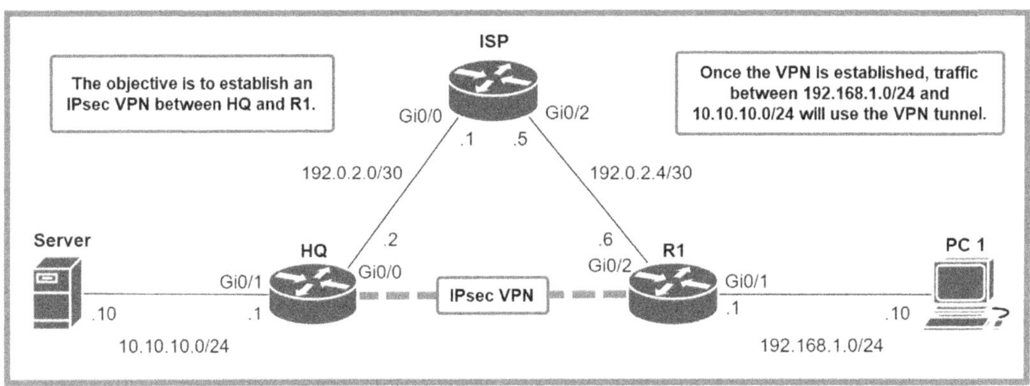

Figure 15.35: Site-to-site VPN topology

To follow along with this exercise, please download the pre-built lab template: `https://packt.link/CCNArepoCh15fourth`.

Ensure you assign IP addresses to each device as shown in *Table 15.1*:

Device	Interface	IP address	Subnet mask	Default gateway
PC 1	Fa0	192.168.1.10	255.255.255.0	192.168.1.1
Server	Fa0	10.10.10.10	255.255.255.0	10.10.10.1
R1	Gi0/1	192.168.1.1	255.255.255.0	N/A
	Gi0/2	192.0.2.6	255.255.255.252	N/A
HQ	Gi0/1	10.10.10.1	255.255.255.0	N/A
	Gi0/0	192.0.2.2	255.255.255.252	N/A
ISP	Gi0/0	192.0.2.1	255.255.255.252	N/A
	Gi0/2	192.0.2.5	255.255.255.252	N/A

Table 15.1: IP scheme

Now that you're lab-ready, use the following instructions to configure an IPsec site-to-site VPN between R1 and the HQ router:

1. Configure the following static routes on each router to simulate the internet:

```
HQ(config)# ip route 0.0.0.0 0.0.0.0 192.0.2.1
R1(config)# ip route 0.0.0.0 0.0.0.0 192.0.2.5
ISP(config)# ip route 10.10.10.0 255.255.255.0 192.0.2.2
ISP(config)# ip route 192.168.1.0 255.255.255.0 192.0.2.6
```

2. Use the following command on the `HQ` and `R1` routers to boot the `securityk9` license. This command enables the VPN capabilities on each device:

```
HQ(config)# license boot module c2900 technology-package
securityk9
```

3. Accept the user agreement by entering `yes` and hit `Enter`.
4. Save the device configurations and reboot each router for the license to take effect:

```
HQ# copy running-config startup-config
HQ# reload
```

5. Once each router has been rebooted, use the `show version` command to verify that the security technology package has been enabled on the `HQ` and `R1` routers, as shown in *Figure 15.36*:

```
----------------------------------------------------------------
Technology    Technology-package           Technology-package
              Current       Type           Next reboot
-----------------------------------------------------------------
ipbase        ipbasek9      Permanent      ipbasek9
security      securityk9    Evaluation     securityk9
uc            disable       None           None
data          disable       None           None

Configuration register is 0x2102
```

Figure 15.36: Verifying the security package

6. Create an **access control list** (**ACL**) on `HQ` to identify traffic that is allowed between the LAN on `HQ` and the LAN on `R1`. This traffic will be encrypted and sent across the IPsec VPN tunnel between the LANs:

```
HQ(config)# ip access-list extended VPN-Traffic
HQ(config-ext-nacl)# permit ip 10.10.10.0 0.0.0.255 192.168.1.0
0.0.0.255
HQ(config-ext-nacl)# exit
```

7. Configure the IKE phase 1 ISAKMP policy on the `HQ` router:

```
HQ(config)# crypto isakmp policy 5
HQ(config-isakmp)# encryption aes 256
HQ(config-isakmp)# authentication pre-share
HQ(config-isakmp)# group 5
HQ(config-isakmp)# exit
HQ(config)# crypto isakmp key myipseckey address 192.0.2.6
```

8. Configure the IKE phase 2 IPsec policy on the `HQ` router. Create the transform set, name it `IPsec-VPN`, and use `esp-aes` and `esp-sha-hmac` for confidentiality and integrity:

```
HQ(config)# crypto ipsec transform-set IPsec-VPN esp-aes
esp-sha-hmac
```

9. Create a crypto map on the HQ router, name it `IPsec-Map`, and bind it to the `VPN-Traffic` ACL:

```
HQ(config)# crypto map IPsec-Map 5 ipsec-isakmp
HQ(config-crypto-map)# description IPsec VPN between HQ and R1
HQ(config-crypto-map)# set peer 192.0.2.6
HQ(config-crypto-map)# set transform-set IPsec-VPN
HQ(config-crypto-map)# match address VPN-Traffic
HQ(config-crypto-map)# exit
```

10. Assign the crypto map to the outbound interface on the `HQ` router:

```
HQ(config)# interface gigabitEthernet 0/0
HQ(config-if)# crypto map IPsec-Map
HQ(config-if)# exit
```

To configure the IPsec site-to-site VPN on `R1`, use the following instructions:

1. Create an ACL on `R1` to identify traffic that is allowed between the LAN on `R1` and the LAN on `HQ`. This traffic will be encrypted and sent across the IPsec VPN tunnel between the LANs:

```
R1(config)# ip access-list extended VPN-Traffic
R1(config-ext-nacl)# permit ip 192.168.1.0 0.0.0.255 10.10.10.0
0.0.0.255
R1(config-ext-nacl)# exit
```

2. Configure the IKE phase 1 ISAKMP policy on the `R1` router:

```
R1(config)# crypto isakmp policy 5
R1(config-isakmp)# encryption aes 256
R1(config-isakmp)# authentication pre-share
R1(config-isakmp)# group 5
R1 (config-isakmp)# exit
R1(config)# crypto isakmp key myipseckey address 192.0.2.2
```

3. Configure the IKE phase 2 IPsec policy on the `HQ` router. Create the transform set, name it `IPsec-VPN`, and use `esp-aes` and `esp-sha-hmac` for confidentiality and integrity:

```
R1(config)# crypto ipsec transform-set IPsec-VPN esp-aes
esp-sha-hmac
```

4. Create a crypto map, name it `IPsec-Map`, and bind it to the `VPN-Traffic` ACL:

```
R1(config)# crypto map IPsec-Map 5 ipsec-isakmp
R1(config-crypto-map)# description IPsec VPN between R1 and HQ
R1(config-crypto-map)# set peer 192.0.2.2
R1(config-crypto-map)# set transform-set IPsec-VPN
R1(config-crypto-map)# match address VPN-Traffic
R1(config-crypto-map)# exit
```

5. Assign the crypto map to the outbound interface on the `R1` router:

```
R1(config)# interface gigabitEthernet 0/2
R1(config-if)# crypto map IPsec-Map
R1(config-if)# exit
```

6. At this point, both the `R1` and `HQ` routers should have established an IPsec tunnel. On `PC 1`, open the command prompt and send ping to the server at `10.10.10.10`. A few packets may drop since the IPsec tunnel may still be initializing.

7. To verify the status of the IPsec tunnel, perform a `traceroute` test between `PC 1` and the server, as shown in *Figure 15.37*:

```
C:\>tracert 10.10.10.10

Tracing route to 10.10.10.10 over a maximum of 30
hops:

  1   1 ms      0 ms      0 ms      192.168.1.1
  2   11 ms     0 ms      10 ms     192.0.2.2
  3   11 ms     13 ms     0 ms      10.10.10.10

Trace complete.
```

Figure 15.37: traceroute between PC 1 and the server

Based on the preceding results, the packet went from `PC 1` to `R1`, then from `R1` to `HQ`, and finally from `HQ` to the server. Notice the packet did not go to the ISP router but rather straight from `R1` to `HQ`; this is because the packet was encrypted and sent across the IPsec tunnel on the network.

8. To view the IKE phase 1 tunnel, use the `show crypto isakmp sa` command as shown in *Figure 15.38*:

```
R1#show crypto isakmp sa
IPv4 Crypto ISAKMP SA
dst             src             state          conn-id slot status
192.0.2.2       192.0.2.6       QM_IDLE           1076    0 ACTIVE
```

Figure 15.38: IKE phase 1 tunnel

9. To view the IPsec phase 2 tunnel, which transports the users' traffic, use the `show crypto ipsec sa` command as shown in *Figure 15.39*:

```
R1#show crypto ipsec sa

interface: GigabitEthernet0/2
    Crypto map tag: IPsec-Map, local addr 192.0.2.6

   protected vrf: (none)
   local  ident (addr/mask/prot/port): (192.168.1.0/255.255.255.0/0/0)
   remote  ident (addr/mask/prot/port): (10.10.10.0/255.255.255.0/0/0)
   current_peer 192.0.2.2 port 500
    PERMIT, flags={origin_is_acl,}
   #pkts encaps: 17, #pkts encrypt: 17, #pkts digest: 0
   #pkts decaps: 14, #pkts decrypt: 14, #pkts verify: 0
   #pkts compressed: 0, #pkts decompressed: 0
   #pkts not compressed: 0, #pkts compr. failed: 0
   #pkts not decompressed: 0, #pkts decompress failed: 0
   #send errors 1, #recv errors 0
```

Figure 15.39: IPsec phase 2 tunnel

10. To view the details about the crypto map on the local router, use the `show crypto map` command, as shown in *Figure 15.40*:

```
R1#show crypto map
Crypto Map IPsec-Map 5 ipsec isakmp
        Peer = 192.0.2.2
        Extended IP access list VPN-Traffic
            access-list VPN-Traffic permit ip 192.168.1.0 0.0.0.255 10.10.10.0 0.0.0.255
        Current peer: 192.0.2.2
        Security association lifetime: 4608000 kilobytes/3600 seconds
        PFS (Y/N): N
        Transform sets={
                IPsec-VPN,
        }
        Interfaces using crypto map IPsec-Map:
                GigabitEthernet0/2
```

Figure 15.40: Crypto map

Having completed this lab, you have gained the hands-on skills needed to implement an IPsec site-to-site VPN in a Cisco environment. In the next lab, you will learn how to configure a Cisco IOS router to support a remote access VPN between a client device and a corporate network.

Lab: Configuring a Remote Access VPN

In this hands-on lab, you will learn how to configure a Cisco IOS router to act as a VPN gateway to support a remote access VPN. In this lab, you will be using the topology in Cisco Packet Tracer shown in *Figure 15.41*:

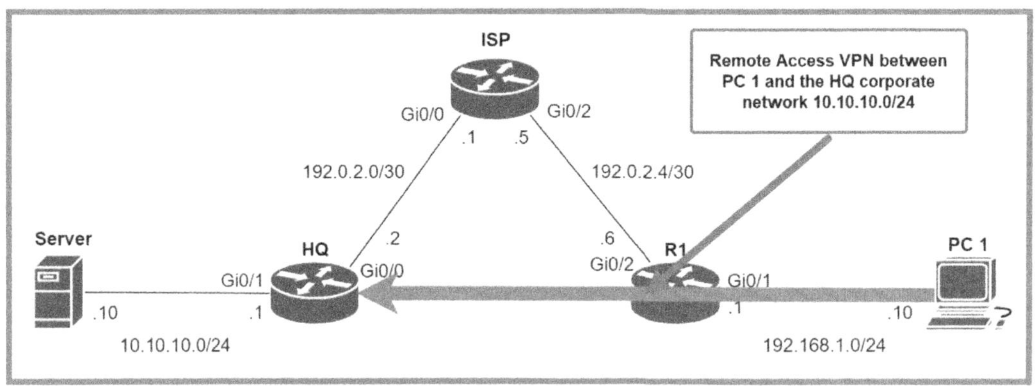

Figure 15.41: Remote access VPN lab topology

To follow along with this exercise, please download the pre-built lab template: `https://packt.link/CCNArepoCh15fifth`.

Ensure that you assign IP addresses to each device as shown in *Table 15.2*:

Device	Interface	IP address	Subnet mask	Default gateway
PC 1	Fa0	192.168.1.10	255.255.255.0	192.168.1.1
Server	Fa0	10.10.10.10	255.255.255.0	10.10.10.1
R1	Gi0/1	192.168.1.1	255.255.255.0	N/A
	Gi0/2	192.0.2.6	255.255.255.252	N/A
HQ	Gi0/1	10.10.10.1	255.255.255.0	N/A
	Gi0/0	192.0.2.2	255.255.255.252	N/A
ISP	Gi0/0	192.0.2.1	255.255.255.252	N/A
	Gi0/2	192.0.2.5	255.255.255.252	N/A

Table 15.2: IP scheme

Now that you are lab-ready, use the following instructions to configure an IPsec remote access VPN on the HQ router:

1. Configure the following static routes on each router to simulate the internet:

```
HQ(config)# ip route 0.0.0.0 0.0.0.0 192.0.2.1
R1(config)# ip route 0.0.0.0 0.0.0.0 192.0.2.5
ISP(config)# ip route 10.10.10.0 255.255.255.0 192.0.2.2
ISP(config)# ip route 192.168.1.0 255.255.255.0 192.0.2.6
```

2. Use the following command on HQ to boot the `securityk9` license. This command enables VPN capabilities on each device:

```
HQ(config)# license boot module c2900 technology-package
securityk9
```

3. Accept the user agreement by entering `yes` and hitting *Enter*.

4. Save the device configurations and reboot each for the license to take effect:

```
HQ# copy running-config startup-config
HQ# reload
```

5. Once each device has been rebooted, use the `show version` command to verify that the security technology package has been enabled on the HQ router:

```
------------------------------------------------------------------
Technology    Technology-package                Technology-package
              Current          Type             Next reboot
-------------------------------------------------------------------
ipbase        ipbasek9         Permanent        ipbasek9
security      securityk9       Evaluation       securityk9
uc            disable          None             None
data          disable          None             None

Configuration register is 0x2102
```

Figure 15.42: Verifying the security package

6. Create an IP address pool for remote access users via the VPN; the range is within the HQ corporate network:

```
HQ(config)# ip local pool RA-VPN-Pool 10.10.10.100 10.10.10.110
```

7. Enable the AAA services on the HQ router and configure the `authentication login` method to use the `local` user database:

```
HQ(config)# aaa new-model
HQ(config)# aaa authentication login RA-UserVPN local
```

8. Configure AAA authorization for network services on the HQ corporate network to use the `local` user database:

```
HQ(config)# aaa authorization network RA-Group-VPN local
```

9. Create a username and password for the remote access user:

```
HQ(config)# username user1 secret ciscovpn1
```

10. Configure the IKE phase 1 ISAKMP policy on the HQ router:

```
HQ(config)# crypto isakmp policy 10
HQ(config-isakmp)# encryption aes 256
HQ(config-isakmp)# authentication pre-share
HQ(config-isakmp)# group 5
HQ(config-isakmp)# exit
```

11. Create the remote user client configurations and the password for the group (`RA-Group-VPN`) on the HQ router:

```
HQ(config)# crypto isakmp client configuration group RA-Group-
VPN
HQ(config-isakmp-group)# key remoteaccessvpn
HQ(config-isakmp-group)# pool RA-VPN-Pool
HQ(config-isakmp-group)# exit
```

12. Configure the IKE phase 2 IPsec policy on the HQ router. Create the transform set, name it `RA-VPN`, and use `esp-aes` and `esp-sha-hmac` for confidentiality and integrity:

```
HQ(config)# crypto ipsec transform-set RA-VPN esp-aes esp-sha-
hmac
```

13. Create a dynamic crypto map on the HQ router, name it `RemoteAccessVPN`, and set the sequence number as `100`:

```
HQ(config)# crypto dynamic-map RemoteAccessVPN 100
HQ(config-crypto-map)# set transform-set RA-VPN
HQ(config-crypto-map)# reverse-route
HQ(config-crypto-map)# exit
```

14. Create the static crypto map for the client configuration for both authentication and authorization:

```
HQ(config)# crypto map StaticVPNMap client configuration address respond
HQ(config)# crypto map StaticVPNMap client authentication list RA-UserVPN
HQ(config)# crypto map StaticVPNMap isakmp authorization list RA-Group-VPN
```

15. Specify a sequence number to insert the crypto map entry:

```
HQ(config)# crypto map StaticVPNMap 20 ipsec-isakmp dynamic RemoteAccessVPN
```

16. Configure the internet-facing interface on HQ with the crypto map:

```
HQ(config)# interface gigabitEthernet 0/0
HQ(config-if)# crypto map StaticVPNMap
HQ(config-if)# exit
```

17. On `PC 1`, open the `Desktop` tab and client on the VPN client as shown in *Figure 15.43*:

Figure 15.43: VPN client on PC 1

18. Enter the configurations shown in *Figure 15.44* into the VPN client interface and click `Connect`:

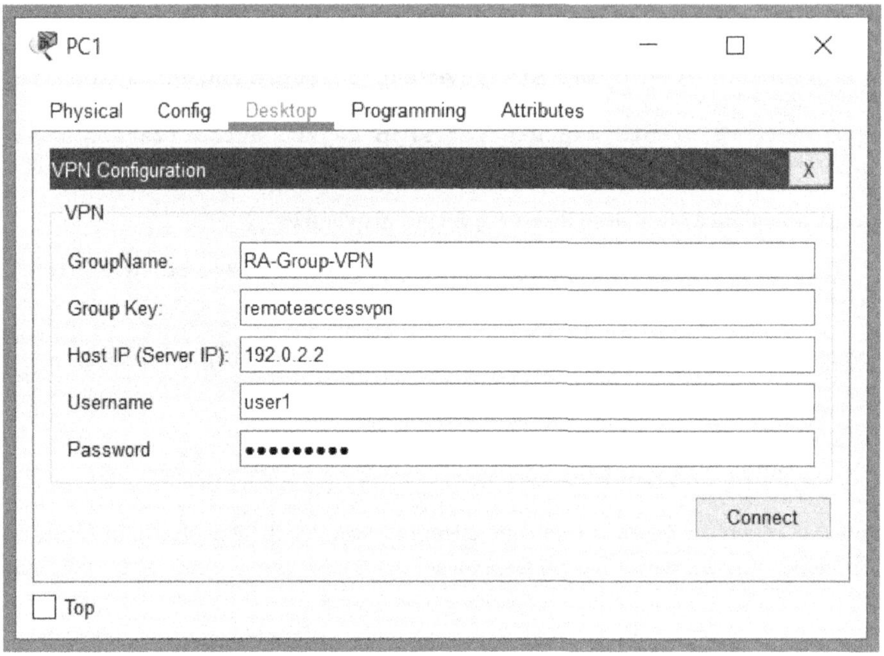

Figure 15.44: VPN client configurations

It may take some time to establish the VPN tunnel between the `PC` and `HQ` routers.

19. Once the VPN tunnel is established, open the command prompt and use the `ipconfig /all` command to verify that `PC 1` has a VPN tunnel interface with an IP address from the `HQ` network, as shown in *Figure 15.45*:

```
C:\>ipconfig /all

FastEthernet0 Connection:(default port)

   Connection-specific DNS Suffix..:
   Physical Address................: 0010.11AD.54B7
   Link-local IPv6 Address.........: FE80::210:11FF:FEAD:54B7
   IP Address......................: 192.168.1.10
   Subnet Mask.....................: 255.255.255.0
   Default Gateway.................: 192.168.1.1
   DNS Servers.....................: 0.0.0.0
   DHCP Servers....................: 0.0.0.0
   DHCPv6 Client DUID..............: 00-01-00-01-AB-C8-B7-7D-00-10-11-AD-54-B7

   Tunnel Interface IP Address.....: 10.10.10.100
```

Figure 15.45: VPN tunnel

20. Perform a connectivity test from `PC 1` to the server on the `HQ` network using the `ping` command, as shown in *Figure 15.46*:

```
C:\>ping 10.10.10.10

Pinging 10.10.10.10 with 32 bytes of data:

Reply from 10.10.10.10: bytes=32 time=1ms TTL=127
Reply from 10.10.10.10: bytes=32 time=1ms TTL=127
Reply from 10.10.10.10: bytes=32 time=1ms TTL=127
Reply from 10.10.10.10: bytes=32 time<1ms TTL=127

Ping statistics for 10.10.10.10:
    Packets: Sent = 4, Received = 4, Lost = 0 (0% loss),
Approximate round trip times in milli-seconds:
    Minimum = 0ms, Maximum = 1ms, Average = 0ms
```

Figure 15.46: Connectivity test

21. To verify that the packets are going via the remote access VPN tunnel, perform `traceroute` from `PC 1` to the server:

```
C:\>tracert 10.10.10.10

Tracing route to 10.10.10.10 over a maximum of 30 hops:

  1   0 ms      0 ms      0 ms      192.0.2.2
  2   0 ms      0 ms      0 ms      10.10.10.10

Trace complete.
```

Figure 15.47: Checking the VPN tunnel

As shown in the results, the packet was sent from `PC 1` to `192.0.2.2`, which is the `HQ` router. Because the VPN tunnel is established between `PC 1` and the `HQ` router, all packets from `PC 1` to the `10.10.10.0/24` network will be encrypted and sent through the remote access VPN tunnel. Hence, the `R1` and ISP routers were not shown as any hops along the path.

Having completed this lab, you have gained the hands-on skills needed to implement a remote access VPN on a Cisco IOS router.

Summary

In this chapter, you have learned how to secure access to the console and AUX ports and VTY lines, how to set up secure remote access, and how to lock down administrative access on a Cisco device. Furthermore, you have discovered how to establish a secure tunnel between two remote sites by extending the LAN at the HQ corporate office using a VPN.

The skills gained from this chapter will play an important role in your future career as a network professional. There are many organizations with unsecured networking devices that pose a significant security risk; therefore, it's important to understand how to secure administrative access to such devices on a network. Furthermore, an organization may be looking into an alternative solution for interconnecting their remote offices and permitting remote work; using site-to-site and remote access VPNs helps organizations reduce their expenditure on managed services.

In the next chapter, *Chapter 16, Implementing Access Controls Lists (ACLs)*, you will learn how to create and implement layer 3 security controls on a Cisco IOS router to filter traffic.

Additional Reading

The following links are recommended for additional reading:

- Cisco guide to hardening Cisco IOS devices: `https://www.cisco.com/c/en/us/support/docs/ip/access-lists/13608-21.html`
- Configuring site-to-site IPsec VPNs: `https://www.cisco.com/c/en/us/support/docs/cloud-systems-management/configuration-professional/113337-ccp-vpn-routerA-routerB-config-00.html`

Exam Readiness Drill – Chapter Review Questions

Apart from mastering key concepts, strong test-taking skills under time pressure are essential for acing your certification exam. That's why developing these abilities early in your learning journey is critical.

Exam readiness drills, using the free online practice resources provided with this book, help you progressively improve your time management and test-taking skills while reinforcing the key concepts you've learned.

HOW TO GET STARTED

- Open the link or scan the QR code at the bottom of this page
- If you have unlocked the practice resources already, log in to your registered account. If you haven't, follow the instructions in *Chapter 19* and come back to this page.
- Once you log in, click the START button to start a quiz
- We recommend attempting a quiz multiple times till you're able to answer most of the questions correctly and well within the time limit.
- You can use the following practice template to help you plan your attempts:

Working On Accuracy		
Attempt	Target	Time Limit
Attempt 1	40% or more	Till the timer runs out
Attempt 2	60% or more	Till the timer runs out
Attempt 3	75% or more	Till the timer runs out
Working On Timing		
Attempt 4	75% or more	1 minute before time limit
Attempt 5	75% or more	2 minutes before time limit
Attempt 6	75% or more	3 minutes before time limit

The above drill is just an example. Design your drills based on your own goals and make the most out of the online quizzes accompanying this book.

First time accessing the online resources?
You'll need to unlock them through a one-time process. **Head to** *Chapter 19* **for instructions**.

Open Quiz	
https://packt.link/ccnachap15 OR scan this QR code →	

16
Implementing Access Controls Lists (ACLs)

Whenever you need to interconnect two or more different networks, the router is always the preferred choice. This is simply because the primary function of a router is to forward packets between networks. However, the Cisco IOS router has many more features than simply forwarding. One major feature is that it filters traffic based on its source and destination. This feature enables the Cisco IOS router to perform **packet filtering** similarly to a firewall appliance on the network.

During the course of this chapter, you will learn how **access control lists** (**ACLs**) can be applied on a Cisco IOS router to filter both inbound and outbound traffic. Furthermore, you will discover the various types of ACLs and how they can be used in various situations to allow or deny traffic between networks.

This chapter covers *Domain 5: Security Fundamentals*, objective *5.6 Configure and verify access control lists*, of the *200-301 CCNA v1.1 Certification* exam.

In this chapter, we will cover the following topics:

- What are ACLs?
- ACL operation
- ACL wildcard mask
- Creating standard ACLs
- Creating extended ACLs

Let's dive in!

What Are ACLs?

As you have learned thus far, routers are used to forward traffic between different networks. As a packet enters an inbound interface of a router, the operating system has to read the layer 3 header information, such as the source and destination IP addresses, and check the **routing table** for a suitable route. Once a route has been found, the router forwards the packet through an outbound interface to its destination. Ensuring all users are able to send and receive messages is excellent in terms of connectivity, but what are some of the security and traffic flow restrictions between certain networks?

The Cisco IOS router has many amazing features and can perform a variety of roles on a network. One such feature is performing traffic filtering between networks. This is done using a very special method that firewall appliances use to filter traffic – **ACLs**.

> **Note**
> Firewall appliances use various methods to filter inbound and outbound traffic. ACLs are simply one of many methods.

The process that a Cisco IOS router uses to determine the best match when forwarding packets to their destination, ACLs, can be applied on the interfaces of routers to filter traffic based on their source or destination information. ACLs are typically rules created on a router that determines how traffic should be filtered. For instance, should it be allowed or denied? Implementing ACLs on a Cisco IOS router does not convert the router into a firewall appliance, nor does it replace the need for a dedicated firewall on your network. ACLs are simply used to filter traffic passing through your router, such as filtering messages between IP subnets and **Virtual Local Area Networks** (**VLANs**).

By default, the Cisco IOS router is not configured with an ACL, and traffic is able to flow without any restrictions. However, when an ACL is created, it must be applied to an interface to take effect. ACLs can be used to filter inbound or outbound traffic on a router's interface. When applied to an inbound interface, the router has to perform additional checks on all traffic entering the interface before checking the routing table for a suitable path. Additionally, when an ACL is applied to an outbound interface, the router still has to perform additional checks before allowing the message to leave the router.

There are two primary types of ACLs:

- **Standard ACLs**: A standard ACL is used to filter all traffic types of a source host or network. This type of ACL is very straightforward in application. If you want to deny all traffic originating from a single host or network, a standard ACL is the better choice.
- **Extended ACLs**: An extended ACL allows you to be more granular when filtering traffic. This type of ACL allows you to filter packets based on the following criteria:
    - Protocol type
    - Source IP address

- Source port number (TCP or UDP)
- Destination IP address
- Destination port number (TCP or UDP)

The extended ACL is the better choice when filtering specific traffic types between a source and a destination.

Benefits of Using ACLs

There are many benefits of using ACLs to filter traffic within an organization. In this section, you will learn about the various scenarios in which ACLs can help improve security and traffic flow in a network.

Imagine that, within your organization, there are many users who frequently stream online videos during their work schedule. The video traffic can consume a lot of bandwidth simply by increasing the load on the network. By implementing an ACL, you can enforce and restrict video traffic within the organization and increase network performance. Additionally, by implementing ACLs on a corporate network, you can restrict or limit access to various network resources to a specific group of users. This adds a layer of network security by granting access to resources to only authorized users.

ACLs can be used to filter unwanted network services and traffic. Some organizations may have security policies to prevent unsecured communication protocols on their network. An example of an unsecured protocol is Telnet. An ACL can be used to enforce this policy within the organization and restrict all Telnet traffic.

In *Chapter 16, Device Access Controls and VPNs*, you learned how to implement secure remote access to your Cisco devices. Imagine configuring remote access on all your devices and anyone is able to establish an SSH session with your routers and switches. By implementing an ACL, you can restrict remote access, granting it to a specific user group, such as those within the IT department of your organization. The ACL can be applied on the **virtual terminal** (**VTY**) lines to filter inbound traffic.

When applying **quality of service** (**QoS**) to a network, it's important to identify the traffic types correctly for classification and prioritization. ACLs can be used with QoS to identify various traffic types, such as **voice over IP** (**VoIP**), enabling the QoS tools to process the traffic quickly.

ACL Operation

ACLs are rules created by a network professional on the router or firewall appliance to filter traffic either entering or leaving the device. ACLs are a list of security rules, and each ACL contains either a **permit** or **deny** statement. Each statement within an ACL is called an **access control entry** (**ACE**). ACEs are the real workers that allow and block packets between networks. When a router receives packets on an interface, the router checks each ACE, starting with the first entry at the top of the list and moving down until a match is found. Once an ACE match is found, the router stops searching and executes the rule on the ACE – whether to permit or deny the traffic. This process is known as packet filtering.

> **Note**
>
> If no matches are found in the ACLs, the packet is discarded by the router. The last ACE within all ACLs is an implicit deny statement. An implicit deny statement simply says that if no matches are found in the previous ACEs, deny the packet. The implicit deny statement is automatically inserted as the last entry within an ACL. It's usually invisible.

With packet filtering, you can configure the Cisco IOS router to analyze traffic and control access between networks. ACLs can be used to filter inbound or outbound traffic and permit or deny traffic based on its source and destination IP address (layer 3) and/or by the source and destination port numbers (layer 4).

> **Note**
>
> Standard ACLs are designed to filter traffic based on layer 3 only. Extended ACLs are able to filter traffic at layer 3 and layer 4 of the OSI model.

ACLs can be configured on a router to filter inbound traffic or outbound traffic. There are two types of ACLs for this purpose:

- Inbound ACLs
- Outbound ACLs

With inbound ACLs, packets entering a router are processed before they are forwarded to their destination. The placement of the inbound ACLs allows the router to conserve its resources, such as performing routing lookups since the inbound ACL can filter packets as they enter the device. If the packet is allowed by the inbound ACL, the router will then perform a route lookup and forward the packet to its destination. It's recommended to use inbound ACLs to perform packet filtering when the source of the traffic is attached or connected to the inbound interface of a router.

Figure 16.1 shows the concepts of inbound and outbound ACLs on a router:

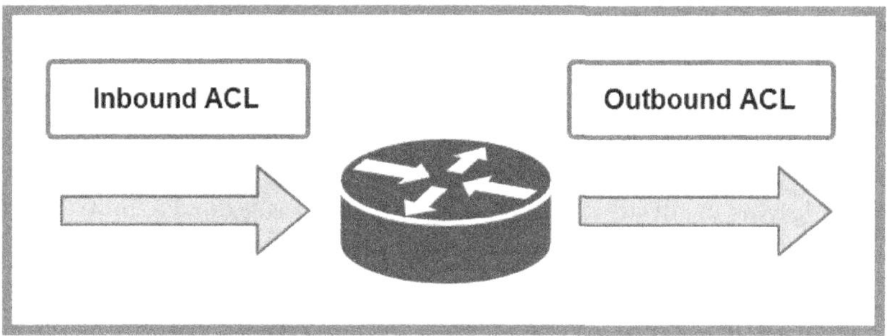

Figure 16.1: Inbound and outbound ACLs

Outbound ACLs are placed on the outgoing interface of a router. Outbound ACLs filter packets after they have been processed by the router. The placement of these ACLs is useful when filtering traffic that originates from multiple interfaces or sources.

To get a better understanding of how ACLs are applied to a router, take a look at *Figure 16.2*:

```
HQ#show ip interface GigabitEthernet 0/2
GigabitEthernet0/2 is up, line protocol is up (connected)
  Internet address is 172.16.1.1/24
  Broadcast address is 255.255.255.255
  Address determined by setup command
  MTU is 1500 bytes
  Helper address is not set
  Directed broadcast forwarding is disabled
  Outgoing access list is 10
  Inbound  access list is Restrict-FTP
  Proxy ARP is enabled
  Security level is default
```

Figure 16.2: Verifying ACLs on an interface

The `show ip interface` command is used to verify whether an ACL is applied on an interface and its direction to filter traffic. As shown in the preceding snippet, there are two ACLs applied on the `GigabitEthernet 0/2` interface. There's a numbered ACL, `10`, applied to filter outbound packets leaving the interface and a named ACL, `Restrict-FTP`, that is applied to filter inbound packets on the router's interface.

Figure 16.3 shows the ACEs for the outbound ACL on the `GigabitEthernet 0/2` interface:

```
HQ#show access-lists 10
Standard IP access list 10
    permit host 192.168.1.10
    permit 10.1.1.0 0.0.0.255

HQ#
```

Figure 16.3: Verifying ACEs within ACL 10

As shown in *Figure 16.3*, ACL 10 contains two ACEs. The first ACE is a `permit` statement to only allow traffic from the host device with the IP address 192.168.1.10. The `host` command is used to specify a single IP address in this statement, therefore a wildcard mask is not required when the `host` command is invoked. The second ACE is a `permit` statement to allow all traffic originating from the `10.1.1.0/24` network. When specifying a network range, wildcard masks are used to tell the router which bits to match in the address and which bits to ignore.

Next, you can examine the contents of the inbound ACL on interface `GigabitEthernet 0/2` in *Figure 16.4*:

```
HQ#show access-lists Restrict-FTP
Extended IP access list Restrict-FTP
    deny tcp host 172.16.1.10 any eq ftp
    permit ip any any

HQ#
```

Figure 16.4: Verifying ACEs within ACL Restrict-FTP

As shown in *Figure 16.4*, there are two ACEs within the inbound ACL. The first ACE is a `deny` statement to prevent any TCP traffic originating from the host IP address `172.16.1.10` to any destination network or destination with a destination port of `21`.

> **Note**
>
> The keyword `ftp` is also used to indicate port `21` within an ACL.

The second ACE is a `permit` statement to allow all IP traffic from any source to any destination. Since neither a source nor destination port was specified within the ACE, all ports are automatically considered. Keep in mind there are 65,535 logical network ports.

Additionally, to view all the ACLs on a router, the `show access-lists` command can be executed without specifying an ACL name or number. *Figure 16.5* shows a list of all the ACLs present on a Cisco IOS router:

```
HQ#show access-lists
Standard IP access list 10
    10 permit host 192.168.1.10
    20 permit 10.1.1.0 0.0.0.255
Standard IP access list INT_Access
    10 permit 172.16.1.0 0.0.0.255
Standard IP access list Secure-VTY
    10 permit host 172.16.1.10
    20 deny any
Extended IP access list Restrict-FTP
    10 deny tcp host 172.16.1.10 any eq ftp
    20 permit ip any any
HQ#
```

Figure 16.5: Viewing all ACLs

The output is a bit different as it contains placement values such as 10, 20, and 30. When creating an ACL, it's important that the ACEs are placed in order as you want the router to process each packet. To put it simply, the router reads an ACL from top to bottom each time it has to reference an ACL on an interface. It's recommended to place more specific ACEs at the top of the ACL and less specific ACEs at the bottom. As an example, take a look at *Figure 16.6*:

```
HQ#show access-lists
Extended IP access list Restrict-FTP
    10 deny tcp host 172.16.1.10 any eq ftp
    20 permit ip any any
HQ#
```

Figure 16.6: Analyzing an ACL

As shown in *Figure 16.6*, the ACEs are placed according to their numerical value. By default, the router automatically inserts a placement value for new ACEs under an ACL with increments of 10. This allows a network engineer to insert ACEs between each other on an ACL.

ACL Wildcard Mask

When creating an ACE, you may need to specify a network ID and the subnet mask. However, within an ACL and an ACE, you cannot use a subnet mask as the Cisco IOS router was not built or designed to accept subnet masks as part of an ACE. ACLs use a wildcard mask, which is a 32-bit binary string used by the Cisco IOS router to determine which bits within the address to match and which bits to ignore.

As with a subnet mask, the 1s and 0s are used to indicate the network and host portions of an IP address. The 1s within a subnet mask are used to identify the network portion of an address, while the 0s are used to identify the host portion. Within a wildcard mask, these bits are used for a different purpose. The 1s and 0s are used to filter either a group of addresses or a single IP address - whether to permit or deny access to a network resource.

In a wildcard mask, the 0s are used to match the corresponding bit value in the address, while the 1s are used to ignore the corresponding bit value in the address. You can think of a wildcard mask as the inverse of a subnet mask.

To get a better idea, take a look at the following examples of using wildcard masking:

- `00000000` – Since all bits are 0s, this wildcard indicates to match all corresponding bits in the address
- `11110000` – Ignore the first 4 address bits
- `00001111` – Match the last 4 address bits
- `11111111` – Ignore all bits within the octet

- `11111100` – Ignore the first 6 address bits

Take a look at *Table 16.1*, applying a `0.0.255.255` wildcard mask to a 32-bit address:

	Decimal	**Binary**			
IP Address	192.168.1.0	11000000	10101000	00000001	00000000
Wildcard	0.0.0.255	00000000	00000000	11111111	11111111
Result Address	192.168.0.0	11000000	10101000	00000000	00000000

Table 16.1: Wildcard masking example 1

As shown in *Table 16.1*, the wildcard mask of `0.0.255.255` is used to match the first 16 bits in the address. The 0s within the wildcard mask indicate a match, while the 1s indicate the router should ignore the corresponding bits in the address.

Take a look at *Table 16.2* to learn how to match all corresponding bits in an address:

	Decimal	**Binary**			
IP Address	172.16.10.1	10101100	00010000	00001010	00000001
Wildcard	0.0.0.0	00000000	00000000	00000000	00000000
Result Address	172.16.10.1	10101100	00010000	00001010	00000001

Table 16.2: Wildcard masking example 2

As shown in *Table 16.2*, the wildcard mask of `0.0.0.0` is used to match all corresponding bits in the address. This ensures the exact IP address of `172.16.10.1` must match the ACL.

Calculating the Wildcard Mask

Calculating the wildcard mask is an easy technique that will quickly provide you with a wildcard when configuring ACLs. To calculate the wildcard mask, simply subtract the subnet mask from `255.255.255.255`.

In this example, imagine you want to permit access to all users within the `192.168.20.0/24` network. Since the subnet mask is `255.255.255.0`, we can subtract the subnet mask from the address `255.255.255.255`, as shown in *Figure 16.7*:

Broadcast Address	255	255	255	255
Subnet Mask	– 255	255	255	0
Wildcard Mask	0	0	0	255

Figure 16.7: Calculating wildcard mask

Your resulting wildcard mask is `0.0.0.255`. This allows you to create the following ACL statement:

```
Router(config)#access-list 10 permit 192.168.20.0 0.0.0.255
```

In the next example, imagine you want to deny traffic from all users within the `172.16.24.64/28` network. The subnet mask is `255.255.255.240`. You can use the same technique as the previous example:

Broadcast Address		255	255	255	255
Subnet Mask	−	255	255	255	240
Wildcard Mask		0	0	0	15

Figure 16.8: Calculating wildcard mask

The resulting wildcard mask is `0.0.0.15`. This allows you to create the following ACL statement:

```
Router(config)#access-list 10 deny 172.16.24.64 0.0.0.15
```

Sometimes, working with wildcard masks can be a bit complex. What if you need to allow a specific single-host device, such as `192.168.1.10`, within an ACL? Rather than using the `0.0.0.0` wildcard mask, you can use the `host` keyword command, as shown here:

```
Router(config)#access-list 20 permit host 192.168.1.10
```

The `host` keyword command simply states that all bits within the address must match within the ACL.

In another scenario, you may need to create an ACL to ignore the entire IPv4 address or accept any addresses. Your typical ACE statement will be `0.0.0.0 255.255.255.255`; however, we can use the `any` keyword command as a shortcut to represent the entire statement, as shown:

```
Router(config)#access-list 30 permit any
```

The preceding ACL simply states to permit any traffic from any source address or network. In the next section, we will discuss some important guidelines and best practices when creating ACLs.

ACL Guidelines and Best Practices

Creating and configuring ACLs on a router can be somewhat complex and a bit confusing at first until you get the hang of it. In this section, you will learn about some guidelines and best practices to help you create and implement ACLs efficiently on a Cisco IOS router.

The first rule of thumb is that you need to know the three Ps when applying ACLs on a router:

- One ACL per protocol (IPv4 or IPv6)
- One ACL per direction (in or out)
- One ACL per interface

You cannot have two ACLs on the same interface filtering inbound IPv4 traffic. You cannot have the same ACL filtering inbound and outbound traffic on the same interface. However, you can have two different ACLs on the same interface, where one ACL is filtering inbound traffic while the other is filtering outbound traffic.

Use the following guidelines when considering ACLs on a router:

- ACLs should be applied on your edge router on the network to filter traffic between your internal network and the internet
- ACLs should be applied on a router that is connected between two or more different networks for the purpose of controlling traffic entering and leaving a network
- Use ACLs to filter specific traffic types between networks

The following are some best practices when creating ACLs on your network routers:

- The ACLs should be aligned with your organization's security policies
- When creating an ACL, ensure you use the `remark` command to insert a description and the purpose of the ACL for future reference
- Use a text editor to help you create, edit, and save ACLs
- Before creating ACLs, ensure they are tested within a lab or development environment before applying them to a production network

After you have created ACLs on your router, the next step is to apply them to the appropriate interface. ACL placement is very important. The following are some recommendations based on the type of ACL:

- **Standard ACLs** are configured to filter (permit or deny) traffic originating from a single host or network. This type of ACL should be placed closest to the destination of the packets on the network.
- **Extended ACLs** are configured to filter specific traffic types on a network. Therefore, it's recommended to place this type of ACL closest to the source where the traffic is originating. This method will simply filter the denied traffic type before it is processed and forwarded by the router.

Take a look at the network topology shown in *Figure 16.9* to gain a better understanding of ACL placement:

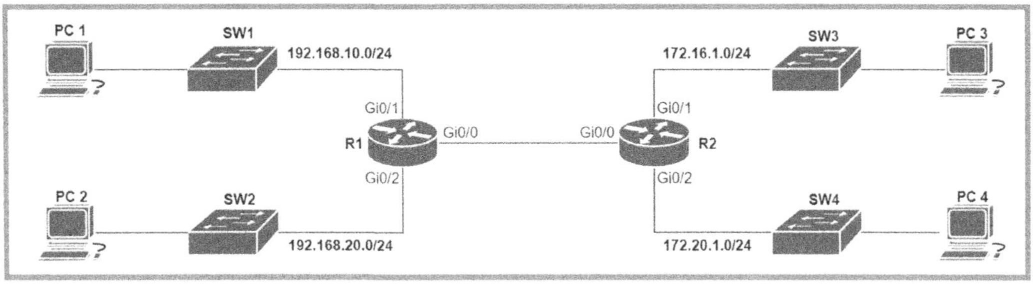

Figure 16.9: ACL placement

Based on the preceding topology, let's create the following scenarios to better understand the most suitable place ACLs should be applied on a router:

- If you want to filter traffic from only the `192.168.20.0/24` network to the `172.16.1.0/24` network, the best place to apply the standard ACL will be on R2's outbound `GigabitEthernet 0/2` interface. The placement of this ACL will filter traffic that is destined only to the `172.20.1.0/24` network. If the ACL is placed on the R2's inbound `GigabitEthernet 0/0` interface, the ACL will filter traffic from `192.168.10.0/24` and `192.168.20.0/24`.
- If you want to filter FTP traffic originating from the `172.16.1.0/24` network to any destination, the most suitable place to apply the extended ACL will be on R2's inbound `GigabitEthernet 0/1` interface. The placement of this ACL will filter all FTP traffic originating from the `172.16.1.0/24` network only. If the ACL is placed on R2's outbound `GigabitEthernet 0/2` interface, it will filter traffic from both `172.16.1.0/24` and `172.20.1.0/24` networks.

In the next section, you will learn how to configure and apply standard ACLs on a Cisco IOS router.

Creating Standard ACLs

When creating a numbered standard ACL on a Cisco IOS router, the ACL must first be created on the device and then applied to an interface to filter traffic. Numbered standard ACLs use the following range of numbers:

- 1 to 99
- 1,300 to 1,999

To create a numbered standard ACL on a Cisco IOS router, use the `access-lists` global configuration command followed by a number within the range **1 to 99** or **1300 to 1999** on the device. With this range of numbers, there can be up to 798 unique standard ACLs on a single router.

The following is the full syntax used to create a numbered standard ACL:

```
Router(config)# access-list access-list-number [ deny | permit |
remark ] source [ source-wildcard ][ log ]
```

> **Note**
>
> The `remark` command will allow you to insert a description for the ACL and the `log` command will generate a syslog message when matches are found. Additionally, there can be more than one ACE within an ACL.

The following are some examples of numbered standard ACLs:

- `Router(config)#` access-list 10 permit host `172.16.1.5`
- `Router(config)#` access-list 20 deny `192.168.20.0 0.0.0.255`

To remove an ACL from a Cisco router, use the following instructions:

1. Use the `show access-lists` command within privileged EXEC mode to verify the exact ACL and its number that you want to remove.
2. Enter global configuration mode and use the `no access-lists` command with the ACL number. *Figure 16.10* shows an example of removing a numbered standard ACL:

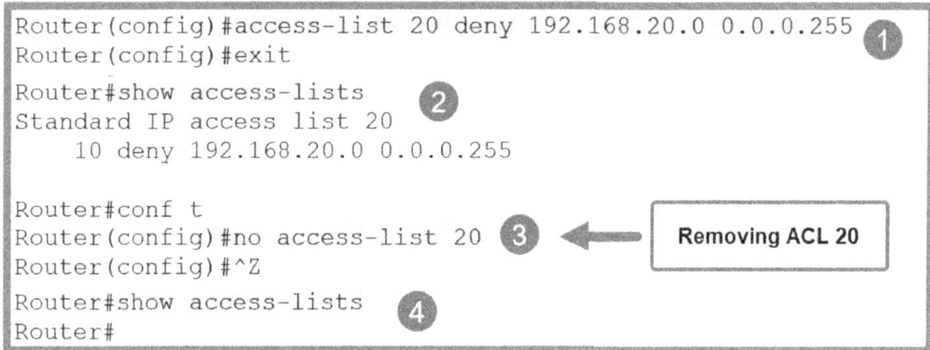

Figure 16.10: Removing an ACL

There is no need to specify the entire ACE or ACL; simply use the `no` command and the ACL number to delete an entire ACL from the `running-config` file.

After creating an ACL, you need to apply it to a router's interface to filter either inbound or outbound traffic. The following is the syntax to apply the ACL under `interface mode`:

```
Router(config-if)# ip access-group [ access-list-number | access-list-
name ] [ in | out ]
```

Figure 16.11 shows an example of applying a numbered ACL to an interface:

```
Router(config)#access-list 20 deny 192.168.20.0 0.0.0.255
Router(config)#interface GigabitEthernet 0/1
Router(config-if)#ip access-group 20 in
Router(config-if)#exit
```

Figure 16.11: Applying an ACL to an interface

To remove an ACL from a Cisco IOS router, use the following instructions:

1. Remove the ACL from the interface by using the `no ip access-group` command with the ACL number and its direction (in or out).
2. Enter global configuration mode and use the `no access-lists` command with the ACL number to remove the entire ACL from the device.

Sometimes, numbered ACLs can be slightly confusing when there are many ACLs on a router. The Cisco IOS allows us to create named standard ACLs, which make things easier for us.

The following are some guidelines when creating a named ACL:

- A named ACL can contain both letters and numbers
- It is recommended to use capital letters
- Named ACLs cannot have any spaces or punctuation characters

To create a named standard ACL, follow the given instructions:

1. Enter global configuration mode, and use the following syntax to create a named standard ACL:

   ```
   Router(config)#ip access-list standard name
   ```

   You will then enter a new mode – standard (`std`) named ACL (`nacl`) configuration mode.
2. Next, use the following syntax to create ACEs within the ACL:

   ```
   Router(config-std-nacl)# [ deny | permit | remark ] source [
   source-wildcard ][ log ]
   ```

Figure 16.12 shows an example of creating and applying a named standard ACL:

```
Router(config)#ip access-list standard Named-STD-ACL
Router(config-std-nacl)#permit 192.168.10.0 0.0.0.255
Router(config-std-nacl)#exit
Router(config)#interface GigabitEthernet 0/2
Router(config-if)#ip access-group Named-STD-ACL in
Router(config-if)#exit
```

Figure 16.12: Creating a named standard ACL

Having completed this section, you have gained an essential understanding of standard ACL operations and how to configure and apply them correctly on a Cisco device. In the next section, we will take a deeper look at creating extended ACLs.

Creating Extended ACLs

Extended ACLs are sometimes the preferred choice as they allow you to filter specific traffic types, in contrast with standard ACLs. Extended ACLs use the following range of numbers:

- 100 to 199
- 2,000 to 2,699

To create a numbered extended ACL on a Cisco IOS router, use the `access-lists` global configuration command followed by a number within the range 100 to 199 or 2,000 to 2,699 on the device.

The following is the full syntax used to create a numbered extended ACL:

```
Router(config)# access-list access-list-number [ deny | permit |
remark ] protocol [source source-wildcard] [operator port] [port-
number or name] [destination destination-wildcard] [operator port]
[port-number or name]
```

The following is a description of the new syntax used within an extended ACL:

- **Protocol**: Specifies the protocol type, such as IP, ICMP, TCP, UDP, and so on.
- **Operator**: Used to compare the source or destination ports. The `eq` operator means equal, `gt` means greater than, `lt` means less than, `neq` means not equal, and `range` allows you to specify a range of ports.
- **Port**: Allows you to indicate a source or destination port number.

The following are some examples of numbered extended ACLs:

- The following command will deny all FTP traffic from source network `192.168.1.0/24` that is going to any destination:

```
Router(config)# access-lists 100 deny tcp 192.168.1.0 0.0.0.255
any eq 20
Router(config)# access-lists 100 deny tcp 192.168.1.0 0.0.0.255
any eq 21
```

- The following command will block all ICMP traffic originating from the `172.16.1.0/24` that has a destination of `10.0.0.0/8`:

```
Router(config)# access-lists 101 deny icmp 172.16.1.0 0.0.0.244
10.0.0.0 0.255.255.255
```

To create a named extended ACL, use the following instructions:

1. Enter global configuration mode and use the following syntax to create a named extended ACL:

```
Router(config)#ip access-list extended name
```

   You will then enter a new mode – extended (`ext`) named ACL mode (`nacl`) configuration mode.

2. Next, use the following syntax to create ACEs within the ACL:

```
Router(config-ext-nacl)# [ deny | permit | remark ] protocol
[source source-wildcard] [operator port] [port-number or name]
[destination destination-wildcard] [operator port] [port-number
or name]
```

Figure 16.13 shows an example of creating and applying a named extended ACL:

```
Router(config)#ip access-list extended Ext-ACL
Router(config-ext-nacl)#permit tcp 192.168.1.0 0.0.0.255 172.16.1.0 0.0.0.255 eq 20
Router(config-ext-nacl)#permit tcp 192.168.1.0 0.0.0.255 172.16.1.0 0.0.0.255 eq 21
Router(config-ext-nacl)#exit
Router(config)#interface GigabitEthernet 0/2
Router(config-if)#ip access-group Ext-ACL in
Router(config-if)#exit
```

Figure 16.13: Creating a named extended ACL

Additionally, you can use various keywords rather than specifying an actual TCP/UDP port number after the operator (`eq`) command. *Figure 16.14* shows an example of some keywords that can be used in place of a TCP/UDP port number:

```
Router(config-ext-nacl)#permit tcp 192.168.1.0 0.0.0.255 172.16.1.0 0.0.0.255 eq ?
  <0-65535>  Port number
  domain     Domain Name Service (DNS, 53)
  ftp        File Transfer Protocol (21)
  pop3       Post Office Protocol v3 (110)
  smtp       Simple Mail Transport Protocol (25)
  telnet     Telnet (23)
  www        World Wide Web (HTTP, 80)
```

Various Keywords that can be used other than port numbers

Figure 16.14: Keywords

Please keep in mind that these keywords are only applicable to extended ACLs and their configurations. Having completed this section, you have gained essential knowledge on how to create extended ACLs. In the following section, you will gain hands-on experience of creating and applying both standard and extended ACLs in a Cisco environment.

Lab: Implementing a Standard Numbered ACL

In this hands-on lab, you will learn how to implement standard ACLs to filter traffic from a source host and network. *Figure 16.15* shows an organization network on the left that is connected to the internet via an **internet service provider** (**ISP**) on the right:

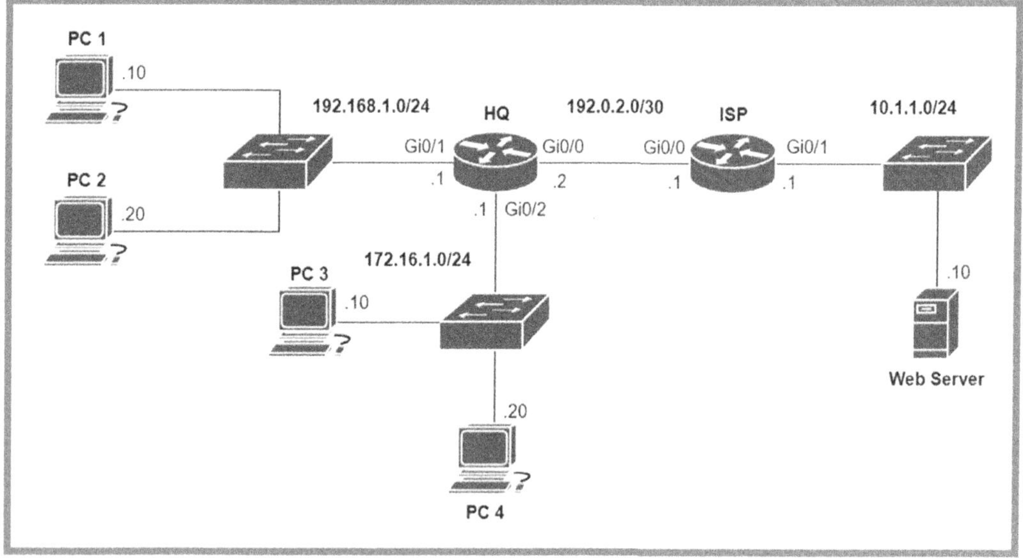

Figure 16.15: Standard ACL lab topology

The objective of this lab is to demonstrate how to apply standard number ACLs on a Cisco router to filter traffic between devices and networks. You'll use a numbered ACL to restrict traffic originating from all devices on the `192.168.1.0/24` network except PC 1, which is going to the `172.16.1.0/24` network.

For this lab, you will be using Cisco Packet Tracer to simulate the Cisco environment. To follow along, please download the pre-built lab template from the following link: `https://packt.link/CCNArepoCh16first`

Having opened the pre-built lab environment using Cisco Packet Tracer, use the following instructions to implement a standard numbered ACL on our HQ router:

1. Create a numbered ACL to only allow traffic from **PC 1** on the `192.168.1.0/24` network to the `172.16.1.0/24` network while restricting all other devices:

   ```
   HQ(config)# access-list 10 permit host 192.168.1.10
   HQ(config)# access-list 10 permit 10.1.1.0 0.0.0.255
   ```

   Please keep in mind that if you did not create a second ACE to permit traffic from the `10.1.1.0/24` network to `172.16.10/24`, **PC 3** and **PC 4** will not be able to reach devices on the internet side of the topology.

2. Apply ACL 10 to the interface closest to the destination of the traffic and configure it to filter outbound traffic only:

   ```
   HQ(config)# interface GigabitEthernet 0/2
   HQ(config-if)# ip access-group 10 out
   HQ(config-if)# exit
   ```

3. Using the `show access-lists` command, you can verify the ACEs and their sequential order as shown in *Figure 16.16*:

   ```
   HQ#show access-lists
   Standard IP access list 10
       10 permit host 192.168.1.10
       20 permit 10.1.1.0 0.0.0.255

   HQ#
   ```

   Figure 16.16: Verifying ACLs

4. Using the `show ip interface` command, you can verify the ACL that is assigned on an interface and the direction it is filtering traffic:

```
HQ#show ip interface gigabitethernet 0/2
GigabitEthernet0/2 is up, line protocol is up (connected)
  Internet address is 172.16.1.1/24
  Broadcast address is 255.255.255.255
  Address determined by setup command
  MTU is 1500 bytes
  Helper address is not set
  Directed broadcast forwarding is disabled
  Outgoing access list is 10
  Inbound  access list is not set
  Proxy ARP is enabled
```

ACL 10

Figure 16.17: Verifying ACLs on an interface

As shown in the preceding snippet, ACL 10 is applied to filter traffic leaving interface `GigabitEthernet 0/2` on the router.

5. Check whether ACL 10 will allow **PC 1** to communicate with devices on the `172.16.1.0/24` network:

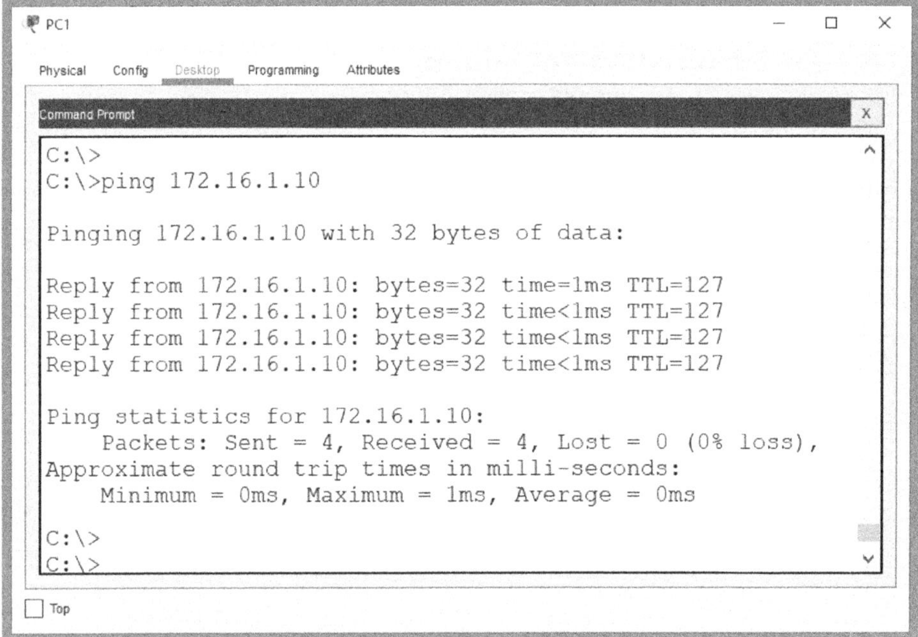

Figure 16.18: Verifying connectivity

As shown in *Figure 16.18*, **PC 1** is able to communicate with **PC 3** on the `172.16.1.0/24` network.

6. Test whether your ACL is working correctly to restrict other devices on `192.168.1.0/24`. Try to ping from **PC 2** to any device within the `172.16.1.0/24` network:

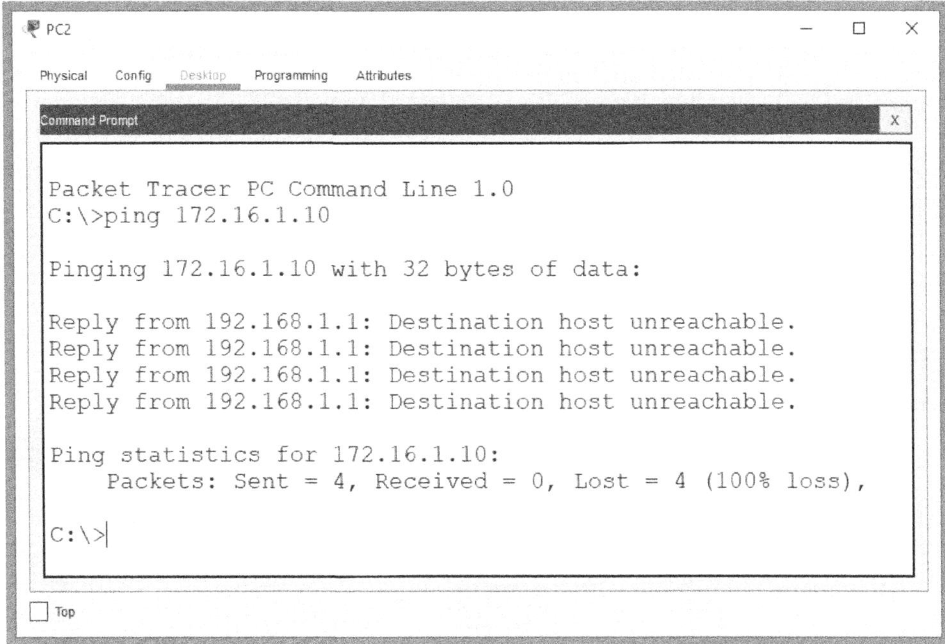

Figure 16.19: Checking connectivity

As expected, PC 2 is unable to communicate with devices on the `172.16.1.0/24` network, simply because your ACL was configured to allow only PC 1 with the host address of `192.168.1.10`.

7. You can use the `show access-lists` command once more to verify which ACEs have been matched within an ACL:

```
HQ#show access-lists
Standard IP access list 10
    10 permit host 192.168.1.10 (4 match(es))
    20 permit 10.1.1.0 0.0.0.255

HQ#
```

Figure 16.20: Verify matches on ACEs

As shown in the preceding snippet, the `permit` ACE in ACL 10 has been matched four times simply because 4 ICMP messages were sent from **PC 1** to **PC 3**. To clear the ACL counters, use the `clear access-list counters` command.

During this lab, you have learned how to create a standard numbered ACL on a Cisco IOS router to filter traffic between networks. In the next lab, you will use a named ACL to only permit traffic from the `172.16.1.0/24` network to access devices on the internet side of the topology.

Lab: Configuring a Standard Named ACL

In this lab, you will learn how to configure a standard named ACL to allow devices on the `172.16.1.0/24` network to communicate with devices on the internet side of your network topology. Your ACL will ensure devices on the `192.168.1.0.24` network will be denied. To complete this exercise, you will be continuing from where you left off in the previous lab.

You will be using the topology shown in *Figure 16.21* and the same guidelines as before:

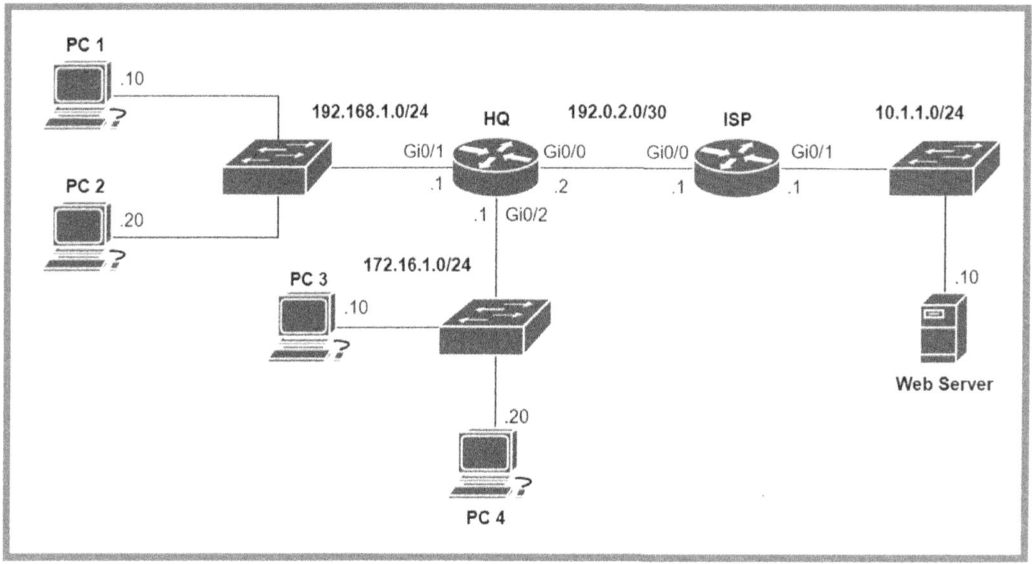

Figure 16.21: Standard ACL lab topology

The objective of this lab is to demonstrate how to apply standard named ACLs on a Cisco router to filter traffic between devices and networks. To follow along, please download the pre-built lab template from the following link: `https://packt.link/CCNArepoCh16second`

To get started with configuring a standard named ACL to meet our objective, use the following instructions:

1. Use the following command to create a standard named ACL, named `INT_Access`, as shown here:

```
HQ(config)# ip access-list standard INT_Access
```

2. Use the `remark` command to insert a description for the ACL:

```
HQ(config-std-nacl)# remark Allowing devices on the
172.16.1.0/24 network only.
```

3. Create an ACE with a placement of `10` to allow all traffic from the `172.16.1.0/24` network:

```
HQ(config-std-nacl)# 10 permit 172.16.1.0 0.0.0.255
HQ(config-std-nacl)# exit
```

4. Assign the `INT_Access` ACL to the outbound interface and configure it to filter traffic leaving the HQ router:

```
HQ(config)# interface GigabitEthernet 0/0
HQ(config-if)# ip access-group INT_Access out
HQ(config-if)# exit
```

Verify whether devices on the `172.16.1.0/24` network are able to communicate with devices on the internet side of the topology. On PC 3, perform a ping test to the web server:

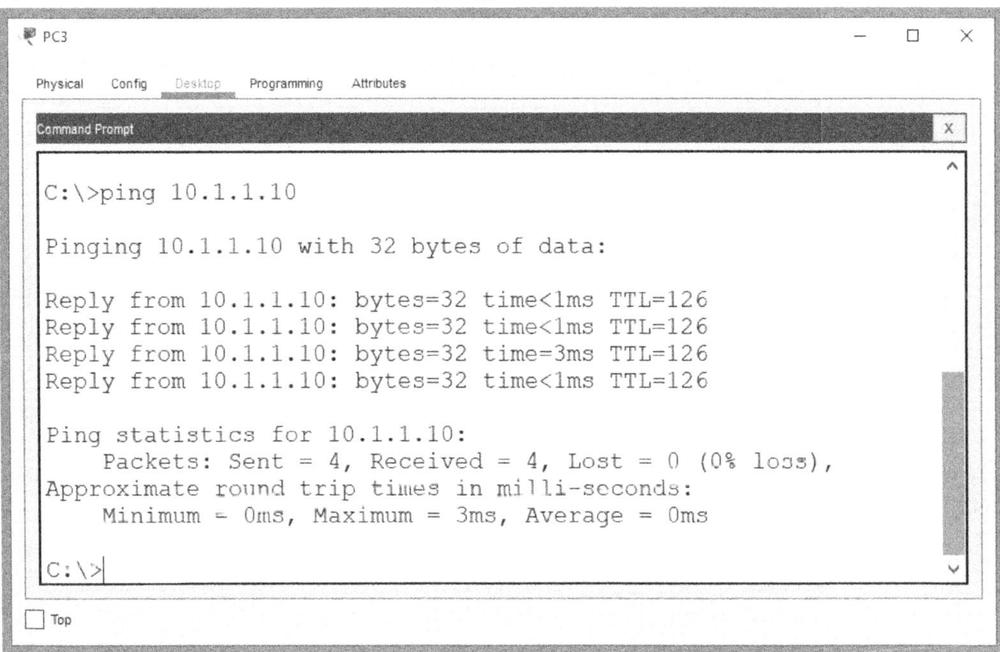

Figure 16.22: Connectivity test

As shown in the preceding snippet, PC 3 is able to communicate with the `10.1.1.0/24` network successfully.

5. Verify whether devices on the `192.168.1.0/24` network are able to reach devices on the `10.1.1.0/24` network. On PC 1, perform a ping test to the web server, as shown in *Figure 16.23*:

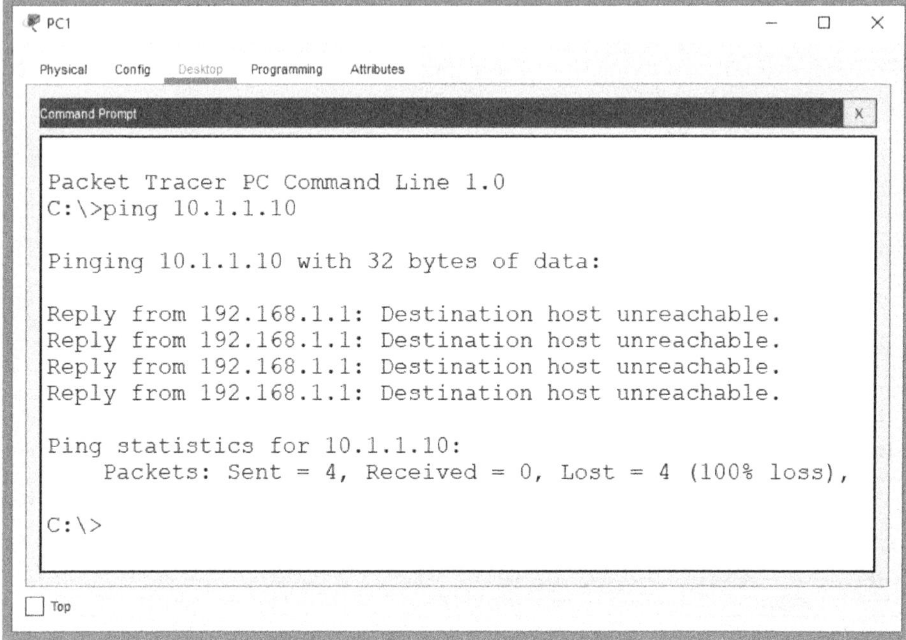

Figure 16.23: Connectivity restricted

As expected, your new ACL is working perfectly as devices on the `172.16.1.0/24` network are permitted to access and communicate with devices on the `10.1.1.0/24` network, while all other networks on the HQ router are denied.

6. Once more, we can use the `show ip interface` command to verify the ACL has been applied correctly on the interface as intended:

```
HQ#show ip interface gigabitEthernet 0/0
GigabitEthernet0/0 is up, line protocol is up (connected)
  Internet address is 192.0.2.2/30
  Broadcast address is 255.255.255.255
  Address determined by setup command
  MTU is 1500 bytes
  Helper address is not set
  Directed broadcast forwarding is disabled
  Outgoing access list is INT_Access
  Inbound  access list is not set
  Proxy ARP is enabled
  Security level is default
```

***INT_Access* ACL applied on the interface**

Figure 16.24: Verifying ACL placement on an interface

7. You can use the `show access-lists` command to verify the number of hits an ACE is receiving for an ACL:

```
HQ#show access-lists
Standard IP access list 10
    10 permit host 192.168.1.10
    20 permit 10.1.1.0 0.0.0.255 (4 match(es))
Standard IP access list INT_Access
    10 permit 172.16.1.0 0.0.0.255 (8 match(es))

HQ#
```

Figure 16.25: Verifying ACEs

Having completed this lab, you have gained the essential skills to configure and implement standard named ACLs on a Cisco IOS router. In the next lab, you will gain hands-on experience in restricting access to VTY lines on a router.

Lab: Securing VTY Lines Using ACLs

In this lab, you will learn how to use ACLs to restrict remote access on your Cisco IOS router to only specific hosts or devices on a network. To complete this exercise, you will be continuing from where you left off in the previous lab.

You will be using the following topology and the same guidelines as before:

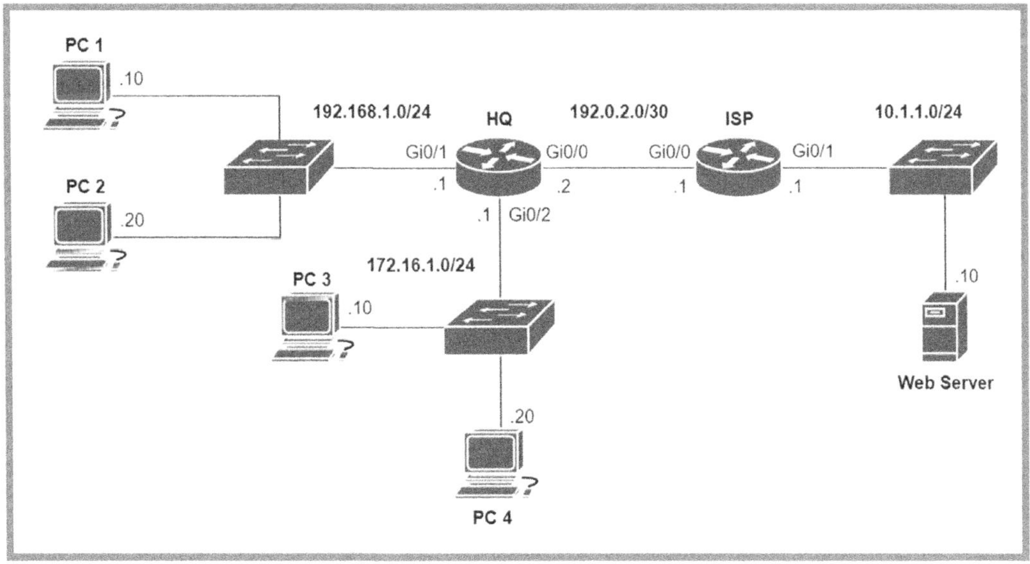

Figure 16.26: Standard ACL lab topology

To follow along, please download the pre-built lab template from the following link: `https://packt.link/CCNArepoCh16third`

To get started setting up secure remote access and implementing ACLs on the VTY lines, use the following instructions:

1. Configure a password on the **HQ** router using the `enable secret` command to restrict access to Privilege Exec mode:

```
Router(config)# enable secret cisco456
```

2. Change the default hostname of the HQ router:

```
Router(config)# hostname HQ
```

3. Join the HQ router onto a domain:

```
HQ(config)# ip domain-name ccnalab.local
```

4. Create a user account for remote access on the HQ router:

```
HQ(config)# username user1 secret sshpass
```

5. Generate RSA encryption keys to secure the SSH traffic:

```
HQ(config)# crypto key generate rsa general-keys modulus 1024
```

6. Configure the VTY lines on the HQ router to accept only SSH connections and check the local user database for authentication:

```
HQ(config)# line vty 0 15
HQ(config-line)# transport input ssh
HQ(config-line)# login local
HQ(config-line)# exit
```

Now that we have configured remote access with SSH on the HQ router, the following instructions will outline how to create an ACL to permit only PC 3 to SSH into the HQ router.

7. Create a standard named ACL using the name `Secure-VTY` as shown here:

```
HQ(config)# ip access-list standard Secure-VTY
```

8. Use the `remark` command to insert a description of the ACL and the ACEs:

```
HQ(config-std-nacl)# remark Securing incoming connections on VTY
lines
```

9. Create a `permit` statement to allow only PC 3 access to the HQ router:

```
HQ(config-std-nacl)# permit host 172.16.1.10
```

10. Insert another ACE to deny all other devices from establishing a remote session with the HQ router:

```
HQ(config-std-nacl)# deny any
HQ(config-std-nacl)# exit
```

11. Next, apply the `Secure-VTY` ACL on the VTY lines on the HQ router to filter inbound traffic on the virtual terminal lines:

```
HQ(config)# line vty 0 15
HQ(config-line)# access-class Secure-VTY in
HQ(config-line)# exit
```

12. Use the `show access-lists` command to verify the newly created ACL and its ACEs on the HQ router:

```
HQ#show access-lists
Standard IP access list 10
    10 permit host 192.168.1.10
    20 permit 10.1.1.0 0.0.0.255
Standard IP access list INT_Access
    10 permit 172.16.1.0 0.0.0.255
Standard IP access list Secure-VTY
    10 permit host 172.16.1.10
    20 deny any

HQ#
```

Figure 16.27: Verifying ACLs

13. We can use the `show running-config` command to also verify the ACLs on the router and the interface/lines they have been applied to:

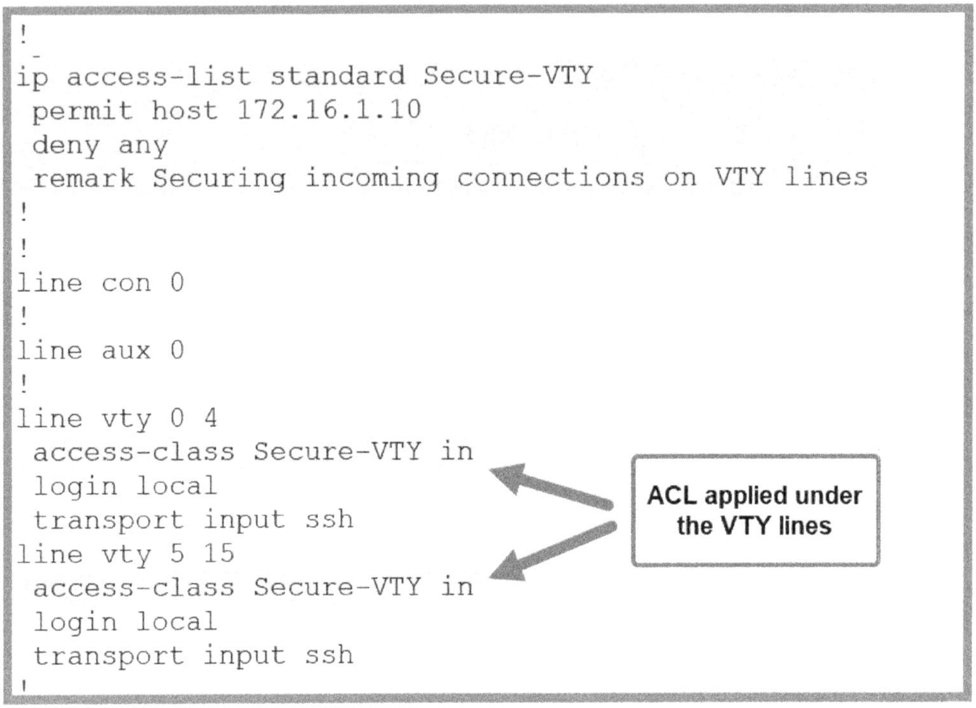

```
!
ip access-list standard Secure-VTY
 permit host 172.16.1.10
 deny any
 remark Securing incoming connections on VTY lines
!
!
line con 0
!
line aux 0
!
line vty 0 4
 access-class Secure-VTY in
 login local
 transport input ssh
line vty 5 15
 access-class Secure-VTY in
 login local
 transport input ssh
!
```


Figure 16.28: Checking the running-config file

14. Establish an SSH session from PC 1 to the HQ to verify whether the Secure-VTY ACL is working as expected. Click on `PC 1`, select the `Desktop` tab, and click on `Telnet/SSH Client`:

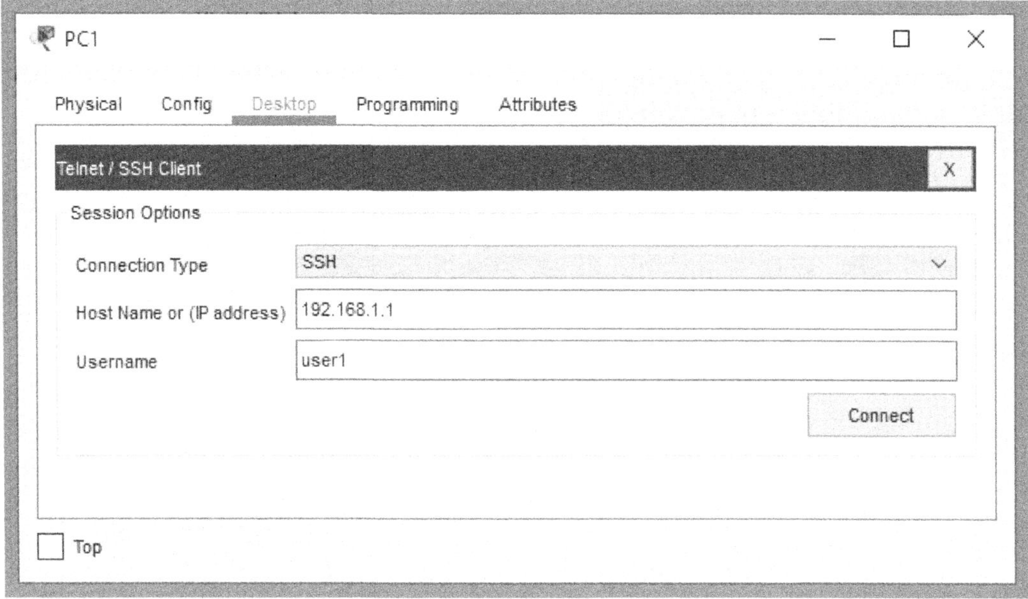

Figure 16.29: Telnet/SSH client

Insert the IP address of the router, choose the SSH protocol, and set the username, as shown in the preceding snippet. The HQ router will deny the connection from PC 1 or any device that is located on the `192.168.1.0/24` network.

Figure 16.30 shows the HQ router has terminated the SSH session because the ACL on the VTY lines restricted access to the router:

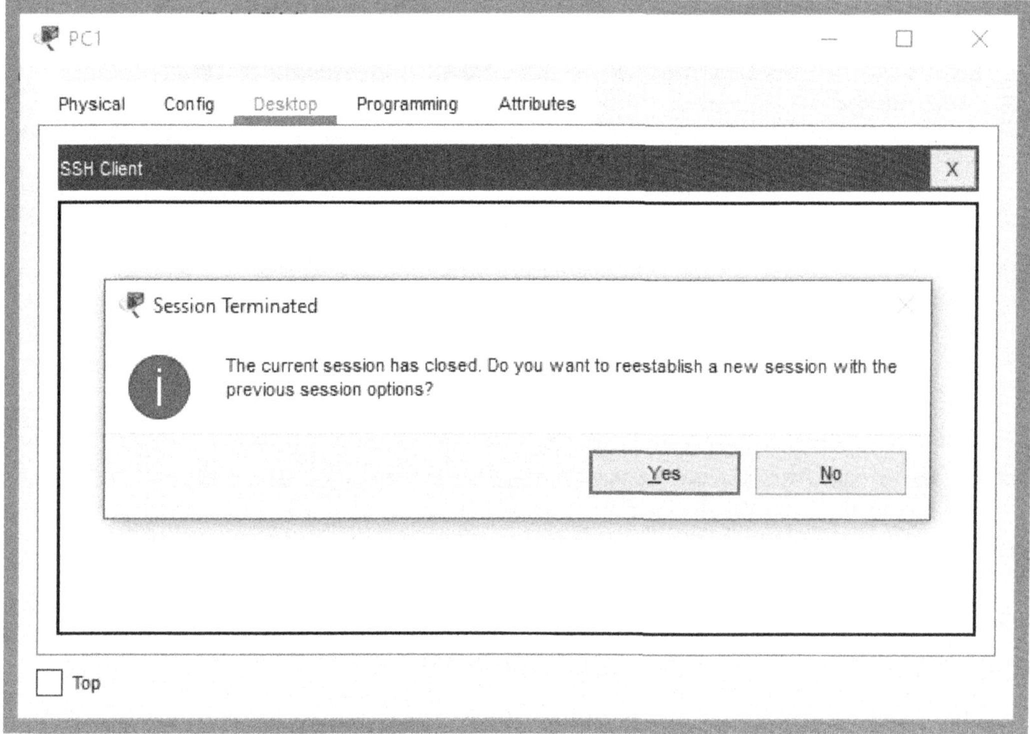

Figure 16.30: Session terminated

15. Attempt to establish an SSH session from PC 3 to the HQ router:

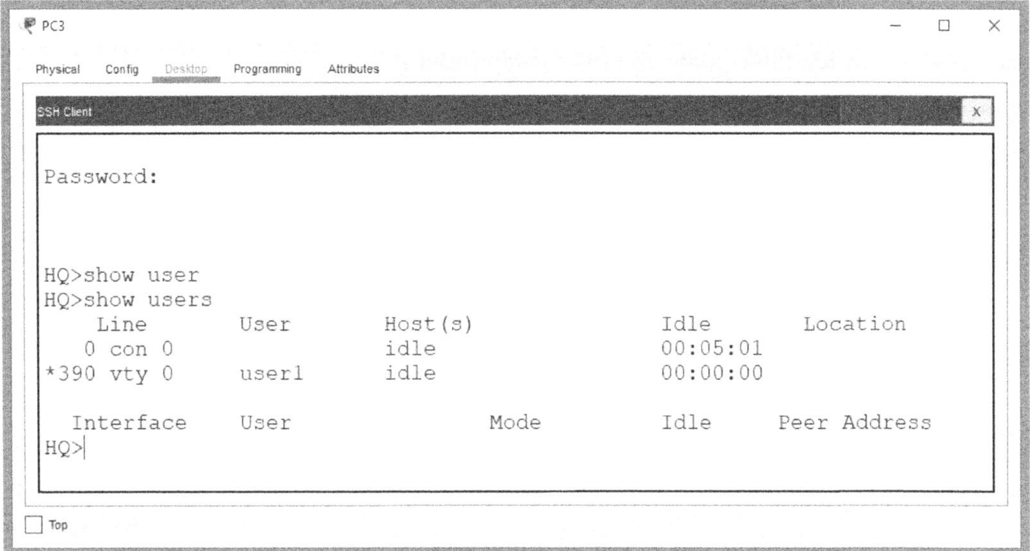

Figure 16.31: Remote access

As shown in *Figure 16.31*, PC 3 is able to remotely connect to the HQ router.

16. Use the `show access-lists` command to verify the ACLs and their entries on a router:

```
HQ#show access-lists
Standard IP access list 10
    10 permit host 192.168.1.10
    20 permit 10.1.1.0 0.0.0.255
Standard IP access list INT_Access
    10 permit 172.16.1.0 0.0.0.255
Standard IP access list Secure-VTY
    10 permit host 172.16.1.10 (2 match(es))
    20 deny any (32 match(es))

HQ#
```

Figure 16.32: Verifying ACLs

Having completed this lab, you have gained the hands-on skills to implement ACLs to secure the VTY lines on a Cisco IOS router. In the next lab, you will learn how to implement extended ACLs.

Lab: Implementing Extended ACLs

In this lab, you will learn how to configure an extended ACL to restrict certain traffic types between networks. To complete this exercise, you will continue from where we left off in the previous lab.

You will be using the topology shown in *Figure 16.33* and the same guidelines as before:

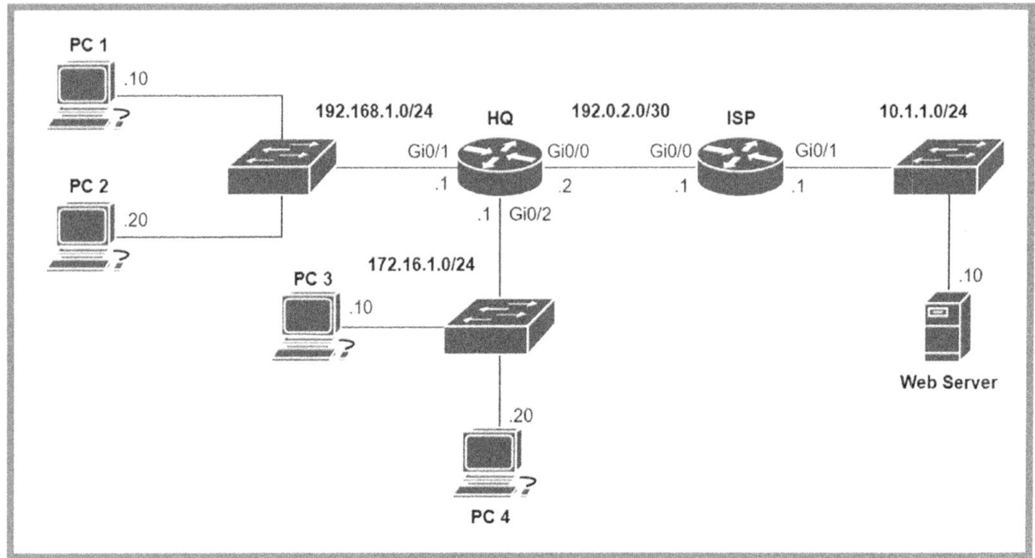

Figure 16.33: Standard ACL lab topology

The objective of this lab is to filter FTP traffic between the `172.16.1.0/24` network and the web server. However, we want to permit only PC 4 to use FTP while blocking all others within the network. To follow along with this exercise, please download the pre-built lab topology using the following link: `https://packt.link/CCNArepoCh16fourth`

To get started setting up secure remote access and implementing ACLs on the VTY lines, use the following instructions:

1. Configure the FTP service on the server. Click on `Server`, select the `Services` tab, then `FTP`, create a user account with the privileges shown in *Figure 16.34*, and click `Save`:

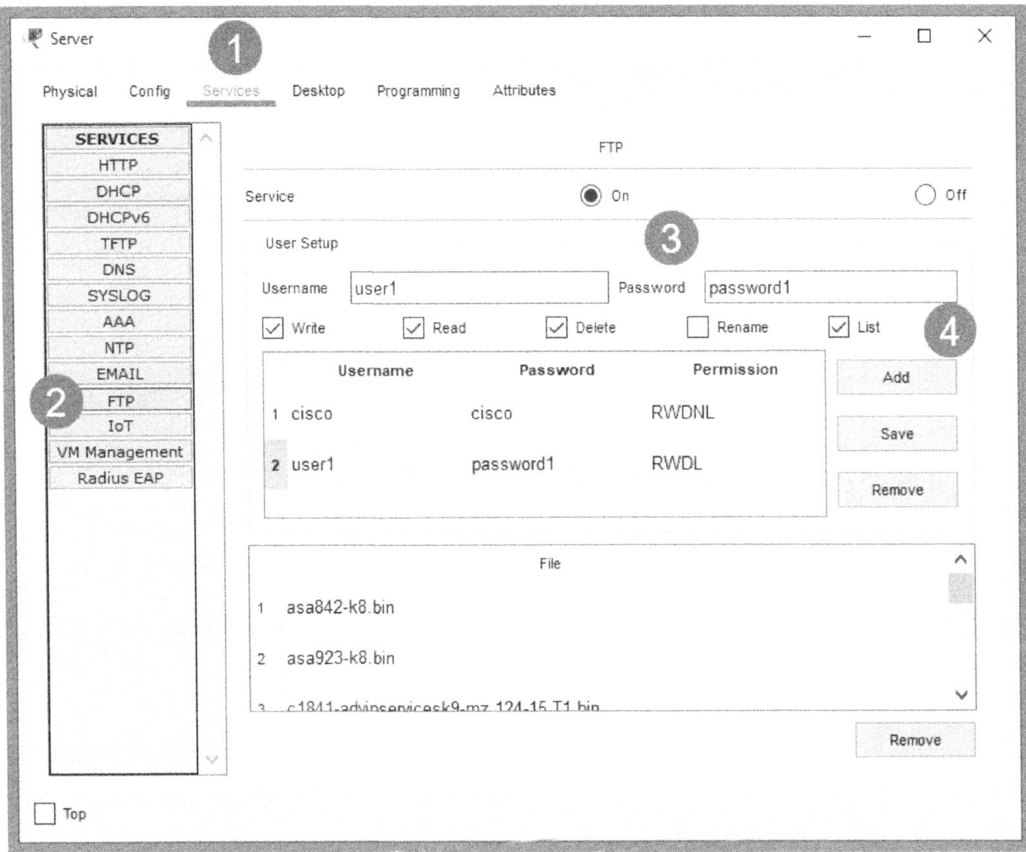

Figure 16.34: FTP server configuration

2. Attempt to remotely access the FTP server from PC 4 to verify connectivity and that FTP is working correctly, as shown in *Figure 16.35*:

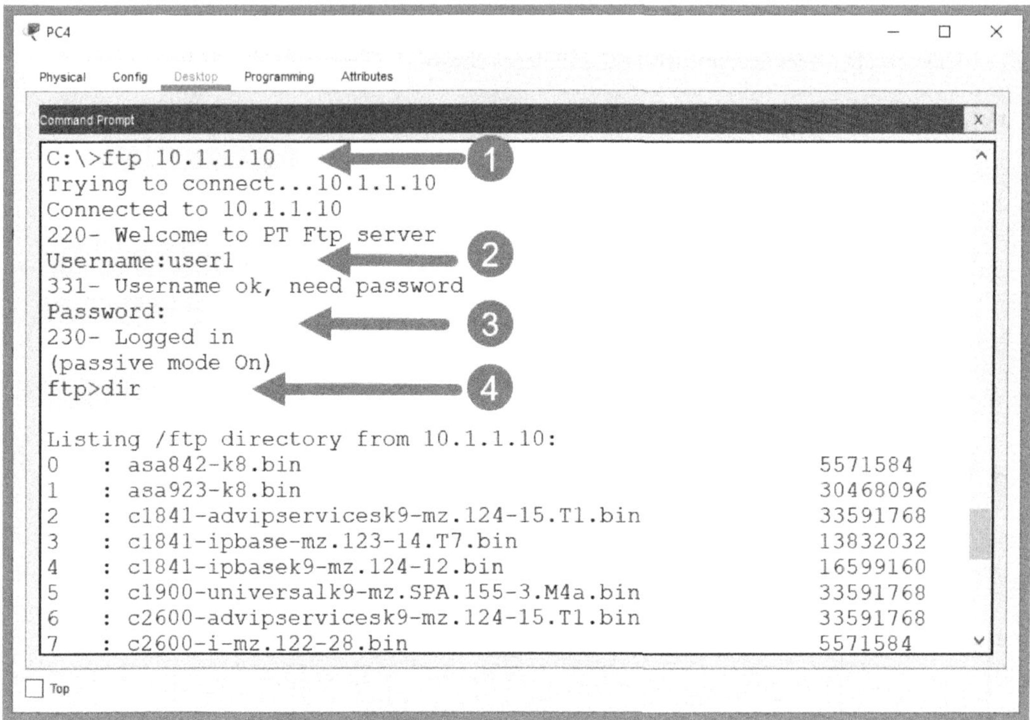

Figure 16.35: Verifying FTP

As shown in *Figure 16.35*, we are able to authenticate to the FTP server and execute various FTP commands.

3. Use the following commands to create an extended named ACL and add a description:

```
HQ(config)# ip access-list extended Restrict-FTP
HQ(config-ext-nacl)# remark Restricting FTP service to only PC 4
```

Create an ACE with a placement value of 10 to deny only PC 3 from accessing any remote FTP servers:

```
HQ(config-ext-nacl)# 10 deny tcp host 172.16.1.10 any eq 20
HQ(config-ext-nacl)# 10 deny tcp host 172.16.1.10 any eq 21
```

1. Create another ACE using a placement value of 20 to allow all other IP traffic types originating from the `172.16.1.0/24` network:

   ```
   HQ(config-ext-nacl)# 20 permit ip any any
   HQ(config-ext-nacl)# exit
   ```

2. Apply the extended ACL on the inbound interface `GigabitEthernet 0/2` on the HQ router:

```
HQ(config)# interface gigabitEthernet 0/2
HQ(config-if)# ip access-group Restrict-FTP in
HQ(config-if)# exit
```

   Please keep in mind that it's recommended to apply extended ACLs close to the source of the traffic, while standard ACLs are to be applied closest to the destination of the traffic.

3. Let's use the `show access-lists` command to verify the ACLs, as shown in *Figure 16.36*:

```
HQ#show access-lists Restrict-FTP
Extended IP access list Restrict-FTP
    deny tcp host 172.16.1.10 any eq ftp
    deny tcp host 172.16.1.10 any eq 20
    permit ip any any

HQ#
```

Figure 16.36: Verifying ACLs

4. Next, head on over to PC 3 to verify connectivity to the server and check whether PC 3 is able to access the FTP service, as shown in *Figure 16.37*:

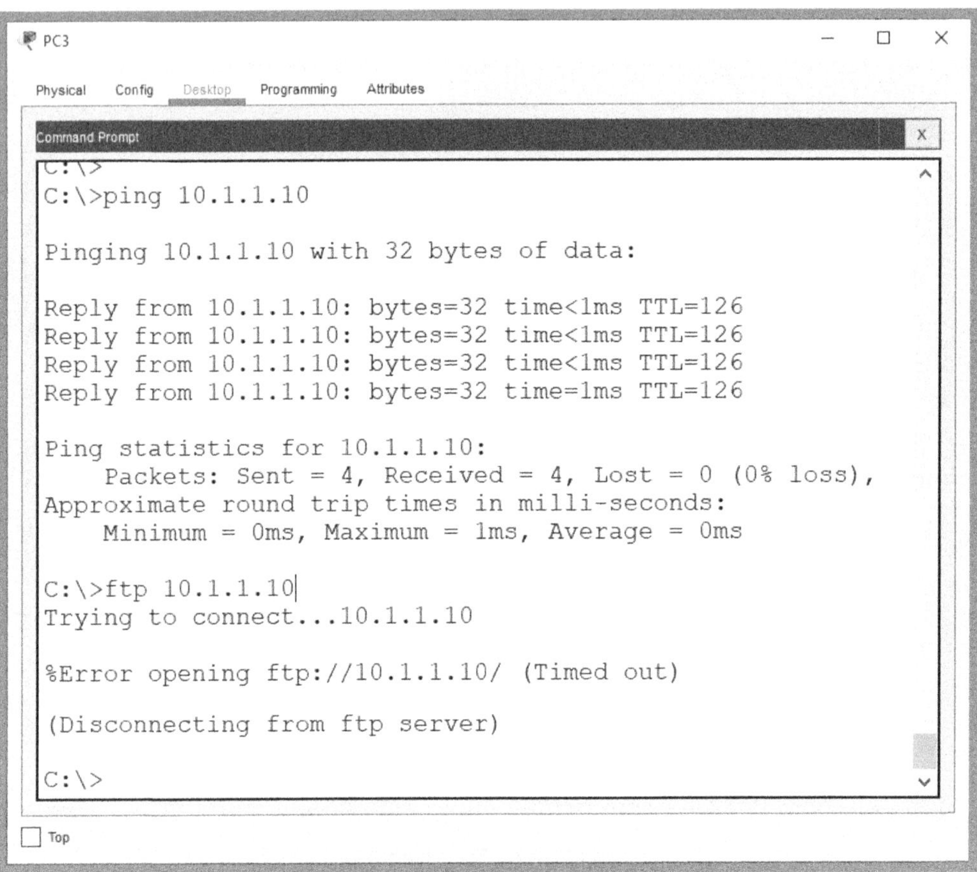

Figure 16.37: PC 3 checking FTP

As shown in *Figure 16.37*, ICMP messages and other IP traffic are permitted between the `172.16.1.0/24` network and any remote networks. However, the ACL does not allow FTP traffic from PC 3 to any other remote devices.

5. Check whether PC 4 is able to access the remote FTP server:

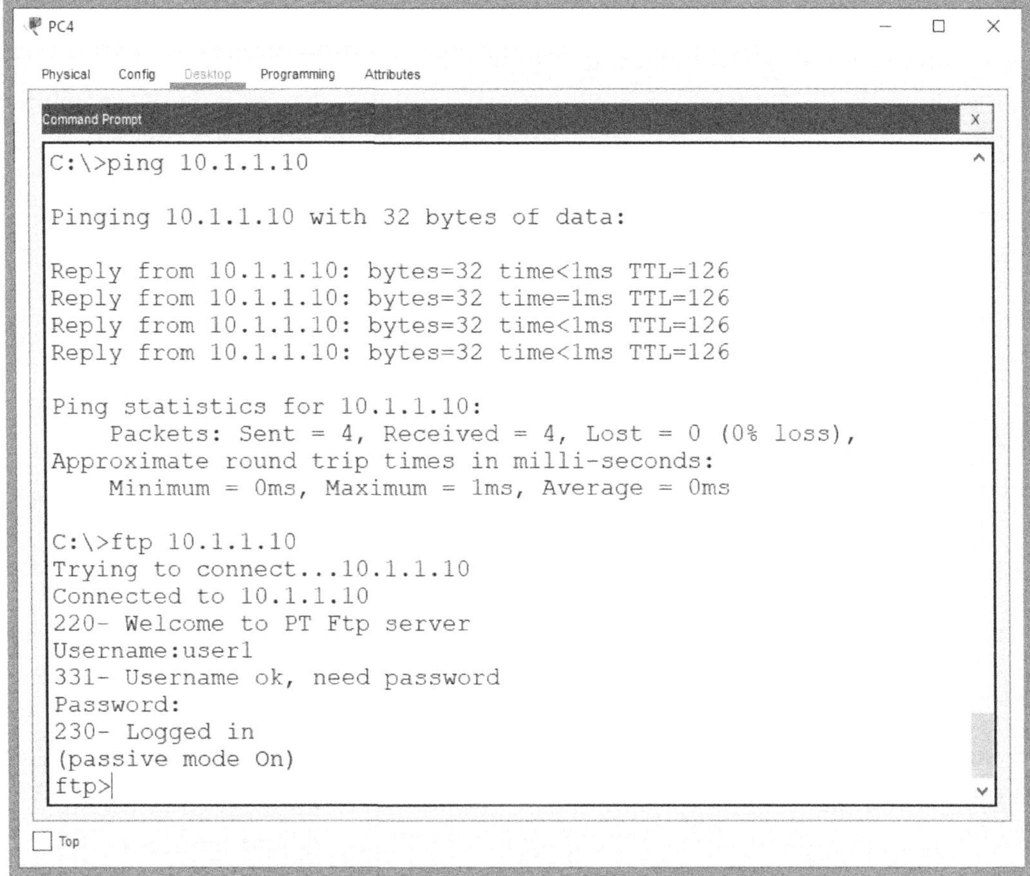

Figure 16.38: PC 4 checking FTP

As shown in *Figure 16.38*, PC 4 is able to access the FTP service on the remote server. This validates our extended ACL is configured correctly and working as expected.

6. Lastly, verify whether the number matches (hits/counts) on your extended ACL by using the `show access-lists` command shown in *Figure 16.39*:

```
HQ#show access-lists Restrict-FTP
Extended IP access list Restrict-FTP
    deny tcp host 172.16.1.10 any eq ftp (24 match(es))
    deny tcp host 172.16.1.10 any eq 20
    permit ip any any (11 match(es))
```

Figure 16.39: Verifying ACE matches

Having completed this lab, you have gained hands-on experience of configuring and implementing extended ACLs on a Cisco network to filter various traffic types between devices and networks.

Summary

In this chapter, you learned about the roles and functions that ACLs have in an enterprise network. Furthermore, you took a dive into discussing the operations of ACLs on a Cisco IOS router and how they are applied to an interface. The benefits of implementing ACLs help network professionals filter traffic between networks using a Cisco IOS router and perform basic packet-level filtering. In addition, you have learned how to efficiently configure and troubleshoot ACL operations on a network and determine the appropriate wildcard mask when setting up complex ACLs on a router. Lastly, you read about both standard and extended ACLs and how they can be used in various situations.

Having completed this chapter, you have learned how to configure both standard and extended ACLs on a Cisco router. Furthermore, you have learned how ACLs function and filter traffic based on their ACEs.

In the next chapter, Implementing Layer 2 and Wireless Security, you will learn about various layer 2 attacks and how to implement mitigation techniques and countermeasures.

Additional Reading

- Configuring IP ACLs: `https://www.cisco.com/c/en/us/support/docs/security/ios-firewall/23602-confaccesslists.html`
- Commonly used IP ACLs: `https://www.cisco.com/c/en/us/support/docs/ip/access-lists/26448-ACLsamples.html`

Exam Readiness Drill – Chapter Review Questions

Apart from mastering key concepts, strong test-taking skills under time pressure are essential for acing your certification exam. That's why developing these abilities early in your learning journey is critical.

Exam readiness drills, using the free online practice resources provided with this book, help you progressively improve your time management and test-taking skills while reinforcing the key concepts you've learned.

HOW TO GET STARTED

- Open the link or scan the QR code at the bottom of this page
- If you have unlocked the practice resources already, log in to your registered account. If you haven't, follow the instructions in *Chapter 19* and come back to this page.
- Once you log in, click the START button to start a quiz
- We recommend attempting a quiz multiple times till you're able to answer most of the questions correctly and well within the time limit.
- You can use the following practice template to help you plan your attempts:

Working On Accuracy		
Attempt	**Target**	**Time Limit**
Attempt 1	40% or more	Till the timer runs out
Attempt 2	60% or more	Till the timer runs out
Attempt 3	75% or more	Till the timer runs out
Working On Timing		
Attempt 4	75% or more	1 minute before time limit
Attempt 5	75% or more	2 minutes before time limit
Attempt 6	75% or more	3 minutes before time limit

The above drill is just an example. Design your drills based on your own goals and make the most out of the online quizzes accompanying this book.

First time accessing the online resources? 🔓

You'll need to unlock them through a one-time process. **Head to** *Chapter 19* **for instructions.**

Open Quiz	
`https://packt.link/ccnachap16`	
OR scan this QR code →	

17
Implementing Layer 2 and Wireless Security

Implementing network security practices and configurations should be second nature to network engineers. As a professional, it is important that you learn about various Layer 2 threats and how a threat actor can take advantage of vulnerabilities found within various Layer 2 network protocols.

In this chapter, you will learn about the need to use a Defense in Depth approach to secure both your users and devices on a network. Furthermore, you will learn how to identify various Layer 2 threats and attacks that are used to compromise an organization. Lastly, you will gain the knowledge and hands-on experience to implement various Layer 2 security controls to prevent and mitigate such attacks.

This chapter covers *Domain 5: Security Fundamentals*, objectives *5.7 Configure and verify Layer 2 security features (DHCP snooping, dynamic ARP inspection, and port security)*, *5.9 Describe wireless security protocols (WPA, WPA2, and WPA3)*, and *5.10 Configure and verify WLAN within the GUI using WPA2 PSK* of the *200-301 CCNA v1.1 Certification* exam.

In this chapter, you will learn about the following topics:

- Types of Layer 2 attacks on a network
- Protecting against Layer 2 threats
- Wireless network security

Let's dive in!

Types of Layer 2 Attacks on a Network

Throughout your journey, you will be exposed to many exciting technologies and environments. One such area an IT professional needs to know about is cybersecurity and network security. As a network engineer, you will not always be designing and implementing networking technologies but will also be responsible for the security of the network and its users. Newly emerging threats are surfacing as hackers are developing new strategies and tools to compromise their targets.

Nowadays, hackers do not just hack for fun. Some hackers create sophisticated malware such as ransomware to encrypt all the data on your computer and request that you pay a ransom to release your assets (data). Currently, there is a shortage of cybersecurity professionals in the world to combat the growing number of cyber threats on the internet. As a network engineer, you also play an important role in helping organizations secure their network and prevent various types of cyber threats and attacks.

In the following sections, you will learn about various network attacks and how using a multilayered approach such as Defense in Depth can be used to reduce the risk of a cyber attack.

Network Attacks

Every day, you read about how large and small organizations becoming victims of cyber attacks. As the former CEO of Cisco, John Chambers, once said back in 2015, *"There are two types of companies: those who have been hacked, and those who do not yet know they have been hacked."* This statement is accurate, as many organizations do not pay a great amount of attention to their network security posture. Some think that their organization is 100% protected or that their network has nothing valuable for attackers.

In reality, no system or network is 100% secure. There are many vulnerabilities that exist – those we know about and others we have not yet discovered. The great challenge we face as security professionals is to discover all hidden vulnerabilities before a threat actor such as a hacker has the opportunity to do so.

Each system and network has something valuable. A smartphone has gigabytes of valuable data about its user – geolocation, contact details, images and videos, logs about all activities, and much more. On a network, your network devices and systems store data as they exchange messages. Your network switches and routers store **media access control** (**MAC**) and IP addresses, contain user accounts for remote access, log messages of various transactions such as forwarding of frames and packets, and so on. To a hacker, such data is very valuable.

> **Note**
>
> Staying up to date with the latest cybersecurity news can be somewhat challenging. Checking the **Hacker News** website for the latest cyber news is one way to stay in the loop: https://thehackernews.com.

Organizations are usually victims of the following cyber attacks:

- Data breaches
- Malware
- **Distributed denial of service** (**DDoS**)

The most valuable asset in any organization today is data. Hackers are not just hacking for fun anymore. Well, some still do, but others are changing hacking into an organized crime. Threat actors aim to gain access to your network and steal your data. Once an attacker is able to exfiltrate data from your computers or servers, the hacker can publish or sell your organization's confidential records on the **Dark web** or to your competitor.

Sometimes, a threat actor such as a hacker, may develop malware to compromise your systems and networks. Some malware can hold your data hostage, such as ransomware and crypto-malware. These types of malware are designed to exploit a vulnerability within your system, compromise the host machine, and encrypt all the data on the local disk drive, except the operating system. One such ransomware is **WannaCry**, which exploited a vulnerability within the Microsoft Windows operating system and took advantage of a security weakness in SMB 1.0, as defined by Microsoft Security Bulletin **MS17-010**. Once the system was compromised, the ransomware presented a window on the user's desktop, requesting a ransom to be paid in bitcoins.

> **Note**
> To learn more about Microsoft Security Bulletin **MS17-010**, please see the following URL: https://docs.microsoft.com/en-us/security-updates/securitybulletins/2017/ms17-010.

Sometimes, threat actors may not want to gain access or compromise a system. Some hackers may want to disrupt an organization's services or resources. They may execute their idea by launching a DDoS attack from multiple geographic sources. Sometimes, the attack may be coordinated by a group of hackers or perhaps be done using a botnet.

> **Note**
> To view recorded DDoS attacks around the globe, check out **Digital Attack Map** using this URL: www.digitalattackmap.com.

For instance, an organization's website may be the target of a threat action. Sometimes, hacktivists organize among themselves to take down various websites and disrupt services as a way of protesting online about a social or political cause.

Preventing all types of cyber attacks is challenging. In the following section, you will learn about a strategic approach to reduce the risk of cyber threats and attacks on a network.

Defense in Depth

Having a single layer of security to protect your organization is no longer efficient in stopping newly emerging threats. Many organizations implement a network-based firewall within their enterprise network and think they are well protected from all cyber threats. Others only implement a host-based anti-virus and host-based firewall on their employees' devices and think they are safe as well. These are just some examples of using a single-layer approach to protecting assets within an organization. This method of using a single component such as a network-based firewall or anti-malware simply does not cut it anymore to combat cyber attacks and threats.

Using a Defense in Depth approach is where a multi-layered strategy can help safeguard an organization and its users. A Defence in Depth approach ensures multiple security components are implemented to protect all assets, including data, and secure communication methods. In addition to using a network-based firewall and anti-malware protection, you could implement email and web security appliances to filter both inbound and outbound threats and a **network-based and host-based intrusion prevention system** (**NIPS and HIPS**) to detect any threats as they pass through your network.

One recommended security appliance is a **next-generation firewall** (**NGFW**). This security appliance has the ability to perform stateful packet inspection and application visibility/control for all inbound and outbound network traffic.

Within some companies, there are employees who work remotely and require access to the corporate network. One such solution for remote workers is using either a VPN-enabled router or a firewall appliance with remote access VPN capabilities. Accessing the corporate network over an untrusted network is not a good thing. A **virtual private network** (**VPN**) is the solution to ensure your remote workers access the corporate network securely.

In the following sub-sections, you will learn more about endpoint protection, and Cisco's email and web security appliances.

Layer 2 Threats

Network professionals commonly implement various network security solutions to keep their corporate network safe from threat actors. Such network solutions may include network-based firewall appliances, **intrusion prevention systems** (**IPSes**), and even VPNs for remote workers. However, such devices and components usually protect data between Layer 3 and Layer 7 of the OSI model.

If layers such as Layer 2 of the OSI model are compromised by an attacker, the upper layers are also compromised. Imagine an attacker is able to intercept all traffic such as frames at Layer 2 within your corporate network. Then, the security implemented to protect the upper layers will not be able to prevent the attack.

Figure 17.1 shows both the OSI reference model and the TCP/IP protocol suite:

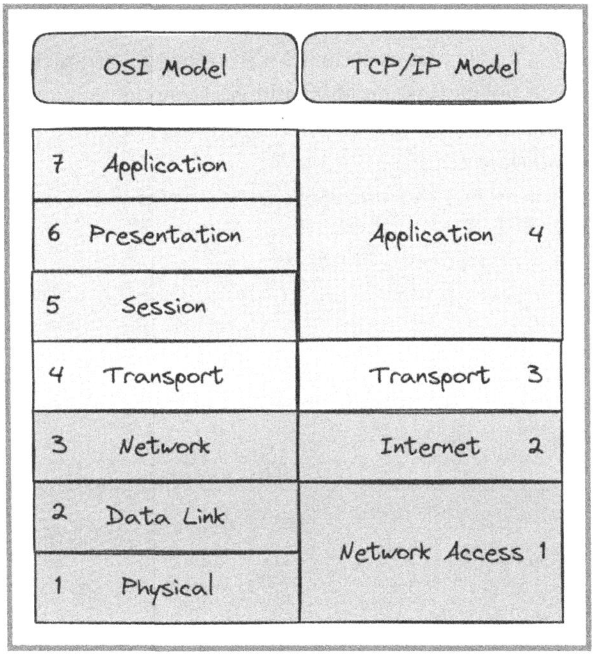

Figure 17.1: Data Link layer

To protect Layer 2, Cisco has implemented several Layer 2 attack mitigation features in their switches. As a network engineer, it is important that you learn about the various types of attacks that occur at Layer 2 and how to implement security features on Cisco switches to mitigate such attacks.

In the following sections, you will learn about various types of Layer 2 attacks that can occur on an enterprise network and how to implement countermeasures to safeguard your network.

CAM Table Overflow

Switches are networking devices that allow you to connect end devices such as computers to a network and access resources. Additionally, switches can forward messages (frames) to their destination by simply recording the source and destination MAC address found in each inbound message. For each frame to enter a switch's interface, the source MAC address is populated within the switch's MAC address table, as shown in *Figure 17.2*:

```
SW1#show mac address-table dynamic
          Mac Address Table
-------------------------------------------

Vlan    Mac Address       Type        Ports
----    -----------       --------    -----

  10    0006.2a88.7218    DYNAMIC      Fa0/24
  10    00d0.ffbc.7202    DYNAMIC      Fa0/24
  10    00e0.b098.d202    DYNAMIC      Fa0/1
  20    0006.2a88.7218    DYNAMIC      Fa0/24
  20    00d0.ffbc.7202    DYNAMIC      Fa0/24
  20    00e0.f72b.9a51    DYNAMIC      Fa0/2
  30    0006.2a88.7218    DYNAMIC      Fa0/24
  30    00d0.ffbc.7202    DYNAMIC      Fa0/24
SW1#
```

Figure 17.2: MAC address table

As shown, the `show mac address-table` command is used to view a list of MAC addresses that were learned on a specific interface and VLAN. However, a switch stores MAC addresses on the **content addressable memory** (**CAM**) table. To put it simply, the CAM table does not have infinite storage capacity, and each switch has a limit to the number of MAC addresses it is able to store. An example is a Cisco switch, which may be able to store 8,000 addresses, while another model may be able to store more. Cisco IOS switches have a default aging/inactivity timer of 300 seconds (5 minutes) for any MAC address within the CAM table. If a switch detects no activity from a MAC address after 300 seconds, it will automatically remove it from the CAM table to make storage available for new addresses.

Figure 17.3 shows an example of the size of the CAM table for a Cisco IOSvL2 switch:

```
Switch#show mac address-table count

Mac Entries for Vlan 1:
---------------------------
Dynamic Address Count  : 0
Static  Address Count  : 0
Total Mac Addresses    : 0

Total Mac Address Space Available: 77818696

Switch#
```

Figure 17.3: Checking CAM table capacity

Keep in mind that not all models of Cisco switches have the same capacity of storage on their CAM table. Even though the figure seems to be very large in the preceding snippet, it is still a finite number. One vulnerability that exists is that if a switch receives more MAC addresses than it can possibly store, it will begin to flood all inbound messages (frames) out of all ports. Technically speaking, the switch becomes a hub on the network.

Attackers can flood unsolicited frames with fake source MAC addresses into a switch to fill the CAM table. When the CAM table is filled, the attacker does not stop the attack. The switch will begin to forward all inbound traffic out of all other interfaces. The attacker can capture all network traffic that is being forwarded out of the switch. This is known as a **CAM table overflow** attack.

> **Note**
>
> Since each interface can be assigned to a **virtual local area network** (**VLAN**), if an attacker floods unsolicited, bogus frames into a switch, during a CAM table overflow, the switch will only forward traffic to all other ports on the same VLAN.

Figure 17.4 shows an example of a network implant injecting bogus frames into a switch:

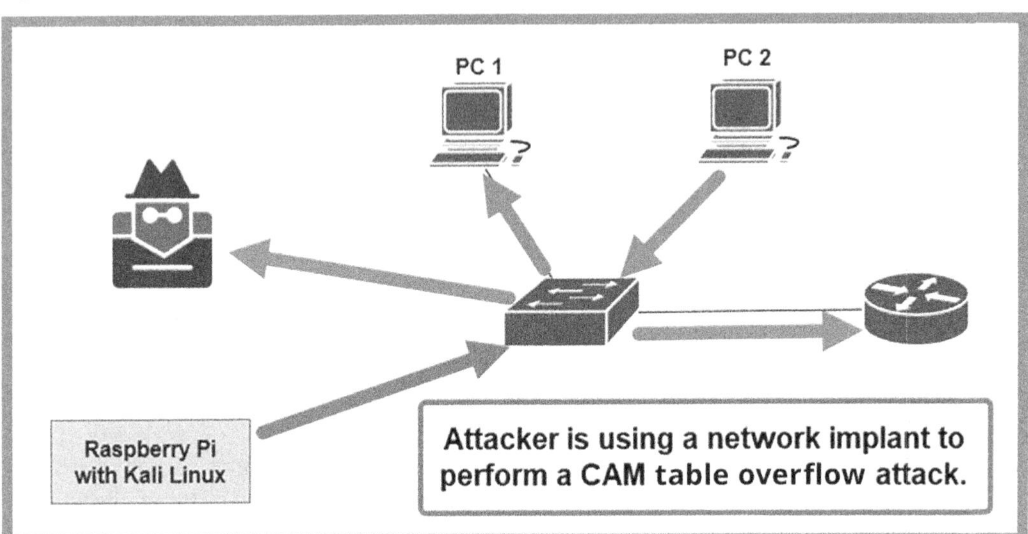

Figure 17.4: Cam table overflow

In *Figure 17.4*, the attacker has implanted a Raspberry Pi with Kali Linux and used special tools such as **macof** or **yersinia** to flood the switch with unsolicited frames.

Figure 17.5 shows macof generating bogus frames:

```
root@kali:~# macof -i eth0
e1:80:f9:45:98:9 6:52:70:39:eb:a1 0.0.0.0.19006 > 0.0.0.0.4320: S 710988111:710988111(0) win 512
1c:c:8a:50:21:a7 e8:31:d7:2d:1e:37 0.0.0.0.35536 > 0.0.0.0.48231: S 1540156923:1540156923(0) win 512
ca:40:59:65:9e:45 9:df:d7:39:65:12 0.0.0.0.16661 > 0.0.0.0.43605: S 1569897595:1569897595(0) win 512
a5:1d:98:6a:e8:60 1e:14:46:61:b4:93 0.0.0.0.61026 > 0.0.0.0.52498: S 1701381115:1701381115(0) win 512
5e:fd:d1:5e:a:46 4e:0:e6:10:ef:3b 0.0.0.0.42122 > 0.0.0.0.34809: S 1692649512:1692649512(0) win 512
75:43:94:29:2f:53 3e:36:b2:7d:eb:85 0.0.0.0.63383 > 0.0.0.0.9898: S 1183917742:1183917742(0) win 512
7d:be:f8:53:7c:75 c2:c4:cc:2d:da:7 0.0.0.0.24670 > 0.0.0.0.30611: S 976029769:976029769(0) win 512
ae:9d:f7:43:a6:1e 5a:7:73:8:d9:f2 0.0.0.0.25470 > 0.0.0.0.32543: S 210634849:210634849(0) win 512
c2:a7:af:45:f8:81 5f:d8:59:b:63:21 0.0.0.0.58444 > 0.0.0.0.32636: S 982725989:982725989(0) win 512
a6:c0:7c:50:6e:2 31:2f:d7:17:b2:3 0.0.0.0.63764 > 0.0.0.0.60069: S 611132256:611132256(0) win 512
7:b1:61:3:74:29 10:f6:20:64:36:c4 0.0.0.0.53548 > 0.0.0.0.32715: S 294560344:294560344(0) win 512
```

Figure 17.5: Macof tool

During the attack, the switch's CAM table will exceed its limitation and begin flooding all incoming traffic out of all other interfaces. In *Figure 17.4*, you can see that PC 2 is sending traffic to the switch, but the switch is forwarding it to unintended destinations and the attacker is able to capture PC 2's traffic.

VLAN Attacks

By default, each interface on a Cisco IOS switch uses **Dynamic Trunking Protocol** (**DTP**) to automatically negotiate the interface mode for connecting to other devices. In *Chapter 7, Implementing VLANs and Inter-Switch Connectivity*, DTP was covered in detail, and you saw how it is applied to automatically negotiate either an **access** or **trunk** interface on Cisco switches. Since all interfaces on a Cisco IOS switch use the default mode, `dynamic auto`, an attacker can use their machine and create an unauthorized trunk between the attacker's machine and the switch.

Figure 17.6 shows that an attacker has enabled an unauthorized trunk on a small network:

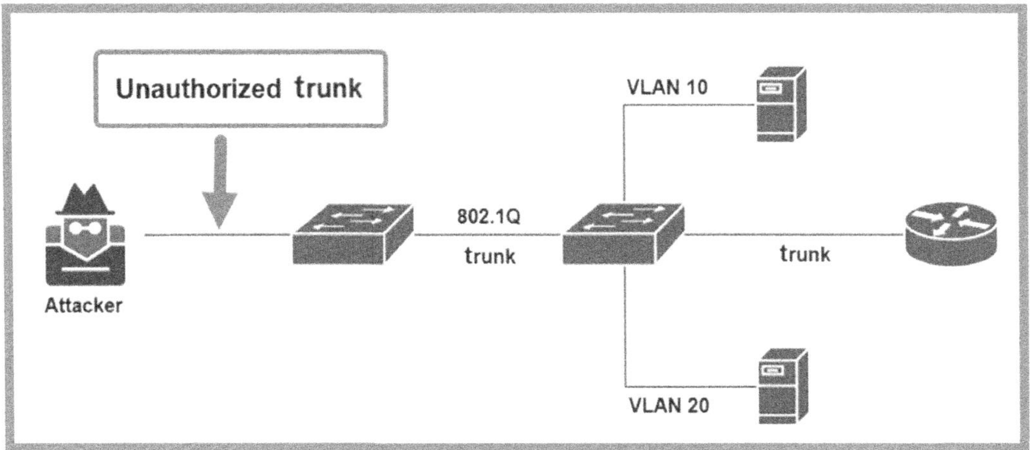

Figure 17.6: Unauthorized trunk

As shown in *Figure 17.6*, the attacker will be able to access any VLANs on the switch. Furthermore, the attacker will be able to send and receive traffic on any VLANs on the switch. This is known as a **VLAN hopping** attack.

Figure 17.7 shows how easily an attacker can attempt to enable trunking using a tool such as Yersinia:

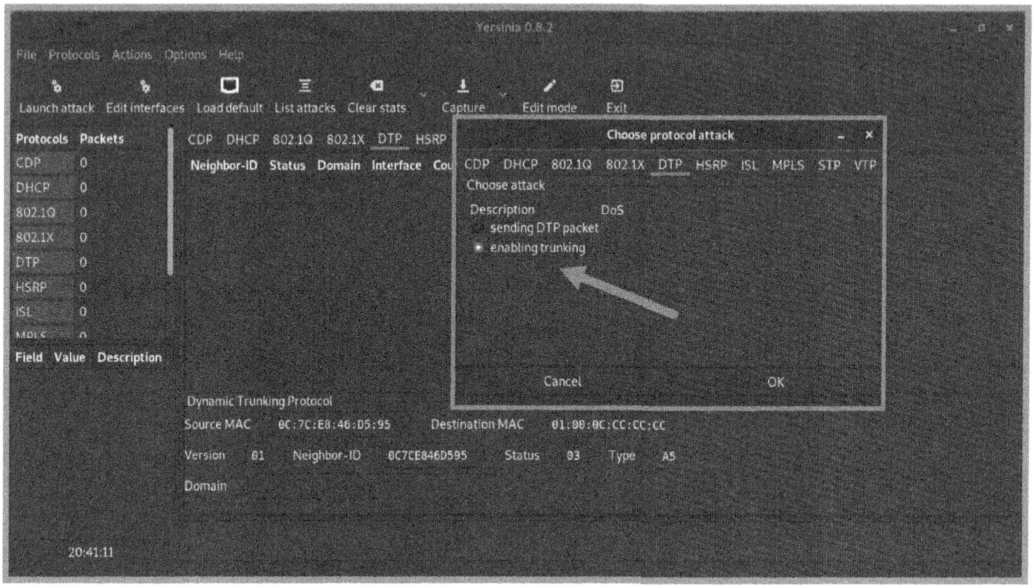

Figure 17.7: Yersinia DTP attacks

An attacker can also insert another VLAN tag in an already tagged frame. This is known as **VLAN double-tagging**. To put it simply, the attacker embeds their own 802.1Q tag within a frame that has an 802.1Q tag already. To get a better understanding of how this attack works, take a close look at *Figure 17.8*:

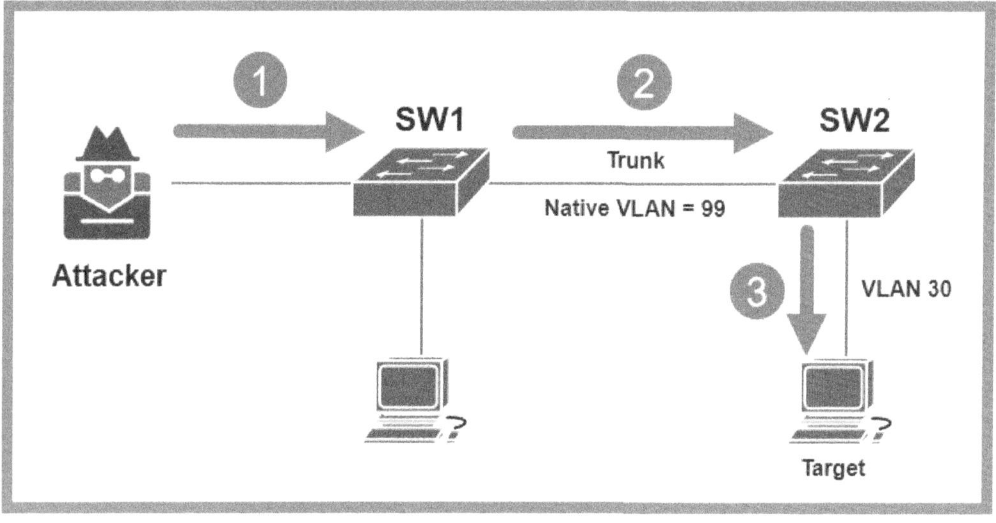

Figure 17.8: VLAN double-tagging

Based on *Figure 17.8*, the following is the sequence of actions that occur on the network:

1. The attacker sends a double-tagged frame into SW1. The outer tag of the frame contains the VLAN ID of the interface the attacker is connected to, which is Native VLAN (99). The inner 802.1Q tag (30) of the frame is also inserted by the attacker.
2. When SW1 receives the double-tagged frame, it inspects only the outer tag (VLAN 99) and forwards the frame out of all VLAN 99 interfaces after removing the outer tag (99). The inner VLAN tag, VLAN 30, is still intact and was not inspected by the first switch.
3. When SW2 receives the frame, it inspects the inner 802.1Q tag that was inserted by the attacker (VLAN 30). The switch will then forward the frame to the target VLAN by flooding it out of all VLAN 30 interfaces or directly to the target machine if the MAC address of the target is known.

In a VLAN double-tagging attack, the transmission is always unicast. This attack works only if the attacker's machine is connected to an interface that is assigned the same native VLAN as the trunk interfaces. Additionally, this attack allows the attacker to communicate with a target on a VLAN that is restricted or blocked by security controls on the network.

To prevent both VLAN hopping and VLAN double-tagging attacks, use the following recommendations:

- Ensure you disable trunking on all your access ports on the switches. To do this, use the following interface mode command on your access ports:

  ```
  Switch(config-if)# switchport mode access
  ```

- Ensure you disable DTP on all interfaces by using the following interface mode command:

  ```
  Switch(config-if)# switchport nonegotiate
  ```

- Configure your trunk interfaces manually by using the following interface mode command:

  ```
  Switch(config-if)# switchport mode trunk
  ```

- Ensure the native VLAN is used only on your trunk links.
- Ensure you do not use VLAN 1 as the native VLAN.

In *Chapter 7, Implementing VLANs and Inter-Switch Connectivity*, the labs utilized all the recommendations mentioned here as good practice. Feel free to revisit the chapter and the labs to gain hands-on experience, applying these configurations in a Cisco environment.

DHCP Attacks

In *Chapter 13, Implementing Network Services and IP Operations*, you learned about the purpose and operations of many IP services, such as **Dynamic Host Configuration Protocol** (**DHCP**). Like many TCP/IP network protocols, DHCP was not designed with security mechanisms. On a network, an attacker can perform two types of DHCP attacks. They are explained here.

DHCP Starvation

In a **DHCP starvation attack**, the goal of the attacker is to create a **denial of service** (**DoS**) for any client machine that requests IP configurations from a DHCP server. The attacker can use a tool such as Yersinia to generate unsolicited fake DHCP discover messages with spoofed source MAC addresses. When the DHCP server receives each DHCP discover message, it will attempt to provide an IP address from the DHCP pool. By flooding the DHCP server with hundreds or even thousands of bogus DHCP discover messages, the DHCP pool will eventually be exhausted. Therefore, any connected client machine that requires a lease IP address will be denied and will not be able to communicate on the network without a valid IP address.

Figure 17.9 shows various DHCP attacks that can be performed using Yersinia:

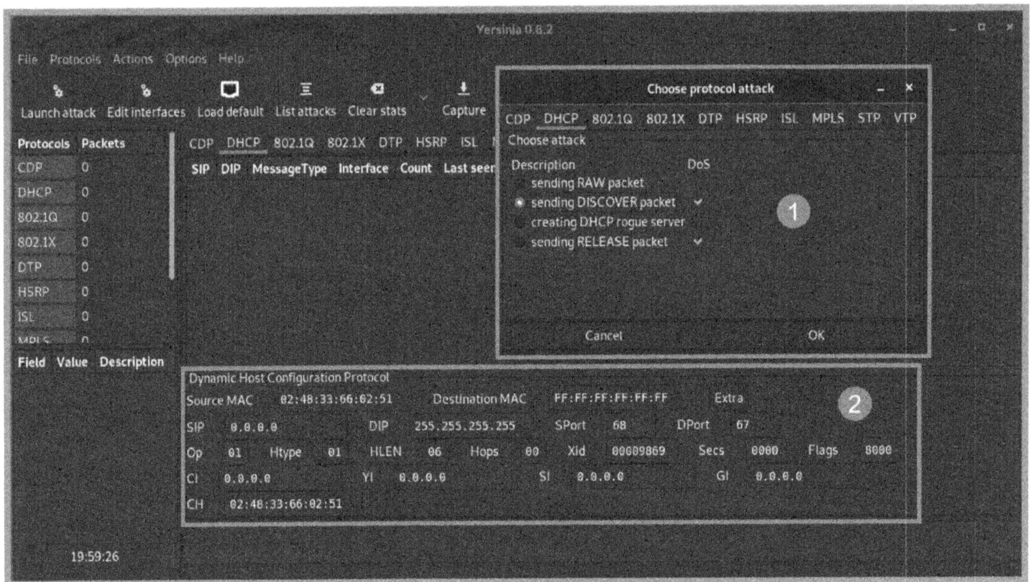

Figure 17.9: Yersinia interface

As shown in *Figure 17.9*, window 1 allows a penetration tester or an attacker to execute various types of DHCP attacks on a network. Window 2 allows you to further customize the source DHCP messages from the attacker machine.

DHCP Spoofing

In a **DHCP Spoofing attack**, the attacker inserts a rogue DHCP server in the network to provide false IP configurations to legitimate clients. A rogue DHCP server can provide the following to clients:

- **Incorrect default gateway**: This will cause legitimate hosts to forward their internet-based traffic to the attacker's machine and create the effect of a **man-in-the-middle** (**MiTM**) attack as well.
- **Incorrect IP addressing**: This involves providing an incorrect IP address and subnet mask to clients on the network. An incorrect IP address and/or subnet mask will prevent a host from communicating with other devices.
- **Incorrect DNS server**: By providing clients with a rogue DNS server, the attack can control the hostname to IP address lookup information. Thus, clients can be redirected to malicious websites.

To get a better understanding of what occurs when an attacker connects a rogue DHCP server on a network, take a look at *Figure 17.10*:

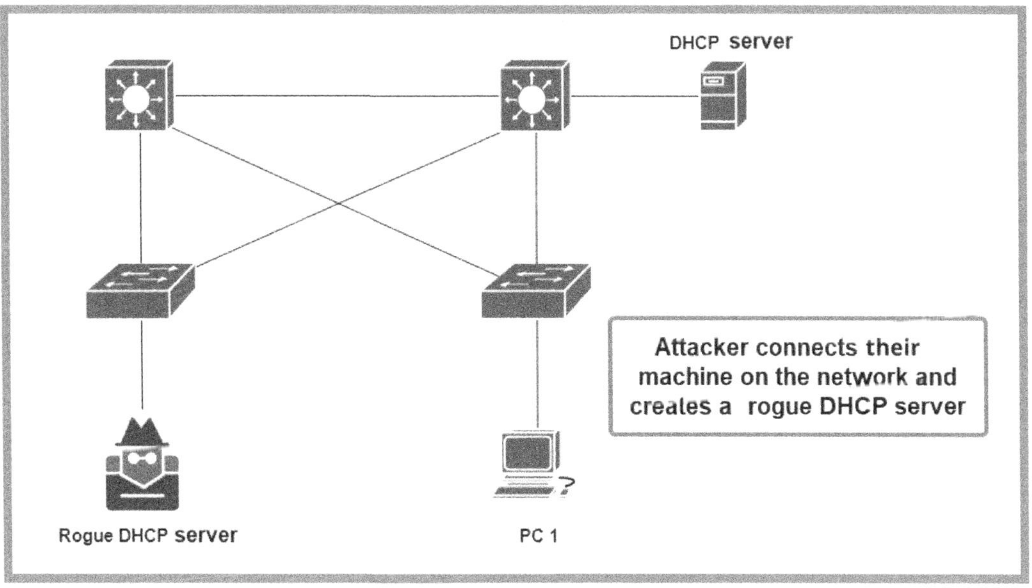

Figure 17.10: Rogue DHCP server

Based on *Figure 17.10*, there is a legitimate DHCP server, and the attacker has connected a rogue DHCP server on the same network. The following is the sequence of events that will take place when a client device such as PC 1 joins the network:

1. When PC 1 connects to the network, it will broadcast a **DHCP discover** message.
2. Both the legitimate and rogue DHCP servers will receive this **DHCP discover** message from PC 1.
3. Both the legitimate and rogue DHCP servers will respond with their **DHCP offer** message containing IP configurations.
4. PC 1 will respond with a **DHCP request** to the first **DHCP offer** message it receives. PC 1 will accept the IP configurations from the first DHCP Offer message. Therefore, if PC 1 receives a **DHCP offer** from the rogue DHCP server first, it will respond with a **DHCP request** (broadcast).
5. Both the legitimate and rogue DHCP servers will receive the broadcast **DHCP request** message from PC 1 and only the rogue DHCP server will respond with a unicast **DHCP acknowledgement** message. The legitimate DHCP server will cease to communicate with PC 1, simply because PC 1 accepted the IP configurations from the rogue DHCP server and has established trust with the device.

Additionally, an attacker can use a tool such as Yersinia to create a rogue DHCP server on a corporate network. In later sections of this chapter, you will learn how **DHCP snooping** can be used to prevent both DHCP starvation and DHCP spoofing attacks on a corporate network.

ARP Attacks

As we have learned throughout this book, the **Address Resolution Protocol** (**ARP**) is a layer 2 protocol that is designed to resolve IP addresses to MAC addresses. As mentioned in *Chapter 6, Wireless Architectures and Virtualization*, switches are used to connect end devices such as PCs and servers to the network. ARP is needed as all devices within a subnet or LAN forward messages to their destination by using the MAC address of the intended recipient.

> **Note**
>
> IP addresses within the Layer 3 header of the packet are utilized when a host is attempting to communicate with another device on a different subnet or network.

Whenever a host wants to send a message to another device on the same network, if the sender does not know the MAC address of the destination device, it will broadcast an **ARP request** message. The ARP request contains the destination device IP address and is sent to all devices on the LAN or subnet. The message simply is a request for the MAC address of the destination device. The ARP request message is received and processed by all devices on the subnet; however, only the device with the matching IP address will respond with an **ARP reply** containing its MAC address.

Like other TCP/IP network protocols, the ARP was not designed with security in mind. Host devices such as computers are able to send unsolicited ARP replies. These are known as **gratuitous ARP**. An attacker can send a gratuitous ARP message to a host on the same subnet. The message will contain a MAC address and IP address mapping that informs the destination device to update its ARP table.

Figure 17.11 is the ARP cache on a Windows operating system:

```
C:\>arp -a

Interface: 172.16.17.11 --- 0x1a
  Internet Address      Physical Address      Type
  172.16.17.2           f8-54-b8              dynamic
  172.16.17.6           f8-54-b8              dynamic
  172.16.17.18          9c-3d-cf              dynamic
  172.16.17.255         ff-ff-ff              static
  224.0.0.22            01-00-5e              static
  224.0.0.251           01-00-5e              static
  224.0.0.252           01-00-5e              static
  239.255.255.250       01-00-5e              static
  255.255.255.255       ff-ff-ff              static

C:\>
```

Figure 17.11: ARP cache

As shown in *Figure 17.11*, the host device will only populate its ARP cache with a device's MAC address that it has recently exchanged messages with. An attacker can send spoofed MAC addresses using gratuitous ARP messages to clients on a network, thus causing them to update ARP tables automatically. As a result, the attacker can trick clients into thinking the attacker's machine is their default gateway and create a MiTM attack.

To get a better understanding of ARP spoofing, take a look at *Figure 17.12*:

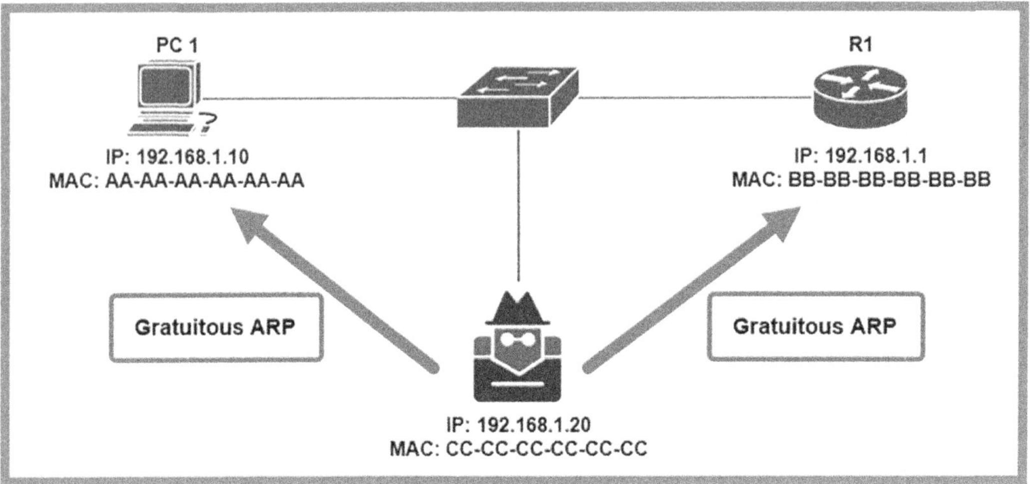

Figure 17.12: ARP attack

Based on *Figure 17.12*, an attacker connects to the network and attempts to send gratuitous ARP messages to PC 1 and R1. The objective is to inform PC 1 that the MAC address of R1 has been updated to `CC-CC-CC-CC-CC-CC`. This will cause PC 1 to update its ARP table and all traffic that is destined for `192.168.1.1` will be sent to the attacker's machine.

> **Note**
>
> When an attacker is attempting to cause a victim to update their ARP cache with false ARP entries, this is referred to as **ARP poisoning**.

Additionally, the same is done to R1 as the attacker tricks the router into thinking PC 1's new MAC address has been updated to `CC-CC-CC-CC-CC-CC`, as shown in *Figure 17.13*:

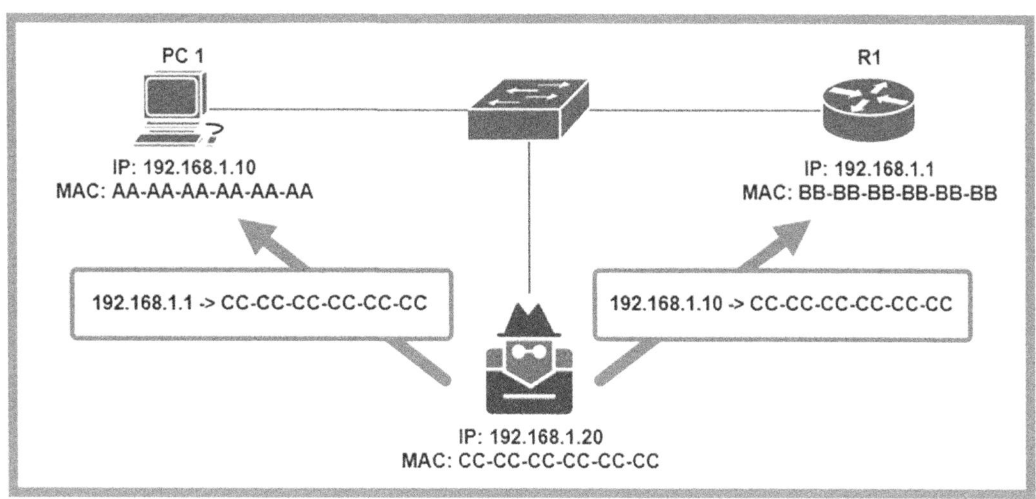

Figure 17.13: ARP spoofing

This will ensure that all traffic between PC 1 and R1 will be sent to the attacker's machine and vice versa. *Figure 17.14* shows the effect of ARP spoofing to chain a MiTM attack:

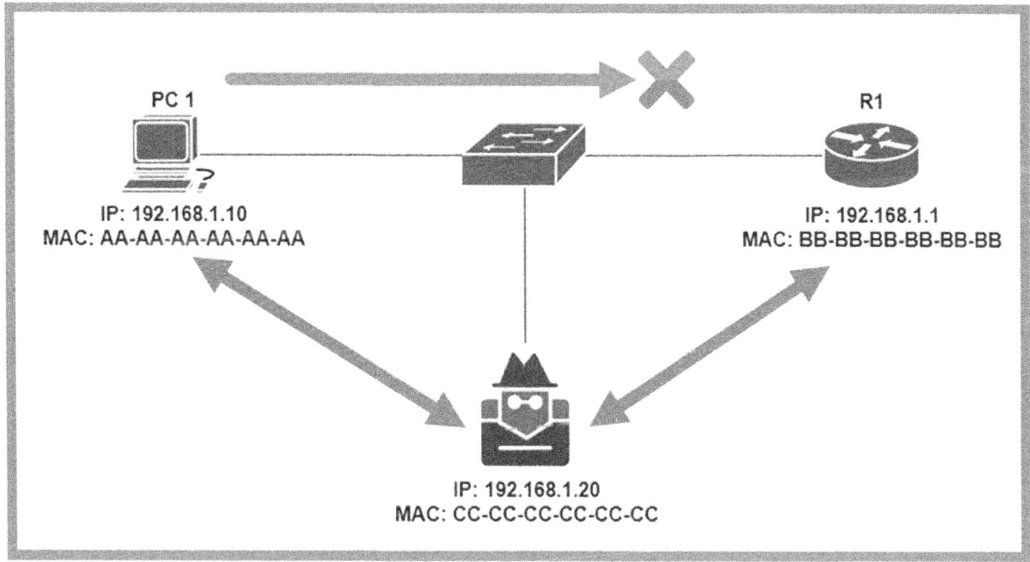

Figure 17.14: MiTM attack

In this attack, all the victim's (PC 1) traffic will be intercepted and captured. If any sensitive data is being exchanged, the messages will be compromised.

Spanning Tree Attacks

On a switch network, the **Spanning Tree Protocol** (**STP**) is used to prevent Layer 2 loops. It does this by electing a root bridge that will then instruct all other switches within the same VLAN to block certain ports while leaving others in a forwarding state.

> **Note**
>
> If you would like a recap on Spanning Tree, please see *Chapter 9, Understanding and Configuring Spanning Tree.*

In *Chapter 9, Understanding and Configuring Spanning Tree*, you learned how the root bridge plays an important role in the network. One key point to always remember is that the root bridge also acts as the central reference point for all traffic within a VLAN. However, once again, STP is another Layer 2 network protocol that was not designed with security mechanisms. An attacker can simply connect their machine to a switch and inject customized STP **bridge protocol data units** (**BPDUs**) with a lower priority value. If the attack is successful, the STP topology will change, making the attacker machine the new root bridge and central reference point on the network. Furthermore, if the attacker's machine is the root bridge, the attacker can capture all traffic on the VLAN, hence acting as a MiTM on the network.

Figure 17.15 shows how an attacker is attempting to become the root bridge:

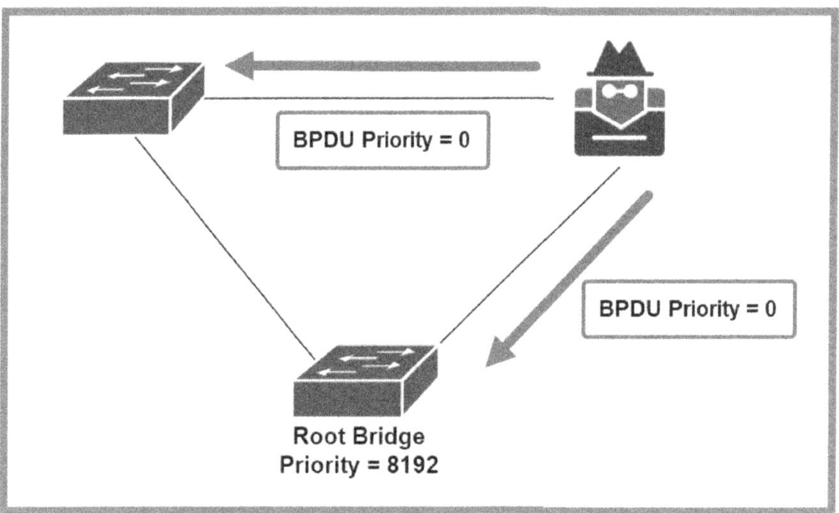

Figure 17.15: STP attack

To prevent STP attacks, it's recommended to implement **BPDU guard** on all access points on your switches. In *Chapter 6, Wireless Architectures and Virtualization,* you read how to implement BPDU guard in the *Configuring PortFast and BPDU Guard* lab.

CDP Attacks

Cisco Discovery Protocol (**CDP**) is a Cisco proprietary Layer 2 protocol that is designed to share information with other Cisco devices on the same network. CDP is enabled by default on all Cisco devices and shares information such as device models, hostname, IOS version, device capabilities, IP addresses, and even the native VLAN with other devices.

CDP was designed to help network engineers with troubleshooting and determining a network topology. As an example, imagine you are unable to ping a directly connected device, but you are still able to receive CDP messages from the same device. This is an indication that Layer 2 is operating properly but Layer 3 may require further investigation.

> **Note**
>
> To recap the topics and operations of CDP, please revisit *Chapter 8, EtherChannels and Layer 2 Discovery Protocols.*

CDP messages are sent out of all CDP-enabled interfaces on a device every 60 seconds. These CDP messages are unencrypted. Such information found within a CDP message can be very valuable to an attacker on the network. The attacker can use the information to create a map of the network infrastructure, determine the type of devices on the network, their capabilities, and IP addresses, and so on.

Figure 17.16 shows the contents of a CDP message using Wireshark:

Figure 17.16: CDP messages on Wireshark

In *Figure 17.16*, the CDP messages were captured with a Cisco IOSv router and a Cisco IOSvL2 switch. The body of packet #7 contains sensitive information about the Cisco IOSv router on the network such as its management IP address, IOS version, and so on. Since CDP was not designed with security in mind, an attacker can also inject fake CDP messages into a network with fake information.

To mitigate this vulnerability within CDP, use the following guidelines:

- Disable CDP globally on your device using the `no cdp run` command.
- Enable CDP on interfaces that are connected to other CDP-enabled devices.
- CDP-enabled interfaces should only be connected to other networking devices and not end devices.
- CDP messages should not be sent to the internet or your **internet service provider** (**ISP**).

Furthermore, the **Link Layer Discovery Protocol** (**LLDP**) is also vulnerable to the same type of attacks as CDP. To disable LLDP globally, use the `no lldp run` command within global configuration mode. To disable LLDP on an interface, use both the `no lldp transmit` and `no lldp receive` commands on the interface mode.

In this section, you have learned about various Layer 2 threats and attacks that can occur within an organization's network. In the next section, you will discover various switch security controls to prevent various Layer 2 attacks.

Protecting Against Layer 2 Threats

Quite often, many organizations think cyber threats and attacks originate from outside of their organization, such as the internet. However, some of these threats and attacks can occur from inside. These threats can be in the form of an innocent employee connecting an unauthorized device to the network, such as a switch or even a wireless router, or even a disgruntled employee who wants to take down the company's network infrastructure for personal reasons. Your responsibility as a network engineer is not only to design and build networks for connectivity but also to ensure you secure the network.

In this section, you will learn how to implement security controls on your switches to prevent various Layer 2 attacks such as those mentioned in the previous sections.

Port Security

Sometimes, when implementing a newly configured switch on a production network, the network engineer may honestly forget to secure any unused interfaces/ports on the switch. Leaving unused ports active is like leaving a doorway wide open for anyone to access your property. Sometimes, when implementing a switch and not all ports are in use, it is recommended to disable all unused ports to prevent any unauthorized access to the Layer 2 network.

> **Note**
>
> Disable all interfaces on a switch and only enable those that are required.

To secure any unused port on a Cisco IOS switch, use the `shutdown` command within interface mode to set the port into an administrative down state, as shown in *Figure 17.17*:

```
Switch(config)#interface FastEthernet 0/1
Switch(config-if)#shutdown
Switch(config-if)#exit
Switch#show ip interface brief
Interface              IP-Address      OK? Method Status                Protocol
FastEthernet0/1        unassigned      YES manual administratively down down
FastEthernet0/2        unassigned      YES manual down                  down
FastEthernet0/3        unassigned      YES manual down                  down
```

Figure 17.17: Securing an unused port

The `shutdown` command changes the interface to an *administratively down* state, which will disable the electrical circuitry on that interface only. However, if you have to disable a range of interfaces, you can use the `interface range` command, as shown in *Figure 17.18*:

```
Switch(config)#interface range FastEthernet 0/5 - FastEthernet 0/10
Switch(config-if-range)#shutdown
Switch(config-if-range)#exit
Switch(config)#exit
Switch#
%SYS-5-CONFIG_I: Configured from console by console

Switch#show ip interface brief | include administratively
FastEthernet0/1        unassigned      YES manual administratively down down
FastEthernet0/5        unassigned      YES manual administratively down down
FastEthernet0/6        unassigned      YES manual administratively down down
FastEthernet0/7        unassigned      YES manual administratively down down
FastEthernet0/8        unassigned      YES manual administratively down down
FastEthernet0/9        unassigned      YES manual administratively down down
FastEthernet0/10       unassigned      YES manual administratively down down
Switch#
```

Figure 17.18: Disabling a range of interfaces

In the earlier parts of this chapter, you read about many types of Layer 2 attacks. One of which was the CAM table overflow attack, which is designed to exhaust the storage capacity of a switch's CAM table. Cisco has implemented a security control known as **Port Security** to limit the number of trusted MAC addresses that are allowed on a switch's interface.

As a network engineer, this feature allows you to either manually configure trusted MAC addresses per interface or allow the switch to dynamically learn a limited number of MAC addresses. When Port Security is enabled on an interface, the source MAC addresses of all inbound frames are compared to a list of secure source MAC addresses. By implementing Port Security, you can control which devices are able to connect to an interface and your network.

Before enabling Port Security on an interface or a range of interfaces, ensure the interface(s) are not using the default DTP mode, that is, **dynamic auto** because the port security feature will not work. Ensure your interface is statically configured as either an **access port** for end devices or a **trunk port**.

To enable port security on an interface, use the following commands:

```
Switch(config)# interface fastEthernet 0/1
Switch(config-if)# switchport mode access
Switch(config-if)# switchport port-security
Switch(config-if)# no shutdown
Switch(config-if)# exit
```

To verify the port security status on an interface, use the `show port-security interface` command, as shown in *Figure 17.19*:

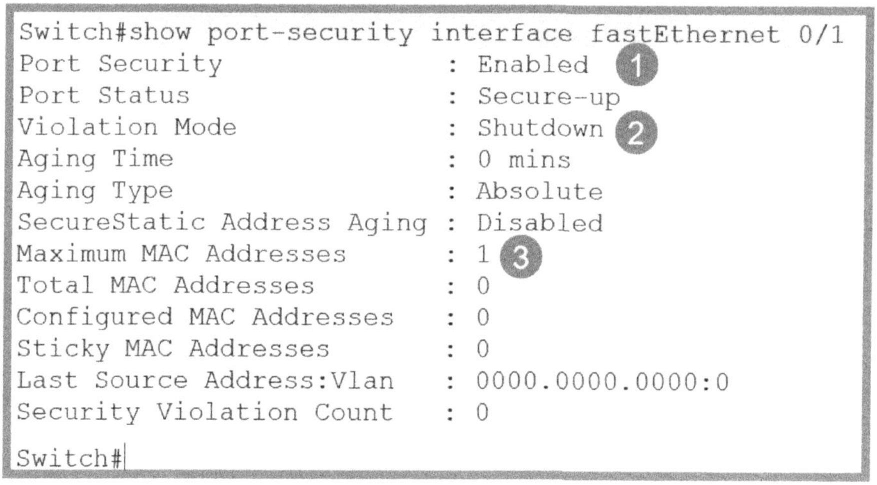

```
Switch#show port-security interface fastEthernet 0/1
Port Security              : Enabled  (1)
Port Status                : Secure-up
Violation Mode             : Shutdown  (2)
Aging Time                 : 0 mins
Aging Type                 : Absolute
SecureStatic Address Aging : Disabled
Maximum MAC Addresses      : 1  (3)
Total MAC Addresses        : 0
Configured MAC Addresses   : 0
Sticky MAC Addresses       : 0
Last Source Address:Vlan   : 0000.0000.0000:0
Security Violation Count   : 0

Switch#
```

Figure 17.19: Verify port-security interface status

We can determine the following key points from *Figure 17.19*:

- Port security is enabled on the `FastEthernet 0/1` interface.
- The violation mode is set to **Shutdown**.

- The maximum number of source MAC addresses that are permitted on this interface is 1. If more than one device is connected to this interface, and the same interface receives frames with 2 or more different source MAC addresses, a security violation will be triggered and the interface will be transitioned into an error-disabled state.
- Currently, no source MAC addresses are learned on the interface. If a device connects and sends traffic into this port, the switch will automatically add the source MAC address as a secure MAC address.

> **Note**
> When port security is turned on, the default configurations are maximum secure MAC addresses is **1**, default violation mode is **shutdown**, and sticky address learning is **disabled**.

Limiting the number of MAC addresses allowed on an interface can prevent unauthorized devices from connecting to the network and prevent malicious users from injecting unsolicited frames into a switch. To limit the number of MAC addresses permitted on an interface, use the following syntax:

```
Switch(config-if)# switchport port-security maximum number
```

There may be a situation that requires you to manually configure a static MAC address on a switch interface. To statically assign/associate a secure MAC address on a switch port, use the following syntax:

```
Switch(config-if)# switchport port-security mac-address mac-address
```

Manually configuring a secure MAC address on an interface ensures only the end device with that same MAC address is permitted to connect on the same interface and send traffic. However, this task can be overwhelming if you have to do this on all switches for the entire organization. One method is to configure the switch to dynamically learn the source MAC addresses on each interface and store them on the running configuration.

To dynamically learn and store the source MAC address on an interface, use the `sticky` command with the following port security syntax:

```
Switch(config-if)# switchport port-security mac-address sticky
```

The source MAC addresses learned using the sticky command will be associated with the interface only and will be saved in the `running-config` file. If the switch loses power or is rebooted, the secure MAC address will be lost. Therefore, ensure you save the configurations to NVRAM (`startup-config`).

The following is an example demonstrating how to configure port security on an interface to limit up to two secure MAC addresses, statically configure one secure MAC address, and enable dynamic learning for additional secure MAC addresses:

```
Switch(config-if)# interface GigabitEthernet 0/1
Switch(config-if)# switchport mode access
Switch(config-if)# switchport port-security
Switch(config-if)# switchport port-security maximum 2
Switch(config-if)# switchport port-security mac-address B881.98D3.B223
Switch(config-if)# switchport port-security mac-address sticky
Switch(config-if)# no shutdown
Switch(config-if)# exit
```

Figure 17.20 verifies our port security status and configurations on the interface:

```
Switch#show port-security interface GigabitEthernet 0/1
Port Security               : Enabled
Port Status                 : Secure-up
Violation Mode              : Shutdown
Aging Time                  : 0 mins
Aging Type                  : Absolute
SecureStatic Address Aging  : Disabled
Maximum MAC Addresses       : 2
Total MAC Addresses         : 2
Configured MAC Addresses    : 1
Sticky MAC Addresses        : 1
Last Source Address:Vlan    : bad4.e05d.fbdf:1
Security Violation Count    : 0

Switch#
```

Figure 17.20: Verify port-security interface status

As shown in *Figure 17.20*, a secure source MAC (*Last Source Address*) address has been dynamically learned on the interface and on the VLAN. Furthermore, you can also use the `show port-security` command to verify statistics on all secure interfaces and the size of the CAM table, as shown in *Figure 17.21*:

```
Switch#show port-security
Secure Port  MaxSecureAddr  CurrentAddr  SecurityViolation  Security Action
                (Count)        (Count)          (Count)
---------------------------------------------------------------------------
      Gi0/1              2            2                  0         Shutdown
---------------------------------------------------------------------------
Total Addresses in System (excluding one mac per port)     : 1
Max Addresses limit in System (excluding one mac per port) : 4096
Switch#
```

Figure 17.21: Verifying port security statistics

Since the `sticky` command was used to dynamically learn and store source MAC addresses, the `show running-config` command shows you sticky MAC addresses, if any, as shown in *Figure 17.22*:

```
Switch#show running-config | begin interface
interface GigabitEthernet0/0
 negotiation auto
!
interface GigabitEthernet0/1
 switchport mode access
 switchport port-security maximum 2
 switchport port-security mac-address sticky
 switchport port-security mac-address b881.98d3.b223
 switchport port-security mac-address sticky bad4.e05d.fbdf
 switchport port-security
 negotiation auto
!
```

Figure 17.22: Verifying sticky MAC addresses

When the maximum number of secure MAC addresses has been learned on an interface, if any frames with new source MAC addresses are sent to a secure port, a violation will occur. There may be times when you need to manually remove a secure MAC address from a secure interface without deleting the existing secure MAC addresses. For this task, the **port security aging** feature allows us to configure an interface with aging time limits to ensure old secure MAC addresses remain while new MAC addresses are added.

Port security uses the following types of aging on a secure interface:

- Absolute: Secure MAC addresses are deleted after a defined aging time
- Inactivity: Secure MAC addresses are deleted only when they are inactive for a defined aging time

To configure port security aging on a secure interface, use the following syntax:

```
Switch(config-if)# switchport port-security aging { static | time time
| type [ absolute | inactivity ] }
```

The following is a description of each parameter for the port security aging command:

- `static`: Enables aging for a secure MAC address that is statically configured on the interface.
- `time time-in-minutes`: Allows you to specify the aging time on the interface. The time ranges between 0 and 1,440 minutes. If the time is set to 0, aging is disabled on the interface.
- `type absolute`: Secure MAC addresses age out and are removed from the secure address list on the switch when the specified time is reached.
- `type inactivity`: Secure MAC addresses will age out only if there is no traffic from a secure MAC address for the specified time.

The following commands are examples to demonstrate how to secure MAC addresses to age out after five minutes of inactivity on an interface:

```
Switch(config)# interface gigabitEthernet 0/1
Switch(config-if)# switchport mode access
Switch(config-if)# switchport port-security
Switch(config-if)# switchport port-security aging time 5
Switch(config-if)# switchport port-security aging type inactivity
Switch(config-if)# exit
```

Using the `show port-security` interface command, you will notice `Aging Time` has been changed to five minutes and `Aging Type` has been changed to `Inactivity`, as shown in *Figure 17.23*:

```
Switch#show port-security interface GigabitEthernet 0/1
Port Security              : Enabled
Port Status                : Secure-up
Violation Mode             : Shutdown
Aging Time                 : 5 mins
Aging Type                 : Inactivity
SecureStatic Address Aging : Disabled
Maximum MAC Addresses      : 2
Total MAC Addresses        : 2
Configured MAC Addresses   : 1
Sticky MAC Addresses       : 1
Last Source Address:Vlan   : bad4.e05d.fbdf:1
Security Violation Count   : 0

Switch#
```

Figure 17.23: Verifying Port Security aging configurations

If a secure port receives a source MAC address that is different from the list of secure MAC addresses, a security violation will occur and the interface will transition into an `error-disabled` state. The following are the three different violation modes when configuring port security:

- `shutdown`: This is the default violation mode. If a violation occurs, the port changes to an `error-disabled` state. The violation counter is increased. This helps network professionals to determine how many security violations have occurred since the last boot of the device. To re-enable the interface, the network engineer must first use the `shutdown` command, wait a few seconds, and then use the `no shutdown` command within the affected interface.
- `restrict`: If a violation occurs, this mode drops any message with an unknown source address. The security violation counter increases and a Syslog message is generated.

- `protect`: If a violation occurs, this mode will drop any message with an unknown source address. However, it does not increase the security violation counter nor does it send a Syslog message. This mode is considered to be the least secure among the three violation modes.

To configure port security violation on an interface, use the following syntax:

```
Switch(config-if)# switchport port-security violation shutdown |
restrict | protect
```

The following is an example of configuring the restrict violation on an interface with port security:

```
Switch(config)# interface GigabitEthernet 0/1
Switch(config-if)# switchport mode access
Switch(config-if)# switchport port-security
Switch(config-if)# switchport port-security violation restrict
Switch(config-if)# exit
```

Using the `show port-security interface` command, you can see the violation mode has changed to `Restrict`, as shown in *Figure 17.24*:

```
Switch#show port-security interface GigabitEthernet 0/1
Port Security              : Enabled
Port Status                : Secure-up
Violation Mode             : Restrict
Aging Time                 : 5 mins
Aging Type                 : Inactivity
SecureStatic Address Aging : Disabled
Maximum MAC Addresses      : 2
Total MAC Addresses        : 2
Configured MAC Addresses   : 1
Sticky MAC Addresses       : 1
Last Source Address:Vlan   : bad4.e05d.fbdf:1
Security Violation Count   : 0

Switch#
```

Figure 17.24: Verifying violation modes

In the next section, you will gain hands-on experience in implementing port security on a Cisco IOS switch.

Lab: Implementing Port Security

In this lab, you will learn how to implement port security to limit the number of secure source MAC addresses that are permitted on the interfaces of a Cisco IOS switch. To get started, you will be using the Cisco Packet Tracer application, which allows us to simulate a Cisco environment. For this lab, please build the network topology shown in *Figure 17.25*:

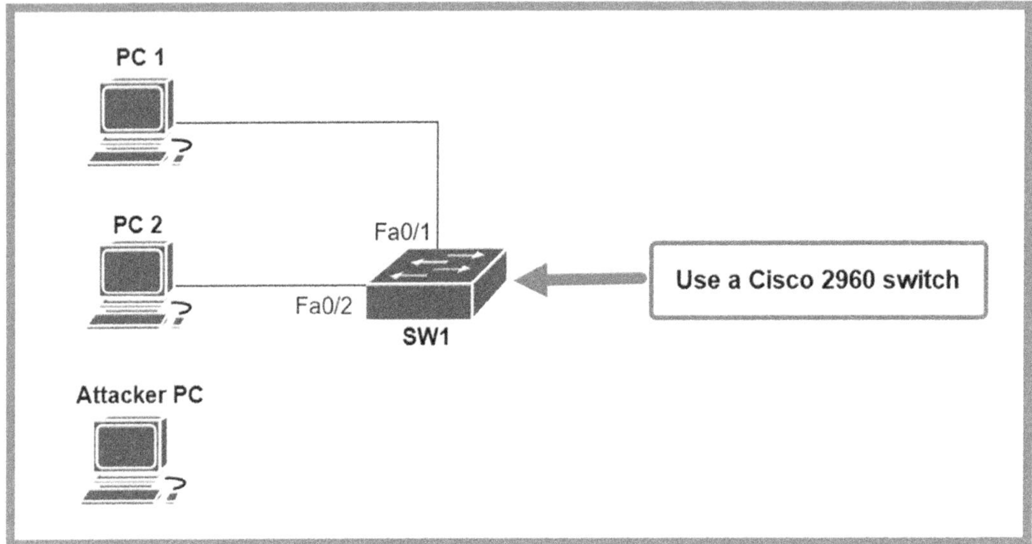

Figure 17.25: Port security lab topology

Ensure that you have assigned the IP addresses on each device according to *Table 17.1*:

Device	Interface	IP Address	Subnet Mask	Default Gateway
PC 1	Fa0	172.16.1.10	255.255.255.0	172.16.1.1
PC 2	Fa0	172.16.1.20	255.255.255.0	172.16.1.1
Attacker PC	Fa0	172.16.1.30	255.255.255.0	172.16.1.1

Table 17.1: IP address scheme

Now that your lab is ready, follow the given instructions to implement port security:

1. On SW1, enable port security on interfaces `FastEthernet 0/1` and `FastEthernet 0/2` using the following commands:

```
SW1(config)# interface range FastEthernet 0/1 - FastEthernet 0/2
SW1(config-if-range)# switchport mode access
SW1(config-if-range)# switchport port-security
```

2. Configure the secure ports to permit a maximum of one device per interface:

```
SW1(config-if-range)# switchport port-security maximum 1
```

3. Configure the secure ports to dynamically learn and store secure source MAC addresses to the running configuration file:

```
SW1(config-if-range)# switchport port-security mac-address
sticky
```

4. Next, enable the secure ports only and exit:

```
SW1(config-if-range)# no shutdown
SW1(config-if-range)# exit
```

5. Secure any unused ports on the switch:

```
SW1(config)# interface range FastEthernet 0/3 - FastEthernet
0/24
SW1(config-if-range)# shutdown
SW1(config-if-range)# exit
SW1(config)# interface range GigabitEthernet 0/1 -
GigabitEthernet 0/2
SW1(config-if-range)# shutdown
SW1(config-if-range)# exit
```

6. Ping between PC 1 and PC 2 to ensure their source MAC addresses are learned and stored on the running configuration file. Use the `show port-security interface` command to validate the configurations on your interfaces, as shown in *Figure 17.26*:

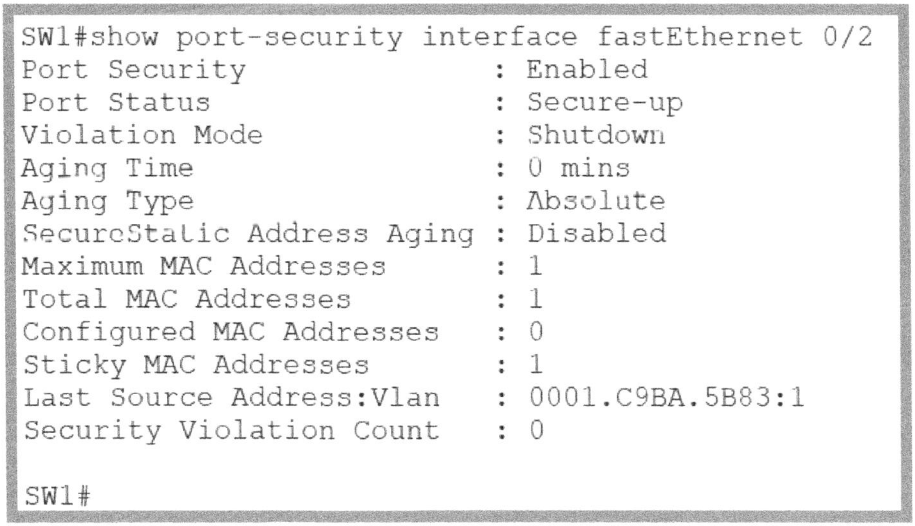

```
SW1#show port-security interface fastEthernet 0/2
Port Security              : Enabled
Port Status                : Secure-up
Violation Mode             : Shutdown
Aging Time                 : 0 mins
Aging Type                 : Absolute
SecureStatic Address Aging : Disabled
Maximum MAC Addresses      : 1
Total MAC Addresses        : 1
Configured MAC Addresses   : 0
Sticky MAC Addresses       : 1
Last Source Address:Vlan   : 0001.C9BA.5B83:1
Security Violation Count   : 0

SW1#
```

Figure 17.26: Validating port security

As shown in *Figure 17.26*, port security is enabled on the interface, the violation mode is set to shutdown (default), aging is disabled, the maximum secure MAC addresses allowed on the interface is 1, the total number of secure MAC addresses learned is 1, sticky is enabled and has stored 1 address on the `running-config`, and the last MAC address learned is 0001.C9BA.5B83 on VLAN 1.

7. Next, use the `show running-config` command to view the port security configurations and the sticky addresses that are automatically added to the running configuration:

```
SW1#show running-config
Building configuration...

Current configuration : 1629 bytes
!
!
interface FastEthernet0/1
 switchport mode access
 switchport port-security
 switchport port-security mac-address sticky
 switchport port-security mac-address sticky 0001.966B.B95A
!
interface FastEthernet0/2
 switchport mode access
 switchport port-security
 switchport port-security mac-address sticky
 switchport port-security mac-address sticky 0001.C9BA.5B83
!
```

Figure 17.27: Verifying the sticky addresses

As shown in *Figure 17.27*, PC1's MAC address is bound to `FastEthernet 0/1` and PC2's MAC address is bound to `FastEthernet 0/2`.

8. Trigger a violation on the network. Connect the attacker PC to `FastEthernet 0/2` on SW1. Then attempt to ping from the attacker PC to PC 1, as shown in *Figure 17.28*:

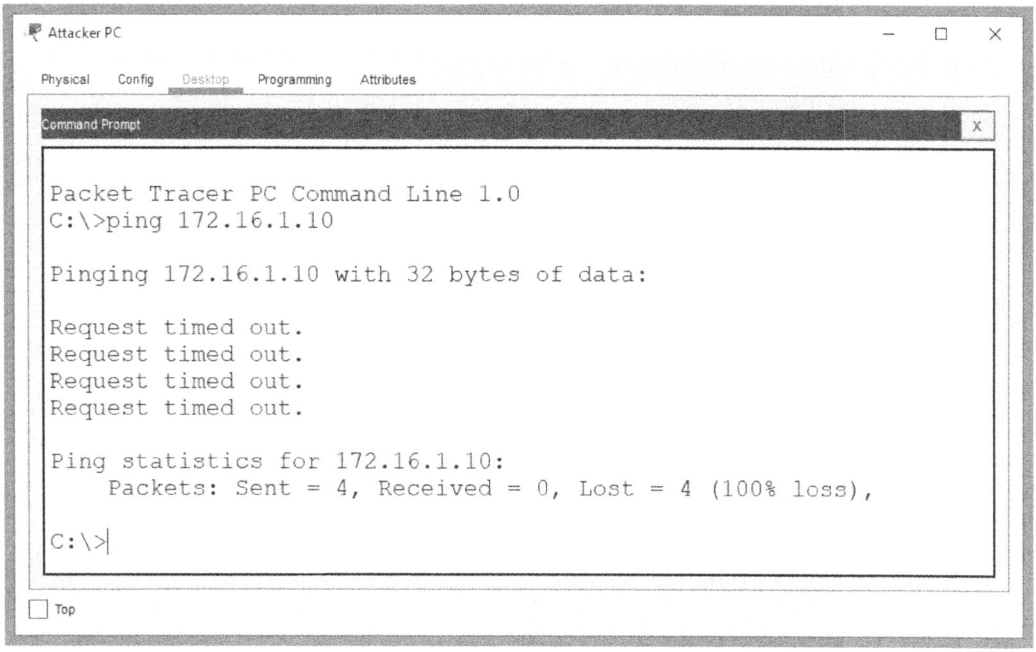

Attacker PC

Physical Config Desktop Programming Attributes

Command Prompt

```
Packet Tracer PC Command Line 1.0
C:\>ping 172.16.1.10

Pinging 172.16.1.10 with 32 bytes of data:

Request timed out.
Request timed out.
Request timed out.
Request timed out.

Ping statistics for 172.16.1.10:
    Packets: Sent = 4, Received = 0, Lost = 4 (100% loss),

C:\>
```

Top

Figure 17.28: Triggering a violation

9. As expected, since the attacker's source MAC address does not match the secure MAC address on `FastEthernet 0/2`, the traffic is not permitted and the interface has been disabled, as shown in *Figure 17.29*:

```
SW1#show port-security interface fastEthernet 0/2
Port Security              : Enabled
Port Status                : Secure-shutdown
Violation Mode             : Shutdown
Aging Time                 : 0 mins
Aging Type                 : Absolute
SecureStatic Address Aging : Disabled
Maximum MAC Addresses      : 1
Total MAC Addresses        : 1
Configured MAC Addresses   : 0
Sticky MAC Addresses       : 1
Last Source Address:Vlan   : 00E0.F9E9.5E39:1
Security Violation Count   : 1

SW1#
```

Figure 17.29: Verifying violation

The port status has been changed to `secure-shutdown`, the attacker's source MAC address is shown, and the violation counter has increased to `1`.

10. To verify which interfaces are in error-disabled state, use the `show interfaces status` command, as shown in *Figure 17.30*:

```
SW1#show interfaces status
Port      Name               Status       Vlan       Duplex  Speed Type
Fa0/1                        connected    1          auto    auto  10/100BaseTX
Fa0/2                        err-disabled 1          auto    auto  10/100BaseTX
Fa0/3                        disabled 1          auto    auto  10/100BaseTX
Fa0/4                        disabled 1          auto    auto  10/100BaseTX
Fa0/5                        disabled 1          auto    auto  10/100BaseTX
```

Figure 17.30: Verifying error-disabled interfaces

Another useful command to verify whether a port is in error-disabled state is the `show interfaces` command.

11. Fix the issue by physically reconnecting PC 2 to `FastEthernet 0/2` on SW1 and re-enabling the interface using the following commands:

```
SW1(config)# interface FastEthernet 0/2
SW1(config-if)# shutdown
SW1(config-if)# no shutdown
SW1(config-if)# exit
```

Having completed this lab, you have gained the hands-on skills to implement port security in a Cisco environment. In the next section, you will learn how to mitigate and prevent rogue DHCP servers on a network.

DHCP Snooping

DHCP snooping is a security feature available within Cisco IOS switches that allows you to prevent and mitigate against rogue DHCP servers. DHCP snooping is not dependent on source MAC addresses like port security but rather determines whether DHCP messages originate from a trusted device or trusted source on the network. With DHCP snooping implemented on a corporate network, it can filter DHCP messages and perform rate-limiting on DHCP messages from untrusted sources. Rate-limiting is used to control the number of messages entering a device's interface.

On a private network, devices such as routers, servers, and switches are considered to be trusted devices. They are trusted devices simply because you, as a network engineer, have administrative control over those networking devices. However, devices that are outside of your network are considered to be untrusted. When DHCP snooping is enabled, all ports are untrusted by default.

> **Note**
>
> Since DHCP clients are expected to send only **DHCP discover** and **DHCP request** messages into an untrusted port, if an untrusted port receives a **DHCP offer** or **DHCP acknowledgement** message, then a violation will occur.

A trusted port must be explicitly configured by the network engineer. Additionally, all access ports should be untrusted simply because the access layer is where an attacker can insert their rogue DHCP server. Trusted interfaces should be trunk interfaces and ports that are connected to the organization's DHCP server.

> **Note**
>
> On a trusted port, **DHCP offer** and **DHCP acknowledgment** messages are permitted.

When DHCP snooping is enabled, the switch creates a special table known as a **DHCP snooping binding table**. This table keeps track of the source MAC addresses of devices that are connected to untrusted ports and their IP addresses that were assigned by the legitimate DHCP server. The MAC addresses and IP addresses are bound together.

To configure DHCP snooping, use the following steps:

1. Use the `ip dhcp snooping` command within global configuration mode to turn on DHCP snooping.
2. Configure trusted interfaces by using the `ip dhcp snooping trust` command within interface mode.
3. Configure rate limiting on untrusted ports using the `ip dhcp snooping rate limit number` command. Specify the number of **packets per second** (**pps**).
4. Assign DHCP snooping for either a single VLAN or a range of VLANs by using the `ip dhcp snooping vlan vlan-id` command in global configuration mode. The following is an example of entering multiple VLANs in the command: `ip dhcp snooping vlan 5,15,20-22`.

In the next section, you will gain hands-on experience in implementing DHCP snooping to prevent and mitigate rogue DHCP servers in a Cisco environment.

Lab: Implementing DHCP Snooping

In this lab, you will learn how to implement DHCP snooping to prevent and mitigate rogue DHCP servers and DHCP attacks on a network. This lab is simply an extension of the previous exercise on *implementing port security*. For this lab, ensure you add the additional devices to the network topology shown in *Figure 17.31*:

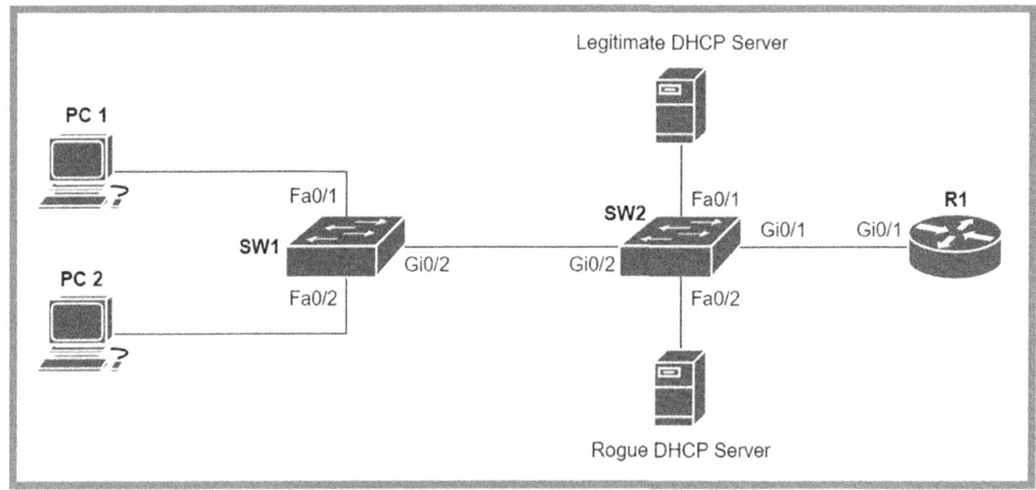

Figure 17.31: DHCP snooping lab topology

Ensure that you have assigned the IP addresses on each device according to *Table 17.2*:

Device	Interface	IP Address	Subnet Mask	Default Gateway
PC 1	Fa0	DHCP		
PC 2	Fa0	DHCP		
DHCP Server	Fa0	172.16.1.100	255.255.255.0	172.16.1.1
Rogue DHCP Server	Fa0	172.16.1.110	255.255.255.0	172.16.1.1
R1	Gi0/1	172.16.1.1	255.255.255.0	

Table 17.2: IP addressing scheme

Before starting the exercise, please configure `GigabitEthernet 0/2` on SW1 and SW2 as a trunk port and enable the interface.

Now that your lab is ready, use the following instructions for DHCP snooping:

1. On SW1, use the `ip dhcp snooping` command to enable DHCP snooping as shown here:

```
SW1(config)# ip dhcp snooping
```

2. Configure `GigabitEthernet 0/2` as a trunk port and as a trusted port using the following commands:

```
SW1(config)# interface GigabitEthernet 0/2
SW1(config-if)# switchport mode trunk
SW1(config-if)# ip dhcp snooping trust
SW1(config-if)# no shutdown
SW1(config-if)# exit
```

3. Assign DHCP snooping to the VLAN in use, VLAN 1, using the following command:

```
SW1(config)# ip dhcp snooping vlan 1
```

Note

A network may contain DHCP relay agents that will insert information about themselves before forwarding a DHCP discover message to the DHCP server. When DHCP snooping is enabled, it prevents the forwarding of the DHCP messages via relay agents. To prevent **DHCP relay option 82 information** from being inserted in the DHCP relay messages, you can use the `no ip dhcp snooping information option` command within global configuration mode.

4. Use the following command to enable DHCP snooping on SW2:

```
SW2(config)# ip dhcp snooping
```

5. Configure `GigabitEthernet 0/1`, `GigabitEthernet 0/2`, and `FastEthernet 0/1` as trusted ports using the following commands:

```
SW2(config)# interface range GigabitEthernet 0/1 -
GigabitEthernet 0/2
SW2(config-if-range)# switchport mode trunk
SW2(config-if-range)# ip dhcp snooping trust
SW2(config-if-range)# no shutdown
SW2(config-if-range)# exit
SW2(config)# interface FastEthernet 0/1
SW2(config-if)# ip dhcp snooping trust
SW2(config-if)# no shutdown
SW2(config-if)# exit
```

6. Assign DHCP snooping to the VLAN in use on SW2, VLAN 1, using the following command:

```
SW2(config)# ip dhcp snooping vlan 1
```

7. Click on `Legitimate DHCP Server` and select **Services** | **DHCP**. Ensure you enable the service and assign the IP details to create a DHCP pool on the server, as shown in *Figure 17.32*:

Figure 17.32: Configuring the Legitimate DHCP Server dialog

Ensure you configure all the IP addresses: `Default Gateway` = `172.16.1.1`, `DNS Server` = `8.8.8.8`, `Start IP Address` = `172.16.1.10`, `Subnet mask` = `255.255.255.0`, `WLC Address` = `172.16.1.40`, and click on `Save`. The **wireless LAN controller** (**WLC**) address will be used in the next lab, on wireless security.

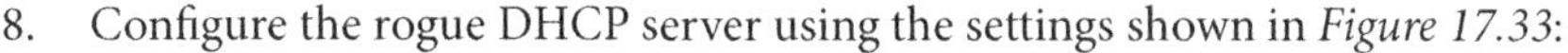

8. Configure the rogue DHCP server using the settings shown in *Figure 17.33*:

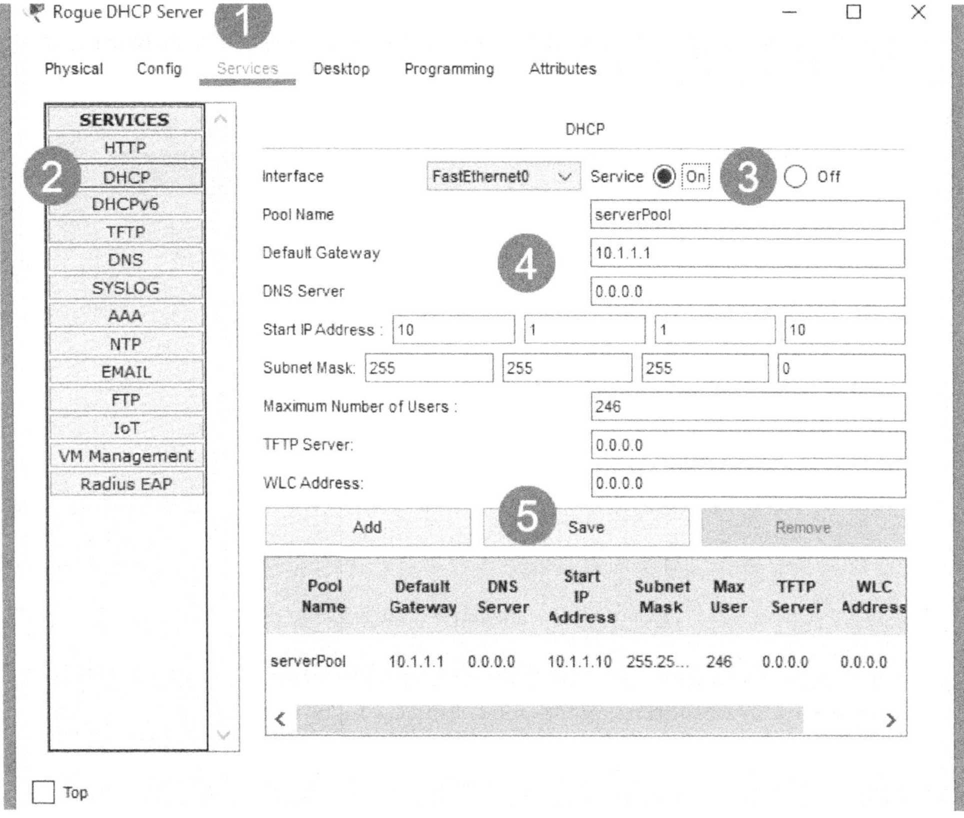

Figure 17.33: Rogue DHCP server settings

9. Next, enable DHCP on both PC 1 and PC 2, as shown in *Figure 17.34*:

PC1

Physical Config Desktop Programming Attributes

IP Configuration

Interface FastEthernet0

IP Configuration

DHCP Static DHCP request successful.

IP Address 172.16.1.10

Subnet Mask 255.255.255.0

Default Gateway 172.16.1.1

DNS Server 0.0.0.0

Figure 17.34: Verifying PC1's IP address

If you disconnect the legitimate DHCP server from the network, you will notice that the PCs do not receive any IP address configurations from the rogue DHCP server.

10. Next, use the `show ip dhcp snooping` command to verify whether DHCP snooping is enabled on the VLAN and whether `Option 82` is enabled. Additionally, this command allows you to verify both trusted and untrusted interfaces on the local switch:

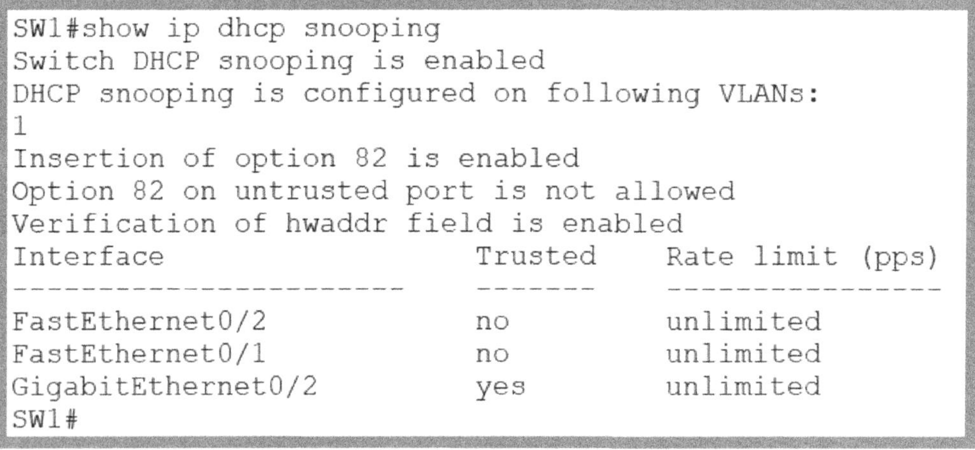

```
SW1#show ip dhcp snooping
Switch DHCP snooping is enabled
DHCP snooping is configured on following VLANs:
1
Insertion of option 82 is enabled
Option 82 on untrusted port is not allowed
Verification of hwaddr field is enabled
Interface                  Trusted    Rate limit (pps)
-----------------------    -------    ----------------
FastEthernet0/2            no         unlimited
FastEthernet0/1            no         unlimited
GigabitEthernet0/2         yes        unlimited
SW1#
```

Figure 17.35: Verify DHCP snooping status

11. Lastly, use `show ip dhcp snooping binding` to view the DHCP snooping binding table:

```
SW1#show ip dhcp snooping binding
MacAddress          IpAddress        Lease(sec)  Type           VLAN  Interface
------------------  ---------------  ----------  -------------  ----  -----------------
00:01:C9:BA:5B:83   172.16.1.2       86400       dhcp-snooping  1     FastEthernet0/2
00:01:96:6B:B9:5A   172.16.1.10      86400       dhcp-snooping  1     FastEthernet0/1
Total number of bindings: 2
SW1#
```

Figure 17.36: Viewing the DHCP snooping binding table

Having completed this lab, you have gained hands-on skills to implement DHCP snooping to prevent and mitigate DHCP attacks on a Cisco environment. In the next section, you will learn how to mitigate and prevent IP spoofing and MiTM attacks on a network.

Dynamic ARP Inspection

During a MiTM attack, an attacker uses ARP spoofing to send an unsolicited ARP message with their source MAC address with the IP address of a default gateway to other hosts on the network. By implementing **Dynamic ARP Inspection** (**DAI**) on Cisco IOS switches, you can prevent and mitigate ARP spoofing and man-in-the-middle attacks on your enterprise network. DAI ensures that only legitimate ARP Requests and ARP Replies are sent on the network.

To ensure DAI is effective on a network, it requires DHCP snooping to be configured and enabled on the switch as well. With DHCP snooping and DAI enabled, ARP attacks can be prevented through the following means:

- Preventing ARP request and ARP reply messages on untrusted interfaces
- Intercepting all ARP messages on untrusted interfaces
- Validating all intercepted messages contain a valid IP-to-MAC address binding
- Discarding and logging all ARP reply messages that originate from invalid sources
- Whenever a violation occurs, the interface transitions into an error-disabled state

> **Note**
>
> All access ports on a switch should be configured as untrusted interfaces. All trunk ports that are connected to other switches or routers should be configured as trusted ports.

To configure DAI, use the following steps:

1. Enable DHCP snooping because DAI requires the DHCP snooping binding table to validate IP-MAC addresses. Use the `ip dhcp snooping` command in global configuration mode.
2. Assign DHCP snooping to a VLAN. Use the `ip dhcp snooping vlan` *vlan-id* command in global configuration mode.
3. Configure the trunk links as trusted interfaces. Use the `ip dhcp snooping trust` command and the `ip arp inspection trust` command in interface mode.
4. Enable DAI on a VLAN. Use the `ip arp inspection vlan` *vlan-id* command in global configuration mode.

DAI also has the capability to inspect both the source and destination MAC and IP addresses of each message. It does this by using the following command:

```
Switch(config)# ip arp inspection validate [ src-mac | dst-mac | ip ]
```

The following is a description of each parameter for the ARP inspection command:

- `src-mac`: Enables DAI to check the source MAC address in the Layer 2 header against the sender's MAC address within the ARP body
- `dst-mac`: DAI checks the destination MAC address in the Layer 2 header against the target's MAC address within the ARP body
- `ip`: DAI checks the ARP body for any invalid IP addresses such as `0.0.0.0`, `255.255.255.255`, and all multicast IP addresses

In the next section, you will gain hands-on experience in implementing DAI in a Cisco environment.

Lab: Implementing DAI

In this lab, you will learn how to implement DAI to prevent and mitigate IP spoofing and MiTM attacks on a network. This lab is simply an extension of the previous exercise, *Implementing DHCP Snooping*. For this lab, you will be using the same lab topology from the previous exercise, shown in *Figure 17.37*:

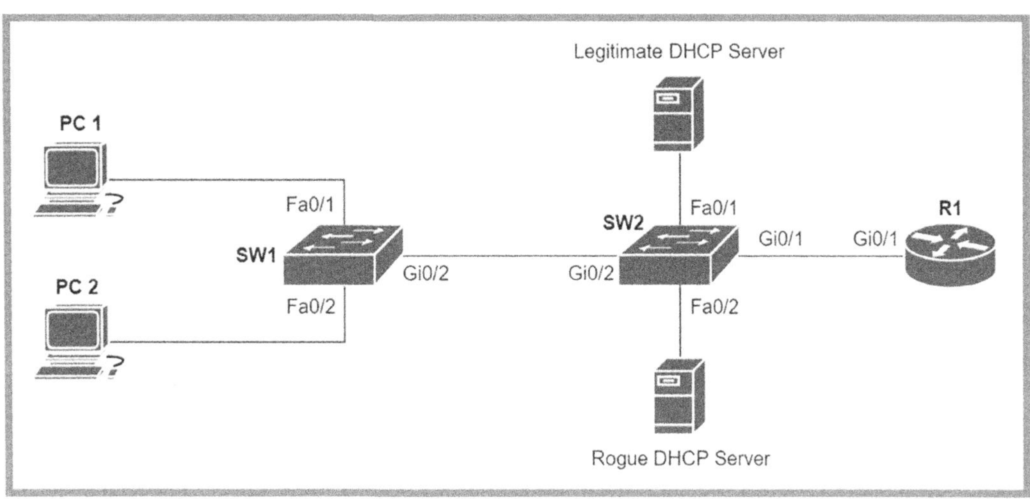

Figure 17.37: DAI lab topology

Since you implemented DHCP snooping in the last lab exercise, you can proceed to apply only the DAI configurations on the network by using the following steps:

1. On SW1, configure the uplink (trunk) interface as an ARP trusted port:

```
SW1(config)# interface GigabitEthernet 0/2
SW1(config-if)# ip arp inspection trust
SW1(config-if)# exit
```

2. Enable DAI on VLAN 1:

```
SW1(config)# ip arp inspection vlan 1
```

3. Configure DAI to inspect both the source or destination MAC and IP addresses of each message on SW1:

```
SW1(config)# ip arp inspection validate src-mac dst-mac ip
```

4. On SW2, configure the trunk interfaces and the port connected to the legitimate DHCP server as ARP trusted ports:

```
SW2(config)# interface range gigabitEthernet 0/1 -
gigabitEthernet 0/2
SW2(config-if-range)# ip arp inspection trust
SW2(config-if-range)# exit
SW2(config)# interface FastEthernet 0/1
SW2(config-if)# ip arp inspection trust
SW2(config-if)# exit
```

5. Enable DAI on VLAN 1:

```
SW2(config)# ip arp inspection vlan 1
```

6. Configure DAI to inspect both the source and destination MAC and IP addresses of each message on SW2:

```
SW2(config)# ip arp inspection validate src-mac dst-mac ip
```

7. Use the `show ip arp inspection` command to verify ARP inspection statistics, as shown in *Figure 17.38*:

```
Vlan     Configuration     Operation    ACL Match          Static ACL
----     -------------     ---------    ---------          ----------
   1     Enabled           Inactive

Vlan     ACL Logging       DHCP Logging       Probe Logging
----     -----------       ------------       -------------
   1     Deny              Deny               Off

Vlan      Forwarded         Dropped      DHCP Drops        ACL Drops
----      ---------         -------      ----------        ---------
   1              0               0               0                0

Vlan   DHCP Permits    ACL Permits  Probe Permits    Source MAC Failures
----   ------------    -----------  -------------    -------------------
   1              0              0              0                      0

Vlan   Dest MAC Failures    IP Validation Failures   Invalid Protocol Data
----   -----------------    ----------------------   ---------------------
   1                   0                         0                       0
```

Figure 17.38: Verifying ARP inspection details

8. The `show ip arp inspection vlan` command can be used to verify whether DAI is inspecting both the source and destination MAC and IP addresses of each message, as shown in *Figure 17.39*:

```
SW1#show ip arp inspection vlan 1

Source Mac Validation      : Enabled
Destination Mac Validation : Enabled
IP Address Validation      : Enabled

 Vlan     Configuration    Operation   ACL Match          Static ACL
 ----     -------------    ---------   ---------          ----------
    1     Enabled          Inactive

 Vlan     ACL Logging      DHCP Logging      Probe Logging
 ----     -----------      ------------      -------------
    1     Deny             Deny              Off

SW1#
```

Figure 17.39: Verifying additional ARP inspection configurations

Having completed this lab, you have gained hands-on experience and skills to implement DAI to prevent and mitigate IP spoofing and MiTM attacks in a Cisco environment. In the next section, you will learn how to secure a wireless network.

Wireless Security

Many organizations implement a wireless network to support the mobility of their users. A **wireless LAN** (**WLAN**) provides convenience to users with mobile devices, allowing them to roam around the building and work from anywhere. A WLAN is open to anyone within the range of the wireless signal generated by **access points** (**APs**) and with the correct user credentials to access the corporate network. WLANs create an entire landscape of threats and attacks by threat actors and even disgruntled employees.

The following are some threats on a wireless network:

- A threat actor can intercept traffic on a wireless network. The threat actor does not need to be within the building but rather within range of the wireless signal. It's recommended that all wireless traffic should be encrypted to prevent any eavesdropping.
- There can be an intruder on the wireless network. This is one who is not authorized to access the wireless network or resources.
- A threat actor can create a DoS attack to prevent legitimate users from accessing the wireless network.
- A threat actor can set up an **evil twin** or **rogue access point** to capture legitimate users' traffic.

A rogue access point is an unauthorized access point connected to an organization's network without permission, potentially allowing attackers direct access to the internal network. An evil twin is a fraudulent access point set up by an attacker outside the organization to mimic a legitimate one, tricking users into connecting and intercepting their data.

> **Note**
>
> To learn about wireless security penetration testing, you can check out the book *The Ultimate Kali Linux Book, Third Edition* at https://www.amazon.com/Ultimate-Kali-Linux-Book-Cutting-Edge/dp/1835085806/. The book also covers various aspects of ethical hacking and penetration testing.

One method to reduce the possibility of hiding your wireless network is disabling **service set identifier** (**SSID**) broadcast. This feature does not protect your network from a threat actor as there are techniques to discover a hidden wireless network, but it does reduce the possibility of a novice hacker detecting it. When SSID broadcast is disabled, the wireless router or AP will not send the SSID within its beacon messages.

Figure 17.40 is an example of how to disable SSID broadcast on a Linksys 160N device:

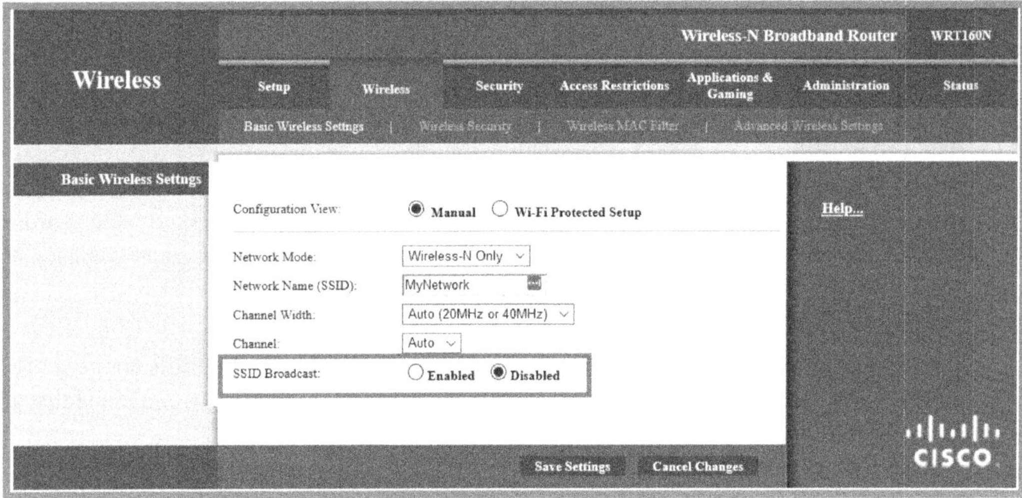

Figure 17.40: Disabling SSID broadcast

Additionally, you can enable **MAC address filtering** to create an access control list of permitted or denied devices. *Figure 17.41* shows an example of the MAC filtering interface on a Linksys 160N wireless router:

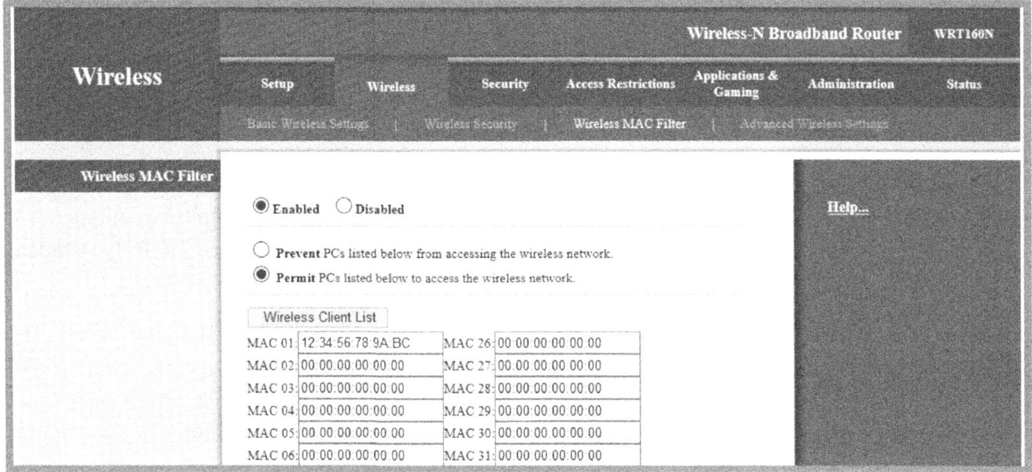

Figure 17.41: MAC filtering

Keep in mind that an experienced hacker can find ways to bypass MAC filtering controls on a wireless network. However, it is better to have security on your network than to have no security at all. In the next section, you will discover various methods of authentication that can be implemented on a wireless network.

Authentication Methods

A wireless router or AP provides a few options to configure how users are authenticated onto the network. One method is **open authentication**, which disables any authentication mechanisms on the wireless device. This method allows anyone to connect to the wireless network freely. This authentication method is commonly used in shopping malls, coffee shops, restaurants, and public areas.

> **Note**
>
> WPA3 is currently the only wireless security standard that encrypts messages on an open network using **Opportunistic Wireless Encryption** (**OWE**). This technology allows the encryption of traffic between the client and the access point on an open network. This type of implementation is useful for public Wi-Fi deployments.

Another method is **shared key authentication**, also referred to as **pre-shared key** (**PSK**). With PSK authentication, the wireless router is configured with a passphrase for the wireless network. Therefore, anyone attempting to access the wireless network will be prompted to provide the correct pre-shared key. There are various wireless security standards that use PSK:

- **Wired Equivalent Privacy** *(***WEP***)*: WEP is the first official standard used to secure data transmission using the **Rivest Cipher 4** *(***RC4***)* encryption algorithm on an IEEE 802.11 network. Due to various security vulnerabilities found in this standard, it's no longer recommended.
- **Wi-Fi Protected Access** *(***WPA***)*: This standard uses WEP with a more secure encryption algorithm known as **Temporal Key Integrity Protocol** *(***TKIP***)*. TKIP applies a unique key to each packet on the wireless network, thus making it difficult to compromise. TKIP also validates the integrity of each message by using **message integrity checks** (**MICs**).
- **WPA2**: WPA2 is currently the industry standard for securing IEEE 802.11 networks. This standard uses the **Advanced Encryption Standard** (**AES**) for data encryption, which is a lot stronger than those previously mentioned. AES uses the **Counter Cipher Mode with Block Chaining Message Authentication Code Protocol** (**CCMP**), which enables the destination device to validate confidentiality and integrity.
- **WPA3**: As of the writing of this book, WPA3 is the latest wireless security standard. WPA3 uses the most up-to-date security protocols and has discontinued outdated and legacy protocols. WPA3 uses **Simultaneous Authentication of Equals** (**SAE**) to mitigate vulnerabilities found in WPA2. WPA3 uses the **Commercial National Security Algorithm** (**CNSA**) in WPA3-Enterprise authentication.

Figure 17.42 shows an example of configuring the authentication methods on a wireless router:

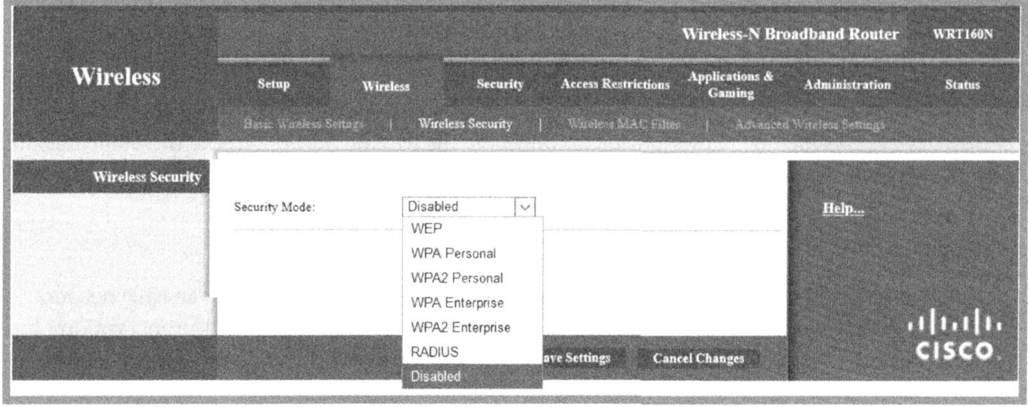

Figure 17.42: Authentication methods

WPA and WPA2 use two additional authentication methods:

- **Personal**: This method is commonly used on a home wireless network, which allows you to configure the pre-shared key directly on the wireless router.
- **Enterprise**: This method allows you to associate the wireless router with an AAA server. The wireless router does not handle the authentication of users on the network but hands the responsibility over to an AAA server such as RADIUS.

Having completed this section, you have learned about various wireless security threats and security mechanisms. In the next section, you will learn how to implement a wireless network and apply wireless security.

Lab: Implementing Wireless Security Using a WLC

In this lab, you will learn how to implement wireless security using a Cisco WLC. This lab is simply an extension of the previous exercise on *implementing dynamic ARP inspection*. For this lab, ensure you add the additional devices to the network topology shown in *Figure 17.43*:

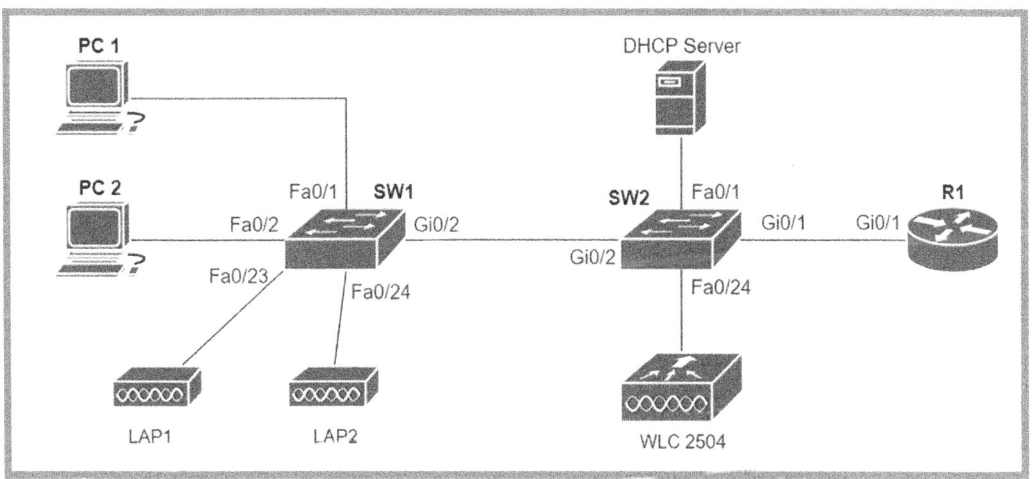

Figure 17.43: Wireless security lab topology

Please ensure you use the following guidelines when creating this lab to ensure you get the same results:

- For the WLC, use the **Cisco 2504** controller. On Cisco Packet Tracer, click on **Network Devices | Wireless** to select the Cisco 2504 controller.
- For the **lightweight access points** (**LAPs**), use the **LAP-PT** devices. *Figure 17.44* shows the location of both the WLC and LAPs on the Cisco Packet Tracer application:

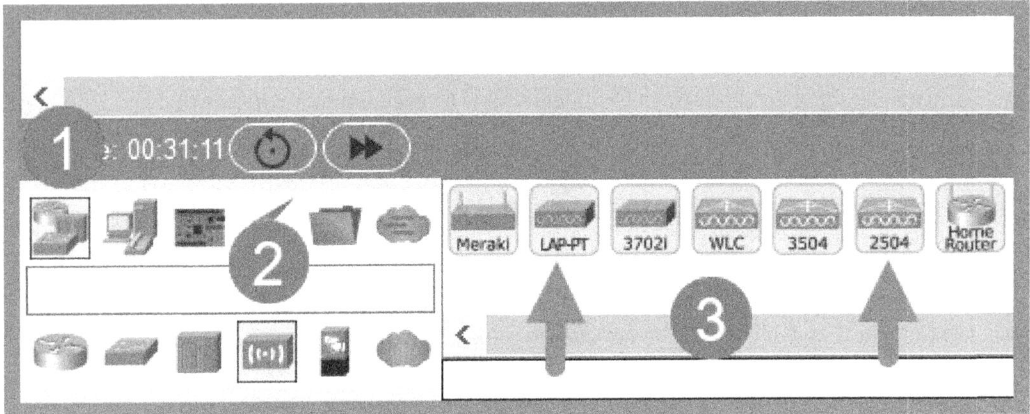

Figure 17.44: Wireless components

The numbered labels in *Figure 17.44* show the buttons to click on.

Now that your topology is ready, use the following instructions to set up the WLC and implement the wireless section on the network:

1. Click on the WLC and select `Config` | `Management` interface to assign the following addresses, as shown in *Figure 17.45*:

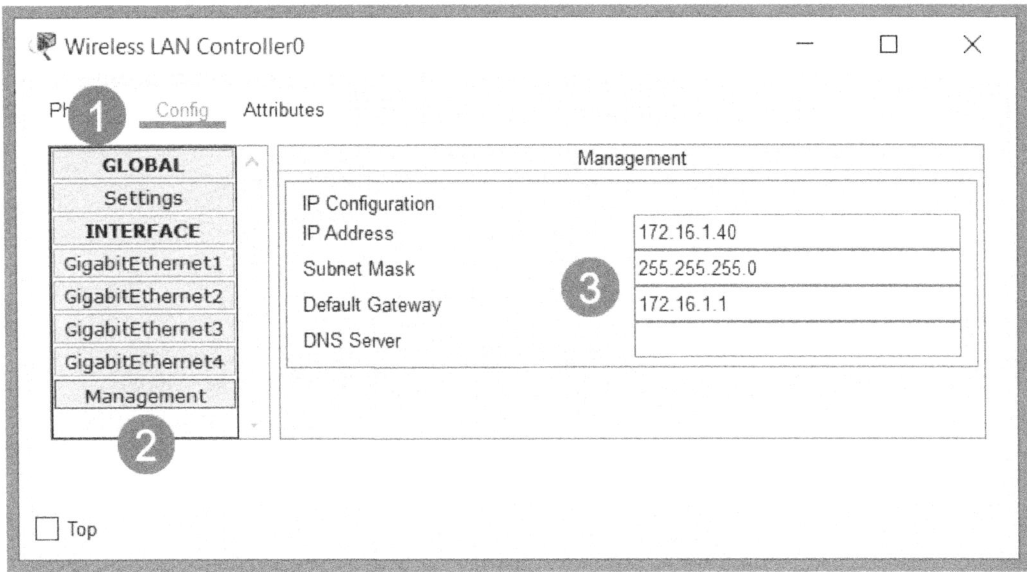

Figure 17.45: WLC IP configurations

2. Click on `PC 1`, select the `Desktop` tab, and open the web browser. Enter the URL http://172.16.1.40 and click `Go` to load the WLC home page.

3. Create a username, `admin`, set a password, `Cisco123`, and click `Start` as shown in *Figure 17.46*:

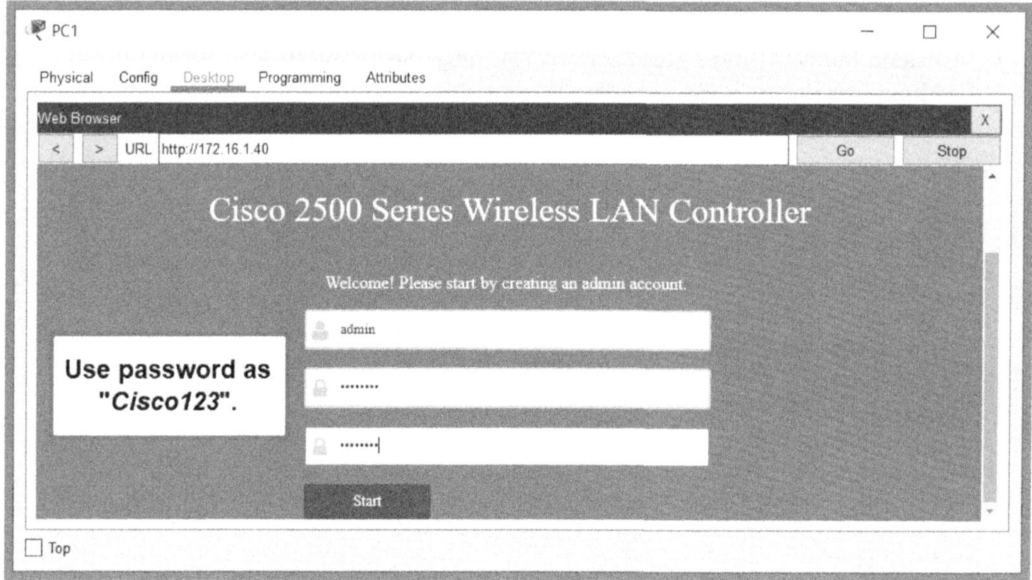

Figure 17.46: WLC welcome page

4. Configure the management IP address, subnet mask, and default gateway, as shown in *Figure 17.47*:

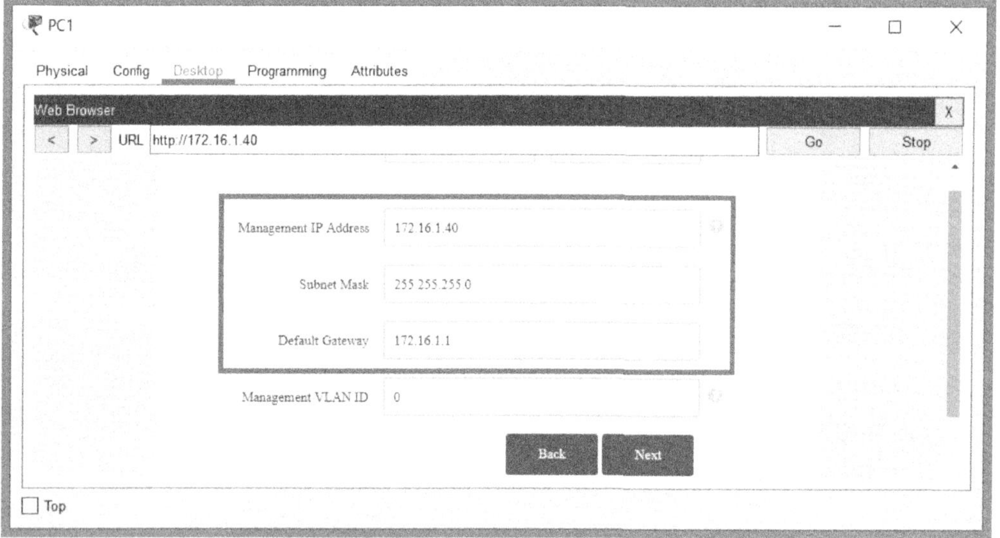

Figure 17.47: Management IP on WLC

The IP settings are the same as defined in Step 1. Click `Next` to continue.

5. On the next page, create a wireless network named `WLAN-Corp`, set `Security` to `WPA2-Personal` and `Passphrase` to `cisco456`, as shown in *Figure 17.48*:

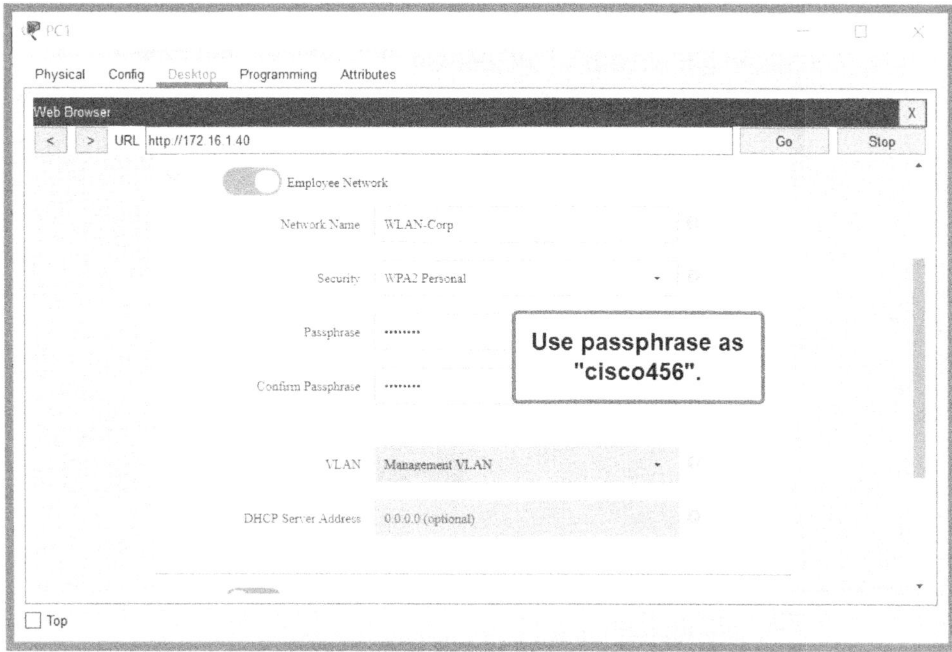

Figure 17.48: Creating a wireless network on WLC

6. You will be asked to configure a virtual IP address that allows the LAPs to communicate with the WLC on the network. Leave this configuration as the default and click `Next`.

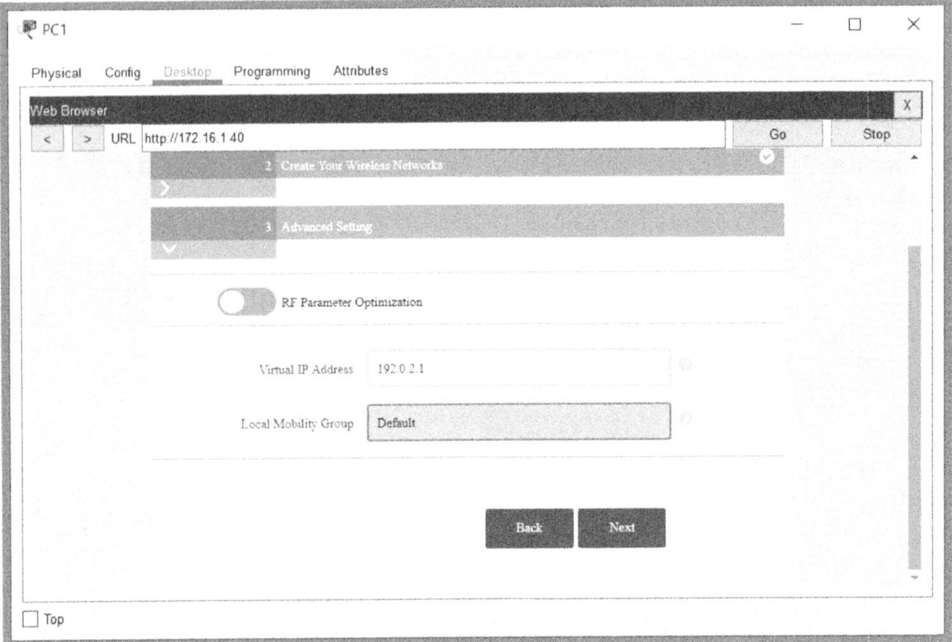

Figure 17.49: Virtual IP configuration on WLC

7. Next, the WLC will present a summary page with the configurations you have made, click `Apply`. The WLC will reboot. To access the WLC after it has rebooted, use the URL https://172.16.1.40.
8. While the WLC is rebooting, click on each LAP and drag the power adapter (1) to the power interface (2) as shown in *Figure 17.50*:

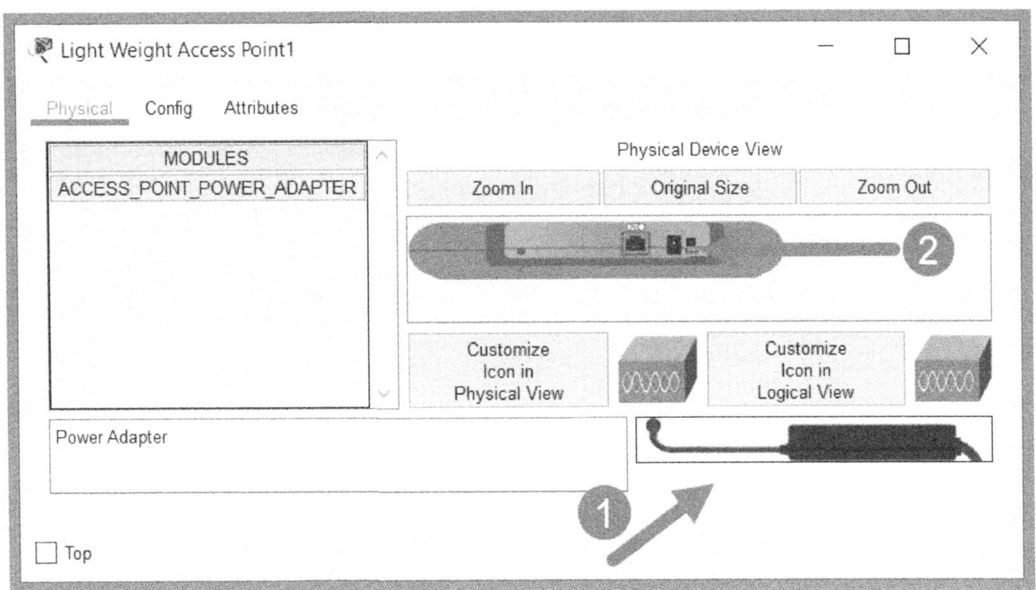

Figure 17.50: Connecting power adapter to AP

By default, the LAPs do not have power. Connecting the power adapter via Cisco Packet Tracer will supply power to the device.

9. You need to re-enable the interfaces associated with the LAPs on SW1. Use the following commands to enable the interfaces:

```
SW1(config)# interface range FastEthernet 0/23 - FastEthernet
0/24
SW1(config-if-range)# no shutdown
SW1(config-if-range)# exit
```

The interfaces may take a few seconds before they transition into a forwarding state.

10. It is time to test whether the wireless network is configured properly by connecting a mobile device. On Cisco Packet Tracer, click on `End Devices` and drag `Smart Device (phone)` near to a LAP.

11. Click on `Smart Device (phone)`, select `Config` | `Wireless0` interface, and apply the SSID `WLAN-Corp`, set `Authentication` to `WPA2-PSK`, and set `PSK Pass Phrase` to `cisco456` as shown in *Figure 17.51*:

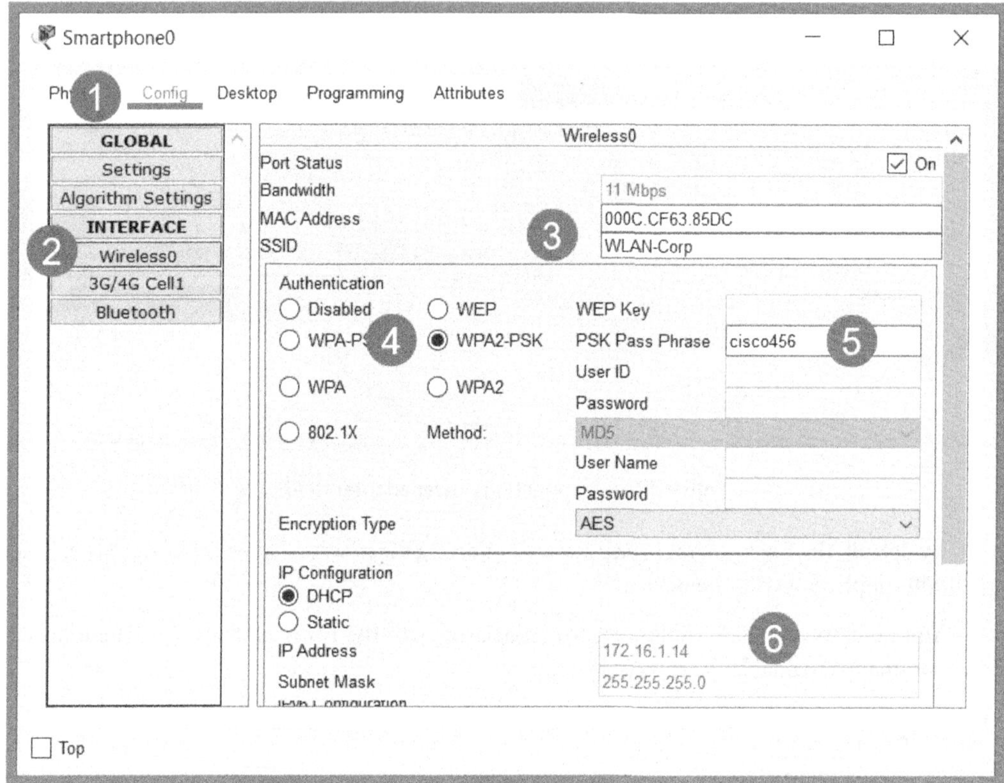

Figure 17.51: Wireless configuration on smart device

After applying the wireless configurations, the smart device will automatically associate itself with one of the LAPs and receive an IP address from the DHCP server on the network.

12. Lastly, you can validate the IP configurations on the smart device. Click on `Desktop` | `Command Prompt` and execute the `ipconfig` command, as shown in *Figure 17.52*:

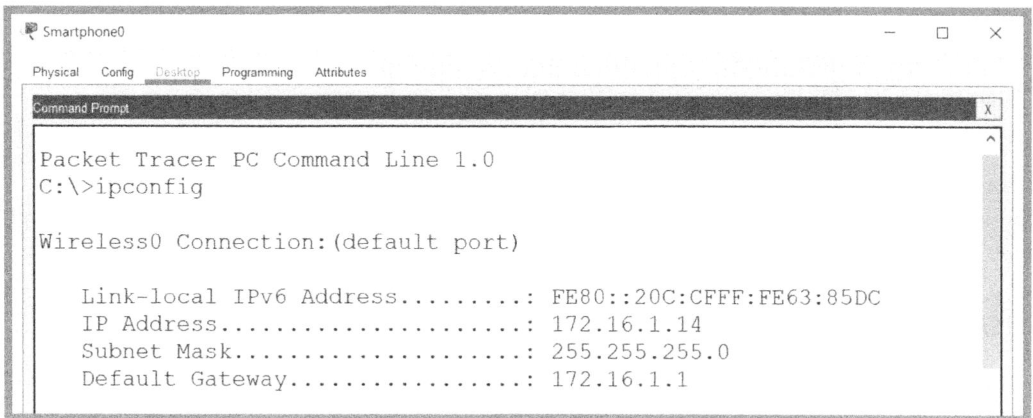

Figure 17.52: Validating IP configurations

Having completed this section, you have gained hands-on experience implementing a Cisco WLC and LAPs, and implemented wireless security in a Cisco environment.

Summary

In this chapter, you learned about the need to use a multi-layered approach known as **Defense in Depth** to improve the security posture of your network and organization. Furthermore, you learned how threat actors can use various Layer 2 threats and attacks to compromise our enterprise network. You then learned how to implement Layer 2 security controls on your Cisco IOS switches to prevent and mitigate Layer 2 attacks and wireless security to secure your network. By better understanding common Layer 2-based attacks and threats, network professionals can leverage such information and improve their network defenses from potential attacks. Implementing common Layer 2 security mechanisms such as DHCP snooping, DAI, and port security can proactively prevent unauthorized devices from joining your network.

In the next chapter, *Chapter 18, Network Automation and Programmability Techniques*, you will learn how automation and programmability can improve efficiency in network deployment and management.

Additional Reading

- Configuring port security: `https://www.cisco.com/c/en/us/td/docs/switches/lan/catalyst4500/12-2/25ew/configuration/guide/conf/port_sec.html`
- Configuring DHCP snooping: `https://www.cisco.com/c/en/us/td/docs/switches/lan/catalyst6500/ios/12-2SX/configuration/guide/book/snoodhcp.html`
- Configuring DAI: `https://www.cisco.com/c/en/us/td/docs/switches/lan/catalyst6500/ios/12-2SX/configuration/guide/book/dynarp.html`

Exam Readiness Drill – Chapter Review Questions

Apart from mastering key concepts, strong test-taking skills under time pressure are essential for acing your certification exam. That's why developing these abilities early in your learning journey is critical.

Exam readiness drills, using the free online practice resources provided with this book, help you progressively improve your time management and test-taking skills while reinforcing the key concepts you've learned.

HOW TO GET STARTED

- Open the link or scan the QR code at the bottom of this page
- If you have unlocked the practice resources already, log in to your registered account. If you haven't, follow the instructions in *Chapter 19* and come back to this page.
- Once you log in, click the START button to start a quiz
- We recommend attempting a quiz multiple times till you're able to answer most of the questions correctly and well within the time limit.
- You can use the following practice template to help you plan your attempts:

Working On Accuracy		
Attempt	Target	Time Limit
Attempt 1	40% or more	Till the timer runs out
Attempt 2	60% or more	Till the timer runs out
Attempt 3	75% or more	Till the timer runs out
Working On Timing		
Attempt 4	75% or more	1 minute before time limit
Attempt 5	75% or more	2 minutes before time limit
Attempt 6	75% or more	3 minutes before time limit

The above drill is just an example. Design your drills based on your own goals and make the most out of the online quizzes accompanying this book.

First time accessing the online resources? 🔓

You'll need to unlock them through a one-time process. **Head to** *Chapter 19* **for instructions.**

Open Quiz

https://packt.link/ccnachap17

OR scan this QR code →

18

Network Automation and Programmability Techniques

In 2019, Cisco made a huge announcement about its certification tracks and examination structure. One notable update was the inclusion of automation and programmability within the *CCNA*, *CCNP*, and *CCIE* certification tracks. You are probably wondering what this means for current and new network engineers. Put simply, automation and programmability are being integrated into network engineering, creating a new type of network professionals, which are referred to as **network developers**.

In this chapter, you will learn how programmability and automation are being integrated into network engineering. Furthermore, you will gain the knowledge to understand various data formats of programming languages, such as **JavaScript Object Notation** (**JSON**), **YAML Ain't Markup Language** (**YAML**), and **Extensible Markup Language** (**XML**).

This chapter covers *Domain 6: Automation and Programmability*, specifically the *6.1 Explain how automation impacts network management*, *6.2 Compare traditional networks with controller-based networking*, *6.3 Describe controller-based, software defined architecture (overlay, underlay, and fabric)*, *6.4 Explain AI (generative and predictive) and machine learning in network operations*, *6.5 Describe characteristics of REST-based APIs (authentication types, CRUD, HTTP verbs, and data encoding)*, *6.6 Recognize the capabilities of configuration management mechanisms, such as Ansible and Terraform*, and *6.7 Recognize components of JSON-encoded data* objectives of the *200-301 CCNA v1.1 Certification* exam.

In this chapter, you will cover the following topics:

- Understanding automation
- Understanding data formats
- Understanding APIs
- Understanding network configuration management
- Understanding **intent-based networking** (**IBN**)

Let's dive in!

Understanding Automation

Automation is any process that is self-driven without the need for human intervention. In many manufacturing plants around the world, machines (or robots) are used during the building and assembly process. Imagine a car manufacturer using machines that can operate on a 24/7/365 continuous schedule that is being controlled by a computer. The computer provides the instructions for the machines to interpret and execute on the manufacturing line. These machines can work continuously without the need to stop and rest. They perform jobs in a precise manner without errors or faults. Having machines in a production line removes the need for human workers, as higher production output is achieved while reducing the risk of human injuries on the job.

Keep in mind that all machines are being controlled using a computer system that instructs the machines when to start, end, and perform tasks all in a systemic process. This is an example of an assembly line being automated using machines and computer systems all working together while eliminating the need for human intervention.

Automation was most used within manufacturing plants where it was more effective to implement machines to perform certain tasks while the working environment may be hazardous to humans. Today, automation has been expanding to many industries, such as **information technology** (**IT**). An example is home automation, where you can use a Raspberry Pi (a small, affordable, single-board computer) with its native operating system and the Python programming language with a few other components to automate various processes at home. Automation is such an awesome topic to learn, especially because many tasks within our jobs in network engineering and even other areas of IT can benefit a lot.

Have you ever wondered how one system is able to communicate with another system? Take the scenario where the computer system is managing the machines to produce a car. Both the computer system and the machines are different altogether, and they are not designed with the same operating system or applications. Hence, natively, they are not able to work together. From the point of view of network engineers, it would seem the computer system is able to communicate fluently with the machines and vice versa, as they are executing the tasks as coordinated by the computer. When the computer sends instructions to the machines, they are able to connect all the instructions received and then use it to perform an action. The computer must send the instructions using a structured **data format** that will contain all the information the machines need to understand for the task and perform their jobs.

Understanding Data Formats

Imagine there are two different systems on a network, such as a computer and a router. The computer was to share data with the router, but since these are two different devices altogether, the router may not understand or be able to interpret the message it receives from the computer. To solve this issue, data formats are used to ensure that the data being exchanged between systems is presented in a format that is easy to understand by another system. Think of data format like a person's handwriting: a document handwritten by a person who has legible handwriting that can be read by another, as compared to a document written by a person who has illegible handwriting.

Data format goes a step further to ensure computers, network devices, and applications are all able to understand the data that is being shared among themselves. As an example, take a look at a simple web page written in **Hypertext Markup Language** (**HTML**), as shown in *Figure 18.1*:

```
HTMLPage1.html
<!DOCTYPE html>

<html lang="en" xmlns="http://www.w3.org/1999/xhtml">
<head>
    <meta charset="utf-8" />
    <title>TEST Web Page</title>
</head>
<body>
    <h1> This is the Heading for the webpage</h1>
    <p>This page is simply used to demonstrate HTML coding </p>
</body>
</html>
```

Figure 18.1: HTML code

HTML is known as one of the standard markup languages used to create web pages. The data format of HTML ensures that an application, such as a web browser, is able to read and understand the data easily. Additionally, a structured data format allows humans to read and understand most of the data, as shown in *Figure 18.1*. Notice how the data is presented between tags (elements). The title of the web page is placed between the `<title></title>` tags. This format is used throughout the remainder of the HTML code. This is an example of the structured data format.

Figure 18.2 shows how the HTML code is presented within a web browser:

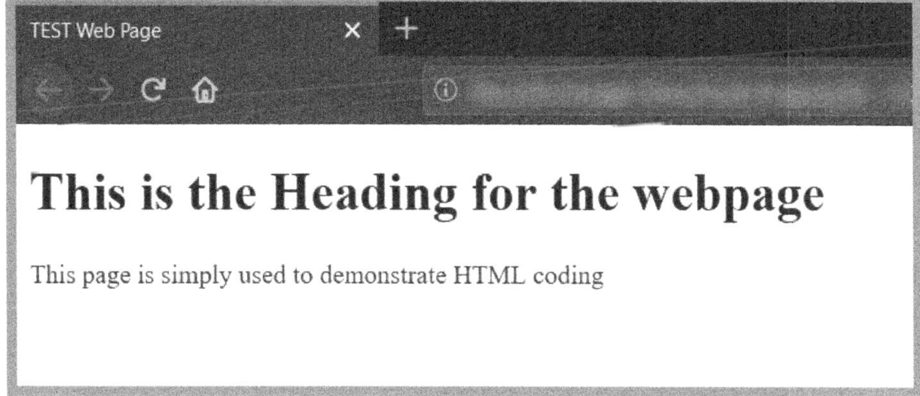

Figure 18.2: HTML web page

Data formats are very important to understand as they play a vital role in network automation and programmability. The following are the various data formats that are used in computer applications to assist with automation and programmability:

- XML
- JSON
- YAML

These data formats are not just for computers and applications to understand but being a structured data format also allows people to read and interpret the data and values just like a system, such as a computer or application, would.

Data formats use the following rules and structure:

- JSON, XML, and YAML use a key/value pair to represent data. The key is always on the left and is used to identify the data. The value is always on the right and is the actual data itself. Additionally, the key and value are always separated using a colon (`:`), such as `key:value`.
- Like programming languages, there are various syntaxes that are used with data formats. These are square braces (`[]`), curve braces (`()`), curly braces (`{ }`), commas, quotation marks, whitespaces, and even indentations.
- The objects within a data format can be characters (`a-z`) or strings, such as words, lists, and arrays.

Over the next few sections, you will learn and understand the characteristics of JSON, XML, and YAML and how data is formatted using each of these data formats.

Extensible Markup Language

The XML data format is designed for the internet, as it closely resembles HTML. The challenge with formatting data using XML is the difficulty we have as humans to read and understand the data. The XML data format was designed to transport or carry data from one system to another, not to present or display it.

The following are some important guidelines when formatting data with XML:

- XML uses tags to structure its data. These tags use the following format: `<key> value </key>`.
- XML has the capability to use attributes with a key/value pair, such as `<key name="MyName"> value </key>`.

- Some whitespaces used within an XML data format are ignored. In XML, whitespace within element content is preserved unless explicitly marked otherwise or processed by an application that interprets the XML data.
- Both configuration files and websites' sitemap use XML.

> **Note**
>
> If you're interested in learning more about the XML data format, please see the following URL for *W3 Schools*: https://www.w3schools.com/xml/default.asp.

Figure 18.3 shows a simple note written in the XML data format:

```
<?xml version="1.0" encoding="UTF-8" ?>
<note>
    <to>Alice</to>
    <from>Bob</from>
    <heading>CCNA Study Group</heading>
    <body>We have received a new assignment.</body>
</note>
```

Figure 18.3: XML data format

As shown in *Figure 18.3*, on each line, the values are placed between their corresponding keys. Additionally, some lines within the data format are indented to improve readability by humans, but this is not mandatory for systems and applications. XML is also used to store, transfer, and read data between systems and applications.

JavaScript Object Notation

JavaScript Object Notation (**JSON**) is another human-readable data format used by systems and applications to store, transfer, and read data. JSON has gained a lot of popularity for its use cases with many web services and **application programming interfaces** (**APIs**) to retrieve data from publicly accessible devices.

To better understand the JSON data form, take a look at the output from `show interface GigabitEthernet 0/1` on a Cisco **Internetwork Operating System** (**IOS**) router:

```
GigabitEthernet0/1 is up, line protocol is up (connected)
  Description: Connected to Wide Area Network (WAN)
  Internet address is 172.16.1.1/24
```

The preceding output provided via the console of a Cisco IOS router can be represented in JSON data format, as shown in *Figure 18.4*:

```
{
    "ietf-interfaces:interface": {
        "name": "GigabitEthernet0/1",
        "description": "Connected to Wide Area Network (WAN)",
        "enabled": true,
        "ietf-ip:ipv4": {
            "address": [
                {
                    "ip": "172.16.1.1",
                    "netmask": "255.255.255.0"
                }
            ]
        }
    }
}
```

Figure 18.4: JSON data format

As shown in *Figure 18.4*, each key/value pair contains a different piece of data about the device's interface, such as name, description, whether the interface is enabled or disabled, and the IP address and subnet mask.

To better understand how data is formatted in JSON, take a look at the following characteristics:

- JSON uses a hierarchical tree structure that contains nested values and objects.
- JSON uses curly braces ({ }) to contain/hold objects.
- An object in JSON is data that is enclosed within curly braces ({ }).
- JSON uses square braces ([]) to contain/hold arrays. An array is used to represent a list of data in programming. An example of a list can be a shopping list.
- Data represented in JSON is written using a **key/value** pair. The key/value pairs are written in the `key:value` format. A colon is used to separate the key and value.
- Whitespaces are ignored but used to improve human readability.

The following are some key points to help you interpret JSON:

- All keys are written in double quotation marks. Values must be either other objects, arrays, strings, numbers, or Boolean expressions. The following is an example of a key/value pair in JSON:

  ```
  { "certification":"CCNA 200-301" }
  ```

  Since the key/value pair is enclosed in curly braces, the entire format is known as a JSON object.

- You can have more than one key/value pair within a single object; a comma is used to separate each key/value pair from each other.
- A key may contain more than one value. Think of it like a list of items for shopping. In the programming world, this is known as an array. An **array** is defined as an ordered list of values enclosed in square braces ([]). Each value within a key is separated by a comma. Each array within an object is also separated by a comma.

  Figure 18.5 is an example of a list of IT certifications represented in JSON:

```
{
  "ITCerts":[
    {
      "Networking":"Cisco Certified Network Associate"
    },
    {
      "Cybersecurity":"Cisco Certified CyberOps Associate"
    },
    {
      "NetworkDeveloper":"Cisco Certified DevNet Associate"
    }
  ]
}
```

Figure 18.5: Array in JSON

From *Figure 18.5*, you can determine the following:

- The key in this code is `ITCerts`.
- Square braces ([]) are used to create an array (list) of three objects. These three objects are `Networking`, `Cybersecurity`, and `NetworkDeveloper`.
- Each object is enclosed with a curly brace ({ }) and is separated by a comma. The last object within the array does not end with a comma because it is the last item on the list.
- Each object contains one key/value pair.

> **Note**
>
> If you are interested in learning more about the JSON data format, please see the following URL for W3 Schools: https://www.w3schools.com/js/js_json_intro.asp.

As you have noticed with JSON, it is another human-readable data format for representing and exchanging data between systems and applications.

YAML Ain't Markup Language (YAML)

YAML is another human-readable data format that is also used to store, transfer, and read data between systems and applications. The following are the characteristics of YAML:

- YAML uses a very minimalistic format, thus making it super easy to read and write
- YAML uses indentations to define the data structure without the need for commas and braces of any kind
- Whitespaces define the structure of the YAML file
- YAM uses a dash (-) to represent a list of items within an array
- It is newer than XML and JSON and is gaining popularity

Compare the JSON data format shown in *Figure 18.6* with YAML:

```
{
  "ITCerts":[
    {
      "Networking":"Cisco Certified Network Associate"
    },
    {
      "Cybersecurity":"Cisco Certified CyberOps Associate"
    },
    {
      "NetworkDeveloper":"Cisco Certified DevNet Associate"
    }
  ]
}
```

Figure 18.6: JSON data format

Now, take a look at the same data written in YAML, as shown in *Figure 18.7*:

```
ITCerts:
    - Networking: Cisco Certified Network Associate
    - Cybersecurity: Cisco Certified CyberOps Associate
    - NetworkDeveloper: Cisco Certified DevNet Associate
```

Figure 18.7: YAML data format

Notice how key/value pairs written in YAML do not use any command or quotation mark and each object within the array is indicated using a dash (-).

> **Note**
>
> If you are interested in learning more about the YAML data format, please see the following URL for Tutorials Point: https://www.tutorialspoint.com/yaml/index.htm.

YAML has become the preferred data format in the networking industry because it is very easy for humans and systems to understand.

Having completed this section, you have gained the essential skills to interpret various data formats, such as XML, JSON, and YAML. In the next section, you will discover the vital role the API plays in a network, especially in network development and operations.

Understanding API

An API allows data formats to be shared between different systems or devices. APIs allow an application to send and retrieve data from another system. APIs are used almost everywhere, from cloud services, such as Microsoft Azure or Amazon AWS, to even social media platforms, such as Facebook.

To understand how APIs operate, imagine you visit your favorite restaurant to have dinner with your family or significant other. At the restaurant, you are given a menu to choose your meal from, before it is prepared in the kitchen. As a customer, you will not be allowed to visit the kitchen to retrieve your meal when it is ready, a waiter or waitress is assigned this role. When you (the user) are ready to place your order, the request is made via the waiter/waitress (API), and this is known as an **API call**. The waiter/waitress then goes to the kitchen with your order (request). When the food (data) is ready, the waiter/waitress (API) delivers it to you (response).

Figure 18.8 shows the concept of an API retrieving data from a system for a user:

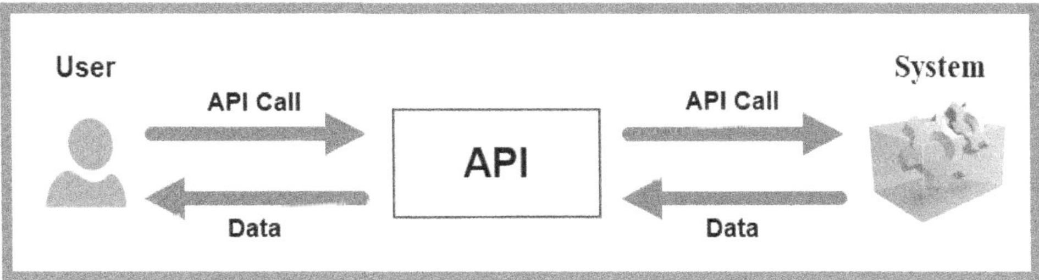

Figure 18.8: API operations

You can think of an API like a messenger that is used for requesting and retrieving data from a system or an application. When one system requests information from another, an API call is used to make the request.

Types of APIs

There are different types of APIs used for specific scenarios. Each type of API has its own unique purpose and role. The following are the various types of APIs:

- **Open/Public APIs**: The open or public APIs are designed to be used without any restrictions on a system. An example of a public API is the YouTube Data API, which allows a person to add YouTube functionality to their application or website.
- **Internal/Private APIs**: An internal or private API is used within an organization by its employees. An example is an internal API that can allow authorized persons from the sales team to access/retrieve internal sales information on their smart devices.
- **Partner APIs**: This type of API is used between different organizations or companies. An organization will gain authorization (permission from another company to use the API to retrieve data from their application or system). An example is a travel agency using APIs to retrieve information about airline schedules, and hotel booking for their customers.

Next, you will learn about **Representational State Transfer** (**REST**) APIs.

RESTful APIs

A REST API uses **Hypertext Transfer Protocol** (**HTTP**) to send or retrieve data to a system or application. Before diving in further, it is important to understand the fundamentals of HTTP communication between a client device, such as a computer, and a web server. For a client device to interface with a web server, a standard web browser is required, which allows the user to view web pages in a human-readable format. When a user wants to view a web page, the user opens their preferred web browser, which then uses either HTTP or **HTTP Secure** (**HTTPS**) to request (`HTTP GET`) the web page from the web server.

Figure 18.9 shows a client machine requesting a web page from a server:

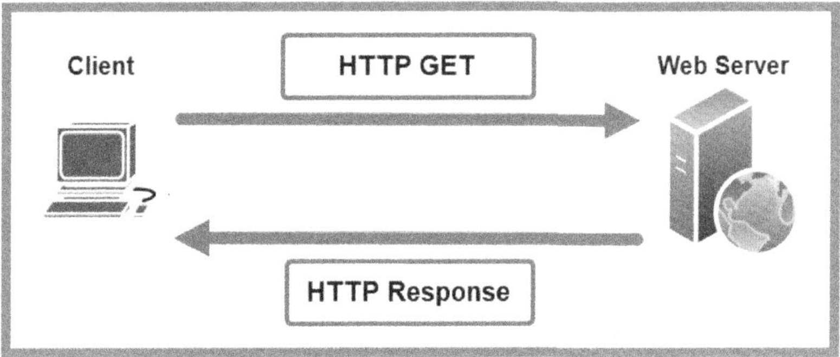

Figure 18.9: HTTP operation

When the server receives the `HTTP GET` message, it will respond with the HTTP `200` status code, and the web page is returned to the client. HTTP uses various status codes that can be used while troubleshooting. However, the HTTP `200` status code simply means the request is successful and the server provides the data.

A **REST API** is a type of API that operates on top of the HTTP, and therefore it defines the rules and instructions developers can use to execute tasks, such as request data and update or modify records on a system or application. All this is done using the HTTP protocol messages, such as `GET` and `POST`.

> **Note**
>
> An `HTTP GET` message is used to request data from a device, such as a server, while the `HTTP POST` message is used to update information on a server.

APIs that abide by the rules and guidelines of the REST structure are referred to as **RESTful APIs**. The following criteria must be met for an API to be considered RESTful:

- A RESTful API uses a **client-server model**. The client device is typically the frontend, where the user is able to interface with the server. The server is responsible for backend operations, such as hosting applications and servers and storing data. The benefit of using this model is that it allows each device to operate independently from each other. This means that either the client or the server can be replaced.
- RESTful APIs are **stateless** in nature. Being stateless means the server does not store any data between requests from any clients. All the session information, such as states, is stored only on the client machine. An example is that if a client sends an API call to a server, asking, "What is the weather like today?", the server will respond with the data. If the client sends a second API call, such as a follow-up to the previous request: "Will it be hot or cold?", the server will not be able to respond to the second request simply because it does not keep track of any states. In addition, the server can respond to the second request if the client includes the necessary context in the request. The statelessness means the server does not retain the state between requests, not that it cannot handle related queries if provided with the right data.
- RESTful APIs are considered **cacheable**. Since the server is not able to store any session states, information such as responses can be cached on the client machine simply to improve the overall performance of communication between clients and the server.

Since RESTful APIs use HTTP to request and respond to messages between systems, it is important to understand the types of HTTP methods, such as `POST`, `GET`, `PUT/PATCH`, and `DELETE`. For HTTP to request a resource, it needs to know where the resource is located, such as a web page on a web server. This is referred to as the **Uniform Resource Identifier** (**URI**). An example of a URI is https://www.netacad.com/courses/packet-tracer. Web services often support various data formats, such as the ones in the previous section: XML, JSON, and YAML. When a client machine wants to request a web page, it will send an `HTTP GET` message to the URI; if successful, the server will respond with the HTTP `200` status code and the web page in HTML.

RESTful API uses HTTP methods (verbs), such as `POST`, `GET`, `PATCH`, and `DELETE`, to send and retrieve data formats between a client and server. These HTTP methods also correspond to RESTful operations, such as **Create, Read, Update, and Delete** (**CRUD**).

Table 18.1 provides a side-by-side comparison between HTTP methods and RESTful operations with their description of CRUD:

HTTP Method	Restful Operations	Description
`POST`	Create	Allows a client to update data on the destination server
`GET`	Request	Allows a client to request or retrieve data from a destination server
`PUT/PATCH`	Update	Allows a client to update the records on a destination server
`DELETE`	Delete	Allows a client to delete data from a destination server

Table 18.1: CRUD

When a client machine is requesting (`HTTP GET`) data from a system such as a server, if the client uses a properly structured JSON request, the server will respond with the JSON data. The JSON data in the responses can then be presented in a client-side application.

For a RESTful API to interact perfectly with a system or application, it is important that the RESTful API correctly identifies web resources using a URI. A URL, which is a specific type of URI, is typically a string of text that identifies the location of a specific network resource.

A URI has the following two specifications:

- **Uniform Resource Name (URN)**: A URN is used to identify only the namespace of the resource. An example of a resource is a web page, image, or document without specifying a protocol. The following is an example of a URN: www.cisco.com/c/en/us/index.html.
- **Uniform Resource Locator (URL)**: A URL is a bit similar to a URN except it is used to specify the location of a resource on a network and specifies a protocol. There are many application layer protocols, such as HTTP, HTTPS, **File Transfer Protocol** (**FTP**), **Secure File Transfer Protocol** (**SFTP**), and so on. The following is an example of a URL: https://www.cisco.com/c/en/us/index.html.

Additionally, a URI is made up of the following components:

- **Protocol (Scheme)**: The protocol simply defines the application layer protocol, which is used by an application to access a resource. An example of a protocol is HTTP or HTTPS.
- **Hostname**: The hostname simply defines the **fully qualified domain name** (**FQDN**), such as www.cisco.com.
- **Path and File Name**: The path and file identify the location and name of the resource. An example of a path and file name is `/c/en/us/training-events/training-certifications/certifications/associate/ccna.html`.
- **Fragment**: The fragment identifies a specific area on a web page. An example of a fragment is `#~exams`.

The following is an example of a URI containing all the components mentioned:

```
https://www.cisco.com/c/en/us/training-events/training-
certifications/certifications/associate/ccna.html#~exams
```

If you click or visit the preceding URI, it will carry you to the examination section on the *CCNA* page of the Cisco website.

In another example, the following shows a RESTful API request sent from a client to Cisco DNA Center to request data on any interface that has the IPv4 address of `10.10.22.253`. The URI is as follows:

```
https://sandboxdnac.cisco.com/dna/intent/api/v1/interface/ip-
address/10.10.22.253
```

The server responded in the JSON data format, providing the response shown in *Figure 18.10*:


```
{
    "response": [
        {
            "pid": "ASR1001-X",
            "deviceId": "1cfd383a-7265-47fb-96b3-f069191a0ed5",
            "portName": "TenGigabitEthernet0/0/0",
            "ifIndex": "1",
            "mediaType": "unknown",
            "speed": "10000000",
            "status": "up",
            "adminStatus": "UP",
            "macAddress": "00:c8:8b:80:bb:00",
            "duplex": "FullDuplex",
            "interfaceType": "Physical",
            "ipv4Address": "10.10.22.253",
            "ipv4Mask": "255.255.255.252",
            "isisSupport": "false",
            "mappedPhysicalInterfaceId": null,
            "mappedPhysicalInterfaceName": null,
            "nativeVlanId": null,
            "ospfSupport": "false",
            "portMode": "routed",
            "portType": "Ethernet Port",
            "serialNo": "FXS1932Q1SE",
            "voiceVlan": null,
            "lastUpdated": "2020-06-30 13:37:16.891",
            "series": "Cisco ASR 1000 Series Aggregation Services Routers",
            "description": "Uplink to WAN Distribution - main-switch ten 1/1/1",
            "className": "EthrntPrtclEndpntExtndd",
            "vlanId": "0",
            "instanceTenantId": "5dc444d31485c5004c0fb20b",
            "instanceUuid": "15fe6fc3-f6e7-45d8-94f9-e89a0bdba9b1",
            "id": "15fe6fc3-f6e7-45d8-94f9-e89a0bdba9b1"
        }
    ],
    "version": "1.0"
}
```


Figure 18.10: Response in JSON data format

Cisco DNA Center returned all data regarding the interface that was assigned the specific IPv4 address as stated in the URI. As shown in *Figure 18.10*, you are able to read and interpret almost all the information presented in JSON, simply because JSON is a human-readable data format.

The RESTful API request consists of the following parts:

- **API Server**: This identifies the URL of the API server, which is as follows: `https://sandboxdnac.cisco.com`.
- **Resources**: This identifies the resources that are being requested by the client, such as `/dna/intent/api/v1/interface/ip-address/10.10.22.253`.
- **Query**: The query is used to specify the data format and the data that the client is requesting from the server. A query can include the format, which indicates whether the request is XML, JSON, or YAML. Additionally, a query can contain a key, which is used to identify an API key to authenticate the client to the server. Lastly, the query may also contain parameters, which are used to end specific information from the client to the server; this helps the API to know exactly what to return to the client.

> **Note**
>
> Systems that offer publicly accessible information, such as Google Maps, allow a user to generate a public API (key) on their platform to use the services. These keys provide a form of authentication between the client and the server, and it allows the server to track the number of persons using the API, limit the number of requests being sent by users, capture and keep track of the data clients are requesting, and gather information about the persons who are using the API.

For a user to make a RESTful API request to a system, the user can only use one of the following methods and tools:

- **Developer Website**: Many online application vendors usually have a developer website that they often maintain and publish procedures on how users are able to create and use their systems with APIs. An example is the Cisco DevNet website (https://developer.cisco.com), which contains many API documentation for various Cisco platforms.
- **Postman**: This tool allows a user to interact with a system using various HTTP verbs to perform actions such as CRUD. Postman also allows a user to construct and send RESTful API requests with additional query parameters, such as keys and format type. To learn more about Postman, please see the following URL: https://www.postman.com.
- **Python**: This programming language allows a developer to integrate RESTful API into their code to perform actions such as automation.
- **Network Operating Systems**: Network operating systems use various protocols, such as **Network Configuration Protocol** (**NETCONF**) and **Representational State Transfer Configuration Protocol** (**RESTCONF**), which allow a network developer to interact with a network device via an API. The NETCONF protocol allows a user to perform network configurations while the RESTCONF protocol allows the application to format the data before parsing it between the client and server machines.

Note

To learn more about **network programmability**, check out the free course on Cisco DevNet at `https://developer.cisco.com/video/net-prog-basics/`.

Having completed this section, you have gained the skills to identify and understand the purpose and role RESTful APIs play in accessing data between different systems. In the next section, you will learn about configuration management tools.

Understanding Network Configuration Management

At the opening of this chapter, we discussed automation and how it helps network engineers work more efficiently when configuring, deploying, and troubleshooting issues on a large network. An important factor with network automation is it saves us a lot of time from performing manual tasks on our network devices. In becoming a network developer, it is important to understand how various configuration management tools can improve how we automate configurations on our switches, routers, firewalls, and many other network devices.

In a traditional scenario, a network engineer will access and manage a network device, such as a router or switch, via a **command-line interface** (**CLI**). This is how everyone learns to manage their devices. If there is a change on the network, you would need to log in to the CLI and manually make the change. As this method has worked for many years, and it is the primary method that is used, it is also vulnerable to human error, where a person may misconfigure a device and it can be very time-consuming if the network engineer has to apply the same configurations to multiple devices. Sometimes, you may think that copying and pasting the configurations between devices is a form of automation. However, in reality, it is still a manual and time-consuming task.

The **Simple Network Management Protocol** (**SNMP**) allows you to manage various devices on your network, such as desktops computers, servers, networking devices, and security appliances, all on an IP-based network. A network engineer will need a **network management station** (**NMS**), which will function as the SNMP manager to interact with the SNMP agents on the nodes (desktops, switches, etc.). With SNMP, you will be able to update configurations on network devices. However, it is not recommended to use older versions of SNMP, such as SNMPv1 and SNMPv2, for network management due to security vulnerabilities found within the protocol suite. SNMP is also used to retrieve information about devices that help networking professionals gather useful data such as statistics and performance details on devices that make SNMP better for network monitoring than automating device configuration.

With APIs, a network developer can quickly automate configurations and deploy devices more efficiently on a network. With APIs, you can use automation configuration tools to configure changes on multiple devices, simultaneously, without having to manually log in to each device individually. With configuration management tools, you are able to use RESTful APIs to perform the automation of configurations on all your devices within your organization. These tools will help you to maintain consistency with system and network device configurations, such as security settings, IP protocol settings, interface configurations, and so on. Common configuration management tools are Ansible and Terraform.

Ansible is created by Red Hat and works with the Python programming language and YAML data format. It is **agentless**, which means an agent is not required to be installed or configured on a network device that you want to control. Being agentless allows the user to push configurations to a node on a network. In addition, you can manage any number of devices using Ansible. As the network grows, you can designate a dedicated machine known as an **Ansible controller** for centralized management of Ansible on the network. Since Ansible is agentless, any device can be a controller on the network. Lastly, all the instructions are created using a playbook.

Terraform is commonly used by developers for **infrastructure as code** (**IaC**) and it's being leveraged by network professionals to perform network automation of large network architectures and manage cloud environments. To define an infrastructure using Terraform, it uses the **HashiCorp Configuration Language** (**HCL**) and works with multiple vendors, not only Cisco.

An important factor of Terraform is its ability to maintain the state of a network or cloud infrastructure and keep track of changes that occur over time. This enables network professionals to maintain consistency of their network configurations and deployment, manage version control of devices' configurations, and reduce the risk of misconfigurations.

Having completed this section, you have gained the knowledge and understanding of various configuration management tools and have learned how each tool is different from the other. In the next section, you will take a deep dive, discovering IBN and Cisco DNA Center.

Understanding Intent-Based Networking

During the course of this chapter, you have learned about many amazing technologies that work together to help you as a network engineer automate many tasks on your enterprise network. In this section, you will learn about two additional pieces of technology that bring everything together for network automation. These are known as IBN and Cisco **Digital Network Architecture** (**DNA**) Center.

In the past, network engineers would implement a concept known as a **software-defined network** (**SDN**) to virtualize a network and provide a new method to offer network administration and management tasks. With SDN, the goal was to ensure network operations tasks were made simple and streamlined for network engineers.

Within a network device, such as a switch, a router or a security appliance contains three planes. Each plane has a unique role and function on the network. The following is a description of each plane:

- **Management Plane**: This plane is responsible for allowing an administrator to manage a device. As a typical network engineer, we would use various protocols, such as **Secure Shell** (**SSH**), HTTPS, **Trivial File Transfer Protocol** (**TFTP**), and SNMP, to help us manage our devices. This management place simply defines how we are able to access a network device.
- **Data Plane**: This plane is responsible for sending and receiving messages on a network device. It's like the forwarding plane on the device itself.
- **Control Plane**: This plane controls the entire network device and how it operates. This is the brain of the device. Within the control plane of a network device, Layer 2 and even Layer 3 forwarding mechanisms, routing protocols, IPv4 and IPv6 routing tables, the **Spanning Tree Protocol** (**STP**), and so on all exist in the control plane.

Since each device has all these planes, each device can think and make forwarding decisions on its own while operating on a production network. An example is an OSPF-enabled router that is able to make its forwarding decision of inbound packets independently, and all OSPF-enabled routers within a single area can establish neighbor adjacencies to exchange information with each other. Enabling OSPF on routers does not happen automatically. A network engineer needs to configure each router on the network with OSPF and the OSPF-enabled routers will attempt to create neighbor adjacencies. With SDN and controller-based networks, the entire overall deployment and configuration of OSPF on the network can be automated and managed.

To put it simply, you are using an SDN controller to manage the brain of all the network devices all together. Therefore, the control plane moves from the switches, routers, firewalls, and so on to the SDN controller on the network. The SDN controller enables a centralized control plane for all devices on the network while the data plane remains on the network devices as they will need to forward Layer 2 and Layer 3 messages.

Figure 18.11 shows the concept of an SDN controller acting as the centralized control plane for all the networking devices in a corporate environment:

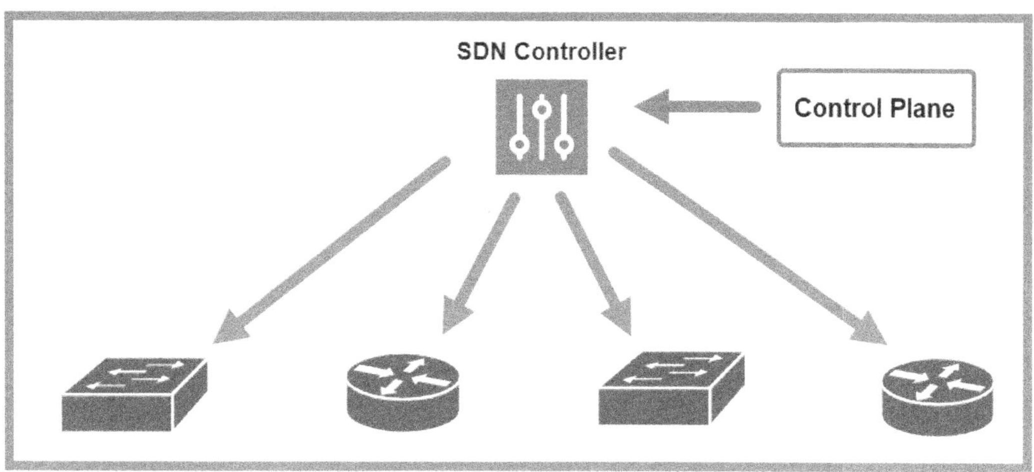

Figure 18.11: SDN controller

The SDN controller is able to control all the nodes (switches, routers, etc.) by using a **southbound interface** (**SBI**). The SDN controller needs to use some type of method to actually manage the network devices; the following is a list of technologies that the controller uses:

- NETCONF
- OpenFlow
- CLI
- SNMP
- OpFlex

The **northbound interface** (**NBI**) on the controller allows the network engineer to access and control everything on the network using a single pane of glass. As a network engineer or network developer, you can access the NBI using either a **graphical user interface** (**GUI**) or RESTful APIs.

Figure 18.12 shows the NBI of Cisco DNA Center on the Cisco DevNet platform:

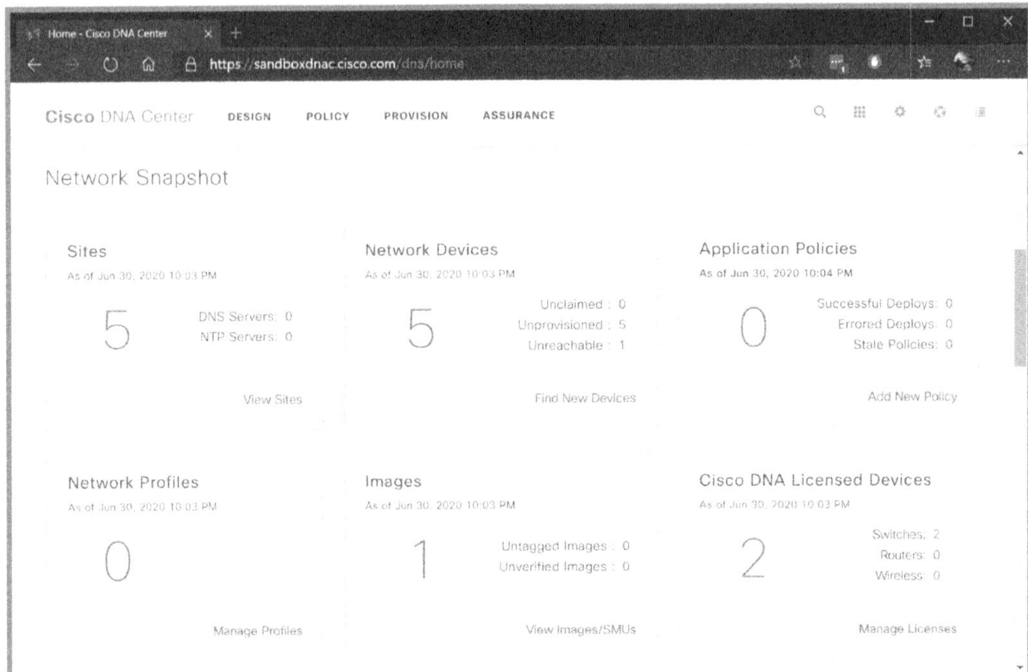

Figure 18.12: Cisco DNA Center NBI

IBN is the newest and latest technology that builds on top of SDN and allows all manual and hardware-centric tasks and operations to be designed to a full-fledge automated system that is software-centric. IBN makes all this happen by using Cisco DNA Center. With IBN, you do not need to log in to your routers or switches individually to configure **access control lists** (**ACLs**) to allow or deny traffic between networks or even manually configure the OSPF routing protocol on a group of routers.

With Cisco DNA Center, as a network developer, you will not need to worry too much about the actual CLI configuration. Cisco DNA Center, the centralized brain of the network, will automatically apply the configurations to all devices to make your thoughts a reality regarding how you want the network to operate, hence the term **intent-based networking**.

IBN contains the following three functions:

- **Translation**: This function is used to gather information about the business intent and translate it into policies. With this feature, a network engineer or developer is able to tell Cisco DNA Center their intention for the network and Cisco DNA Center will translate into supporting policies for the network.

- **Activation**: This function takes the policies it received from Translation, then coordinates the policies and configures the network devices, such as switches, routers, and so on, to meet the intent of the business.
- **Assurance**: This function is used to continuously gather insights about the network, which will allow Cisco DNA Center to manage and perform any adjustments to the network.

Figure 18.13 shows how these three functions all work together in Cisco DNA Center:

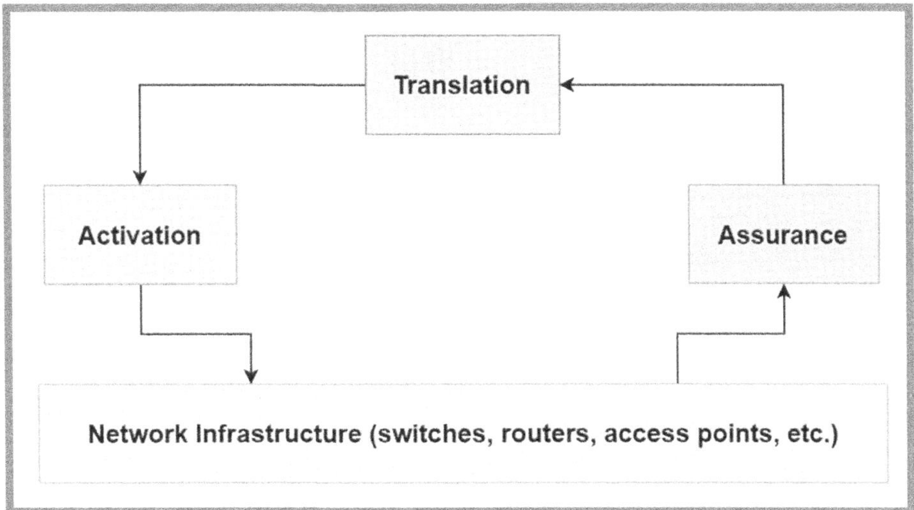

Figure 18.13: The three functions of IBN

With IBN on a network architecture, both physical and virtual devices are known as **fabric**. The term fabric is used to describe the entire topology of an enterprise network. Fabric is everything in a network, such as the devices, applications, and technologies used to forward traffic between networks and devices.

Fabric, Overlay, and Underlay

With SDNs and IBNs, Cisco DNA Center controller is not too concerned about how the network devices are interconnected or about the protocols they are using to forward traffic along the network. Cisco DNA Center uses an **overlay** to manage the logical topology. The overlay reduces the number of network devices a network engineer has to manually configure on the network; also, Cisco DNA Center is responsible for the services and how network devices forward traffic.

To put it simply, a network engineer can specify their intent to Cisco DNA Center, which will be translated into policies, and then be applied to the devices on the network via the overlay control plane to make it happen.

Figure 18.14 shows a typical physical network topology without seeing the overlay:

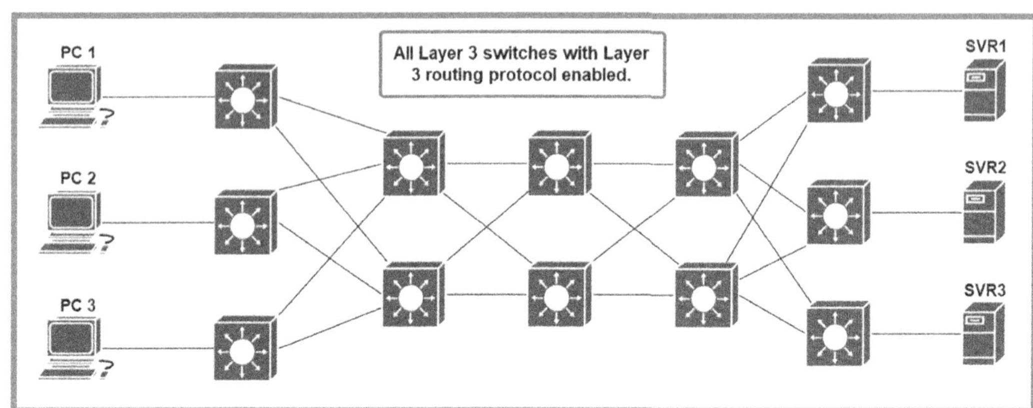

Figure 18.14: Physical network topology

Based on the physical topology in *Figure 18.14*, there are multiple hops between PC 1 and SVR1. If PC 1 wants to communicate with SVR1, the traffic can take many paths. With an overlay, a tunnel known as **Virtual Extensible LAN** (**VXLAN**) is established between both devices, therefore PC 1 will see SVR1 as a single hop away on the network.

Figure 18.15 shows the concept of VXLAN established between PC 1 and SVR1 on the network:

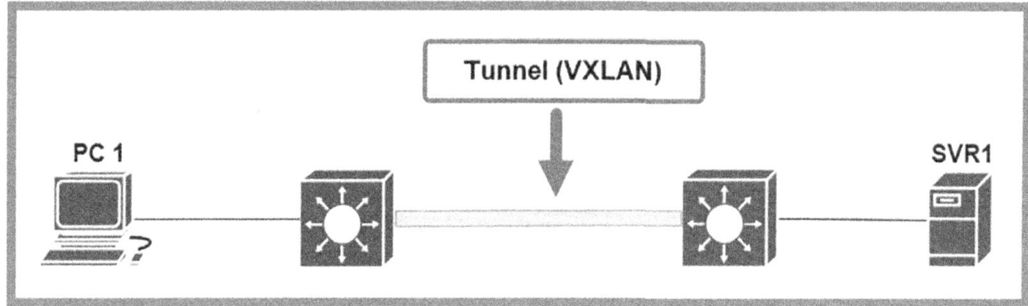

Figure 18.15: VXLAN tunnel

With Cisco DNA Center, the controller makes it seem that PC 1 and SVR1 are on a network only with those two devices.

> Note
>
> Think of the overlay as the area in which encapsulation protocols, such as **Control and Provisioning of Wireless Access Points** (**CAPWAP**), exist, which allows a **wireless LAN controller** (**WLC**) to manage its **lightweight access points** (**LAPs**).

The **underlay** is the actual physical network that provides connectivity for the overlay. This is typically the physical network topology that includes the switches, routers, servers, firewalls, and so on. Within the underlay, the control plane is responsible for the forwarding of traffic between devices on the topology.

Within a larger topology, such as a data center, such technologies are used to improve traffic flow between endpoints on the network. Cisco uses its **Application Policy Infrastructure Controller (APIC)** to manage all the network devices within the data center network.

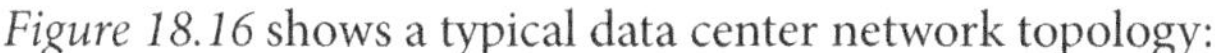

Figure 18.16 shows a typical data center network topology:

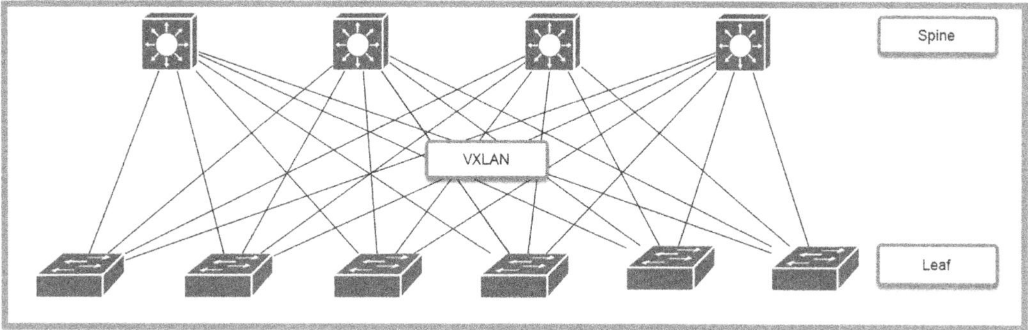

Figure 18.16: Spine-leaf topology

The lower switches (leaf) are connected to the upper layer switches (spine) to create a full-mesh design. The lower layer is made up of access switches that operate as both the Access and Distribution layer, and each leaf switch is connected to every spine switch. This model, with the implementation of VXLAN, allows the network to scale easily and takes care of issues that are related to cloud deployments.

Cisco DNA Center

Cisco DNA Center provides you with the following five key functions:

- **Design**: This function allows you to create an entire model of your intent network with buildings and office locations. You can also include both physical and virtual devices, LANs, WANs, and even cloud technologies.
- **Policy**: The policies allow the automation of network management and help us reduce the overall cost and risk while rolling out new services quickly on our enterprise network.
- **Provision**: This feature enables Cisco DNA Center to provide new network services quickly and efficiently on the network, whether it's a small or larger enterprise network Cisco DNA Center gets it done.

- **Assurance**: This feature enables Cisco DNA Center to take a proactive approach to monitoring and gathering intelligence on the network. Such information helps Cisco DNA Center predict potential network issues quickly and ensure the policies applied to the underlay are aligned with the business intent.
- **Platform**: This feature allows a network engineer to use APIs to interact between Cisco DNA Center and vendor devices.

> **Note**
>
> To learn more about the Cisco DNA Center user interface, please be sure to check out the free Cisco DNA Center online sandbox at Cisco DevNet using this URL: `https://developer.cisco.com/docs/sandbox/`.

With Cisco DNA Center, you can implement IBN within your organization. As you have learned, with this controller, you are able to securely deploy devices on your network. Additionally, with Cisco DNA Center, you can implement the following solutions:

- **Software-Defined Access (SD-Access)**: With SD-Access, access to network resources is made available within a matter of minutes to users or devices without security being a concern.
- **Software-Defined WAN (SD-WAN)**: This solution allows organizations to gain a better user experience when accessing their applications that are hosted in the cloud or even locally on an on-premises platform.
- **Cisco DNA Security**: This provides an entire 360 view of all real-time analytics and security intelligence on the network. It helps reduce the risk of threats while protecting your organization.
- **Cisco DNA Assurance**: This allows a network engineer to determine the cause of issues on the network quickly and provides recommended actions to resolve issues.

Having completed this section, you have learned about IBN, and its operations and components to make everything work together. Additionally, you discovered how Cisco DNA Center became the brain behind the entire operation of your network and its functionalities to improve everything on an enterprise network.

AI and ML in Network Operations

With the rise of **artificial intelligence** (**AI**) and **machine learning** (**ML**), network professionals are leveraging these technologies in network operations. AI enables network professionals to perform tasks that traditionally require manual action by human intelligence. For instance, **generative AI** enables network professionals to improve the creation and development of new solutions based on existing datasets.

The following are some common applications of generative AI in network operations:

- **Optimize Network Configurations**: Network professionals can use generative AI to create more efficient and optimized network configurations on devices, such as routers and switches. This enables network professionals to also leverage industry best practices in their network infrastructure.
- **Optimize Network Topology**: Generative AI can help network professionals get insights from existing datasets for designing an efficient and optimized network topology to provide the best performance for an organization.
- **Create Predictive Maintenance Schedules**: Since generative AI analyzes existing datasets and collects data quickly, network professionals can create a proactive maintenance schedule while predicting when the next failure may occur.
- **Create and Optimize Security Policies**: Generative AI can assist with creating optimized network security policies and configurations that are aligned with best practices and security requirements based on the business objectives.

Predictive AI helps network professionals analyze both historical and real-time data to predict potential future events on a network. The following are some common use cases of predictive AI in network operations:

- **Predicting Failures**: Predictive AI helps network professionals predict when the next potential network failure may occur based on the past performance issues that were recorded
- **Forecasting of Bandwidth**: Using past and current data, network professionals can leverage predictive AI to forecast their network bandwidth usage and assist with determining whether additional bandwidth is needed for critical applications
- **Cyber Threats Predication**: Predictive AI can be used to analyze network activities using past and real-time data to identify anomalies and patterns of a possible cyber-attack or threat
- **Optimization**: Predictive AI helps network professionals by suggesting preemptive actions to ensure their network infrastructure is operating efficiently

Being a subset of AI, ML focuses more on creating algorithms used by computing systems to improve their performance based on experiences. ML helps network professionals detect network anomalies, such as learning normal network traffic behavior patterns and looking for any deviations that would indicate a possible issue or security incident. In addition to this, network professionals can leverage ML to accurately perform traffic classification when working with QoS. Furthermore, ML can learn about issues based on past incidents and experiences to provide automated solutions to network professionals for common network issues, with insights into the root cause of the issue.

While AI and ML are trending topics and exciting fields with many signification benefits, there are some important factors to consider when using these technologies. For instance, the data quality and quantity may not be sufficient to provide the best solution. AL and ML usually require a lot of high-quality datasets to provide more accurate results and predictions; the lack of such quality and quantity may result in poor predictions. When using AI and ML technologies, there is little to no transparency in the decision-making process by the model. This can lead to a lack of interpretability by network professionals.

Having completed this section, you have learned about the essentials and the roles that AL and ML play in the field of network operations.

Summary

In this chapter, you learned about the new era of networking where automation and programmability can greatly help network engineers improve the time spent on deployment and configurations while reducing the need to manually perform repetitive tasks in their daily jobs. Additionally, you gained the skills in understanding various data formats, such as XML, JSON, and YAML, and learned how they are used to request data from a system using APIs.

Furthermore, you learned about the functions of various types of APIs and the components of RESTful APIs. You learned about the characteristics of configuration management tools and the roles they play in assisting us in network automation. Then, you learned how IBN and Cisco DNA Center can be used to help us fully automate our enterprise network using a controller-based model.

Although the journey of preparing for the 200-301 CCNA v1.1 examination can be tough, and there are many challenges along the path on the road to success, thank you very much for your support in purchasing a copy of this book, and congratulations on making it to end while acquiring all these amazing new skills on learning about network engineering. Everything you have learned in this book has been designed to be informative and helpful in your journey toward implementing and administering Cisco solutions and preparing for the 200-301 CCNA v1.1 certification.

Additional Reading

- Cisco DNA Center: `https://www.cisco.com/c/en/us/products/collateral/cloud-systems-management/dna-center/nb-06-dna-center-so-cte-en.html?oid=sowen000306`
- Learn JSON: `https://www.w3schools.com/js/js_json_intro.asp`
- Learn YAML: `https://www.tutorialspoint.com/yaml/index.htm`

Exam Readiness Drill – Chapter Review Questions

Apart from mastering key concepts, strong test-taking skills under time pressure are essential for acing your certification exam. That's why developing these abilities early in your learning journey is critical.

Exam readiness drills, using the free online practice resources provided with this book, help you progressively improve your time management and test-taking skills while reinforcing the key concepts you've learned.

HOW TO GET STARTED

- Open the link or scan the QR code at the bottom of this page
- If you have unlocked the practice resources already, log in to your registered account. If you haven't, follow the instructions in *Chapter 19* and come back to this page.
- Once you log in, click the START button to start a quiz
- We recommend attempting a quiz multiple times till you're able to answer most of the questions correctly and well within the time limit.
- You can use the following practice template to help you plan your attempts:

Working On Accuracy		
Attempt	**Target**	**Time Limit**
Attempt 1	40% or more	Till the timer runs out
Attempt 2	60% or more	Till the timer runs out
Attempt 3	75% or more	Till the timer runs out
Working On Timing		
Attempt 4	75% or more	1 minute before time limit
Attempt 5	75% or more	2 minutes before time limit
Attempt 6	75% or more	3 minutes before time limit

The above drill is just an example. Design your drills based on your own goals and make the most out of the online quizzes accompanying this book.

First time accessing the online resources?

You'll need to unlock them through a one-time process. **Head to** *Chapter 19* **for instructions.**

Open Quiz	
`https://packt.link/ccnachap18`	
OR scan this QR code →	

19
Accessing the Online Practice Resources

Your copy of *Implementing and Administering Cisco Solutions 200-301 CCNA Exam Guide* comes with free online practice resources. Use these to hone your exam readiness even further by attempting practice questions on the companion website. The website is user-friendly and can be accessed from mobile, desktop, and tablet devices. It also includes interactive timers for an exam-like experience.

How to Access These Materials

Here's how you can start accessing these resources depending on your source of purchase.

Purchased from Packt Store (packtpub.com)

If you've bought the book from the Packt store (`packtpub.com`) eBook or Print, head to `https://packt.link/ccnaunlock`. There, log in using the same Packt account you created or used to purchase the book.

Packt+ Subscription

If you're a *Packt+ subscriber*, you can head over to the same link (`https://packt.link/ccnapractice`), log in with your `Packt ID`, and start using the resources. You will have access to them as long as your subscription is active.

If you face any issues accessing your free resources, contact us at `customercare@packt.com`.

Purchased from Amazon and Other Sources

If you've purchased from sources other than the ones mentioned above (like *Amazon*), you'll need to unlock the resources first by entering your unique sign-up code provided in this section. **Unlocking takes less than 10 minutes, can be done from any device, and needs to be done only once**. Follow these five easy steps to complete the process:

STEP 1

Open the link `https://packt.link/ccnaunlock` OR scan the following **QR code** (*Figure 19.1*):

Figure 19.1: QR code for the page that lets you unlock this book's free online content

Either of those links will lead to the following page as shown in *Figure 19.2*:

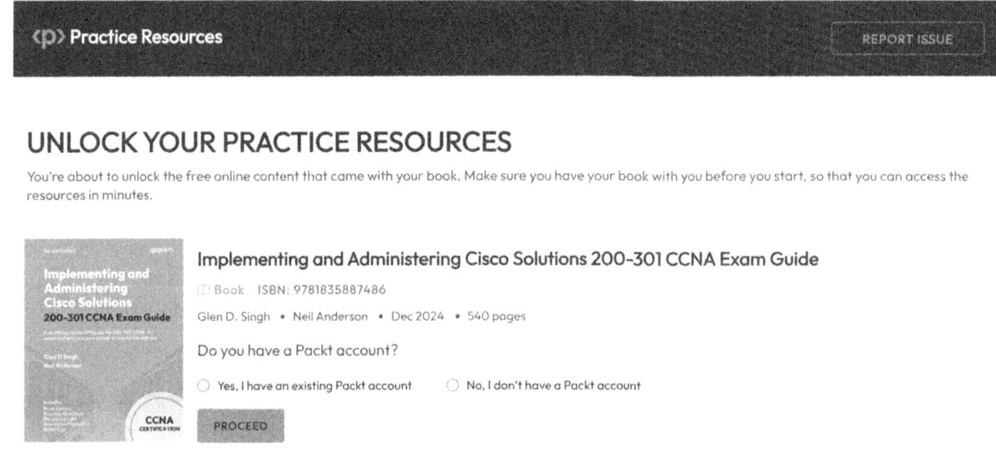

Figure 19.2: Unlock page for the online practice resources

STEP 2

If you already have a Packt account, select the option `Yes, I have an existing Packt account`. If not, select the option `No, I don't have a Packt account`.

If you don't have a Packt account, you'll be prompted to create a new account on the next page. It's free and only takes a minute to create.

Click `Proceed` after selecting one of those options.

STEP 3

After you've created your account or logged in to an existing one, you'll be directed to the following page as shown in *Figure 19.3*.

Make a note of your unique unlock code:

```
FNO3042
```

Type in or copy this code into the text box labeled 'Enter Unique Code':

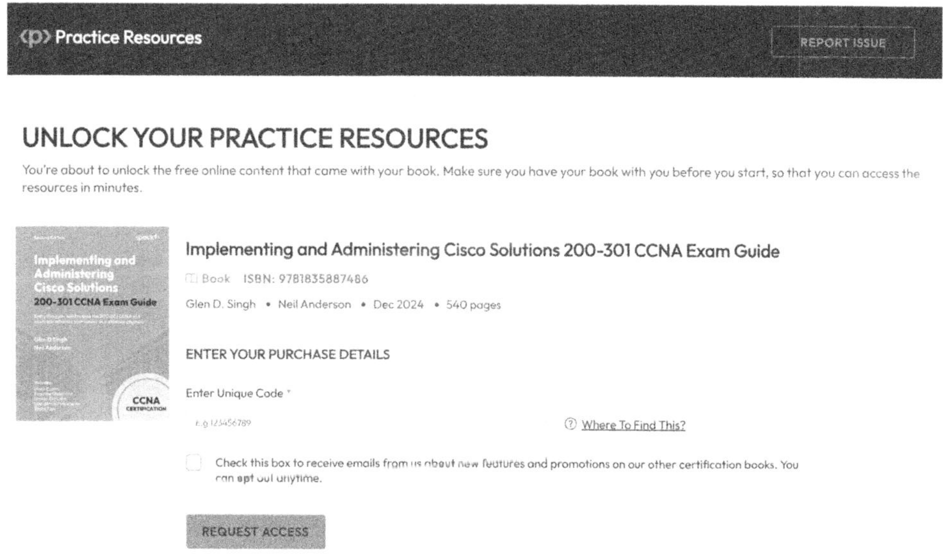

Figure 19.3: Enter your unique sign-up code to unlock the resources

Troubleshooting tip

After creating an account, if your connection drops off or you accidentally close the page, you can reopen the page shown in *Figure 19.2* and select `Yes, I have an existing account`. Then, sign in with the account you had created before you closed the page. You'll be redirected to the screen shown in *Figure 19.3*.

STEP 4

Note

You may choose to opt into emails regarding feature updates and offers on our other certification books. We don't spam, and it's easy to opt out at any time.

Click `Request Access`.

STEP 5

If the code you entered is correct, you'll see a button that says, `OPEN PRACTICE RESOURCES`, as shown in *Figure 19.4*:

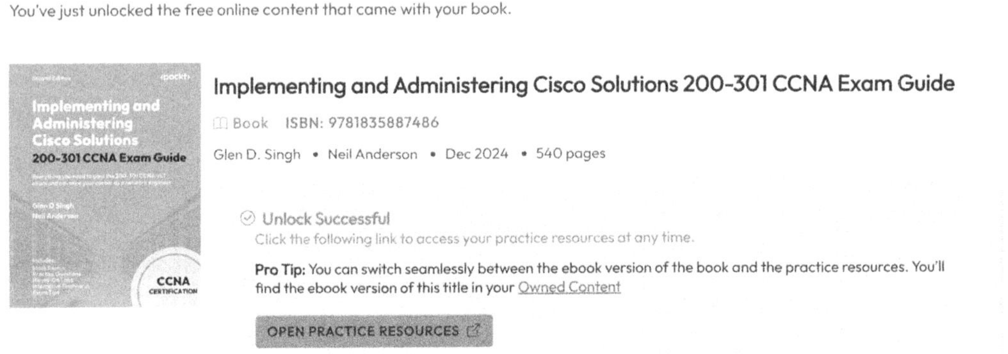

Figure 19.4: Page that shows up after a successful unlock

Click the `OPEN PRACTICE RESOURCES` link to start using your free online content. You'll be redirected to the Dashboard shown in *Figure 19.5*:

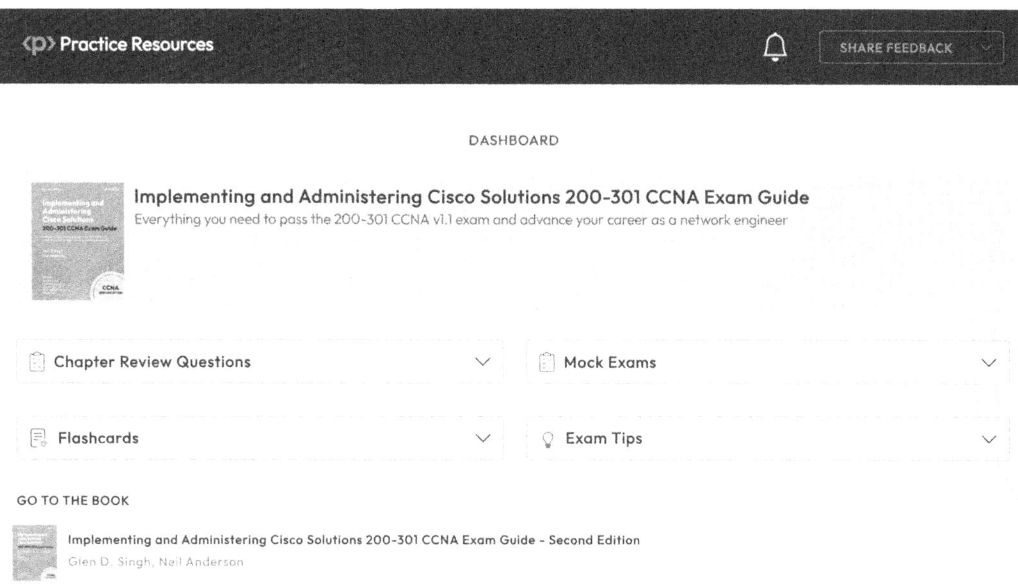

Figure 19.5: Dashboard page for CCNA practice resources

> **Bookmark this link**
>
> Now that you've unlocked the resources, you can come back to them anytime by visiting `https://packt.link/ccnapractice` or scanning the following QR code provided in *Figure 19.6*:

Figure 19.6: QR code to bookmark practice resources website

Troubleshooting Tips

If you're facing issues unlocking, here are three things you can do:

- Double-check your unique code. All unique codes in our books are case-sensitive and your code needs to match exactly as it is shown in *STEP 3*.
- If that doesn't work, use the `Report Issue` button located at the top-right corner of the page.
- If you're not able to open the unlock page at all, write to `customercare@packt.com` and mention the name of the book.

Share Feedback

If you find any issues with the platform, the book, or any of the practice materials, you can click the `Share Feedback` button from any page and reach out to us. If you have any suggestions for improvement, you can share those as well.

Back to the Book

To make switching between the book and practice resources easy, we've added a link that takes you back to the book (*Figure 19.7*). Click it to open your book in Packt's online reader. Your reading position is synced so you can jump right back to where you left off when you last opened the book.

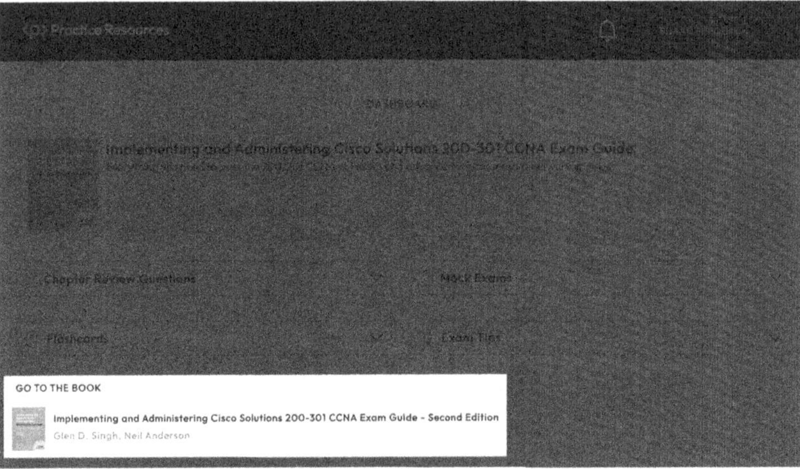

Figure 19.7: Dashboard page for CCNA practice resources

> **Note**
>
> Certain elements of the website might change over time and thus may end up looking different from how they are represented in the screenshots of this book.

Index

A

B

C

D

E

H

I

J

L

M

N

O

P

Q

R

S

T

U

V

W

X

Y

www.packtpub.com

Subscribe to our online digital library for full access to over 7,000 books and videos, as well as industry leading tools to help you plan your personal development and advance your career. For more information, please visit our website.

Why subscribe?

- Spend less time learning and more time coding with practical eBooks and Videos from over 4,000 industry professionals
- Improve your learning with Skill Plans built especially for you
- Get a free eBook or video every month
- Fully searchable for easy access to vital information
- Copy and paste, print, and bookmark content

At www.packtpub.com, you can also read a collection of free technical articles, sign up for a range of free newsletters, and receive exclusive discounts and offers on Packt books and eBooks.

Other Books You May Enjoy

If you enjoyed this book, you may be interested in these other books by Packt:

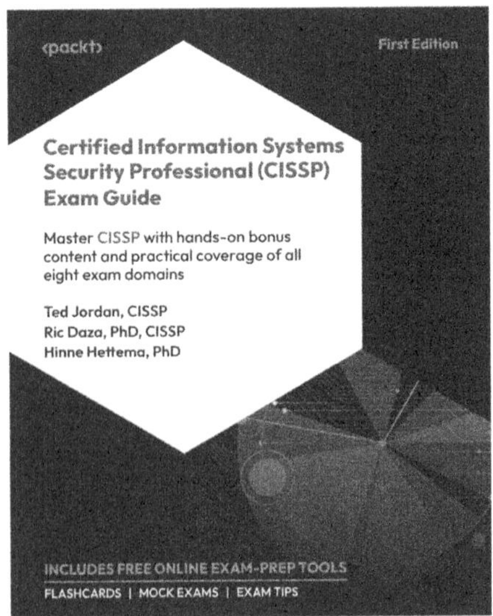

Certified Information Systems Security Professional (CISSP) Exam Guide

Ted Jordan, Ric Daza and Hinne Hettema

ISBN: 978-1-80056-761-0

- Get to grips with network communications and routing to secure them best
- Understand the difference between encryption and hashing
- Know how and where certificates and digital signatures are used
- Study detailed incident and change management procedures
- Manage user identities and authentication principles tested in the exam
- Familiarize yourself with the CISSP security models covered in the exam
- Discover key personnel and travel policies to keep your staff secure
- Discover how to develop secure software from the start

<packt>

SY0-701
Certification Guide

Third Edition

Master cybersecurity fundamentals and pass the SY0-701 exam on your first attempt

Ian Neil

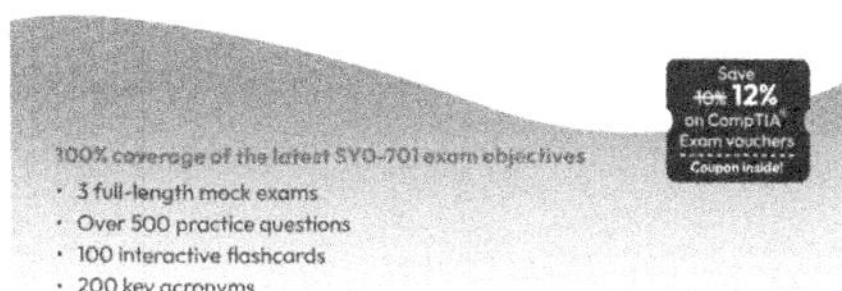

CompTIA Security+ SY0-701 Certification Guide

Ian Neil

ISBN: 978-1-83546-153-2

- Differentiate between various security control types
- Apply mitigation techniques for enterprise security
- Evaluate security implications of architecture models
- Protect data by leveraging strategies and concepts
- Implement resilience and recovery in security
- Automate and orchestrate for running secure operations
- Execute processes for third-party risk assessment and management
- Conduct various audits and assessments with specific purposes

Share Your Thoughts

Now you've finished *Implementing and Administering Cisco Solutions 200-301 CCNA Exam Guide, Second Edition*, we'd love to hear your thoughts! Scan the QR code below to go straight to the Amazon review page for this book and share your feedback or leave a review on the site that you purchased it from.

`https://packt.link/r/183588749X`

Your review is important to us and the tech community and will help us make sure we're delivering excellent quality content.

Download a Free PDF Copy of This Book

Thanks for purchasing this book!

Do you like to read on the go but are unable to carry your print books everywhere? Is your eBook purchase not compatible with the device of your choice?

Don't worry! With every Packt book, you now get a DRM-free PDF version of that book at no cost.

Read anywhere, any place, on any device. Search, copy, and paste code from your favorite technical books directly into your application.

The perks don't stop there. You can get exclusive access to discounts, newsletters, and great free content in your inbox daily.

Follow these simple steps to get the benefits:

1. Scan the QR code or visit the link below:

`https://packt.link/free-ebook/9781835887486`

2. Submit your proof of purchase.
3. That's it! We'll send your free PDF and other benefits to your email directly.

Made in the USA
Coppell, TX
12 August 2025

53182445R00385